The Anthropolog

Wiley Blackwell Anthologies in Social and Cultural Anthropology

Series Editor: Parker Shipton, Boston University

Drawing from some of the most significant scholarly work of the nineteenth and twentieth centuries, the *Wiley Blackwell Anthologies in Social and Cultural Anthropology* series offers a comprehensive and unique perspective on the ever-changing field of anthropology. It represents both a collection of classic readers and an exciting challenge to the norms that have shaped this discipline over the past century.

Each edited volume is devoted to a traditional subdiscipline of the field such as the anthropology of religion, linguistic anthropology, or medical anthropology; and provides a foundation in the canonical readings of the selected area. Aware that such subdisciplinary definitions are still widely recognized and useful – but increasingly problematic – these volumes are crafted to include a rare and invaluable perspective on social and cultural anthropology at the onset of the twenty-first century. Each text provides a selection of classic readings together with contemporary works that underscore the artificiality of subdisciplinary definitions and point students, researchers, and general readers in the new directions in which anthropology is moving.

Series Advisory Editorial Board:

1. *Linguistic Anthropology: A Reader, 2nd Edition*
   Edited by Alessandro Duranti
2. *A Reader in the Anthropology of Religion, 2nd Edition*
   Edited by Michael Lambek
3. *The Anthropology of Politics: A Reader in Ethnography, Theory, and Critique*
   Edited by Joan Vincent
4. *Kinship and Family: An Anthropological Reader*
   Edited by Robert Parkin and Linda Stone
5. *Law and Anthropology: A Reader*
   Edited by Sally Falk Moore
6. *The Anthropology of Development and Globalization: From Classical Political Economy to Contemporary Neoliberalism*
   Edited by Marc Edelman and Angelique Haugerud
7. *The Anthropology of Art: A Reader*
   Edited by Howard Morphy and Morgan Perkins
8. *Feminist Anthropology: A Reader*
   Edited by Ellen Lewin
9. *Ethnographic Fieldwork: An Anthropological Reader, 2nd Edition*
   Edited by Antonius C. G. M. Robben and Jeffrey A. Sluka
10. *Environmental Anthropology*
    Edited by Michael R. Dove and Carol Carpenter
11. *Anthropology and Child Development: A Cross-Cultural Reader*
    Edited by Robert A. LeVine and Rebecca S. New
12. *Foundations of Anthropological Theory: From Classical Antiquity to Early Modern Europe*
    Edited by Robert Launay
13. *Psychological Anthropology: A Reader on Self in Culture*
    Edited by Robert A. LeVine
14. *A Reader in Medical Anthropology: Theoretical Trajectories, Emergent Realities*
    Edited by Byron J. Good, Michael M. J. Fischer, Sarah S. Willen, and Mary-Jo DelVecchio Good
15. *Sexualities in Anthropology*
    Edited by Andrew Lyons and Harriet Lyons
16. *The Anthropology of Performance: A Reader*
    Edited by Frank J. Korom
17. *The Anthropology of Citizenship: A Reader*
    Edited by Sian Lazar

The Anthropology of Citizenship

A Reader

Edited by

Sian Lazar

WILEY Blackwell

This edition first published 2013
© 2013 John Wiley & Sons, Inc

Registered Office
John Wiley & Sons, Ltd, The Atrium, Southern Gate, Chichester, West Sussex, PO19 8SQ, UK

Editorial Offices
350 Main Street, Malden, MA 02148-5020, USA
9600 Garsington Road, Oxford, OX4 2DQ, UK
The Atrium, Southern Gate, Chichester, West Sussex, PO19 8SQ, UK

For details of our global editorial offices, for customer services, and for information about how
to apply for permission to reuse the copyright material in this book please see our website at
www.wiley.com/wiley-blackwell.

Library of Congress Cataloging-in-Publication Data

Lazar, Sian.
The anthropology of citizenship: a reader / Sian Lazar. – First edition.
pages cm
Includes index.
ISBN 978-1-118-41291-6 (hardback) – ISBN 978-1-118-42445-2 (paper)   1. Citizenship –
Cross-cultural studies.   2. Civil society – Cross-cultural studies.   I. Title.
JF801.L39 2013
323.6–dc23

2013016703

A catalogue record for this book is available from the British Library.

Cover image: Protest in support of immigrant rights, Portland, Oregon, 2006. © Rick Bowmer/AP/
Press Association Photos.
Cover design by Nicki Averill Design.

Set in 9/11pt Sabon by SPi Publisher, Services, Pondicherry, India
Printed in Malaysia by Ho Printing (M) Sdn Bhd

1   2013

Contents

Introduction

Sian Lazar

Whether it is the World Bank talking about citizen engagement or Latin American feminists arguing that domestic violence inhibits full citizenship for women, political actors all over the world have embraced the language of citizenship. But the context of this language is not only states and nations, it is also local communities, cities, global organizations and social movements, and as a result the theory of citizenship has had to expand and develop to encompass this variety. Anthropologists have made significant contributions to this process, and this reader draws together the existing body of work in this vein.

What is citizenship? The word itself is now used in a wide range of arenas, from citizenship education in schools to multilateral development agencies' programmes of good governance and public statements from BP, Microsoft or Coca-Cola about their 'corporate citizenship'.[1] It is being used, it seems, to evoke virtues such as equality in rights, respectful engagement between citizen (individual or corporate) and wider national society, participation in and knowledge about institutions of government, the right to vote and be elected, etc. Yet at its most fundamental, citizenship names political belonging, and in this introductory essay I argue that to study citizenship is to study how we live with others in a political community.

The sociologist T. H. Marshall gave the following definition of citizenship in 1950: 'Citizenship is a status bestowed on those who are full members of a community. All who possess the status are equal with respect to the rights and duties with which the status is endowed' (Marshall 1983 [1950]: 253) (see also this volume, Chapter 8).

This definition is at the heart of almost all contemporary social theories of citizenship, including many anthropologies of citizenship, and Marshall's essay is a common starting point for critics and adherents alike. He equated community with the nation, and viewed membership of that community as primarily an individual ownership of a set of rights and corresponding duties. His version of citizenship has a distinguished pedigree: from Locke onwards, liberal citizenship has been seen as a status of the individual. The rights associated with this status in theory allow individuals to pursue their own conceptions of the good life, as long as they do not hinder others' similar pursuits, and the state protects this status quo. In return citizens have minimal responsibilities, which revolve primarily around keeping the state running, such as paying taxes or participating in military service.

However, insights from ethnography complicate this normative picture of liberal citizenship, as anthropologists have insisted on the specificity of citizenship in different contexts. This reader brings together some of the very best of this work. Through their disciplinary emphasis on lived experiences anthropologists have revealed the contingencies of political membership, its relationship to day-to-day practices of politics and how citizenship is a mechanism for making claims on different political communities, of which the state is just one. One important consequence of this is that anthropologists denaturalize *liberal* citizenship and ask questions about the actual constitution of political membership and subjectivity in a given context.

The anthropology of citizenship is at a critical juncture. A coherent body of ethnographic work explicitly on citizenship has coalesced around a series of themes, organized here as follows: citizenship as subject-formation, both top-down and bottom-up; the interplay of citizenship regimes at local, national and global scales; and the relation between citizen and non-citizen. As scholars move from current concerns into new territory, anthropology of citizenship's future has the potential to make extremely exciting contributions to anthropology, political economy, sociology and social theory.

In this introduction, I trace two genealogies of the anthropology of citizenship, beginning with its emergence out of political anthropology more broadly. Next, I give a brief intellectual history of normative understandings of citizenship as a concept, through an exploration of some of the key debates on the theme within political philosophy. This is potentially one of the most productive areas of interdisciplinary overlap and dialogue between anthropology and philosophy. I then move to a more detailed discussion of recent ethnographic work on citizenship itself.

From Political Anthropology to the Anthropology of Citizenship

The problem of how human beings live with others is a fundamental concern of anthropological enquiry. One might indeed want to claim it as *the* concern of *all* anthropological enquiry, but I will focus here specifically on political anthropology, in order to trace the emergence of an anthropology of citizenship out of the anthropology of the political. This is of necessity a partial survey, with the aim of highlighting specific elements to contextualize the more detailed discussions below. Texts I refer to here are not extracted in this particular reader, because they are in most cases widely taught in anthropology and easily found in other collections (for example Vincent 2002; Sharma and Gupta 2006; Goodale 2008).

Some of the earliest anthropological attempts to grapple explicitly with politics come from the British Structural Functionalist tradition. As Radcliffe-Brown's Foreword to *African Political Systems* (Fortes and Evans-Pritchard 1940) outlines, these scholars viewed the study of politics as the study of social order. In the Introduction, Fortes and Evans-Pritchard distinguished between stateless societies and primitive states, demonstrating that for them political order was intimately linked to the state. If order existed in societies without an identifiable state it had to be accounted for, usually through the discovery of some other institutional structure to take its place. For Evans-Pritchard in his famous study of the Nuer (1940), that other structure was kinship – and the blood feud. Until some of the ideas about 'small politics' (Bailey 1971) and transactionalism (Barth 1965) emerged, much anthropological concern was directed to studying the maintenance of the most evidently political structures in any given society. This meant in practice the political communities that looked most like modern states. As a more diachronic emphasis gradually entered into the analysis these included states in development or indeed collapse (Leach 1954). The verifiably 'political' nature of any given grouping was most obviously evident when violence was concerned. Thus, for the authors of *African Political Systems*, social order was maintained through the use of coercion, and the sanctioning of violence was a key aspect of political control. This echoes the Weberian notion of the state as the entity with the monopoly over the legitimate use of force across a given territory.

Later anthropologists began to study practices of political activity as well as the structures within which such activity was thought to occur. In a collection first published in 1966, Swartz, Turner and Tuden described the shift from a preoccupation with 'taxonomy, structure and function of the political system' (2006 [1966]: 1) towards a concern with process and change, especially under decolonization. The work of the Manchester School was crucial in this regard, particularly in the prominence that anthropologists such as Gluckman and Turner gave to the explanation of political conflict and rapid change. F. G. Bailey (1969, 1971) had also long explored what he argued were the 'rules' of the political 'game' in different societies. He focused both on the rules and patterns of political competition at leadership level and on the 'small politics' of gossip and reputation in local communities. Fredrik Barth's work on the different political groupings led by 'chiefs' and 'saints' in northern Pakistan also focused on the agency of political participants. He argued that political organization was an outcome of the tactical choices and alignments made by both leaders and followers, choices which were both rational and the result of much discussion (Barth 1965, 2007). Talal Asad (2002 [1972]) subsequently pointed out that he had rather downplayed the structural elements limiting the choices available to tenant farmers. However, Barth's emphasis on the ways that groupings coalesced and demonstrated their strength to others illustrates an important move from structure to practice, and this particular analytical movement has special relevance for the anthropology of citizenship, since participation in politics understood as practice is a central element of many understandings of citizenship, as I discuss below.

Another relevant trend within political anthropology is the study of ethnicity and ethnic groups. Here, Barth's introduction to *Ethnic Groups and Boundaries* (1969) provides a bridge between the concerns of earlier US cultural anthropology with the localized development of specific cultures and the more general approach of political anthropology. He argued that ethnic units are not natural but ascriptive groups and therefore culturally constituted through the maintenance of a boundary between members and outsiders, even while the features that signal the boundary may change over time (1969: 14). The key is the construction of the boundary, through multiple means – economic, social, cultural and so on. To put it in more contemporary phrasing, Barth saw that the 'self' needs the 'other' to constitute and understand itself, and that interaction takes place within a complex space of power relations, including those shaped by legal and economic regimes at global and local scales. This again has considerable relevance for our understanding of citizenship, as the citizen and the non-citizen exist in a similar relationship. Earlier Manchester School anthropology had explored the self–other dynamic with respect to ethnicity in the context of the complex political economic and cultural relations of colonialism. For example, J. Clyde Mitchell's (1959) discussion of the kalela dance in the Zambian Copperbelt provoked significant debate about the role of mimicry in the relationship between colonizer and colonized, between 'Africa' and 'the West' (see Ferguson 2002). Bruce Kapferer's (1995) insightful analysis of this debate also highlighted the importance of the *urban* colonial context in the development of ethnic identifications, another theme of considerable importance for the discussion of citizenship.

With the post-colonial turn in political anthropology, attention shifted more explicitly towards two fronts successively, beginning with the study of *global* political economic and cultural formations and moving to the study of the state. From the early 1980s onwards, anthropologists developed their analysis of globalization through a political economy approach initially inspired by World Systems Theory (e.g. Mintz 1985; Wolf 1997 [1982]) and still influential today. This line of study has been complemented by the development of contemporary tropes of globalization such as 'flows', 'scapes' and so on (see Inda and Rosaldo 2008). Today, anthropologists study a wide range of global entities, including social movements (Juris 2008), the financial system (LiPuma and Lee 2004), international financial institutions such as the IMF (Harper 2000) and multinational corporations (Rajak 2011). Around the same time as the first turn to the global, political anthropologists also began to engage in a more conscious discussion of the state itself. Rather than taking for granted the nature of the state as Weberian entity for the promotion of social order or simply turning their gaze elsewhere as early anthropologists had, they began to see the modern state as an object of study, often influenced by Foucault's work on governmentality, as well as more historical and political science work on the development of the state (e.g. Corrigan and Sayer 1985; Skocpol 1985). Thus, the scale of the political community or communities studied by anthropologists moved rapidly from the village to the globe, taking in the national along the way.

Work on the anthropology of the state has expanded exponentially since the 1990s (see Sharma and Gupta 2006). The wide variety of approaches include those that drew on Marxist discussions of the state (Abrams 1988 [1977]); culturalist discussions of the fetishization of the state as idea (Taussig 1992, 1997; Coronil 1997); those on the centrality of ritual and theatre to the making of the state (Geertz 1980); day-to-day ethnographies of bureaucratic spaces (Gupta 1995); and engagement with state bureaucracies (Hetherington 2011). Begoña Aretxaga (2003) argued that the state comes into being in a series of 'encounters' between state officials and citizens, both violent and non-violent, thereby summarizing what has become a very productive and important approach, particularly for the study of citizenship in practice.

What the idea of citizenship has enabled is a focus on the state or bureaucracy's others: the citizen and the non-citizen. The concept allows for the examination of who is fetishizing the state as idea, or who is being managed by the bureaucracy, how successfully and under what conditions. To date, these questions have most prominently been discussed through the optic of the expert cultures that sustain certain ideas of 'state', 'government', 'politics', 'the economy', 'society' and so on (Mitchell 2002, 2006 [1999]); and the interweaving of technology with politics remains an important anthropological theme today (Ong and Collier 2005). The writings collected in this reader show the contribution that is possible through ethnographies of non-expert cultures.

Something similar has happened with respect to the burgeoning anthropology of democracy, which studies popular understandings of democracy – liberal or not – and ordinary people's engagement with democratic institutions (Gutmann 2002; Michelutti 2008; Nugent 2008). Like anthropology of citizenship, anthropology of democracy explores the meanings, practices and languages of political action, as well as the interplay between formal and informal political spaces in specific contexts. Anthropologists study both the obvious spaces of democratic politics, like elections, and less institutionalized ones, such as social movements (Paley 2001) or day-to-day conversations about politics in the times between elections (Banerjee 2008). This is of course one of the most important methodological advantages of an ethnographic approach to such matters: the 'analytic openness' (Paley 2008: 19) that allows for emergent rather than predefined objects of study. Thus, as Paley argues, the anthropology of democracy does not take a definition of democracy as its starting point but allows meanings to surface through a 'dialogic engagement with people in the places we study' (Paley 2008: 19). This is a key aspect of the very best anthropology of citizenship. And, like ethnographies of citizenship, ethnographic study of democracy requires us not to take normative definitions for granted. One result of this has been the scholarly investigation of democratic potentials inherent in illiberal political structures, including populist regimes (Hetherington 2011).

Theorists might wish to link the question of citizenship specifically to democratic political regimes, however democracy might itself be defined (e.g. Isin 2002; Holston 2008). An alternative position is to suggest that anthropology of citizenship overlaps with the anthropology of democracy but is not a subset of it. This is because citizenship broadly defined as a set of practices understood to constitute membership of a political community can be found in non-democratic spaces as well. One good example of this is in contemporary Africanist anthropologists' reconsideration of chieftaincies. Mahmood Mamdani (1996) had argued that under colonial regimes of direct and indirect rule, urban areas in Africa were governed according to practices of citizenship (albeit restricted racially to a limited number of citizens) whereas in the countryside indirect rule through 'traditional authorities' meant that Africans there were and could only ever be subjects. He has been criticized on a number of grounds (see Spear 2003), but those most suggestive for my purposes here are ethnographies that recognize the continuing importance of 'traditional chiefs' to ordinary people without attributing it to false consciousness. Thus, Englund (2012) points to the perceived 'empowering potential of subjection' of villagers to traditional village headmen, while Nyamnjoh (2003) argues that chieftainship is not incompatible with liberal democracy in Botswana. Mamdani's argument is important for reminding us of the need to bring a historical perspective to examinations of contemporary political practice and the importance of variable histories of colonialism to the development of citizenship. However, as Robins *et al.* (2008) argue, anthropologists must also aim at grounded analyses of political practices as what people actually *do*, as opposed to reading political practice through normative ideologies. This enables a recognition of citizens' attachment to multiple and often counter-intuitive political strategies.

Still, the commitment to a democratic politics has been an important feature of contemporary anthropology of citizenship. It remains definitional of the field for many, not least because it is a fundamental aspect of the critical potential of citizenship language as deployed in the contemporary world (see Wittman, this volume, Chapter 16). Yet assuming that proper citizenship can only exist in liberal representative democracies is two-edged: on the one hand such a position can and does help advocacy for greater democratic freedoms as defined in liberal regimes, freedoms which are desired by many if not most people worldwide. On the other, such an assumption runs the ethnographic and analytical risk of narrowing the ethnographer's gaze to the point that she does not see the full range of possibilities for the organization of political life that exist in any given context.

Anthropologies of state institutions such as law courts, bureaucracies and development interventions can give considerable insight into the conditions for action by citizens, non-citizens and those claiming (full) citizenship. Legal anthropologists in particular have had to develop conceptual tools for analysing expert or institutional cultures and popular understandings of law. Specific legal regimes are linked to citizenship experience, often with regard to immigration and naturalization law (see de Genova 2005, and this volume, Chapter 25), but also property rights (Hetherington 2011). James Holston's (2008) work in particular has broken new ground by using the conceptual language of citizenship to examine bureaucratic-legal spaces, the history of property relations and the lived experiences of slum dwellers.

The extent of the range of topics covered in political anthropology today indicates the complexities of studying political life in contemporary society. We can no longer examine politics exclusively in small-scale political structures or national states, if indeed we ever could. How far the institutional, legal, bureaucratic or material frameworks that define the conditions for political action are shaped by state institutions and how far they are influenced by NGOs or other private actors also significantly complicates the understanding of political membership. Recent work on neoliberal government has highlighted this complexity, one good example being that of the study of privatization of security in cities, through gated communities protected by private security companies, state-sanctioned community policing, organized vigilante groups or lynchings (see Pratten and Sen 2007).

For people are members of varying political communities, not just those governed by national or even local states, and they are subject to forms of government that originate from different entities. This is especially true when we take globalization into account, as Michel Rolph Trouillot (2001) pointed out. Given the contemporary importance of transnational and sometimes global political entities such as corporations or religious networks in the government of citizens of different national states, can we argue that citizenship is merely the relationship between the individual and the state as normative definitions suggest? If we wish to take an Aristotelian position and argue that citizenship is participation in government, in the taking of decisions that affect our lives, then the citizen's position regarding a range of governing entities becomes crucial in an assessment of the quality of his or her citizenship under a given political regime. Studying citizenship enables contemporary political anthropologists to grapple with these questions.

The Political Community

If the anthropology of citizenship has grown out of the developments of political anthropology more broadly, the concept of citizenship has a much longer trajectory. In this section, I give a brief intellectual history of the idea of citizenship, to explore ways that anthropologists can situate themselves theoretically with regard to political theory. I do so, first, to help identify our own normative assumptions – about citizenship, liberal citizenship, political subjectivity and so on – and second, to suggest some ways that anthropological theory can be brought to bear on philosophical debates.

This continues a longstanding intellectual dialogue between anthropology and philosophy, which has also flourished in areas other than the political, such as ethics, moral philosophy and philosophy of mind. With respect to political philosophy of citizenship, the results of this interdisciplinary engagement are threefold. First, anthropologists make the obvious but no less important analytical shift from the normative to the descriptive, from what citizenship and citizens should be to a critical analysis of what they are. Second, there are some significant commonalities between political philosophy of citizenship and anthropological approaches. They have developed largely naturally, yet a more conscious and explicit recognition of the connections could lead to productive future lines of enquiry. Examples of these common concerns include the morality of the subject, the nature of liberty, the relationship between individuality and collectivity in political subjecthood, and the nature of the urban political community. Finally, there are some recurring themes in political philosophy of citizenship that anthropologists have not yet explored in this light, one such being the relationship between property and persons.

As with political anthropology, one of the basic questions of political philosophy is: how should we live with others in a political community? This section traces some key moments in this enduring debate. Aristotle is my starting point, as the most celebrated proponent of a civic republican tradition of citizenship that began in the early Greek city-states. I begin by highlighting three main aspects of his writing on citizenship and the *polis*, which have proved central to subsequent Anglo-American theories of citizenship. The first is the question of how precisely to constitute membership and its corollary exclusion. This was a particular issue for early Greek philosophers because of the presence of slaves, often in important bureaucratic positions in the government of the city. Therefore, membership of the *polis* itself was contested, having an internal other right at its heart. So, when Aristotle wrote that 'man is a political animal', he was confronted with the limits to that phrase, and needed to define which 'men' he was referring to (women were quickly dismissed and then ignored, along with children). Hence his concern to define who is the citizen: a member of the *polis* who participates in government – 'gives judgement and holds office'. A second crucial thread in Aristotle's work is the constitution of the citizen as a particular kind of person capable of living in the collectivity. As the extracts in this reader from both Aristotle and Pericles show, virtue was central to citizenship, and that virtue consisted in – amongst other qualities – respect for law and for others and a passion for politics. Finally, politics itself was intimately linked with speech, and discussion and debate was absolutely key to Athenian politics and personhood (see Arendt 1951, 1998 [1958]). Thus, citizenship was constituted through political practice, and political practice was constituted through speech and deliberation.

Aristotle's work highlights two important analytical themes common to anthropology and philosophy of citizenship. They are, first, that citizenship is more than simply a status denoting membership of a polity but is constituted through a set of practices associated with participation in politics. Second, he points to the importance of conceptualizing political subjectivity as something that cannot be assumed to exist but that must be created. For Aristotle, political subjects – citizens – are inherently collective and also eminently moral; they are constituted according to particular ethical concerns or virtues. This speaks to contemporary anthropological explorations not only of education, but also of morality, virtue and ethics more broadly conceived (Laidlaw 2002; Faubion 2011).

The second set of foundational philosophical texts I want to highlight as important for understanding the anthropology of citizenship are those of the social contract philosophers. For Rousseau and Locke, social order cannot be achieved through violence, but through the acceptance of all to live via the agreement of the majority for the benefit of all. The social contract between people and ruler or state protects property rights, a point I will return to below. In the state of 'natural freedom' (Rousseau) prior to the establishment of a state, property is always subject to the threat of what Locke called 'the Invasion of others'. To overcome this danger each individual 'puts into the community his person and all his powers under the supreme direction of the general will', thus creating 'civil freedom' (Rousseau). The *polis* is therefore created when individuals voluntarily subject themselves to the collectivity, that is, the state and the rule of law. As with Aristotle, political subjectivity is not to be assumed, but is created, and is intimately linked to moral questions of personal virtue.

The radical natures of the American Declaration of Independence (1776) and the French Declaration of the Rights of Man (1789) lay in their willingness to question the inevitability of the existing regime of state power and sovereignty, and then to actively claim sovereignty for 'the people'. They did so by claiming the equality of men in the name of individual rights, especially those to 'Life, Liberty and the pursuit of Happiness' and 'liberty, property, security, and resistance to oppression.' The political context meant that they needed to claim liberty in order to change sovereign power, but the question of liberty could also be interpreted in the light of Rousseau's and Locke's position that true freedom comes through the respect for the rule of law, not through the absence of law.

The question of property was foundational for the authors of these declarations, as for Rousseau and Locke. The role of the state as guarantor of individual property rights became a central question of citizenship in republican and liberal regimes from the late eighteenth century onwards. Property was a criterion for membership, when only male property holders were defined as citizens. Questions of property-holding often created practical difficulties for the implementation of individual, universal ideals of citizenship. For example, Latin American constitutions and legislation of the nineteenth century often attempted to abolish collective land-holding in favour of individual property rights, but this proved a much contested policy in some parts of the region, especially the Andes. The contestation becomes more readily understandable in modern eyes when we acknowledge the importance of collective traditions of citizenship among indigenous communities, especially those connected to collective property-holding.

Anthropologists have done a great deal to illuminate our understanding of the complexities of these processes in the contemporary world, giving due import to their historical, economic and political background. This has always been a highly politicized discussion (e.g. Povinelli 2002). However, the debates within a broader anthropology of property have yet to be explicitly connected to a discussion of citizenship, even though for some time, different understandings of property and ownership have been important concerns for anthropologists with regard both to land and to persons. The latter body of work has at its most radical criticized the notion of the rights-bearing political subject by putting into question the assumption that persons cannot be property (Strathern 2004). It also prompts us to look anew at the centrality of questions of slavery to the early history of the development of citizenship as a concept, not least in recognizing that citizens have been constructed in contrast not only to subjects (Mamdani 1996) but to slaves, from Aristotle onwards.

In the dominant liberal narrative of the nineteenth century, liberty in one's own person would be achieved through citizenship based on individual rights, which superseded institutions perceived as backward, such as slavery or collective property-holding. However, in practice, citizenship was continually negotiated, and collective traditions were not peculiar only to indigenous communities. In fact, the historical development of citizenship is linked to the coalescing of modern nation-states – which often took liberal forms – out of earlier city-state formations built on civic republican traditions. But even the most radical of modern nation-states mixed the two traditions of citizenship together. The 1805 constitution of Haiti is a good example of the mixing of civic republicanism and liberalism in practice. Again, slavery is crucial, as the second article simply abolishes it 'forever'; and articles 3–6 promote liberal values of equality in the eyes of the law, the rule of law itself and the protection of property rights. Article 9, though, brings out beautifully and succinctly a more Aristotelian notion of the virtuous citizen: 'No person is worthy of being a Haitian who is not a good father, good son, a good husband, and especially a good soldier.'

Most versions of liberalism, such as that of John Stuart Mill, also incorporated conceptions of the importance of the virtue of the citizen and the morality of political institutions into their theories of the relationship between states and individual freedom. Mill's famous principle of liberty stated that 'the sole end for which mankind are warranted, individually or collectively, in interfering with the liberty of action of any of their number, is self-protection' (1991: 14). This did not prevent him from powerfully advocating a strong form of representative government, one of the purposes of which was the moral improvement of its citizens: 'We may consider as one criterion of the goodness of a government, the degree in which it tends to increase the sum of good qualities in the governed, collectively and individually' (1991: 227). In an Aristotelian turn, this moral improvement at a societal level came from individual participation in government and the exercise of social functions, such as jury service. So, although for Mill the individual was very much the core political subject, his or her fulfilment as a political subject required in practice the collective context of participation in public life. But in contrast to Aristotle, for Mill this could be done through institutional mechanisms of representation rather than more direct political participation through speech and discussion. This assumes a particular theory of subjectivity as individual and prior to the collectivity. Such a theory of the subject is one of the most normative in contemporary political life, one that even anthropologists often assume to be true cross-culturally, and yet it has been a considerable source of debate within anthropology of the self since Marcel Mauss' influential essay on the topic (Mauss 1979 [1938]; Morris 1994).

The gendered language of most of the historical writings discussed here makes obvious the inherent connection of citizenship to exclusion from membership in both civic republican and the most liberal, universal and individualistic formulations. Exclusion has been one of the most important aspects of anthropological discussion of citizenship, as I illustrate below, but it has also been a significant area of debate within political philosophy. The exclusion of women from liberal citizenship was denounced from its beginnings by early feminists (Wollstonecraft 1975 [1792]; de Gouges 2003 [1791]). Contemporary feminist political philosophers, historians and other social theorists have argued that the abstract individual citizen of liberal ideals is in fact a very particular white male property-holding individual citizen (see Barron 1993).

Feminists and others have also criticized contemporary liberal political theory for promoting the abstracted individual as a basis for political theory and thus making universal what is in actuality a rather particular form of subjecthood. An example of such a critique is one of the most celebrated debates within recent political theory, that between liberals and communitarians. Michael Sandel criticized the model of the subject proposed by the procedural liberal John Rawls (1972) as 'a self understood as prior to and independent of purposes and ends' (Sandel 1984: 86). This subject is conceptually already constituted before it enters into any kind of social or interrelational space; but for the communitarian and also feminist critics of procedural liberalism, such a theory of the subject does not hold (Moller Otkin 1991). The communitarians – like many anthropologists – place much more emphasis on the embedding of subjects within collectivities (e.g. Walzer 1982), and their influence can be seen in the work of more political communitarians.[2]

The extract from Hannah Arendt's *The Origins of Totalitarianism* (1951) included in this reader predates the liberal–communitarian debate but emphasizes the importance of belonging to a community, indeed the pain of being outside a political community. Her example is that of post-World

War II refugees in Europe who had no home to return to, or state to belong to. Contemporary anthropology of migration (forced and not) and human rights speaks strongly to her analysis of exclusion from the political community, but also broadens Arendt's focus to explore the differential incorporation of refugees and migrants within modern polities, an incorporation that can also be an internal exclusion. Arendt provides a genealogical link between civic republicanism and present-day communitarianism, in part because she stresses the naturalness of community belonging, as well as its importance. Her work also has enormous relevance for discussions about the relationships between cosmopolitanism, human rights, migration and national citizenship, which problematize the scale of the political community at stake (see below). Debates about internationally applicable human rights and the nature of the boundaries around specific membership rights such as national citizenship continue to be extremely important today (Benhabib 2004).

The critique of communitarianism emerged rapidly, even from theorists who may have agreed with its criticism of the liberal theory of the subject. Theorists, especially feminist political theorists (Young 1990, and this volume, Chapter 9; Pateman and Shanley 1991), took issue with the reification of 'community' or 'group', not least because community very strongly conceived leaves little space for individual variability and internal differentiation, and, more importantly, for the internal power relations that constrain the ability to define what 'a community' is and what 'it' thinks. For anthropologists, this is a crucial point, which has come out in debates as varied as those centred on individual or collective (sociocentric) notions of the self, the interplay between 'indigenous' or 'customary' legal jurisdictions and national ones, human and property rights and the development interventions.[3] While their traditional affinity with subaltern groups has led many anthropologists to the defence of group rights from a perspective of cultural relativism, it has long been acknowledged that societal and legal recognition of group rights may inhibit individual claims to justice. Indigenous legal jurisdiction is one group right that exposes these difficulties (Sullivan and Brunnegger 2011). Anthropological study takes the discussion beyond abstract principles, not least through the recognition that conflicts between group rights and legal regimes based upon liberal notions of individual rights often happen in grey zones imbued with complex power relations, such as land rights and the exploitation of natural resources (e.g. Behrends *et al.* 2011).

In a classically liberal approach, individual rights constitute citizenship of the national political community and group rights undermine that civic belonging, while in political thought more influenced by communitarianism, smaller communities define their members. Contemporary liberals such as Will Kymlicka (1995) and Seyla Benhabib (2004) have modified the first position, to argue for liberal versions of community membership that protect both individual and group rights. Yet the tension remains largely unresolved. In an important essay, Iris Marion Young (1990, and this volume, Chapter 9) opposes the reification of 'face-to-face' community without entirely falling back on the individual *a priori* subject. She critiques the dichotomy of individualism/ community, seeking a politics of difference that resists the 'urge to unity'. In resisting this urge, such a politics resists the subsumption of the individual within the whole that happens when the individual is defined and organized politically only through membership of either a national community or some smaller face-to-face community. Instead, she argues that an 'openness to unassimilated others' is the political ideal, one found today in the 'unoppressive city'. Thus 'radical politics must begin from the existence of urban life' (317). And here we have come full circle in this section, back to Aristotle's city-state *polis*, reimagined for the current moment. Subsequent theorists have extended the idea of the city as key locus for contemporary political economy and radical politics (Harvey 2012) and citizenship (Holston and Appadurai 1999; Isin 2000). Anthropologists are well placed to explore these contrastive notions of political community in both urban and rural spaces, as the contents of the second part of this reader make clear. We should resist the urge to ally strongly with either liberal or communitarian political thinking, and ensure that we recognize the complexities within both bodies of theory – complexities to which it is impossible to do justice in a short introduction.[4] By engaging in a dialogue with the full range of both communitarian and liberal political thought (classical and revisionist), anthropology has potentially a great deal to contribute in moving the debate beyond the communitarian alternative to liberal formulations.

The Anthropology of Citizenship

Citizenship as subject-formation

An ethnographic focus on the practices of citizenship has proved to be one of anthropology's distinctive contributions to the theory of citizenship over recent years, and in the remainder of this Introduction I discuss this in more detail. This section focuses on processes of political subject-formation, both top-down and bottom-up. In an important early article, Aihwa Ong argued that citizenship is a 'process of self-making and being-made' (1996: 737); one prominent thread in the anthropology of citizenship uses a Foucauldian analysis to examine how states and other entities make citizens under various citizenship regimes (Buffington 2003; Baitenmann 2005). This can be analysed through the exploration of a series of encounters between people and state officials or policy, following Aretxaga's (2003) suggested analytical approach. Immigration has been an important area for this kind of study, not least because it is where boundaries between citizen and non-citizen are most contested. But immigration encounters are not solely punitive and exclusionary: Ong's studies (1996, 2003) among others show the work that governments put in to 'assimilate' different groups of migrants and refugees.

The interaction between assimilation and respect for difference was investigated early on through the concept of 'cultural citizenship', first brought to an anthropological audience by Renato Rosaldo (1994a, and this volume, Chapter 10). For Rosaldo, cultural citizenship 'refers to the right to be different (in terms of race, ethnicity or native language) with respect to the norms of the dominant national community, without compromising one's right to belong, in the sense of participating in the nation-state's democratic processes' (1994: 57). In a series of research and activist projects with Latino immigrants to the USA, he and his collaborators discussed immigrants' experiences of second-class citizenship and their struggles for better citizenship quality, the latter often defined through values such as respect and dignity. He firmly located the struggle for cultural citizenship within a political struggle of dissidence and for rights in the face of exclusionary definitions of national identity.

Yet states' policies towards immigrants are not the only form of cultural citizenship regime in operation today. By citizenship regime, I refer to legal, bureaucratic, ideological and material frameworks that condition practices of and ideas about government and participation in politics. While citizenship regimes may define the limits of citizenship activities and identities, they are constantly shifting and dynamic. Work on welfare and development points to contemporary attempts to construct particular kinds of citizen through governmental and non-governmental action (Cruikshank 1999; Robins et al. 2008). Under contemporary neoliberal regimes such a citizen ideally behaves in a certain way, expressing and enacting values of entrepreneurship and self-reliance, especially with respect to her welfare and that of her family. A range of state and non-state agencies are involved in these processes, as illustrated by the example of micro-credit NGOs and their international donors (Lazar, this volume, Chapter 13). Much of the work on development interventions shows the creation of a particular citizenship regime through a complex interaction between a range of actors, including the local state, NGOs, national governments and transnational para-statal agencies such as the UN or the World Bank.

Although not always directly acknowledged, a similar range of actors come together in one of the most important ways that states create citizens, that is, education – or, better, schooling. National schooling systems have long been recognized as central to the development of national identity and civic commitment (Gellner 1983). Although so closely associated with nation-building projects, today education is transnational, and a key area for development intervention: from provision of universal primary education to human rights education programmes. The virtues promoted through schooling vary from country to county, valuing different languages, bodily and emotional dispositions (Benei 2008, and this volume, Chapter 14). The reproduction school of educational sociologists pointed out the connection between schooling and the creation of certain types of economic actors (Bourdieu and Passeron 1977; Willis 1977). These are citizenship regimes, attempts to create citizens with particular moral, political and economic attributes.

States try to create specific kinds of citizens through schooling by including civics classes in national curricula, but also in the ways that schools and pupil–teacher relationships are constructed and students' bodies disciplined (Lazar 2010; Levinson 2011). They may promote certain gender roles, a hierarchical relationship with authority or a commitment to democracy as a value in itself, but schooling is always a moral project, even when that moral quality is hidden behind seemingly technocratic language as with the example of 'human capital' discourses. Schools may also not always succeed in producing the kinds of citizens envisaged by normative ideologies, and anthropological analysis is very good at exposing the unintended consequences of such policies.

The moral nature of citizenship regimes associated with education should come as no surprise, since citizenship has always been understood in part as a project to work on the self in order to create good citizens. In Athens, creating a sense of duty towards the *polis* was considered an absolutely crucial element of citizenship, and implied the creation of particular kinds of persons with the sense that the individual was part of the collectivity and defined by it (Castoriadis 1992). Rousseau also advocated a programme of citizenship education in *Emile* (1762). Today, education continues to be inherent to citizenship whether implemented through political participation, schooling, participation in local voluntary projects or citizenship classes for immigrants. Education can be added to other cultural and moral projects of citizenship construction in the interface between people, policy, markets and the state. These include the citizen as consumer – of public services, goods, lifestyles (García Canclini 2001; Lukose 2005), as knowledge worker in the information economy (Ong 2005), as auditor of transparent government (Hetherington 2011), as soldier or ex-soldier (Gill 1997).

A further important contribution of anthropological work has been to investigate how these processes of citizen construction are embodied, and thus gendered and ethnicized. Military service is of course a central institution of citizen education and construction (Gill 1997; Yuval-Davis 1997; Benei 2008). Historically, defending the state militarily was a key responsibility for citizens (recall article 9 of the 1805 Haiti constitution quoted earlier), and one of the ways that women were excluded from full citizenship (Yuval-Davis 1997). In contemporary Israel, military service is restricted not so much by gender as by ethnicity, since Israeli Arab citizens are not conscripted as Israeli Jewish citizens are, and many Israeli Arabs therefore do not perform military service (also for political reasons). The link between military service and many citizenship entitlements as well as a sense of belonging to the national project of Israel is one way, then, that citizenship has historically been restricted for Israeli Arabs (Kaplan 2000; Kanaaneh and Nusair 2010). Military service is only one example of the myriad ways that citizenship comes into being through the creation of embodied and emotional dispositions according to specific understandings of gender, ethnicity and sexuality.

Importantly, though, the processes of subject construction are not only top-down. This is possibly the most significant contribution of Aihwa Ong's (1996) seminal article, where she explicitly connected the more top-down 'being-made' to 'self-making'. This aspect is important because it keeps an analytical focus on the agency of citizens, as well as of those claiming citizenship or claiming better citizenship. A body of work has thus emerged on how people frame and make claims of the state – for example for disability benefits for those affected by the explosion of the Chernobyl nuclear reactor (Petryna 2002), or for regularization of land titles in the peripheral neighbourhoods of São Paulo (Holston 2008). These studies bring out the complex relationships between people and state bureaucracy, and between people and law, as citizens operate in the gaps between expectations of resolution, certainty and buttressing of privilege that are usually associated with the public face of the legal system and realities of specific legal processes. As the ethnographies illustrate, the room for manoeuvre that citizens enjoy is not completely free, but constrained by legal and political regimes and by the languages of political action available to actors.

In some spaces, the processes of claims-making are articulated through a local language of citizenship, as in Latin America, especially Brazil (Dagnino 2003), or South Africa, where HIV/AIDS activists have successfully mobilized using the language of citizenship to demand antiretroviral treatment from the state (Robins and von Lieres 2004). The language of citizenship as a means of articulating claims usually names a claim to rights: rights to medical treatment, to legalization of property, to self-government, etc. As a result, for many theorists of citizenship, including anthropologists, the link between citizenship claims-making and rights is irrefutable and exclusive (Mandel 2008; Isin 2009). However, although the connection between citizenship and rights is often assumed, citizenship is in fact linked to languages of rights in quite specific (liberal) political contexts. Indeed, some anthropological work demonstrates that political claims and talk of membership – i.e. citizenship – can also be articulated through different languages, such as obligations (Englund 2008), or the naturalized membership of a collectivity (Lazar 2008, 2012). This may reflect a non-liberal, possibly communitarian vision of citizenship. The recognition of languages of citizenship other than that of rights opens up analytical space for research into non-normative citizenships.

The scales of citizenship

The move away from a theory of citizenship as purely a legal status towards a position where citizenship is analysed as a complex bundle of practices constituting political membership is now well established. However, it is less common to question exactly what the political community of which citizens are citizens is, or of which non-citizens are claiming citizenship. The dominant version of that political community remains the nation-state, following Marshall. Hence, anthropologists such as Ruth Mandel (2008, and this volume, Chapter 24), Trevor Stack (2003) and Richard Werbner (2004) have explored citizenship extremely productively as a way of discussing the relationship between the nation(-state) and immigrants, town-dwellers and elites respectively. In practice, though, there is no reason to yoke citizenship solely to the nation-state, and indeed the scale at which we perceive a given political community has been opened to question by other anthropological and historical work.

In modern times the dominant political community is most often the (nation-)state, but in early modern Europe it was the city, and today some of the most relevant political communities of advanced capitalism operate on a supra-national scale. This may be global, as in the ideas of cosmopolitanism, world citizenship and human rights, but also transnational, as for activist groups, citizen-migrants, diasporic groups and religious networks (Hannerz 1990; Ong 1999; Glick Schiller 2005, and this volume, Chapter 19; Nguyen 2005; Siu 2005, and this volume, Chapter 18). The work on transnational migrants links many of the questions of citizenship discussed in this Introduction, including membership, nationality, identity, cultural citizenship and political practice. The dual or even multiple nature of people's citizenship in practice highlights cultural aspects of political belonging and denaturalizes the automatic equation of citizenship with the nation-state of residence. Still other political communities may be non-state or stateless, as in the citizenship formations resulting from humanitarian aid management in post-1948 Gaza (Feldman 2007, and this volume, Chapter 20). So, what the *polis* is at any given point and in any given context needs to be established.

As with the transnational dimension, local citizenship of the city is of equal theoretical importance to citizenship of the nation. Engin Isin (2007) has argued that the state must articulate itself through the city: states, empires, leagues and republics have all been performances enacted in practices that can happen only in the city. One might not wish to go quite this far for the case of countries with considerable rural populations, but political theorists are increasingly highlighting the city as a focus and locus of political action today. David Harvey (2012) argues that claiming the right to define the city is a crucial contemporary site for resistance to capital. Such action may not simply be urban protest or social movements, but, as Dorothy Solinger shows, may also be constituted by citizens making a life for themselves in the city (1999, and this volume, Chapter 22). James Holston (2008) demonstrates how slum dwellers' dogged persistence with legal claims to regularize their property rights constitute a claim for citizenship. Yet the contests over city space may also expose undemocratic citizenship formations, such as the privatization of space in gated communities and through fear of crime (Caldeira 2000, and this volume, Chapter 21). This is all the more acute in conditions of contemporary neoliberalism, leading to new forms of urban governmentality in policing and service provision (Robins 2002).

The recognition of the importance of local and urban citizenship of the city pushes us into a consideration of how it operates and interacts with national citizenship in particular contexts. In modern Western political thought, which Isin characterizes as 'scalar', spaces and territories are conceived of as nested scales: cities subordinated to provinces, which are subordinated to the nation-state in a hierarchical and exclusive relationship. National citizenship thus is supposed to overtake and replace urban citizenship. In Europe, for example, modern (nation-)states emerged from states that were a conglomeration of separate self-governing towns, and states attempted to remove layers of allegiances between them and the individual, but failed to do so, leaving what is often called 'civil society' as intermediary. That intermediary sphere is often concentrated in the city; it is the local public sphere, which incorporates much more than the institutions of government. Urban public spheres include the streets, where people demonstrate and work, as well as the many forms of association where citizens negotiate the building and defining of society, even act violently towards one another (Holston 1999, and this volume, Chapter 12). Thus, the location for the practices of citizenship is a key question for the analysis of citizenship. The logical realm for political action for most citizens has always been their local area, and people are often suspicious of those who choose to extend their political action beyond that, and become professional politicians rather than citizens (Lister 1997). Furthermore, as Nikolas Rose (2000) argued, urban governmentality inheres in various arenas, and the 'new games of citizenship' often coalesce around politicized notions of community, that are negotiated, enacted and resisted in the public spheres of the city. Iris Marion Young's (1990) proposal of the 'unoppressive city' to counter this version of communitarianism is therefore an ideal type worthy of further examination. What ethnography can do is put into question such ideal types – of community or city – and examine which political collectivities are important in citizens' lives at any given time and place.

Citizenship and membership

However we define the political community under study, it is clear that citizenship as a language names membership, and this is the final important theme of the anthropology of citizenship I will review here. It is also a means of claiming membership, and commenting on the quality (or content, extent) of that membership. We can see the latter clearly with the distinctions between full and second-class citizenship (Rosaldo 1994b; Dagnino 1998) or formal and substantive citizenship (Holston 2001; Sassen 2003). James Holston (2001) understands substantive citizenship as the ability that citizens have in reality to claim rights that they possess through their formal status as citizen, 'formal membership, based on principles of incorporation into the nation-state', which contrasts with 'the substantive distribution of the rights, meanings, institutions, and practices that membership entails to those deemed citizens' (Holston 2008: 7). As I discussed earlier, liberal citizenship has held out the promise of universal equality achieved through universal formal citizenship, at least for particular categories of persons; but despite this promise, citizenship regimes have developed differently in different historical contexts. This recognition is one of the most important contributions that anthropologists and historians have made to understanding citizenship.

Holston (2008) argues that Brazilian citizenship developed as differentiated, but suggests that the developments of the peripheral settlements of São Paulo from the mid-twentieth century onwards have challenged that differential treatment. They did so by basing an 'insurgent citizenship', a claim to rights, precisely on a form of the quality of property ownership that had shaped differentialization in civil citizenship historically. This has been facilitated by the rise in literacy that resulted from widespread urbanization, and is therefore a matter of urban citizenship. Evelina Dagnino (1998, 2005) describes the social movement politics that emerged around the concept of citizenship in urban Brazil, where activists argued that the concept of citizenship amplified the concept of politics itself, to demand active social subjects with the right to have rights and to define what those rights are. This Arendtian formulation (of the right to have rights) was also particularly powerful for Latin American feminists in the 1990s (Molyneux and Lazar 2003).

In some contexts, substantive (urban) citizenship does not necessarily require formal (national) citizenship status, as in the case of illegal Mexican immigrants in California who have successfully gained some social and civil rights even when they lack political rights (Holston 2001). Saskia Sassen (2003) makes a similar distinction, when she outlines two types of citizens: 'unauthorized yet recognized' and 'authorized yet not recognized'. She uses the example of undocumented immigrants to illustrate the former category, and explains as follows:

> The daily practices by undocumented immigrants as part of their daily life in the community where they reside – such as raising a family, schooling children, holding a job – earn them citizenship claims in the US even as the formal status and, more narrowly, legalization may continue to evade them. There are dimensions of citizenship, such as strong community ties and participation in civic activities, which are being enacted informally through these practices. These practices produce an at least partial recognition of them as full social beings. (Sassen 2003: 12)

For the second category, Sassen uses the example of women as housewives, as a case of 'those who are full citizens yet not recognized as political subjects'. A number of different groups of citizens also fall into this latter category, such as indigenous peoples who achieved full formal citizenship status well before they were recognized as full political subjects on their own terms (if that recognition has in fact yet occurred); migrants who gained their citizenship through naturalization; or their children and grandchildren (de Genova 2005; Mandel 2008; Fikes 2009).

In the processes of non-citizens' claims to citizenship (or of second-class citizens' claims for full citizenship), the nature of citizenship itself changes. For Sassen (2003), citizenship is therefore an 'incomplete' category, which develops through a dialectic whereby the practices of those excluded from full citizenship come to define and/or influence the terms of their subsequent inclusion. Indeed, often the struggle for inclusion (or against exclusion) is what changes the nature of the political system, by creating new laws or constitutions, new categories of people and political subjects, or by changing public opinion. Social and political practices of membership are a crucial part of this dynamic.

But if citizenship is a means of claiming membership or better-quality membership, it is also a means of excluding others from that membership or shaping them in contrast to the normative citizen. Engin Isin argues that 'citizenship and otherness are … really not two different conditions, but two aspects of the ontological condition that makes politics possible' (2002: x) and that citizenship is 'that kind of identity within a city or state that certain agents constitute as virtuous, good, righteous, and superior, and differentiate it from strangers, outsiders, and aliens who they constitute as their alterity via various solidaristic, agonistic, and alienating strategies and technologies. Citizenship exists through its alterity and strategies' (Isin 2002: 35–36). Citizenship is thus constituted by both the virtue of the individual citizen as political actor and the nature of political practice. Constituting non-citizens as other can lead to a positive politics of dissent and resistance and to the broadening of citizenship, as discussed above, but can also be highly restrictive, not to say violent.

The archetypal non-citizen is the foreign migrant, but 'migrant' is in practice not a simple identity category, not least because migration is often constituted within the force field of colonial and neocolonial relations. The transformation from colonial subject to imperial citizen and then immigrant other is the contingent outcome of a set of political choices, as Fred Cooper (2009) has shown for France. Most migrants have travelled to their host country for reasons of labour, and restrictions on their citizenship status that keep them as resident aliens often facilitate exploitation in the form of low wages and poor working conditions. They are especially vulnerable to government by state officials (Fikes 2009), and where migrants are kept wholly illegal they are subject to the insecurity of constant risk of deportation (de Genova 2005, and this volume, Chapter 25). Culturally, the presence of 'outsiders' within an imagined 'national body' is not constituted as a problem for the dominant group of citizens, but for the non-citizens themselves (Mandel 2008, and this volume, Chapter 24). They become ciphers, representing threat, hypersexuality (Partridge 2008), cultural backwardness or diversity and multiculturalism. They are marked out, subject to discrimination and racism, even when they have become fully legal citizens, over generations (Gilroy 2002 [1987]). Kesha Fikes (2009) points out that even antiracism campaigns constitute the migrant as outsider rather than (black) citizen.

Such operations of sovereignty are the other side of the coin to the operations of governmentality discussed earlier. They may become violent, as when groups use languages of autochthony to justify attacks on others, who are constituted as migrant interlopers in the hegemonic sovereign discourse regardless of longstanding histories of mobility and transnationalism (Marshall-Fratani 2006, and this volume, Chapter 23). Thus, as boundaries are drawn between citizens and non-citizens, and legal frameworks mobilized to emphasize some group's otherness, the status of citizen and non-citizen can become hardened, and citizenship restricted, not amplified.

Future Directions

One of the results of the growth in the anthropology of citizenship has been a proliferation of new concepts derived from the addition of a qualifying adjective to the word citizenship. We have biological citizenship, flexible citizenship, agrarian citizenship, insurgent citizenship, therapeutic citizenship, urban citizenship, pharmaceutical citizenship, formal and substantive citizenship, etc. The specificity of the qualifying adjective is an important conceptual move, since it recognizes the diversity in modalities of citizenship today and acknowledges that liberal citizenship is one modality among many. However, in the proliferation of adjectives we still risk assuming that we know what citizenship itself is, that the key is the 'biological', 'urban', 'differentiated' aspects, and that citizenship does not require explanation as a concept in its own right. Indeed, we should be wary of all essentialisms and acknowledge that 'liberal citizenship' must itself be plural, as attested by the varieties of liberalism both in historical reality and political thought.

At its most elemental a focus on citizenship is a way of approaching the political; hence the inclusion in this reader of some of the most foundational texts in political philosophy. As a charter for ethnographic explorations of political membership, subjectivity and agency, they are unrivalled; but they can also be a foil against which to develop the distinctive contribution that anthropology can bring to the field. Much has already been achieved within the hugely vibrant area of ethnography of citizenship, as reflected in the contents of this reader. There are, however, many equally exciting threads that future ethnographers could pursue, and possible directions for the future include using citizenship as an optic onto agency, work, the self, collectivity, democracy, the state and political subjectivity more generally.

This may involve a decoupling of citizenship from normative formulations, such as its connection to rights and democracy. If so, anthropologists will need to bear in mind two important questions. First, although it is important to take a critical position to those understandings of citizenship perceived as normative, we do risk ending up in an enclave of cultural relativism where the only argument we can make is that citizenship *there* is different from citizenship *here*. While this is undoubtedly an important argument, anthropology has significantly more to contribute to our understanding of citizenship. Second, it will be important not to lose sight of the political implications of such a strategy. Studying citizenship as political practice often obliges us to take a political stand, perhaps alongside those advocating for rights at individual or group level, or critical of mainstream or counter-hegemonic notions of citizenship. However, a non-normative perspective could allow a future anthropology of citizenship to profitably explore the languages and practices of political membership, agency, and constitution of varied political communities, without assuming liberal parameters for either.

The most productive avenue for anthropologists is undoubtedly that of continuing to follow the ethnographic material, deriving new concepts for analysis from the real-life political experiences of our informants. If we recognize that from time to time our view of what citizenship *is* can be heavily coloured by a normative assumption about what it *should be*, we are then better placed to see how citizenship is configured in practice, and to explore the historical, material and cultural reasons for that configuration. Furthermore, a better understanding of the development of those normative assumptions and ideas will open space for fresh approaches to some of the important questions also discussed within the political philosophy of citizenship. There is enormous potential for creative dialogue between anthropological work on questions such as subjectivity, selfhood, ethics, property and political practice and the understandings of rights, individuality, subjecthood, property and slavery embedded in political theory and contemporary practice. Through such a dialogue, we should be able to derive new questions and analytical approaches to political life.

This reader thus takes up the challenge to draw together the existing body of work on citizenship in a way that opens up new possibilities for future research. It covers a wide range of analytical approaches to citizenship, organized by means of a two-pronged strategy: theoretical foundations and ethnographic explorations. The readings in Part I are drawn from political philosophy, historical texts and anthropology. They are organized in part through a division into two dominant traditions of liberal and civic republicans, although in practice most tend to mix elements of the two. They finish with some of the early and foundational texts in anthropological theory of citizenship. Philosophers such as Aristotle, Rousseau, Locke and Arendt are thus placed side by side with more contemporary political theorists such as Marshall and Young and key anthropologists of citizenship such as Ong, Holston and Rosaldo. We see the commonalities between anthropological analyses that view citizenship as a set of practices especially related to participating in politics and the approaches of key political theorists, particularly those in the civic republican tradition.

By titling Part II 'Ethnographic Explorations', I do not mean to imply that there is a distinction between theory and ethnography (Englund and Leach 2000). Indeed, the readings here are both ethnographically detailed and cross different theoretical perspectives. The emphasis is on detailed ethnographic discussion of citizenship in specific contexts. The readings cover the following broad areas: the relationship between citizens and the state, both in terms of citizenship regimes enacted upon citizens and in terms of more 'bottom-up' uses of citizenship and other idioms to make claims of the state; the constitution of political communities at different scales, from sub- to supra-national; and finally the relationship between the citizen and the non-citizen in the constitution of modern political entities. Each section has a very brief introduction, which includes suggestions for further reading on the topic.

NOTES

1 http://www.thecoca-colacompany.com/citizenship/; http://www.microsoft.com/about/corporatecitizen-
  ship/en-us/; http://www.cnbc.com/id/38426553/New_Chief_Pledges_BP_Will_Be_Good_Corporate_
  Citizen (article dated 27 July 2010). All accessed 22 August 2012.
2 The distinction between philosophical communitarians and political communitarians comes from
  Elizabeth Frazer (1998). Members of the latter group could also include many US and UK politicians
  from the 1990s onwards, especially those attempting to enact 'Third Way' politics (Gledhilll 2004) or
  promote 'social capital' (Putnam 2001).
3 See, for example, Morris (1994) on the anthropology of the self, Spear (2003) and Sullivan and
  Brunnegger (2011) on customary law in Africa and indigenous law in Latin America, Goodale
  (2008) on human rights and Cooke and Kothari (2001) on development.
4 Although see Avineri and de-Shalit (1992), Shafir (1998) and Rosen and Wolff (1999) for good
  collections of relevant texts in political theory that can serve as starting points. Discussions of
  citizenship in political theory include Biener (1995), van Steenbergen (1994) and Heater (1999).

REFERENCES

Abrams, Philip, 1988 [1977]. Notes on the difficulty of studying the state. *Journal of Historical Sociology* 1: 58–89.

Arendt, Hannah, 1951. The decline of the nation-state and the end of the rights of man. In *The Origins of Totalitarianism*. New York: Harcourt, Brace, and Company, pp. 266–298.

Arendt, Hannah, 1998 [1958]. *The Human Condition*. Chicago and London: University of Chicago Press.

Aretxaga, Begoña, 2003. Maddening states. *Annual Review of Anthropology* 32: 393–410.

Asad, Talal, 2002 [1972]. Market model, class structure and consent: a reconsideration of Swat political organization. In *The Anthropology of Politics: A Reader in Ethnography, Theory, and Critique*, J. Vincent, ed. Oxford: Blackwell, pp. 65–82.

Avineri, S., and A. de-Shalit, 1992. *Communitarianism and Individualism*. Oxford: Oxford University Press.

Bailey, F. G., 1969. *Stratagems and Spoils: A Social Anthropology of Politics*. Oxford: Blackwell.

Bailey, F. G., 1971. Gifts and poisons. In *Gifts and Poisons: The Politics of Reputation*, F. G. Bailey, ed. Oxford: Blackwell, pp. 1–26.

Baitenmann, Helga, 2005. Counting on state subjects: state formation and citizenship in twentieth-century Mexico. In *State Formation: Anthropological Perspectives*, C. Krohn-Hansen and K. G. Nustad, eds. Anthropology, Culture and Society. London and Ann Arbor MI: Pluto Press, pp. 171–194.

Banerjee, Mukulika, 2008. Democracy, sacred and everyday: an ethnographic case from India. In *Democracy: Anthropological Approaches*, J. Paley, ed. Santa Fe: School for Advanced Research Press, pp. 63–96.

Barron, Anne, 1993. The illusions of the 'I': citizenship and the politics of identity. In *Closure or Critique: New Directions in Legal Theory*, A. Norrie, ed. Edinburgh: Edinburgh University Press, pp. 80–100.

Barth, Fredrik, 1965. *Political Leadership among Swat Pathans*. London: Athlone.

Barth, Fredrik, 1969. *Ethnic Groups and Boundaries: The Social Organization of Culture Difference*. Bergen: Universitetsforlaget; London: Allen and Unwin.

Barth, Fredrik, 2007. Overview: sixty years in anthropology. *Annual Review of Anthropology* 36(1): 1–16.

Behrends, A., S. P. Reyna and G. Schlee, 2011. *Crude Domination: An Anthropology of Oil*. Oxford: Berghahn Books.

Benei, Véronique, 2008. *Schooling Passions: Nation, History, and Language in Contemporary Western India*. Stanford, California: Stanford University Press.

Benhabib, Seyla, 2004. *The Rights of Others: Aliens, Residents and Citizens*. Cambridge: Cambridge University Press.

Biener, R., 1995. Introduction. In *Theorizing Citizenship*, R. Beiner, ed. Albany: State University of New York Press.

Bourdieu, Pierre, and Jean-Claude Passeron, 1977. *Reproduction in Education, Society, and Culture*. R. Nice, trans. London: Sage.

Buffington, Robert, 2003. *Forjando patria*: anthropology, criminology, and the post-revolutionary discourse on citizenship. In *Emancipating Cultural Pluralism*, C. E. Toffolo, ed. SUNY Series in National Identities. Albany NY: State University of New York Press, pp. 81–104.

Caldeira, Teresa, 2000. *City of Walls: Crime, Segregation, and Citizenship in São Paulo*. Berkeley: University of California Press.

Castoriadis, Cornelius, 1992. *Philosophy, Politics, Autonomy*. D. Curtis, trans. New York: Oxford University Press.

Cooke, Bill, and Uma Kothari, 2001. *Participation: The New Tyranny?* London and New York: Zed Books.

Cooper, Frederick, 2009. From imperial inclusion to republican exclusion? France's ambiguous postwar trajectory. In *Frenchness and the African Diaspora: Identity and Uprising in Contemporary France*, C. Tshimanga, D. Gondola and P. Bloom, eds. Bloomington: Indiana University Press, pp. 91–119.

Coronil, Fernando, 1997. *The Magical State: Nature, Money, and Modernity in Venezuela*. Chicago: University of Chicago Press.

Corrigan, Philip, and Derek Sayer, 1985. *The Great Arch: State Formation, Cultural Revolution and the Rise of Capitalism*. Oxford: Blackwell.

Cruikshank, Barbara, 1999. *The Will to Empower: Democratic Citizens and Other Subjects*. Ithaca, New York and London: Cornell University Press.

Dagnino, Evelina, 1998. Culture, citizenship and democracy: changing discourses and practices of the Latin American left. In *Cultures of Politics, Politics of Cultures: Re-visioning Latin American Social Movements*, S. E. Alvarez, E. Dagnino and A. Escobar, eds. Boulder, Colorado: Westview Press, pp. 33–63.

Dagnino, Evelina, 2003. *Citizenship in Latin America*. Special issue, *Latin American Perspectives* 30(2).

Dagnino, Evelina, 2005. 'We all have rights, but ...' Contesting concepts of citizenship in Brazil. In *Inclusive Citizenship: Meanings and Expressions*, N. Kabeer, ed. London: Zed Books, pp. 149–163.

de Genova, Nicholas, 2005. *Working the Boundaries: Race, Space, and 'Illegality' in Mexican Chicago*. Durham, North Carolina and London: Duke University Press.

de Gouges, Olympe, 2003 [1791]. *Déclaration des droits de la femme et de la citoyenne*. Paris: Mille et une nuits.

Englund, Harri, 2008. Extreme poverty and existential obligations: beyond morality in the anthropology of Africa? *Social Analysis* 52(3): 33–50.

Englund, Harri, 2012. Human rights and village headmen in Malawi: translation beyond vernacularisation. In *Law against the State: Ethnographic Forays into Law's Transformations*, J. Eckert, Brian Donahoe, C. Strümpell and Z. Özlem Biner, eds. Cambridge: Cambridge University Press, pp. 70–93.

Englund, Harri, and James Leach, 2000. Ethnography and the meta-narratives of modernity. *Current Anthropology* 41(2): 225–248.

Evans-Pritchard, Edward, 1940. *The Nuer*. Oxford: Clarendon Press.

Faubion, James D., 2011. *An Anthropology of Ethics*. Cambridge: Cambridge University Press.

Feldman, Ilana, 2007. Difficult distinctions: refugee law, humanitarian practice, and political identification in Gaza. *Cultural Anthropology* 22(1): 129–169.

Ferguson, James G., 2002. Of mimicry and membership: Africans and the 'New World Society'. *Cultural Anthropology* 17(4): 551–569.

Fikes, Kesha, 2009. *Managing African Portugal: The Citizen-Migrant Distinction*. Durham, North Carolina: Duke University Press.

Fortes, Meyer, and Edward Evans-Pritchard, 1940. *African Political Systems*. London: Oxford University Press, for the International African Institute.

Frazer, Elizabeth, 1998. Communitarianism. In *New Political Thought: An Introduction*, A. Lent, ed. London: Lawrence & Wishart, pp. 112–125.

García Canclini, Nestor, 2001. *Consumers and Citizens: Globalization and Multicultural Conflicts*, G. Yudice, trans. Minneapolis and London: University of Minnesota Press.

Geertz, Clifford, 1980. *Negara: The Theatre State in Nineteenth-Century Bali*. Princeton, New Jersey: Princeton University Press.

Gellner, Ernest, 1983. *Nations and Nationalism*. Oxford: Blackwell.

Gill, Lesley, 1997. Creating citizens, making men: the military and masculinity in Bolivia. *Cultural Anthropology* 12(4): 527–550.

Gilroy, Paul, 2002 [1987]. *'There Ain't no Black in the Union Jack': The Cultural Politics of Race and Nation*. London: Routledge.

Gledhilll, John, 2004. 'Disappearing the poor?' A critique of the new wisdoms of social democracy in an age of globalization. In *The Anthropology of Development and Globalization*, M. Edelman and A. Haugerud, eds. Oxford: Blackwell, pp. 382–390.

Glick Schiller, Nina, 2005. Transborder citizenship: an outcome of legal pluralism within transnational social fields. In *Mobile People, Mobile Law: Expanding Legal Relations in a Contracting World*, F. von Benda-Beckmann, K. von Benda-Beckmann and A. Griffiths, eds. London: Ashgate, pp. 27–49.

Goodale, Mark, ed., 2008. *Human Rights: An Anthropological Reader*. Oxford: Blackwell.

Gupta, Akhil, 1995. Blurred boundaries: the discourse of corruption, the culture of politics, and the imagined state. *American Ethnologist* 22(2): 375–402.

Gutmann, Matthew, 2002. *The Romance of Democracy: Compliant Defiance in Contemporary Mexico*. Berkeley: University of California Press.

Hannerz, Ulf, 1990. Cosmopolitans and locals in world culture. In *Global Culture: Nationalism, Globalization and Modernity*, M. Featherstone, ed. London: Sage, pp. 237–252.

Harper, Richard, 2000. The social organisation of the IMF's mission work. In *Audit Cultures: Anthropological Studies in Accountability, Ethics and the Academy*, M. Strathern, ed. London: Routledge, pp. 21–53.

Harvey, David, 2012. *Rebel Cities: From the Right to the City to the Urban Revolution*. London: Verso.

Heater, Derek, 1999. *What is Citizenship?* Cambridge: Polity Press.

Hetherington, Kregg, 2011. *Guerrilla Auditors: The Politics of Transparency in Neoliberal Paraguay*. Durham, North Carolina and London: Duke University Press.

Holston, James, 1999. Spaces of insurgent citizenship. In *Cities and Citizenship*, J. Holston and A. Appadurai, eds. Durham, North Carolina: Duke University Press, pp. 155–173.

Holston, James, 2001. Urban citizenship and globalization. In *Global City-Regions*, A. J. Scott, ed. New York: Oxford University Press, pp. 325–348.

Holston, James, 2008. *Insurgent Citizenship: Disjunctions of Democracy and Modernity in Brazil*. Princeton, New Jersey: Princeton University Press.

Holston, James, and Arjun Appadurai, eds, 1999. *Cities and Citizenship*. Durham, North Carolina: Duke University Press.

Inda, Jonathan Xavier, and Renato Rosaldo, eds, 2008. *The Anthropology of Globalization: A Reader*, 2nd edn. Oxford: Blackwell.

Isin, Engin, 2000. *Democracy, Citizenship and the Global City*. London: Routledge.

Isin, Engin, 2002. *Being Political: Genealogies of Citizenship*. Minneapolis: University of Minnesota Press.

Isin, Engin, 2007. City.state: critique of scalar thought. *Citizenship Studies* 11(2): 211–228.

Isin, Engin, 2009. Citizenship in flux: the figure of the activist citizen. *Subjectivity* 29: 367–388.

Juris, Jeffrey S., 2008. *Networking Futures: The Movements against Corporate Globalization*. Experimental Futures: Technological Lives, Scientific Arts, Anthropological Voices. Durham, North Carolina and London: Duke University Press.

Kanaaneh, Rhoda Ann, and Isis Nusair, 2010. *Displaced at Home: Ethnicity and Gender among Palestinians in Israel*. Albany: State University of New York Press.

Kapferer, Bruce, 1995. The performance of categories: plays of identity in Africa and Australia. In *The Urban Context: Ethnicity, Social Networks and Situational Analysis*, A. Rogers and S. Vertovec, eds. Oxford: Berg, pp. 55–80.

Kaplan, Danny, 2000. The military as a second Bar Mitzvah: combat service as an initiation-rite to Zionist masculinity. In *Imagined Masculinities: Male Identity and Culture in the Modern Middle East*, M. Ghoussoub and E. Sinclair-Webb, eds. London: El-Saqi Books, pp. 127–144.

Kymlicka, Will, 1995. *Multicultural Citizenship: A Liberal Theory of Minority Rights*. Oxford: Clarendon Press.

Laidlaw, James, 2002. For an anthropology of ethics and freedom. *Journal of the Royal Anthropological Institute* 8(2): 311–332.

Lazar, Sian, 2008. *El Alto, Rebel City: Self and Citizenship in Andean Bolivia*. Durham, North Carolina: Duke University Press.

Lazar, Sian, 2010. Schooling and critical citizenship: pedagogies of political agency in El Alto, Bolivia. *Anthropology and Education Quarterly* 41(2): 181–205.

Lazar, Sian, 2012. Disjunctive comparison: citizenship and trade unionism in Bolivia and Argentina. *Journal of the Royal Anthropological Institute* 18(2): 349–368.

Leach, Edmund, 1954. *Political Systems of Highland Burma: A Study of Kachin Social Structure*. London: London School of Economics and Political Science.

Levinson, Bradley, 2011. Toward an anthropology of (democratic) citizenship education. In *A Companion to the Anthropology of Education*, B. Levinson and M. Pollock, eds. Chichester: Wiley Blackwell, pp. 279–298.

LiPuma, Edward, and Benjamin Lee, 2004. *Financial Derivatives and the Globalization of Risk*. Durham, North Carolina: Duke University Press.

Lister, Ruth, 1997. *Citizenship: Feminist Perspectives*. London: Macmillan.

Lukose, Ritty, 2005. Empty citizenship: protesting politics in the era of globalization. *Cultural Anthropology* 20(4): 506–533.

Mamdani, Mahmood, 1996. *Citizen and Subject: Contemporary Africa and the Legacy of Late Colonialism*. Kampala: Fountain; London: James Currey.

Mandel, Ruth, 2008. *Cosmopolitan Anxieties: Turkish Challenges to Citizenship and Belonging in Germany*. Durham, North Carolina and London: Duke University Press.

Marshall, T. H., 1983 [1950]. Citizenship and social class. In *States and Societies*, D. Held *et al.*, eds. Oxford: Martin Robertson, in association with The Open University, pp. 248–260.

Marshall-Fratani, Ruth, 2006. The war of 'who is who': autochthony, nationalism, and citizenship in the Ivoirian crisis. *African Studies Review* 49(2): 9–43.

Mauss, Marcel, 1979 [1938]. A category of the human mind: the notion of person, the notion of 'self'. Part III of *Sociology and Psychology*, Ben Brewer, trans. London: Routledge, pp. 57–94.

Michelutti, Lucia, 2008. *The Vernacularisation of Democracy: Politics, Caste and Religion in India*. London and Delhi: Routledge.

Mill, John Stuart, 1991. *On Liberty and Other Essays*. Oxford: Oxford University Press.

Mintz, Sidney W., 1985. *Sweetness and Power: The Place of Sugar in Modern History*. New York: Elisabeth Sifton Books.

Mitchell, James Clyde, 1959. *The Kalela Dance: Aspects of Social Relationships among Urban Africans in Northern Rhodesia*. Manchester: Manchester University Press.

Mitchell, Timothy, 2002. *Rule of Experts: Egypt, Techno-Politics, Modernity*. Berkeley: University of California Press.

Mitchell, Timothy, 2006 [1999]. Society, economy, and the state effect. In *Anthropology of the State: A Reader*. A. Sharma and A. Gupta, eds. Oxford: Blackwell, pp. 169–186.

Moller Otkin, Susan, 1991. John Rawls: *Justice as Fairness* – for whom? In *Feminist Interpretations and Political Theory*, M. L. Shanley and C. Pateman, eds. London: Polity Press, pp. 181–198.

Molyneux, Maxine, and Sian Lazar, 2003. *Doing the Rights Thing: Rights-Based Development and Latin American NGOs*. London: Intermediate Technology.

Morris, Brian, 1994. *Anthropology of the Self: The Individual in Cultural Perspective*. London: Pluto Press.

Nguyen, Vinh-Kim, 2005. Antiretroviral globalism, biopolitics, and therapeutic citizenship. In *Global Assemblages: Technology, Poltics and Ethics as Anthropological Problems*, A. Ong and S. Collier, eds. Oxford: Blackwell, pp. 124–144.

Nugent, David, 2008. Democracy otherwise: struggles over popular rule in the northern Peruvian Andes. In *Democracy: Anthropological Approaches*, J. Paley, ed. Santa Fe: School for Advanced Research Press, pp. 21–62.

Nyamnjoh, Francis B., 2003. Chieftaincy and the negotiation of might and right in Botswana democracy. *Journal of Contemporary African Studies* 21(2): 233–250.

Ong, Aihwa, 1996. Cultural citizenship as subject-making: immigrants negotiate racial and cultural boundaries in the United States [and Comments and Reply]. *Current Anthropology* 37(5): 737–762.

Ong, Aihwa, 1999. *Flexible Citizenship: The Cultural Logics of Transnationality.* Durham, North Carolina: Duke University Press.

Ong, Aihwa, 2003. *Buddha is Hiding: Refugees, Citizenship, the New America.* Berkeley: University of California Press.

Ong, Aihwa, 2005. Ecologies of expertise: assembling flows, managing citizenship. In *Global Assemblages: Technology, Politics, and Ethics as Anthropological Problems,* A. Ong and S. J. Collier, eds. Oxford: Blackwell, pp. 337–354.

Ong, Aihwa, and Stephen J. Collier, 2005. *Global Assemblages: Technology, Politics, and Ethics as Anthropological Problems.* Oxford: Blackwell.

Paley, Julia, 2001. *Marketing Democracy: Power and Social Movements in Post-Dictatorship Chile.* Berkeley and London: University of California Press.

Paley, Julia, 2008. Introduction. In *Democracy: Anthropological Approaches,* J. Paley, ed. Santa Fe: School for Advanced Research Press, pp. 3–21.

Partridge, Damani, 2008. We were dancing in the club, not on the Berlin Wall: black bodies, street bureaucrats, and exclusionary incorporation into the new Europe. *Cultural Anthropology* 23(4): 660–687.

Petryna, Adriana, 2002. *Life Exposed: Biological Citizens after Chernobyl.* Princeton, New Jersey: Princeton University Press.

Povinelli, Elizabeth A., 2002. *The Cunning of Recognition: Indigenous Alterities and the Making of Australian Multiculturalism.* Durham, North Carolina and London: Duke University Press.

Pratten, David, and Atreyee Sen, 2007. *Global Vigilantes.* London: Hurst.

Putnam, Robert, 2001. *Bowling Alone: The Collapse and Revival of American Community.* New York: Simon & Schuster.

Rajak, Dinah, 2011. *In Good Company: An Anatomy of Corporate Social Responsibility:* Stanford, California: Stanford University Press.

Rawls, John, 1972. *A Theory of Justice.* Oxford: Clarendon Press.

Robins, Steven, 2002. At the limits of spatial governmentality: a message from the tip of Africa. *Third World Quarterly* 23(4): 665–689.

Robins, Steven, Andrea Cornwall and Bettina von Lieres, 2008. Rethinking 'citizenship' in the post-colony. *Third World Quarterly* 29(6): 1069–1086.

Robins, Steven, and Bettina von Lieres, 2004. Remaking citizenship, unmaking marginalization: the treatment action campaign in post-apartheid South Africa. *Canadian Journal of African Studies / Revue Canadienne des Etudes Africaines* 38(3): 575–586.

Rosaldo, Renato, 1994a. Cultural citizenship and educational democracy. *Cultural Anthropology* 9(3): 402–411.

Rosaldo, Renato, 1994b. Cultural citizenship in San Jose, California. *PoLAR* 17(2): 57–63.

Rose, Nikolas, 2000. Governing cities, governing citizens. In *Democracy, Citizenship and the Global City,* E. Isin, ed.. London: Routledge, pp. 95–109.

Rosen, Michael, and Jonathan Wolff, eds, 1999. *Political Thought.* Oxford Reader. Oxford: Oxford University Press.

Rousseau, Jean-Jacques, 1762. *Emile.* Project Gutenberg, http://www.gutenberg.org/ebooks/5427.

Sandel, Michael, 1984. The procedural republic and the unencumbered self. *Political Theory* 12(1): 81–96.

Sassen, Saskia, 2003. The repositioning of citizenship: emergent subjects and spaces for politics. *Berkeley Journal of Sociology* 46: 4–25.

Shafir, Gershon, ed., 1998. *The Citizenship Debates: A Reader.* Minneapolis and London: University of Minnesota Press.

Shanley, Mary Lyndon, and Carole Pateman, 1991. *Feminist Interpretations and Political Theory.* University Park: Pennsylvania State University Press.

Sharma, Aradhana, and Akhil Gupta, eds, 2006. *The Anthropology of the State: A Reader.* Oxford: Blackwell.

Siu, Lok, 2005. *Memories of a Future Home: Diasporic Citizenship of Chinese in Panama.* Stanford, California: Stanford University Press.

Skocpol, Theda, 1985. Bringing the state back in: strategies of analysis in current research. In *Bringing the State Back In,* P. B. Evans, D. Rueschemeyer, T. Skocpol and F. H. Hinsley, eds. Cambridge and New York: Cambridge University Press, pp. 3–42.

Solinger, Dorothy, 1999. *Contesting Citizenship in Urban China: Peasant Migrants, the State, and the Logic of the Market.* Berkeley: University of California Press.

Spear, Thomas, 2003. Neo-traditionalism and the limits of invention in British colonial Africa. *Journal of African History* 44(1): 3–27.

Stack, Trevor, 2003. Citizens of towns, citizens of nations: the knowing of history in Mexico. *Critique of Anthropology* 23(2): 193–208.

Strathern, Marilyn, 2004. Losing (out on) intellectual resources. In *Law, Anthropology, and the Constitution of the Social,* A. Pottage and M. Mundy, eds. Cambridge: Cambridge University Press, pp. 201–233.

Sullivan, Kathleen, and Sandra Brunnegger, 2011. Introduction. *Studies in Law, Politics, and Society* 55: 3–17.

Swartz, M. J., V. W. Turner and A. Tuden, 2006 [1966]. *Political Anthropology.* New Brunswick, New Jersey: AldineTransaction.

Taussig, Michael, 1992. *The Nervous System.* New York and London: Routledge.

Taussig, Michael, 1997. *The Magic of the State.* London: Routledge.

Trouillot, Michel-Rolph, 2001. The anthropology of the state in the age of globalization. *Current Anthropology* 42(1): 125–138.

van Steenbergen, Bart, 1994. *The Condition of Citizenship.* London: Sage.

Vincent, Joan, 2002. *The Anthropology of Politics: A Reader in Ethnography, Theory, and Critique,* P. Shipton, ed. Oxford: Blackwell.

Walzer, Michael, 1982. *Spheres of Justice: A Defence of Pluralism and Equality.* Oxford: Martin Robertson.

Werbner, Richard, 2004. *Reasonable Radicals and Citizenship in Botswana: The Public Anthropology of Kalanga Elites.* Bloomington: Indiana University Press.

Willis, Paul, 1977. *Learning to Labour: How Working Class Kids Get Working Class Jobs.* Farnborough, Hants: Saxon House.

Wolf, Eric R., 1997 [1982]. *Europe and the People without History.* Berkeley: University of California Press.

Wollstonecraft, Mary, 1975 [1792]. *A Vindication of the Rights of Woman.* London: Penguin.

Young, Iris Marion, 1990. The ideal of community and the politics of difference. In *Feminism/Postmodernism,* L. Nicholson, ed. London: Routledge, pp. 300–323.

Yuval-Davis, Nira, 1997. *Gender and Nation.* London: Sage.

Part I
Theoretical Foundations

Introduction

By putting liberal theories of citizenship and political belonging after civic republicanism, the selection of readings for this part seeks to counteract assumptions in both popular conception and scholarly thought in the West that equate liberal citizenship with citizenship. If citizenship is a series of practices associated with the individual's relationship with the state (or political community), one constellation of those practices constitutes liberal citizenship – the right to vote and be elected, citizenship as the legal status of belonging to a specific nation-state, representative politics based on political parties and so on. However, one of the aims of this reader is to argue that this is only *one* possible constellation, and the pertinent question is what kinds of citizenship practices constitute a person's relationship with the *polis* or state in any particular context.

Although dominant lay understandings of citizenship in Anglo-Saxon and European countries have tended to privilege liberal traditions, from the American Declaration of Independence and the French Revolution onwards, in fact, citizenship in practice as well as in political thought has usually been characterized by an articulation between liberal ideas of political belonging and civic republican ones, as well as ideas of exclusion. The civic republican

texts have been chosen to illustrate their emphasis on the nature of the citizen as a particular political subject: the virtuous man who imagines and enacts his political agency as part of a given collective. The liberal texts included here promote a slightly different relationship between individual and collective. Although the ability to subsume individual interests for the good of the collective is also crucial, the relationship begins from individual interest or subjecthood. The section on liberal political thought thus includes extracts from pieces that are crucial to an understanding of liberal notions of citizenship. The key is to denaturalize these as 'citizenship' and recognize them as 'liberal citizenship'. However, it also includes historical texts that show the mixing of the two traditions in historical practice, such as the French Declaration of the Rights of Man of 1789 and the Haitian Constitution of 1805. The section culminates with Marshall's foundational essay on liberal citizenship as a property of the person, a kind of basket of rights and responsibilities that go along with the status of membership of the national community.

The liberal–communitarian debate has been discussed in the Introduction, and is explored in this section in Iris Marion Young's chapter.

The Anthropology of Citizenship: A Reader, First Edition. Edited by Sian Lazar.
© 2013 John Wiley & Sons, Inc. Published 2013 by John Wiley & Sons, Inc.

It exposes some of the tensions between ideas of the political subject as individual or community, and anthropology has much to contribute to such a debate, as the following section and Part II of this reader demonstrate. Section I.3, on early anthropological theories of citizenship, is organized more or less chronologically. It gives the most important early discussions of citizenship in anthropology, where explicit discussion of citizenship began with Rosaldo's early work on cultural citizenship in the USA. Aihwa Ong developed that in her 1996 article, and she has subsequently been an extremely influential anthropologist of citizenship. James Holston has been at the forefront of anthropological discussions of citizenship for some time now, and this extract crystallizes the anthropological emphasis on the agency of people claiming citizenship through his notion of 'insurgent citizens', and the importance of his discussion of formal and substantive citizenship.

SUGGESTIONS FOR FURTHER READING

Arendt, Hannah, 1998 [1958] *The Human Condition*. Chicago and London: University of Chicago Press.

Aretxaga, Begoña, 2003 Maddening states. *Annual Review of Anthropology* 32: 393–410.

Avineri, S., and A. de-Shalit, 1992 *Communitarianism and Individualism*. Oxford: Oxford University Press.

Barron, Anne, 1993 The illusions of the 'I': citizenship and the politics of identity. In *Closure or Critique: New Directions in Legal Theory*, A. Norrie, ed. Edinburgh: Edinburgh University Press, pp. 80–100.

Hall, Stuart, and David Held, 1989 Citizens and citizenship. In *New Times*, S. Hall and M. Jacques, eds. London: Lawrence & Wishart, pp. 173–188.

Heater, Derek, 1999 *What is Citizenship?* Cambridge: Polity Press.

Isin, Engin, 2002 *Being Political: Genealogies of Citizenship*. Minneapolis: University of Minnesota Press.

Isin, Engin, and Greg M. Nielsen, eds, 2008 *Acts of Citizenship*. London: Zed Books.

Kymlicka, Will, 1995 *Multicultural Citizenship: A Liberal Theory of Minority Rights*. Oxford: Clarendon Press.

Kymlicka, Will, and W. Norman, 1994 Return of the citizen: a survey of recent work on citizenship theory. *Ethics* 104(2): 352–381.

Laclau, Ernesto, and Chantal Mouffe, 1985 Hegemony and radical democracy. In *Hegemony and Socialist Strategy: Towards a Radical Democratic Politics*, E. Laclau and C. Mouffe, eds. London: Verso, pp. 149–194.

Lister, Ruth, 1997 *Citizenship: Feminist Perspectives*. London: Macmillan.

Mouffe, Chantal, 1992 *Dimensions of Radical Democracy: Pluralism, Citizenship, Community*. London and New York: Verso.

Pateman, Carole, 1988 *The Sexual Contract*. Stanford, California: Stanford University Press.

Rancière, Jacques, 2004 Who is the subject of the Rights of Man? *South Atlantic Quarterly* 103(2–3): 297–310.

Rawls, John, 1972 *A Theory of Justice*. Oxford: Clarendon Press.

Rose, Nikolas, 1999 *Powers of Freedom: Reframing Political Thought*. Cambridge: Cambridge University Press.

Sandel, Michael, 1984 The procedural republic and the unencumbered self. *Political Theory* 12(1): 81–96.

Shafir, Gershon, ed., 1998 *The Citizenship Debates: A Reader*. Minneapolis: University of Minnesota Press.

Taylor, Charles, 1995 *Philosophical Arguments*. Cambridge, Massachusetts and London: Harvard University Press.

Turner, Bryan, 1993 *Citizenship and Social Theory*. London: Sage.

Twine, Fred, 1994 *Citizenship and Social Rights*. London: Sage.

I.1 Civic Republican Traditions

1
The Democratic Citizen

Pericles

'Let me say that our system of government does not copy the institutions of our neighbours. It is more the case of our being a model to others, than of our imitating anyone else. Our constitution is called a democracy because power is in the hands not of a minority but of the whole people. When it is a question of settling private disputes, everyone is equal before the law; when it is a question of putting one person before another in positions of public responsibility, what counts is not membership of a particular class, but the actual ability which the man possesses. No one, so long as he has it in him to be of service to the state, is kept in political obscurity because of poverty. And, just as our political life is free and open, so is our day-to-day life in our relations with each other. We do not get into a state with our next-door neighbour if he enjoys himself in his own way, nor do we give him the kind of black looks which, though they do no real harm, still do hurt people's feelings. We are free and tolerant in our private lives; but in public affairs we keep to the law. This is because it commands our deep respect.

'We give our obedience to those whom we put in positions of authority, and we obey the laws themselves, especially those which are for the protection of the oppressed, and those unwritten laws which it is an acknowledged shame to break.

[…]

'Our love of what is beautiful does not lead to extravagance; our love of the things of the mind does not make us soft. We regard wealth as something to be properly used, rather than as something to boast about. As for poverty, no one need be ashamed to admit it: the real shame is in not taking practical measures to escape from it. Here each individual is interested not only in his own affairs but in the affairs of the state as well: even those who are mostly occupied with their own business are extremely well-informed on general politics – this is a peculiarity of ours: we do not say that a man who takes no interest in politics is a man who minds his own business; we say that he has no business here at all. We Athenians, in our own persons, take our decisions on policy or submit them to proper discussions: for we do not think that there is an

'Pericles' Funeral Oration'. In Thucydides, *History of the Peloponnesian War*, Rex Warner, trans., with introd. by M. I. Finley (Harmondsworth: Penguin Books, 1972), pp. 145, 147–148.

The Anthropology of Citizenship: A Reader, First Edition. Edited by Sian Lazar.
© 2013 John Wiley & Sons, Inc. Published 2013 by John Wiley & Sons, Inc.

incompatibility between words and deeds; the worst thing is to rush into action before the consequences have been properly debated. And this is another point where we differ from other people. We are capable at the same time of taking risks and of estimating them beforehand. Others are brave out of ignorance; and, when they stop to think, they begin to fear. But the man who can most truly be accounted brave is he who best knows the meaning of what is sweet in life and of what is terrible, and then goes out undeterred to meet what is to come.

'Again, in questions of general good feeling there is a great contrast between us and most other people. We make friends by doing good to others, not by receiving good from them. This makes our friendship all the more reliable, since we want to keep alive the gratitude of those who are in our debt by showing continued good-will to them: whereas the feelings of one who owes us something lack the same enthusiasm, since he knows that, when he repays our kindness, it will be more like paying back a debt than giving something spontaneously. We are unique in this. When we do kindnesses to others, we do not do them out of any calculations of profit or loss: we do them without afterthought, relying on our free liberality. Taking everything together then, I declare that our city is an education to Greece, and I declare that in my opinion each single one of our citizens, in all the manifold aspects of life, is able to show himself the rightful lord and owner of his own person, and do this, moreover, with exceptional grace and exceptional versatility.'

2

The Politics

Aristotle

[...]

The State and the Individual

1253a1 It follows that the state belongs to the class of objects which exist by nature, and that man is by nature a political animal. Any one who by his nature and not simply by ill-luck has no state is either too bad or too good, either subhuman or superhuman – he is like the war-mad man condemned in Homer's words as 'having no family, no law, no home'; for he who is such by nature is mad on war: he is a non-cooperator like an isolated piece in a game of draughts.

1253a7 But obviously man is a political animal in a sense in which a bee is not, or any other gregarious animal. Nature, as we say, does nothing without some purpose; and she has endowed man alone among the animals with the power of speech. Speech is something different from voice, which is possessed by other animals also and used by them to express pain or pleasure; for their nature does indeed enable them not only to feel pleasure and pain but to communicate these feelings to each other. Speech, on the other hand, serves to indicate what is useful and what is harmful, and so also what is just and what is unjust. For the real difference between man and other animals is that humans alone have perception of good and evil, just and unjust, etc. It is the sharing of a common view in *these* matters that makes a household and a state.

[...]

1253a29 Among all men, then, there is a natural impulse towards this kind of association; and the first man to construct a state deserves credit for conferring very great benefits. For as man is the best of all animals when he has reached his full development, so he is worst of all when divorced from law and justice. Injustice armed is hardest to deal with; and though man is born with weapons which he can use in the service of practical wisdom and virtue, it is all too easy for him to use them for the opposite purposes. Hence man without virtue is the most savage, the most unrighteous, and the worst in regard to sexual licence

Aristotle, *The Politics*, T. A. Sinclair, trans., revised and re-presented by Trevor J. Saunders (Harmondsworth: Penguin Books, 1962, 1981), pp. 59–61, 169–171, 179–185.

The Anthropology of Citizenship: A Reader, First Edition. Edited by Sian Lazar.
© 2013 John Wiley & Sons, Inc. Published 2013 by John Wiley & Sons, Inc.

and gluttony. The virtue of justice is a feature of a state; for justice is the arrangement of the political association, and a sense of justice decides what is just.

III i   How Should We Define 'Citizen'?

[...]

1275a22 What effectively distinguishes the citizen proper from all others is his participation in giving judgement and in holding office. Some offices are distinguished in respect of length of tenure, some not being tenable by the same person twice under any circumstances, or only after an interval of time. Others, such as membership of a jury or of an assembly, have no such limitation. It might be objected that such persons are not really officials, and that these functions do not amount to participation in office. But they have the fullest sovereign power, and it would be ridiculous to deny their participation in office. In any case nomenclature ought not to make any difference; it is just that there is no name covering that which is common to a juryman and to a member of an assembly, which ought to be used of both. For the sake of a definition I suggest that we say 'unlimited office'. We therefore define citizens as those who participate in this. Such a definition seems to cover, as nearly as may be, those to whom the term citizen is in fact applied.

[...]

1275b5 Our definition of citizen is best applied in a democracy; in the other constitutions it *may* be applicable, but it need not necessarily be so. For in some constitutions there is no body comprising the people, nor a recognized assembly, but only an occasional rally; and justice may be administered piecemeal. For example, at Sparta contract cases are tried by the Ephors, one or other of them, cases of homicide by the Elders, and other cases doubtless by other officials. Similarly at Carthage all cases are tried by officials.

1275b13 But our own definition of a citizen can be amended so as to apply to the other constitutions also. We simply replace our 'unlimited' office of juror or member of assembly by 'limited'. For it is to all or some of these that the task of judging or deliberating is assigned, either on all matters or on some. From these considerations it has become clear who a citizen is: as soon as a man becomes entitled to participate in office, deliberative or judicial, we deem him to be a citizen of that state; and a number of such persons large enough to secure a self-sufficient life we may, by and large, call a state.

III iv   How Far Should the Good Man and the Good Citizen be Distinguished?

1276b16 Connected with the matters just discussed is the question whether we ought to regard the virtue of a good man and that of a sound citizen as the same virtue, or not. If this is a point to be investigated, we really must try to form some rough conception of the virtue of a citizen.

1276b20 So then: we say a citizen is a member of an association, just as a sailor is; and each member of the crew has his different function and a name to fit it – rower, helmsman, look-out, and the rest. Clearly the most exact description of each individual will be a special description of his virtue; but equally there will also be a general description that will fit them all, because there is a task in which they all play a part – the safe conduct of the voyage; for each member of the crew aims at securing that. Similarly the task of all the citizens, however different they may be, is the stability of the association, that is, the constitution. Therefore the virtue of the citizen must be in relation to the constitution; and as there are more kinds of constitution than one, there cannot be just one single *and perfect* virtue of the sound citizen. On the other hand we do say that the good *man* is good because of one single virtue which *is* perfect virtue. Clearly then it is possible to be a sound citizen without having that virtue which makes a sound man.

1276b35 Look now at the problem from another angle and consider the same point in relation to the best constitution. That is to say, if it is impossible for a state to consist entirely of sound *men*, still each of them must do, and do well, his proper work; and doing it well depends on his virtue. But since it is impossible for all the *citizens* to be alike, there cannot be one virtue of citizen and good man alike. For the virtue of the sound citizen must be possessed by all (and if it is, then that state is necessarily best). *But* if it is inevitable that not all the citizens in a sound state are good, it is impossible for all to have the virtue of the good man.

1277a5 Again, a state is made up of unlike parts. As an animate creature consists of body and soul, and soul consists of reasoning and desiring, and a household consists of husband and wife, and property consists of master and slave, so also a state is made up of these and many other sorts of people besides, all different. The virtue of all the citizens cannot, therefore, be *one*, any more than in a troupe of dancers the goodness of the leader and that of the followers are one.

1277a12 Now while all this shows clearly that they are not the same in general, the question may be asked whether it is not possible in a particular case for the same virtue to belong both to the sound citizen and the sound man. We would answer that there is such a case, since we maintain that a sound ruler is both good and wise, whereas wisdom is not essential for a citizen. Some say that from the very start there is a different kind of education for rulers. They instance (a) the obvious training of the sons of royalty in horsemanship and war, and (b) a saying of Euripides, which is supposed to refer to the education of a ruler: 'No frills in education, please ... only what the state doth need.'[1] But though we may say that the virtue of good ruler and good man is the same, yet, since he too that is ruled is a citizen, we cannot say in general that the virtue of citizen and man are one, but only that they may be in the case of a particular citizen. For certainly the virtue of ruler and citizen are not the same. And that doubtless is the reason why Jason of Pherae said that he went hungry whenever he ceased to be tyrant, not knowing how to live as a private person.

1277a25 But surely men praise the ability to rule and to be ruled, and the virtue of a citizen of repute seems to be just this – to be able to rule and be ruled well. If then we say that the virtue of the good man is to do with ruling, and that of the citizen to do with both ruling and being ruled, the two things cannot be praiseworthy to the same degree.

1277a29 So since on occasions they seem different, and ruler and ruled ought not to learn the same things, whereas the citizen ought to know both and share in both, one could see from the following.

1277a33 For there is such a thing as rule by a master, which we say is concerned with necessary tasks; but the master has no necessity to know more than how to *use* such labour. Anything else, I mean to be able actually to be a servant and do the chores, is simply slavelike. (We speak of several kinds of slave, corresponding to the several varieties of operation. One variety is performed by manual workers, who, as the term itself indicates, live by their hands; among these are the skilled mechanics.) Hence, in some places, only with the arrival of extreme democracies have workmen attained to participation in office. The work then of those who are subject to rule is not work which either the good statesman or the good citizen ought to learn, except occasionally for the personal use he may require to make of it. For then the distinction *between* master and slave just ceases to apply.

1277b7 But there is another kind of rule – that exercised over men who are free, and similar in birth. This we call rule by a statesman. It is this that a ruler must first learn through being ruled, just as one learns to command cavalry by serving under a cavalry-commander and to be a general by serving under a general, and by commanding a battalion and a company. This too is a healthy saying, namely that it is not possible to be a good ruler without first having been ruled. Not that good ruling and good obedience are the same virtue – only that the good citizen must have the knowledge and ability both to rule and be ruled. That is what we mean by the virtue of a citizen – understanding the governing of free men from both points of view.

[...]

III v   Ought Workers to be Citizens?

1277b33   There remains still a question about the citizen. Is a citizen really 'one who has the chance to participate in offices', or are we to count mechanics too as citizens? If we do the latter, i.e. give them the title citizen though they do not share in government, then the virtue of the citizen ceases to be that of every citizen, since the mechanic too is a citizen. On the other hand, if he is not a citizen, where *does* he belong, since he is not a foreign resident or a visitor either? But perhaps this kind of reasoning does not really result in any absurdity. After all, slaves do not belong to any of the above-mentioned categories, nor do freed slaves: true it is that we must not give the name citizen to all persons whose presence is necessary for the existence of the state. (Nor yet are children citizens in an unqualified sense, like grown men; children can be called citizens only in a hypothetical sense: they *are* citizens, but incomplete ones.) Indeed, in ancient times in certain countries the mechanics *were* slaves or foreigners, and therefore mostly still are. But the best state will not make the mechanic a citizen. But if even he is to be a citizen, then at any rate what we have called the virtue of a citizen cannot be ascribed to everyone, nor yet to free men alone, but simply to those who are in fact relieved of necessary tasks. Some tasks of this kind are discharged by services to an individual, by slaves, others by mechanics and hired labourers, who serve the public at large.

1278a13   A little further examination will show how it stands with these people, and our earlier statement of the position will itself suffice to make matters clear: as there are several constitutions, so there must be several kinds of citizen, particularly of citizen under a ruler. Thus in one constitution it will be necessary, in another impossible, for the mechanic and the hired labourer to be a citizen. It would, for example, be impossible in any constitution called aristocratic or any other in which honours depend on merit and virtue; for it is quite impossible, while living the life of mechanic or hireling, to occupy oneself as virtue demands. In oligarchies it is

not possible for a hireling to be a citizen, because of the high property-qualifications required for participating in office; but it may be possible for a mechanic, since in fact most skilled workers become rich. In Thebes, however, there was a law requiring an interval of ten years to elapse between giving up trade and participating in office.

1278a26   In many constitutions the law admits to citizenship a certain number even of foreigners; in some democracies the son of a citizen mother is a citizen, and in many places the same applies to illegitimate children. Lack of population is the usual reason for resorting to laws such as these. But when, after making such persons citizens because of a dearth of legitimate citizens, the state has filled up its numbers, it gradually reduces them, dropping first the sons of slave father or slave mother, then sons of citizen mother but not father, and finally they confine citizenship to those of citizen birth on both sides.

1278a34   From all this two points emerge clearly: first, that there are several kinds of citizen, but second, that a citizen in the fullest sense is one who has a share in honours. We are reminded of Homer's 'Like some immigrant settler, without honour'.[2] For he who has no share in honours is no better than a resident alien. (Sometimes such efforts are concealed, so that the fellow-inhabitants may be deceived.)

1278a40   We have now answered the question whether it is the same or a different virtue that makes a good man and a sound citizen, and have shown that in one state they will be the same person, and in another different; and that where they are the same, not every sound citizen will be a good man, but only the statesman, that is one who is in sovereign control, or capable of being in control, either alone or in conjunction with others, of the administration of public affairs.

NOTES

1   From Euripides' *Aeolus*: part of lines 2 and 3 of fr. 16 in A. Nauck, *Tragicorum Graecorum Fragmenta* (2nd ed., Leipzig, 1889).
2   *Iliad*, IX 648, XVI 59.

3

The Social Contract, 1762

Jean-Jacques Rousseau

Chapter 1   The Subject of Book I

Man was born free, and he is everywhere in chains. Those who think themselves the masters of others are indeed greater slaves than they. How did this transformation come about? I do not know. How can it be made legitimate? That question I believe I can answer.

If I were to consider only force and the effects of force, I should say: 'So long as a people is constrained to obey, and obeys, it does well; but as soon as it can shake off the yoke, and shakes it off, it does better; for since it regains its freedom by the same right as that which removed it, a people is either justified in taking back its freedom, or there is no justifying those who took it away.' But the social order is a sacred right which serves as a basis for all other rights. And as it is not a natural right, it must be one founded on covenants. The problem is to determine what those covenants are.

[...]

Chapter 5   That We Must Always Go Back to an Original Covenant

[...] There will always be a great difference between subduing a multitude and ruling a society. If one man successively enslaved many separate individuals, no matter how numerous, he and they would never bear the aspect of anything but a master and his slaves, not at all that of a people and their ruler; an aggregation, perhaps, but certainly not an association, for they would neither have a common good nor be a body politic. Even if such a man were to enslave half the world, he would remain a private individual, and his interest, always distinct from that of the others, would never be more than a personal interest. When he died, the empire he left would be scattered for lack of any bond of union, even as an oak crumbles and falls into a heap of ashes when fire has consumed it.

'A people,' says Grotius, 'may give itself to a king.' Therefore, according to Grotius a people is *a people* even before the gift to the king is made. The gift itself is a civil act; it presupposes

Jean-Jacques Rousseau, *The Social Contract* [1762], Maurice Cranston, trans. (Harmondsworth: Penguin Books, 1968), pp. 49–50, 58–62, 64–65.

public deliberation. Hence, before considering the act by which a people submits to a king, we ought to scrutinize the act by which people become *a* people, for that act, being necessarily antecedent to the other, is the real foundation of society.

In fact, if there were no earlier agreement, how, unless the election were unanimous, could there be any obligation on the minority to accept the decision of the majority? What right have the hundred who want to have a master to vote on behalf of the ten who do not? The law of majority-voting itself rests on an agreement, and implies that there has been on at least one occasion unanimity.

Chapter 6   The Social Pact

I assume that men reach a point where the obstacles to their preservation in a state of nature prove greater than the strength that each man has to preserve himself in that state. Beyond this point, the primitive condition cannot endure, for then the human race will perish if it does not change its mode of existence.

Since men cannot create new forces, but merely combine and control those which already exist, the only way in which they can preserve themselves is by uniting their separate powers in a combination strong enough to overcome any resistance, uniting them so that their powers are directed by a single motive and act in concert.

Such a sum of forces can be produced only by the union of separate men, but as each man's own strength and liberty are the chief instruments of his preservation, how can he merge his with others' without putting himself in peril and neglecting the care he owes to himself? This difficulty, in terms of my present subject, may be expressed in these words:

'How to find a form of association which will defend the person and goods of each member with the collective force of all, and under which each individual, while uniting himself with the others, obeys no one but himself, and remains as free as before.' This is the fundamental problem to which the social contract holds the solution.

The articles of this contract are so precisely determined by the nature of the act, that the slightest modification must render them null and void; they are such that, though perhaps never formally stated, they are everywhere the same, everywhere tacitly admitted and recognized; and if ever the social pact is violated, every man regains his original rights and, recovering his natural freedom, loses that civil freedom for which he exchanged it.

These articles of association, rightly understood, are reducible to a single one, namely the total alienation by each associate of himself and all his rights to the whole community. Thus, in the first place, as every individual gives himself absolutely, the conditions are the same for all, and precisely because they are the same for all, it is in no one's interest to make the conditions onerous for others.

Secondly, since the alienation is unconditional, the union is as perfect as it can be, and no individual associate has any longer any rights to claim; for if rights were left to individuals, in the absence of any higher authority to judge between them and the public, each individual, being his own judge in some causes, would soon demand to be his own judge in all; and in this way the state of nature would be kept in being, and the association inevitably become either tyrannical or void.

Finally, since each man gives himself to all, he gives himself to no one; and since there is no associate over whom he does not gain the same rights as others gain over him, each man recovers the equivalent of everything he loses, and in the bargain he acquires more power to preserve what he has.

If, then, we eliminate from the social pact everything that is not essential to it, we find it comes down to this: 'Each one of us puts into the community his person and all his powers under the supreme direction of the general will; and as a body, we incorporate every member as an indivisible part of the whole.'

Immediately, in place of the individual person of each contracting party, this act of association creates an artificial and corporate body composed of as many members as there are voters in the assembly, and by this same act that body acquires its unity, its common *ego*, its life and its will. The public person thus formed by the union of all other persons was once called the *city*,[1] and is now known as the *republic* or the *body politic*. In its passive role it is called the *state*, when it plays an active role it is the *sovereign*; and when it is compared to others of its own kind, it is a *power*. Those who are associated in it take collectively the name of *a people*, and call themselves individually *citizens*, in that they share in the sovereign power, and *subjects*, in that they put themselves under the laws of the state. [...]

Chapter 8 Civil Society

The passing from the state of nature to the civil society produces a remarkable change in man; it puts justice as a rule of conduct in the place of instinct, and gives his actions the moral quality they previously lacked. It is only then, when the voice of duty has taken the place of physical impulse, and right that of desire, that man, who has hitherto thought only of himself, finds himself compelled to act on other principles, and to consult his reason rather than study his inclinations. And although in civil society man surrenders some of the advantages that belong to the state of nature, he gains in return far greater ones; his faculties are so exercised and developed, his mind is so enlarged, his sentiments so ennobled, and his whole spirit so elevated that, if the abuse of his new condition did not in many cases lower him to something worse than what he had left, he should constantly bless the happy hour that lifted him for ever from the state of nature and from a stupid, limited animal made a creature of intelligence and a man.

Suppose we draw up a balance sheet, so that the losses and gains may be readily compared. What man loses by the social contract is his natural liberty and the absolute right to anything that tempts him and that he can take; what he gains by the social contract is civil liberty and the legal right of property in what he possesses. If we are to avoid mistakes in weighing the one side against the other, we must clearly distinguish between *natural* liberty, which has no limit but the physical power of the individual concerned, and *civil* liberty, which is limited by the general will; and we must distinguish also between *possession*, which is based only on force or 'the right of the first occupant', and *property*, which must rest on a legal title.

We might also add that man acquires with civil society, moral freedom, which alone makes man the master of himself; for to be governed by appetite alone is slavery, while obedience to a law one prescribes to oneself is freedom. However, I have already said more than enough on this subject, and the philosophical meaning of the word 'freedom' is no part of my subject here.

NOTE

1 The real meaning of this word has been almost entirely lost in the modern world, when a town and a city are thought to be identical, and a citizen the same as a burgess. People forget that houses may make a town, while only citizens can make a city. The Carthaginians once paid dearly for this mistake. I have never read of the title *cives* being given to the subject of any prince, not even to the Macedonians in ancient times or the English today, in spite of their being closer to liberty than any other people. The French alone treat the same 'Citizen' with familiarity, and that is because they do not know what it means, as their Dictionaries prove; if they did know, they would be guilty, in usurping it, of *lèse-majesté*; as it is, they use the word to designate social status and not legal right. When Bodin wanted to speak of citizens and burgesses, he made the gross error of mistaking the one for the other. Monsieur d'Alembert avoids this mistake; and in his article on 'Geneva' he correctly distinguishes between the four orders of men (five, if aliens are included) which are found in our town, and of which only two compose the republic. No other French author to my knowledge has understood the real meaning of the word 'citizen'.

4

The Decline of the Nation-State and the End of the Rights of Man, 1951

Hannah Arendt

The calamity of the rightless is not that they are deprived of life, liberty, and the pursuit of happiness, or of equality before the law and freedom of opinion – formulas which were designed to solve problems *within* given communities – but that they no longer belong to any community whatsoever. Their plight is not that they are not equal before the law, but that no law exists for them; not that they are oppressed but that nobody wants even to oppress them. Only in the last stage of a rather lengthy process is their right to live threatened; only if they remain perfectly "superfluous," if nobody can be found to "claim" them, may their lives be in danger. Even the Nazis started their extermination of Jews by first depriving them of all legal status (the status of second-class citizenship) and cutting them off from the world of the living by herding them into ghettos and concentration camps; and before they set the gas chambers into motion they had carefully tested the ground and found out to their satisfaction that no country would claim these people. The point is that a condition of complete rightlessness was created before the right to live was challenged.

The same is true even to an ironical extent with regard to the right of freedom which is sometimes considered to be the very essence of human rights. There is no question that those outside the pale of the law may have more freedom of movement than a lawfully imprisoned criminal or that they enjoy more freedom of opinion in the internment camps of democratic countries than they would in any ordinary despotism, not to mention in a totalitarian country. But neither physical safety – being fed by some state or private welfare agency – nor freedom of opinion changes in the least their fundamental situation of rightlessness. The prolongation of their lives is due to charity and not to right, for no law exists which could force the nations to feed them; their freedom of movement, if they have it at all, gives them no right to residence which even the jailed criminal enjoys as a matter of course; and their freedom of opinion is a fool's freedom, for nothing they think matters anyhow.

Hannah Arendt, The decline of the nation-state and the end of the rights of man. In *The Origins of Totalitarianism* (New York: Harcourt, Brace and Company, 1951), pp. 266–298.

The Anthropology of Citizenship: A Reader, First Edition. Edited by Sian Lazar.

These last points are crucial. The fundamental deprivation of human rights is manifested first and above all in the deprivation of a place in the world which makes opinions significant and actions effective. Something much more fundamental than freedom and justice, which are rights of citizens, is at stake when belonging to the community into which one is born is no longer a matter of course and not belonging no longer a matter of choice, or when one is placed in a situation where, unless he commits a crime, his treatment by others does not depend on what he does or does not do. This extremity, and nothing else, is the situation of people deprived of human rights. They are deprived, not of the right to freedom, but of the right to action; not of the right to think whatever they please, but of the right to opinion. Privileges in some cases, injustices in most, blessings and doom are meted out to them according to accident and without any relation whatsoever to what they do, did, or may do.

We became aware of the existence of a right to have rights (and that means to live in a framework where one is judged by one's actions and opinions) and a right to belong to some kind of organized community, only when millions of people emerged who had lost and could not regain these rights because of the new global political situation. The trouble is that this calamity arose not from any lack of civilization, backwardness, or mere tyranny, but, on the contrary, that it could not be repaired, because there was no longer any "uncivilized" spot on earth, because whether we like it or not we have really started to live in One World. Only with a completely organized humanity could the loss of home and political status become identical with expulsion from humanity altogether.

Before this, what we must call a "human right" today would have been thought of as a general characteristic of the human condition which no tyrant could take away. Its loss entails the loss of the relevance of speech (and man,

since Aristotle, has been defined as a being commanding the power of speech and thought), and the loss of all human relationship (and man, again since Aristotle, has been thought of as the "political animal," that is one who by definition lives in a community), the loss, in other words, of some of the most essential characteristics of human life. This was to a certain extent the plight of slaves, whom Aristotle therefore did not count among human beings. Slavery's fundamental offense against human rights was not that it took liberty away (which can happen in many other situations), but that it excluded a certain category of people even from the possibility of fighting for freedom – a fight possible under tyranny, and even under the desperate conditions of modern terror (but not under any conditions of concentration-camp life). Slavery's crime against humanity did not begin when one people defeated and enslaved its enemies (though of course this was bad enough), but when slavery became an institution in which some men were "born" free and others slave, when it was forgotten that it was man who had deprived his fellow-men of freedom, and when the sanction for the crime was attributed to nature. Yet in the light of recent events, it is possible to say that even slaves still belonged to some sort of human community; their labor was needed, used, and exploited, and this kept them within the pale of humanity. To be a slave was after all to have a distinctive character, a place in society – more than the abstract nakedness of being human and nothing but human.

Not the loss of specific rights, then, but the loss of a community willing and able to guarantee any rights whatsoever, has been the calamity which has befallen ever-increasing numbers of people. Man, it turns out, can lose all so-called Rights of Man without losing his essential quality as man, his human dignity. Only the loss of a polity itself expels him from humanity.

I.2   Liberal Traditions

Two Treatises of Government, 1689

John Locke

Chap. VIII   Of the Beginning of Political Societies

95. Men being, as has been said, by Nature, all free, equal and independent, no one can be put out of this Estate, and subjected to the Political Power of another, without his own *Consent*. The only way whereby any one devests himself of his Natural Liberty, and *puts on the bonds of Civil Society* is by agreeing with other Men to joyn and unite into a Community, for their comfortable, safe, and peaceable living one amongst another, in a secure Enjoyment of their Properties, and a greater Security against any that are not of it. This any number of Men may do, because it injures not the Freedom of the rest; they are left as they were in the Liberty of the State of Nature. When any number of Men have so *consented to make one Community* or Government, they are thereby presently incorporated, and make *one Body Politick*, wherein the *Majority* have a Right to act and conclude the rest.

96. For when any number of Men have, by the consent of every individual, made a *Community*, they have thereby made that *Community* one Body, with a Power to Act as one Body, which is only by the will and determination of the *majority*. For that which acts any Community, being only the consent of the individuals of it, and it being necessary to that which is one body to move one way; it is necessary the Body should move that way whither the greater force carries it, which is the *consent of the majority*: or else it is impossible it should act or continue one Body, *one Community*, which the consent of every individual that united into it, agreed that it should; and so every one is bound by that consent to be concluded by the *majority*. And therefore we see that in Assemblies impowered to act by positive Laws where no number is set by that positive Law which impowers them, the *act of the Majority* passes for the act of the whole, and of course determines, as having by the Law of Nature and Reason, the power of the whole.

97. And thus every Man, by consenting with others to make one Body Politick under one Government, puts himself under an Obligation

John Locke, *Two Treatises of Government*, Peter Laslett, ed., Cambridge Texts in the History of Political Thought (Cambridge: Cambridge University Press, 1988), pp. 330–333, 347–349, 350–353.

The Anthropology of Citizenship: A Reader, First Edition. Edited by Sian Lazar.

to every one of that Society, to submit to the determination of the *majority*, and to be concluded by it; or else this *original Compact*, whereby he with others incorporates into *one Society*, would signifie nothing, and be no Compact, if he be left free, and under no other ties, than he was in before in the State of Nature. For what appearance would there be of any Compact? What new Engagement if he were no farther tied by any Decrees of the Society, than he himself thought fit, and did actually consent to? This would be still as great a liberty, as he himself had before his Compact, or any one else in the State of Nature hath, who may submit himself and consent to any acts of it if he thinks fit.

98. For if *the consent of the majority* shall not in reason, be received, as *the act of the whole*, and conclude every individual; nothing but the consent of every individual can make any thing to be the act of the whole: But such a consent is next impossible ever to be had, if we consider the Infirmities of Health, and Avocations of Business, which in a number, though much less than that of a Common-wealth, will necessarily keep many away from the publick Assembly. To which if we add the variety of Opinions, and contrariety of Interests, which unavoidably happen in all Collections of Men, the coming into Society upon such terms, would be only like *Cato's* coming into the Theatre, only to go out again. Such a Constitution as this would make the mighty *Leviathan* of a shorter duration, than the feeblest Creatures; and not let it outlast the day it was born in: which cannot be suppos'd, till we can think, that Rational Creatures should desire and constitute Societies only to be dissolved. For where the *majority* cannot conclude the rest, there they cannot act as one Body, and consequently will be immediately dissolved again.

99. Whosoever therefore out of a state of Nature unite into a *Community*, must be understood to give up all the power, necessary to the ends for which they unite into Society, to the *majority* of the Community, unless they expressly agreed in any number greater than the majority. And this is done by barely agreeing to *unite into one Political Society*, which is *all the Compact* that is, or needs be, between the Individuals, that enter into, or make up a *Common-wealth*. And thus that, which begins and actually *constitutes any Political Society*, is

nothing but the consent of any number of Freemen capable of a majority to unite and incorporate into such a Society. And this is that, and that only, which did, or could give *beginning* to any *lawful Government* in the World.
[...]

119. *Every Man* being, as has been shewed, *naturally free*, and nothing being able to put him into subjection to any Earthly Power, but only his own Consent; it is to be considered, what shall be understood to be *a sufficient Declaration of a Mans Consent, to make him subject* to the Laws of any Government. There is a common distinction of an express and a tacit consent, which will concern our present Case. No body doubts but an *express Consent*, of any Man, entring into any Society, makes him a perfect Member of that Society, a Subject of that Government. The difficulty is, what ought to be look'd upon as a *tacit Consent*, and how far it binds, *i.e.* how far any one shall be looked on to have consented, and thereby submitted to any Government, where he has made no Expressions of it at all. And to this I say, that every Man, that hath any Possession, or Enjoyment, of any part of the Dominions of any Government, doth thereby give his *tacit Consent*, and is as far forth obliged to Obedience to the Laws of that Government, during such Enjoyment, as any one under it; whether this his Possession be of Land, to him and his Heirs for ever, or a Lodging only for a Week; or whether it be barely travelling freely on the Highway; and in Effect, it reaches as far as the very being of any one within the Territories of that Government.
[...]

122. But submitting to the Laws of any Country, living quietly, and enjoying Priviledges and Protection under them, *makes not a Man a Member of that Society*: This is only a local Protection and Homage due to, and from all those, who, not being in a state of War, come within the Territories belonging to any Government, to all parts whereof the force of its Law extends. But this no more *makes a Man a Member of that Society*, a perpetual Subject of that Commonwealth, than it would make a Man a Subject to another in whose Family he found it convenient to abide for

some time; though, whilst he continued in it, he were obliged to comply with the Laws, and submit to the Government he found there. And thus we see, that *Foreigners*, by living all their Lives under another Government, and enjoying the Priviledges and Protection of it, though they are bound, even in Conscience, to submit to its Administration, as far forth as any Denison; yet do not thereby come to be *Subjects or Members of that Commonwealth.* Nothing can make any Man so, but his actually entering into it by positive Engagement, and express Promise and Compact. This is that, which I think, concerning the beginning of Political Societies, and that *Consent which makes any one a Member* of any Commonwealth.

Chap. IX   Of the Ends of Political Society and Government

123.   IF Man in the State of Nature be so free, as has been said; If he be absolute Lord of his own Person and Possessions, equal to the greatest, and subject to no Body, why will he part with his Freedom? Why will he give up this Empire, and subject himself to the Dominion and Controul of any other Power? To which 'tis obvious to Answer, that though in the state of Nature he hath such a right, yet the Enjoyment of it is very uncertain, and constantly exposed to the Invasion of others. For all being Kings as much as he, every Man his Equal, and the greater part no strict Observers of Equity and Justice, the enjoyment of the property he has in this state is very unsafe, very unsecure. This makes him willing to quit this Condition, which however free, is full of fears and continual dangers : And 'tis not without reason, that he seeks out, and is willing to joyn in Society with others who are already united, or have a mind to unite for the mutual *Preservation* of their Lives, Liberties and Estates, which I call by the general Name, *Property.*

124.   The great and *chief end* therefore, of Mens uniting into Commonwealths, and putting themselves under Government, *is the Preservation of their Property.* To which in the state of Nature there are many things wanting.

First, There wants an *establish'd*, settled, known *Law*, received and allowed by common consent to be the Standard of Right and Wrong, and the common measure to decide all Controversies between them. For though the Law of Nature be plain and intelligible to all rational Creatures; yet Men being biassed by their Interest, as well as ignorant for want of study of it, are not apt to allow of it as a Law binding to them in the application of it to their particular Cases.

125.   *Secondly,* In the State of Nature there wants *a known and indifferent Judge,* with Authority to determine all differences according to the established Law. For every one in that state being both Judge and Executioner of the Law of Nature, Men being partial to themselves, Passion and Revenge is very apt to carry them too far, and with too much heat, in their own Cases; as well as negligence, and unconcernedness, to make them too remiss, in other Mens.

126.   *Thirdly,* In the state of Nature there often wants *Power* to back and support the Sentence when right, and to *give* it due *Execution.* They who by any Injustice offended, will seldom fail, where they are able, by force to make good their Injustice: such resistance many times makes the punishment dangerous, and frequently destructive, to those who attempt it.

127.   Thus Mankind, notwithstanding all the Priviledges of the state of Nature, being but in an ill condition, while they remain in it, are quickly driven into Society. Hence it comes to pass, that we seldom find any number of Men live any time together in this State. The inconveniencies, that they are therein exposed to, by the irregular and uncertain exercise of the Power every Man has of punishing the transgressions of others, make them take Sanctuary under the establish'd Laws of Government, and therein seek *the preservation of their Property.* 'Tis this makes them so willingly give up every one his single power of punishing to be exercised by such alone as shall be appointed to it amongst them; and by such Rules as the Community, or those authorised by them to that purpose, shall agree on. And in this we have the original *right and rise* of both *the Legislative and Executive Power,* as well as of the Governments and Societies themselves.

128. For in the State of Nature, to omit the liberty he has of innocent Delights, a Man has two Powers.

The first is to do whatsoever he thinks fit for the preservation of himself and others within the permission of the *Law of Nature*: by which Law common to them all, he and all the rest of *Mankind are one Community*, make up one Society distinct from all other Creatures. And were it not for the corruption, and vitiousness of degenerate Men, there would be no need of any other; no necessity that Men should separate from this great and natural Community, and by positive agreements combine into smaller and divided associations.

The other power a Man has in the State of Nature, is the *power to punish the Crimes* committed against that Law. Both these he gives up, when he joyns in a private, if I may so call it, or particular Political Society, and incorporates into any Commonwealth, separate from the rest of Mankind.

129. The first *Power, viz. of doing whatsoever he thought fit for the Preservation of himself*, and the rest of Mankind, *he gives up* to be regulated by Laws made by the Society, so far forth as the preservation of himself, and the rest of that Society shall require; which Laws of the Society in many things confine the liberty he had by the Law of Nature.

130. *Secondly*, the *Power of punishing* he wholly *gives up*, and engages his natural force, (which he might before imploy in the Execution of the Law of Nature, by his own single Authority, as he thought fit) to assist the Executive Power of the Society, as the Law thereof shall require. For being now in a new State, wherein he is to enjoy many Conveniencies, from the labour, assistance, and society of others in the same Community, as well as protection from its whole strength; he is to part also with as much of his natural liberty in providing for himself, as the good, prosperity, and safety of the Society shall require: which is not only necessary, but just; since the other Members of the Society do the like.

131. But though Men when they enter into Society, give up the Equality, Liberty, and Executive Power they had in the State of Nature, into the hands of the Society, to be so far disposed of by the Legislative, as the good of the Society shall require; yet it being only with an intention in every one the better to preserve himself his Liberty and Property; (For no rational Creature can be supposed to change his condition with an intention to be worse) the power of the Society, or *Legislative* constituted by them, *can never be suppos'd to extend farther than the common good*; but is obliged to secure every ones Property by providing against those three defects abovementioned, that made the State of Nature so unsafe and uneasie. And so whoever has the Legislative or Supream Power of any Commonwealth, is bound to govern by establish'd *standing Laws*, promulgated and known to the People, and not by Extemporary Decrees; by *indifferent* and upright *Judges*, who are to decide Controversies by those Laws; And to imploy the force of the Community at home, *only in the Execution of such Laws*, or abroad to prevent or redress Foreign Injuries, and secure the Community from Inroads and Invasion. And all this to be directed to no other *end*, but the *Peace, Safety*, and *publick good* of the People.

6

Declaration of the Rights of Man, France, 1789

Approved by the National Assembly of France, August 26, 1789

The representatives of the French people, organized as a National Assembly, believing that the ignorance, neglect, or contempt of the rights of man are the sole cause of public calamities and of the corruption of governments, have determined to set forth in a solemn declaration the natural, unalienable, and sacred rights of man, in order that this declaration, being constantly before all the members of the Social body, shall remind them continually of their rights and duties; in order that the acts of the legislative power, as well as those of the executive power, may be compared at any moment with the objects and purposes of all political institutions and may thus be more respected, and, lastly, in order that the grievances of the citizens, based hereafter upon simple and incontestable principles, shall tend to the maintenance of the constitution and redound to the happiness of all. Therefore the National Assembly recognizes and proclaims, in the presence and under the auspices of the Supreme Being, the following rights of man and of the citizen:

Articles:

1. Men are born and remain free and equal in rights. Social distinctions may be founded only upon the general good.
2. The aim of all political association is the preservation of the natural and imprescriptible rights of man. These rights are liberty, property, security, and resistance to oppression.
3. The principle of all sovereignty resides essentially in the nation. No body nor individual may exercise any authority which does not proceed directly from the nation.
4. Liberty consists in the freedom to do everything which injures no one else; hence the exercise of the natural rights of each man has no limits except those which assure to the other members of the society the enjoyment of the same rights. These limits can only be determined by law.
5. Law can only prohibit such actions as are hurtful to society. Nothing may be prevented which is not forbidden by law, and no one

The Anthropology of Citizenship: A Reader, First Edition. Edited by Sian Lazar.
© 2013 John Wiley & Sons, Inc. Published 2013 by John Wiley & Sons, Inc.

may be forced to do anything not provided for by law.

6. Law is the expression of the general will. Every citizen has a right to participate personally, or through his representative, in its foundation. It must be the same for all, whether it protects or punishes. All citizens, being equal in the eyes of the law, are equally eligible to all dignities and to all public positions and occupations, according to their abilities, and without distinction except that of their virtues and talents.

7. No person shall be accused, arrested, or imprisoned except in the cases and according to the forms prescribed by law. Any one soliciting, transmitting, executing, or causing to be executed, any arbitrary order, shall be punished. But any citizen summoned or arrested in virtue of the law shall submit without delay, as resistance constitutes an offense.

8. The law shall provide for such punishments only as are strictly and obviously necessary, and no one shall suffer punishment except it be legally inflicted in virtue of a law passed and promulgated before the commission of the offense.

9. As all persons are held innocent until they shall have been declared guilty, if arrest shall be deemed indispensable, all harshness not essential to the securing of the prisoner's person shall be severely repressed by law.

10. No one shall be disquieted on account of his opinions, including his religious views, provided their manifestation does not disturb the public order established by law.

11. The free communication of ideas and opinions is one of the most precious of the rights of man. Every citizen may, accordingly, speak, write, and print with freedom, but shall be responsible for such abuses of this freedom as shall be defined by law.

12. The security of the rights of man and of the citizen requires public military forces. These forces are, therefore, established for the good of all and not for the personal advantage of those to whom they shall be Intrusted.

13. A common contribution is essential for the maintenance of the public forces and for the cost of administration. This should be equitably distributed among all the citizens in proportion to their means.

14. All the citizens have a right to decide, either personally or by their representatives, as to the necessity of the public contribution; to grant this freely; to know to what uses it is put; and to fix the proportion, the mode of assessment and of collection and the duration of the taxes.

15. Society has the right to require of every public agent an account of his administration.

16. A society in which the observance of the law is not assured, nor the separation of powers defined, has no constitution at all.

17. Since property is an inviolable and sacred right, no one shall be deprived thereof except where public necessity, legally determined, shall clearly demand it, and then only on condition that the owner shall have been previously and equitably indemnified.

7

The Second Constitution of Haiti (Hayti), May 20, 1805

Promulgated by Emperor Jacques I (Dessalines)

[...]

Preliminary Declaration

1. Art. 1.   The people inhabiting the island formerly called St. Domingo, hereby agree to form themselves into a free state sovereign and independent of any other power in the universe, under the name of empire of Hayti.
2. Slavery is forever abolished.
3. The Citizens of Hayti are brothers at home; equality in the eyes of the law is incontestably acknowledged, and there cannot exist any titles, advantages, or privileges, other than those necessarily resulting from the consideration and reward of services rendered to liberty and independence.
4. The law is the same to all, whether it punishes, or whether it protects.
5. The law has no retroactive effect.
6. Property is sacred, its violation shall be severely prosecuted.
7. The quality of citizen of Hayti is lost by emigration and naturalization in foreign countries and condemnation to corporal or disgrace punishments. The first case carries with it the punishment of death and confiscation of property.
8. The quality of Citizen is suspended in consequence of bankruptcies and failures.
9. No person is worthy of being a Haitian who is not a good father, good son, a good husband, and especially a good soldier.
10. Fathers and mothers are not permitted to disinherit their children.
11. Every Citizen must possess a mechanic art.
12. No whiteman of whatever nation he may be, shall put his foot on this territory with the title of master or proprietor, neither shall he in future acquire any property therein.
13. The preceding article cannot in the smallest degree affect white women who have been naturalized Haytians by Government, nor does it extend to children already born, or that may be born of the said women. The Germans and Polanders naturalized by government are also comprized (sic) in the dispositions of the present article.
14. All acception (sic) of colour among the children of one and the same family, of whom the chief magistrate is the father,

Source in English, http://www.webster.edu/~corbetre/haiti/history/earlyhaiti/1805-const.htm (accessed 9 April 2013), originally published in the *New York Evening Post*, 15 July 1805.

The Anthropology of Citizenship: A Reader, First Edition. Edited by Sian Lazar.
© 2013 John Wiley & Sons, Inc. Published 2013 by John Wiley & Sons, Inc.

being necessarily to cease, the Haytians shall hence forward be known only by the generic appellation of Blacks.

[...]
Of the Government

19. The Government of Hayti is entrusted to a first Magistrate, who assumes the title of Emperor and commander in chief of the army.
20. The people acknowledge for Emperor and Commander in Chief of the Army, Jacques Dessalines, the avenger and deliverer of his fellow citizens. The title of Majesty is conferred upon him, as well as upon his august spouse, the Empress.
21. The persons of their Majesties are sacred and inviolable.
22. The State will appropriate a fixed annual allowance to her Majesty the Empress, which she will continue to enjoy even after the decease of the Emperor, as princess dowager.
23. The crown is elective not hereditary.
24. There shall be assigned by the state an annual income to the children acknowledged by his Majesty the Emperor.
25. The male children acknowledged by the Emperor shall be obliged, in the same manner as other citizens, to pass successively from grade to grade, with this only difference, that their entrance into service shall begin at the fourth demi-brigade, from the period of their birth.
26. The Emperor designates, in the manner he may judge expedient, the person who is to be his successor either before or after his death.

[...]

30. The Emperor makes seals and promulgates the laws; appoints and revokes at will, the Ministers, the General in Chief for the Army, the Counselors of State, the Generals and other agents of the Empire, the sea offices, the members of the local administrations, the Commissaries of Government near the Tribunals, the judges, and other public functionaries.

31. The Emperor directs the receipts and expenditures of the State, Surveys the Mint of which he alone orders the emission, and fixes the weight and the model.
32. To him alone is reserved the power of making peace or war, to maintain political intercourse, and to form treaties.
33. He provides for the interior safety and for the defense of the State: and distributes at pleasure the sea and land forces.

[...]
Of Worship

50. The law admits of no predominant religion.
50. The freedom of worship is tolerated.
51. The state does not provide for the maintenance of any religious institution, nor any minister.

[...]
General Dispositions

1. Art. 1. To the Emperor and Empress belong the choice, the salary, and the maintenance of the persons composing their court.
2. After the decease of the reigning Emperor, when a revision of the constitution shall have been judged necessary, the council of state will assemble for that purpose, and shall be presided by the oldest member.
3. The crimes of high treason, the dilapidations of the ministers and generals shall be judged by a special council called and presided by the emperor.
4. The armed force is essentially obedient: no armed body can deliberate.
5. No person shall be judged without having been legally heard in his defense.
6. The house of every citizen is an inviolable asylum.
7. It cannot be entered but in case of conflagration, inundation, reclamation from the interior, or by virtue of an order from the emperor, or from any other authority legally constituted.
8. He deserves death who gives it to his fellow.
9. Every judgment to which the pain of death or corporal punishment is annexed shall not be carried into execution until it has been confirmed by the emperor.

10. Theft shall be punished according to the circumstances which may have preceded, accompanied or followed it.

11. Every stranger inhabiting the territory of Hayti shall be, equally with the Haytians, subject to the correctional and criminal laws of the country.

12. All property which formerly belonged to any white Frenchmen, is incontestably and of right confiscated to the use of the state.

13. Every Haytian, who, having purchased property from a white Frenchman, may have paid part of the purchase money stipulated in the act of sale, shall be responsible to the domains of the state for the remainder of the sum due.

14. Marriage is an act purely civil, and authorized by the government.

15. The law authorises (sic) divorce in all cases which shall have been previously provided for and determined.

16. A particular law shall be issued concerning children born out of wedlock.

17. Respect for the chiefs, subordination and discipline are rigorously necessary.

18. A penal code shall be published and severely observed.

19. Within each military division a public school shall be established for the instruction of youth.

20. The national colours shall be black and red.

21. Agriculture, as it is the first, the most noble, and the most useful of all the arts, shall be honored and protected.

22. Commerce, the second source of the prosperity of states, will not admit of any impediment; it ought to be favored and specially protected.

23. In each military division a tribunal of commerce shall be found, whose members shall be chosen by the Emperor from the class of merchants.

24. Good faith and integrity in commercial operations shall be religiously maintained.

25. The government assures safety and protections to neutral nations and friends who may be desirous of establishing a commercial intercourse with this island, they conforming to the regulations and customs of the country.

26. The counting houses and the merchandize of foreigners shall be under the safeguard and guarantee of the state.

27. There shall be national festivals for celebrating independence, the birth day of the emperor and his august spouse, that of agriculture and of the constitution.

28. At the first firing of the alarm gun, the cities will disappear and the nation rise.

We, the undersigned, place under the safeguard of the magistrates, fathers and mothers of families, the citizens, and the army the explicit and solemn covenant of the sacred rights of man and the duties of the citizen.

We recommend it to our successors, and present it to the friends of liberty, to philanthropists of all countries, as a signal pledge of the Divine Bounty, who in the course of his immortal decrees, has given us an opportunity of breaking our fetters, and of constituting ourselves a people, free civilized and independent.

[...]

8
Citizenship and Social Class, 1950

T. H. Marshall

The sociological hypothesis latent in Alfred Marshall's essay[1] postulates that there is a kind of basic human equality associated with the concept of full membership of a community – or, as I should say, of citizenship – which is not inconsistent with the inequalities which distinguish the various economic levels in the society. In other words, the inequality of the social class system may be acceptable provided the equality of citizenship is recognized. [...]

He recognizes only one definite right, the right of children to be educated, and in this case alone does he approve the use of compulsory powers by the state to achieve his object. He could hardly go further without imperilling his own criterion for distinguishing his system from socialism in any form – the preservation of the freedom of the competitive market. [...] His sociological hypothesis lies as near to the heart of our problem today as it did three-quarters of a century ago – in fact nearer. The basic human equality of membership [...] has been enriched with new substance and invested with a formidable array of rights. It has developed far beyond what he foresaw, or would have

wished. It has been clearly identified with the status of citizenship. [...]

Is it still true that basic equality, when enriched in substance and embodied in the formal rights of citizenship, is consistent with the inequalities of social class? I shall suggest that our society today assumes that the two are still compatible; so much so that citizenship has itself become, in certain respects, the architect of legitimate social inequality. Is it still true that the basic equality can be created and preserved without invading the freedom of the competitive market? Obviously it is not true. Our modern system is frankly a socialist system[2] not one whose authors are, as Marshall was, eager to distinguish it from socialism. But it is equally obvious that the market still functions – within limits. Here is another possible conflict of principles which demands examination. And thirdly, what is the effect of the marked shift of emphasis from duties to rights? Is this an inevitable feature of modern citizenship – inevitable and irreversible? [...]

I shall ask whether there appear to be limits beyond which the modern drive towards social

T. H. Marshall, Citizenship and social class. In *States and Societies*, David Held, ed. (Oxford: Martin Robertson, in association with The Open University, 1983), pp. 248–260.

The Anthropology of Citizenship: A Reader, First Edition. Edited by Sian Lazar.
© 2013 John Wiley & Sons, Inc. Published 2013 by John Wiley & Sons, Inc.

equality cannot, or is unlikely to pass, and I shall be thinking, not of the economic cost (I leave that vital question to the economists), but of the limits inherent in the principles that inspire the drive. But the modern drive towards social equality is, I believe, the latest phase of an evolution of citizenship which has been in continuous progress for some 250 years. [...]

The Development of Citizenship to the End of the Nineteenth Century

[...] I shall be running true to type as a sociologist if I begin by saying that I propose to divide citizenship into three parts. But the analysis is, in this case, dictated by history even more clearly than by logic. I shall call these three parts, or elements, civil, political and social. The civil element is composed of the rights necessary for individual freedom – liberty of the person, freedom of speech, thought and faith, the right to own property and to conclude valid contracts, and the right to justice. The last is of a different order from the others, because it is the right to defend and assert all one's rights on terms of equality with others and by due process of law. This shows us that the institutions most directly associated with civil rights are the courts of justice. By the political element I mean the right to participate in the exercise of political power, as a member of a body invested with political authority or as an elector of the members of such a body. The corresponding institutions are Parliament and councils of local government. By the social element I mean the whole range from the right to a modicum of economic welfare and security to the right to share to the full in the social heritage and to live the life of a civilized being according to the standards prevailing in the society. The institutions most closely connected with it are the educational system and the social services. [...]

By 1832 when political rights made their first infantile attempt to walk, civil rights had come to man's estate and bore, in most essentials, the appearance that they have today.[3] 'The specific work of the earlier Hanoverian epoch', writes Trevelyan, 'was the establishment of the rule of law; and that law, with all

its grave faults, was at least a law of freedom. On that solid foundation all our subsequent reforms were built.' This eighteenth-century achievement, interrupted by the French Revolution and completed after it, was in large measure the work of the courts, both in their daily practice and also in a series of famous cases in some of which they were fighting against Parliament in defence of individual liberty. The most celebrated actor in this drama was, I suppose, John Wilkes, and, although we may deplore the absence in him of those noble and saintly qualities which we should like to find in our national heroes, we cannot complain if the cause of liberty is sometimes championed by a libertine.

In the economic field the basic civil right is the right to work, that is to say the right to follow the occupation of one's choice in the place of one's choice, subject only to legitimate demands for preliminary technical training. This right had been denied by both statute and custom; on the one hand by the Elizabethan Statute of Artificers, which confined certain occupations to certain social classes, and on the other by local regulations reserving employment in a town to its own members and by the use of apprenticeship as an instrument of exclusion rather than of recruitment. The recognition of the right involved the formal acceptance of a fundamental change of attitude. The old assumption that local and group monopolies were in the public interest, because 'trade and traffic cannot be maintained or increased without order and government', was replaced by the new assumption that such restrictions were an offence against the liberty of the subject and a menace to the prosperity of the nation. [...]

By the beginning of the nineteenth century this principle of individual economic freedom was accepted as axiomatic. You are probably familiar with the passage quoted by the Webbs from the report of the Select Committee of 1811, which states that:

> no interference of the legislature with the freedom of trade, or with the perfect liberty of every individual to dispose of his time and of his labour in the way and on the terms which he may judge most conducive to his

own interest, can take place without violating general principles of the first importance to the prosperity and happiness of the community.⁴ [...]

The story of civil rights in their formative period is one of the gradual addition of new rights to a status that already existed and was held to appertain to all adult members of the community – or perhaps one should say to all male members, since the status of women, or at least of married women, was in some important respects peculiar. This democratic, or universal, character of the status arose naturally from the fact that it was essentially the status of freedom, and in seventeenth-century England all men were free. Servile status, or villeinage by blood, had lingered on as a patent anachronism in the days of Elizabeth, but vanished soon afterwards. This change from servile to free labour has been described by Professor Tawney as 'a high landmark in the development both of economic and political society', and as 'the final triumph of the common law' in regions from which it had been excluded for four centuries. Henceforth the English peasant 'is a member of a society in which there is, nominally at least, one law for all men'.⁵ The liberty which his predecessors had won by fleeing into the free towns had become his by right. In the towns the terms 'freedom' and 'citizenship' were interchangeable. When freedom became universal, citizenship grew from a local into a national institution.

The story of political rights is different both in time and in character. The formative period began, as I have said, in the early nineteenth century, when the civil rights attached to the status of freedom had already acquired sufficient substance to justify us in speaking of a general status of citizenship. And, when it began, it consisted, not in the creation of new rights to enrich a status already enjoyed by all, but in the granting of old rights to new sections of the population. [...]

It is clear that, if we maintain that in the nineteenth century citizenship in the form of civil rights was universal, the political franchise was not one of the rights of citizenship. It was the privilege of a limited economic class, whose limits were extended by each successive Reform Act. [...]

It was, as we shall see, appropriate that nineteenth-century capitalist society should treat political rights as a secondary product of civil rights. It was equally appropriate that the twentieth century should abandon this position and attach political rights directly and independently to citizenship as such. This vital change of principle was put into effect when the Act of 1918, by adopting manhood suffrage, shifted the basis of political rights from economic substance to personal status. I say 'manhood' deliberately in order to emphasize the great significance of this reform quite apart from the second, and no less important, reform introduced at the same time – namely the enfranchisement of women. [...]

The original source of social rights was membership of local communities and functional associations. This source was supplemented and progressively replaced by a Poor Law and a system of wage regulation which were nationally conceived and locally administered. [...]

As the pattern of the old order dissolved under the blows of a competitive economy, and the plan disintegrated, the Poor Law was left high and dry as an isolated survival from which the idea of social rights was gradually drained away. But at the very end of the eighteenth century there occurred a final struggle between the old and the new, between the planned (or patterned) society and the competitive economy. And in this battle citizenship was divided against itself; social rights sided with the old and civil with the new. [...]

In this brief episode of our history we see the Poor Law as the aggressive champion of the social rights of citizenship. In the succeeding phase we find the attacker driven back far behind his original position. By the Act of 1834 the Poor Law renounced all claim to trespass on the territory of the wages system, or to interfere with the forces of the free market. It offered relief only to those who, through age or sickness, were incapable of continuing the battle, and to those other weaklings who gave up the struggle, admitted defeat, and cried for mercy. The tentative move towards the concept of social security was reversed. But more than that, the minimal social rights that remained were detached from the status of citizenship. The Poor Law treated the claims of the poor, not as an integral part of the rights of the citizen, but as an alternative to them – as claims which could be met only if the claimants ceased to be citizens in any true sense of the word. For paupers forfeited in practice the civil right of personal liberty, by internment in the workhouse, and they forfeited by law any political rights they might possess. This disability of defranchisement remained in being until 1918, and the significance of its final removal has, perhaps, not been fully appreciated. The stigma which clung to poor relief expressed the deep feelings of a people who understood that those who accepted relief must cross the road that separated the community of citizens from the outcast company of the destitute.

The Poor Law is not an isolated example of this divorce of social rights from the status of citizenship. The early Factory Acts show the same tendency. Although in fact they led to an improvement of working conditions and a reduction of working hours to the benefit of all employed in the industries to which they applied, they meticulously refrained from giving this protection directly to the adult male – the citizen *par excellence*. And they did so out of respect for his status as a citizen, on the grounds that enforced protective measures curtailed the civil right to conclude a free contract of employment. Protection was confined to women and children, and champions of women's rights were quick to detect the implied insult. Women were protected because they were not citizens. If they wished to enjoy full and responsible citizenship, they must forgo protection. By the end of the nineteenth century such arguments had become obsolete, and the factory code had become one of the pillars in the edifice of social rights. [...]

By the end of the nineteenth century, elementary education was not only free, it was compulsory. This signal departure from *laissez faire* could, of course, be justified on the grounds that free choice is a right only for mature minds, that children are naturally subject to discipline, and that parents cannot be trusted to do what is in the best interests of their children. But the principle goes deeper than that. We have here a personal right combined with a public duty to exercise the right. Is the public duty imposed merely for the benefit of the individual – because

children cannot fully appreciate their own interests and parents may be unfit to enlighten them? I hardly think that this can be an adequate explanation. It was increasingly recognized, as the nineteenth century wore on, that political democracy needed an educated electorate, and that scientific manufacture needed educated workers and technicians. The duty to improve and civilize oneself is therefore a social duty, and not merely a personal one, because the social health of a society depends upon the civilization of its members. And a community that enforces this duty has begun to realize that its culture is an organic unity and its civilization a national heritage. It follows that the growth of public elementary education during the nineteenth century was the first decisive step on the road to the re-establishment of the social rights of citizenship in the twentieth. [...]

The Impact of Citizenship on Social Class

Citizenship is a status bestowed on those who are full members of a community. All who possess the status are equal with respect to the rights and duties with which the status is endowed. There is no universal principle that determines what those rights and duties shall be, but societies in which citizenship is a developing institution create an image of an ideal citizenship against which achievement can be measured and towards which aspiration can be directed. The urge forward along the path thus plotted is an urge towards a fuller measure of equality, an enrichment of the stuff of which the status is made and an increase in the number of those on whom the status is bestowed. Social class, on the other hand, is a system of inequality. And it too, like citizenship, can be based on a set of ideals, beliefs and values. It is therefore reasonable to expect that the impact of citizenship on social class should take the form of a conflict between opposing principles. If I am right in my contention that citizenship has been a developing institution in England at least since the latter part of the seventeenth century, then it is clear that its growth coincides with the rise of capitalism, which is a system, not of equality, but of inequality. Here is something that needs explaining. How is it that these two opposing principles could grow and flourish side by side in the same soil? What made it possible for them to be reconciled with one another and to become, for a time at least, allies instead of antagonists? The question is a pertinent one, for it is clear that, in the twentieth century, citizenship and the capitalist class system have been at war. [...]

It is true that class still functions. Social inequality is regarded as necessary and purposeful. It provides the incentive to effort and designs the distribution of power. But there is no overall pattern of inequality, in which an appropriate value is attached, *a priori*, to each social level. Inequality therefore, though necessary, may become excessive. As Patrick Colquhoun said, in a much-quoted passage: 'Without a large proportion of poverty there could be no riches, since riches are the offspring of labour, while labour can result only from a state of poverty ... Poverty therefore is a most necessary and indispensable ingredient in society, without which nations and communities could not exist in a state of civilization.'[6] [...]

The more you look on wealth as conclusive proof of merit, the more you incline to regard poverty as evidence of failure – but the penalty for failure may seem to be greater than the offence warrants. In such circumstances it is natural that the more unpleasant features of inequality should be treated, rather irresponsibly, as a nuisance, like the black smoke that used to pour unchecked from our factory chimneys. And so in time, as the social conscience stirs to life, class-abatement, like smoke-abatement, becomes a desirable aim to be pursued as far as is compatible with the continued efficiency of the social machine.

But class-abatement in this form was not an attack on the class system. On the contrary it aimed, often quite consciously, at making the class system less vulnerable to attack by alleviating its less defensible consequences. It raised the floor-level in the basement of the social edifice, and perhaps made it rather more hygienic than it was before. But it remained a basement, and the upper stories of the building were unaffected. [...]

There developed, in the latter part of the nineteenth century, a growing interest in equality as a principle of social justice and an appreciation of the fact that the formal recognition of an equal capacity for rights was not enough. In theory even the complete removal of all the barriers that separated civil rights from their remedies would not have interfered with the principles or the class structure of the capitalist system. It would, in fact, have created a situation which many supporters of the competitive market economy falsely assumed to be already in existence. But in practice the attitude of mind which inspired the efforts to remove these barriers grew out of a conception of equality which overstepped these narrow limits, the conception of equal social worth, not merely of equal natural rights. Thus although citizenship, even by the end of the nineteenth century, had done little to reduce social inequality, it had helped to guide progress into the path which led directly to the egalitarian policies of the twentieth century. [...]

This growing national consciousness, this awakening public opinion, and these first stirrings of a sense of community membership and common heritage did not have any material effect on class structure and social inequality for the simple and obvious reason that, even at the end of the nineteenth century, the mass of the working people did not wield effective political power. By that time the franchise was fairly wide, but those who had recently received the vote had not yet learned how to use it. The political rights of citizenship, unlike the civil rights, were full of potential danger to the capitalist system, although those who were cautiously extending them down the social scale probably did not realize quite how great the danger was. They could hardly be expected to foresee what vast changes could be brought about by the peaceful use of political power, without a violent and bloody revolution. The 'planned society' and the welfare state had not yet risen over the horizon or come within the view of the practical politician. The foundations of the market economy and the contractual system seemed strong enough to stand against any probable assault. In fact, there were some grounds for expecting that the working classes, as they became educated, would accept the basic principles of the system and be content to rely for their protection and progress on the civil rights of citizenship, which contained no obvious menace to competitive capitalism. Such a view was encouraged by the fact that one of the main achievements of political power in the later nineteenth century was the recognition of the right of collective bargaining. This meant that social progress was being sought by strengthening civil rights, not by creating social rights; through the use of contract in the open market, not through a minimum wage and social security.

But this interpretation underrates the significance of this extension of civil rights in the economic sphere. For civil rights were in origin intensely individual, and that is why they harmonized with the individualistic phase of capitalism. By the device of incorporation groups were enabled to act legally as individuals. This important development did not go unchallenged, and limited liability was widely denounced as an infringement of individual responsibility. But the position of trade unions was even more anomalous, because they did not seek or obtain incorporation. They can, therefore, exercise vital civil rights collectively on behalf of their members without formal collective responsibility, while the individual responsibility of the workers in relation to contract is largely unenforceable. These civil rights became, for the workers, an instrument for raising their social and economic status, that is to say, for establishing the claim that they, as citizens, were entitled to certain social rights. But the normal method of establishing social rights is by the exercise of political power, for social rights imply an absolute right to a certain standard of civilization which is conditional only on the discharge of the general duties of citizenship. Their content does not depend on the economic value of the individual claimant. There is therefore a significant difference between a genuine collective bargain through which economic forces in a free market seek to achieve equilibrium and the use of collective civil rights to assert basic claims to the elements of social justice. Thus the acceptance of collective bargaining was not simply a natural extension of civil rights; it represented the transfer of an important process from the political to the civil sphere of

citizenship. But 'transfer' is, perhaps, a misleading term, for at the time when this happened the workers either did not possess, or had not yet learned to use, the political right of the franchise. Since then they have obtained and made full use of that right. Trade unionism has, therefore, created a secondary system of industrial citizenship parallel with and supplementary to the system of political citizenship. [...]

A new period opened at the end of the nineteenth century, conveniently marked by Booth's survey of Life and Labour of the People in London and the Royal Commission on the Aged Poor. It saw the first big advance in social rights, and this involved significant changes in the egalitarian principle as expressed in citizenship. But there were other forces at work as well. A rise of money incomes unevenly distributed over the social classes altered the economic distance which separated these classes from one another, diminishing the gap between skilled and unskilled labour and between skilled labour and non-manual workers, while the steady increase in small savings blurred the class distinction between the capitalist and the propertyless proletarian. Secondly, a system of direct taxation, ever more steeply graduated, compressed the whole scale of disposable incomes. Thirdly, mass production for the home market and a growing interest on the part of industry in the needs and tastes of the common people enabled the less well-to-do to enjoy a material civilization which differed less markedly in quality from that of the rich than it had ever done before. All this profoundly altered the setting in which the progress of citizenship took place. Social integration spread from the sphere of sentiment and patriotism into that of material enjoyment. The components of a civilized and cultured life, formerly the monopoly of the few, were brought progressively within reach of the many, who were encouraged thereby to stretch out their hands towards those that still eluded their grasp. The diminution of inequality strengthened the demand for its abolition, at least with regard to the essentials of social welfare.

These aspirations have in part been met by incorporating social rights in the status of citizenship and thus creating a universal right to real income which is not proportionate to the market value of the claimant. Class-abatement is still the aim of social rights, but it has acquired a new meaning. It is no longer merely an attempt to abate the obvious nuisance of destitution in the lowest ranks of society. It has assumed the guise of action modifying the whole pattern of social inequality. It is no longer content to raise the floor-level in the basement of the social edifice, leaving the superstructure as it was. It has begun to remodel the whole building, and it might even end by converting a skyscraper into a bungalow. It is therefore important to consider whether any such ultimate aim is implicit in the nature of this development, or whether, as I put it at the outset, there are natural limits to the contemporary drive towards greater social and economic equality. [...]

The degree of equalization achieved [by the modern system of welfare benefits] depends on four things: whether the benefit is offered to all or to a limited class; whether it takes the form of money payment or service rendered; whether the minimum is high or low; and how the money to pay for the benefit is raised. Cash benefits subject to income limit and means test had a simple and obvious equalizing effect. They achieved class-abatement in the early and limited sense of the term. The aim was to ensure that all citizens should attain at least to the prescribed minimum, either by their own resources or with assistance if they could not do it without. The benefit was given only to those who needed it, and thus inequalities at the bottom of the scale were ironed out. The system operated in its simplest and most unadulterated form in the case of the Poor Law and old age pensions. But economic equalization might be accompanied by psychological class discrimination. The stigma which attached to the Poor Law made 'pauper' a derogatory term defining a class. 'Old age pensioner' may have had a little of the same flavour, but without the taint of shame. [...]

The extension of the social services is not primarily a means of equalizing incomes. In some cases it may, in others it may not. The question is relatively unimportant; it belongs to a different department of social policy. What matters is that there is a general enrichment of the concrete substance of civilized life, a general reduction of risk and insecurity, an equalization between the more and the less fortunate at all levels – between the healthy and the sick, the employed and the unemployed, the old and the active, the bachelor and the father of a large family. Equalization is not so much between classes as between individuals within a population which is now treated for this purpose as though it were one class. Equality of status is more important than equality of income. [...]

I said earlier that in the twentieth century citizenship and the capitalist class system have been at war. Perhaps the phrase is rather too strong, but it is quite clear that the former has imposed modifications on the latter. But we should not be justified in assuming that, although status is a principle that conflicts with contract, the stratified status system which is creeping into citizenship is an alien element in the economic world outside. Social rights in their modern form imply an invasion of contract by status, the subordination of market price to social justice, the replacement of the free bargain by the declaration of rights. But are these principles quite foreign to the practice of the market today, or are they there already, entrenched within the contract system itself? I think it is clear that they are. [...]

Conclusions

I have tried to show how citizenship, and other forces outside it, have been altering the pattern of social inequality. [...] We have to look, here, for the combined effects of three factors. First, the compression, at both ends, of the scale of income distribution. Second, the great extension of the area of common culture and common experience. And third, the enrichment of the universal status of citizenship, combined with the recognition and stabilization of certain status differences chiefly through the linked systems of education and occupation. [...]

I asked, at the beginning, whether there was any limit to the present drive towards social equality inherent in the principles governing the movement. My answer is that the preservation of economic inequalities has been made more difficult by the enrichment of the status of citizenship. There is less room for them, and there is more and more likelihood of their being challenged. But we are certainly proceeding at present on the assumption that the hypothesis is valid. And this assumption provides the answer to the second question. We are not aiming at absolute equality. There are limits inherent in the egalitarian movement. But the movement is a double one. It operates partly through citizenship and partly through the economic system. In both cases the aim is to remove inequalities which cannot be regarded as legitimate, but the standard of legitimacy is different. In the former it is the standard of social justice, in the latter it is social justice combined with economic necessity. It is possible, therefore, that the inequalities permitted by the two halves of the movement will not coincide. Class distinctions may survive which have no appropriate economic function, and economic differences which do not correspond with accepted class distinctions. [...]

NOTES

1 Alfred Marshall, a distinguished Professor of Economics at Cambridge, whose lecture on 'The future of the working classes' (1873) provided T. H. Marshall with his point of departure.
2 Marshall, writing in 1949, in the heyday of the welfare state, means by this 'social democratic'.
3 G. M. Trevelyan, 1942. *English Social History*, p. 351.
4 Sidney Webb, and Beatrice Webb, 1920. *History of Trade Unionism*, p. 60.
5 R. H. Tawney, 1916. *The Agrarian Problem in the Sixteenth Century*, pp. 43–4.
6 P. Colquhoun, 1806. *A Treatise in Indigence*, pp. 7–8.

The Liberal–Communitarian Debate

9

The Ideal of Community and the Politics of Difference, 1986

Iris Marion Young

Prologue

The ideal of community, I suggest in this chapter, privileges unity over difference, immediacy over mediation, sympathy over recognition of the limits of one's understanding of others from their point of view. Community is an understandable dream, expressing a desire for selves that are transparent to one another, relationships of mutual identification, social closeness and comfort. The dream is understandable, but politically problematic, I argue, because those motivated by it will tend to suppress differences among themselves or implicitly to exclude from their political groups persons with whom they do not identify. The vision of small, face-to-face, decentralized units that this ideal promotes, moreover, is an unrealistic vision for transformative politics in mass urban society.

[...]

Introduction

Radical theorists and activists often appeal to an ideal of community as an alternative to the oppression and exploitation that they argue, characterizes capitalist patriarchal society. Such appeals often do not explicitly articulate the meaning of the concept of community but rather tend to evoke an affective value. Even more rarely do those who invoke an ideal of community as an alternative to capitalist patriarchal society ask what it presupposes or implies, or what it means concretely to institute a society that embodies community. I raise a number of critical questions about the meaning, presuppositions, implications, and practical import of the ideal of community.

As in all conceptual reflections, in this case there is no universally shared concept of community, only particular articulations that overlap, complement, or sit at acute angles to one another.[1] I will rely on the definitions and

Iris Marion Young, The ideal of community and the politics of difference. In *Feminism/Postmodernism*, Linda J. Nicholson, ed. (London: Routledge, 1990), pp. 300–323 (originally published in *Social Theory and Practice* 12(1) (1986): 1–26).

The Anthropology of Citizenship: A Reader, First Edition. Edited by Sian Lazar.

expositions of a number of writers for examples of conceptualizations about community as a political ideal. All these writers share a critique of liberal individualist social ontology, and most think democratic socialism is the best principle of social organization. I claim acceptance for my analysis only within this general field of political discourse, although I suspect that much of the conceptual structure I identify applies to an ideal of community that might be appealed to by more conservative or liberal writers.

I criticize the notion of community on both philosophical and practical grounds. I argue that the ideal of community participates in what Derrida calls the metaphysics of presence and Adorno calls the logic of identity, a metaphysics that denies difference. The ideal of community presumes subjects can understand one another as they understand themselves. It thus denies the difference between subjects. The desire for community relies on the same desire for social wholeness and identification that underlies racism and ethnic chauvinism on the one hand and political sectarianism on the other.

Insofar as the ideal of community entails promoting a model of face-to-face relations as best, it devalues and denies difference in the form of temporal and spatial distancing. The ideal of a society consisting of decentralized face-to-face communities is undesirably utopian in several ways. It fails to see that alienation and violence are not only a function of mediation of social relations but also can and do exist in face-to-face relations. It implausibly proposes a society without the city. It fails to address the political question of the relations among face-to-face communities.

The ideal of community, finally, totalizes and detemporalizes its conception of social life by setting up an opposition between authentic and inauthentic social relations. It also detemporalizes its understanding of social change by positing the desired society as the complete negation of existing society. It thus provides no understanding of the move from here to there that would be rooted in an understanding of the contradictions and possibilities of existing society.

I propose that instead of community as the normative ideal of political emancipation, that radicals should develop a politics of difference.

A model of the unoppressive city offers an understanding of social relations without domination in which persons live together in relations of mediation among strangers with whom they are not in community.

The Metaphysics of Presence

[...]

Community usually appears as one side of a dichotomy in which individualism is the opposite pole, but as with any such opposition, each side is determined by its relation to the other. I argue that the ideal of community exhibits a totalizing impulse and denies difference in two primary ways. First, it denies the difference within and between subjects. Second, in privileging face-to-face relations it seeks a model of social relations that are not mediated by space and time distancing. In radically opposing the inauthentic social relations of alienated society with the authentic social relations of community, moreover, it detemporalizes the process of social change into a static before and after structure.

The Opposition between Individualism and Community

Critics of liberalism frequently invoke a conception of community to project an alternative to the individualism and abstract formalism they attribute to liberalism.[2] This alternative social ontology rejects the image of persons as separate and self-contained atoms, each with the same formal rights, the rights to keep others out, separate. In the idea of community, critics of liberalism find a social ontology which sees the attributes of a person as coeval with the society in which he or she lives.

For such writers, the ideal of community evokes the absence of the self-interested competitiveness of modern society. In this ideal of community, critics of liberalism find an alternative to the abstract, formal methodology of liberalism. Existing in community with others entails more than merely respecting their rights, but rather attending to and sharing in the particularity of their needs and interests.

For example, in his critique of Rawls, Michael Sandel argues that liberalism's emphasis on the primacy of justice presupposes a self as an antecedent unity existing prior to its desires and goals, whole unto itself, separated and bounded. This is an unreal and incoherent conception of the self, he argues, better replaced by a constitutive conception of self as the product of an identity it shares with others, all of whom mutually understand and affirm one another. This constitutive conception of self is expressed by the concept of community.[3]

[...]

In contemporary political discussion, for the most part, the ideal of community arises in this way as a response to the individualism perceived as the prevailing theoretical position, and the alienation and fragmentation perceived as the prevailing condition of society. Community appears, that is, as part of an opposition, individualism/community, separated self/shared self. In this opposition each term comes to be defined by its negative relation to the other, thus existing in a logical dependency. I suggest that this opposition, however, is integral to modern political theory and is not an alternative to it.

The opposition individualism/community receives one of its expressions in bourgeois culture in the opposition between masculinity and femininity. The culture identifies masculinity with the values associated with individualism – self-sufficiency, competition, separation, the formal equality of rights. The culture identifies femininity, on the other hand, with the values associated with community-affective relations of care, mutual aid, and cooperation.

Carol Gilligan has recently posed this opposition between masculine and feminine in terms of the opposition between two orientations on moral reasoning.[4] The "ethic of rights" that Gilligan takes to be typical of masculine thinking emphasizes the separation of selves and the sense of fair play necessary to mediate the competition among such separated selves. The "ethic of care," on the other hand, which she takes to be typical of feminine thinking, emphasizes relatedness among persons and is an ethic of sympathy and affective attention to particular needs, rather than formal measuring of each according to universal rules. This ethic of care expresses the relatedness of the ideal of community as opposed to the atomistic formalism of liberal individualism.

The opposition between individualism and community, then, is homologous with and often implies the opposition masculine/feminine, public/private, calculative/affective, instrumental/aesthetic, which are also present in modern political thinking.[5] This thinking has always valued the first side of these oppositions more highly than the second, and it has provided them with a dominant institutional expression in the society. For that reason asserting the value of community over individualism, the feminine over the masculine, the aesthetic over the instrumental, the relational over the competitive, does have some critical force with respect to the dominant ideology and social relations. The oppositions themselves, however, arise from and belong to bourgeois culture, and for that reason merely reversing their valuation does not constitute a genuine alternative to capitalist patriarchal society.

Like most such oppositions, moreover, individualism and community have a common logic underlying their polarity, which makes it possible for them to define each other negatively. Each entails a denial of difference and desire to bring multiplicity and heterogeneity into unity, although in opposing ways. Liberal individualism denies difference by positing the self as a solid, self-sufficient unity, not defined by or in need of anything or anyone other than itself. Its formalistic ethic of rights denies difference by leveling all such separated individuals under a common measure of rights. Community, on the other hand, denies difference by positing fusion rather than separation as the social ideal. Community proponents conceive the social subject as a relation of unity composed by identification and symmetry among individuals within a totality. As Sandel puts it, the opacity of persons tends to dissolve as ends, vocabulary, and practices become identical. This represents an urge to see persons in unity with each other in a shared whole.

As is the case with many dichotomies, in this one the possibilities for social ontology and social relations appear to be exhausted in the two categories. For many writers, the rejection of individualism logically entails asserting community, and conversely any rejection of community entails that one necessarily supports individualism. In their discussion of the debate between Elshtain and Ehrenreich, for example, Sara Evans and Harry Boyte claim that Ehrenreich promotes individualism because she rejects the appeal to community that Elshtain makes.[6] The possibility that there could be other conceptions of social organization does not appear because all possibilities have been reduced to the mutually exclusive opposition between individualism and community.

Ultimately, however, for most radical theorists the hard opposition of individualism and community breaks down. Unlike reactionary appeals to community which consistently assert the subordination of individual aims and values to the collective, most radical theorists assert that community itself consists in the respect for and fulfillment of individual aims and capacities. The neat distinction between individualism and community thus generates a dialectic in which each is a condition for the other.

[...]

Denial of Difference as Time and Space Distancing

Many political theorists who put forward an ideal of community specify small-group, face-to-face relations as essential to the realization of that ideal. Peter Manicas expresses a version of the ideal of community that includes this face-to-face specification.

Consider an association in which persons are in face-to-face contact, but where the relations of persons are not mediated by "authorities," sanctified rules, reified bureaucracies or commodities. Each is prepared to absorb the attitudes, reasoning and ideas of others and each is in a position to do so. Their relations, thus, are open, immediate and reciprocal. Further, the total conditions of their social lives are to be conjointly determined with each having an equal voice and equal power. When these conditions are satisfied and when as a result, the consequences and fruits of their associated and independent activities are perceived and consciously become an object of individual desire and effort, then there is a democratic community.[7]

Roberto Unger argues that community requires face-to-face interaction among members within a plurality of contexts. To understand other people and to be understood by them in our concrete individuality, we must not only work together but play together, take care of children together, grieve together, and so on.[8] Christian Bay envisions the good society as founded upon small face-to-face communities of direct democracy and many-sided interaction.[9] Michael Taylor specifies that in a community, relations among members must be direct and many-sided. Like Manicas, he asserts that relations are direct only when they are unmediated by representatives, leaders, bureaucrats, state institutions, or codes.[10] While Gould does not specify face-to-face relations as necessary, some of her language suggests that community can only be realized in such face-to-face relations. In the institutionalization of democratic socialism, she says, "social combination now becomes the *immediate* subjective relations of mutuality among individuals. The relations again become *personal* relations as in the precapitalist stage, but no longer relations of domination and no longer mediated, as in the second stage, by external objects."[11]

I take there to be several problems with the privileging of face-to-face relations by theorists of community. It presumes an illusory ideal of unmediated social relations and wrongly identifies mediation with alienation. It denies difference in the sense of time and space distancing. It implies a model of the good society as consisting of decentralized small units, which is both unrealistic and politically undesirable. Finally, it avoids the political question of the relation among the decentralized communities.

All the writers cited previously give primacy to face-to-face presence because they claim that only under those conditions can the social relations be *immediate*. I understand them to mean several things by social relations that are immediate. They are direct, personal relations, in which each understands the other in her or his individuality. Immediacy here means relations of co-presence in which persons experience a simultaneity of speaking and hearing and are in the same space, that is, have the possibility to move close enough to touch.[12]

This ideal of the immediate presence of subjects to one another, however, is a metaphysical illusion. Even a face-to-face relation between two people is mediated by voice and gesture, spacing and temporality. As soon as a third person enters the interaction, the possibility arises of the relation between the first two being mediated through the third, and so on. The mediation of relations among persons by speech and actions of still other persons is a fundamental condition of sociality. The richness, creativity, diversity, and potential of a society expand with growth in the scope and means of its media, linking persons across time and distance. The greater the time and distance, however, the greater the number of persons who stand between other persons.

The normative privileging of face-to-face relations in the ideal of community seeks to suppress difference in the sense of the time and space distancing of social processes, which material media facilitate and enlarge. Such an ideal dematerializes its conception of interaction and institutions. For all social interaction takes place over time and across space. Social desire consists in the urge to carry meaning, agency, and the effects of agency beyond the moment and beyond the place. As laboring subjects we separate the moment of production from the moment of consumption. Even societies confined to a limited territory with few institutions and a small population devise means of their members communicating with one another over distances, means of maintaining their social relationships even though they are not face to face. Societies occupy wider and wider territorial fields and increasingly differentiate their activity in space, time, and function, a movement that, of course, accelerates and takes on qualitatively specific form in modern industrial societies.[13]

I suggest that there are no conceptual grounds for considering face-to-face relations more pure, authentic social relations than relations mediated across time and distance. For both face-to-face and non-face-to-face relations are mediated relations, and in both there is as much the possibility of separation and violence as there is communication and consensus.

[...]

By positing a society of immediate face-to-face relations as ideal, community theorists generate a dichotomy between the "authentic" society of the future and the "inauthentic" society we live in, which is characterized only by alienation, bureaucratization, and degradation. Such a dichotomization between the inauthentic society we have and the authentic society of community, however, detemporalizes our understanding of social change. On this understanding, social change and revolution consist in the complete negation of this society and the establishment of the truly good society. In her scheme of social evolution, Gould conceives of "the society of the future" as the negated sublation of capitalist society. This understands history not as temporal process but as divided into two static structures: the before of alienated society and the after of community.

The projection of the ideal of community as the radical other of existing society denies difference in the sense of the contradictions and ambiguities of social life. Instead of dichotomizing the pure and the impure into two stages of history or two kinds of social relations, a liberating politics should conceive the social process in which we move as a multiplicity of actions and structures which cohere and contradict, some of them exploitative and some of them liberating. The polarization between the impure, inauthentic society we live in and the pure, authentic society we seek to institute detemporalizes the process of change because it fails to articulate how we move from one to the other. If institutional change is possible at all, it must begin from intervening in the contradictions and tensions of existing society. No telos of the final society exists, moreover; society understood as a moving and contradictory process implies that change for the better is always possible and always necessary.

The requirement that genuine community embody face-to-face relations, when taken as a model of the good society, carries a specific vision of social organization. Since the ideal of community demands that relations between members be direct and many-sided, the ideal society is composed of small locales, populated by a small enough number of persons so that each can be personally acquainted with all the others. For most writers, this implies that the ideal social organization is decentralized, with small-scale industry and local markets. Each community aims for economic self-sufficiency, and each democratically makes its own decisions about how to organize its working and playing life.

[...]

Such a model of the good society as composed of decentralized, economically self-sufficient, face-to-face communities functioning as autonomous political entities is both wildly utopian and undesirable. To bring it into being would require dismantling the urban character of modern society, a gargantuan physical overhaul of living space, work places, places of trade and commerce. A model of a transformed better society must in some concrete sense begin from the concrete material structures that are given to us at this time in history, and in the United States these are large-scale industry and urban centers. The model of society composed of small communities is not desirable, at least in the eyes of many. If we take seriously the way many people live their lives today, it appears that people enjoy cities, that is, places where strangers are thrown together.

One final problem arises from the model of face-to-face community taken as a political goal. The model of the good society as usually articulated leaves completely unaddressed the question of how such small communities are to relate to one another. Frequently, the ideal projects a level of self-sufficiency and decentralization which suggests that proponents envision few relations among the decentralized communities except those of friendly visits. But surely it is unrealistic to assume that such decentralized communities need not engage in extensive relations of exchange of resources, goods, and culture. Even if one accepts the notion that a radical restructuring of society in the direction of a just and humane society entails people living in small democratically organized units of work and neighborhood, this has not addressed the important political question: How will the relations among these communities be organized so as to foster justice and prevent domination? When we raise this political question the philosophical and practical importance of mediation re-emerges. Once again, politics must be conceived as a relationship of strangers who do not understand one another in a subjective and immediate sense, relating across time and distance.

City Life and the Politics of Difference

I have claimed that radical politics must begin from historical givens and conceive radical change not as the negation of the given but rather as making something good from many elements of the given. The city, as a vastly populated area with large-scale industry and places of mass assembly, is for us a historical given, and radical politics must begin from the existence of modern urban life. The material surroundings and structures available to us define and presuppose urban relationships. The very size of populations in our society and most other nations of the world, coupled with a continuing sense of national or ethnic identity with millions of other people, all support the conclusion that a vision of dismantling the city is hopelessly utopian.

Starting from the given of modern urban life is not simply necessary, moreover, it is desirable. Even for many of those who decry the alienation, massification, and bureaucratization of capitalist patriarchal society, city life exerts a powerful attraction. Modern literature, art, and film have celebrated city life, its energy, cultural diversity, technological complexity, and the multiplicity of its activities. Even many of the most staunch proponents of decentralized community love to show visiting friends around the Boston or San Francisco or New York in which they live, climbing up towers to see the glitter of lights and sampling the fare at the best ethnic restaurants. For many people deemed deviant in the closeness of the face-to-face community in which they lived, whether "independent" women or socialists or gay men and lesbians, the city has often offered a welcome anonymity and some measure of freedom.[14] To be sure, the liberatory possibilities of capitalist cities have been fraught with ambiguity.

Yet, I suggest that instead of the ideal of community, we begin from our positive experience of city life to form a vision of the good society. Our political ideal is the unoppressive city. In sketching this ideal, I assume some material premises. We will assume a productivity level in the society that can meet everyone's needs, and a physical urban environment that is cleaned up and renovated. We will assume, too, that everyone who can work has meaningful work and those who cannot are provided for with dignity. In sketching this ideal of city life, I am concerned to describe the city as a *kind of relationship* of people to one another, to their own history and one another's history. Thus, by "city" I am not referring only to those huge metropolises that we call cities in the United States. The kinds of relationship I describe obtain also ideally in those places we call towns, where perhaps 10,000 or 20,000 people live.

As a process of people's relating to one another, city life embodies difference in all the senses I have discussed in this chapter. The city obviously exhibits the temporal and spatial distancing and differentiation that I have argued, the ideal of community seeks to collapse. On the face of the city environment lies its history and the history of the individuals and groups that have dwelt within it. Such physical historicity, as well as the functions and groups that live in the city at any given time, create its spatial differentiation. The city as a network and sedimentation of discretely understood places, such as particular buildings, parks, neighborhoods, and as a physical environment offers changes and surprises in transition from one place to another.

The temporal and spatial differentiation that mark the physical environment of the city produce an experience of aesthetic *inexhaustibility*. Buildings, squares, the twists and turns of streets and alleys offer an inexhaustible store of individual spaces and things, each with unique aesthetic characteristics. The juxtaposition of incongruous styles and functions that usually emerge after a long time in city places contribute to this pleasure in detail and surprise. This is an experience of difference in the sense of always being inserted. The modern city is without walls; it is not planned and coherent. Dwelling in the city means always having a sense of beyond, that there is much human life beyond my experience going on in or near these spaces, and I can never grasp the city as a whole.

City life thus also embodies difference as the contrary of the face-to-face ideal expressed by most assertions of community. City life is the "being-together" of strangers. Strangers encounter one another, either face to face or through media, often remaining strangers and yet acknowledging their contiguity in living and the contributions each makes to the others. In such encountering people are not "internally" related, as the community theorists would have it, and do not understand one another from within their own perspective. They are externally related, they experience each other as other, different, from different groups, histories, professions, cultures, which they do not understand.

The public spaces of the city are both an image of the total relationships of city life and a primary way those relationships are enacted and experienced. A public space is a place accessible to anyone, where people engage in activity as individuals or in small groups. In public spaces people are aware of each other's presence and even at times attend to it. In a city there are a multitude of such public spaces: streets, restaurants, concert halls, parks. In such public spaces the diversity of the city's residents come together and dwell side by side, sometimes appreciating one another, entertaining one another, or just chatting, always to go off again as strangers. City parks as we now experience them often have this character.

City life implies a social exhaustibility quite different from the ideal of the face-to-face community in which there is mutual understanding and group identification and loyalty. The city consists in a great diversity of people and groups, with a multitude of subcultures and differentiated activities and functions, whose lives and movements mingle and overlap in public spaces. People belong to distinct groups or cultures and interact in neighborhoods and work places. They venture out from these locales, however, to public places of entertainment, consumption, and politics. They witness one another's cultures and functions in such public interaction, without adopting them as their own. The appreciation of ethnic foods or professional musicians, for example, consists in the recognition that these transcend the familiar everyday world of my life.

In the city strangers live side by side in public places, giving to and receiving from one another social and aesthetic products, often mediated by a huge chain of interactions. This instantiates social relations as difference in the sense of an understanding of groups and cultures that are different, with exchanging and overlapping interactions that do not issue in community, yet which prevent them from being outside of one another. The social differentiation of the city also provides a positive inexhaustibility of human relations. The possibility always exists of becoming acquainted with new and different people, with different cultural and social experiences; the possibility always exists for new groups to form or emerge around specific interests.

The unoppressive city is thus defined as openness to unassimilated otherness. Of course, we do not have such openness to difference in our current social relations. I am asserting an ideal, which consists in a politics of difference. Assuming that group differentiation is a given of social life for us, how can the relationships of group identities embody justice, respect, and the absence of oppression? The relationship among group identities and cultures in our society is blotted by racism, sexism, xenophobia, homophobia, suspicion, and mockery. A politics of difference lays down institutional and ideological means for recognizing and affirming differently identifying groups in two basic senses: giving political representation to group interests and celebrating the distinctive cultures and characteristics of different groups.

Many questions arise in proposing a politics of difference. What defines a group that deserves recognition and celebration? How does one provide representation to group interests that avoids the mere pluralism of liberal interest groups? What are institutional forms by which the mediations of the city and the representations of its groups in decision making can be made democratic? These questions, as well as many others, confront the ideal of the unoppressive city. They are not dissimilar from questions of the relationships that ought to exist among communities. They are questions, however, which appeal to community as the ideal of social life appears to repress or ignore. Some might claim that a politics of difference

does express what the ideal of community ought to express, despite the meaning that many writers give the concept of community. Fred Dallmayr, for example, reserves the term *community* for just this openness toward unassimilated otherness, designating the more totalistic understanding of social relations I have criticized as either "communalism" or "movement."

As opposed to the homogeneity deliberately fostered in the movement, the communitarian mode cultivates diversity – but without encouraging willful segregation or the repressive preponderance of one of the social subsectors. … Community may be the only form of social aggregation which reflects upon, and makes room for, otherness or the reverse side of subjectivity (and inter-subjectivity) and thus for the play of difference – the difference between ego and Other and between man and nature.[15]

In the end it may be a matter of stipulation whether one chooses to call such politics as play of difference "community." Because most articulations of the ideal of community carry the urge to unity I have criticized, however, I think it is less confusing to use a term other than community rather than to redefine the term. Whatever the label, the concept of social relations that embody openness to unassimilated otherness with justice and appreciation needs to be developed. Radical politics, moreover, must develop discourse and institutions for bringing differently identified groups together without suppressing or subsuming the differences.

NOTES

1 I examine community specifically as a normative ideal designating how social relations ought to be organized. There are various non-normative uses of the term *community* to which my analysis does not apply. Sociologists engaged in community studies, for example, usually use the term to mean something like "small town" or "neighborhood," and they use the term primarily in a descriptive sense. The questions raised apply to community understood only as a normative model of social organization. See Jessie Bernard, *The Sociology*

of Community (Glenview, IL: Scott, Foresman, and Co., 1973) for a summary of different sociological theories of community in its non-normative sense.

2 R. P. Wolff, *The Poverty of Liberalism* (Boston: Beacon Press, 1978), Chapter 5.

3 Michael Sandel, *Liberalism and the Limits of Justice* (Cambridge: Cambridge University Press, 1982), pp. 172–173.

4 Carol Gilligan, *In a Different Voice* (Cambridge: Cambridge University Press, 1981).

5 I develop more thoroughly the implications of these oppositions in modern political theory and practice and a practical vision of their unsettling in my paper "Impartiality and the Civic Public: Some Implications of Feminist Critics of Modern Political Theory," *Praxis International*, vol. 5, no. 4, 1986, pp. 381–401.

6 Harry C. Boyte and Sara M. Evans, "Strategies in Search of America: Cultural Radicalism, Populism, and Democratic Culture," *Socialist Review* (May to August 1984), pp. 73–100.

7 Peter Manicas, *The Death of the State* (New York: Putnam and Sons, 1974), p. 247.

8 Roberto Unger, *Knowledge and Politics* (New York: Free Press, 1975), pp. 262–263.

9 Christian Bay, *Strategies of Political Emancipation* (South Bend, IL: Notre Dame Press, 1981), Chapters 5 and 6.

10 Michael Taylor, *Community, Anarchy and Liberty* (Cambridge: Cambridge University Press, 1982), pp. 27–28.

11 Carol C. Gould, *Marx's Social Ontology: Individual and Community in Marx's Theory of Social Reality* (Cambridge, MA: MIT Press, 1978), p. 26.

12 Derrida discusses the illusory character of this ideal of immediate presence of subjects to one another in community in his discussion of Levi-Strauss and Rousseau. See *Of Grammatology* (Baltimore: Johns Hopkins University Press, 1976), pp. 101–140.

13 Anthony Giddens, *Central Problems in Social Theory*, pp. 198–233.

14 Marshall Berman presents a fascinating account of the attractions of city life in *All That Is Solid Melts Into Air* (New York: Simon & Schuster, 1982). George Shulman points to the open-endedness of city life as contrasted with the pastoral vision of community in "The Pastoral Idyll of *Democracy*," *Democracy*, vol. 3, 1983, pp. 43–54; for a similar critique, see David Plotke, "Democracy, Modernization, and Democracy," *Socialist Review*, vol. 14, March–April 1984, pp. 31–56.

15 Fred R. Dallmayr, *Twilight of Subjectivity* (Amherst: University of Massachusetts Press, 1981), pp. 142–143.

I.3 Constructing an Anthropology of Citizenship

10
Cultural Citizenship in San Jose, California, 1994[1]

Renato Rosaldo

Cultural Citizenship

The collective project on cultural citizenship in San Jose, California has developed over the past four summers (1990–1993) in coordination with research teams working on the formation of Latino communities, as well as their inter-action with other ethnic groups and the larger civil society, in Los Angeles, New York City, and San Antonio (IUP, 1989).[2] The project studies how Latinos view themselves, how they constitute communities and how they concep-tualize and claim rights.

Cultural citizenship refers to the right to be different (in terms of race, ethnicity, or native language) with respect to the norms of the dominant national community, without com-promising one's right to belong, in the sense of participating in the nation-state's democratic processes. The enduring exclusions of the color line often deny full citizenship to Latinos and other people of color. From the point of view of subordinated communities, cultural citizenship offers the possibility of legitimizing demands made in the struggle to enfranchise themselves. These demands can range from legal, political, and economic issues to matters of human dignity, well-being, and respect.

The focus of this paper is on Latino cultural citizenship; that is, how Latinos conceive of community, where they do and do not feel a sense of "belonging," and how they claim rights to belong to America. In our view, the process of claiming rights both defines communities (Rosaldo 1989) and comprises a renegotiation of belonging in America. Latinos' identity is, in part, shaped by discrimination and by collective efforts to achieve full membership for themselves and their culture.

The concept of cultural citizenship includes and also goes beyond the dichotomous cate-gories of legal documents, which one either has or does not have, to encompass a range of gradations in the qualities of citizenship. Ordinary language distinguishes full from second-class citizens and tacitly recognizes that citizenship can be a matter of degree. Our project, then, is to explore the qualitative dis-tinctions in senses of belonging, entitlement, and influence that vary in distinct situations and in different local communities.

Renato Rosaldo, 1994. Cultural citizenship in San Jose, California. *PoLAR* 17(2): 57–63.

The Anthropology of Citizenship: A Reader, First Edition. Edited by Sian Lazar.
© 2013 John Wiley & Sons, Inc. Published 2013 by John Wiley & Sons, Inc.

Culture in this context refers to how specific subjects conceive of full enfranchisement. It does not refer to culture as either (a) a monolithic, neatly bounded homogeneous social unit, or (b) a realm of art and expressive production as opposed to, for example, the economy. Project interviews with Latinos and other ethnic groups reveal differences in perceptions of rights and in the very definition of first-class citizenship. Such differences occur within as well as between groups because of internal differentiations and inequalities that roughly correspond with divergent perceptions of social reality. Similarly, the perceived elements of full citizenship can range in varying mixtures from dignity, well-being, and respect to wages, housing, health care, and education. The definition of first-class citizenship cannot be taken as a given, but rather must be a central focus of research.

Identity, Respect, and Rights

Through the interviews, we have gained an understanding of how Latinos view their place in society and how they associate their sense of enfranchisement with cultural concepts such as *respeto* (respect) or *humilicion* (humiliation). An interview with a Chicana activist may prove instructive. She has lived in San Jose for more than forty years and currently is a community worker in a social service agency. In one of the interviews, she explained her concept of respect and its connection to rights and entitlements. Her notion of respect began with her father as she explains:

My father was full of wisdom. One time Dad asked me: "Do you love me?" "Yes," I said, "I really love you." "Why do you love me?" "Because you're my father." "That is the last reason you should love me. Many people should not love their fathers." When he asked me on other days I said, "Because you're kind ... gentle ... understanding."

About *respeto*, my father gave me this advice: the first, first thing about *respeto* is to listen to the person. Second, don't tell them that they don't feel something just because you don't. Even if the temperature is 106

degrees, we can't tell you that you're not cold when you tell us that you are. Third, if you see something and they see something different, accept what they tell you. Fourth, ask a lot of questions to make sure you respect and understand. Fifth, you can be angry, but show respect. Do not raise your voice, break things, or belittle the other person. Do not put yourself in the position where you have to apologize for yourself. Sixth, don't lie. All these *consejos* were taught by my father.

The Chicana activist conceives of respect as a series of *consejos*, roughly, paternal pieces of advice that are presented verbally in the form of a numbered list. The advice underlines that different individuals are capable of experiencing the world in very different ways and that being respectful has to do with finding out what another individual sees and feels. Abundant evidence in interviews and observations confirms that *respeto* is a key term in how Chicanos/Mexicanos understand human dignity, both as conveying a sense of full citizenship and as a potential area of violation.

The interviews moved from vocabulary items and their meanings to specific examples of how such matters worked out in everyday life. The researchers asked for concrete stories about occasions when the interviewees felt both respected and humiliated. The woman who spoke about respect went on, at the interviewer's request, to tell of a concrete instance that could clarify how respect functions, not at the level of advice but in her daily life. She answered in the following way:

My reputation in this town is that I'm real tough. My dad taught me to be real tough. I've tangled with the major and with Reagan, when he was governor. This was in the papers. I don't respect either man. When Reagan came into a meeting, I had my feet stretched out and I didn't move them so that he had to walk over them. He looked at me real funny. I wanted him to look at me so he would remember me when I asked him questions. I asked him, "Why are you using prison inmates to break the farmworkers union?" Reagan got angry. He asked me my name. I said, "Answer my question." We went back and forth like this until he got so angry he broke his pencil. Then he said something and I told him, "My name is Chela Ramirez. I'll repeat my name because I know you can't pronounce it." Then I spelled it. Then, while I was in Sacramento with the Poor People's March, he said, "Hello, Chela Ramirez." He did it with respect. I got more out of him by acting with respect than if I'd cussed him out.

This interplay between Chela Ramirez (a pseudonym) and then-governor Ronald Reagan reflects an effort to elicit respect for those traditionally seen as powerless. By refusing to move her legs or answer Reagan's questions, she angered him, even came close to insulting him, but she earned his respect. Not only did he finally respond to her questioning, but he also remembered her name the next time they met.

The New Politics of Citizenship

Not unlike a number of European countries, the United States has witnessed the recent return of citizenship as a site of political struggle.
[...]
The new politics of citizenship arises not from abstract theoretical reflection, but from a combination of rightist national politics bent on exclusion and from new social movements determined to expand legitimate claims for rights to include a broader range of forms of subordination. The cultural citizenship project attempts to analyze the possibilities for change from a progressive political vantage point and aspires to articulate new claims for entitlements.

The central hypothesis of the cultural citizenship project has been that people in subordinated communities struggle to achieve full enfranchisement and that they search for well-being, dignity, and respect in their ordinary everyday lives. The notion of a micropolitics that seeks cultural citizenship in one's plural communities – neighborhoods, workplaces, churches, and activist groups – has been borne out in observations and interviews over the past four summers. What impact these emergent politics will have (and they are already abundantly

apparent in interviews and observations) will only become clear over time.

The politics of citizenship gains its force in part through its location within long-term dissident and progressive traditions in the United States. The Constitution itself defined a number of exclusions that formed the basis for social movements over the last two centuries. Perhaps this form of exclusion can be understood by imagining the revolutionary slogan, not as "Liberty, Equality, Fraternity," but as "Liberty, Equality, Sorority." Denial of the vote to women formed the impetus for women's suffrage movements in the nineteenth century which, in turn, prepared the ground for feminist movements in the second half of the twentieth century. Denial of citizenship to slaves provided the basis for anti-slavery movements in the nineteenth century and civil rights movements among communities of color in the twentieth century. Their goals and strategies remade with each successive generation, these dissident traditions of the politics of citizenship have been progressive, at times radical, and have achieved certain enduring changes. Despite backlash, today only the most extreme sects would reinstitute slavery or deny the vote to women. Contemporary "new social movements" and the politics of citizenship emerge from such oppositional traditions that make possible a generally accepted legitimacy and a widely recognized political force.

Cultural citizenship is a process by which rights are claimed and expanded. It is only one process among many, but it is an important one. And, in an America that is increasingly diverse racially and ethnically, the manner by which groups claim cultural citizenship may very well affect a renegotiation of the basic social contract of America. So-called new citizens – people of color, recent immigrants, women, gays, and lesbians – are not only "imagining" America; they are creating it anew.

NOTES

1   This paper was presented at the invited session "Citizenship Contested" at the American Anthropological Association Meetings, Washington, DC, November 20, 1993.

2 Researchers at the Centro de Estudios Puertorriqueños at Hunter College, University of Texas at Austin, Stanford University and University of California, Los Angeles are: Rina Benmayor, Richard Chabrán, Richard Flores, William Flores, Ana Juarbe, Pedro Petraza, Ray Rocco, Luis Rubalcava, Blanc Silvestrini, and Rosa Torruellas.

REFERENCES

IUP Working Group on Latino Cultural Studies, 1989. *The Concept of Cultural Citizenship*. Centro de Estudios Puertorriqueños. Hunter College, City University of New York.

Rosaldo, Renato, 1989. *Culture and Truth: The Remaking of Social Analysis*. Boston: Beacon Press.

11
Cultural Citizenship as Subject-Making

Immigrants Negotiate Racial and Cultural Boundaries in the United States, 1996

Aihwa Ong

In the fall of 1970, I left Malaysia and arrived as a freshman in New York City. I was immediately swept up in the antiwar movement. President Nixon had just begun his "secret" bombing of Cambodia. Joining crowds of angry students marching down Broadway, I participated in the "takeover" of the East Asian Institute building on the Columbia University campus. As I stood there confronting policemen in riot gear, I thought about what Southeast Asia meant to the United States. Were Southeast Asians simply an anonymous mass of people in black pajamas? Southeast Asia was a far-off place where America was conducting a savage war against "communism." American lives were being lost, and so were those of countless Vietnamese, Cambodians, Laotians, and others. This rite of passage into American society was to shape my attitude toward citizenship. As a foreign student I was at a disadvantage, ineligible for most loans, fellowships, and jobs. My sister, a naturalized American, could have sponsored me for a green card, but the bombing of Cambodia, symptomatic of wider disregard

for my part of the world, made American citizenship a difficult moral issue for me.

Much writing on citizenship has ignored such subjective and contradictory experiences, focusing instead on its broad legal-political aspects. [...] Seldom is attention focused on the everyday processes whereby people, especially immigrants, are made into subjects of a particular nation-state.

Citizenship as Subjectification

Taking an ethnographic approach, I consider citizenship a cultural process of "subject-ification," in the Foucaldian sense of self-making and being-made by power relations that produce consent through schemes of surveillance, discipline, control, and administration (Foucault 1989, 1991). Thus formulated, my concept of cultural citizenship can be applied to various global contexts (see Ong 1993; Ong and Nonini 1996), but in this paper I will discuss the making of cultural citizens in Western democracies like the United States. Philip

Aihwa Ong, 1996. Cultural citizenship as subject-making: immigrants negotiate racial and cultural boundaries in the United States. *Current Anthropology* 37(5): 737–762.

The Anthropology of Citizenship: A Reader, First Edition. Edited by Sian Lazar.

Corrigan and Derek Sayer (1985), in their analysis of the state as a cultural formation, speak of "governmentality," by which they mean the state's project of moral regulation aimed at giving "unitary and unifying expression to what are in reality multifaceted and differential experiences of groups within society" (1985: 4–5). This role of the state in universalizing citizenship is paradoxically attained through a process of individuation whereby people are constructed in definitive and specific ways as citizens – taxpayers, workers, consumers, and welfare-dependents.

This notion of citizenship as dialectically determined by the state and its subjects is quite different from that employed by Renato Rosaldo (1994), who views cultural citizenship as the demand of disadvantaged subjects for full citizenship in spite of their cultural difference from mainstream society.[1] While I share Rosaldo's sentiments, his concept attends to only one side of a set of unequal relationships. It gives the erroneous impression that cultural citizenship can be unilaterally constructed and that immigrant or minority groups can escape the cultural inscription of state power and other forms of regulation that define the different modalities of belonging. Formulated in this manner, Rosaldo's concept of cultural citizenship indicates subscription to the very liberal principle of universal equality that he seeks to call into question.

In contrast, I use "cultural citizenship" to refer to the cultural practices and beliefs produced out of negotiating the often ambivalent and contested relations with the state and its hegemonic forms that establish the criteria of belonging within a national population and territory. Cultural citizenship is a dual process of self-making and being-made within webs of power linked to the nation-state and civil society. Becoming a citizen depends on how one is constituted as a subject who exercises or submits to power relations; one must develop what Foucault (cited by Rabinow 1984: 49) calls "the modern attitude," an attitude of self-making in shifting fields of power that include the nation-state and the wider world.

Furthermore, in analyzing the pragmatic struggle towards an understanding of cultural citizenship, one must attend to the various regulatory regimes in state agencies and civil society. Michel Foucault (1991) notes that in modern Western democracies control of subjects is manifested in rituals and rules that produce consent; "governmentality" refers to those relations that regulate the conduct of subjects as a population and as individuals in the interests of ensuring the security and prosperity of the nation-state. A major problem with Corrigan and Sayer's (1985) approach is its restriction to the state sector, ignoring civil institutions and social groups as disciplinary forces in the making of cultural citizens. Indeed, it is precisely in liberal democracies like the United States that the governmentality of state agencies is often discontinuous, even fragmentary, and the work of instilling proper normative behavior and identity in newcomers must also be taken up by institutions in civil society. For instance, hegemonic ideas about belonging and not belonging in racial and cultural terms often converge in state and nonstate institutional practices through which subjects are shaped in ways that are at once specific and diffused. These are the ideological fields within which different criteria of belonging on the basis of civilized conduct by categorically distinguishable (dominant) others become entangled with culture, race, and class (Williams 1991: 2–29).

Race, Class, and Economic Liberalism

My approach constitutes an intervention into the conventional theorizing of American citizenship solely in terms of racial politics within the framework of the nation-state (Omi and Winant 1986; Gregory and Sanjek 1994). What is urgently needed is a broader conception of race and citizenship shaped by the history of European imperialism. African slavery and colonial empires were central to the making of modern Western Europe and the Americas. Encounters between colonizers and the colonized or enslaved gave rise to the view that white-black hierarchies are homologous with levels of civilization, a racist hegemony that pervades all areas of Western consciousness (Memmi 1967; Fanon 1967; Alatas 1977; Said 1978; Nandy 1983; Gilman 1985; Stoler 1995). [...]

Another lacuna in theories of racism and citizenship is the effect of class attributes and property rights on citizenship status (see Harrison 1991). As we shall see, the interweaving of ideologies of racial difference with liberal conceptions of citizenship is evident in popular notions about who deserves to belong in implicit terms of productivity and consumption. For instance, in the postwar United States, neoliberalism, with its celebration of freedom, progress, and individualism, has become a pervasive ideology that influences many domains of social life. It has become synonymous with being American, and more broadly these values are what the world associates with Western civilization. There is, however, a regulatory aspect to neoliberalism whereby economics is extended to cover all aspects of human behavior pertaining to citizenship. An important principle underlying liberal democracy emphasizes balancing the provision of security against the productivity of citizens. In other words, neoliberalism is an expression of the biopolitics of the American state as well as setting the normative standards of good citizenship in practice. In the postwar era, such thinking has given rise to a human-capital assessment of citizens (Becker 1965), weighing those who can pull themselves up by their bootstraps against those who make claims on the welfare state. Increasingly, citizenship is defined as the civic duty of individuals to reduce their burden on society and build up their own human capital – to be "entrepreneurs" of themselves (Gordon 1991: 43–45). Indeed, by the 1960s liberal economics had come to evaluate nonwhite groups according to their claims on or independence of the state. Minorities who scaled the pinnacles of society often had to justify themselves in such entrepreneurial terms. A rather apt example was the 1990s nomination of Clarence Thomas to the Supreme Court of the United States, a move widely viewed as the token appointment of an African American to the powerful white-dominated institution. In his confirmation hearings, Judge Thomas painted himself as a deserving citizen who struggled out of a hardscrabble past by "pulling himself up by his bootstraps." The can-do attitude is an inscription of ideal masculine citizenship; its legitimating power was more than sufficient to overcome the ugly stain of sexual harassment that plagued the judge's confirmation.

Attaining success through self-reliant struggle, while not inherently limited to any cultural group, is a process of self-development that in Western democracies becomes inseparable from the process of "whitening." This racializing effect of class and social mobility has evolved out of historical circumstances whereby white masculinity established qualities of manliness and civilization itself against the "Negro" and the "Indian" (Bederman 1993). [...]

Although one need not imagine a contemporary synchrony of views on intrepid individualism, the white man, and deserving citizenship, the convergences and overlaps between hegemonies of race, civilization, and market behavior as claims to citizenship are too routine to be dismissed. Hegemonies of relative racial contributions often conflated race and class, as, for example, in the polarizing contrast between the "model minority" and the "underclass" (Myrdal 1994), both economic terms standing for racial ones. As I will show, the different institutional contexts in which subjects learn about citizenship often assess newcomers from different parts of the world within given schemes of racial difference, civilization, and economic worth. Because human capital, self-discipline, and consumer power are associated with whiteness, these attributes are important criteria of nonwhite citizenship in Western democracies. Indeed, immigrant practices earlier in the century also subjected immigrants from Europe to differential racial and cultural judgments (see, e.g., Archdeacon 1983). The racialization of class was particularly evident in the construction of Irish-American (and Southern European) immigrants whose whiteness was in dispute (Roediger 1991: 14). This racializing logic of class attributes is applied even to current flows of immigrants from the South and East who seem obviously nonwhite; discriminatory modes of perception, reception, and treatment order Asian immigrants along a white-black continuum. Although immigrants come from a variety of class and national

backgrounds, there is a tendency, in daily institutional practices, towards interweaving of perceived racial difference with economic and
cultural criteria, with the result that long-term
residents and newcomers are ideologically constructed as "the stereotypical embodiments" of
ethnicized citizenship (Williams 1989: 437).

Of course, these processes of implicit racial
and cultural ranking do not exhaust the conditions that go into processes of subjectification
as citizens. [...] I will present ethnographic
accounts of interactions between key institutions and newcomers, the drawing of lines
against Asian others, and the struggles over
representations that are part of the ideological
work of citizen-making in the different domains
of American life. While I will be dealing with the
making of immigrants into American citizens,
I maintain that the processes of explicit and
implicit racial and cultural ranking pervading
institutional and everyday practices are but a
special case of similar constructions in Western
democracies in general.

New Asian Immigrants
in Metropolitan Countries

[...]

The San Francisco Bay area was one of the
major sites of resettlement for refugees from all
over the Third World, the majority of whom
were Southeast Asians.[2] Most arrived in two
waves: in the aftermath of the communist takeover of Saigon in 1975 and following the
Vietnamese invasion of Cambodia in 1979. At
about the same time, another flow of immigrants,
mainly professionals and upper-middle-class
people seeking investments in stable markets in
the West, arrived from Southeast Asia and India.
The combined impact of these flows greatly
exceeded that of earlier arrivals from Asia,
increasing the Asian population in America by
80% to 6.88 million by the end of the decade.
Asians are "far and away the most rapidly
growing minority in the country" (*New York
Times*, February 24, 1991). They have fanned
out across the country to establish sizable Asian
American communities outside the Chinatowns
of the east and west coasts, spreading to the
Southern states and the Midwest. There are

Vietnamese fishing villages in Texas, Cambodian
crab farmers in Alabama, and Asian professionals in fields such as electronics, medicine,
and mathematics. The number of Chinese restaurants has increased in smaller towns all over
the country. In major cities such as Queens,
Houston, and Los Angeles, investments by
Koreans and Chinese immigrants have raised
real estate prices to stratospheric levels (see, e.g.,
Wall Street Journal, January 15, 1991).

The new Asian demographics are so striking
that today Asians make up a third of the
population of San Francisco and 30% of the
student body at the University of California,
Berkeley. Overall, the Bay Area, with a population
of over 6 million, has "emerged as the Western
Hemisphere's first genuine Pacific metropolis,"
with one out of every five residents being of
Asian background (*San Francisco Chronicle*,
December 5, 1988). The increasing importance
of the economic boom in Asia and the influx of
Pacific Rim capital as well as boat people into the
Western democracies make Asian immigration a
highly charged issue that is framed differently
from the issue of immigration from other parts of
the world.

[...]

I will examine institutional practices that differently receive and socialize Asian immigrants
depending on their gender, position within racial
hierarchies, and class and consumption. Drawing
on ethnographic research, I will explore the
ways in which Cambodian refugees, on the one
hand, and affluent Chinese cosmopolitans, on
the other, explore the meanings and possibilities
of citizenship in California. By contrasting Asian
groups from different class backgrounds I hope
to show how despite and because of their racialization as Asian Americans, they are variously
socialized by and positioned to manipulate state
institutions, religious organizations, civilian
groups, and market forces inscribing them as citizens of differential worth.

Disciplining Refugees in
an Age of Compassion Fatigue

The moral imperative to offer refugees shelter
has been a hallmark of US policy since 1945,
breaking from earlier policies that privileged

race, language, and assimilation above concerns about human suffering (Loescher and Scanlan 1986: 210). During the cold war, refugees from communist regimes were treated with special kindness because of the ideological perception that they had undergone great suffering as symbolic or literal "freedom fighters" (p. xviii). This policy continued more or less even after the United States ended its intervention to prevent the spread of communism in Indochina, setting off waves of boat people fleeing Vietnam. In 1979, tens of thousands of Cambodians fled to the Thai border after the Vietnamese invasion of Kampuchea. President Carter, in the spirit of his human rights campaign, signed a refugee act to increase immigration quotas for them. Between 1975 and 1985, almost 125,000 Cambodians arrived in the United States. [...]

From the beginning, a political ambiguity dogged Cambodian refugees because of the immigration authorities' suspicion that many Khmer Rouge communist-sympathizers managed to slip through screening by the Immigration and Naturalization Service (INS) and gain entry to the country (Golub 1986; Ngor 1987). This morally tainted image was accompanied by the perception of Cambodian refugees as mainly peasants, unlike the boat people, who were by and large unambiguously anticommunist Sino-Vietnamese and middle-class, despite significant numbers of fishermen and peasants among them. Cambodians in refugee-processing camps were quickly separated out as destined for lower-class status. At the Philippine Refugee Processing Center, classes trained US-bound Cambodians to be dependent on Americans, who dealt with refugees only from their positions as superiors, teachers, and bosses (Mortland 1987: 391). One teacher charged that, from the very beginning, training programs were "ideologically motivated to provide survival English for entry-level jobs" in the United States (Tollefson 1990: 546). Khmers were socialized to expect limited occupational options and taught subservient behavior, as well as a flexible attitude towards frequent changes of jobs which would help them adapt to cycles of employment and unemployment. Thus, the camp training of Cambodian refugees as dependent on Americans and as potential low-wage workers initiated the

minoritization process even before they set foot in the country. This ideological construction of Khmers as a dependent minority channeled them into the same economic situations as other refugees from poor countries: "Policy and ideology underlying the [Overseas Refugees Training Program] ensure that refugees serve the same function as African Americans and Latinos" (p. 549).

Furthermore, once immigrants arrived in the country, whatever their national origin or race, they were ideologically positioned within the hegemonic bipolar white-black model of American society. The racialization of Southeast Asian refugees depended on differential economic and cultural assessment of their potential as good citizens. Although all relied on refugee aid for the first two years after their arrival, Cambodians (together with Laotians and Hmongs) found themselves, by acquiring an image of "welfare-dependent" immigrants, quickly differentiated from the Vietnamese, who had arrived in this country out of the same war. Cambodian and Laotian immigrants were ethnicized as a kind of liminal Asian American group that has more in common with other poor refugees of color like Afghans and Ethiopians than with the Vietnamese. They were often compared to their inner-city African American neighbors in terms of low-wage employment, high rates of teenage pregnancy, and welfare-dependent families.

[...]

By 1987, well over half of the 800,000 Indochinese refugees in the country had settled down in California, and there was widespread fear that there would be "perpetual dependence on the welfare system for some refugees" (New York Times, April 27, 1987). This positioning of Cambodians as black Asians is in sharp contrast to the model-minority image of Chinese, Koreans, and Vietnamese (including Sino-Vietnamese), who are celebrated for their "Confucian values" and family businesses. Although there have been racist attacks on Vietnamese fishermen in Texas and California and exploitation of Vietnamese workers in chicken-processing plants in the South, the general perception of them is as possessed of "can-do" attitudes closer to the white ideal standards of American citizenship.[3] It is therefore not surprising that Cambodians are almost always referred to as "refugees" whereas Vietnamese refugees are viewed as immigrants. Regardless of the actual, lived cultures of the Khmers before they arrived in the United States, dominant ideologies clearly distinguish among various Asian nationalities, assigning them closer to the white or the black pole of American citizenship.

As I will show, the disciplining of the welfare state, combined with the feminist fervor of many social workers, actually works to weaken or reconstitute the Cambodian family. My own research on the welfare adjustments of Khmers, described below, may seem to reinforce the hegemonic picture of their dependency, but my goal is actually a critique of the effects of the welfare system as it operates now in an increasingly low-waged, service-oriented economy. Earlier generations of poor immigrants have managed to establish basic security for their families through blue-collar employment (Komorovsky 1967). The welfare system continues to operate by withdrawing support from families with a single wage-earner, whereas for most poor immigrants like the Cambodians, part-time and unsteady low-wage employment are needed to supplement welfare aid. Like ghetto blacks and poor Puerto Rican immigrants, Cambodians are in a continual struggle to survive in a low-wage economy in which they cannot depend on earnings alone and, despite their organizational skills, everyday problems of survival and social interventions often adversely affect family relations and dynamics (Harrington 1962; Valentine 1971; Stack 1974).

Within the refugee population, there are frequent reports of marital conflict, often attributed to the suffering and dislocation engendered by war and exile. However, I maintain that most of the tensions are exacerbated by the overwhelming effort to survive in the inner city, where most of the Cambodian refugees live. Many of the men, with their background in farming and inability to speak English, cannot make the leap into job training and employment in the United States. Their wives often lose respect for them because of their inability to make a living and their refusal to share "women's" household and child-care chores at home. Cambodian customs regarding family roles and gender norms have become if not irrelevant at

least severely undermined as men fail to support their families and wives become more assertive in seeking help. Relations between husband and wife, parents and children have come to be dictated to a significant degree not by Khmer culture as they remember it but by pressing daily concerns to gain access to state resources and to submit to the rules of the welfare state.

Male informants complain that "in America, men feel they have lost value because they are no longer masters in their own families." A *kru khmer* (shaman) who is often consulted by unhappy couples noted that "money is the root cause of marital problems in the United States." Welfare has become a system which provides families with material support and women with increased power and a bargaining position vis-à-vis their husbands and children. The shaman explained:

For instance, most of us who came to the United States are recipients of welfare assistance; the majority of us are supported by the state. It is usually the wife who gets the welfare check but not the husband. She is the one who takes care of the kids. But when she receives the check, her husband wants to spend it. When she refuses, and wants to keep the money for the children, that's what leads to wife abuse.

Some Khmer men lash out at their wives, perhaps to restore the sense of male privilege and authority they possessed in Cambodia. In many instances, they beat their wives in struggles to gain control over particular material and emotional benefits. Besides fights over welfare checks, the beatings may be intended to compel wives to resume their former deferential behavior despite their newly autonomous role in supporting the children. Many women try to maintain the male-dominated family system despite the threats and abuse. A woman confided:

There are many cases of wife abuse. Yes, everyone gets beaten, myself included. But sometimes we have to just keep quiet even after a disagreement. Like in my case, I don't want to call the police or anything. As the old saying goes, "It takes two hands to clap. One hand cannot sound itself." I just shed a few tears and let it go. If it gets out of hand, then you can call the police. But the men still think more of themselves than of women. They never lower themselves to be our equals.

This acknowledgment of a shift in the balance of domestic power, linked to dependency on state agencies, indicates that Khmer women do not think of themselves as passive victims but are aware of their own role in marital conflicts. The speaker seems to imply that she tolerates the occasional beating because men cannot adjust to their change in status and she always has the option of calling the police. Like their counterparts among European immigrants in the early-twentieth-century United States, Cambodian women are often caught in their "double position" as victims of wife abuse and guardians of their children (Gordon 1988: 261); they stand up to their husbands in order to ensure their children's economic survival.

Some women who can manage on their own with welfare aid abandon their spouses. A social worker reported cases involving couples over 65 years old in which the wives kicked their husbands out and then applied for SSI (Supplementary Security Income). Informants told me that there were Cambodian women who, having fallen in love with American co-workers, left their husbands and even their children; this was something, they claimed, that happened in Florida and Long Beach, not in their own community. Speaking of her former neighbors, a woman noted that many Cambodian women had left their husbands because they "look down on them ... for not working, for not being as clever as other men." They felt free to do so because Aid to Families with Dependent Children (AFDC) supported them and their children in any case. In an optimistic tone, she continued, "That's why Khmer women are very happy living in America, because they now have equal rights. ... We can start up business more easily here. If we want to work, we can pay for day care."

One of the indirect effects of the welfare system is to promote rather complex strategies for manipulating and evading rules, thus affecting household composition. Cambodian households, often composed of mother-child

units, routinely pool incomes from different sources, and many households depend on a combination of different welfare checks received by family members and both part- and full-time employment. Through the pooling of income from multiple sources, household heads hope to accumulate savings to buy a home outside the violent neighborhoods in which many live. As has been reported among inner-city blacks, such strategies for coping with the welfare system increase the networking among female kin and neighbors but contribute to the shifting membership of households (Stack 1974: 122–23).

Many Khmers seek to prolong the time they can receive welfare support by disguising the age of children and by concealing their marital status and income-generating activities. In some cases, young girls who become pregnant are allowed to keep their babies so that the latter can receive financial aid that helps to support the entire family. Many girls who get pregnant marry the fathers of their babies but fail to register their change of status in order to avoid revealing that their husbands are working and thus forfeiting their chance to get AFDC for the babies. For instance, Madam Neou[4] lived with two sons, seven daughters, and a son-in-law in her one-bedroom apartment. Her eldest daughter was 18 and pregnant. She had married her boyfriend according to Khmer ceremonies but had not registered her marriage, and therefore she continued to receive her General Assistance (GA) check. Her husband, who worked in a fast-food restaurant, disguised the fact that they were living together by giving a false address. They hoped to have saved enough money by the time their GA stipends ended to move out and rent a home of their own. Thus, although parents try to discourage their daughters from having premarital sex, they also tolerate and support those who do become pregnant. Not all pregnant girls get married or receive their mothers' support. However, those who do marry are taken in to enable them to save on rent and perhaps continue to accumulate welfare benefits so that they can ultimately become an independent household.

Social workers are frustrated by the mixed motivations and strategies that, in their view, promote teenage pregnancy. A social worker complains about Cambodians "working the system" and says that young girls "become pregnant again and again and have no time to go to school." However, it appears that peer pressure and street culture are primarily responsible for the few pregnancies in girls younger than 16 (well below the average marriage age of 18 for women in Cambodia before the upheavals of war and diaspora). In one case, a social worker intervened and advised a Khmer mother to let her recently married daughter use contraceptives so that she could continue to go to school and have a career later on. However, the girl's husband, who was employed as a mechanic, refused to practice family planning and wanted her to get on welfare. They lived with her mother in exchange for a small monthly payment. The social worker threatened to expose the mother's strategy of combining welfare checks across households, thus exercising the disciplinary power of the state that threatens family formation among people at the mercy of the welfare system and a chronic low-wage market. The withdrawal of welfare support at a point in young people's lives when they are first breaking into the labor market thus compels poor families to scheme to prolong welfare dependency so that they can save towards economic independence. The dual structure of supporting poor mothers, on the one hand, while disciplining chronic underemployment, on the other, contributes to a particular minoritization process of Cambodian refugees that is not so very different from that experienced by other poor people of color (Valentine 1971; Stack 1974). Welfare policy promotes the "blackening" of the underprivileged by nurturing and then stigmatizing certain forms of coping strategies.

An academic cottage industry on refugee affairs, ignoring the disciplinary effects of the welfare state and the low-wage economy, has emerged to provide cultural explanations for the presumed differential economic and moral worth of different Asian immigrant groups. Cambodians (together with Hmongs and Laotians) are identified as culturally inferior to Vietnamese and Chinese and thus to be targeted for "civilizing" attention by state agents

and church groups. In a report to the Office of Refugee Settlement, social scientists elaborated a "sociocultural" portrait of Khmers (and Laotians) as more "Indian" than "Chinese" among the "Indochinese" (Rumbaut and Ima 1988: 73) – a term that is itself the creation of French imperialism. This artifact drew upon the anthropological model of the "loosely structured" society (Embree 1950), noting that Cambodians were more individualistic, prone to place feelings and emotions above obligations, and likely to use Americans as role models than the Vietnamese (who were "more Chinese") (p. 76) – in other words, Cambodians were more deferential and susceptible to socialization by US institutions than groups that possessed Confucian culture. Cambodians were viewed as "affectively oriented"; their "love of children" and "nonaggressive" behavior seem in implicit contrast to the "more pragmatic" Vietnamese. This moral discrimination among Asian groups becomes a diffused philosophy that informs the work of agencies dealing with immigrants, thus demonstrating that in mechanisms of regulation, hierarchical cultural evaluations assign different populations places within the white-black polarities of citizenship.

The disciplinary approach to Cambodians often takes the form of teaching them their rights and needs as normative lower-class Americans. In the Bay Area, the refugee and social service agencies are driven by a feminist ethos that views immigrant women and children as especially vulnerable to patriarchal control at home. Implicit in social workers' training is the goal of fighting Asian patriarchy – "empowering" immigrant women and "teaching them their rights in this country," as one lawyer-activist explained. Perhaps influenced by essentializing statements that Khmers are "more prone to divorce and separation" than the Vietnamese (Rumbaut and Ima 1988: 75–76), service workers tend to view the Khmer family as rife with patriarchal domination and violence. At the same time, service agents working with Cambodians frequently complain about their "primitive culture," especially as expressed in male control and a tendency to be swayed by emotions rather than by rationality and objectivity.

This ideological construction often puts Sam Ngor, a Cambodian social worker, in the uncomfortable position of being caught between his sympathy for the plight of Cambodian men and the social worker's implicit unfavorable comparison of them with white men. At a Cambodian self-help group meeting, Sam was trying to explain why a married couple gave contradictory accounts of their conflict. He noted that there was a difference between "oral and literate cultures"; in oral cultures, "people always change their minds about what happened" (presumably, in a literate society they do not). Furthermore, in a literate society like the United States, men can be jailed for abusing their wives and children. Covert smiles lit up the faces of the women, while the men looked down. The man fighting with his wife crossed his arms and said, "I respect her, but it is she who controls me."

Indeed, Cambodian men complain that service workers are not only eager to interfere in their family affairs but favor women and children over men in domestic battles. Another social worker notes that "often, among refugees of all nationalities, men have lost their place in society. They don't like to ask for help, and it seems they've lost control over their families. Women tend to ask for help more." Sam added that both the welfare system and affirmative action favored women of color over men, so that the former had easier access to resources and jobs.

Some Khmer women, emboldened by service workers and the disciplining of refugee men, routinely call for outside intervention in settling domestic disputes. In one example, Mae, a woman in her thirties, called the police after claiming that her husband, an alcoholic, had hit her. A few days later she came to the self-help group and wanted assistance in getting him released from jail. She insisted that the policeman had misunderstood her and that she had never claimed that she was abused. Meanwhile, she called her husband in jail, boasting that she would try to "free" him if he promised, when he came out, to stop drinking and to attend the self-help group regularly. Mae's husband, it was reported, charged her with delusions of power: "I think that the judge is the one who will decide to release me,

but she thinks she is the one who is controlling the situation. She thinks that by telling the police that I did not beat her she is securing my release." A couple of months later, Mae dropped the charges, and her husband was set free and prevailed upon by the group to join Alcoholics Anonymous. Although the marriage remained rocky, Mae apparently had manipulated the police, the self-help group, and the court system to discipline her husband. A neighbor reported that Mae's daughter said she wanted her mum to be in jail and her dad home. Public interventions in such domestic battles implicitly devalue men of color while upholding white masculinity, as presented by police and judge, as the embodiment of culturally correct citizenship and privilege.

[...]

Chinese Cosmopolitans: Class Property and Cultural Taste

In Northern California, the so-called Hong Kong money elite resides in an exclusive community on the flank of the San Francisco Peninsula mountain range. All the homes in this suburb cost over a million dollars. The choicest are set into the hillsides, with mountains as a backdrop and a view of the bay. Mansions in an Asian-Mediterranean style stand amidst clearings where few trees remain unfelled. This was a sore point with locals, along with the fact that many of the houses were paid for in hard cash, sometimes before the arrival of their new occupants. The driveways are parked with Mercedes Benzes, BMWs, and even a Rolls Royce or two.

The *feng-shui* ("wind-water" propitious placement) of the place is excellent. Fleeing the impending return of Hong Kong to China's rule or merely seeking to tap into US markets, overseas Chinese crossed the Pacific to make this former white enclave their new home. Led initially by real estate agents and later by word of mouth, the influx of wealthy Chinese from Hong Kong, Taiwan, and Southeast Asia has spread to cities and up-scale communities all over the state and the country. While many of the newcomers are well-educated professionals who work in the Silicon Valley, an increasing number are property developers, financiers, and industrialists who work on both sides of the Pacific. [...]

What kinds of processes are making such cosmopolitan subjects into citizens? Although the affluent immigrant Chinese appear to be able to evade disciplining by the state, they are not entirely free of its citizenship requirements, on the one hand, and local mediations over what being part of the imagined American community (or the Northern Californian version of it) is all about. [...] [T]here are cultural limits to the ways in which they can negotiate the hegemonic production of Chineseness in California and the local values about what constitutes civilized conduct and appropriate citizenship.

[...]

Bad taste or the homeless in an affluent neighborhood?

Whereas poor Asians are primarily disciplined by state agencies, affluent Chinese immigrants, as home buyers and property developers, have encountered regulation by civic groups upset at the ways in which their city is being changed by transnational capital and taste. In wealthier San Franciscan neighborhoods, residents pride themselves on their conservation consciousness, and they jealously guard the hybrid European ambiance and character of particular neighborhoods. In their role as custodians of appropriate cultural taste governing buildings, architecture, parks, and other public spaces, civic groups routinely badger City Hall, scrutinize urban zoning laws, and patrol the boundaries between what is aesthetically permissible and what is intolerable in their districts. By linking race with habitus, taste, and cultural capital (Bourdieu 1984), such civic groups set limits to the whitening of Asians, who, metaphorically speaking, still give off the whiff of sweat despite arriving with starter symbolic capital.

Public battles over race/taste have revolved around the transformation of middle-class neighborhoods by rich Asian newcomers. At issue are boxy houses with bland facades – "monster houses" – erected by Asian buyers to accommodate extended families in low-density,

single-family residential districts known for their Victorian or Mediterranean charm. Protests have often taken on a racialist tone, registering both dismay at the changing cultural landscape and efforts to educate the new arrivals to white upper-class norms appropriate for the city. While the activists focus on the cultural elements – aesthetic norms, democratic process, and civic duty – that underpin the urban imagined community, they encode the strong class resentment against large-scale Asian investment in residential and commercial properties throughout the city (see Mitchell 1996). A conflict over one of these monster houses illustrates the ways in which the state is caught between soothing indignant urbanites seeking to impose their notion of cultural citizenship on Asian nouveaux riches while attempting to keep the door open for Pacific Rim capital.

In 1989 a Hong Kong multimillionaire, a Mrs. Chan, bought a house in the affluent Marina district. Chan lived in Hong Kong and rented out her Marina property. A few years later, she obtained the approval of the city to add a third story to her house but failed to notify her neighbors. When they learned of her plans, they complained that the third story would block views of the Palace of Fine Arts as well as cut off sunlight in an adjoining garden. The neighbors linked up with a citywide group to pressure City Hall. The mayor stepped in and called for a city zoning study, thus delaying the proposed renovation. At a neighborhood meeting, someone declared, "We don't want to see a second Chinatown here." Indeed, there is already a new "Chinatown" outside the old Chinatown, based in the middle-class Richmond district. This charge thus raised the specter of a spreading Chinese urbanscape encroaching on the heterogeneous European flavor of the city. The remark, with its implied racism, compelled the mayor to apologize to Chan, and the planning commission subsequently approved a smaller addition to her house.

However, stung by the racism and the loss on her investment and bewildered that neighbors could infringe upon her property rights, Chan, a transnational developer, used her wealth to mock the city's self-image as a bastion of liberalism. She pulled out all her investments in the United States and decided to donate her million-dollar house to the homeless. To add insult to injury, she stipulated that her house was not to be used by any homeless of Chinese descent. Her architect, an American Chinese, told the press, "You can hardly find a homeless Chinese anyway" (*Asia Week*, May 6, 1995). Secure in her overseas location, Chan fought the Chinese stereotype by stereotyping American homeless as non-Chinese, while challenging her civic-minded neighbors to demonstrate the moral liberalism they professed. Mutual class and racial discrimination thus broke through the surface of what initially appeared to be a negotiation over normative cultural taste in the urban milieu. A representative of the major's office, appropriately contrite, remarked that Chan could still do whatever she wanted with her property; "We just would like for her not to be so angry." The need to keep overseas investments flowing into the city had to be balanced against neighborhood groups' demands for cultural standards. The power of the international real estate market, as represented by Mrs. Chan, thus disciplined both City Hall and the Marina neighbors, who may have to rethink local notions of what being enlightened urbanites may entail in the "era of Pacific Rim capital" (Mitchell 1996).

Other Chinese investor-immigrants, unlike Mrs. Chan, try to negotiate the tensions between local and global forces and to adopt the cultural trappings of the white upper class so as to cushion long-term residents' shock at the status change of the racial other, until recently likely to be a laundry or garment worker. Chinese developers who live in San Francisco are trying harder to erase the image of themselves as "economic animals" who build monster houses, as well as the perception that they lack a sense of civic duty and responsibility. They try to maintain their Victorian homes and English gardens, collect Stradivari violins and attend the opera, play tennis in formerly white clubs, and dress up by dressing down their nouveaux riches appearances. I have elsewhere talked about the limits to cultural accumulation of Chinese gentrification in Western metropolitan circles (Ong 1992). Perhaps realizing the limits to how they can be accepted through these whitening practices, some Chinese investors are for the first time making significant philanthropic contribu-

tions outside the old Chinatown. I interviewed a surgeon who was the first Chinese American to sit on the board of the city symphony. When he complained about the lack of Chinese contributions to the symphony, I had to remind him that there were hardly music lessons in Chinatown or other poor urban schools.

But the effort to funnel Pacific Rim money upwards continues. Hong Kong–based companies are making generous donations to major public institutions such as universities and museums. Leslie Tang-Schilling (her real name), the daughter of a Hong Kong industrialist, married into a prominent San Franciscan family, and a commercial developer in her own right, leads the move to soften the hard-edged image of Chinese investor-immigrants. The Tang family name is emblazoned on an imposing new health center on the Berkeley campus. Other overseas Chinese and Asian businesses have donated large sums to the construction of buildings devoted to chemistry, life sciences, computer science, and engineering. An East Coast example is the gift of $20 million to Princeton University by Gordon Wu, a Hong Kong tycoon whose money could perhaps better have benefited long-neglected universities on the Chinese mainland.

Whereas an earlier generation of overseas Chinese tycoons went home to build universities in China, today Asian investors wish to buy symbolic capital in Western democracies as a way to ease racial and cultural acceptance across the globe. Like earlier European immigrant elites looking for symbolic real estate, overseas Chinese donors show a preference for "hardware" (impressive buildings bearing their names) over "software" (scholarships and programs that are less visible to the public eye). The difference is that subjects associated with Third World inferiority have scaled the bastions of white power. Such showcase pieces have upgraded Asian masculinity, layered over the hardscrabble roots of the Asian *homo economicus*, and proclaimed their arrival on the international scene. Nevertheless, there are limits to such strategies of symbolic accumulation, and white backlash has been expressed in a rise in random attacks on Asians. By placing an Asian stamp on prestigious "white" public space, the new immigrants

register what for over a century – one thinks of
the plantation workers and railroad men,
maids and garment workers, gardeners and
cooks, shopkeepers and nurses, undocumented
workers laboring in indentured servitude,
whether in the colonies or in cities like New
York and Los Angeles – has been a space of
Asia-Pacific cultural production within the
West.

Are the New Asians Asian Americans?

Through an ethnographic examination of
cultural citizenship as subjectification and
cultural performance, I argue that the ideological entanglements of race and culture operate
both to locate and to marginalize immigrants
from the metaphorical South and East. This
approach thus suggests that while "cultural
fundamentalism" may have replaced racism
in rhetorics of exclusion (Stolcke 1995), in
practice racial hierarchies and polarities continue to inform Western notions of cultural
difference and are therefore inseparable from
the cultural features attributed to different
groups. I maintain that the white-black polarities emerging out of the history of European-
American imperialism continue to shape
attitudes and encode discourses directed at
immigrants from the rest of the world that are
associated with racial and cultural inferiority.
This dynamic of racial othering emerges in a
range of mechanisms that variously subject
nonwhite immigrants to whitening or blackening processes that indicate the degree of
their closeness to or distance from ideal white
standards.

The contrasting dynamics of the subjectification experienced by new immigrants demonstrate the critical significance of institutional
forces, both domestic and international, in making different kinds of minorities. Cambodian
refugees and Chinese business people did not
arrive as ready-made ethnics. Through the
different modes of disciplining – the primacy
of state and church regulation in one and the
primacy of consumption and capitalist instrumentality in the other – Cambodian refugees
and Chinese immigrants are dialectically

positioned at different ends of the black-white
spectrum. The racialization of class, as well
as the differential othering of immigrants,
constitutes immigrants as the racialized embodiments of different kinds of social capital.

Thus, the category "Asian American" must
acknowledge the internal class, ethnic, and
racial stratifications that are both the effect
and the product of differential governmentalities
working on different populations of newcomers.
It must confront the contradictions and insta-
bilities within the imposed solidarity and temporary alliances of what has been prematurely
called an "Asian American panethnicity"
(Espiritu 1992). The two new Asian groups
represent different modalities of precarious
belonging – one as ideologically blackened subjects manipulating state structures in order to
gain better access to resources and the other
expressing an ultramodern instrumentality
that is ambivalently caught between whitening
social practices and the consumer power that
spells citizenship in the global economy. They
are thus not merely new arrivals passively
absorbed into an overarching Asian American
identity, nor can they be easily subsumed within
the inter-Asian coalitions that emerged among
college students in the 1960s or united simply
on the basis of having been treated "all alike"
as biogenetic others sharing a history of
exclusion (Chan 1991: xiii). The entanglement
of ideologies of race, culture, nation, and
capitalism shapes a range of ethnicized
citizenship in different fields of power. Given all
these factors, the heterogeneity and instability
of Asian American identities (Lowe 1991) suggest that a dramatic shift in coalitions may cut
across racial lines – for example, Asian-Anglo
partnerships in business or linkages between
Cambodian and other refugees of color in
dealing with the welfare state.

I end by returning to the moral predicament
of my own passage into American society.
Twenty years later, and only after the birth of
my first child (whose father is a fourth-genera-
tion Japanese- and Spanish-speaking Chinese
American) did I feel ready to mark my long
apprenticeship in cultural citizenship
by becoming a legal citizen. I continue to view
the term "Asian American" with ambivalence,
as much for its imposed racialized normativity

as for what it elides about other-Asians/other-Americans and for what it includes as well as excludes within the American scheme of belonging. One learns to be fast-footed, occasionally glancing over one's shoulder to avoid tripping over – while tripping up – those lines.

The unbearable lightness of being a nonwhite American means that the presumed stability and homogeneity of the Asian American identity must, in this era of post–civil-rights politics (Takagi 1994) and globalization, be open to the highly particularized local reworkings of global forces. In California these forces have been dramatically played out in domestic, racial terms as well as in transnational, class ones, foreshadowing the reconfiguration of citizenship in the West in the new global era.

NOTES

1 According to Rosaldo (1994: 57), cultural citizenship is "the right to be different (in terms of race, ethnicity, or native language) with respect to the norms of the dominant national community, without compromising one's right to belong, in the sense of participating in the nation-state's democratic processes. The enduring exclusions of the color line often deny full citizenship to Latinos and other people of color. From the point of view of subordinate communities, cultural citizenship offers the possibility of legitimizing demands made in the struggle to enfranchise themselves. These demands can range from legal, political and economic issues to matters of human dignity, well-being, and respect."

2 In 1988, the Bay Area was the third-most-favored destination for legal immigrants, after New York and Los Angeles. Nearly 41,000 immigrants arrived in the Bay Area that year, 60% of them Asian (*San Francisco Chronicle*, July 6, 1989).

3 See Kelly (1980), Nicholson (1989), Welaratna (1993), and Ong (1995a, b) for studies of how, after their arrival in the United States, Southeast Asian refugees are differently socialized in a range of institutional contexts to the requirements of the dominant white culture.

4 All the names of informants are fictive to protect their privacy.

REFERENCES

Alatas, Syed Hussein, 1977. *The Myth of the Lazy Native*. London: Cass.

Archdeacon, Thomas J., 1983. *Becoming American: An ethnic history*. New York: Free Press.

Becker, Gary C. 1965. A theory of the allocation of time. *Economic Journal* 75: 493–517.

Bederman, Gail, 1993. Civilization, the decline of middle-class manliness, and Ida B. Wells's anti-lynching campaign (1892–94). In *Gender in American History since 1890*, Barbara Melosh, ed. New York: Routledge, pp. 207–239.

Bourdieu, Pierre, 1984. *Distinction: A social critique of the judgement of taste*. Cambridge: Harvard University Press.

Chan, Sucheng, 1991. *Asian Americans: An interpretive history*. Boston: Twayne.

Corrigan, Philip, and Derek Sayer, 1985. *The Great Arch: English state formation as cultural revolution*. London: Basil Blackwell.

Embree, John F., 1950. Thailand – a loosely structured social system. *American Anthropologist* 52: 181–193.

Espiritu, Yen Le, 1992. *Asian American Panethnicity: Bridging institutions and identities*. Philadelphia: Temple University Press.

Fanon, Frantz, 1967. *Black Skin, White Masks*. Translated by C. L. Markman. New York: Grove Press.

Foucault, Michel, 1989. The subject and power. In *Michel Foucault: Beyond structuralism and hermeneutics*, H. L. Dreyfus and P. Rainbow, eds. Chicago: University of Chicago Press, pp. 208–228.

Foucault, Michel, 1991. On governmentality. In *The Foucault Effect*, G. Burchell, C. Gordon, and P. Miller, eds. Chicago: University of Chicago Press, pp. 87–104.

Gilman, Sander, 1985. *Difference and Pathology: Stereotypes of sexuality, race, and madness*. Ithaca: Cornell University Press.

Golub, Stephens, 1986. *Looking for Phantoms: Flaws in the Khmer Rouge health screening process*. Washington, DC: US Committee for Refugees.

Gordon, Colin, 1991. Governmental rationality: An introduction. In *The Foucault Effect*, G. Burchell, C. Gordon, and P. Miller, eds. Chicago: University of Chicago Press, pp. 1–51.

Gordon, Tamar, 1994. Constructing authenticities and modernities at the Polynesian Cultural Center. Paper presented at the American Anthropological Association meetings, Atlanta, November 30–December 3.

Gregory, Steven, and Roger Sanjek, eds, 1994. *Race*. New Brunswick: Rutgers University Press.

Harrington, Michael, 1962. *The Other America*. New York: Macmillan.

Harrison, M. L., 1991. Citizenship, consumption, and rights: A comment on B. S. Turner's theory of citizenship. *Sociology* 25: 215–218.

Kelly, Gail P., 1980. The schooling of Vietnamese immigrants: Internal colonialism and its impact on women. In *Comparative Perspectives on Third World women: The impact of race, sex, and class*, New York: Praeger, pp. 276–296.

Komorovsky, Mirra, 1967. *Blue-collar Marriage*. New York: Vintage Books.

Loescher, Gil, and John A. Scanlan, 1986. *Calculated Kindness: Refugees and America's half-open door: 1945 to the present*. New York: Free Press.

Lowe, Lisa, 1991. Heterogeneity, hybridity, and multiplicity: Masking Asian American differences. *Diaspora* 1: 24–44.

Memmi, Albert, 1967. *The Colonizer and the Colonized*. Translated by Howard Greenfield. New York: Beacon Press.

Mitchell, Katharyne, 1994. Multiculturalism, or The united colors of capitalism? *Antipode* 25: 263–294.

Mortland, Carol, 1987. Transforming refugees in refugee camps. *Urban Anthropology* 16: 375–404.

Myrdal, Gunnar, 1944. *An American Dilemma: The Negro problem and modern democracy*. New York: Harper and Row.

Nandy, Ashis, 1983. *The Intimate Enemy: Loss and the recovery of self under colonialism*. Delhi: Oxford University Press.

Ngor, Haing, 1987. *A Cambodian Odyssey*. New York: Macmillan.

Nicholson, Barbara, 1989. The influence of culture on teaching Southeast Asian paraprofessionals: A challenge to social work education. *Journal of Teaching in Social Work* 3: 73–86.

Omi, Michael, and Howard Winant, 1986. *Racial Formation in the United States: From the 1960s to the 1990s*. New York: Routledge and Kegan Paul.

Ong, Aihwa, 1992. Limits to cultural accumulation: Chinese capitalists on the American Pacific Rim. *Annals of the New York Academy of Sciences* 645: 125–145.

Ong, Aihwa, 1993. On the edges of empires: Flexible citizenship among cosmopolitan Chinese. *Positions* 1: 745–778.

Ong, Aihwa, 1995a. Making the biopolitical subject: Khmer immigrants, refugee medicine, and cultural citizenship in California. *Social Science and Medicine* 40: 1243–1257.

Ong, Aihwa, 1995b. Mother's milk in war and diaspora. *Cultural Survival Quarterly* 19: 61–64.

Ong, Aihwa, and Don Nonini, eds, 1996. *Ungrounded Empires: The cultural politics of modern Chinese transnationalism*. New York: Routledge.

Rabinow, Paul, ed., 1984. *The Foucault Reader*. New York: Pantheon.

Rosaldo, Renato, 1994. Cultural citizenship in San Jose, California. *Polar* 17: 57–63.

Rumbaut, Ruben G., and Kenji Ima, 1988. *The Adaptation of Southeast Asian Youth: A comparative study (Final report to the Office of Refugee Settlement, US Department of Health and Human Services, Family Support Administration)*. Washington, DC: Office of Refugee Settlement.

Said, Edward, 1978. *Orientalism*. New York: Pantheon.

Stack, Carol, 1974. *All Our Kin: Strategies for survival in a black community*. New York: Harper and Row.

Stolcke, Verena, 1995. Talking culture: New boundaries, new rhetorics of exclusion in Europe. *Current Anthropology* 36: 1–24.

Stoler, Ann L., 1995. *Race and the Education of Desire*. Durham: Duke University Press.

Takagi, Dana Y., 1994. Post-civil rights politics and Asian-American identity: Admissions and higher education. In *Race*, Steven Gregory and Roger Sanjek, eds. New Brunswick: Rutgers University Press, pp. 229–42.

Tollefson, J. W., 1990. Response to Ranard and Gilzow: The economics and ideology of overseas refugee education. *TESOL Quarterly* 24: 543–555.

Valentine, Charles A., 1971. Deficit, difference, and bicultural models of Afro-American behavior. *Harvard Educational Review* 41(2).

Welaratna, Usha, 1993. *Beyond the Killing Fields: Voices of nine Cambodian survivors in America*. Stanford: Stanford University Press.

Williams, Brackette F., 1989. A class act: Anthropology and the race across ethnic terrain. *Annual Review of Anthropology* 18: 401–444.

Williams, Brackette F., 1991. *Stains on my Name, War in my Veins: Guyana and the politics of cultural struggle*. Durham: Duke University Press.

12

Spaces of Insurgent Citizenship, 1999

James Holston

Insurgent Citizenship

My criticism of modernist planning is not that it presupposes a nonexistent egalitarian society or that it dreams of one. To deny that dream is also to conceal or encourage a more totalitarian control of the present. It is rather that modernist planning does not admit or develop productively the paradoxes of its imagined future. Instead, it attempts to be a plan without contradiction, without conflict. It assumes a rational domination of the future in which its total and totalizing plan dissolves any conflict between the imagined and the existing society in the imposed coherence of its order. This assumption is both arrogant and false. It fails to include as *constituent* elements of planning the conflict, ambiguity, and indeterminacy characteristic of actual social life. Moreover, it fails to consider the unintended and the unexpected as part of the model. Such assumptions are common to master plan solutions generally and not only to those in urban planning. Their basic feature is that they attempt to fix the future – or the past, as in

historical preservation – by appealing to precedents that negate the value of present circumstance. The crucial question for us to consider, therefore, is how to include the ethnographic present in planning, that is, the possibilities for change encountered in existing social conditions.

Not all master plans negate the present as a means to get to the imagined future (or past) of planning. A powerful counterexample is the US Constitution. It is certainly a master plan and certainly modern in proposing a system of national government "in order to form a more perfect union" (Preamble). Yet its great strength is precisely that its provisions are imprecise and incomplete. Moreover, it is distrustful of the very institutions of government it creates. As a blueprint, it does not try to legislate the future. Rather, its seven original articles and twenty-six amendments embody a few guiding principles – for example, federalism, separation of powers, and checks and balances – that not only channel conflict into mediating institutions but also protect against possible abuses of the governmental powers they create. Above all, they establish a trust that future generations of citizens have the

James Holston, Spaces of insurgent citizenship. In *Cities and Citizenship*, J. Holston and A. Appadurai, eds (Durham, North Carolina: Duke University Press, 1999), pp. 165–173.

The Anthropology of Citizenship: A Reader, First Edition. Edited by Sian Lazar.

ability and the right to make their own histories by interpreting what the master plan means in light of their own experience.

The US Constitution has, therefore, two kinds of planning projects: state building and citizenship building. The key point for our discussion is that the latter is conditioned by the former but not reducible to it because the Constitution secures for citizens a real measure of insurgence against the state. On the one hand, it designs a state with the minimum conditions necessary to institutionalize both order and conflict. On the other hand, it guarantees the necessary conditions for social mobilization as a means to include the unintended and the unforeseeable as possible sources of new constitutional interpretation.

This frame of complementary perspectives offers an important suggestion for thinking about a new production of the city. If modernist planning relies on and builds up the state, then its necessary counteragent is a mode of planning that addresses the formations of insurgent citizenship. Planning theory needs to be grounded in these antagonistic complements, both based on ethnographic and not utopian possibility: on one side, the project of state-directed futures, which can be transformative but which is always a product of specific politics; and, on the other, the project of engaging planners with the insurgent forms of the social that often derive from and transform the first project but are in important ways heterogeneous and outside the state. These insurgent forms are found both in organized grassroots mobilizations and in everyday practices that, in different ways, empower, parody, derail, or subvert state agendas. They are found, in other words, in struggles over what it means to be a member of the modern state – which is why I refer to them with the term citizenship. Membership in the state has never been a static identity, given the dynamics of global migrations and national ambitions. Citizenship changes as new members emerge to advance their claims, expanding its realm, and as new forms of segregation and violence counter these advances, eroding it. The sites of insurgent citizenship are found at the intersection of these processes of expansion and erosion.

These sites vary with time and place. Today, in many cities, they include the realm of the homeless, networks of migration, neighborhoods of Queer Nation, autoconstructed peripheries in which the poor build their own homes in precarious material and legal conditions, ganglands, fortified condominiums, employee-owned factories, squatter settlements, suburban migrant labor camps, sweatshops, and the zones of the so-called new racism. They are sites of insurgence because they introduce into the city new identities and practices that disturb established histories. These new identities and the disturbances they provoke may be of any social group, elite or subaltern. Their study views the city as not merely the container of this process but its subject as well – a space of emergent identities and their social organization. It concentrates on practices that engage the problematic nature of belonging to society. It privileges such disturbances, emergences, and engagements because it is at the fault lines of these processes that we perceive the dynamism of society – that is, the "multiplicity" that van Eyck could not discern. This perception is quite different, however, from a sociological accretion of data, and its register includes the litter and not only the monuments of urban experience.

This dynamism and its perception are the theoretical objectives of a planning linked to insurgent forms of the social. It differs from the modernist objectives of planning because it aims to understand society as a continual reinvention of the social, the present, and the modern and their modes of narrative and communication. What planners need to look for are the emergent sources of citizenship – and their repression – that indicate this invention. They are not hard to find in the wake of this century's important processes of change: massive migration to the world's major cities, industrialization and deindustrialization, the sexual revolution, democratization, and so forth. The new spaces of citizenship that result are especially the product of the compaction and reterritorialization in cities of so many new residents with histories, cultures, and demands that disrupt the normative and assumed categories of social life. This disruption is the source of insurgent citizenship and the object of a planning theory that includes the ethnographic present in its constitution.

The distinction between formal and substantive citizenship is useful in identifying this object because it suggests how the forms of insurgent citizenship appear as social practice and therefore how they may be studied. Formal citizenship refers to membership in a political community – in modern history, preeminently, the nation-state. Substantive citizenship concerns the array of civil, political, and social rights available to people. In a much-quoted essay, T. H. Marshall links these two aspects: "Citizenship is a status bestowed on those who are full members of a community. All who possess the status are equal with respect to the rights and duties with which the status is endowed" ([1950] 1977: 92). As new kinds of residents occupy cities – southern blacks in Chicago, Turks in Frankfurt, Nordestinos in São Paulo, Candangos in Brasília – these formal and substantive conditions shape their urban experience. In turn, this experience becomes a principal focus of their struggle to redefine those conditions of belonging to society.

Notions of formal citizenship have become problematic especially in the context of the massive urban migrations of recent decades. As new and more complex kinds of ethnic diversity dominate cities, the very notion of shared community becomes increasingly exhausted. What now constitutes that "direct sense of community membership based on loyalty to a civilization which is a common possession" that Marshall ([1950] 1977: 101) considered essential to citizenship – essential because only direct participation secures the rights, responsibilities, and liberties of self-rule? In the past, this sense has been a supralocal, indeed, national consciousness. But both national participation and community have become difficult notions for citizenship in the context of the new urban and, often at the same time, global politics of difference, multiculturalism, and racism. One indication of this problem is that in many cases formal citizenship is neither a necessary nor a sufficient condition for substantive citizenship. In other words, although in theory full access to rights depends on membership, in practice that which constitutes citizenship substantively (rights and duties) is often independent of its formal status. Indeed, it is often inaccessible to those who are formal citizens (e.g., the native poor), yet available to those who are not

(e.g., legally resident "aliens"). These kinds of problems challenge the dominant notion of citizenship as national identity and the historic role of the nation-state as the preeminent form of modern political community.

But in so doing, they indicate a new possibility that could become an important focus for urban planning: they suggest the possibility of multiple citizenships based on the local, regional, and transnational affiliations that aggregate in contemporary urban experience. Although this possibility represents a significant change in the recent history of citizenship, it is not a new arrangement. Multiple and overlapping jurisdictions predominated in Europe until the triumph of national citizenship obliterated other forms, among them the urban citizenships that organized so many regions of the ancient and the premodern world. The modern state explicitly competed with the city for the primary affiliation of its citizens. Moreover, it usurped their differences, replacing the local management of history with the national. That is, the state reorganized local diversity under the banner of national heritage. One of the most widely shared projects of modern states, this nationalization of diversity legitimates a *singular* state citizenship as the best condition for securing a society of plural cultural identities. But the recent worldwide multiplication of "rights to difference" movements profoundly challenges this claim. Their new ethnocultural politics and violence are in large part a response to the perceived failures of a singular national citizenship. In this reevaluation, the local and the urban reappear as the crucial sites for articulating not only new fanaticisms and hooliganisms but also new transnational and diasporic identities. If planning theory, as I suggest, can conceptualize this collision between state citizenship and these insurgent alternatives, planning practice can respond to this articulation first by expressing its heterogeneity – the social condition we actually live – and then by developing some of the ethnographic possibilities that are, by definition, embedded in heterogeneous conditions.

In terms of substantive issues, the insurgence of new citizenship is no less dramatic. Over the last few decades, many societies have experienced great expansions and erosions of rights. The expansions are particularly evident in the new social movements of the urban poor for "rights to the city" and of women, gays, and ethnic and racial minorities for "rights to difference." These movements are new not only because they force the state to respond to new social conditions of the working poor – in which sense they are, indeed, one important consequence of massive urban poverty on citizenship. They are also unprecedented in many cases because they create new kinds of rights, based on the exigencies of lived experience, outside the normative and institutional definitions of the state and its legal codes.

These rights generally address the social dramas of the new collective and personal spaces of the city, especially its impoverished residential neighborhoods. They focus on housing, property, sanitation, health, education, and so forth, raising basic questions about the scope of entitlements. Is adequate housing a right? Is employment? Moreover, they concern people largely excluded from the resources of the state and are based on social demands that may not be constitutionally defined but that people perceive as entitlements of general citizenship. The organization of these demands into social movements frequently results in new legislation, producing an unprecedented participation of new kinds of citizens in making law and even in administering urban reform and local government. Thus, as the social movements of the urban poor expand citizenship to new social bases, they also create new sources of citizenship rights and new forms of self-rule.

Yet if the city is in this sense an arena for a Rousseauian self-creation of new citizens, it is also a war zone for this very reason: the dominant classes meet the advances of these new citizens with new strategies of segregation, privatization, and fortification. Although the city has always been a place of such contestations, they have taken on new and especially intense forms in recent decades. Where the repressive structures of the state are especially effective, as in the United States, or especially murderous, as in Brazil, the resulting erosions of citizenship are particularly evident in the city's disintegrating public spaces and abandoned public spheres. This contemporary war zone includes not only the terror of death squads and gangs but also the terror of corporate fortresses and suburban enclaves. The latter too are insurgent forms of the social, subverting the proclaimed equalities and universals of national citizenship. Thus, the city-as-war-zone threatens the articulation of formal state membership as the principal universalizing norm for managing the simultaneity of modern social identities. As the war escalates, this threat ignites ever deeper anxieties about what form such coordination might take if national citizenship no longer has that primary role. As much as optimism may radiate from the city's social movements, this anxiety hovers over its war zone, structuring its possible futures.

Planning the Ethnographically Possible

In this essay, I have raised the problem of developing a new social imagination in planning and architecture. I have suggested that when citizenship expansions and erosions focus on urban experience, they constitute an insurgent urbanism that informs this development in several ways. First, they present the city as both the text and the context of new debates about fundamental social relations. In their localism and strategic particularism, these debates valorize the constitutive role of conflict and ambiguity in shaping the multiplicity of contemporary urban life. In a second sense, this heterogeneity works against the modernist absorption of citizenship into a project of state building, providing alternative, possible sources for the development of new kinds of practices and narratives about belonging to and participating in society. This "working against" defines what I called an insurgent citizenship; and its spatial mode, an insurgent urbanism. This insurgence is important to the project of rethinking the social in planning because it reveals a realm of the possible that is rooted in the heterogeneity of lived experience, which is to say, in the ethnographic present and not in utopian futures.

But in advocating a move to the ethnography of the present, I do not suggest that planning abandon the project of state building that modernist doctrine defined and that is basic to the notion of modernity itself. Excessive attention to the local has its own dangers. Although I argue, for example, that ethnographic investigation is the best way to establish the terms by which residents participate in the planning of their communities, such participation can be paradoxical: residents across the economic spectrum will often decide, by the most democratic of processes, to segregate their communities "from the evil outside," closing, fortifying, and privatizing their spaces in relation to those deemed outsiders. Hence, throughout the United States, it is common to find home-owner associations trying to use the powers and privileges of democratic organization to exclude and discriminate. Local enactments of democracy may thereby produce anti-democratic results. [For examples from Los Angeles, see Davis 1990.]

The lesson of this paradox is that planning needs to engage not only the development of insurgent forms of the social but also the resources of the state to define, and occasionally impose, a more encompassing conception of right than is sometimes possible to find at the local level. An example of this transformative power of the state comes from the conflict over legal segregation in the southern United States during the 1960s, when the federal government eventually intervened in local affairs and acted against local authorities. Above all, planning needs to encourage a complementary antagonism between these two engagements. It needs to operate simultaneously in two theaters, so to speak, maintaining a productive tension between the apparatus of state-directed futures and the investigation of insurgent forms of the social embedded in the present.

In developing the latter as the counter of the former, planners and architects engage a new realm of the possible with their professional practice. But this realm requires a different kind of practice, different in both objective and method, and this difference amounts to a reconceptualization of the fields. In terms of methods, I mean to emphasize those of an urban ethnographer – or of a detective, which are similar: methods of tracing, observing, decoding, and tagging, at one moment of the investigation, and those of reconstructing, identifying, presenting, and rearticulating, at another. Both the trace and the reconstruction compose this engagement with the ethnographic present. In this proposal, I am not suggesting that planners and architects

become anthropologists, for anthropology is not reducible to ethnography. Rather, I suggest that they learn the methods of ethnographic detection and also learn to work with anthropologists.

As for its objective, it is the very heterogeneity of society that baffles the architect van Eyck. To understand this multiplicity is to learn to read the social against the grain of its typical formations. The typical are the obvious, assumed, normative, and routine, and these are – as Poe illustrates so well in *The Purloined Letter* – hardest to detect. Rather, it is often by their deformations and counters that we learn about them. But countersites are more than just indicators of the norm. They are themselves possible alternatives to it. They contain the germ of a related but different development. Embedded in each of the facets of the multiple relations we live, such possibility accounts for the feeling we have that social life and its spaces are heterogeneous. This possibility is like a bog just beneath the surface of experience, at every step threatening to give way to something different if we let it. But generally we do not, because the technology of the normative keeps us from doubting the taken-for-granted on which we depend. Reading the social against the grain of its typical formations means showing that this surface is indeed doubly encoded with such possibility, and it means identifying the sites at which it seeps through.

To understand society's multiplicity is to learn to recognize "its counter-form" at these sites – to return to van Eyck's critical mission – and "to form a more perfect union" without sacrificing this double-encoding that is the vitality of present circumstance. As I have suggested here, one path to this understanding is to hunt for situations that engage, in practice, the problematic nature of belonging to society and that embody such problems as narratives about the city. But this kind of investigation amounts to a redefinition of the practice of planning and architecture as long as these fields remain obsessed with the design of objects and with the execution of plans and policies. Even though very few architects or planners conduct their professional practice in ways that correspond to this obsession, it remains a powerfully seductive mirage. To reengage the social after the debacle of modernism's utopian attempts, however, requires expanding the idea of planning and architecture beyond this preoccupation with execution and design. It requires looking into, caring for, and teaching about lived experience as lived. To plan the possible is, in this sense, to begin from an ethnographic conception of the social and its spaces of insurgence.

REFERENCES

Davis, Mike, 1990. *City of Quartz: Excavating the Future in Los Angeles*. London: Verso.

Marshall, T. H., 1977 [1950]. Citizenship and Social Class. In *Class, Citizenship, and Social Development*. Chicago: University of Chicago Press, pp. 71–134.

Part II
Ethnographic Explorations

II.1   Citizenship Regimes, Subject-Formation and the State

Introduction

The readings in Section II.1 explore how citizenship is constructed through encounters between citizens and the state, in particular how states create regimes of subject-making by means of welfare policy (Petryna), development projects (Lazar) and education (Benei). Sian Lazar's chapter shows how microcredit NGOs participate in an international yet highly localized project of citizen construction through the distribution of credit and programmes in human development education. Véronique Benei discusses the nature of citizenship-construction through schooling in Western India. While several discussions of schooling could have been extracted for this reader, Benei's ethnography is distinctive because of its very detailed focus on the phenomenological aspects of daily life and education in schools. She shows that bodily and emotional dispositions are as much a part of citizenship education as knowledge transfer. Adriana Petryna's chapter draws on some of the material discussed in her highly acclaimed and influential book on biological citizenship after the explosion of the Chernobyl reactor in Ukraine. She shows how people as political subjects must constitute themselves through particular scientific, technological and political categories in order to make claims on the state for welfare support and compensation for harm.

The element of self-construction made evident in Petryna's article provides a bridge to the second part of this section, which emphasizes more the bottom-up processes of 'self-making' through making claims on the state. The readings here focus very much on citizenship as political claims-making, for land reform (Wittman) and medical treatment (Nguyen). In Latin America, languages of citizenship have featured most prominently in academic and activist discourse, and Wittman's chapter discusses one of the key actors in that process, the MST (Landless Workers' Movement) in Brazil, who have defined their social movement activity as in part – although not exclusively – a struggle for full citizenship. She introduces the notion of agrarian citizenship, and details the intricate ways that MST activists claim citizenship through their daily political practice. Nguyen examines another process, in Côte d'Ivoire, whereby HIV+ individuals create themselves as particular kinds of political subjects – able to be empowered, to confess and inspire through speech – in order to gain access to antiretroviral treatment. He coins the phrase 'therapeutic citizenship' to describe the constellation of political relations around antiretroviral treatment and HIV/AIDS in the contemporary context. The relevant actors constitute a complex assemblage of government, commercial, non-governmental, philanthropic, research science and social movement actors as well as affected individuals, and the chapter extracted here is part of his recent book on the subject.

SUGGESTIONS FOR FURTHER READING

Albro, Robert, 2005. 'The water is ours, carajo!' Deep citizenship in Bolivia's water war. In *Social Movements: An Anthropological Reader*, J. Nash, ed. Oxford: Blackwell, pp. 249–271.

Alvarez, Sonia E., Evelina Dagnino and Arturo Escobar, 1998. *Cultures of Politics, Politics of Cultures: Revisioning Latin American Social Movements*. Boulder, Colorado: Westview Press.

Castle, Tomi, 2008. Sexual citizenship: articulating citizenship, identity, and the pursuit of the good life in urban Brazil. *PoLAR* 31(1): 118–133.

Chalfin, Brenda, 2008. Sovereigns and citizens in close encounter: airport anthropology and customs regimes in neoliberal Ghana. *American Ethnologist* 35(4): 519–538.

Cody, Francis, 2009. Inscribing subjects to citizenship: petitions, literacy activism, and the performativity of signature in rural Tamil India. *Cultural Anthropology* 24(3): 347–380.

Cornwall, Andrea, 2003. Whose voices? Whose choices? Reflections on gender and participatory development. *World Development* 31(8): 1325–1342.

Cruikshank, Barbara, 1999. *The Will to Empower: Democratic Citizens and Other Subjects*. Ithaca, New York and London: Cornell University Press.

Dagnino, Evelina, 2005. 'We all have rights, but …' Contesting concepts of citizenship in Brazil. In *Inclusive Citizenship: Meanings and Expressions*, N. Kabeer, ed. London: Zed Books, pp. 149–163.

de la Peña, Guillermo, 2002. Social citizenship, ethnic minority demands, human rights and neoliberal paradoxes: a case study in western Mexico. In *Multiculturalism in Latin America*, R. Sieder, ed. London: Palgrave, pp. 129–156.

Dewey, John, 1941. *Democracy and Education: An Introduction to the Philosophy of Education*. London: Allen & Unwin.

Ecks, Stefan, 2005. Pharmaceutical citizenship: antidepressant marketing and the promise of demarginalization in India. *Anthropology and Medicine* 12(3): 239–254.

Garcia Canclini, Nestor, 2001. *Consumers and Citizens: Globalization and Multicultural Conflicts*, G. Yudice, trans. Minneapolis and London: University of Minnesota Press.

Gutmann, Matthew, 2002. *The Romance of Democracy: Compliant Defiance in Contemporary Mexico*. Berkeley: University of California Press.

Hall, Kathleen, 2002. *Lives in Translation: Sikh Youth as British Citizens*. Philadelphia: University of Pennsylvania Press.

Hetherington, Kregg, 2011. *Guerrilla Auditors: The Politics of Transparency in Neoliberal Paraguay*. Durham, North Carolina and London: Duke University Press.

Levinson, Bradley, 2011. Toward an anthropology of (democratic) citizenship education. In *A Companion to the Anthropology of Education*, B. Levinson and M. Pollock, eds. Chichester: John Wiley & Sons, pp. 279–298.

Lukose, Ritty, 2005. Empty citizenship: protesting politics in the era of globalization. *Cultural Anthropology* 20(4): 506–533.

Luykx, Aurolyn, 1999. *The Citizen Factory: Schooling and Cultural Production in Bolivia*. New York: State University of New York Press.

Maeckelbergh, Marianne, 2009. *The Will of the Many: How the Alterglobalisation Movement is Changing the Face of Democracy*. London: Pluto Press.

Ong, Aihwa, 2003. *Buddha is Hiding: Refugees, Citizenship, the New America*. Berkeley, California: University of California Press.

Pan, Tianshu, 2006. 'Civilizing' Shanghai: government efforts to cultivate citizenship among impoverished residents. In *Chinese Citizenship: Views from the Margins*, V. Fong and R. Murphy, eds. London and New York: Routledge, pp. 96–122.

Petryna, Adriana, 2002. *Life Exposed: Biological Citizens after Chernobyl*. Princeton, New Jersey: Princeton University Press.

Postero, Nancy, 2007. *Now We Are Citizens: Indigenous Politics in Post-Multicultural Bolivia*. Stanford, California: Stanford University Press.

Sieder, Rachel, 2002. *Multiculturalism in Latin America: Indigenous Rights, Diversity and Democracy*. Basingstoke: Palgrave Macmillan.

Song, Jesook, 2009. *South Koreans in the Debt Crisis: The Creation of a Neoliberal Welfare Society*. Durham, North Carolina and London: Duke University Press.

Sørensen, Birgitte Refslund, 2008. The politics of citizenship and difference in Sri Lankan schools. *Anthropology and Education Quarterly* 39(4): 423–443.

13

Education for Credit

Development as Citizenship Project in Bolivia, 2004

Sian Lazar

This article investigates economic aspects of citizenship in El Alto, Bolivia through an exploration of microcredit NGOs working with female Aymara rural–urban migrants. Such NGOs operate from a basis of transnational discourses of citizenship conceived in an individualized neoliberal framework. Their activities can be viewed as a set of citizenship projects which attempt to modify the ways in which individuals act as economic agents. In recent years, the domain of the informal economy has become one of the key fields in which differing conceptions of individuality and citizenship are worked on by local people, the state and international agencies. In the last decade, microcredit NGOs for women have become one of the most important spaces where these projects of government operate (Rose 1999, 2000). Their focus on entrepreneurial activity operates on the assumption of a market-based (or disembedded) economic rationality, and is combined with capacity-building in a 'human development' model. This combination tells us much about the kinds of female citizens that governments and development agencies

seek to create, namely (crudely), 'empowered' individual, entrepreneurial, active citizens who will take responsibility for their own and their families' welfare, and who are prepared for the market rather than the state to provide for them.

I would argue that citizenship is best analysed as a dynamic and contested set of practices and projects, and that microcredit in Bolivia is an example of the meeting of development as a citizenship project from above with people's individual and collective economic strategies from below. In more normative anthropological terms, this meeting is an interaction between embedded and disembedded economic rationalities. Citizenship has always had an important economic dimension, from the Liberal emphasis on property rights to Marshallian social rights (Marshall 1983/1950). The end of the twentieth century saw a shift in understandings of citizenship, nowhere more keenly than in the economic dimension. From economic citizenship based on a bottom line of social rights collectively respected, the global trend now is a return to the focus on civil rights and more individual entrepreneurial responsibilities. Microcredit is

Sian Lazar, 2004. Education for credit: development as citizenship project in Bolivia. *Critique of Anthropology* 24(3): 301–319.

a form of development intervention perfectly in line with neoliberal philosophies of the entrepreneurial, individual citizen and the privatization of citizenship. The privatization of citizenship is not just illustrated by the issue of state responsibility for social welfare/rights, but also in the ways politics intervenes in what Foucault identified as the central issue for government, the 'conduct of conduct' (Rose 1999) and the disciplining of bodies. In the case of microcredit, it is not the state that is trying to measure and thus fix a certain set of subjects/citizens; rather, the NGOs and donor agencies do this work in its stead.

Citizenship and the Economy in Twentieth-Century Bolivia

Although Bolivia has never had anything that could be called a welfare state, there has been a shift in understandings of citizenship from one based upon collective social rights recognized by the state and delivered through corporatist mechanisms towards a more individualized focus (see Roberts 1995, for a discussion of this for Latin America). From the 1980s, the economic crisis, precipitated in part by over-reliance on foreign debt, led to structural adjustment programmes that greatly reduced the role of the state in the provision of economic security, particularly in the city of El Alto.[1] The neoliberal restructuring of Decree 21060 in 1985 led to thousands of miners losing their jobs, or being 'relocalized', as the euphemism of the time put it. Many went to the Chapare region in the Department of Cochabamba, to grow coca for cocaine; others went into commerce in El Alto. Between 1976 and 1992, the population of El Alto grew at a rate of 9.23 percent annually, to 405,492 in 1992, and in 2001 its population was 647,350 (Instituto Nacional de Estadísticas [INE], Bolivia). The dual imperatives of excess labour supply in the formal sector and increased amounts of drug money that needed laundering led to an explosion in commercial activity in the informal sector during the 1990s, which was focused particularly on El Alto.[2] The majority of the vendors in the street markets there are women, and most of the clients of microcredit organizations are female market-traders, shop-owners, or small-scale artisans.

By 1999, most people in El Alto were experiencing the consequent increased competition that made making a living very much more difficult than 'before'. By 2003, the economic crisis had become even more acute, due to the global economic slowdown and the situation in Argentina from 2001 onwards. Frequently, people told me that life was especially hard, and complained that there were more vendors than consumers. The comment I heard most frequently from friends when talking about business was 'no hay venta' – there are no sales. In this context, setting up in economic activity is extremely difficult, and requires flexibility and the ability to adapt to many different means of earning a living. The informal market operates on a knife-edge. The unfettered operation of the laws of supply and demand, with no subsidies in place, as well as fierce competition, mean that profit margins are tiny, and those who operate in this sector are highly vulnerable to economic downturn or recession. They are what Nikolas Rose has called 'entrepreneurs of the self' (1999: 164). Unfortunately, for a large proportion of 'active, responsible' citizens in contemporary societies shaped by advanced liberalism, this enterprise relies upon a willingness to super-exploit themselves and their families (Rivera Cusicanqui 2002), and the lack of state-provided safety nets is possible only because families and NGOs take up the slack. Kinship networks, in particular, play a vital role in the various economic strategies available to families, in terms of provision of credit, labour assistance and finding work. These networks are part of what is fashionably called the 'social capital' of the poor. In the absence of state assistance, it is this 'social capital' that ensures that people do not become utterly destitute. In other words, the economic strategies available to the poor of El Alto today are necessarily embedded in social and kinship relations but also respond to more disembedded, market-based forms of allocating resources.

Worldwide, liberal (and neoliberal) responses to the problems of poverty associated with advanced liberalism have been two-fold: deregulation of the informal sector and the provision of loans to 'microentrepreneurs' (see de Soto 1989, 2000). From the late 1970s onwards, microfinance has been an increasingly important form of development intervention aimed particularly at women, following the success of the Grameen Bank in Bangladesh. Bolivia's microfinance industry is often held up as a model for other parts of the world: a 'true development success story' according to Elizabeth Rhyne (2001). It incorporates a wide range of microfinance institutions, from development NGOs based closely on the Grameen bank model, to commercial institutions that are more like banks and which offer various financial services such as savings and current accounts. This article focuses on three institutions at the less commercial end of the sector, called ProMujer, Crecer and Diakonía, all of who target their efforts at the very poor. ProMujer and Crecer were both started by activists associated respectively with Acción and Freedom from Hunger, both American NGOs (Mosely 2001; Rhyne 2001). Their donors include USAID and the Inter-American Development Bank. Diakonía is run by an association of Norwegian Churches, and funded through them by NORAD (the Norwegian government development agency).

Although all three NGOs continue to operate on the 'village banking' model, they have had to become increasingly professional and efficient because of the rigour demanded by what Rhyne (2001) calls the dominant 'financial systems paradigm' of the more commercial bodies. The 'village banking' NGOs continue to focus their efforts on microcredit, with savings functioning principally as insurance against non-payment of the loans. Advocates have argued that microcredit is a very effective form of poverty alleviation, and most effective if targeted at women. Some claim that it can also lead to women's empowerment (Berger and Buvinic 1989), but it is probable that targeting women is less about female empowerment than about ensuring repayment of the loans, because of greater reliability on the part of women borrowers. There are, of course, significant debates about the effectiveness of microcredit in the alleviation of poverty and the empowerment of women (Hulme 2000; Kabeer 2001; Rogaly 1996). Most scholars nowadays agree that microcredit can aid those near the poverty line,

but that it does not alleviate extreme poverty. Nonetheless, development agencies such as the World Bank, DFID (Department for International Development, UK) and NORAD continue to view microcredit as a key part of their poverty alleviation strategies (Short 2000; Strand 2000; Wolfensohn 2000).

Microcredit NGOs in Rosas Pampa and El Alto: Navigating Market-Based and Kinship-Based Economic Rationalities

Most of the material for this article comes from Rosas Pampa, a neighbourhood in the south of El Alto. Rosas Pampa has about 1,000 households, and the majority of its adult residents are first- or second-generation Aymara-speaking migrants from the countryside of the Andean high plain. The first microcredit NGO to come to Rosas Pampa while I was there in 2000 was ProMujer. An educator came to the zone to run two weeks of training, which the women had to attend in order to get loans. During the first week, the women learned basic business administration. The course covered topics such as calculation of capital, earnings and profit, as well as increasing competitiveness, quality of products and what to do when 'no hay venta'. Presented within an entrepreneurial framework, the stress was on maintaining a stable level of profit, so that the loan can be paid back. The second week covered the running of a Communal Association, and how their credit scheme ran, what the interest rates were and so on. Crecer did not conduct as much training prior to giving out the loans, but spent time on it throughout the first loan cycle.

The director of one of the El Alto branches of ProMujer said in an interview with me that she thought that women who progress through the loan cycles to the point where they have loans of US $1,000 are extremely good future clients of ordinary banks; as she said, it is impressive that they pay US $150 a fortnight without fail and punctually. She thought it important to create a 'credit culture', i.e. one where recipients of credit know that they have to pay it back on time and responsibly:

At the national level, there isn't much of a credit culture, people aren't responsible. Here, I think that the majority of people think that you're clever if you swindle the bank; and you're a fool if you're honest.

However, ProMujer's position is somewhat disingenuous. They are not really training women for access to formal credit, since formal financial institutions do not have such demanding repayment terms. It is also a rather patronizing position, since there is already a perfectly vibrant credit culture in Rosas Pampa. As Hernando de Soto (2000) points out, one of the most important ways in which the poor bank the assets they have is through making loans to friends, neighbours and family, often at high rates of interest. I knew of people who lent out money on the basis of the collateral of title deeds to houses or cars. At interest rates of around 5 percent per month, this was the best way to invest any large sums of money they received, such as redundancy payments. Most people I knew borrowed from family members, to set up a small shop or to cover general living expenses. It is also common to sell building materials, food and other provisions on credit. The issue is not whether there exists a credit culture but whether it is regulated by government and/or large private financial institutions, and whether that credit culture is inside, or on the edges, of the formal economy.

People managed extremely delicate webs of credit, but as they were very private I was only allowed a glimpse of a small part of them. Microcredit NGOs are just another available resource, with lower interest rates than neighbours might charge, but more onerous repayment arrangements, and less flexibility than family. Often, women would borrow from family members to make the loan repayments to the NGO. Given all these resources to tap into, the relatively low levels of loans meant that some women decided that it was not worth the trouble for them. Others I knew thought it might be a convenient source for money to enable them to spread payment for their children's dental work, or their military service; what one might term embedded use of economic resources. And others did actually spend it on their businesses, as they were supposed to.

Women's responses therefore varied, from 'misuse' of the money to using it 'correctly', although members of each solidarity group (see below) usually had no idea of what exactly individual women spent the money on. This despite the NGOs' request that the women monitor how they all spent their loan money.

The use of networks and self-regulation to enforce repayment

Despite a rhetorical insistence on the market-based, instrumental rationality of individual entrepreneurship and accumulation of capital, the microcredit NGOs are constructed and understood using cultural codes that are very familiar to the women involved. Principally, they rely upon the women's existing networks of family and friends, and associated cultural understandings and obligations, in order to ensure loan repayment. As with the women themselves, the microcredit NGOs navigate effectively between disembedded and embedded economic rationalities. All three organizations discussed here function more or less on the model of the Grameen bank: the NGO lends to the 'association', a group of about 20 women from the same neighbourhood or village, which is split into small solidarity groups of 4–8 women who know each other very well. If one member of a solidarity group does not pay, then her fellow group members are in the first place responsible. The leadership committee will help the solidarity group chase up an errant member, and the whole association may help with payment. If one solidarity group does not pay, the association must cover their payment. The facilitator from the third microcredit NGO to operate in Rosas Pampa, Diakonía, frequently said that the repayment quotas for the Diakonía loans were 'sacred'. There was a little more flexibility with paying back money loaned from the association's savings, as long as the weekly payment to the bank was covered.

Repayment rates for schemes such as this are legendarily high, given the supposed high-risk nature of loans to those without a great deal of material collateral. This probably has much to do with the rather egregious terms of repayment, what the ProMujer Director called their 'credit technology'. All of the organizations operating in Rosas Pampa demanded weekly repayment meetings during the first loan cycle, which became fortnightly thereafter. At the beginning, these meetings were held at lunchtime, when the women have family responsibilities. If they were one minute late, they had to pay a small fine. I found it hard arranging my time so that I could go to the meetings each week, and a number of the women had other clashing commitments, quite apart from the responsibility to feed their husbands and to get their children ready for afternoon school. For example, one woman had to go on a demonstration with her union at the time of two payment meetings. Since both organizations would have fined her for non-attendance, she had to weigh up which fine to pay. As the groups became more established, they changed the meeting times so that they were more convenient, but the meetings continued to last several hours each fortnight.

Repayment is also enforced through the use of the women's existing social networks, based on, for example, *compadrazgo*,[3] marriage, economic relationships (such as that between landlady and tenant), occupational friendships and being neighbours. More generally, being '*conocida*', or 'known', was extremely important for the women of Rosas Pampa. If someone is *conocida*, it means that they can be placed through their connection to others via various types of important relationships. Its importance was demonstrated in the first meeting of the ProMujer Credit Committee, which consisted of the leaders of each solidarity group. They met with the director to discuss confidentially the amount each woman would get as a loan. This involved considerable bargaining, as the group leaders were generally unwilling to allow the director to lower the amount of loan available to each woman. For them, the criteria for credit-worthiness were whether someone was *conocida*, whereas the director's criteria were more business-oriented. Where someone was not a homeowner, she was unwilling to lend large amounts, whereas the leaders of the solidarity groups were far more ready to defend requests for large loans from women who were *conocidas*. Even if they

did not know someone personally, if someone they did know could place her in a kinship network then that was *conocida* enough for them. The ProMujer director later told me that the women become more active in controlling the credit as the loan cycles progress. They become more wary of allowing new women into the group, even if they are *conocidas*, and police non-payment more strictly. I heard that by the meeting of the Credit Committee at the beginning of the second loan cycle, the group leaders had become much stricter, and gave a friend of mine a smaller loan than she had applied for. So, in addition to the NGO workers hectoring any non-payers, in theory the women eventually self-regulate as a group in order to achieve the NGO's goals of reliable repayment of credit, and the structures gradually function more efficiently, as the less reliable women are weeded out over the loan cycle.

In practice, this can be quite a stressful process. The Diakonía group went through a small crisis when three borrowers (one man and two women) defaulted at the end of the group's third loan cycle. The group had been going for one and a half years, and the Diakonía facilitators had left the group to regulate itself. The chair ('Don Pablo') had allowed people, including himself, to borrow rather large internal loans[4] on the basis of only one guarantor. One woman in particular ('Doña Maria') had overcommitted herself and was unable to pay. She also owed money to the Crecer group in the neighbourhood. She (and others) didn't turn up to the meeting when the repayment was due, so the group faced the prospect of not being able to pay their full quota to the bank. The facilitator said that they would have to go into '*mora*', an official status meaning defaulter, but the other women objected to this because they wanted their next loan. So they agreed to pay the amount lacking from the group's quota themselves. Some began to grumble that they had known that Doña Maria wasn't entirely trustworthy, and a number of people had said that she shouldn't join their group. However, the Diakonía facilitator had said that they should go ahead and let her join. For her part, the facilitator was unhappy that they had approved such large internal loans, and on the basis of only one guarantor. There were recriminations on both sides, but eventually a small group of people, led by the guarantors of the defaulters and the members of their solidarity group, went to the defaulters' houses. Doña Maria was not in, but they went to her mother's house and her mother came to the meeting, to face the group. Her presence appeased the women somewhat. They felt that even if you couldn't pay, you should come and explain yourself: 'She has to confront the situation, you can't just disappear.'

Over the next couple of weeks, the commissions tracked down Doña Maria and Don Pablo and managed to persuade them to come to a meeting and explain their situation, so that the group and the facilitator could remonstrate with them. They were all very angry, and the arguments went on for hours, as the defaulters tried to defend their position and find a way to delay payment. Don Pablo left a TV and radio to prove his intention to pay, but Doña Maria had nothing worth leaving. Eventually, the defaulters were permitted by the other women to withdraw a new loan from Diakonía in order to pay back their internal loans little by little, a process development scholars call 'debt recycling', and certainly not what the loans are meant to be used for (Rahman 1999). The capital from that new loan was added to the group's savings and earnings (from interest on the internal loans) to pay the final quota to the bank. The group did not therefore enter into defaulter status, but at the end of that loan cycle, the women earned no dividend on their loans and had no savings returned to them.

The strategy of getting the defaulters to face the group was central to enforcing their responsibility to pay. In what F. G. Bailey (1971) called the 'small politics' of reputation, this publicized their action and emphasized the attendant social disapproval. The facilitator said to Doña Maria that 'our husband's prestige depends on us – if we behave wrongly, it reflects badly on him', and exhorted her 'come on, let's not make a scandal out of this'. She also told her mother that she would 'come and paint [Doña Maria's] house', referring to a practice common to informal lenders: I once saw large letters painted on someone's house saying 'Marco C—, pay back your debt'. When groups went to defaulters' houses, they demonstrated that they

knew where they lived, and would be able to create problems for them with their landlords or family. Rahman calls this kind of organized pressure from other group members 'social collateral', and points out its deleterious effects on group cohesion and solidarity, because loan group members cannot pay defaulters' debts easily. He argues that:

The failure in building mutual trust and support with each other in loan centers compels peer loan group borrowers and the bank workers to impose certain forms of repayment discipline – coercion and even debt recycling [i.e. using a new loan to pay off a previous loan] – that contradict the social objectives of generating trust, mutual support, and solidarity. (Rahman 1999: 149)

Microfinance institutions maintain that difficulties in repaying loans are overcome by 'social support' from other members of the group, but in fact it is a very stressful situation for all concerned. In some parts of the world, debtors have been arrested by the police, threatened with physical violence and have even reportedly committed suicide as a result of being unable to repay their loans (Hulme 2000).

In Bolivia, it is unclear whether the involvement of microcredit NGOs in the small-scale money lending 'market' has intensified the stresses that are part of money lending more generally. The social tensions associated with the inability to make loan payments may have been exacerbated by the greater availability of credit. On the other hand, the economic crisis of the last few years has increased defaults on all kinds of loans. This has even led to the development of an increasingly voluble protest movement of 'small debtors' of the more commercial microfinance institutions, raising the prospect of wider social instability. Although the situation was stressful, the women in the Diakonía credit group were able to understand the defaulters and reach a settlement with them. Perhaps of more concern is the underlying stress for those women who worry that they might not be able to pay back their loans, either because of a change in their personal situation or because they over-committed themselves in the first place. What we can say is that microcredit is not the panacea for poverty that many of its advocates assume.

Microcredit NGOs use the cultural and embedded nature of economic relationships to enhance their success in market-oriented terms of profit, repayment of loans and accumulation of capital. All over the world, they have created structures whereby women's social networks can even eventually make a profit for those lending to the women. Their talk of lending on the basis of 'trust' is somewhat misleading, as they rely on their clients to do the trusting, and to enforce their trust through social disapproval and pressure. This is an illustration of one of the ways in which 'social capital' grounds success in the market.

'La parte social': Human Development Education

As the above section shows, the microcredit NGOs under discussion here considered it their role to educate the women in 'credit culture', but ProMujer and Crecer's educational goals went further. As if the repayment terms were not onerous enough, a further requirement was added to the weekly or fortnightly sessions, in the form of 'capacity-building' for the women. These NGOs are a complicated hybrid of business logic and education in what I call a 'human development model'. I use this to refer to training sessions on family planning, nutrition, infant health, women's sexual health, women's health, women's rights, self-esteem and other issues. These sessions are a necessary complement to the economic citizenship project described above, because they attempt to get the women to work on their bodies in order to construct themselves as particular kinds of gendered citizens.

The whole package combines to form a fairly conservative take on women's empowerment. From the earliest days of the fashion for women's empowerment as a development goal, it has meant different things to different people (Kabeer 1999). One position sees female empowerment as residing essentially in access to markets (Ackerly, in Kabeer 2001), a position with which most feminist and/or women's organizations in Latin America would certainly

disagree. Activists in the Latin American women's movement tend to see empowerment as a complex range of changes in women's self-perceptions and in their abilities to be involved in decisions that affect them, at all sorts of levels. This is the essence of full citizenship for women as demanded by the women's movement in Latin America since the run-up to the Beijing Conference of 1995 (Molyneux and Lazar 2003). Obstacles to empowerment range from structural issues such as inequitable wealth distribution to more intimate questions of self-esteem. Different women's NGOs have different ways of approaching empowerment, but few ignore them. Hence the social programmes of ProMujer and Crecer.

The administrators of both ProMujer and Crecer highlighted the educational function of their credit schemes to me in interviews. Crecer maintain that they provide 'credit with education' and have even applied to trademark the phrase (Rhyne 2001). In the first cycle, they conduct sessions on vaccinating children, and in later cycles they work on themes such as infant nutrition, family planning, women's health and self-esteem. ProMujer in El Alto moved from providing business training for women into credit provision, and later incorporated the 'parte social' ('social part'), namely training in healthcare as well as healthcare service provision. According to the director there, they brought the 'parte social' into their credit programmes to 'make their institution more attractive to clients in a competitive market'. In the long run, she plans to jettison the training and provision of healthcare services and become a bank, on the basis that the funding for their social programmes won't last forever. In this, she is probably being very astute: two of her principal donors are USAID and the IDB, both of whom favour promoting sustainability in NGOs. 'Sustainability' tends to mean that users of NGOs should pay for their services, and social programmes in this context will inevitably suffer.

One might argue that the social programmes are mainly there to enable donor agencies to justify the subsidy they give to microcredit NGOs. The mantra that microcredit for the poor is good business, although often repeated, is widely known to be a fiction. As Ben Rogaly (1996) points out, if it were so profitable then the big banks and commercial financial institutions would have moved in a long time ago. A number of the larger private microfinance institutions in Bolivia are profitable, but they do not target the poor. When BancoSol moved from being a microcredit NGO to become a self-sustaining financial institution, its interest rates doubled in order to cover administrative costs (Rivera Cusicanqui 2002).

Reproduction, empowerment and women's citizenship

Social programmes also enable the NGOs to say that they are empowering women, and thus they can gain access to development agency funds set aside for that purpose. International donor agencies may also have other unstated goals that are fulfilled by many 'women's empowerment' and training sessions. For example, in women's training there is often a strong emphasis on healthy but not excessive reproduction. In prac-tice, family planning is stressed by a number of agencies, especially USAID, ostensibly because it empowers women to control the size of their families and therefore their lives. It is positively correlated with other indicators generally held to denote development (such as income, maternal mortality, infant mortality, infant nutritional levels and education). There is also a clear demand from many women for access to family planning. However, the emphasis placed upon it by NGOs in their training sessions seemed to me disproportionate. I was struck when the ProMujer director said to me and to health representatives for each Communal Association that 'we must get them [i.e. the ordi-nary members] to stop reproducing'. I could not help wondering if the contemporary focus on family planning in part reflects earlier eugenicist population control ideas (Stepan 1991). This may at first sound far-fetched, but the recent scandal of forced sterilizations in rural Peru dur-ing the 1990s attests to the persistence of some rather unpleasant Malthusian approaches to women's 'health'.[5] Mayra Buvinic (1989) argues that the prime aim for donors of most 'women in development' projects has been to control female fertility.

The content of the 'capacity-building' sessions provided by ProMujer and Crecer was based around a particular image of womanhood that may or may not have been consonant with the women's actual lived experience. That image was overwhelmingly one of monogamy (usually), responsibility for family, fearfulness, ignorance and abnegation. We can see examples of this in the ways the ProMujer trainer explained cancer susceptibility. She said that single women and nuns often get breast cancer because 'they did not make these organs function. God created us with these, not to have curves, but to feed children'; and she implicitly presented womb cancer as a punishment for many abortions/miscarriages, promiscuity and having had lots of children. More generally, she aimed to encourage the women to take an interest in their own health, to look after themselves and not to feel shame; and a slogan I often heard was 'If we don't look after our health, who else is going to?' This responds to a generalized feminist consensus that women tend to disregard their health in favour of that of their families.

Encouraging women to look after their health is not something that most people would object to, but for both ProMujer and Crecer, this meant that the women should go regularly to a doctor. *Curanderos* (traditional healers) or home-based remedies were never advocated in any capacity-building session I attended, despite the fact that they are one of the most common types of health-care for residents of El Alto. For example, ProMujer runs a system where each Communal Association appoints a Popular Health Representative (PHR). Her responsibility is to advise the women on health problems, accom-pany them to the doctor and, on occasion, give talks. I went along to their training session, which ran over five days at the office. Throughout the course, the emphasis was on attending formal, 'modern' healthcare services, despite the often bitter complaints made by participants and trainers about the quality of care provided in the health centres. One nurse was particularly dis-missive of 'traditional remedies', saying:

We're going to think here, we'll be logical. I apply x, and I get better. But it's only thanks to God that it healed. Or it's actually advancing on the inside.

Her paranoia was a further feature of the training. She maintained that the common remedies of putting dog hair or burnt material on a graze might cause serious bone disease in the future, for example. She did not discount the appropriateness of 'household medicine' for small things, but was much more in favour of hospital treatment. The Rosas Pampa PHR agreed, saying 'it's good to know. Sometimes we make very serious mistakes.' Nonetheless, many of the women remained sceptical of the vehement condemnation of traditional medicine. One former auxiliary nurse present, who had previously been very dismissive of the ignorance of indigenous women, asked at the final course evaluation for more teaching about herbal remedies.

The PHR training responded to donor agencies' demands for quantitative measurement of NGO activity, an example of the 'audit culture' (Shore and Wright 1999) operating in the NGO sector. The stated aim of the training was that each one could then be a health promoter and give talks to her loan group. However, they received no training in how to teach, so it is not surprising that factors such as age, force of personality, numbers of people and even the acoustics in the room made the difference between whether people listened or not to their talks. In fact, the NGO was more concerned about having trained the PHRs than about whether the women listened to them later. During the last day of the training session, we were told that the external evaluators wanted ProMujer to train more health promoters. Our centre was behind other ProMujer ones, such as Alto Lima, where of the 60 different loan groups, all the PHRs are trained. In ours there were 58 loan groups, but only 22 PHRs came for their training sessions. Since not all 22 PHRs in my session were actually effectively trained, I assume that the same is true for the 60 in Alto Lima. Nonetheless, ProMujer is able to say that they have trained these numbers of health promoters, because they attended the classes and passed the exams, which were brief and certainly did not require 100 percent correct answers in order to pass. The women have their certificates, and everyone is happy. Empowerment and training are reduced to target figures for those attending courses, meetings, capacity-building sessions and talks. This is by no means exceptional: charities and NGOs all over the world have to respond to quantitative targets set by donors or they lose their funding. This 'audit culture' is the form of government to which they are subject; the way in which politics regulates the provision of what used to be public services (Rose 1999; Shore and Wright 1999).

Although charities/NGOs are not profit-making outfits in the sense of providing dividends to shareholders, when they reach a certain size, other profit-making motives may come into play. Funding may become necessary for its own sake: rather than growth allowing the charity to provide a better service to more beneficiaries, more services to more beneficiaries become the means to justify growth. This 'corporatization' of charities/NGOs is perhaps inevitable, if not intentional. It means that it is probably incorrect to ask whether organizations such as ProMujer and Crecer are empowering women, since although that is their aim, it is not the way in which they measure, or are forced to measure, their performance. Maia Green (2003) makes the point with regard to DFID, using the project-based logframe as an example: regardless of 'higher' development aims, each project has to be defined in terms of achievable objectives, which are then met, because they are essentially self-fulfilling. Whether meeting those particular objectives leads to the 'higher aims' is functionally irrelevant, because this is simply how accountability works.

The end result is that capacity-building sessions are not tailored to the women's needs, essentially because they are conceived of as chats or programmes that are delivered to a large number of listeners. This tends to respond not only to quantitative measurement of activity, but also to a transmissive notion of education still dominant in Bolivia (Luykx 1999). Furthermore, the NGOs appear to think that the women do not get this knowledge from anywhere else, and thus begin from a position of complete ignorance. In addition, or as a result, the women were not particularly interested in learning the often overly technical and irrelevant information, for example the name of the TB bacterium, which was one of the main focuses of a Crecer session on the vaccination of children. The majority of women paid only polite attention to the training, and forgot the details very quickly. This was illustrated when the ProMujer group were 'trained' in 'women's health' twice, but did not realize that they had already covered that topic until well into the second session. Nonetheless, these projects are an example of government that attempts to operate in very intimate spheres. Through them, the women are encouraged to work on their selves within a particular image of womanhood linked to responsible reproduction. Empowerment and citizenship are thus, in practice, available to them only on certain terms.

Microcredit NGOs exploit women's sociability through making them come to so many meetings in order to ensure repayment of loans; and to be the subjects of capacity-building sessions that in turn gain the NGO funding from donor agencies. However, it is important not to overstate the case against these NGOs. Although the meetings are sometimes inconvenient, on the whole, the women enjoyed getting together every so often, away from their home or market stall. My abiding memories of the meetings are not the training sessions, but of everyone talking about how their babies were growing and developing, of women knitting, dozing, catching up with friends, gossiping, talking about illnesses, about pregnancies, problems, hangovers. The training and paying were in many ways background to the real business of the day for the majority of women there, including myself. Doña Emiliana once said to me that she really enjoyed the meetings, because the women get together and laugh and talk. They are also important business opportunities, as members of both Diakonía and Crecer would cook and sell lunch or supper, along with drinks and other snacks. Selling food during the meetings draws on an important cultural link between commensality and solidarity in Andean societies (Harris 1982), and is one of the ways in which the women themselves mould the microcredit NGOs into collective enterprises.

In practice, this is one of the ways in which women from El Alto gather together and reinforce a collective sense of self through maintaining their social networks. A collective sense of agency and political subjectivity is important for citizenship more generally in El Alto because the relationship between citizens and the state is mediated through membership in collective entities such as neighbourhood associations and trade unions (Lazar 2002). So, in a general sense, the experience of being part of a microcredit group does reinforce the women's vision of their identity as based upon collective organization. In a slightly different sphere (that of the more commercial microcredit institutions), this has even been translated into a political movement of small debtors who are demanding lower interest on their loans. However, it is true that the kinds of collective organization encouraged by microcredit groups are on the whole extremely depoliticized when compared with others, such as the trade unions of street traders. They are perhaps evidence of the development of what Nikolas Rose calls 'networks of allegiance' (1999: 177), that is a neoliberal model of collectivity that complements individual active citizenship. The feminist project of the empowerment of women viewed as a crucial precondition for effective political participation is diluted into depoliticized and temporary collectivities based upon common interest and the regulation of credit. So, while the dominant 'citizenship project' of the microcredit NGOs encourages a self-reliant and individualized approach to economic success, this sits alongside competing notions of collectivity, which are played out in the everyday dramas of debt repayments and collective meetings.

Conclusions

Microcredit is a complex issue, and not as uncomplicatedly good and efficient as it is sometimes made out to be by the 'microcredit evangelicals' (Rogaly 1996). The dual strategy of provision of credit and credit education alongside human development education is an attempt to create gendered citizens who are 'empowered' to access formal markets on certain terms, and who do not expect the state to provide them with social rights. They should also, ideally, monitor their own health and reproduction and learn to discipline their own bodies by subjecting them to the modern healthcare system. Development scholars debate whether microcredit fulfils its promise of empowerment and poverty alleviation (Hulme 2000; Kabeer 2001; Mayoux 1998; Mosely 2001; Rahman 1999; Rhyne 2001; Rogaly 1996), but often fail to address the question of whether it is appropriate to exploit women's resources in order to fulfil the NGOs' own development targets, such as sustainability (or profit) and the ability to attract further funds from development agencies. The demand that exists may in fact be for money rather than specifically for credit, but whichever it is, that demand is rather exploited, and there are plenty of women who do not consider it worth their while. The NGOs are not only exploiting women's social networks and pressures to conform, but they also exploit the women's time, patience and, ultimately, their inability to get credit from other private financial institutions.

Nonetheless, the women subject to these 'citizenship projects' respond to them in different ways. They may, for example, use the loans for 'incorrect' purposes that do not aid the accumulation of capital, such as paying for dental work for their children; or they may lend to other people or default on their payments. Most ignore or imperfectly understand the content of the 'human development' training sessions, and only a very few use the loans for their intended purpose and listen carefully in the capacity-building sessions. In this article I have discussed microcredit NGOs in order to explore how some of the citizenship projects devised by international development agencies and favoured by government policy operate in practice. I wanted to show the mix of their attempts at creating the women as particular kinds of agents alongside education in a specific version of womanhood. The women's patchy responses to such projects mean that they are only partially successful in meeting their explicit aims. Their success in other terms, specifically ensuring repayment of loans, has much to do with their contradictory reliance upon the embedded economic rationalities that, on the surface, they seek to modify.

In this sense, the microcredit NGOs discussed here reflect two aspects of a wider process of alteration of the terms of economic citizenship at the beginning of the twenty-first century. First, the individual–collective tension is playing itself out in development such that the rhetoric of individual citizen responsibility is moving towards a greater focus on 'social capital' and collective responsibility for social welfare, but a collective responsibility not channelled through the state. The privatization of citizenship in Latin America is not solely an individualizing process but, as with microcredit NGOs, draws upon deeply rooted collective traditions of organization, community and kinship for its strength. Second, although the *state* has abdicated responsibility for social welfare, the 'human development education' described here is an example of a process through which *government* extends to very intimate spheres, as, in the name of capacity-building, parastatal organizations such as NGOs and donor agencies seek to create and 'empower' gendered citizens through the disciplining of their bodies within a particular image of womanhood.

NOTES

1   El Alto lies on the Andean high plain at 4100 m above sea level. It began in the early twentieth century as a suburb of the city of La Paz, but became a city in its own right in 1985.

2   Here I am using a broad definition of the 'informal economy' as characterized by small-scale commerce, production or transport that is unregulated and untaxed by government, with people mostly self-employed rather than receiving a wage. I acknowledge that it is difficult to define precisely; and that there is no clear distinction between 'formal' and 'informal' sectors, since they rely so much upon each other. See Rivera Cusicanqui (2002) and Ypeij (1999).

3   *Compadrazgo* is the relationship between parents of a child and the child's godparents. It is a very common means of formalizing a friendship between adults.

4 These are extra loans drawn from the group's savings. The 'internal bank' from which these loans are drawn grows through the weekly amount that each woman is obliged to save, and also from accumulated interest charged on the internal loans. At the end of each loan cycle, Diakonía distributes the earnings of this 'internal bank' as dividends to each member of the group.

5 See BBC News Wednesday, 24 July 2002, 11:33 GMT 12:33 UK, 'Mass sterilisation scandal shocks Peru'. http://news.bbc.co.uk/1/hi/world/americas/2148793.stm.

REFERENCES

Bailey, F. G., 1971. Gifts and poisons. In *Gifts and Poisons: The Politics of Reputation*, F. G. Bailey, ed. Oxford: Blackwell, pp. 1–26.

Berger, M. and M. Buvinic, eds, 1989. *Women's Ventures: Assistance to the Informal Sector in Latin America*. West Hartford, CT: Kumarian Press.

Buvinic, M., 1989. Investing in poor women: The psychology of donor support. *World Development* 17: 1045–1057.

de Soto, H., 1989. *The Other Path: The Invisible Revolution in the Third World*. London: I. B. Tauris.

de Soto, H., 2000. *The Mystery of Capital: Why Capitalism Triumphs in the West and Fails Everywhere Else*. New York: Basic Books.

Green, M., 2003. Globalizing development in Tanzania: Policy franchising through participatory project management. *Critique of Anthropology* 23: 123–143.

Harris, O., 1982. Labour and produce in an ethnic economy, Northern Potosí. In *Ecology and Exchange in the Andes*, D. Lehmann, ed. Cambridge: Cambridge University Press, pp. 70–96.

Hulme, D., 2000. Is microdebt good for poor people? A note on the dark side of microfinance. *Small Enterprise Development* 11: 26–28.

Kabeer, N., 1999. Resources, agency, achievements: Reflections on the measurement of women's empowerment. *Development and Change* 30: 435–464.

Kabeer, N., 2001. Conflicts over credit: Re-evaluating the empowerment potential of loans to women in rural Bangladesh. *World Development* 29: 63–84.

Lazar, S., 2002. Cholo Citizens: Negotiating Personhood and Building Communities in El Alto, Bolivia. PhD thesis, Goldsmiths College, University of London.

Luykx, A., 1999. *The Citizen Factory: Schooling and Cultural Production in Bolivia*. SUNY series, Power, Social Identity, and Education. New York: State University of New York Press.

Marshall, T. H., 1983 [1950]. Citizenship and social class. In *States and Societies*, D. Held, ed. Oxford: Martin Robertson, in association with Open University, pp. 248–260.

Mayoux, L., 1998. Women's empowerment and micro-finance programmes: Strategies for increasing impact. *Development in Practice* 8: 235–241.

Molyneux, M., and S. Lazar, 2003. *Doing the Rights Thing: Rights-based Development and Latin American NGOs*. London: Intermediate Technology.

Mosely, P., 2001. Microfinance and poverty in Bolivia. *Journal of Development Studies* 37: 101–132.

Rahman, A., 1999. *Women and Microcredit in Rural Bangladesh: Anthropological Study of the Rhetoric and Realities of Grameen Bank Lending*. Boulder, CO: Westview Press.

Rhyne, E., 2001. *Mainstreaming Microfinance: How Lending to the Poor Began, Grew, and Came of Age in Bolivia*. West Hartford, CT: Kumarian Press.

Rivera Cusicanqui, S., 2002. *Bircholas: Trabajo de mujeres: explotación capitalista y opresión colonial entre las migrantes aymaras de La Paz y El Alto*, 2nd edn. La Paz: Mama Huaco.

Roberts, B. R., 1995. *The Making of Citizens: Cities of Peasants Revisited*. London: Arnold.

Rogaly, B., 1996. Micro-finance evangelism, "destitute women" and the hard-selling of a new anti-poverty formula. *Development in Practice* 6: 100–112.

Rose, N., 1999. *Powers of Freedom: Reframing Political Thought*. Cambridge: Cambridge University Press.

Rose, N., 2000. Governing cities, governing citizens. In *Democracy, Citizenship and the Global City*, E. Isin, ed. London: Routledge, pp. 95–109.

Shore, C., and S. Wright, 1999. Audit culture and anthropology: Neo-liberalism in British higher education. *Journal of the Royal Anthropological Institute* 5: 557–576.

Short, C., 2000. Influencing the policy framework for enterprise development. *Small Enterprise Development* 11: 8–10.

Stepan, N., 1991. *The Hour of Eugenics: Race, Gender and Nation in Latin America*. Ithaca, NY: Cornell University Press.

Strand, T., 2000. Norwegian support for small enterprises in the fight against poverty. *Small Enterprise Development* 11: 11–12.

Wolfensohn, J., 2000. How the World Bank is attacking poverty through small enterprise development and microfinance. *Small Enterprise Development* 11: 5–7.

Ypeij, A., 1999. *Producing against Poverty: Female and Male Micro-entrepreneurs in Lima, Peru*. Amsterdam: Amsterdam University Press.

14

Producing Good Citizens

Languages, Bodies, Emotions, 2008

Véronique Benei

[A]nd the body is our anchorage in a world.
        Maurice Merleau-Ponty, *Phenomenology*
                                of Perception

Political integration has already taken place to some extent, but what I am after is something much deeper than that – an emotional integration of the Indian people so that we might be welded into one, and made into one strong national unit.
                    Jawaharlal Nehru

Just like you have sucked your mother's milk, you have at the same time imbibed your mother's language.
        Shantabai Vankudre, mother of
                    Sushila, Class 3

The classroom is rather bare, with four to five rows of wooden planks aligned on the floor for the pupils to sit on, a few posters of the national and regional leaders (*nete*) stuck onto the dark painted walls, and an uneven board covered in neatly chalked words. These would hardly be legible in the room darkened by the stormy, cloudy skies of a March afternoon were it not for the light filtering in through the half-closed shutters. At times, a slight breeze gently pushes the shutters back and forth, relieving the fanless room's occupants from the humid heat. Behind the small desk to the right of the board is sitting Mr. Pawar. The young Class 3 teacher, in his early thirties, was posted two years before, in 1997, at Marathi Corporation School. The school is one of seventy-two run by the municipality of Kolhapur. Located in the slum area of Sachar Bazar, the institution is also competing with the All India Marathi School, founded and run by the progressive socialist Antar Bharati society, and the Urdu Corporation School that caters to most of the Muslim students of the area. Apart from its small size, however, nothing really distinguishes Marathi Corporation School from its counterparts: the teachers have undergone the same training as their colleagues and are equally paid by the state government. Their schooling years have been similarly shaped by a patriotic education geared toward national "emotional

Véronique Benei, Producing good citizens: languages, bodies, emotions. In *Schooling Passions: Nation, History, and Language in Contemporary Western India* (Stanford, California: Stanford University Press, 2008), pp. 70–98.

integration." The latter was deemed "easily the most important component element ... of ... national integration" in a homonymous *Report* (1962: 1) commissioned by Jawaharlal Nehru in the late 1950s. "Emotional integration" has been a staple of the national curriculum for the past forty years. Even today, the report in which the concept first appeared in many ways prefigures and informs much of the ideology undergirding life in primary schools in Maharashtra. Emotional integration is not only instantiated in textbook contents but also permeates routines and procedures of daily national production, whether during morning liturgies or in classrooms like that of Mr. Pawar.

The Marathi lesson has already started. Today, it is devoted to a recapitulation of the vocabulary learned in the course of the past few months. Mr. Pawar has concocted a revision schedule of his own based on the syllabus. His neat and clear handwriting covers the entire board: words in four columns on the left-hand side face whole sentences on the right. Armed with a ruler, he points to each word methodically, column after column, the pupils repeating the words in chorus. At times the teacher interrupts his enumeration to call for a distracted pupil's attention, firing copious chalk bullets at the recalcitrant pupils; at other times he selects several students to repeat words and sentences one after another. And so the repetition goes:

"My school is very nice, my village is beautiful, I like my country very much, I have pride and respect in my country, in my country live people from different jāt,[1] in my country people live happily." [Majhi shala chan ahe, Majhe gaon sundar ahe, Majha desh mala khup avadto, Majhya deshaca mala abhiman ahe, Majhya deshat vividh jatice lok rahat, Majhya deshatil lok anandane rahat.]

Mr. Pawar's choice of words and sentences is nothing exceptional in this part of India. Rather, his examples are integral to the daily iterations of devotion to the Indian nation in the Marathi language. Although the lexical selection here is clearly informed by the official textbook in use in every Class 3 across the regional state, it also partly stems from Mr. Pawar's own inspiration.

For there exists no stipulation of procedures for vocabulary revisions along such explicitly national lines. Asked why he chose these examples in the first place, Mr. Pawar seemed somewhat puzzled. He had not really given it much thought. Wasn't it obvious that children had to be taught how to love their country (deshvar prem thevayce) and become good citizens (cangle nagarik huvayce)? Was it not the same where I came from? This, then, is an illustration of Maharashtrian and Indian nationalism at its most banal level of quotidian experience.

How does the nation become this natural object of devotion, and what are the modalities of this "affective shaping of nationhood" (Yano 1995: 20)? How are political emotions constructed? In the previous chapter we conducted a conceptual and ethnographic exploration of "what moves people" and of the ways in which political discourses and practices of *deshbhakti* play upon regional traditions of devotionalism in the production of a national devotional sensorium. This exploration brought home the usefulness of the notion of political emotion for envisaging the emotive dimension inherent in political and social processes. I now turn to the phenomenological entailments of such a notion by addressing the issue of the intertwined production of ideals of love of nation and good citizenship feeding into the construction of national citizens. This requires identifying the kind of labor that goes into the naturalizing objectification of the nation, and through what mediations. This chapter explores the mediation of language, both as ideology and incorporated practice. Rather than confining my analysis to the level of linguistic performance, I also examine the embodiedness of discourse on language. My reflection is situated at the crossroads of three main anthropological trends: an anthropology of emotions, of bodies, and of language ideology. Anthropology, and the other social sciences to varying extents, has been marked by various genealogies of works reinstating the body as a primary medium for socialization. That socialization does take place largely through social actors' bodies – however these are to be defined and located, socially, culturally, historically, and politically – has by now become a commonplace. Similarly, it has been firmly established that language and emotion are social, cultural, and political practices. Yet little work has sought to explore the intersections of the production of language ideologies and emotions with any notion of embodiment in the formation of national attachment. In this chapter, I seek to illuminate the crucial dimension of *embodied* linguistic emotions of national belonging nurtured through schooling.

Elsewhere (Benei 2001b) I showed how children through morning liturgies create their physical selves while enacting and embodying the nation into existence. I want to pursue this approach here and explore the ways in which the body is not only one of the main sites of inscription of a national project of citizenship through the disciplining procedures extant in everyday life at school but, as crucially, a phenomenological site of feeling and experiencing the construction of the nation. In other words, the body is not solely acted upon and acting in a subjected rapport to discipline and inscription of the law; it is a *felt and feeling* body. Arguably, much of the production of national bonds in the early years of socialization, especially schooling, involves teaching and learning how to "feel" the nation. Here I aim to unravel the joint modalities of embodied self-formation and instantiation of the nation, and its articulation with idioms of citizenship. As I will also suggest, the plasticity of the body is, however, not exhausted by either this national emotional sensorium or its associated project of collective and individual self-formation.

First, I want to take you out of Mr. Pawar's classroom on the periphery of Kolhapur and drive you fast-forward in time, to another, more popular school situated in the bustling heart of town. It is a year later, at the Varsity Marathi School, one of the oldest privately run Marathi primary schools. It is Saturday noon, and the school day has just ended. We are in the teachers' room. The new Congress government in the regional state has just announced its decision to introduce compulsory English from Class 1 onward. Ms. Kirari, the school headmistress, who, like many of her colleagues, has always voiced her pride in her "Indian culture," is strongly opposed to such a measure. She is vehemently discussing

the government's intention with her staff. I have known Kirari Bai well for over two years. She is a strong-willed and generous lady in her early fifties and is often rather outspoken. Never have I seen her behave so passionately. Her face is red with anger, her hair flying loose as she gestures forcefully in the course of her diatribe against the new government's "populist policy."

A few days later, when we meet again, Kirari Bai takes up the topic afresh on her own initiative. Although she has cooled down by now, she makes no mystery of how dear to her heart the issue of language is, shaking her head in negation: "No, it is definitely not good, one should not do it." "Why not?" I prompt her. Her answer is pat:

"Before, we had the Moghuls, in the times of the Muslims, and we had to learn the Persian [*Farsi*] language. Then with the advent of Shivaji the Marathi language was successfully imposed. But then, later on, the English came and forced their English language on us. Then we got our independence, and our Marathi, our own language [*swabhasha*] back again. Now, what is the point of imposing the firangi [English] language on us again? Besides, learning in a foreign tongue is just so unnatural [*aswābhāvik*]. Learning in a foreign language is not right [*barobar nāhī*]; it hinders the child's development. It is more natural [*swābhāvik*] to learn in one's mother tongue [*mātr bhāṣā*]."

Throughout this chapter I will use Kirari Bai's visceral linguistic performance as a guiding thread and tease out its underlying understandings, assumptions, and implications. [...]

Public Emotions or Private Feelings? Toward Phenomenological Reconciliations

[...]

Bodies, as is by now established, are as much the principal medium for most socialization processes as they are social and cultural constructions. Bourdieu's notion of "bodily hexis" as a "set of body techniques and postures that are learned habits or deeply ingrained dispositions that both reflect and reproduce the social relations that surround and constitute them" (as summarized by Abu-Lughod and Lutz 1990: 12) has become received wisdom in the social sciences. Other works have made much of Foucault's insights into disciplinary processes (1979) and the notion of individuals', agents', subjects', actors' bodies as the site of the "inscription of the law."[2] Arguably, heeding the embodied dimension of socialization also illuminates the processes at play in the quotidian production of national imaginings and senses of belonging. Among other things, an emotional, embodied discourse of the nation is produced in the morning rituals as much as in the ordinary school day routine in Kolhapur. It does not consist only of words, verbal utterances, and gestures, through which emotion, however defined, is expressed at every level of language, from intonation to inflection, grammar – especially syntax – and vocabulary (Ochs and Schieffelin 1989; Besnier 1990; Irvine 1990; Errington 1998a, 1998b). It is also concrete, physical, embodied. For this reason, it is as much a collective discourse as an individuated one (or whatever finer continuum of experientiality between these two arbitrary extremes is available as a cultural resource), without any necessary implication of primacy or authenticity of one over the other.

Bodies, Emotions, Nations

[O]ur mental life is knit up with our corporeal frame, in the strictest sense of the term.
William James, "What is an Emotion?"

[...] Michelle Rosaldo's article (1984) inspired a large part of the intellectual approach to be found in later work on emotion. However, such inspiration has been partial, for Rosaldo was genuinely interested in the notion of embodiment. She explicitly referred to "flushes, pulses, 'movements' of our livers, minds, hearts, stomachs, skin" as *"embodied* thoughts, thoughts seeped with the apprehension that 'I am involved'" (1984: 143). Such a phenomenological awareness seems to have been lost in much subsequent work. I want to pause on Rosaldo's comment of "I am involved," which resonates

with the approach developed by Maurice Merleau-Ponty in his *Phenomenology of Perception* (1989). Drawing upon earlier conceptions that emerged in the late nineteenth century (especially Husserl's notion of "I-can"), Merleau-Ponty expanded on the notion of the body as the medium of involvement in the world. Rather than the objective body, he saw the "phenomenal body," that which has a representation/consciousness/image of itself, as our medium for relating to the world: "The body is the vehicle of being in the world, and having a body is, for a living creature, to be intervolved in a definite environment, to identify oneself with certain projects and be continually committed to them" (1989: 82). This conceptualization of human beings anchored in the world through their bodies parted with a dualistic – and still prevalent – assumption of disjunction between organism and psyche (88). Here I want to take this insight into an exploration of the ways in which bodies are, through what might at first sight appear "mere" disciplining, also made to feel the nation in the space of school.

Even in schools where the morning assembly would regularly take no more than ten minutes, the body always operated as a fundamental vehicle for producing a national attachment, with different drills being practiced at each stage. In the process, the idea of the body of the nation (Assayag 1997) was enacted by the pupils, congruently with the idea advanced more than a century ago by the historian of religions Ernest Renan (1996: Prologue). In all the schools visited, pupils would sing the national anthem while standing, keeping their bodies upright and stiff, arms alongside. This would be followed by the recitation of the pledge (*pratidnya*) in Marathi, with the children holding their right arm horizontally as if taking a pledge in court. After the *pratidnya* would ensue the school prayer, other *shloks*, and more contemporary songs, promoting various topics ranging from national unity to girls' schooling. All these sung items were often interspersed with simple calisthenics, involving arm raising, repeatedly putting the legs apart and together, sideways movements of the arms, and so on. Orchestrating the session, the teacher in charge – often a middle-aged Brahmin

or Maratha woman – would lead the children
into gymnastic movements while singing along
with them. In many schools, this was accompanied by continuous drumming performed by
an office boy, a teacher, or a pupil while the
other teachers stood by their divisions and
joined in the singing, their bodies stiff and their
facial expressions grave, adding to the martial
physicality of the ceremony. What we have
here is an exemplification of incorporation
of a "spontaneous" national sentiment, also
acknowledged – yet hardly documented – in
Europe (Thiesse 1999: 14). This incorporation
is integral to the child's everyday life, blending
patriotic sentiment with other, ordinary
matters.

Moreover, the idea of this national physical
integration is made very explicit in the official
textbooks produced by the Maharashtra State
Bureau and in some of the supplementary ones
used for physical education prepared for each
class by private educational publishers. Thus,
the textbook *Vocal and Physical Education*
(*Sangit ani Sharirik shikshan*) designed for
Class 4 and published by Vikas (literally,
"progress") starts with the *pratidnya* and the
rashtragit. It includes the song "Jay Bharta,"
inspired by the national anthem and additionally
glorifying Hindu gods and all the various revolu-
tionaries and builders of modern and independent
India. The song also appears as the first lesson in
the official Class 3 Marathi-language book,
together with explicit instructions as to how it
should be practiced and repeated individually
and collectively, accompanied by, or interspersed
with, calisthenics.

This disciplining of bodies, both at the time
of the morning liturgy and later on in the classroom, is regulated by the concept of *śista*.
Commonly translated as "discipline," the term
also refers to the controlled immobility and
stiffness that pupils are expected to adopt,
whether during phenomenological experiences
of daily assembly in alternating drills and
physical training (PT) movements with rigid,
standing postures or in classroom situations. A
teacher calling for pupils' silence or attention,
for instance, will often shout: "Shistit basayce;
gap basayce" (Sit properly; shut up [literally,
"sit quiet"]). As important, the notion of *shista*
encompasses the meaning of moral rectitude

and is explicitly enacted as such in everyday
school life as well as in the official pedagogy.
To give an example, the Class 3 Marathi book
mentioned contains another instance of incorporation of the nation: the very first story in
the language manual emphasizes the bodily
and moral rectitude to be observed while
singing the *rashtragit*. It is a masterpiece of the
nationalist pedagogical genre and a wonderful
Bourdieusian illustration of how "obedience is
belief and belief is what the body grants even
when the mind says no." The story is narrated
by a schoolteacher and is about untrained
schoolchildren on their first school day. The
narrative adroitly weaves another story into
the plot, that of a retired army officer (*subhe-
dar*) walking past the school with a water jug
in hand. As he hears the shouting of the call to
attention (*sāwadhān*, the call marking the
beginning of both military and nationalist
school drills, as well as ending the first ritual in
wedding ceremonies; see Benei 1996), the
retired officer "instinctively" straightens himself up to adopt the *shista* position and drops
his jug to the ground. The last words of the
story provide an excellent illustration of the
intricate relationship between the teaching of
the nation and the disciplining of bodies:

Like [that of] the *subhedhar*, the body of each
schoolchild should become proper, fit ....
While singing the *rashtragit*, correctness
should be displayed. Whenever and wherever
our country's *rashtragit* is started playing, we
must stop and stand in the *sawdhan* position;
we must show respect to our *rashtragit*!
(*Marathi Bal Bharati* 1998: 11)

This intricate interplay of bodily and moral
rectitude undergirds the attempted production
of a social body of future generations of Indian
citizens: a social body that should ideally be
unconditionally devoted to loving and serving
the nation. These last two aims of unity of and
love for the nation are made explicit in the
pledge [...]. In many ways, this example of
schooling projects draws attention to the
embodied kind of morality integral to the
formation of personhood and citizenship, and to
which language socialization practices crucially
contribute while shaping notions of ethnicity

and cultural identity (Garrett and Baquedano-Lopez 2002: 350). I now turn to these language socialization practices.

Language Ideologies, Standardization, and Nationalism

Language invites people to unite, but it does not force them to do so.

Ernest Renan, *Qu'est-ce qu'une nation?*

Language acquisition obviously entails more than a child simply learning to produce "well-formed referential utterances" (Garrett and Baquedano-Lopez 2002: 342). It involves the child's developing skills in order to use language in socially appropriate ways and make meaning of culturally relevant contexts and activities. These are determined by language ideologies, that is, "self-evident ideas and objectives a group holds concerning roles of language in the social experiences of members as they contribute to the expression of the group" (Heath 1989: 53, quoted in Woolard 1998: 4). In other words, ideologies of language articulate historical constructions with the developmental process of language acquisition, as well as with local notions of cultural and group identity, nationhood, personhood, and childhood (Garrett and Baquedano-Lopez 2002: 353–64). Working with the notion of language ideology has rendered possible a "debunking" of the claims to pristine purity and authenticity inherent in most nationalist language ideologies. In particular, it has highlighted the contingency and arbitrariness of language as a referent and mediation for the imagination of the nation. Despite Ernest Renan's comment of over a century ago upon the arbitrary equation of language and nation, fetishization of language as a referential system for a national community of speakers has been the consequence of Lockean and Herderian ideologies (although distinct as language philosophies) and their profound impact on the modern theories of linguistic nationalism prevalent since the nineteenth century in Europe and elsewhere (Kroskrity 2000: 11). Many studies of nationalism across the world stressed

the prominent part linguistic factors have since played in the cultural formation of the nation – whether at a national or a regional level (Anderson 1991; Gellner 1983; Hobsbawm 1992; Hastings 1997). Linguistic movements in the formation of ethno-nationalisms have also been documented in the subcontinent (King 1996; Rahman 1996, 2004; King 1998). In India, regional nationalisms have been intricately associated with regional languages, particularly in Bengal, Tamilnadu, and Maharashtra (see Phadke 1979; Cohn 1987; Ramaswamy 1997). The case of Maharashtrian nationalism and Marathi language offers a particularly rich historical instance of a linguistic and cultural regionalism mediating national sentiment.

The very issue of how languages come to be naturalized in locutors' representations requires further probing. Why are conceptions of languages as "discrete, distinctive entities ... emblematic of self and community" so universally prominent (Fishman 1989, quoted in Woolard 1998: 18)? Here I seek to reach an understanding of such emblematization through Marathi discourses of belonging. The mediatory role of linguistic ideologies in relation to language and emotion (Wilce 2004: 11) also calls for a phenomenological exploration of language ideologies and their physicality as indigenous discursive practices as well as lived, embodied experiences. In Maharashtra, as we shall see, social actors both possess and share a language ideology of Marathi and have a linguistic discourse on the physicality of emotion. The first step of the demonstration, however, requires probing into the idea of an imagined, homogeneous language for national purposes.

At first glance, there may appear a contradiction between Marathi linguistic belonging and Indian nationalism. Yet the two are intricately related: the notion of a Marathi/Maratha nation stands in Maharashtrian conceptualizations as *the* precondition for the possibility of the Indian nation. Marathi-predicated Maharashtrian nationalism owes much to the processes of homogenization that have accompanied the development of the language into a nationalist/regionalist ideology. Indeed, Marathi nationalism clearly instantiates the notion that if language alone suggests – mostly in the form of poetry and songs – "a kind of contemporaneous community" (Anderson 1991: 145), "homogeneous language is as much imagined as is community" (Irvine and Gal 2000: 76). Marathi's normalization and homogenization were enabled by the philological efforts of British linguists and educationists working closely with local Sanskrit pundits in the mid-nineteenth century (McDonald 1968a, 1968b; Nemade 1990; Benei 2001b; Naregal 2002). In the process, the Marathi spoken by Pune Brahmins emerged as *the* sanctioned legitimate standard. The colonial concern for codifying and standardizing Marathi and its (written) usages later proved indigenously instrumental in its development into a medium of communication for Marathi speakers whose "dialectal" varieties had heretofore made it difficult for them to communicate with one another.[3] Consequently, official Marathi today is to some extent a modern creation, and the underlying standardization process was at the core of the birth of a vernacular print literature providing reconceptualization of social and political space on the basis of a unified "imagined community": through this literature were produced common ideas about Maharashtra as a region celebrating a glorious martial past and *bhakti* tradition. The (re)definition of a modern Marathi and Maharashtrian identity thus participated in the emergence of a regionalist consciousness in the last decades of the nineteenth century. This regional consciousness was also largely nationalist.

Marathi provided the medium for celebrating at length the "idea of India." Indeed, despite full recognition within the regional state of the role Hindi played as a linguistic and national unifier, the notion of "Marathi language" (*Marathi bhasha*) operated as a powerful, rallying trope and a crucial mediation for the production, assertion, and defense of a sense of both regional and national belonging. Evidence of this in the space of school lies in the contents of the language textbooks designed by the regional state's production bureau for Classes 1 to 5, and in the wealth of poems and songs pupils learned and were made to recite, sing, and mime. The primary Marathi language manuals are replete with poems, stories, and songs glorifying India.

Even the Class 1 Marathi textbook has its fair share of devotional national contents. In addition to reproducing the words of the national anthem on the last page of the book under the title "Our National Song" (Aple rashtragit), it has a twelve-line poem entitled "This Is My Country of India" (Ha majha Bharat desh). These are the poem's first and last lines:

This is my country of India	Ha majha Bharat desh
Superb, superb is my country	Chhan chhan majha desh
...	...
My country is superb	Majha desh chhan ahe
India is my country.	Bharat majha desh ahe.

This kind of poetic declaration is reiterated throughout the day, whether by rote learning of the textbook contents and recitation at the time of the paripath; by teachers selecting examples "at random" for the purpose of illustrating a point, grammatical, geographical, historical, or otherwise; or, as we saw in Mr. Pawar's class, merely practicing acquired vocabulary. Among the examples selected, the stories of independence heroes and nationalist fighters, especially Mahatma Gandhi and Subhas Chandra Bose, figure prominently. Telling these stories provides occasions for teachers to proffer side commentaries, often ending with an exhortation for the pupils to emulate these edifying models. These moments are clear instances of affect being linguistically mediated, permeating talk and "infusing words with emotional orientations" (Garrett and Baquedano-Lopez 2002: 352; see also Ochs and Schieffelin 1989; Besnier 1990), and in which the very celebration of the nation occurs in the intricate folds of a linguistic intimacy with the region.

Such an intimacy is further undergirded by the concept of "one's own language" (*swabhasha*). The notion may have already existed prior to the colonial encounter; yet it was reinscribed as a political and nationalist one in the throes of redefining and strengthening a sense of *communitas* predicated upon a sense of belonging to the soil as *swadesh* (one's own country) and sharing *swadharma* (one's own religion [...]) in the late nineteenth and early twentieth centuries.[4] In Maharashtra today, this trinitarian conceptualization meaningfully informs the reworking and reproduction of emotional structures of feeling. In Kolhapur, in the late 1990s and early 2000s, Marathi-speaking parents of both English- and Marathi-educated children often expressed their attachment to Maharashtra as a whole in those very terms. This connection between language and the (re)production of a sense of belonging (to both a community of speakers and people living on the same soil) is also poignantly revealed in the wording of Kirari Bai's impassioned diatribe and emotional expression, verbal and bodily. Furthermore, in using the notion of *swabhasha* as standing in opposition to other languages (especially English), Kirari Bai was reproducing a pattern common among Marathi speakers today. Many parents and teachers similarly expressed their contrasted attachment to the Marathi language, resorting to the popular expression of *swataci bhasha* – as in "Amci bhasha 'he, swataci" (This is our language, our own). Often, they would utter these words while scanning them, with an emphasis on each syllable; the physicality of the utterance would also be completed with a gesture of the hand (palm flat, or fist) tapping on the chest or heart. Of all the embodied aspects of such a testimony, this gesture, common in many other contexts of claiming, confessing, and pledging faithfulness, best signals emotional involvement.

This emotional involvement vividly resonates with discursive practice where even the pronoun used in discussions of ownership of the Marathi language crucially encapsulates and furthers a sense of cohesiveness of the thus-constituted Marathi-speaking *communitas* in opposition to the linguistic outside. Like most Indian languages, Marathi has two pronouns for the first-person plural pronoun *we* used in English: one is the exclusive *āmhī* (*āmce, -ā, -ī* for neutral, masculine, and feminine possessive forms respectively), which demarcates the speaker from her or his audience. In contexts where the audience is meant to be included in the speaker's reference group, the pronoun used is the inclusive *āpaṇ* (*āple, -ā, -ī* in possessive forms). Hence, there is always

a notion of clear demarcation in ordinary and daily speech and interaction between those who do belong to one's group of elocution and those who do not. Of course, such demarcation is highly fluid, variable, and context specific. When used in discussions of belonging, however, such a lexical marker powerfully contributes to emphasize – and thus reinforces – a collective sentiment of cohesion. Therefore, when, as in political discourses, teachers address their audience referring to "our country" using the phrase *apla desh*, they are clearly calling out to the children as part of the same united, exclusive group. The potentialities of such a deictic marker are obviously vast and need to be borne in mind in a reflection on identity, citizenship, and belonging (see also Billig 1995 on the notion of deictic marker). They have special import given the close association of *swabhasha* with *swadesh*, especially with respect to conceptualizations of members of non-Marathi-speaking, non-Hindu communities in Maharashtra. For the moment, I want to concentrate on the predication of Marathi language ideology upon notions of naturalness mediated and legitimized by the concept of "mother tongue." I wish to illuminate the ways in which schools are sites of language naturalization and homogenization, thereby creating a conscious notion of the mother tongue "already there" as an object and a medium of love and attachment. This "already there," however, is by no means a natural given. Rather, it is itself the product of early childhood socialization processes occurring in the intimacy of home. Schools, therefore, draw upon, amplify, and crystallize senses of linguistic belonging while making the latter's ideology explicit and further anchoring it in lived and experienced bodies.

Mother Tongue, Naturalness, and Philological Explorations

What accounts for the meaningfulness of language ideology as both social practice and pedagogical tool is its experiential association with the concept of "mother tongue." Language ideology crystallizes, almost reifies, Marathias-*swabhasha* as the

naturalized object of motherly love experienced in the infancy of social and family life.
[...]
The felt authenticity of the idea and lived experience of the Marathi language as mother tongue has in many ways been relayed by schooling, not only at an official level with explicit discourses promoting a Marathi-predicated Maharashtrian identity but also, and most important on the ground of everyday practices, intricately linking it to an idiom of motherhood. Thus, the large number of prayers and poems in Marathi addressed to both mother and motherland and officially part of the syllabus are supplemented by primary schoolteachers' own daily pronouncements on the topic.
[...]
Taking Ramaswamy's proposition of the embodied mother tongue literally, I aim to document the cognitive and phenomenological deployment of this trope. In particular, I seek to understand the articulation between the level of somatic imagery and its transposition to "the guts" of its ordinary citizen-subjects. Documenting such a transposition requires that we recognize it as *not* metaphorical (Strathern 1993). [...] Here, I want to emphasize the *physicality* of the mother-tongue ideology for its speakers. This physicality is evidenced in the analogy often drawn between mother language and biological mother. Thus, Mr. Joshi, an art teacher running a cultural center for schoolchildren, explained in the summer of 2003:

> Before traveling abroad, it is important that we should first see our gaon, Maharashtra, our desh, etc. Today, everybody wants to go to America; people are all forgetting their mother tongue.... Yet your mother tongue is like your mother's womb: you cannot forget it. Moreover, it is unique. Just like you only have one mother, so you only have one mother tongue. It cannot be changed.

Mr. Joshi's statement echoes those frequently made by both female and male parents and teachers, who identified other bodily parts and substances, the mother's milk in particular. Thus, Shantabai, Maratha mother of Sushila, a

Class 3 student at Modern Marathi School quoted earlier, states, "Just like you have sucked your mother's milk, you have at the same time imbibed your mother's language."

Both Mr. Joshi's and Shantabai's words are strikingly reminiscent of the views of the eighteenth-century linguist, poet, and philologist Johann Gottfried von Herder, famous for his influential theology of cultural nation building premised on linguistic revelation through one's people (*Volk*). At the core of Herder's vision of national forms lies an organic connection between human language and natural and historical forces that the most enlightened people would realize. The "true character" of a nation, its soul, spirit, and genius, would be reflected in, expressed through, and further strengthened by the uniqueness of its language conceived, produced, and transmitted as mother tongue. Especially noteworthy in the present case is that, if language is more than a mere cognitive tool, it is also associated with motherly substances *and* operates as a material object: it is the very *substance* of one's cultural and national being. Thus, by going away, by leaving one's homeland, one loses one's own culture and, more precisely, the nurturing substance of motherly milk and idiom. In some ways, it is as if the humoral theory of old *patriae* analyzed by C. A. Bayly (1998) had been transposed and transmuted into that of the mother tongue in a triadic association with soil and faith. We need to go one step further and examine how the notion and ideology of mother tongue are embedded in a process that concomitantly naturalizes language. The apparent "obviousness" and "naturalness" – and their emotional implications – of the Marathi language need further attention, especially because they are crucial elements in ordinary Marathi speakers' discursive iterations. Furthermore, paying heed to local understandings of "naturalness" also illuminates the moral dimension associated with somatic and emotional notions of language.

Linguistic ideologies characteristically operate a kind of neutralization or naturalization of language value through semiotic processes erasing both the historical contingency of languages and the relations of power and interest underlying them (Spitulnik 1998: 163).

This begs the question of how ordinary social actors produce, posit, and understand such naturalness. Drawing on discursive constructions of language as well as observations and descriptions of speech acts and performances, I contend that the construction of "naturalness" is premised on an understanding of language as incorporation, both as discourse and practice. We have just encountered Mr. Joshi's views on the substantialization of language and the fear and anxiety attached to the idea of identity loss generated by distance and forgetting. Although such fears and anxieties culminate in comments from expatriate Maharashtrians, they are generally pervasive in discussions "back home," especially of the medium of instruction for schoolchildren, as suggested by Kirari Bai's passionate defense of Marathi over English at the opening of this chapter.

Yet if Kirari Bai's statement was clearly one of the best articulated ever encountered in the course of research, it was in no way exceptional. Many Marathi-speaking parents shared the same fears of potential identity loss associated with the teaching of, and in, the English language. Moreover, the discursive (and pragmatic) favoring of instruction in Marathi was by no means specific to *Hindutva*-sympathetic teachers or parents. In addition, such a preference recurred both among parents of children schooled in the Marathi language and among those whose children attended English-language institutions. In both cases, the discursive preference was primarily couched in an idiom of naturalness associated with the notion of mother tongue: "Learning in one's mother tongue is so much more natural [*swabhavik*]" was a leitmotif among parents who would cite evidence of children having gone through the primary phase of instruction in their native language as being more scholarly grounded than others. Here, the Marathi word used for "natural" crucially illuminates the breadth of the semantic repertoire of emotionality characterizing Marathi language ideology. Naturalness is conceptualized as both an emotional *and* embodied state. The word *swabhavik* (from the root *bhāv*) encompasses many layers of meaning, including that of a natural state of being, innate property, disposition, nature, but also, as important,

sentiment or passion, emotion or feeling, a class of affections, *as well as* the actions, gestures, or postures constituting corporeal expression thereof. When Marathi native speakers elaborate on the naturalness of their language, therefore, they are often – whether consciously or not – playing into an embodied experientiality of linguistic emotion.

Perhaps the best exemplification of such embodied experientiality lies in the expression *trās yene*, as in the phrase "Tras yeto, English maddhe shikayla." Such a statement was often encountered among parents voicing their concern about the difficulty caused by the unnaturalness of learning in any language other than one's mother tongue. Loosely translated, the sentence means "It creates problems, to learn in English." The semantic register is however much wider: *tras* in Marathi may refer as much to emotional as physical issues. Consider, for instance, the common expression *kunala tras dene* (to give a hard time to someone). In the idiom of domesticity, and especially among married women, the expression is used with reference to kin relations within the conjugal family, whose epitome lies in the figure of the mother-in-law. Narratives pertaining to daughters-in-law – young brides in particular – suffering at the hands of their mothers-in-law would often be couched in these terms. In this context as in others, *tras* could be psychological, emotional, and physical. To return to the context of learning, the physical connotation of *tras* must be taken seriously, rather than hastily dismissed as merely metaphorical. As Andrew Strathern argued, the notion of metaphor should not be considered as a heuristic device for the "unfamiliar or the strange." In contrast, Strathern proposed, we should favor an "against metaphor" perspective and take discourses about bodily emotions literally: "A stress on metaphor goes with a textual emphasis, but 'reading the body' may require us to alter our categories more radically" (1993: 6). Here, it must be emphasized that the expression *tras yene* is also used in association with the disruption of the ordinary course of bodily functions, especially that of the digestive system. Important to note is that the verb "to digest" (*pacavne*) itself conveys connotations of harmony, and its use in the negative sense is common to refer to disruption of social and political order and the resulting degradation of moral order. Thus, if a battle is lost, the shame incurred in defeat goes "undigested" (*apacavleli*). When parents or teachers voice their concern about the naturalness of learning in one's mother tongue (and the converse *tras* generated by learning in any other idiom), therefore, they are not just demonstrating the appropriateness of such a conceptual vocabulary in the South Asian context today, despite its historical genealogy of vernacular language ideology rooted in the West (Nemade 1990; Pollock 2006: 318–19). They are also explicitly referring to a phenomenological understanding of language. Both vocabulary and understanding also entail a moral dimension, which requires elaboration.

Anxious Emotions, Idioms of Morality, and Family Tropes of the Nation

Language does not only encode embodied emotions; it also forms the basis for the socialization of morality, that is, the social sanctioning or rejection of actions (one's own and others'). As participants in everyday routines internalize and express emotion, they also learn to make sense of the moral order they are actively constructing through interaction with others. Notions of morality are thus negotiated through linguistically (and corporeally) mediated understandings of daily life and events, providing bearings for one's place in the world, both as an individual and as part of a collective (Abu-Lughod and Lutz 1990: 13). Producing a sense of national belonging, whether through morning school assemblies or throughout the day – during language and history lessons in particular – was mediated by a Marathi vocabulary of kinship. This vocabulary furnishes a moral trope for articulating belonging to the family community of the nation identified by Anderson (1991). Here, in addition to the mother trope analyzed previously, the kinship one of "brothers and sisters" (*bhauband*) informs the pledge daily recited in Marathi. The pledge is taken almost verbatim from the *Report of the Committee on Emotional Integration* commissioned by Nehru in the early 1960s. The national leader envisaged such emotional integration as central to his project of nation building and explicitly resorted to metaphors and rhetoric of kinship: the nation was understood as a mother, whether implicitly or explicitly, and her children, the citizens of India, were to be *bhauband*. The term possesses many layers of meaning in Maharashtra: predicated on *bhāū* (literally, "brother"), *bhauband* defines a kinsman, or in some contexts, all agnatic kinsmen. By extension, it can apply to all the men of a village. In all these senses, the term often conveys a strong sense of emotional and practical commitment, sharing, and friendliness, implying some form of cohesion and loyalty. As suggested earlier, such notions of cohesion and loyalty are integral to the Marathi language ideology, with the result that any move away from the language is conceived by Marathi speakers as a form of betrayal; a betrayal not only of language and its incorporation but also of *desh* and *dharma* (associated with *bhasha*, as discussed earlier) and of the community of the (Marathi-speaking) nation. Thus, parents' affective bodily displays accompanied assertive vocalizations about the necessity to teach in Marathi as against the *firangi* language. This moral imperative was also voiced by social actors who did not abide by this rule, as will be seen shortly. But such are the entailments of Marathi ideology that the moral and embodied emotionality associated with the notion of the language remains a powerful one. This bears elaboration.

In a recent article about the linguistic choices and dilemmas obtaining among Marathi speakers in the face of a so-called English-mediated globalization, I discussed the complex tensions between the educational and professional choices linked to middle-class aspirations and expectations on the one hand, and local and regional linguistic attachments on the other (Benei 2005c). I showed how the notion of morality tied up with the Marathi language ideology is reflected in the contrapuntal conception of "foreign" languages held by many Marathi speakers. English occupies a particular place in this linguistic moral economy. Kirari Bai's virulent statement about

British rule indicates the lingering malaise associated with the "colonial language" in this part of India.[5] In many ways, such a malaise has moral resonances dating back to British educationists' attempts at disciplining and moralizing the Marathi language in the course of their standardizing endeavors (Benei 2001a). Today, this malaise is compounded by the perceived lack of morality associated with American English. Many Marathi-speaking middle-class people in Kolhapur can boast about a – however distant – family connection currently living, studying, or working in America; however, the underlying fascination for the new world's promise of a potential site for better economic opportunities, prosperity, and happiness is also matched by ambivalent imaginings of a land of high rate of divorce, loose morality, and loss of parental and filial values. In these representations, America often emerged as the place of all moral and familial perdition, in a sense, an archetypal site of Kaliyuga. Remarkably, the tensions documented here were as salient in cases of successful exposure to English-language instruction. The decision parents made to have their children learn in a language other than Marathi often gave rise to anxieties of cultural loss similarly couched in an idiom of morality. An example is that of Baba Pankat, the head of a Bhangi (ex-Untouchable) family.

At the beginning of my research, the family was composed of sixteen members spread across three generations living together. Two of the sons ran the prosperous spare-part workshops started by their father decades earlier. Baba, in his mid-seventies at the time of research, recalled the early days when he had to do his caste's calling (scavenging) and had to struggle hard through the educational system, paying for his studies by working as a mechanic. His educational beginnings were harsh and besmirched by the stigma attached to his "caste untouchability." Baba remembered not being allowed to sit within the classroom at the primary school and having to follow the lessons from the threshold. Against all odds, he managed to study up to Class 7 in Marathi at Kolhapur New High School before switching to English Class 5. He left after finishing Class 6. In the following two generations, those of

his children and grandchildren who, regardless of gender, could handle studying in English were sent to English-language institutions, and the less academically able ones went into Marathi instruction. Some of the English-educated children pursued higher education and later secured mid-ranking jobs in a company and the local administration, respectively. Even so, Baba, for whom (particularly English) education was a precious asset representing a means of escaping the socioeconomic status ascribed to him by his caste, sometimes expressed a sense of unresolved tension between the desirability of learning in one's mother tongue and that of acquiring the linguistic proficiency necessary to rise above the condition of one's caste. Over the years that I got to know him, Baba, who had consciously pushed the ablest among his offspring into English-language instruction, would increasingly confide that he "had made a mistake" (majhe cukle), "now felt bad" (atta wait watle) because "one should definitely learn in one's mother tongue" (matru bhashemadhyec shiklec pahije).

Like comments by many Marathi parents and teachers, Baba's were not just an elaboration on the naturalness of learning in one's mother tongue. His formulation also suggested moral self-condemnation, as in English: *cukne* in Marathi bears the dual meaning of "making a mistake or a blunder" and of "being morally wrong, unjust," "straying or wandering," "deviating from a righteous path," or even "falling short of one's duty." By the same token, the concept of "wrong" (*wāiṭ*) also has moral connotations: *wait* can be approximated as "bad," as in "I feel bad," but it can also mean "foul" or "evil." If it was not "wrong" strategically for Baba to have pushed his offspring away from education in their mother tongue, it was so morally, even though the aim of socioeconomic upward mobility had in his eyes been a legitimate one. So Baba concurred in the statement proffered by Kirari Bai at the beginning of this chapter, contrasting the notion of *wait* with that of *barobar*, or "right, correct, good": "It is not right to learn in another language but one's mother tongue." The moral condemnation implicit in these judgments suggests a sense of anguish and betrayal generated by the neglect of the

Marathi language. It is in fact in similar discussions that anxieties and fears about loss of linguistic and cultural substance become explicitly formulated. For, as C. Wright Mills had already written in 1940: "[M]en live in immediate acts of experience and their attentions are directed outside themselves until acts are in some way frustrated. It is then that awareness of self and motive occur" (905). In Kolhapur and elsewhere in western Maharashtra, such anxieties were rarely manifest until parents and teachers made linguistic and educational choices that elicited questions about their implications.

Finally, drawing on Mills's proposition that "typal vocabularies of motives for different situations are significant determinants of conduct" (908), it may be argued that these anxieties are also caused by the tension between *moral* vocabularies of motives associated with Marathi language ideology and strategic choices that run counter to them. There is, as Mills suggests, a sense of self-fulfilling realization in the process of motive enunciation (907), a kind of performative iteration: the act of describing one's motive is not related exclusively to experienced social action. Rather, it is about "influencing others and [one's] self." Mills's argument resonates with the concept of "emotive" inspired by Austin's notion of "performative" and developed by William Reddy in his history of emotions: its heuristic value is to point to the performative (in addition to embodied) character of discursive iteration of emotional attachment (Austin 1962; Reddy 2001, cited in Wilce 2004: 14). In sum, it is as if by reiterating one's emotional attachment to language and nation, one has experienced it more fully. This has yet wider ramifications touching the core of local notions of patriotism associating the *patria* (Bayly 1998: 26) with *dharma*. As Baba and many Marathi speakers of his and younger generations would often proudly assert, "It is our language, our own" (Amci bhasha ahe, swataci). In some ways, then, neglecting "one's own mother tongue" amounted to an act of moral and political deviance, and of potential regional and national treachery. This is so also because of the notion that the correct mastery of the Marathi language, vocabulary, and

grammar is fundamental to the training of proper, fit social and political persons, as I now wish to illustrate by taking you back to Mr. Pawar's classroom, where we began this chapter.

Producing Moral Citizens: Language and Righteousness

We are again in Mr. Pawar's classroom on that hot, humid afternoon, picking up the thread of the vocabulary repetition where we left it earlier. We have just reached the last proposition: "I have pride in and respect for my country" (Majhya deshaca mala abhimaan ahe), which Mr. Pawar suddenly interrupts, barking to a boy pupil: "Sunil, shut up; sit properly; now it's your turn!" Sunil, who had been whispering conspiratorially with his classmate, instinctively straightens up and, with somewhat startled eyes gazing at the board, begins, painfully stuttering upon the next group of words:

"Ma-jh, majh, majhya da."
"Deshat, hurry up, Sunil!" bellows Mr. Pawar impatiently.
"De-shat, vi-vidh ja-tic."
"Vi-vi-dha ja-ti-ce lo-ka raha-tat," the teacher pounds in, accentuating each syllable. "Jatice, Sunil, say it again; say it properly. The pronunciation [*uccār*] must be good. Isn't it so?"

Mr. Pawar now turns to the class.

"Yes!" (Ho!), some children chorus back.
"This is what correct language [*pramanit bhasha*] is about. What does correct language mean? It means proper pronunciation, and to speak nicely. The way we sometimes speak at home, isn't it; well, this is speaking language [*bolī bhāṣā*], but it is not correct [*barobar*]. It is not good [*cāngale*]. How can you grow into good people [*cangle lok*], good citizens [*cangle nagarik*], if you don't pronounce correctly?!"

Silence fills the classroom, while some pupils nod and gesture in vigorous approval, and others seemingly remain noncommitted. The enumeration, led again by the teacher, continues:

"In my country live people from different jat. In my country people live happily." [Majhya deshat vividh jatice lok rahtat. Majhya deshatil lok anandane rahtat.]

Inasmuch as morality, justice, and rectitude are characteristic of the Marathi language ideology, they are also inherent in the project of producing a good, schooled citizen. This is particularly evidenced in the emphasis teachers, like Mr. Pawar, often lay upon the notion of *pramanit bhasha*, in opposition to *boli bhasha*. The distinction between *pramanit* and *boli bhasha* is a recurring one in many Marathi classrooms. At a general level, *pramanit bhasha* represents the "standard" version of the Marathi language officially taught in schools in Maharashtra. It is a version deriving its authority from its legitimacy as "superior knowledge" and, as intimated earlier, is the negotiated product of linguistic encounters between British educational officers and Marathi pundits in the mid-nineteenth century. At a more specific level, *pramanit* (from the Sanskrit *pramān*, "proof, evidence, authority") is used in Marathi to denote a measuring standard, in the sense of what is true, just, right, and authoritative. The phrase *pramanit bhasha* thus translates as "the correct, authoritative language" in contradistinction with *boli bhasha* as the "oral language" spoken at home or more generally in everyday life, without much concern for hard-and-fast rules, whether of pronunciation and grammar, let alone punctuation.

Furthermore, the notion of *pramanit bhasha* encompasses proper pronunciation and utterance, to which meaning becomes secondary. Teachers throughout the day lay emphasis on the proper pronunciation of this standard version of the Marathi language, as Mr. Pawar did. [...] [T]his emphasis culminated in learning the pronunciation of the national anthem, which often superseded a search for meaning. Proper pronunciation and the register of *pramanit bhasha* are also intricately associated with notions of good personhood, more generally predicated upon the notion of *samskar*. Teachers in Marathi primary schools often considered the hymns, prayers, songs, moral stories, and thoughts for the day as fulfilling the purpose of cultivating *samskar*. Such

moral edification was deemed crucial to a child learning "how to behave" (*kase wagayce*), thus growing into a well-rounded, moral person and citizen (*nagarik*). Marathi language ideology, then, is predicated on idioms of morality that play a potent part in shaping the attempts at producing civic persons, as true *samskara*-predicated national citizens. Implicit in the project of schooling is therefore the understanding of school as a space where students, as future proper citizens, should internalize *pramanit bhasha* naturalizing it as their own *boli bhasha*. Whether this is ever really successful, in Indian schools or in those of other nation-states, is of course debatable. A stark opposition exists between this attempted naturalization and the resilience of everyday speech, especially among students of lower-caste or non-Hindu backgrounds, whose spoken idioms are generally the furthest removed from the version acknowledged as "proper and standard" Marathi.

Notes for a Provisional Conclusion

Central to this chapter is the notion that language and the passion it elicits are truly somatic instantiations. They are so not only in a descriptive, deictic sense but in a more profound, embodied one. It is not language that structures a human being but a relationship to body and emotion that is mediated by language as ideology. And because language – and its ideology – is incorporated in everyday bodily experience of the world as well as relayed in schools to acute levels of emotional figuration, it acquires this emotional and passionate quality for its speakers, regardless of the strategic choices they may make for their children's education. Inasmuch as emotions are socially and culturally constructed, then, we should pay closer attention to what local discourses of emotion have to say about their concrete location. Furthermore, such discourses do not necessarily espouse the unhelpful dichotomy of public (emotions) versus private (feelings). Eventually, the extent to which they are conceived as "personal" and "interior" and culturally constructed is almost impossible to assess. Arguably, the imprecision remains precisely because it is so difficult, nay, impossible, to disentangle personal feelings from public emotions, as both are mutually constituted. This, if anything, should already alert us to the illusionary character of the "public/private" dichotomy (to be discussed later). A phenomenological approach to emotions thus provides a way of reconciling what at first glance appear radically, irreconcilable categories acknowledging social actors' perceptions of them as "embodied." Put differently, the notion of embodiment dissolves the conceptual boundary between public and private. This has far-reaching implications, which I want to begin to unravel here.

In what has come to be considered a foundational text, Jean-François Lyotard argued that the end of meta-narratives such as nationalism was the distinctive mark of postmodernity. Lyotard's comment was undoubtedly generated by the observation at the time of the development of discourses counter to those of nationalism, at the levels of regional, international, and transnational movements. Although his voice was a rather specific one, his observation was shared by many scholars who, whether explicitly engaging with his argument or pursuing other lines of inquiry, joined in agreement until the 1990s in tolling the bell of the national formation. Since then, history has, cruelly and often poignantly, disproved these willful yet un-self-fulfilling prophecies. More nations saw the light of day in the last quarter of the twentieth century, often through bloody and traumatic births amid vivid longings and ethnic violence. If anything, these painful engenderings have brought home the notion that, perhaps more than ever before, the nation form is alive and kicking. Despite these ontological realizations, the category has in many scholarly circles acquired a slightly antiquated ring of passé-ness, overridden by more flashy, trendy notions of "globalization" and "global civil society," whether pragmatic or phantasmic. I suggest that, if the notion of the national formation, despite its dramatic enactments and practical translations in the lives of an increasing number of ordinary social actors the world over, has become taken for granted, it is precisely because it has been *naturalized* to an unprecedented extent. The idea, of course, is

not new. Part of the theoretical canvas Benedict Anderson developed was aimed at furnishing the premises for an understanding of how nations become culturally formed, that is, how they come to be produced as cultural, natural units of belonging. Michael Billig later drew attention to the banalization of the nation in people's daily lives, especially through the performative iterations of the nation in the mass media. Yet I want to formulate a different kind of argument and suggest that more than sharing a commonality of nationhood with newspaper readers or "banally flagging" the nation, the naturalization of the idea and experience of the nation entails its "incorporation." It is because of the nation's deep incorporation into who we are as bodied social persons, subjects, and citizens that we can somehow entertain a sense of national belonging, much as this sense may at times be fleetingly vague, and despite a professed lack of patriotic appetence. Remember Bourdieu's pronouncement: "what the body grants even when the mind says no" (1990: 167).

Of course, I do not mean to suggest that this somatization of national emotionality is either ever present or exhausts the potentialities of the body/mind. Such production of an "emotionationality" requires daily labor, as we have seen, and does not determine all social action. Rather, this production allows for the "something recalcitrant in the body" to remain and possibly surface at any time. Embodied emotionationality can never fully exhaust the pliability and resourcefulness of social and cultural agency, whether individual or collective. However absolutist the prevalent ideological structure, any exploration of ideology, both as structure of belief and "interpellative subject positioning," has to allow for some measure of "openness onto heterogeneous realities" (Massumi 2002: 263). Therefore, despite the potency of Marathi native-speaking social actors' emotional social and individual constructions and lived experiences of the Marathi language ideology, a space must be left open for the "conceptual enablement," not necessarily of "resistance" but at least for alternative negotiations "in connection with the real" (263). Thus, for instance, despite teachers' obstinate attempts at impressing a military-like atmosphere during the morning liturgies, much of the school day was characterized more by unruliness than discipline: such unruliness started soon after the classes left the ground of the morning liturgy, as pupils would walk to their classrooms in a sort of stampede. Similarly in overcrowded classrooms, some teachers had relinquished their authority, abandoning any notion of an entirely quiet and disciplined class, and would only mildly, though regularly, "tsa tsa" in vain efforts to impose total silence. Often when teachers under some pretense interrupted their class and momentarily left the room to attend to some more pressing business, general bedlam would ensue. Pupils greatly relished these moments that, in addition to the recesses that punctuated the school day, provided welcome outlets for their energy and vigor. Arguably, these formed as important a part in the production of future Maharashtrian (and Indian) citizens.

The workings of Marathi language ideology therefore have to be understood as both official implementation processes and social actors' agency. Here is the double bind of all processes of language socialization, whether national or otherwise: in the same movement of ideologically shaping, naturalizing, and incorporating language ideologies in the constitution of social and cultural units, language ideologies fail to grasp the totality of agency, unwittingly allowing for interstices and cracks in these processes. On the one hand, even cases of diglossia leave room for negotiating the production of national emotional attachment. In the social production of a schooled self, a readjustment between the language spoken at home and the standardized version taught in school may concomitantly be effected. In particular, variations existing between the official standardized version of the Marathi written in official textbooks and the local brand spoken at home may become erased, especially in the common referent to the notions of "mother" and "motherhood". The mother language might thus be envisaged as uniting her dialectal (school)children in her lap. On the other hand, such union is arguably best realized in cases of convergence of family and school idioms. These generally pertain to upper-caste and upper-class Hindu children. Even in these cases, there may always remain unconquered space and unpredictable agency. Ultimately, because even the mother tongue, for all its instrumentality in negotiating internal divisions between different local varieties of a language, is never totally realized, never fully complete, this linguistic incorporation of the nation generates accrued anxieties and fears of loss of substance and morality. These anxieties and fears are inherent in the pursuit of any project of linguistically premised national (or regional) formation, if only because such projects are de facto predicated upon processes of self-definition athwart other idioms, whether these be local, vernacular "dialects" or "foreign-born" ones. So social actors, while beholden to an emotional attachment to a linguistic nation, are deeply – although rarely explicitly – aware of the fragility of projects of language-predicated nationalisms. As the nation (or the region) is working toward its linguistic realization, it is constantly battling with the possibility of its self-perdition.

What implications does this have for the naturalization of a sense of belonging? What kind of community is thus created, and what room is there for an "other," speaking a different language, in the participation in the life of the polis? The issue is obviously further complicated by the fact that this Marathi-speaking Indian citizen is by default a Hindu-inflected one. I hope to have brought to light in this chapter how the project of Marathi self-formation is potentially always an exclusivist one that seeks to exclude other, improper Marathi- or non-Marathi-speaking locutors. Despite an overtly integrational approach, it is clear that those children deemed less capable of becoming good Indian citizens in this part of Maharashtra are those standing the furthest apart from (standardized) Marathi. [...]

NOTES

1 The word *jat* can refer to both castes and faiths.
2 Butler (1989: 334–35).
3 McDonald (1968a, 1968b).
4 See Goswami (2004); Kumar (1992); Lelyveld (1993).

5 Tariq Rahman (2004) appraises the debates over instruction in English and vernacular in Pakistan. On the colonial period, see also Viswanathan (1989); Kumar (1991); Crook (1996); Zastoupil and Moir (1999); and Kumar (2000), among others. On the issue of authenticity and language politics in contemporary India, see Sadana (2007).

REFERENCES

Abu-Lughod, Lila, and Catherine Lutz, eds, 1990. *Language and the Politics of Emotion*. Cambridge: Cambridge University Press.

Anderson, Benedict, 1991 [1983]. *Imagined Communities: Reflections on the Origin and Spread of Nationalism*. London: Verso.

Assayag, Jackie, 1997. Le corps de l'Inde. La carte, la vache, la nation. *Gradhiva* 22: 14–29.

Austin, John L., 1962. *How to Do Things with Words: The William James Lectures Delivered at Harvard University in 1955*. Oxford: Clarendon Press.

Bayly, C. A., 1998. *Origins of Nationality in South Asia: Patriotism and Ethical Government in the Making of Modern India*. Delhi: Oxford University Press.

Benei, Véronique, 1996. *La dot en Inde: un fléau social? Socio-anthropologie du mariage au Maharashtra*. Paris: Karthala; Pondicherry: French Institute.

Benei, Véronique, 2001a. A Passion for Order: Vernacular Languages, Morality and Race in the Mid-19th Century Bombay Presidency. Paper presented at South Asian Studies Programme, Asian Studies Centre, St. Antony's College, Oxford, January 23.

Benei, Véronique, 2001b. Teaching Nationalism in Maharashtrian Schools. In *The Everyday State and Society in Modern India*, C. J. Fuller and V. Benei, eds. London: Hurst, pp. 194–221. (Orig. pub. Delhi: Social Science Press, 2000.)

Benei, Véronique, 2005c. Of Languages, Passions and Interests: Education, Regionalism and Globalization in Maharashtra, 1800–2000. In *Globalizing India: Locality, Nation and the World*, Jackie Assayag and Chris Fuller, eds. London: Anthem, pp. 141–162.

Besnier, Niko, 1990. Language and Affect. *Annual Review of Anthropology* 19: 419–451.

Billig, Michael, 1995. *Banal Nationalism*. London: Sage Publications.

Bourdieu, Pierre, 1990. *In Other Words: Essays towards a Reflexive Sociology*. Stanford: Stanford University Press.

Butler, Judith, 1989. Gender Trouble, Feminist Theory, and Psychoanalytic Discourse. In *Feminism/Postmodernism*, Linda J. Nicholson, ed. New York: Routledge, pp. 324–40.

Cohn, Bernard S., 1987. Regions Subjective and Objective: Their Relation to the Study of Modern Indian History and Society. In *An Anthropologist among the Historians and Other Essays*. Delhi: Oxford University Press, pp. 100–135.

Crook, Nigel, ed., 1996. *The Transmission of Knowledge in South Asia: Essays in Education, Religion, History and Politics*. Delhi: Oxford University Press.

Errington, J. Joseph, 1998a. Indonesian('s) Development: On the State of a Language of State. In *Language Ideologies: Practice and Theory*, Bambi B. Schieffelin, Kathryn A. Woolard, and Paul V. Kroskrity, eds. New York: Oxford University Press, pp. 271–284.

Errington, J. Joseph, 1998b. *Shifting Languages: Interaction and Identity in Javanese Indonesia*. Cambridge: Cambridge University Press.

Foucault, Michel, 1979. *Discipline and Punish*. London: Harmondsworth. (Orig. pub. 1975.)

Garrett, Paul B., and Patricia Baquedano-Lopez, 2002. Language Socialization: Reproduction and Continuity, Transformation and Change. *Annual Review of Anthropology* 31: 339–361.

Gellner, Ernest, 1983. *Nations and Nationalism*. Ithaca, NY: Cornell University Press.

Goswami, Manu, 2004. *Producing India: From Colonial Economy to National Space*. Chicago: University of Chicago Press.

Hastings, Adrian, 1997. *The Construction of Nationhood: Ethnicity, Religion and Nationalism*. Cambridge: Cambridge University Press.

Hobsbawm, Eric J., 1992. *Nations and Nationalism since 1780: Programme, Myth, Reality*, 2nd edn. Cambridge: Cambridge University Press.

Irvine, Judith T. 1990. Registering Affect: Heteroglossia in the Linguistic Expression of Emotion. In *Language and the Politics of Emotion*, Catherine A. Lutz and Lila Abu-Lughod, eds. Cambridge: Cambridge University Press, pp. 69–91.

Irvine, Judith, and Susan Gal, 2000. Language Ideology and Linguistic Differentiation. In *Regimes of Language: Ideologies, Polities, and*

Identities, Paul V. Kroskrity, ed. Santa Fe, NM: School of American Research Press, SAR Advanced Seminar Series; Oxford: James Currey, pp. 35–83.

King, Christopher R., 1996. *One Language, Two Scripts: The Hindi Movement in 19th C. North India.* Bombay: Oxford University Press.

King, Robert D., 1998 [1997]. *Nehru and the Language Politics of India.* New Delhi: Oxford University Press.

Kroskrity, Paul V., ed., 2000. *Regimes of Language: Ideologies, Polities, and Identities.* Santa Fe, NM: School of American Research Press, SAR Advanced Seminar Series; Oxford: James Currey.

Kumar, Krishna, 1991. *Political Agenda of Education: A Study of Colonialist and Nationalist Ideas.* New Delhi: Sage Publications.

Kumar, Krishna, 1992. Hindu Revivalism and Education in North-Central India. In *Fundamentalisms and Society*, Martin Marty and Scott Appleby, eds. Chicago: University of Chicago Press, pp. 536–557.

Kumar, Nita, 2000. *Lessons from Schools: The History of Education in Banaras.* New Delhi: Sage Publications.

Lelyveld, David, 1993. The Fate of Hindustani. Colonial Knowledge and the Project of a National Language. In *Orientalism and the Postcolonial Predicament: Perspectives on South Asia*, Carol Breckenridge and Peter van der Veer, eds. Philadelphia: University of Pennsylvania Press, pp. 189–214.

Massumi, Brian, 2002. *Parables for the Virtual: Movement, Affect, Sensation.* Durham, NC: Duke University Press.

McDonald, E. E., 1968a. The Growth of Regional Consciousness in Maharashtra. *Indian Economic and Social History Review* 5(3): 223–243.

McDonald, E. E., 1968b. The Modernizing of Communication: Vernacular Publishing in 19th C. Maharashtra. *Asian Survey* 8(7): 589–606.

Merleau-Ponty, Maurice, 1989. *Phenomenology of Perception.* Basingstoke: Macmillan. (Orig. pub. 1945.)

Mills, C. Wright, 1940. Situated Actions and Vocabularies of Motive. *American Sociological Review* 5(6): 904–913.

Naregal, Veena, 2002 [2001]. *Language Politics, Elites, and the Public Sphere: Western India under Colonialism.* London: Anthem; New Delhi: Permanent Black.

Nemade, Bhalchandra, 1990. *The Influence of English of Marathi: A Sociolinguistic Study.* Kolhapur: Rajhans.

Ochs, Elinor, and Bambi Schieffelin, 1989. Language Has a Heart. *Text* 9: 7–25.

Phadke, Y. D., 1979. *Politics and Language.* Bombay: Himalaya Publishing House.

Pollock, Sheldon, 2006 [2007]. *The Language of the Gods in the World of Men: Sanskrit, Culture, and Power in Premodern India.* Berkeley: University of California Press; Delhi: Permanent Black.

Rahman, Tariq, 1996. *Language and Politics in Pakistan.* Karachi: Oxford University Press.

Rahman, Tariq, 2004. *Denizens of Alien Worlds: A Study of Education, Inequality and Polarization in Pakistan.* Karachi: Oxford University Press.

Ramaswamy, Sumathi, 1997. *Passions of the Tongue: Language Devotion in Tamil India, 1891–1970.* Berkeley: University of California Press.

Renan, Ernest, 1996 [1882]. What is a Nation? In *Becoming National: A Reader*, Geoff Eley and Ronald Grigor Suny, eds. New York: Oxford University Press, pp. 41–55.

Rosaldo, Michelle Z., 1984. Toward an Anthropology of Self and Feeling. In *Culture Theory: Essays on Mind, Self, and Emotion*, Richard A. Schweder and Robert A. Le Vine, eds. Cambridge: Cambridge University Press, pp. 137–157.

Sadana, Rashmi, 2007. A Suitable Text for a Vegetarian Audience: Questions of Authenticity and the Politics of Translation. *Public Culture* 19(2): 307–328.

Spitulnik, Debra, 1998. Mediating Unity and Diversity: The Production of Language Ideologies in Zambian Broadcasting. In *Language Ideologies: Practice and Theory*, Bambi B. Schieffelin, Kathryn A. Woolard, and Paul V. Kroskrity, eds. New York: Oxford University Press, pp. 163–188.

Strathern, Andrew, 1993. Organs and Emotions: The Question of Metaphor. *Canberra Anthropology* 16(2): 1–16.

Thiesse, Anne-Marie, 1999. *La création des identités nationales: Europe XVIIIe–XXe siècle.* Paris: Seuil.

Viswanathan, Gauri, 1989. *Masks of Conquest: Literary Study and British Rule in India.* New York: Columbia University Press.

Wilce, James M., Jr, 2004. Passionate Scholarship: Recent Anthropologies of Emotion. *Reviews in Anthropology* 33: 1–17.

Woolard, Kathryn A., 1998. Introduction: Language Ideology as a Field of Inquiry. In *Language Ideologies: Practice and Theory*,

Bambi B. Schieffelin, Kathryn A. Woolard, and Paul V. Kroskrity, eds. New York: Oxford University Press, pp. 3–47.

Yano, Christine R., 1995. Shaping Tears of a Nation: An Ethnography of Emotion in Japanese Popular Song. PhD diss., University of Hawaii.

Zastoupil, Lynn, and Martin Moir, eds, 1999. *The Great Indian Education Debate:* *Documents Relating to the Orientalist-Anglicist Controversy, 1781–1843*. London: Curzon.

Official sources

Report of the Committee on Emotional Integration. 1962. Delhi: Ministry of Education, Government of India.

15

Biological Citizenship

The Science and Politics of Chernobyl-Exposed Populations, 2004

Adriana Petryna

The Event

The Chernobyl nuclear reactor's Unit Four exploded in Ukraine on April 26, 1986. The damages from this disaster have been manifold, including immediate injury in the form of radiation burns and death to plant workers, damaged human immunities and high rates of thyroid cancer among resettled populations, and substantial soil and waterway contamination.[1] Soviet reports attributed the cause of the disaster to a failed experiment. According to one official report, "The purpose of the experiment was to test the possibility of using the mechanical energy of the rotor in a turbo-generator cut off from steam supply to sustain the amounts of power requirements during a power failure."[2] Many of the reactor's safety systems were shut off for the duration of the experiment. A huge power surge occurred as technicians decreased power and shut off the steam. The unit exploded once at 1.23 a.m. and then again. Due to particular wind-pressure gradients that day and in the following weeks, the radioactive plume

moved to an estimated height of eight kilometers. Subsequent attempts to extinguish the flames of the burning graphite core proved only partly successful. By most accounts, they even exacerbated the danger of the situation. For example, an attempt was made to suffocate the flames with tons of boron carbide, dolomite, sand, clay, and lead dropped from helicopters. As a result, the core's temperature increased. The cloud of radiation rose dramatically and moved across Belarus, Ukraine, Russia, Western Europe, and other areas of the Northern Hemisphere.[3]

An official announcement of the disaster came almost three weeks after the event. In that time, roughly 13,000 children in contaminated areas took in a dose of radiation to the thyroid that was more than two times the highest allowable dose for nuclear workers for a year.[4] A massive onset of thyroid cancers in adults and children began appearing four years later. Had nonradioactive iodine pills been made available within the first week of the disaster, the onset of this disease could have been significantly reduced. Soviet administrators

Adriana Petryna, 2004. Biological citizenship: the science and politics of Chernobyl-exposed populations. *Osiris* 19: 250–265.

contradicted assessments of the scale of the plume made by English and American meteorological groups. The Soviets claimed the biomedical aspects of Chernobyl were under control. Dr. Angelina Guskova of the Institute of Biophysics in Moscow initially selected 237 victims to be airlifted to her institute's acute radiation sickness ward. Acute radiation syndrome (ARS) was diagnosed among 134 of them. The official death toll was set at 31 persons, most of them fire fighters or plant workers.

The disaster continued, especially among the groups of workers who were recruited or went voluntarily to work at the disaster site. Among the hundreds of thousands of paid and unpaid laborers,[5] work ranged from bulldozing polluted soil and dumping it in so-called radiation dumpsites (*mohyl'nyky*), to raking and shoveling pieces of the reactor core – radioactive graphite – that had dispersed over a vast area, to constructing fences around the reactor, to cutting down highly contaminated surrounding forests. By far the most dangerous work involved the adjacent reactor's roof. In one-minute intervals, workers (mainly military recruits) ran onto the roof, hurled radioactive debris over parapets into containers below with their shovels, and then left. Many of these volunteers called themselves "bio-robots"; their biologies were exploited "and then thrown out." Based on extensive interviews, some laborers felt trapped and unable to leave the disaster area; this sentiment was particularly felt by unpaid military recruits and local collective farmworkers recruited to do the most menial and dangerous of tasks. Some said they went gladly, believing their tripled salary more than compensated for their risk. However, it cannot be definitively said that money truly compensated them for the suffering that was to come.

Five months after the disaster, a so-called sarcophagus (now simply called the Shelter) was built to contain the 216 tons of uranium and plutonium in the ruined reactor. At present, the power plant is decommissioned. Some fifteen thousand people conduct maintenance work or service the Zone of Exclusion. Most of the exclusion zone is located in Ukraine. The zone circumscribes the disaster site and covers thirty kilometers in diameter. Zone entry is limited to the plant's workers.

Ukraine inherited the power plant and most of the Zone of Exclusion when independence was declared in 1991. The government announced new and ambitious standards of safety. It focused its resources on stabilizing the crumbling Shelter, implementing norms of worker safety, decreasing the possibility of future fallout risk, and decommissioning all units of the Chernobyl plant. These acts were important from a foreign policy standpoint. Showing that it could adhere to strict safety standards, Ukraine became the recipient of European and American technical assistance, loans, and trading partnerships. The legacy of Chernobyl has been used as a means of signaling Ukraine's domestic and international legitimacy and staking territorial claims; and as a venue of governance and state building, social welfare, and corruption. [...]

Constructed Unknowns

In what follows, I address some of the scientific elements that played a key role in measuring and delineating the scope of the disaster and defining remediation and compensation strategies. In this context, matters such as atmospheric dispersion maps, international scientific cooperations, and local scientific responses, as well as people's involvement in bureaucratic and testing procedures, led up to what can be called a "technical and political course of illness." Examples of people's engagement with, and influence on, such courses will then be discussed.

[...]

Chernobyl also became a venue for unprecedented international scientific cooperation and human research. [...]

As this internationalization of science ensued, however, the physical management of contamination at the accident site was internalized – to the sphere of Soviet state control. One policy statement released by the Soviet Health Ministry at the height of these cooperations, for example, directed medical examiners in the Zone of Exclusion to "classify workers who have received a maximum dose" as having "vegetovascular dystonia," that is, a kind of panic disorder, and a novel psychosocial disorder called "radiophobia"

Table 15.1 Symptoms and other inadequately known states (per 10,000).

1982	1983	1984	1985	1986	1987	1988	1989	1990	1991	1992
1.3	1.7	1.7	1.9	2.3	2.7	5.9	34.7	108.3	127.4	141.3

Source: Ministry of Statistics, Kyiv, Ukraine.

(or the fear of the biological influence of radiation). These categories were used to filter out the majority of disability claims.[6] Substantial challenges to this Soviet management came from certain labor sectors in subsequent years. At the end of 1989 only 130 additional persons were granted disability; by 1990, 2,753 more cases had been considered, of which 50 percent were authorized on a neurological basis. Levels of political influence of specific labor sectors are reflected in the order they received disability: coal miners, then Ministry of Internal Affairs workers (the police), and then Transport Ministry workers. These various labor groups would soon realize that in the Ukrainian management of Chernobyl, forms of political leveraging had to be coupled with medical-scientific know-how.

Arguably, the new Ukrainian accounting of the Chernobyl unknown was part and parcel of the government's strategies for "knowledge-based" governance and social mobilization. In 1991 and in its first set of laws, the new parliament denounced the Soviet management of Chernobyl as "an act of genocide." The new nation-state viewed the disaster as (among other things) a key means for instituting domestic and international authority. Legislators assailed the Soviet standard for determining biological risk to populations. The Soviets had established a high of 35 rem (a unit of absorbed dose), spread over an individual's lifetime (understood as a standard seventy-year span), as the threshold of allowable radiation dose intakes. This threshold limited the scale of resettlement actions. Ukrainian law lowered the Soviet threshold dose to 7 rem, comparable to what an average American would be exposed to in his or her lifetime. In effect these lowered measures for safe living increased the size of the labor forces going to the exclusion zone (since workers had to work shorter amounts of time if they were to avoid exceeding the stricter dose standards). The measures also expanded terri-

tories considered contaminated. A significant new sector of the population would want to claim itself as part of a state-protected post-Soviet polity. A biophysicist responsible for conducting retrospective dose assays on resettlers told me: "Long lines of resettlers extended from our laboratory doors. It wasn't enough that they were evacuated to 'clean' areas. People got entangled in the category of victim, by law. They had unpredictable futures, and *each of them wanted to know their dose.*"

Statistics from the Ukrainian Ministry of Health gave evidence of the sharp increase in 1991 of zone workers, resettled persons and inhabitants of contaminated territories registering their disability, and the annual patterns of enrollment of this new population for which the state committed itself to care. The statistics also show that the sharpest increase in the clinical registration of illnesses occurred under the category "symptoms and other inadequately known states," Class 16 in the International Classification of Disease, ICD 10 (see Table 15.1). These states typically include afflictions such as personality changes, premature senility, and psychosis.

Ukrainian claims to a sudden expansion of Chernobyl health effects became a target of international skepticism. Ukrainian scientists were often rebuked for their "failure to use modern epidemiological methods and criteria of causality and a reliable data system." As a World Bank consultant noted, "Right now virtually any disease is attributed to Chernobyl, and no effort is being made either to prove or disprove these claims that would satisfy standard epidemiological criteria of causality."[7] For the government, however, one can argue that these new statistics became a kind of "moral science,"[8] a resolute display of its intention to make visible the effects of the Soviet mismanagement of the disaster and to guarantee its own social legitimacy while keeping world attention on the Chernobyl risk.

In this daily bureaucratic instantiation of Chernobyl, tensions among zone workers, resettled individuals and families, scientists, physicians, legislators, and civil servants intensified. Together, these groups became invested in a new social and moral contract between state and civil society, a contract guaranteeing them the right to know their levels of risk and to use legal means to obtain medical care and monitoring. The sufferers and their administrators were also supported by the nonsuffering citizens, who paid a 12 percent tax on their salaries to support compensations. The hybrid quality of this postsocialist state and social contract comes into view. On the one hand, the Ukrainian government rejected Western neoliberal prescriptions to *downsize* its social welfare domain; on the other hand, it presented itself as informed by the principles of a modern risk society. On the one hand, these Chernobyl laws allowed for unprecedented civic organizing; on the other hand, they became distinct venues of corruption through which informal practices of providing or selling access to state privileges and protections (*blat*) expanded.[9]

Ethnographic accounts have illustrated that postsocialism's future cannot be based in predictive models or treated as unproblematic flows toward free markets. Michael Burawoy and Katherine Verdery point to the links between the socialist and postsocialist worlds as well as growing dependencies between postsocialist state formations and global economics. Such dependencies "have radically shifted the rules of the game, the parameters of action within which actors pursue their daily routines and practices."[10] Ethnographic methods are critical for elucidating such interrelated processes at local levels. This is particularly true with regard to assessing the decisions people make based on limited choices available to them and the informal aspects of power that inform those decisions.

Shifts in aggregate human conditions and the circumstances of citizenship are also at stake in these changing political and economic worlds. The principles of a "classical citizenship" endow citizens with natural and legal rights protected as matters of birthright.[11] Regardless of nationality, such protections were granted to all Ukrainian inhabitants when the country declared independence. Yet birthright remains an insufficient guarantor of protection as the lives of inhabitants of some Ukrainian areas cannot be fully, or even partly, protected owing to long-term environmental challenges. For these inhabitants, the very concept of citizenship is charged with the super-added burden of survival. The acquisition and mastery of certain democratic forms related to openness, freedom of expression, and the right to information are primary goals to be sure. Yet populations are also negotiating for the even more basic goal of protection (i.e., economic and social inclusion) using the constituent matters of life. Such negotiations expose certain patterns that are traceable elsewhere: the role of science in legitimating democratic institutions, increasingly limited access to health care and welfare as the capitalist trends take over, and the uneasy correlation of human rights with biological self-preservation.

Biological Citizenship

In Ukraine, where democratization is linked to a harsh market transition, the injured biology of a population has become the basis for social membership and for staking claims to citizenship. Government-operated radiation research clinics and non-governmental organizations mediate an informal economy of illness and claims to a "biological citizenship" – a demand for, but limited access to, a form of social welfare based on medical, scientific, and legal criteria that recognize injury and compensate for it. These demands are being expressed in the context of losses of primary resources such as employment and state protections against inflation and a deterioration in legal-political categories. Struggles over limited medical resources and the factors that constitute a legitimate claim to citizenship are part of postsocialism's uncharted terrain. Against a stark and overwhelming order of insecurity, there are questions to be asked about how the value of another's life is being judged in this new political economy, about the ability of scientific knowledge to politically empower those seeking to set that value relatively high, and about the kinds of rationalities and biomedical practices emerging with respect to novel social, economic, and somatic indeterminacies. The indeterminacy of scientific knowledge about the afflictions people face and about the nature of nuclear catastrophe materializes here as both a curse and a source of leverage. Ambiguities related to the interpretation of radiation-related injury, together with their inextricable relations to the social and political uncertainties generated by Soviet interventions and current political-economic vulnerability, make the scope of the afflicted population in Ukraine and its claims to injury at once plausible, ironic, and catastrophic.

One instance of how these scientific and political dynamics operated in the everyday: the country's eminent expert on matters related to the disaster, Symon Lavrov, was well-regarded internationally for having developed computerized fallout models and calculating population-wide doses in the post-Soviet period. He told me, however, that "when a crying mother comes to my laboratory and asks me, Professor Lavrov, 'tell me what's wrong with my child?' I assign her a dose and say nothing more. I double it, as much as I can." The offer of a higher dose increased the likelihood that the mother would be able to secure social protection on account of her potentially sick child. Lavrov and the grieving mother were two of the many figures whose efforts I documented. The point is the following: the mother could offer her child a dose, a protective tie with the state, which is founded on a probability of sickness, a biological tie. What she could offer, perhaps the most precious thing she could offer her child in that context, is a specific knowledge, history, and category. The child's "exposure" and the knowledge that would make that exposure an empirical fact were not things to be repressed or denied (as had been tried in the Soviet model) but rather things to be made into a resource and then distributed through informal means.

Specific cases illustrate how these economic and state processes, combined with the technical dynamics already described, have laid the groundwork for such "counter-politics."[12] Citizens have come to depend on obtainable technologies and legal procedures to gain political recognition and admission to some form of welfare inclusion. Aware that they had fewer chances for finding employment and health in the new market economy, these citizens accounted for elements in their lives (measures, numbers, symptoms) that could be linked to a state, scientific, and bureaucratic history of mismanagement and risk. The tighter the connection that could be drawn, the greater the chance of securing economic and social entitlement. This dimension of illness as counter-politics suggests that sufferers are aware of the way politics shapes what they know and do not know about their illnesses and that they are put in a role of having to use these politics to curb further deteriorations of their health, which they see as resulting, in part, from a collapsing state health system and loss of adequate legal protections.

Probability in relation to radiation-related disease became a central resource for local scientific research. This play with probability was being projected back into nature, so to speak, through an intricate local science. Young neuropsychiatrists made the best of the inescapability of their political circumstances (they could not get visas to leave the country) as they integrated international medical taxonomies into Soviet ones and developed classifications of mental and nervous disorders that in expert literatures were considered far too low to make any significant biological contribution. For example, neuropsychiatrists were involved in a project designed to find and assess cases of mental retardation in children exposed in utero in the first year after the disaster. In the case of one such child, a limping nine-year-old boy, researchers and parents pooled their knowledge to reconstruct the child's disorder as having a radiation origin. Even though the boy's radiation dose was low, he was given the status of sufferer because of his mother's occupation-related exposure (she was an emergency doctor who elected to work in the zone until late in her pregnancy) and also because a PET scan did reveal a cerebral lesion that was never hypothesized as being related to anything other than radiation. (It could have been birth trauma.) As researchers constructed a human research cohort, they were also constructing a destiny for the newly designated human research subjects. It was precisely the destiny the parents were intent on offering to this child – a biological citizenship.

These radiation-related claims and practices constituted a form of work in this market transition. A clinical administrator concurred that claims to radiation illness among the Ukrainian population amounted to a form of "market compensation." He told me, "If people could improve their family budgets, there would be a lot less illness. People are now oriented towards one thing. They believe that only through the constitution of illnesses, and particularly difficult illnesses, incurable ones, can they improve their family budgets." Administrators such as he informed me that they should not to be "blamed too much" for fueling an informal economy of diagnoses and entitlements. Complicities could be found at every level, and the moral conflicts they entailed were publicly discussed. Another administrator who authenticated compensation claims told me illnesses had become a form of currency. "There are a lot of people out of work," he said. "People don't have enough money to eat. The state doesn't give medicines for free anymore. Drug stores are commercialized." He likened his work to that of a bank. "The diagnosis we write is money."

The story of Anton and Halia (age forty-two in 1997) shows the ways such complicity functioned in the most personal arenas. The new institutions, procedures, and actors that were at work at the state level, at the research clinic, and at the level of civic organizations were making their way into the couple's *kvartyra* (apartment). Anton's identity as a worker, his sense of masculinity, and his role as a father and breadwinner were being violently dislocated and altered in the process. In 1986, the state recruited Anton to work for six months in the Zone of Exclusion, transporting bags of lead oxide, sand, and gravel to the reactor site. The bags were airlifted and deposited using helicopters. He had no idea how much radiation he absorbed during those six months. From 1991 on, Anton routinely passed through

the clinical system, monitored like any "prospective" invalid. His symptoms mounted over time. He had chronic headaches, lost his short-term memory, exhibited antisocial behavior, developed a speech disorder, and experienced seizures and impotence, as well as many other problems. Despite the growing number and intensity of his symptoms, his diagnosis did not "progress" from an initial listing as a "psycho-social" case.

When I met Anton and his wife, Halia, they were trying to manage on a small pension he received as a sufferer. Anton saw himself as bankrupt, morally as well as economically: "The state took my life away. Ripped me off, gone. What is there to be happy about? An honorable man cannot survive now. For what? For what? We had a life. We had butter. We had milk. I can't buy an iron. Before I could buy fifty irons. The money was there. My wife's salary is less than the cost of one iron." He told me that he did not know "how to trade goods" or to sell petty goods on the market. His meager pension left Anton with few options. He found himself confronting the shameful option of breadwinning with his illness in the Chernobyl compensation system or facing poverty. Over time, and in a concerted effort to remove Anton's psychosocial label, the couple befriended a leader of a disabled workers' activist group in a clinic. Through him they met a neurologist who knew the director of the local medical-labor committee. The couple hoped this individual would provide official support for Anton's claim of Chernobyl-related disability.

The economic motives for these actions were clear. Yet it was difficult for me to see this man giving up everything he knew or thought about himself to prove that his diffused symptoms had an organic basis. Neurology was a key gateway to disability; neurological disorders were most ambiguous but most possible to prove using diagnostic technologies, self-inducements, and bodily display. At each step, Anton was mentally breaking down; he fell into a pattern of abusive behavior. His legal-medical gamble – this gaining of life in the new market economy through illness – reflected the practices of an entire citizenry lacking money or the means of generating it. This approach has become common sense, in Clifford Geertz's words, or that which is "left over when all [the] more articulated sorts of symbol systems have exhausted their tasks."[13]

When I returned in 2000 to Kyiv to conduct further research, I discovered that current democratic politicians, many of whom drafted the original compensation laws as sovereignty-minded nationalists, now saw the Chernobyl compensation system as a dire mistake that has "accidentally" reproduced a socialist-like population. Funds and activist groups were now supported by socialist and communist leaderships, who lobbied for continued aid in an increasingly divided parliament. Meanwhile, international agencies such as the World Bank cited the Chernobyl social apparatus as a "dead weight" to Ukraine's less-than-ideal transition to a market economy. Bank officials were so ill-disposed toward the system that they made its quick extinction a condition of future loan contracting. The disappearance of this exposed population from the state's radar seems ever more likely. Once "protected" by a safety-conscious state, this exposed population is being left alone to their symptoms and social disarray.

Opinions about how the state should address the fate of these Chernobyl victims also serve as a kind of barometer of the country's changing moral fabric. Rural inhabitants who normally received the least in terms of socialist redistribution tended to be sympathetic to the victims' struggles. Among inhabitants of Kyiv and other urban centers, there is a growing consensus that the invalids are "parasites of the state, damaging the economy, not paying taxes." Many youths who had been evacuated from the zone do not want to be associated with groups of sufferers as this association makes it more difficult for them to find employment.

Chernobyl was a key political event, generating many effects, some of which have yet to be known; its truths have been made only partly known through estimates derived from experimental science. The immediate postindependence discourse in Ukraine centered on the "truth" of Chernobyl. Ukrainians tried to put their suffering in perspective vis-à-vis the repres-sive model of science and state: the number of people who died, how the government deceived citizens about the scale of the disaster, how the maps of contamination were misrepresentative, and so on. As harsh market realities entered everyday life, this model of organizing suffering quickly gave way to a different kind of scientific and political negotiation, one which had directly to do with the maintenance, and indeed the remaking, of a postsocialist state and population.

If, at the level of the modern state, spheres of scientific production and politics are in a constant process of exchange and mutual stabilization, then what I have suggested here is that stabilization proves to be a much more difficult task. At stake in the Chernobyl aftermath is a distinctive postsocialist field of power-in-the-making that is using science and scientific categories to establish the state's reach. Scientists and victims are also establishing their own modes of knowledge related to injury as a means of negotiating public accountability, political power, and further state protections in the form of financial compensation and medical care. Biology becomes a resource in a multidimensional sense – versatile material through which the state and new populations can be made to appear. This postsocialist field of power has specific physical, experiential, political, economic, and spatial aspects. It is about knowledge and constructed ignorance, visibility and invisibility, inclusion and exclusion, probabilities and facts, and the parceling out of protection and welfare that do not fit predictive models. It is also about how individuals and populations become part of new cooperative regimes in scientific research and in local state-sponsored forms of human subjects protection. In this context, suffering is wholly appropriated and objectified in its legal, economic, and political dimensions. At the same time, these objectifications constitute a common sense that is enacted by sufferers themselves in ways that can promote protection as well as intensify new kinds of vulnerability in domestic, scientific, and bureaucratic spheres.

NOTES

1 I use pseudonyms for the majority of people interviewed for this essay. Names that appear in scientific and legal print are in some cases actual.

2 See Soviet State Committee on the Utilization of Atomic Energy, *Report to the IAEA* (Vienna, 1986), 16.

3 See Alexander Sich, "The Denial Syndrome (Efforts to Smother the Burning Nuclear Core at the Chernobyl Power Plant in 1986 Were Insufficient)," *Bulletin of Atomic Scientists* 52 (1996): 38–40.

4 See Yurii Shcherbak, "Ten Years of the Chernobyl Era," *Scientific American*, April 1996, 46.

5 Estimates vary from 600,000 to 800,000. These workers came from all over the Soviet Union. The labor pool, however, drew heavily from the Russian and Ukrainian populations.

6 In my interviews, I heard instances of workers mimicking symptoms of ARS (vomiting, for example). This shows the level of desperation on the part of some of them to receive permission to leave the zone.

7 World Bank, *Managing the Legacy of Chernobyl* (Washington, DC, 1994), 7:6.

8 Ian Hacking, *Taming of Chance* (Cambridge, 1990).

9 For an elaboration of the concept of *blat*, see Alena Ledeneva, *Russia's Economy of Favours: Blat, Networking, and Informal Exchange* (Cambridge, 1998).

10 Michael Burawoy and Katherine Verdery, *Uncertain Transition: Ethnographies of Change in the Postsocialist World* (Lanham, MD, 1999), 2.

11 Dominique Schnapper, "The European Debate on Citizenship," *Daedalus* 126 (1997): 201.

12 Colin Gordon, "Government Rationality: An Introduction," in *The Foucault Effect: Studies in Governmentality*, ed. G. Burchell, C. Gordon, and P. Miller (Chicago, 1991), 5.

13 Clifford Geertz, *Local Knowledge: Further Essays in Interpretive Anthropology* (New York, 1983), 92.

Inclusive Citizenship and
Claims-Making from Below

16

Reframing Agrarian Citizenship

Land, Life and Power in Brazil, 2009

Hannah Wittman

1. Introduction

The roots of citizenship practice in urban spaces, coupled with the maintenance of urban political and economic centers of power, have historically marginalized rural actors and spaces to the periphery of political articulation. Within this relation, land, as "the prerequisite of active citizenship" (Wallerstein, 2003, p. 652), has been a constitutive component of political and economic power. Access to land has structured control over labor and material resources even when the ownership and occupation of land are separated, with urban landowners exerting political influence over rural people and the land they work. In this sense, members of rural polities often find themselves in a situation in which they have the technical rights of citizenship, but lack the substantive rights of participation, or the power to govern the development of landed resources. In a citizenship regime based on property ownership, landownership and power structured through individual social actors often absent or external to the rural community thus fractures the potential for collective social action in the countryside.

[...]

With about half the world's population still living and working in rural areas, the resurgence of organizations comprised of rural workers and landless peasants are increasingly referenced as one of the dynamic modern classes operating in the world system (McMichael, 2006, 2008; Petras, 1997; Petras and Veltmeyer, 2001). These organizations are increasingly calling into question long-standing assumptions about the relationships between property, production practices, governance institutions, and political power. Farmer-based movements worldwide are reasserting their physical and political relevance, demanding new guarantees and political rights (Desmarais, 2002, 2007; Edelman, 1999; Navarro, 2005) and calling for the re-valuation of agrarian culture as a "virtuous activity" (Mariola, 2005). In this vein, Brazil's *Movimento dos Trabalhadores Rurais Sem Terra* (Landless Rural Workers Movement, or MST), comprises over one million members that conduct grass-

Hannah Wittman, 2009. Reframing agrarian citizenship: land, life and power in Brazil. *Journal of Rural Studies* 25: 120–130.

roots organization and political action demanding land, agrarian reform, and "a broader social transformation" which, for them, includes promoting family farm production and sustainable agriculture based on a well-developed discourse around rural rights and citizenship. For these rural activists, political change and rural survival are simultaneously pursued through political education and mobilization in both rural and urban spaces to broaden public conceptions of the responsibilities and rights associated with rural life.

This resurgence of rural social movements and their diverse calls for new conceptualizations of citizenship has laid the groundwork for a new research agenda on the contingent relationships between land, power, social organization and citizenship in the countryside within diverse contexts of social and economic restructuring (Moyo and Yeros, 2005; Parker, 2002; Woods, 2006, 2008). [...] In this light, the particular reformulation of rural citizenship advocated here is contained in the concept of agrarian citizenship. It is modeled not solely on the geographic location of rurality but rather on understanding the changing political basis for agrarian social action, which includes differential practices of production and political participation conducted within and beyond rural spaces. This concept provides a framework to explore the emerging demand for, and practice of, modern agrarian citizenship, when peasantries are supposed to be disappearing rather than mobilizing for a reconceptualization of what citizenship means.

This investigation of agrarian citizenship builds on alternative notions of participation and production from the grassroots, and is based on ethnographic fieldwork conducted between 2004 and 2006 in Mato Grosso, Brazil. Land related policies in this region have historically situated political and economic rights in the hands of an elite land-owning minority. This ethnographic research exposes how the relation between land, power, and citizenship is negotiated and reconfigured in the Brazilian countryside as a result of grassroots mobilizations around land access, production practices, and political articulation by rural people. By contesting the equation of property with citizenship, agrarian citizenship, as expressed and enacted by members of the MST, goes beyond traditional

or liberal conceptions of rights linked to individual property, production, or possession. Instead, it foregrounds new collective roles and rights for rural dwellers. De-centering the role of land possession as the historical mediator of citizenship rights, contemporary agrarian actors aim for the diversification of new forms of rural political and production-oriented practices. These are designed to ensure not only the economic survival and political demarginalization of the rural poor but also a broader conception of land stewardship as a social relation that involves all members of society. In what follows, I first examine the historical development of the relationship between landholding, citizenship, and grassroots demands for reform in Brazil. I then explore how particular actors within the land reform movement negotiate the terms of citizenship in discursive and practical ways through the development of alternative forms of political participation.

2. Land and Citizenship in Brazil

The "social" nature of land is particularly evident in Brazil, where centuries of exclusion and discriminatory land administration laws have resulted in a contemporary system in which 3.5% of landowners control over half of Brazil's arable land (MDA, 2003). The link between land possession and political power has been a formative part of Brazilian society since the colonial period (Brannstrom, 2001; Bruno, 2003; Faoro, 2001; Freyre, 1953; Holston, 1991, 2008; Leal, 1977 [1949]). As a result, full appreciation of the new forms of agrarian citizenship emerging in Brazil today requires a reflection on how territorial administration has been related to citizenship status, the exercise of political power and access to material and political rights in Brazil's past.

Based on liberal notions of property as a principal organizer of individual personhood and its relation to land, rights, and the state (Holston, 2008), land administration in Brazil has served a dual purpose: to ensure Brazilian sovereignty over its inland territory, and to ensure access to land and labor for elite sectors of society by excluding workers from direct political participation in the daily affairs of the nation. In colonial Brazil, land grants to elites with political ties to the Crown were a mark of social prestige, with the possession of property guaranteeing political voice and substantive citizenship rights. Eligibility requirements for voting established in 1822 limited suffrage to those with income from property and industry, explicitly excluding wage laborers, women, and the rural landless (da Costa, 2000). Large landholders were important mediators between tenants and the state, making land possession the basis of power and a clear territorial mechanism ensuring a "citizenship gap" (Brysk and Shafir, 2004) by limiting access to political participation.

Facing an imminent labor crisis linked to the strengthened abolition movement, land-owners passed the 1850 Land Law, creating a series of new obstacles to landownership for poor laborers (da Costa, 2000; Silva, 1996). The law established the commodification of land as a system to exclude those who could not pay for a title from land occupation, in the process regulating land tenure and creating individual property rights. Despite a modification in the 1889 Constitution replacing the property requirement for suffrage with a literacy requirement, landholding continued to structure political power and participation. Civil rights were granted to landless populations not by the state, but by the *senhores da terra* (landed elite) through the social relation of *"coronelismo"*, or the hierarchical political relations between the rural elite and other rural people, especially those without land. *Coronelismo* emerged as a combination of violence and patronage as a way to control labor and votes, enforcing widespread exclusion from land ownership and active political participation, and leading to the social exclusion of a reserve labor force comprised of freed slaves and dispossessed peasants lacking capital to invest in expansion (Bruno, 2003; Faoro, 2001; Leal, 1977 [1949]; Mendoça, 1998).

[...]

Grassroots demands for land and citizenship

By the mid 1980s, movements for agrarian reform in Brazil had begun to demand access to land as a material right linked to membership in the nation, associating the struggle for land with the struggle for social incorporation in a way that made sense based on the traditional relationship between land and power in Brazil. Over time, however, the struggle for land became more than about just access to land; rather, it became a political starting point for "defining, deepening, and expanding alternative spaces aimed at pursuing effective forms of democratic citizenship" (Robles, 2002), in addition to the material aims of improving prospects for rural employment and food security. In other words, politicizing the struggle for land began to problematize the territorial relationship between state and society, in which land access historically served as an enfranchisement mechanism.

Responding to grassroots mobilization as part of the return to democracy, the federal Brazilian Government developed the first National Plan for Land Reform in 1985. The new policy included clear references to the grassroots demands for citizenship, illustrated by language that referenced the objectives of reform as not only a rural modernization strategy but also a chance to "create equal opportunities for all" through policies of land distribution and tenure regularization. In 1985, Nelson Ribeiro, Brazil's Minister of Agrarian Development, declared that the "great objective of agrarian reform is to incorporate millions of landless workers into the Brazilian citizenry" (Ribeiro, 1985). But land reform activists were careful to explain that they demanded rights to land as a function of citizenship, not a prerequisite to it. Their mobilization to counter the government cooptation of the grassroots citizenship discourse included gathering over a million signatures advocating for an agrarian reform clause in the 1988 Constitution. They saw in the 1988 Constituent Assembly the possibility to "install new equilibriums in benefit of a collectivity with territory as a back-drop" (Santos, 2002, p. 23). The movements were successful in instigating a public discussion of how the constitution would define the social function of land, resulting in its inclusion in the 1988 constitution as one of the fundamental rights and guarantees of citizenship,[1] adding both discursive and legal weight to the demands of the rural land reform movements.

In Brazil, legislation linking land ownership to responsible and productive use for the benefit of society has been an ongoing way to contest and control property. A social function clause had appeared previously in the 1934 Constitution, (art. 111, n.17), disappearing in the 1937 Constitution and returning in the 1946 Constitution (art. 147) with reference to requiring land use to foster "social well-being" (Pereira, 2000, p. 109). Although liberal land legislation linking ownership to productivity dates back to Portuguese colonial law, in practice this legislation was widely ignored. By the mid 1980s, however, Brazilian rural workers' unions, the MST, and other rural social movements began to promote a concept of the social function of land that went beyond the criteria of economic production. They advocated legislation that required land use to be environmentally sustainable, economically productive, and foster equitable social relations. As related by a rural leader in Mato Grosso, these movements considered a wide spectrum of social rights to be associated with land, including:

> The right to participate, the right to leisure, schools, health, roads ... all the public goods that citizens have a right to. [It is a land relation that] respects labor rights ... a healthy environment preserved for future generations, and democratizes access to land. It is within this democratization that we go beyond the economic vision of productivity that the legislation talks about...We ask 'what productivity is of interest to society'? From the point of view of social gain and from the point of view of necessity, the public interest should be above purely economic interests.[2]

In response to grassroots pressure, Article 186 of the 1988 constitution exhibited a conceptual advance in the content of the social function of land, with four specific legal criteria: rational and adequate use (based on legislated norms of economic productivity); adequate use of available natural resources and preservation of the environment; compliance with labor regulations and landuse that favors the well-being of the owners and laborers. In this formulation, economic productivity is seen as only one component of the social function of land. By legislating a land–society relation that considers community and environmental well-being (in the form of fair labor practices and environmental conservation) as equally important to individual use rights, the Brazilian constitutional assembly recognized that the interests of individuals do not exist separately from those of the community.

All this is to say that by the mid 1980s, a national contestation of the historical meaning of the land–society relation was peaking at the same time that agricultural modernization policies that favored large-scale and export-oriented production practices were leading to record levels of rural displacement. As rural populations continued to be in flux in Brazil, with significant populations forced to leave rural areas to work in urban areas, new settlements were also forming through the agricultural resettlement of thousands of displaced families as a result of the mobilization for agrarian reform.

3. Transforming Citizenship Post-Settlement

The MST, in particular, has continued to act as a national leader in the struggle for agrarian reform in Brazil since its formation in 1984. An important component of this struggle is the changing perception by rural workers of land as a *condition* of citizenship to land as a *right* of an expanded citizenry. Like many modern rural social movements, the MST emerged from a combination of agricultural restructuring which displaced small farmers from their land, Brazil's emergent process of democratization, and the consolidation of isolated agrarian reform movements, many with historic ties to the church.[3] The MST's day-to-day operation is based on political organizing, physical land occupations in rural encampments, and alternative models of post-reform settlement. Between 1984 and 2004, the MST organized over 350,000 families in 2,200 land reform settlements in 23 of Brazil's 27 states, while between 2004 and 2006 another 150,000 families were organized in occupations and camps.[4]

But focusing on national membership numbers or on hectares of land shifted from the hands of elites or the state misses an essential element in the discursive and practical development of agrarian citizenship. For MST leaders, land distribution is necessary to ensure continued food production in rural areas, and to provide jobs for the landless. But unlike many previous attempts at land reform, the objectives of Brazil's contemporary grassroots movements do not stop at the acquisition of land. They frame their struggle around "the social question" of agrarian reform, which not only involves lobbying the state for the broader elements of rural reform (including investment in programs designed to support rural livelihoods, protect the agricultural landscape, and foster local food security), but also seeks political incorporation founded upon participation in ongoing political action post settlement.

Aiming to foster a "broad social transformation" in Brazilian society, the MST and allied movements act simultaneously on several social and political fronts in addition to their struggle to acquire land. In actions as diverse as developing a national plebiscite on the Free Trade Area of the Americas, participating in a nation-wide Popular Assembly to legislate an alternative form of popular sovereignty, and building networks of rural social movements across Latin America and globally, the members and leadership of the MST seek to enact a structure of citizenship that provides a space for all people to participate in constructing a national project while receiving the material benefits of membership in the nation. The formation of alternative ways of organizing at the local, regional, and national levels, rather than linkage to political parties or formal interaction with the legislative structure is a key characteristic that differentiates the MST from traditional political parties and rural workers' unions in Brazil.

After acquiring land in a reform settlement, settlers are required by the Brazilian government to have a membership in some kind of formal organization (whether the MST or an agricultural association) to access material benefits available to the settlement, including agricultural credit payments, housing materials, seeds, or agricultural extension visits. Continued membership in the MST requires ongoing participation in political activities, meetings, and neighborhood groups associated with the movement. When some settlers, as a result of political differences with movement leaders, distance or formally disassociate themselves from the movement after obtaining land, they most often subsequently join one of several agricultural associations linked to Rural Workers' Unions, political parties, or Municipal Agricultural Offices.

An ethnographic examination of how citizenship action is negotiated post settlement offers insights into how settlers characterize and contest forms of citizenship, political participation and the rights and responsibilities associated with land and models of agricultural production. The reconfiguration of land–society relationships post settlement provides the diverse group of settlers an opportunity to engage in debate and political practice over different meanings and experiences attached to land, membership in the MST, and alternative organizations of civil society.

4. The Antonio Conselheiro Settlement

The following ethnographic description is based on six months of participant observation in the Antonio Conselheiro land reform settlement in Mato Grosso in 2004 in addition to follow up visits in 2005 and 2006.[5] Over 100 interviews were conducted within the settlement, half with those designated here as MST activists (settlers who have maintained active participation in the movement for more than 5 years after obtaining land in the settlement) and half with former members of the MST who remain in the settlement but no longer self-identify as members of the movement.

The MST arrived in Mato Grosso in 1994, more than a decade after making significant advances in mobilization and settlement in southeast and northeast Brazil. The movement was in a phase of national expansion, and saw in Mato Grosso evident demand for rural organization combined with the highest land concentration in the country. Building on a national experience of grassroots organization based on the methods of popular education (Freire, 1970), the MST began to integrate physical land occupations in Mato Grosso with political education designed to foster a process of personal transformation linked to the construction of community well-being. The MST's method of organizing differed from the traditional model of rural organization in Mato Grosso, historically based on political membership in rural workers' unions with strong links to political parties. One MST activist who participated in the earliest land occupations in Mato Grosso remembers:

There were several movements here that had already organized the workers, but in a way very much about profit. They had the workers, but sought to gain money. Until then, no one had met any members of the MST. They had heard about us in the press, on the news, around, right? But [through the process of our first occupation in Mato Grosso] they came to know in practice, a new idea, a new discourse, something that was going to bring benefit for the families that organized themselves through this organization.[6]

Key in this statement are two important aspects of membership in the MST – a new organizational praxis, and "something that was going to bring benefit for the families." Most settlers joined the MST simply because they wanted land, and they had heard that the MST members were usually successful at obtaining it. But in the lengthy process of political mobilization leading to the legalization of a settlement, the MST delivers a program of political education about "the movement in theory". This process seeks to teach settlers how to negotiate bureaucracy through collective action to obtain the agricultural supports (land, credit, technical assistance) to which they have rights as rural producers, but also situates their particular agricultural problems as small producers within the larger historical context of global political economy and the influence of

neoliberal policies – including increasing government support for large-scale export agriculture and decreasing support for small farmers – on their agricultural futures. In pre-settlement organizing meetings, the influence of neoliberalism on rural displacement, local food relations and environmental degradation were key topics of discussion. By connecting the individual struggle for survival to a collective agrarian situation beyond local boundaries, this process of political education teaches the importance of a personal responsibility to act in support of the collective good, as an agrarian ideal. As an MST activist involved in organizing the Antonio Conselheiro settlement explains:

We show the other side of the conquest of land, the social question. [Settlers] first have to learn the theory ... politically who is the enemy, who isn't, to understand the political process of the whole society and how it functions. Even those who haven't studied, they must get out of this [political] illiteracy ... to be able to go out of the old into the new. The movement goes through a process of the people conquering a space of their own, with their own force.

The activist continues:

First they come to understand the theory, right, about what is an encampment, what is the movement in theory, to later participate in practice. The person then goes conscious of what is going to happen out in the forest [the occupation] ... They learn before and then they go.[7]

As such, MST activists highlight the significance of political education and conscious recognition of the roots of agricultural and social challenges as a basis for citizenship practice, rather than just the accomplishment of material objectives (land access and agricultural credit), although those material benefits were the primary reason most families joined the movement. For long-term activists, the substantive transformation of agrarian citizenship goes beyond just conquering rural space, to involve a process of personal transformation that occurs through consciously informed strategic action challenging traditional power relations in the countryside that are based on land possession.

Land occupations are the most significant public acts asserting rights to rural land for members of the movement. MST activists identify a property that is deemed to not fulfill a social function – an unproductive estate, a land use that is damaging to the environment, or an estate that uses coercive labor practices. The movement members "occupy" this land by setting up a temporary camp and school facilities and planting subsistence crops. This initial act of occupation requires the construction of a new form of collective social organization comprised of previously isolated individuals and families coming from different spheres of society. It also symbolizes one of the primary objectives of their agrarian mobilization – the production of food for local consumption, part of their vision of the social function of land. Many of the families who joined the MST in Mato Grosso were working as ranch hands, on small plots of lands belonging to extended family, as seasonal and permanent workers on sugar cane or other agroindustrial plantations, or as displaced domestic or day workers in the urban centers.

The structure of social organization in a land encampment is especially instructive regarding the way in which traditional land–society relations are challenged by rural activists. The Antonio Conselheiro families conducted an initial occupation of an idle ranch in 1996 and immediately formed about 40 "family groups" charged with the political and material organization of the settlement. Rather than electing one settlement leader, family groups comprised of "nuclei" of 25–30 families each elect two coordinators (one man and one woman) which sit on a settlement coordination council, and also elect representatives to each of the settlement-wide committees (production and environment, health, security, political formation, education). This organizational structure assigns each individual person a *tarefa*, a task or action that benefits the settlement as a whole, which is intended to foster a process of self-education and responsibility in each person. This way of organizing ensures that political and other survival tasks "should not be centered in the hands of few people." It also functions as a level of decision-making, seeking to break the history of patronage and dependency that characterized the political relationship of landless workers with the rural elites, often their employers and benefactors.

Antonio Conselheiro settlers remained camped for over two years waiting for the legalization of their land claim. During this time, discussions took place among the settlers on strategies of settlement organization, models of production, and ongoing political issues facing agriculture in Brazil. The MST continued to offer courses and workshops on political education, livestock management, agroforestry and agro-ecological systems, cooperative marketing, organic farming and reforestation, and other survival concerns, as well as organizing basic education, adult literacy classes, and improvised health clinics. The MST teaches that land use is for collective benefit, highlighting their focus on peasant food production as the primary economic activity in the countryside.

During the period of encampment families participated in intense discussions about both the political and social direction of the settlement, and divisions began to occur within the movement members that resulted in the withdrawal of over 300 families from the MST, while maintaining their physical stakes in the settlement and continuing to participate in legal negotiations and camp management. Interviews with participants identified several factors in the split, including some settlers who distrusted the leadership, squabbles over organizational finances, and the influence of political outsiders offering alternative organizational options, in the form of traditional rural associations. The ongoing tensions and dialogue between these two sets of settlers over what constitutes participation, and how different forms of participation relate to the relationship between land access and responsibilities illustrates the ongoing dynamism of rural politics and the changing implications of agrarian citizenship in Brazil.

[...]

5. Agrarian Citizenship as Personal and Collective Transformation

Despite differences in day-to-day political organization strategies and objectives, MST members and association settlers both exemplify the changing norms of agrarian citizenship in the Brazilian countryside. They do this by fundamentally challenging a land-based notion of citizenship by developing an autonomous, and sometimes internally contentious, set of settler organizations in the countryside. Now it is political organization and debate (whether via associations or MST), and autonomy in agricultural production that links settlers to their rural identity as citizens, not their exclusion from land. In this vein, a MST leader notes a fundamental difference in political work as a result of the transformative struggle for land.

Before, it was easier for a single farmer to go and talk with the mayor, than for a worker's representative or leader. They isolate you, they isolated people who were struggling for the collective good. Now, collectively we put the greater good on the agenda, we pull [the mayor] out of that small circle that they have there.[8]

The ability of settler associations – whether linked to the MST or not – to engage with rural and urban policy makers stands in direct contrast to the traditional patronage system associated with property colonization in Brazilian history. This engagement stems from the learned forms of political practice and organizing strategies gained during the grassroots mobilization for land experienced by all members of the settlement. Several Antonio Conselheiro MST settlers suggested that an important factor mediating their ability to combine political activities with agricultural settlement practices and to survive as both small producers and political actors in the face of ongoing challenges to small-scale production in Brazil was the level of personal transformation that they had experienced as a result of the ongoing practical struggle to stay on the land. One activist explained: "if the body stops, the consciousness stops, it gets

stagnant."[9] Another settler explained his view that some people leave the settlement altogether because of their inability to experience personal transformation:

People who join the MST and then leave, and hang around defaming the movement, these people did not experience any social transformation. I think that people don't change because they don't want to. You have to have a lot of strength and courage and even sacrifice, because many times we have to leave things aside to enter into this struggle. If you can't do that, you will never be able to carry out a transformation of yourself.[10]

Association members within the settlement pointed out that they were more politically active than they had ever been before joining the settlement, and that they were using different strategies and tactics than currently practiced by the MST in the settlement. As each settlement member learned in the encampment and political education process, the MST's Freirian educational model seeks to engage each individual in a form of political awakening that allows each person to recognize the historical foundations of the obstacles that have prevented previous political participation. This education is then used as a method of understanding how to overcome those obstacles. To the extent that the political awakening is incomplete, the individual remains isolated and not free, subject to continued manipulation. For settlers in the Antonio Conselheiro settlement, opportunities for this kind of informed transformation are continual: the daily opportunities to participate in settlement activities around agricultural production and negotiation of credit, the collective protection of environmental reserve areas, adult education and literacy are simultaneously opportunities to engage in political action. Even the occasional political or settlement management conflicts between sectors of the settlement were a new terrain upon which to settle differences, according to newly installed processes of autonomous political negotiation.
    Another Antonio Conselheiro settler explained his perspective on the relationship between personal transformation and public action:

The most important thing is the change within ourselves, that isn't easy, it doesn't always work in the countryside. You have to wait out a lot of sacrifice. Speaking of myself, when I entered the MST I had a great transformation inside myself, I changed a lot.[11]

Another activist redefined activism as not just "going to the streets with flag and staff, but undergoing permanent changes in our daily life...with the objective not only immediate and material needs like land and credit but also permanent issues like citizenship and class struggle."[12] MST activists explained that settlers commonly focus first on material needs, and only later see the benefits of a transformative political model:

In the beginning there was that strong resistance, like 'No, I want my piece of land'. It's that culture of property, right? So, *Puxa*, 'I have my lot, right'?! Then you put a fence up … but with time you begin to realize that it's not like you thought. It's only later when you see that by yourself things just don't work, that they begin to reflect together again, about coming together.[13]

In the case of the Antonio Conselheiro settlement, the process of personal transformation expressed by settlers gave rise to the development of a demonstrated collective consciousness, despite political differences, that is key in the new reformulation of agrarian citizenship. Through the ongoing collaboration between MST and association members to develop alternative agricultural practices, foster new markets for local food production and to protect a riverine reserve within the settlement, individual settlers become part of a collectivity, as expressed by a movement statement:

Settlements are not just a unit of production. They are above all a social nucleus where people live together and develop a group of community activities in the sphere of culture, leisure, education, religion. We need to be attentive so that the settlements can fulfill their historic mission of seeding change in the rural areas (MST, 2001, 25).

In MST workshops and internal debates, the idea of being "woken up" or "reborn" through political education is a common topic of discussion. But care is made to emphasize the collective nature of individual transformation. As one activist explained,

Collective and individual reflection is one of the principles of struggle coming out of our 20 years of accumulated experience in political and methodological practice. The advancement of consciousness is done collectively, in community, as opposed to a process of individual reflection like that done in a monastery. It is done through a three-legged process of organization, political education, and struggle. Our ideas and our people are reborn every day as we move forward in the struggle that places new challenges before our conscious and permanent participation. We have the commitment to participate.[14]

Creating space for ongoing political organization and participation is a continual task in the process of reframing agrarian citizenship, and an important outcome of the process of personal transformation and the development of a collective rural consciousness. In the Antonio Conselheiro settlement in 2004, the MST undertook an active campaign to politically reorganize the settlement. Families from the settlement carried out the same kind of door-to-door grassroots recruiting, recalling the initial urban work to bring people into the movement before the initial land occupation. Families who had drifted away from the movement towards association membership were encouraged to reformulate their *núcleo* groups and attend general settlement assemblies to discuss both material settlement needs and larger political issues. By reframing organizational goals in collective terms (e.g. accessing credit and agricultural development program, improving settlement schools and infrastructure), MST leaders sought to provide forums for collective debate and political action that could transcend the organizational divisions of previous years. In a follow-up visit to the settlement in 2006, a number of interviewed families indicated that they had reframed their daily political practices within the settlement organization as congruent with the objectives of the MST, and now considered themselves "back in the movement". What is interesting is that this seemed more a transition of discourse, rather than a change in practice. Both self-identified association members and self-identified MST members were speaking the same language of personal transformation and collective action.

In addition to issues of internal organization with the settlement and ongoing political engagement with the state and federal authorities on issues pertaining specifically to agrarian reform, settlement members have played an active role in fostering local and regional political and economic change, as part of the commitment to continued engagement in the public issues. Regular marches and demonstrations at the municipal and state level – organized by both the MST and association groups – have addressed such concerns as the rights of the state workers' unions to better salaries and retirement benefits, protests against the legalization of transgenic seeds and foods, public mobilization for additional support for the local farmer's market, and ongoing mobilization to improve rural schools and health services. Collaboration between Antonio Conselheiro settlers and MST leadership with the State University of Mato Grosso (UNEMAT) since 2002 has led to the organization of an ongoing seminar on Agro-Ecology and Family Agriculture attended by over 800 local farmers and students. A new extension relationship with the UNEMAT Department of Agronomy also fosters agro-ecological production practices, the preservation of several forest reserves, and the implementation of a community-supported agriculture in a nearby city that supports the movement's commitment to increased local control over the food supply.

An MST activist from Antonio Conselheiro summarizes the importance of participation in a broader rural and national social transformation as follows:

No change will exist in our country if the people don't participate. This power of mobilization is found in the willingness to struggle and in the consciousness and the organization of the people. Change requires

the organization of work, it requires indignation. And we understand that this will, this desire for change by the people, needs to be woken up again and again. From the people we need to construct a new space (terreno), a critical consciousness, deepened within us, with our spirit of indignation. That spirit of indignation has many spaces and directions, leading to changes in reality, and changes in ourselves, as subjects of a historical process.[15]

As illustrated here, the concept of citizenship employed by members of rural social movements in Brazil is not derived from just access to land (or simply equating of land possession with citizenship). Rather, it situates land-holding in a complex and changing set of social relations, rights, and responsibilities that are (re)produced through democratizing access to land, as one factor in creating space for political participation. It is a seemingly subtle but fundamental difference that begins with pre-settlement organization and continues with political education during the practice of land occupation. Rural politics in this sense moves from acquiescence to a state- or elite-directed territorial administration to, as one interviewee explained,

participation from the smallest decisions, the small processes ... in order for the small farmer to become the subject of his/her own history. The moment of conquering the right [to land] and to social rights in general, fundamental rights, leads to participation in the history of workers, the history of the settlement, the encampment, as a group and as part of society, in community and collective life and in political life ... in the process of human and social development ... as a citizen of society as a whole.[16]

These words illustrate the changing self-conception of rural workers and the emerging notion of agrarian citizenship. From a set of isolated individuals in rural areas, settlement members have become an organized collectivity that, despite internal political debates and differences, sees itself as part of society "as a whole." This self-conception emphasizes a strategic shift in the notion of agrarian citizenship: the implicit nature of rights and responsibilities associated with rural production and settlement becomes collective, rather than individual. This is further explained by this statement from another rural leader:

> Citizenship from an individual point of view is related to fundamental rights and guarantees of liberty, of the right to a name and title... [and other individual rights enumerated in the constitution]. But from the point of view of social advancement, of improvement in quality of life for small farmers and for the working class, for the earth and for the small ones of the earth, it is a collective project. Because from the individual point of view this confrontation [social change] is impossible.[17]

6. Conclusion

The preceding discussion from movement activists illustrates how changing visions and practices of citizenship enacted by contemporary grassroots actors directly contest the traditional marginalization of rural dwellers from political participation. Challenging liberal notions of the relation between property and citizenship, incorporation into the rural citizenry in Brazil is not accomplished solely through the individual acquisition of land, as demonstrated by the failure of the rural colonization projects implemented by the Brazilian government from the mid-20th century onwards to change social relations and patterns of political participation in the countryside. Instead, the grassroots vision of a particularly agrarian citizenship prioritizes the creation of new rural social relations, in which citizenship is not an assumed right but rather an accomplishment. For grassroots organizers in Brazil, this accomplishment includes using land in accordance with a social function perspective – providing food for the nation, respecting labor rights and the environment, and providing rural space for political action. Agrarian citizenship thus recognizes the agency of rural peoples in challenging the traditional binaries of modernity/peasantry, landed/landless, and subject/citizen.

As shown in the contested organizational practices of settlers who acquire land through the struggle for agrarian reform, the day-to-day construction of this process of change – negotiated by the very settlers involved in its implementation – is a complicated process and one that does not happen overnight. Many settlers, formerly workers on rural estates or living on the margins of urban areas as day laborers, have never accomplished political enfranchisement, with personal and collective histories of patronage and clientelism as foundational to their perception of what is politically possible. The transformation of their personal self-vision and relation to a larger social network, through the collective struggle for land, alters the politics of the possible and broadens horizons for action. The decision to be a dissenter – even from the grassroots network that initiated that very dissent in the countryside – demonstrates that diversity is not only possible, but in itself is transformatory. The ongoing debate between political and organizational strategies between MST and association members has, in the end, contributed to a vibrant rural political community characterized by debate and dissent.

Finally, the discursive and normative political transformations occurring on a day-to-day basis in the Brazilian countryside have demonstrated material consequences of land redistribution in both social and ecological terms. For both activists that continue as members of the MST and those that engage with municipal politicians through rural associations, the experience of political participation that was directly fostered through their struggle for land has changed their lives in a substantive way. They have not just gained a piece of land, but have developed a diverse set of active political voices and socio-ecological practices that comprise a new and alternative vision of agrarian citizenship that resonates beyond the settlement boundaries.

This paper has paid particular attention to how citizenship is expressed and renegotiated around a struggle for land, reframing the meaning and practice of active citizenship in the Brazilian countryside. By unpacking the historical development of the relationship between land and power, and exploring how these relations are contested and reframed by members of land-based rural social movements, this analysis demonstrates the contours of a particularly "agrarian" citizenship, one in which rights are won and practiced not through simple presence in a rural locality but through transformative rural action, with implications for the basis of power beyond the rural spheres. As urban absentee landowners are forced to relinquish control or re-negotiate relations with rural workers, the traditional land base of power is eroded. Thus, a broadened conception of citizenship goes beyond a passive and hierarchical relationship between individual persons and the state, in which the state mediates the awarding of rights discriminately according to particular terms and subjectivities. These terms and subjectivities, in Brazil, have had a tight historical relationship to the possession of land, as demonstrated by long history of linking territorial administration and governing power to political enfranchisement. The new practices of active agrarian citizenship, as developed by grassroots actors through independent production and political activities, address and transform relationships between individuals, rural and urban communities and the state in such a way as to challenge the assumption that access to land alone will lead to the development of new forms of citizenship and rights.

Acknowledgments

The author is grateful for insightful comments from Charles Geisler, Phil McMichael, Gerardo Otero, Raj Patel and Razack Karreim, as well as the two anonymous reviewers.

NOTES

1 Cf. 1988 Constitution, Chapter One, Sec. XIII, on Individual and Collective Rights and Duties: property shall observe its social function.
2 Interview #231, Cuiabá 12/20/2004.
3 There is an extensive literature on the origin and expansion of the MST as a national movement. In English see in particular Branford and Rocha (2002); Robles (2000, 2001); Wright and Wolford (2003). In Brazil, definitive works are Fernandes (1999, 2000); Morissawa (2001); Stédile and Fernandes (1999).
4 For additional information on MST land distribution figures, see www.mst.org.br and the DATALUTA Project recording land reform activity at the University of São Paulo, http://www4.fct.unesp.br/dataluta/.
5 Multi-sited field research was conducted in Brazil during a period of 17 months between 2002 and 2004, including participant observation in nine land reform settlements, numerous meetings and political activities organized by settlement leaders and over 200 interviews with settlers and social movement leaders. The bulk of interviews and observations were carried out in four settlements, two organized by the MST, one organized by a Rural Workers' Union, and one organized by a municipal government.
6 Interview #30, 4/17/2003.
7 Interview #30, 4/17/2003.
8 Interview #30, 4/17/2003.
9 MST activist, interview #164, state workshop, Cuiabá, 12/9/2004.
10 Settler from Antonio Conselheiro, #202, MST state meeting Cuiabá, 12/9/2004.
11 Settler from Antonio Conselheiro, #202, MST state meeting Cuiabá, 12/9/2004.
12 MST meeting participant, Antonio Conselheiro settlement, 3/26/2004.
13 Interview #241, 6/25/2004.
14 Antonio Conselheiro leader, MST state meeting Cuiabá, 12/9/2004.
15 Statement at MST Mato Grosso workshop, 12/10/2004.
16 Interview #231, Cuiabá 12/20/2004.
17 Interview #231, Cuiabá 12/20/2004.

REFERENCES

Branford, S., and Rocha, J., 2002. *Cutting the Wire: The Story of the Landless Movement in Brazil*. London: Latin American Bureau.
Brannstrom, C., 2001. Producing possession: labour, law and land on a Brazilian agricultural frontier, 1920–1945. *Political Geography* 20(7): 859–883.

Bruno, R., 2003. Nova República: a violência patronal rural como prática de classe. *Sociologias* 5(10): 284–310.

Brysk, A., and Shafir, G., 2004. Introduction: globalization and the citizenship gap. In *People out of Place: Globalization, Human Rights, and the Citizenship Gap*. London: Routledge.

da Costa, E. V., 2000. *The Brazilian Empire: Myths and Histories*. Chapel Hill: University of North Carolina Press.

Desmarais, A., 2002. The Vía Campesina: consolidating an international peasant and farm movement. *Journal of Peasant Studies* 29(2): 91–124.

Desmarais, A., 2007. *La Vía Campesina: Globalization and the Power of Peasants*. Fernwood Publishing.

Edelman, M., 1999. *Peasants Against Globalization: Rural Social Movements in Costa Rica*. Stanford: Stanford University Press.

Faoro, R., 2001. *Os Donos do Poder: Formação do Patronato Político Brasileiro*. São Paulo: Globo.

Fernandes, B. M., 1999. *MST: Movimento dos Trabalhadores Rurais Sem Terra: Formação e Territorialização em São Paulo*. São Paulo: Hucitec.

Fernandes, B. M., 2000. *A Formação do MST no Brasil*. Petrópolis: Vozes.

Freire, P., 1970. *Pedagogy of the Oppressed*. New York: Continuum Publishing Company.

Freyre, G., 1953. *The Mansions and the Shanties*. New York: Knopf.

Holston, J., 1991. The misrule of law: land and usurpation in Brazil. *Comparative Studies in Society and History* 33(4): 695–725.

Holston, J., 2008. *Insurgent Citizenship: Disjunctions of Democracy and Modernity in Brazil*. Princeton: Princeton University Press.

Leal, V. N., 1977 [1949]. *Coronelismo: The Municipality and Representative Government in Brazil [Coronelismo, Enxada e Voto]*. Cambridge: Cambridge University Press.

Mariola, M. J., 2005. Losing ground: farmland preservation, economic utilitarianism, and the erosion of the agrarian ideal. *Agriculture and Human Values* 22(2): 209–223.

McMichael, P., 2006. Peasant prospects in the neoliberal age. *New Political Economy* 11(3): 407–418.

McMichael, P., 2008. Peasants make their own history, but not just as they please. *Journal of Agrarian Change* 8(2,3): 205–228.

MDA, 2003. *Plano Nacional de Reforma Agrária, Proposta: Paz, produção e qualidade de vida no meio rural*. Brasília: Ministério de Desenvolvimento Agrícola.

Mendoça, S. R. d., 1998. *Ruralismo Brasileiro (1888–1931)*. São Paulo: Hucitec.

Morissawa, M., 2001. *A História da Luta Pela Terra e o MST*. São Paulo: Expressão Popular.

Moyo, S., and Yeros, P. (eds), 2005. *Reclaiming the Land: The Resurgence of Rural Movements in Africa, Asia, and Latin America*. London and New York: Zed Books.

MST, 2001. *Somos Sem Terra: Pra Soletrar a Liberdade*, Caderno do Educando No. 2. Veranopolis, RS: ITERRA.

Navarro, Z., 2005. Transforming rights into social practices? The landless movement and land reform in Brazil. *IDS Bulletin-Institute of Development Studies* 36(1): 129–142.

Parker, G., 2002. *Citizenships, Contingency, and the Countryside: Rights, Culture, Land and the Environment*. London: Routledge.

Pereira, R. P. C. R., 2000. A teoria da função social da propriedade rural e seus reflexos na acepção clássica de propriedade. In Strozake, J. J. (ed.), *A Questão Agrária e a Justiça*. São Paulo: Editora Revista dos Tribunais, pp. 88–129.

Petras, J., 1997. Latin America – the resurgence of the Left. *New Left Review* 223: 17–47.

Petras, J., and Veltmeyer, H., 2001. Are Latin American peasant movements still a force for change? Some new paradigms revisited. *Journal of Peasant Studies* 28(2): 83–118.

Ribeiro, N. d. F., 1985. *O Estatuto da Terra e o Problema Fundiário*. Brasilia: MIRAD, Coordenadoria de Comunicação Social.

Robles, W., 2000. Beyond the politics of protest: the landless rural workers movement of Brazil. *Canadian Journal of Development Studies* 21(3): 657–691.

Robles, W., 2001. The landless rural workers movement (MST) in Brazil. *Journal of Peasant Studies* 28(2): 146–161.

Robles, W., 2002. Review: Breaking ground: development aid for land reform by Martin Adams. *Canadian Review of Development Studies* 23(1): 159–161.

Santos, M., 2002. *O País Distorcido: O Brasil, A Globalização e a Cidadania*. São Paulo: Publifolha.

Silva, L. O., 1996. *Terras Devolutas e Latifúndio: Efeitos da lei de 1850*. Campinas, SP: Editora da UNICAMP.

Stédile, J. P., and Fernandes, B. M., 1999. *Brava Gente: A Trajetória do MST e a Luta Pela Terra no Brasil*. São Paulo: Editora Fundação Perseu Abramo.

Wallerstein, I., 2003. Citizens all? Citizens some! The making of the citizen. *Comparative Studies in Society and History* 45(4): 650–679.

Woods, M., 2006. Political articulation: the modalities of new critical politics of rural citizenship. In Cloke, P., Marsden, T. and Mooney, P. (eds), *Handbook of Rural Studies*. London: Sage Publications, pp. 457–471.

Woods, M., 2008. Social movements and rural politics. *Journal of Rural Studies* 24: 129–137.

Wright, A., and Wolford, W., 2003. *To Inherit the Earth: The Landless Movement and the Struggle for a New Brazil*. Oakland, CA: Food First Books.

17

Life Itself

Triage and Therapeutic Citizenship, 2010

Vinh-Kim Nguyen

On Monday, 10 July 2000, South African Supreme Court Justice Edwin Cameron, speaking at a plenary session of the International AIDS Conference in Durban, declared "I am here because I can pay for life itself." This chapter explores how with the discovery of effective treatment for HIV in 1995 and in the continuing efforts to organize communities with HIV, practices of forming associations and providing testimonials reformed around a sharply focused goal: life itself. The material I present here draws extensively on my own experiences as an HIV physician in Montréal and Abidjan, where I was involved in the introduction of the new treatments that revolutionized HIV care. I saw firsthand how practices that had tried to foster and nourish solidarity among people with HIV now helped to separate those who would receive treatment and live from those who would not. This was triage, and this chapter chronicles its emergence. In its wake, a therapeutic citizenship has emerged as the hallmark of a "politics of life itself" (Rose 2006)

that defines the struggle to survive in biomedical terms: a politics of life and death.[1]

A Therapeutic Revolution

In 1995, clinicians in North America and Europe began to see the benefits of what was then an experimental treatment paradigm that relied on combining multiple antiretrovirals (ARVs) in the treatment of HIV infection. The paradigm emerged with the development of a new class of drugs, protease inhibitors (PIs), which target a crucial enzyme that the virus requires to reproduce itself. Previous drugs had targeted reverse transcriptase, the virus's "signature" enzyme that allows it to transcribe its RNA back into DNA. These drugs are accordingly referred to as reverse-transcriptase inhibitors (RTIs), which are divided into nucleoside and non-nucleoside type (nRTIs and nnRTIs respectively). Protease inhibitors are remarkably powerful antiretrovirals; however, biological resistance to the drugs was found to emerge very quickly, attenuating their

Vinh-Kim Nguyen, Life itself: triage and therapeutic citizenship. In *The Republic of Therapy: Triage and Sovereignty in West Africa's Time of AIDS* (Durham, North Carolina: Duke University Press, 2010), pp. 89–110.

The Anthropology of Citizenship: A Reader, First Edition. Edited by Sian Lazar.
© 2013 John Wiley & Sons, Inc. Published 2013 by John Wiley & Sons, Inc.

effectiveness. As a result, drawing on the success of combination therapy for the treatment of tuberculosis, the idea of combining RTI-type drugs with the PIs was advanced as a strategy for delaying the emergence of drug resistance and permanently suppressing the virus. The strategy and the new treatment paradigm it defined – combating resistance through strategic drug combinations – revolutionized HIV treatment.

By late 1995, HIV clinicians across the industrialized world had all seen dying patients return to health with the new drug combinations. At the Montreal General Hospital, where I attended as an HIV physician, our patients had been dying at a rate of two a week. Within a few years of the new treatments' introduction, only a handful of patients died each year. New viral load tests showed that the drug cocktails suppressed viral replication to the point that HIV was no longer detectable in the blood, and biological tests showed that with treatment patients' immune systems were being restored. The adoption of what came to be called highly active antiretroviral therapy – HAART, for short – had an enormous impact, reducing deaths from AIDS by over half in industrialized countries during the first few years of their use. After fourteen years of bad news, it was almost too good to be true. At the 1996 World AIDS Conference in Vancouver, optimistic researchers debated the possibility of curing patients with the drug cocktails.

Although eradicating HIV from patient's bodies is no longer considered likely, HAART marked the advent of a therapeutic revolution akin to the discovery of insulin for the treatment of diabetes. An illness that was previously fatal, in most cases, within a few years of diagnosis, is now treatable and has been transformed as a result into a chronic condition. It is not unreasonable, given the current state of knowledge, to expect that those people newly diagnosed with HIV will live lengthy and productive lives: a recent Danish study estimated that with access to treatment, HIV shortens lifespan by about twenty years. A thirty-year-old woman with HIV, for instance, can expect to live to be sixty-five rather than eighty-five (the life expectancy of a woman without HIV) (Lohse, Hansen, Pederson et al. 2007); by early 2010 data had begun to emerge that in the North people with HIV could expect to have a normal life expectancy.

How Activism Produced Treatment: Clinical Trials and Therapeutic Citizenship

The discovery of the efficacy of these drugs – their ability to suspend the ticking time-bomb of viral replication, restore health, and almost indefinitely postpone illness and death – was itself linked to an earlier therapeutic activism that did much more than exercise direct political pressure on the biomedical establishment to find a cure for the disease. Most accounts of drug discovery focus on the process of laboratory research; however, only a fraction of drugs found to be biologically effective in laboratories make it into clinical practice. In the "real world" of patients' bodies, drugs may prove to be ineffective for a range of reasons: they are too poorly absorbed, cause too many side effects, are too toxic, or are metabolized too quickly. Clinical trials, where drugs are tested in real patients, are necessary to weed out the truly effective drugs from those whose promising results in the test tube won't translate into clinical results.

Recruitment into clinical trials for HIV in the early years of the epidemic in North America, Europe, and Australia was facilitated by a strong therapeutic militancy that was rooted in a decade of gay activism, which generated significant expertise about drugs and biomedical research among AIDS activists and people living with HIV. This was accompanied by a strong willingness to participate as research subjects. This readiness drew on a sense of political engagement in the struggle to find a cure for the disease. Participation in clinical trials demonstrated what can be termed a kind of *therapeutic citizenship*. This politicization of research participation has since spread to other diseases, as has been documented by medical anthropologists who have studied the proliferation of patient self-help groups around specific illnesses.[2]

Today, recruitment is the biggest challenge faced by clinical trials and the pharmaceuticals industry that most often sponsors them. Enormous sums of money have to be invested in recruiting and then retaining patients. Because it takes so many patients to statistically tease out a treatment effect from chance, trials have to be run in multiple sites, most often in different countries and can cost hundreds of millions of dollars. As shown by a number of high-profile failures of "blockbuster" drugs that did not succeed once they were tested in clinical trials, the stakes are enormous not only in terms of the potential health of thousands or even millions of patients but also financially. The cost of failure also raises the financial stakes in recruitment efforts. Ironically, such clinical trials benefit from a kind of therapeutic citizenship born of the activism of the grim, early AIDS years. Volunteering to participate in clinical trials grew out of a sense of duty so that others may benefit from treatments eventually found to be effective. This situation is what bioethicists would call altruism; however, I prefer to examine it through the lens of citizenship because of the activist and political dimensions to clinical trials.

The development of a politicized consciousness, and indeed of a form of citizenship, around HIV was a two-edged sword for pharmaceuticals firms. Most visibly, therapeutic activists were quick to accuse the firms of refusing to make drugs accessible, sparking at times highly visible and embarrassing protests. However, therapeutic activism and its corollary of citizenship also made recruitment and retention in trials easier, potentially diminishing drug development costs. Both continue to inform an ambivalent relationship between the industry and the activists. Quietly aware of the benefit of therapeutic citizenship to recruitment in drug trials as well as public relations and tax benefits, the pharmaceuticals industry funds community groups through "community programs," even as they worry about the potential for activists to influence shareholders and cut into profits. In parallel, activists are deeply suspicious of industry's motives even as they are kept alive by the drugs. Until the mid-1990s, therapeutic citizenship remained confined to the North, as there was no significant research on HIV treatment being carried out in the developing world.

The first major trial that took place outside Europe, North America, or Australia was Merck's 1997 "028" study, conducted in Brazil, comparing triple therapy (using two standard HIV drugs alongside the drug indinavir) against monotherapy (indinavir alone). The study generated controversy (though surprisingly little) because some patients were kept on the single therapy arm of the study long after other trials proved that triple therapy was better and was therefore the standard of treatment. In effect, those in the indinavir-only arm likely developed resistance rapidly to the drug, compromising their future options for effective treatment. Normally, when it is determined that patients in a trial are actually receiving inferior treatment, the trial is terminated immediately; however, this was not done in the Brazilian case for reasons that remain unclear (Oliveira, Santos, and Mello 2001).

Another trial, this time conducted in Africa, generated even greater controversy. In Africa, while no trials using ARVs to treat patients were conducted at the time, a number of clinical trials were carried out to test various ARV drugs' efficacy in preventing HIV transmission from mother to child (this is abbreviated as PMTCT, for "Prevention of Mother To Child Transmission"). These trials became the subject of fierce debate in scientific circles in 1997. Although AZT had already been shown to decrease PMTCT by two-thirds in previous experiments, these trials tested a simplified AZT regimen against a placebo. Proponents of the trial argued that the placebo-controlled arm was necessary to quickly prove the effectiveness of AZT in developing country settings. Opponents denounced the placebo as racist and drew ominous comparisons with the Tuskegee experiments of the 1930s–1970s. In this infamous study, African American men with syphilis were never offered penicillin, even after it had been shown to be effective in treating the disease, in order to not interfere with the study's goal of describing the "natural" (that is, without treatment) progression of syphilis.[3] A short time later, a PMTCT trial comparing the new drug nevirapine to AZT was conducted in Uganda, which while showing the effectiveness of the drug, became the focus of a controversy relating to the initial use of, once again, a placebo (which was subsequently dropped), as well as its study design, data management practices, and statistical analyses. These controversies, however, failed to ignite AIDS activists in the West, for whom, by and large, the issue of access to treatment in the South did not gain any traction until 2000. That was to change with the emergence of an indigenous African activism that, in Francophone West Africa, was inadvertently unleashed by two clinical trials.

How West African Clinical Trials Produced Activists

In the mid-1990s, two large clinical trials of AZT for the prevention of mother-to-child transmission of HIV were conducted in West Africa, one sponsored by the French National AIDS Research Agency (ANRS) and the other by the rival American Centers for Disease Control (CDC). The French study tested 14,385 women in Bobo-Dioulasso (Burkina Faso) and Abidjan, while the American study tested 12,668 women in Abidjan. All the women received state-of-the-art pretest counseling for HIV. Of the more than 27,000 women tested, 3,424 (13 percent) were found to be HIV positive. However, in the American study, 618 HIV-positive women never returned for their results and the post-test counseling, while in the French study the figure was 648: that is, 37 percent of HIV-positive women didn't find out their diagnosis. Researchers told me that the rate of nonreturn for results was lower in HIV-negative women, suggesting that women with HIV suspected their diagnosis and decided not to return for results. Of the HIV-positive women who returned for their results, only 711 (32 percent) were included in the actual trials, the remaining 2,182 (68 percent) women having either been excluded for medical reasons (discussed below), or because they did not consent to be in the trial (Dabis, Msellati, Meda *et al.* 1999; Wiktor, Ikpini, Karon *et al.* 1999).

The trials had an enormous impact in shaping the early response to the epidemic in both Burkina Faso and Côte-d'Ivoire – simply because of the sheer number tested. In those early years, HIV testing programs were relatively few and far between – in the Ivoirian metropolis of Abidjan, for example, there was only one site that provided free and anonymous testing in 1995. In Burkina Faso, there was little or no access to HIV screening, including screening blood transfusions. As a result, only a handful of people knew their HIV status. The few who were tested were often not told of their diagnosis; [...] health care workers feared the demoralizing effect that doing so might entail.

The relative lack of HIV testing elsewhere, as well as my own medical experience in Abidjan, led me to believe that the majority of those who knew their HIV status had found out because they were initially recruited to participate in the trials. Of course, only a small minority were actually enrolled in the trials, which needed to screen a very large number to have a significant pool from which to enroll a necessarily smaller number of selected, eligible study-subjects. Women were disqualified from participating in the trials for numerous reasons; not arriving early enough in pregnancy to receive the AZT, and suffering from anemia (which could be dangerously worsened with AZT), were among the most common. Women who had tested positive but who had not been eligible to enroll in the trials complained bitterly to me that they had been "discarded." They resented that they did not have access to the panoply of services offered to the women who had been included in the trials. Indeed, women who were included in the trials did receive medical care and social services that were not available to others.

After having been tested, many women found their way into community groups in search of material and social support. Some even set up organizations for their fellow would-be trial subjects. These women made up the bulk of the membership of early groups of people living with HIV in both countries. Yet, as this account makes clear, the reasons that led them to participate in this clinical trial did not amount to the kind of therapeutic citizenship that drove people with HIV in North America, Europe, or Australia to enlist in clinical trials. It was poverty and fear of the consequences of being HIV positive that made them enlist in the trials in the hope of gaining access to medical care, rather than an abstract notion of solidarity with others suffering from HIV. Nonetheless, within a few years, a more radical kind of therapeutic citizenship emerged from the lack of access to drugs and the work of a few therapeutic pioneers.

Conversion

In late 1997, Abdoulaye traveled to Europe for the first time. He had been invited by a French NGO to attend a workshop there. Traveling to France was enormously exciting – an opportunity that few Burkinabè would ever have. By then Abdoulaye was spending most of his time putting together HIV projects for Jeunes sans frontières. Once in Paris, trips to the Eiffel Tower, the Louvre, and the Champs-Élysées were complemented by visits to the French AIDS organizations whose material Abdoulaye had been reading and whose names were by now important references for him. Abdoulaye took the "exchange and sharing of experiences" purpose of the trip seriously. He visited HIV testing centers and counseling groups that he had read about. He also had an HIV test, which turned out to be positive. Even worse, he had almost no more T4 cells and was classified as having AIDS as a result.[4] Parisian friends found a doctor who was able to supply him with HAART for himself.

After he returned from Europe, inspired by the self-help groups he had seen there, Abdoulaye convened – but did not participate in – a discussion group of people who had come to him because they were HIV positive and had heard that Jeunes sans frontières was involved in the "fight against AIDS." However, at these meetings, no one spoke about being HIV positive. Discussion centered on the details of everyday life and the difficulties of getting by. By 1999, Abdoulaye was faced with a new problem. He realized that some of the people he had invited to the group were better off than others – some of them were even able to pay for some form of medical treatment. This would surely "inhibit" any of the kind of

spontaneous discussion that was important to mutual support; he worried at the time that it would "only create jealousies and frustrations."

During the time he was trying to set up the "talking group," one of Abdoulaye's aunts in the family compound fell ill. She had been sick for some time, and unbeknownst to her she had tested positive for HIV at the local hospital. As was customary at the time, the diagnosis was confided to her father, the head of her household, and he had summoned his knowledgeable Abidjan-educated nephew to discuss the matter. Abdoulaye arranged for medical care and made sure that she was properly looked after and that her medications were paid for. Her diagnosis was never discussed. She died six months later, not having been told she had AIDS. Although I helped care for her, Abdoulaye never spoke to me about the effect her illness and death had on him.

The challenges Abdoulaye faced in starting a self-help group indicate that the process of "telling" and "sharing" was indeed difficult in settings such as these, where sheer poverty could magnify even minor inequalities, lead to jealousy, and undermine solidarity. As we saw with Light for AIDS, Positive Nation, and Abidjan Women against AIDS [...], the resulting rivalries and competition tore groups apart, leading to schisms in many community groups of people living with HIV. In settings of numbing poverty, the Western dream of self-help, characterized by perfect sharing and caring, was more illusion than practical strategy. Uncontained disclosure had the potential to upset social hierarchies, such as those in Abdoulaye's family, that had been negotiated over long periods of time.

For Madame Janvier of the World Bank and other Westerners I interviewed who worked to support community organizations responding to AIDS in Africa, it seemed obvious that self-disclosure was cathartic and a first step to the organization of therapeutic social relations. Although Abdoulaye told me he believed this too, this was belied by the different manner in which disclosure occurred around him. While he was encouraging others to talk about being

HIV positive, until 1999 he himself never spoke about his HIV positivity or of his worries about those who were close to him whom he knew to be ill.

Therapeutic Solidarity

Early in 1999, Jeunes sans frontières embarked on a new project called the "Friendship Center." As the organization developed a higher profile, local physicians and even the National AIDS Control Program began referring people with HIV. Abdoulaye, inspired by what he had seen on his trip to France, conceived of the Friendship Center as a combination drop-in center and dispensary. The Friendship Center was located in a small house with a courtyard in an outlying neighborhood of Ouagadougou. An erratic flow of medicines from concerned friends in Paris made for a small stock for the dispensary – "nothing much," Abdoulaye told me, but certainly better than what was available at the nearby state-run dispensary, where years of World Bank mandated cost-recovery had long ago emptied the pharmacy.

As the volume of patients grew, an informal camaraderie was struck up in the house's living room, which doubled as a waiting room. It was airier than the organization's headquarters and had two wooden benches, a small table, a shelf full of AIDS literature, a large color television, and a VCR. The TV and VCR had been obtained through a World Bank program. The patients often sat watching the television, exchanging long formulaic greetings as others arrived or left. All of them had at some point learned they were HIV positive, and some were visibly ill. They all knew that the others sitting around them were HIV positive. Yet never, in those first months of operation, did they discuss this situation among themselves.

Things began to change, however, in early 2000. By then, Abdoulaye had been on his antiretroviral treatment for almost three years, managing to get by with donations from his Parisian doctor. Together with this doctor, Abdoulaye had devised a treatment plan to deal with erratic supplies; he would just switch medicines according to what he had on hand, making sure that he was taking at least three

different and complementary drugs. He had bought a small fridge to store those medicines that had to be kept cold. As a result, by late 1999 his T4 cells had shot up, from fourteen to over four hundred, and his viral load had been undetectable for almost three years.

He put on weight, regaining the stocky build of his early twenties. His girlfriend Fatou also thrived with a supply of medicines from Montréal, but their daughter Salimata was often ill with fevers. While this is not unusual for a child in West Africa, Abdoulaye was distraught every time she took ill. For the first year of life, HIV tests are unreliable, as infants still have their mother's antibodies at that point. Because Fatou was HIV positive, her daughter Sali would have tested positive too. By the time she was two, Sali still had not had a test, even though at that point it could have been reliably ascertained whether or not she had contracted HIV. By that time, Abdoulaye had resigned himself to preferring uncertainty – punctuated by attacks of anxiety every time Sali had a fever – to the possibility of definitely finding out his daughter had HIV.

Meanwhile, Abdoulaye's visible recovery had an effect on his surroundings. Rumors circulated that he had supernatural healing powers, and this brought a new influx of the ill to the Friendship Center. Those who knew about his consumption of medicines did not suspect HIV, he told me, because he had always been "easy to take medicines," a quirk that his Ouagadougou friends assumed had been acquired in Abidjan. His stock of antiretrovirals did seem ostentatiously modern, laid out in their brightly colored boxes by the foam mattress he slept on in the adobe room in the family courtyard where he lived.

The doctor in Paris was also impressed, telling me that he had "never imagined" that such a striking clinical response could have been obtained with rotating medicines and a long-distance therapeutic relationship. As a result, in early 1999 he began sending Abdoulaye away with armfuls of medicines for other patients in Ouagadougou. By 2000, Abdoulaye was telling some people he was HIV positive but "only my friends who are taking the test or have taken it," he told me, "because only they can understand." That year, he moved out of the family compound. His daughter's frequent illnesses had led the other women in the family compound to accuse his aunt's mother of witchcraft. As I helped him pack up his antiretrovirals in their pristine packages, Abdoulaye told me he was "tired" of these "African stories" and wanted a holiday.

Storytelling and Triage

Faced with the influx of newcomers at the Friendship Center, Abdoulaye tried again to start a "talking group." However, the patients maintained an awkward silence. Discussion invariably turned to the problems of material subsistence. A European psychologist who tried to work with the group told me that these people are "completely overwhelmed by their material needs and difficulties – how can you expect to do any psychological work until these more basic issues get resolved?" But with the arrival of medicines, things began to change. With circumspection, Abdoulaye and an inner circle of Friendship Center staff began carefully – "little by little" – to distribute the medicines.

He explained to me that they used the talking group to identify candidates for the medicines – those who came regularly were more likely to observe the rigorous treatment schedules and those who "contributed" most to the group were favored. These "dynamic" members should have access to treatment, they reasoned, because they would be able to help others more than those who remained passive. The "talking group" began to fulfill a function unintended by those who championed it as a model of self-help: it served as a kind of laboratory for identifying those who should have access to treatment. Thus the self-help group functioned as a *triage* system, a method for determining who would benefit most from medicines – just as in wartime, when military physicians must decide who among the wounded can be saved and who cannot.

Interviews I conducted with other activists during that period confirmed that the story of Abdoulaye and Jeunes sans frontières was not unique. Many members of community groups involved with AIDS prevention in the mid-1990s were HIV positive. Some learned of their

diagnosis before joining, while others did afterward, taking the test (as Abdoulaye did) in order to "practice what they preach." As a result, these organizations, like Jeunes sans frontières, inevitably found themselves drawn into the issue of treatment for their own members as well as for those who came to them for help. Ultimately, access to treatment was contingent on social relations and the ability to capitalize on social networks. Jeunes sans frontières made treatment decisions based on a social calculation: who would translate improved health into the greatest good for others? The few who did get the drugs through this improvised form of triage were initially a minority. Many obtained antiretrovirals through contacts with Westerners. For these individuals, the key to survival was to be able to "tell a good story." Some activists made it to France, where AIDS activists took them in and helped them obtain residency permits. The French authorities, like other European countries, quietly renewed HIV-positive foreigners' residency permits, subsequent to domestic political pressure denouncing early deportations of HIV-positive Africans. Those who stayed behind in Africa viewed those who left as the lucky ones – those whose stories had got them to Europe.

Friends who told me they were HIV positive had differing experiences with the drugs. Ange-Daniel never wanted to go on the drugs. He just didn't think he needed them, and he was right for another ten years. He only started on the drug cocktails in 2008. Kouamé became active in a local HIV group, becoming somewhat of a cause célèbre because of his charismatic testimonials of being HIV positive. His oratorical skills eventually helped him to secure a supply of HIV medicines from a European contact he made through the association. As he became more involved in the group, he confided feeling guilty that he was on medication while others were not. He rationalized to himself that, at least, his being healthy meant he could contribute to getting more drugs for others, which he continued to do for several years. As the supply of donated drugs increased from 1998, however, Kouamé and his colleagues in the group were increasingly faced with the gut-wrenching prospect of deciding who should get the drugs. No matter how many donations they received, demand always outstripped supply.

As already mentioned, the concept of triage was developed on the battlefield, as a way to use scarce treatment resources in the most rational way: those most likely to live are prioritized to receive care, while those whose prognosis is poor are left to die. Kouamé and his group, like most other groups faced with the same situation, made the difficult decision of who should benefit from the limited source of drugs by adopting a form of triage. But how did the groups choose? Kouamé, like Abdoulaye, reasoned that those who were most charismatic, most able to deliver effective testimonials would be the best advocates for getting more drug donations. Gradually, over time, this reasoning subtly introduced another outcome to the discussion groups: what was at stake was no longer "talking and sharing" but the identification of those whose continued health was most likely to translate into increased resources for the group. Sometimes the decision as to who should get the drugs was more directly pragmatic. Prioritizing access to drugs for beneficiaries who would facilitate the group's work in virtue of their professional position, for instance, as a customs officer, was an example of how groups reserved drugs for members they considered valuable.

Over time, those who were gifted communicators also became those with the most direct experience with the drugs. Echoing the experience of AIDS activism in the North, these patients were often the most knowledgeable people around when it came to their treatments. When treatment programs expanded after 2002 in the wake of scaled-up funding for HIV treatment in Africa, they were ideal candidates for assuming leadership roles in the new programs. Others exploited their connections differently. Kouamé managed to get a visa through his HIV contacts to go to France in 2002. Once there, he obtained a permit that allowed him to stay in France "on humanitarian grounds" because he had AIDS. But the permit did not allow him to work legally. When I last spoke to him in 2004, he lived in what was called a "therapeutic apartment" in Marseille that was provided by the French government for those who could not work because of a medical condition. But he was lonely there and talked of

starting a new AIDS group for other Africans who were in the same situation as he was.

The Institutionalization of Triage

For Abdoulaye and those that followed the same therapeutic journey, the improved health that came with antiretrovirals embodied the discourses of empowerment that had up to then been limited to a rhetoric of self-help. Affecting groups of people living with HIV, where many sickened and died, the advent of antiretrovirals meant that it was life itself that was now at stake – for them, and for those around them. Their ability to harness social resources to leverage access to the drugs translated into healthier bodies, a biological transcription of the discourse of empowerment. That skill, produced and tested in the disclosure laboratory of the discussion groups, triaged who would have access. For others, however, personal activism was less of a factor, particularly when they were able to obtain treatments through the handful of African pilot programs that began, somewhat piecemeal, in the late 1990s. These programs institutionalized triage under the cover of administrative procedures, medical criteria, and the need to ration scarce resources.

Launched in 1998, the first program in Africa that sought to provide the general population with access to ARVs was a joint initiative between the Ivoirian Ministry of Public Health and UNAIDS. The UNAIDS initiative was a pilot program coordinated by the agency to improve access to antiretrovirals (similar programs were launched in Uganda, Vietnam, and Chile). Its inception reflected the political pressures that HIV-positive Africans and their allies were putting on the agency. True to the rhetoric of empowerment, UNAIDS had cultivated a constituency of HIV-positive African "stakeholders." Simultaneously, people living with HIV across the continent were being trained using the self-disclosure technologies in the kind of workshops I described [earlier]. This subsequently turned these individuals into effective advocates for an emerging public of HIV-infected and HIV-affected Africans. UNAIDS hired an Irish consulting firm with close ties to the pharmaceuticals industry to negotiate reduced prices for antiretrovirals with pharmaceuticals firms and implement a distribution system in the country. The Ivoirian government pledged one million dollars to a drug-purchasing fund that would be used to subsidize the medicines. Interestingly, UNAIDS did not itself make any financial contribution to drug purchases. According to the officials I interviewed in 1999, this was "beyond their mandate" as a "coordinating and technical support agency."

The program got underway in late 1998, recruiting patients at the Infectious Diseases Service of the Treichville University Hospital, one of the city's TB control clinics, and at a handful of NGO outreach sites. The program quickly became embroiled in controversy. Several hundred people were treated through the initiative; however, the subsidies were insufficient to allow them to afford the recommended three-drug cocktail for more than a few months. Almost all of those who continued could afford only two-drug cocktails. As a result, the majority became resistant to these drugs.

Informants at the American Centers for Disease Control laboratory in Abidjan told me about the irregularity of follow-up, which meant that blood specimens were collected at more or less random intervals, rendering any kind of meaningful epidemiological analysis difficult. It was nonetheless evident in the clinical data I reviewed at the time when I worked in Abidjan that many patients were becoming resistant to the drugs. Prescribing physicians, selected from a variety of public health institutions across the city, had minimal training in using the drugs, limited to a three-day seminar conducted by a French AIDS NGO. I learned this through a workshop on ARV prescription I organized with colleagues in Abidjan in 1999.

The selection criteria for subsidies were never made clear. One group of activists, the splinter group ACT-UP Abidjan, had been quite vocal at the Geneva AIDS Conference in 1998 and was granted an unprecedented 95 percent discount. Its members were therefore able to afford the triple-therapy cocktail with this subsidy. The group ceased to be active on the local AIDS scene from then on, fueling rumors that they had been "bought" with the drug subsidy. The coordinator of the program explained to me that the generous subsidy had been an administrative error. It was never clear what role the drug distribution system set up by UNAIDS with the Irish consulting firm was to play. The prices that had been negotiated by the consulting firm were in fact going market rates, and as prices for antiretrovirals dropped through 2000 and 2001, the program was briefly locked into a higher price.

Complications Arise

By 1999 the program quickly became mired in an ongoing corruption scandal that erupted when several billion francs earmarked for health aid from the European Union went missing – a situation that resulted in the suspension of EU assistance to the country. As political and economic problems mounted, the national Public Health Pharmacy stopped getting reimbursed for its ARV purchases. As unpaid debt mounted, its ability to purchase other essential generic medicines was compromised, and discontinuation of ARV purchases ensued. This, combined with poor inventory management, led to repeated stock-outs of antiretroviral drugs. Thus, throughout 2001, the supply was patchy at best, meaning that almost all of those on the UNAIDS program had intermittent, partial therapy – a situation certain to generate drug resistance in the patients concerned. Although patients complained bitterly about the situation, little could be done.

In retrospect, it seems unreasonable to have expected Abidjan's crumbling public health facilities to shoulder the burden of such an ambitious program. Staff in hospitals and clinics complained that they were not compensated for the extra work that the program entailed. Furthermore, after launching the process, UNAIDS did not follow through as enthusiastically as it might have done with technical support to monitor drug procurement and distribution, as well as the training of physicians. However, it is still debated whether the program can be termed a failure – after all, many patients did obtain the antiretroviral drugs.

The fact that tens of millions suffer from AIDS means that hundreds of thousands die every year. This supports the claim that AIDS is a public health emergency, as the UNAIDS Initiative maintained, and emphasizes the need to develop rapid and at times improvised measures to get drugs to people. Yet, HIV is a slow and chronic condition, which means that the benefits of antiretroviral therapy do not occur until after at least several months of treatment. Thus, while the epidemic may be a political emergency, it is rarely an emergency in clinical terms. That is, unlike a heart attack (which requires treatment in a matter of minutes to save a life), HIV infection does not cause immediate death, and treatment does not immediately save a life; rather, it prolongs survival, as long as treatment continues. Paradoxically, it is HIV's relatively indolent but inevitably fatal course that enabled therapeutic citizenship to arise. This happened as people diagnosed with HIV transformed into activists who demanded access to treatment, articulating their claims based on the official declaration of a state of emergency. [...]

Emergence of Global Treatment Activism

In America and Europe, an important goal of AIDS activism was to obtain treatment for the disease by lobbying for research and speeding up the regulatory process in order to get "drugs into bodies." The result was a blending of activism, clinical research, and medical practice (S. Epstein 1996). Consequently, drug approval and distribution were fast-tracked. Over a decade after the advent of this biomedical activism in the North, the year 2000 marked a watershed in the global fight against AIDS and, arguably, in the broader issue of globalization and public health. The therapeutic revolution heralded by combination antiretroviral therapy catalyzed consciousness of the implications of global health inequities.

When awareness crystallized in 1996 that the drug cocktails were going to let people with HIV live, treating people with HIV in devel-oping countries was almost unthinkable – the cocktails cost upward of fifteen thousand dollars annually, required complex monitoring, and were clearly out of reach for poor countries with health budgets that amounted to no more than a few dollars per person. The issue began to surface in 1998, as symbolized by that year's World AIDS Conference's slogan: "Bridging the gap," a timid acknowledgment that "one world one hope," the slogan of the 1996 Vancouver conference, was certainly not the case. The decision to hold the 2000 conference in Durban, South Africa – the first time this conference had been held outside of a Northern country – catalyzed activists and media interest. Simultaneously, South African president Thabo Mbeki's public skepticism about whether HIV "caused" AIDS precipitated a media storm that focused attention on the catastrophic dimensions of the epidemic in Africa in general, and in South Africa in particular.

The result was unprecedented attention to the issue of access to HIV treatments and, increasingly, the state of public health in Africa and indeed throughout the developing world in the age of globalization. This visibility was largely due to the efforts of a transnational coalition of health and AIDS activist NGOs that had taken up the issue of access to HIV treatment in developing countries. This issue resonated with broader concerns – and coalitions – that sprang up around a number of issues posed by globalization, in effect making access to treatment – and the global intellectual property laws thought to impede this – a signature issue for the antiglobalization movement.

Spearheaded by a professional and effective campaign led by Médecins sans frontières, Health Action International, and the Consumer Project on Technology, public and political attention focused on the prohibitive cost of these drugs (Stolberg 2001). These NGOs had been active advocates for equity in access to health for many years but had gained little support for the issue in international policy circles or with the general public. The lack of access to AIDS medicines gave them a high-profile issue and, most importantly, political traction. Although AIDS activist groups in the North quickly rallied to the campaign, it is unclear why they did not join the bandwagon until a full five years after the therapeutic revolution took place. In 1998 ACT-UP Paris drew attention to the issue at the AIDS Conference in Geneva, but unfortunately, in this case the group's lack of professionalism and their inability to back up rhetoric with solid policy undermined their credibility.

The increasingly professionalized NGOs of the AIDS industry and multilateral organizations such as UNAIDS and WHO belatedly joined the call for greater access to treatment. This was a staggering shift for some organizations, which had historically been supportive of the international consensus on the protection of intellectual property and had consistently backed away from any measures that might threaten pharmaceutical industry profits (Peschard 2001). Claiming the mantle of treatment activism occasionally led to jarring scenes. Spokespeople who had vehemently argued against treatment for people with HIV were just as vehemently arguing the opposite a few months later. Privately, the emphasis on treatment worried the more established NGOs. They believed that treatment was too expensive and would take away money from prevention efforts – an understandable concern to the extent that they believed they were competing for money from a fixed AIDS "pot." People I spoke to who worked for multilateral organizations echoed these concerns.

As a result of the access-to-treatment campaign and the media attention it drew, through 2000 and 2001 a succession of declarations announced dramatic price reductions in the cost of these drugs. Drug prices collapsed once the Indian generic pharmaceuticals manufacturer, CIPLA, offered to make the nine antiretrovirals it produces in India available at cost to African countries. Subsequent price cuts by "big pharma," as the research and development (R&D) pharmaceutical industry that makes patented drugs is called, followed. In early 2008, GlaxoSmithKline, the world's largest pharmaceuticals firm, announced even further price cuts for drugs to the developing world.

Therapeutic Citizenship

I have elaborated on the notion of therapeutic citizenship in this chapter to show how

patients' sense that they were contributing to developing treatments for others motivated participation in the first clinical trials in the North, which led to the discovery of effective therapy. In Burkina Faso and Côte-d'Ivoire, clinical trials were a way of accessing some form of care where it was otherwise nonexistent. Clinical trials, in a sense, produced a population of people who knew they were HIV positive, even as the trials themselves included only a few and excluded many. This injustice triggered an initial AIDS activism that led many to join or set up groups of people living with HIV. Gradually, a trickle of supplies of the life-saving drugs was obtained by therapeutic pioneers like Abdoulaye, who used their contacts and their skills to make the necessary connections and set up the drug pipelines. These were years of triage, where painful decisions had to be made as to who would get the drugs and live, and who would not and as a result eventually die. It became clear that what was at stake was life itself. Triage was initially conducted on a micro scale, within small groups, before expanding to a broader level as pilot programs ramped up supplies that were, nevertheless, insufficient to meet demand. What emerged out of this experience was a powerful sense of rights – to treatment and, in effect, to life – and of responsibilities to others. That sense of responsibility was heightened by the experience of having lived through those early years of drug rationing and the profound conviction that no other person should die for want of drugs. These profoundly ethical predicaments shaped the therapeutic citizenship that emerged in places where other forms of citizenship could not be relied upon to secure life itself.

This therapeutic citizenship contrasts with other forms of "biological citizenship" that are also mediated by biomedical categories (Petryna 2002; Rose and Novas 2004). These authors use the term "biological citizenship" to index the way in which biomedical science and categories are used to categorize and manage individuals and adjudicate their claims for compensation; it also refers to how individuals act on their lives through biomedicine. Central to these notions of biological citizenship has been an understanding of the role of the state and other large, stable institutions as guarantors of health care and social security. Therapeutic citizenship is also conditioned by biological knowledge and biomedical practice. It differs from the "biological citizenship" described by Rose and Novas and Petryna in that it arises where large, stable institutions that can grant access to life-saving therapy are absent. It is a thin citizenship, solely focused on a particular disease. Since it is active in a setting where the disease may be the only way to get any of the material security one usually associates with citizenship, it takes on a particular poignancy.

Triage

Life-saving antiretroviral treatments arrived against a background of crushing poverty. Efforts to organize communities with HIV had put into place technologies used to foster self-help and elicit testimonials. With the arrival of ARVs, these practices were used for selecting those who would receive the treatments and those who would not. This is what I call "triage." Triage is an operation that differentiates people into groups based on specific criteria, such as those who require immediate medical attention from those who do not. We have seen how biomedical criteria occluded subtle forms of evaluating differences and selected people based on their perceived value to organizations, communities, or programs. The prioritizing of those who should be rescued and the forms of value they constituted resulted from dire material circumstances. The pragmatic assemblage of procedures and technologies not intended for this purpose was the rational response to these circumstances. This was life-boat ethics. Life itself was at stake. Tentative forms of solidarity and social relations, anchored by the biomedical predicament of being infected with HIV and shared through testimonials and confessional narratives, gave way to competition and an emerging therapeutic citizenship. Triage thus linked procedures for selecting people, the ways in which people seek to transform themselves, practices of "telling" the truth about the self, and the paradoxical affirmation of citizenship.

The politics of triage are not seamless. They occur at multiple levels: within groups and in practices that, despite the intentions behind their use, selected those that would receive treatment; between international agencies and governments; in policies that used selection criteria to ration treatment in the global arena; and in the political and economic structures that produce and enforce the global inequalities decried by global treatment activists. These are politics that are linked to social and biological practices of self-transformation; the former through narrative and experiential technologies of the self, the latter through pharmaceuticals. What unites them is a central concern with life itself. This concern institutes practices of triage in procedures that explicitly or implicitly separate those who will receive life-giving treatment from those who will not. It is a politics that has leveraged some meaningful political changes; but it remains, for the most part, turned toward the predicament of individual survival.

The notion of citizenship highlights the political dimensions of the patterns of resort that brought people diagnosed with HIV to self-help groups and the social relations that resulted. These trajectories were attempts to influence fate, to enroll others in one's destiny, and to shape how the future played out in the organization of communities around HIV. They recall Harris's prophetic movement and the voluntary associations during colonial times. The historical unfolding of Harris's prophetic movement and colonial voluntary associations revealed the potential for new technologies to unleash political energies.

NOTES

1   Epstein (1996); see also Brown (1997), Petryna (2002), Rose and Novas (2004), Heath, Rapp, and Taussig (2004).
2   Jones (1993), Washington (2006), Wendland (2008).
3   See Institute of Medicine, Board on Population Health and Public Health Practice (2005).
4   A normal T4 cell count is over 600; with less than 50 cells, patients are at high risk of serious opportunistic infections and death within the year.

REFERENCES

Brown, Michael P., 1997. *Replacing Citizenship: AIDS Activism and Radical Democracy.* New York: Guilford Press.

Dabis, François, Philippe Msellati, Nicolas Meda et al., for the DITRAME Study Group, 1999. Six-Month Efficacy, Tolerance, and Acceptability of a Short Regimen of Oral Zidovudine to Reduce Vertical Transmission of HIV in Breastfed Children in Côte-d'Ivoire and Burkina Faso: A Double-Blind Placebo-Controlled Multicentre Trial. *Lancet* 353(6): 786–793.

Epstein, Steve, 1996. *Impure Science: AIDS, Activism, and the Politics of Knowledge.* Berkeley: University of California Press.

Heath, Deborah, Rayna Rapp and Karen-Sue Taussig, 2004. Genetic Citizenship. In *Companion to the Anthropology of Politics,* David Nugent and Joan Vincent, eds. Oxford: Blackwell, pp. 152–167.

Institute of Medicine, Board on Population Health and Public Health Practice, 2005. *Review of the HIVNET 012 Perinatal HIV Prevention Study.* Washington: National Academies Press.

Jones, James H., 1993. *Bad Blood: The Tuskegee Syphilis Experiment,* rev. edn. New York: Free Press.

Lohse, Nicolai, Ann-Brit Eg Hansen, Gitte Pedersen et al., 2007. Survival of Persons with and without HIV Infection in Denmark, 1995–2005. *Annals of Internal Medicine* 146(2): 87–95.

Oliveira, Maria A., Elizabeth M. dos Santos and José M. Mello, 2001. AIDS, Activism and the Regulation of Clinical Trials in Brazil: Protocol 028. *Cad Saude Publica* 17(4): 863–875.

Peschard, Karine, 2001. Access to HIV Treatment from a Historical and Social Perspective. Honor's thesis, Department of Anthropology, McGill University.

Petryna, Adriana, 2002. *Life Exposed: Biological Citizens after Chernobyl.* Princeton: Princeton University Press.

Rose, Nikolas, 2006. *The Politics of Life Itself: Biomedicine, Power, and Subjectivity in the Twenty-First Century.* Princeton: Princeton University Press.

Rose, Nikolas, and Carlos Novas, 2004. Biological Citizenship. In *Global Assemblages: Technology, Politics, and Ethics as Anthropological Problems,* Aihwa Ong and Stephen J. Collier, eds. London: Blackwell, pp. 439–463.

Stolberg, Sheryl Gay, 2001. AIDS Groups Revive a Fight, and Themselves. *New York Times,* 20 March.

Washington, Harriet A., 2006. *Medical Apartheid: The Dark History of Medical Experimentation on Black Americans from Colonial Times to the Present.* New York: Harlem Moon Books.

Wendland, Claire L., 2008. Research, Therapy, and Bioethical Hegemony: The Controversy over Perinatal AZT Trials in Africa. *African Studies Review* 51(3): 1–23.

Wiktor, S. Z., I. Ikpini, J. M. Karon et al., 1999. Short-Course Oral Zidovudine for Prevention of Mother-to-Child Transmission of HIV-1 in Abidjan, Côte-d'Ivoire: A Randomised Trial. *Lancet* 35(6): 781–785.

II.2 Citizenship Beyond the Nation-State

Introduction

This section shows how anthropological work has broken open the easy assumption of congruity between citizenship-as-political-belonging and the nation-state. The first readings explore articulations of citizenship at different scales and in different spaces: diasporic citizenship (Siu); transnational citizenship (Glick Schiller); and citizenship regimes in non-state spaces (Feldman, on Gaza). The following two readings explore urban citizenship more thoroughly, examining local forms of belonging based on the city in São Paulo (Caldeira) and migration to the city in Beijing (Solinger).

Lok Siu explores the construction, contest and reaffirmation of diasporic identities through the deceptively banal institution of the beauty contest. Her ethnography weaves together questions of gender, language, the body and personal connections in affirming 'Chinese', 'Central American' and 'Panamanian' identity to a greater or lesser extent in the person of an individual beauty queen. The passion surrounding the final judgement of who is Queen of the Chinese Colony reveals the contestation between these different elements of identity, all available to diasporic Chinese citizens in Panama. Nina Glick Schiller proposes the concept of the 'transborder

citizen', who 'claims and acts on a relationship to more than one government', utilizing the analytical trope of legal pluralism to explore the transnational practices of citizenship that have developed in US-Haiti and the city of Halle in East Germany. She shows the importance of both the legal regime and matters of cultural and social citizenship for how we understand the experience of transborder citizens. Ilana Feldman's chapter further complicates the picture, by examining a stateless political community that has been created as such through an international legal and political regime that has largely ignored the daily experience of its citizens. She illustrates the importance of humanitarian actors in the constitution of membership or citizenship of the non-state of Gaza; and along the way shows how longstanding some supposedly anomalous citizenship regimes can become.

Urban life is a crucial site of citizenship practice in three senses: first, as space wherein (national) citizenship action often takes place, second, as an object for attempts to change citizenship formations, and third, where the city itself is the primary political community of its citizens. The last two chapters of this section explore all three, although with a focus

The Anthropology of Citizenship: A Reader, First Edition. Edited by Sian Lazar.
© 2013 John Wiley & Sons, Inc. Published 2013 by John Wiley & Sons, Inc.

on the latter two. Nikolas Rose (2000) has argued that the city is the space where projects of governmentality – so, top-down projects of citizenship – are mostly articulated, especially through the 'ethical space' of the community. Teresa Caldeira explores in detail one of these ethical urban spaces in São Paulo, exploring the ambiguities of changes in urban form and their relationship to democratic and undemocratic political and social praxis. Dorothy Solinger's chapter approaches citizenship practice as the practice of making a life in the city, especially for rural–urban migrants. Her chapter illustrates the complex interaction between making a living and struggling for services, including legal accommodation as key sites for the struggle for citizenship, and the importance of local-level political organizations of both elites and ordinary citizens in those processes of recognition.

SUGGESTIONS FOR FURTHER READING

Supra-national or transnational citizenship regimes

Ferme, Marianne, 2004. Deterritorialized citizenship and the resonances of the Sierra Leonean state. In *Anthropology in the Margins of the State*, V. Das and D. Poole, eds. Santa Fe: SAR Press, pp. 81–116.

Fox, Jonathan, 2005. Unpacking 'transnational citizenship'. *Annual Review of Political Science* 8(1): 171–201.

Ong, Aihwa, 1999. *Flexible Citizenship: The Cultural Logics of Transnationality*. Durham, North Carolina: Duke University Press.

Tsing, Anna Lowenhaupt, 2005. *Friction: An Ethnography of Global Connection*. Princeton, New Jersey: Princeton University Press.

Urban citizenship

Holston, James, 2001. Urban citizenship and globalization. In *Global City-Regions*, A. J. Scott, ed. New York: Oxford University Press, pp. 325–348.

Holston, James, 2008. *Insurgent Citizenship: Disjunctions of Democracy and Modernity in Brazil*. Princeton, New Jersey: Princeton University Press.

Holston, James, and Arjun Appadurai, 1999. *Cities and Citizenship*. Durham, North Carolina: Duke University Press.

Isin, Engin, 2007. City.state: critique of scalar thought. *Citizenship Studies* 11(2): 211–228.

Isin, Engin, and Ebru Ustundag, 2008. Wills, deeds, acts: women's civic gift-giving in Ottoman Istanbul. *Gender, Place and Culture* 15(5): 519–532.

Lazar, Sian, 2008. *El Alto, Rebel City: Self and Citizenship in Andean Bolivia*. Durham, North Carolina: Duke University Press.

Rose, Nikolas, 2000. Governing cities, governing citizens. In *Democracy, Citizenship and the Global City*, E. Isin, ed. London: Routledge, pp. 95–109.

Sargeson, Sally, and Yu Song, 2010. Land expropriation and the gender politics of citizenship in the urban frontier. *China Journal* (64): 19–45.

Standing, Guy, 2009. *Work after Globalization: Building Occupational Citizenship*. Cheltenham: Edward Elgar.

Rural citizenship

Pandian, Anand, 2009. *Crooked Stalks: Cultivating Virtue in South India*. Durham, North Carolina: Duke University Press.

Shah, Alpa, 2007. Keeping the state away: democracy, politics and imaginations of the state in India's Jharkhand. *Journal of the Royal Anthropological Institute* 13(1): 129–145.

Wittman, Hannah, 2009. Reworking the metabolic rift: la via campesina, agrarian citizenship, and food sovereignty. *Journal of Peasant Studies* 36(4): 805–826.

18

The Queen of the Chinese Colony

Contesting Nationalism, En-Gendering Diaspora, 2005

Lok C. D. Siu

All the beauty contestants had performed their roles brilliantly – parading gracefully across the stage several times, modeling their national dresses and variations of traditional Chinese gowns, and performing their respective national dances. They had introduced themselves in Spanish and sometimes in Cantonese and/or Mandarin. Finally, they had offered their eloquent responses to the questions asked by the master of ceremonies. The audience of diasporic Chinese from Central America and Panama anxiously waited to hear the final decision of the judges.

Half an hour went by, then an hour, then two. The banquet hall was by now only half full, with about a hundred restless people energized by gossip and suspicion. Why were they taking so long? What was the problem? Finally, the MC took the podium and proclaimed Miss Honduras 1996's "Reina de la Colonia China" (Queen of the Chinese Colony). But before Miss Honduras could reach the stage, the vice president of the Convención de Asociaciones Chinas de Centroamérica y Panamá (Convention of Chinese Associations of Central America and Panama) interjected and announced that there had been a mistake – that, in fact, Miss Costa Rica was the winner, not Miss Honduras.

The audience was confused. They looked around at one another, not knowing how to react, wondering what to make of what had just happened. Judging from the looks on their faces, I could see this was not a common outcome, that something had clearly gone wrong.

Then, suddenly, out of this confused silence, a man in his sixties marched onto the stage. The contrast of his angrily flushed face with his graying hair and formal dark gray suit attracted the crowd's rapt attention. Without a moment's hesitation, his body rose as if preparing for battle, and he unleashed a passionate tirade denouncing what had just happened: "This event is supposed to be a joyous celebration for all those attending this convention. Why do you newcomers insist on betraying the spirit of this convention and break the community in this way?"

Lok C. D. Siu, The Queen of the Chinese Colony: contesting nationalism, en-gendering diaspora. In *Memories of a Future Home: Diasporic Citizenship of Chinese in Panama* (Stanford, California: Stanford University Press, 2005), pp. 54–85.

The Anthropology of Citizenship: A Reader, First Edition. Edited by Sian Lazar.

As reflected in this scene, the annual contest for the "Queen of the Chinese Colony" is not just about beauty, femininity, or friendly competition. The fact that the contest evokes such passionate interest suggests that other issues are at stake. As the anthropologists Colleen Ballerino Cohen, Richard Wilk, and Beverly Stoeltje have argued, "Beauty contests are places where cultural meanings are produced, consumed, and rejected, where local and global, ethnic and national, national and international cultures, and structures of power are engaged in their most trivial but vital aspects" (Cohen *et al.* 1996, 8). Wilk proposes that, as sites where multiple struggles for power and representation are publicly debated, beauty contests mediate difference in order to produce a "structure of common difference" and suggests that "the process of judging beauty is always a process of negotiation, a process of reconciling difference or at least accepting the terms of the disagreement" (Wilk 1996, 117).

I want to extend Wilk's argument further by asserting that not only can this "structure of common difference" be created through beauty contests but, more important here, diasporic communities contest, forge, and reaffirm their identities through gender itself. Moreover, I argue that the contest over who is to be the Queen of the Chinese Colony is a microcosm of broader issues at play among diasporic Chinese in Central America and Panama. Indeed, what is at stake in this beauty contest is the struggle for diasporic citizenship, or for full belonging within the diaspora. By mediating debates about diasporic Chinese femininity, the contest seeks to establish the criteria for idealized diasporic subjectivity, criteria against which belonging in the diaspora is measured. With the beauty contestants embodying and performing specific ways of being diasporic Chinese, their divergent representations not only reflect the wide spectrum of diasporic Chinese in this region but also reveal and disrupt hegemonic constructions of what it means to be "Chinese" and "Central American" or "Panamanian." Furthermore, the contest provides a window onto the regional differences among diasporic Chinese communities, thereby disrupting the simple binary formula of "nation of residence" and "homeland" in understanding diaspora. The contestants' varied presentations and performances reflect the tension not only between their emplacement in specific local contexts and their ongoing engagement with Chineseness but also between their national difference and shared regional affiliation. Overall, their performance helps mediate debates of belonging and cultural identity, and the elected queen is supposed to become the symbol and representative of the Chinese diaspora.

But what happens when there is no agreement, or even acceptance of the terms of disagreement, as in the case I describe above? What does this rupture, or disputed result of the beauty contest, tell us about the tensions and contradictions within the diaspora, and the cultural politics of diaspora? Furthermore, what does it tell us about the nature of diaspora that makes diasporic identifications so contingent and tenuous, yet so provocative and powerful? The ensuing debates about who should be queen and why reveal not only the politics of belonging within the diaspora, but also the shifts in identifications among diasporic Chinese. The question of belonging in diaspora is highly contested and, as we shall see, contingent on local-transnational dynamics.

In the discussion that follows, I briefly outline the historical context of the Federation of Chinese Associations of Central America and Panama, the organization that sponsors the beauty contest and the annual convention, before returning to a more detailed discussion of the 1996 convention and its controversial beauty contest. The final section turns specifically to Panamanian Chinese and examines their interpretations and responses to these debates. By using gender as a category of analysis (Scott 1999) and taking the beauty contest as a focus, I examine how racial-cultural purity, migration, and homeland politics intersect in setting the terms of diasporic citizenship.

Transnational Networks and Diasporic Identifications

The Queen of the Chinese Colony beauty contest takes place at the annual Convention of Chinese Associations of Central America and Panama, which is hosted by the Federation of Chinese Associations of this region. Its participants include Chinese from Panama, Costa Rica, Nicaragua, Guatemala, Honduras, and El Salvador. This transnational organization was founded in 1965, amid intensifying regional instability, by the presidents of the six national Chinese associations of this region. Shortly after its founding, the association leaders requested financial help from the Republic of China (ROC) embassies in order to make the organization a permanent institution of the diaspora. Since then, the organization has become a joint venture between diasporic Chinese and the ROC government, solidifying both their sociopolitical ties and their symbolic ones.

According to the Chinese Panamanian Association's president, Alberto Lee, the Federation of Chinese Associations of Central America and Panama decided to host an annual convention that would bring together representatives of the six nation-based associations to discuss economic and political issues confronting their respective communities. The founders intended this organization to provide

additional resources and support for diasporic Chinese beyond what was available within the borders of their nation-states. For instance, during the Sandinista Revolution in Nicaragua, when diasporic Chinese who had supported the Somoza regime were being systematically captured and imprisoned, the organization raised funds and lobbied government officials on their behalf. As a result, a number of Chinese were able to escape to other parts of Central America. The organization has also provided relief funds for victims of natural disasters and scholarships for underprivileged Chinese.

Given that these Central American countries have been relatively poor and – until recently – politically volatile, it was understandable that diasporic Chinese of the region would pool their resources on a transnational scale to form a safety net for themselves. The fact that diasporic Chinese have experienced long histories of persecution in Central America (and throughout the world), and the realization that they could not rely on China

Figure 18.1 *1996 Chinese of Central America and Panama Beauty Pageant. From left, reigning queen and contestants in the following country order: Panama, Guatemala, Costa Rica, El Salvador, Nicaragua, Honduras. Photograph by author.*

for protection, further motivated the formation
of the organization to help ensure their safety
and survival.

It is also important to remember that there
is not a simple binary relationship between the
nation-state and the diaspora. On the contrary,
diasporas are not only embedded in the system
of nation-states but also partially constituted
by the conditions within those nation-states. In
other words, the marginalization of diasporic
Chinese, manifested in their lack of cultural
and legal-political acceptance in Central
America and Panama, has everything to do
with their desire to maintain ties with a distant
"homeland" and to form transnational organizations that create "safe spaces" and a sense of
community. Indeed, their inability to participate as full citizens of the nation-state has
inspired many to participate in diasporic
politics, where their voice is heard and their
presence matters.

[...]

The Beauty Contest: Performing Nation/Performing Diaspora

Throughout the four days of the convention,
the beauty contestants were at their best. They
knew all too well that their performance
began the moment they arrived and that they
were judged not only on their on-stage
presence but also on their overall demeanor
and comportment throughout the convention.
Since the beauty contest took place during the
last dinner banquet, people were by then
already familiar with the contestants, and
many had chosen their favorite. What follows
is a discussion of the various categories of the
beauty context, with a particular focus on the
two contested queens, Miss Costa Rica and
Miss Honduras, and their different strengths
in the "national dance" and "self-introduc-
tion" categories. As the contestants performed, not only did they present hegemonic
constructions of "Central American/
Panamanian-ness" and "Chineseness," they
also disrupted them by revealing the tensions
and contradictions inherent in diasporic subjectivities. Moreover, their very embodiment
of difference within the diaspora also incited

discussions of idealized diasporic subjectivity,
unveiling in public debate competing notions
of diasporic citizenship.

The beauty contest was divided into four
categories. The contest began with the contestants adorned in their respective national
dresses.[1] Carrying their respective national
flags and marching to their national anthems,
the contestants slowly entered the banquet
room and walked onto the stage. The reigning
queen, who also happened to be my cousin
from Guatemala, marched with the contestants;
but instead of wearing her national dress, she
wore the traditional Chinese cheongsam and
marched to the ROC national anthem. The
symbolism of her Chinese dress in contrast to
the national dresses worn by the contestants
encapsulates the process by which the winner
of the beauty contest shifts from representing
the nation to representing the Chinese diaspora
(and its connection to the Chinese homeland).
The beauty contest in this sense serves to
abstract the differences between the national
communities and reconstitutes them into a
queen whose image emphasizes a shared
Chinese identity. Once all the contestants and
the queen were on stage, the audience
applauded, and the two masters of ceremony
briefly introduced the contestants in Mandarin
and Cantonese.

Following this segment, the contestants
took turns performing their respective national
dances. While a couple of the national dances
used indigenous dance forms popularized as
official representations of national culture, the
others were drawn from colonial contexts.
This category of performance underscored
diasporic identification with the nation of
residence. Yet, even as the contestants performed these dances, they inherently disrupted
the very message they sought to convey – that
of homogenizing the nation. Their embodiment
of racialized difference articulated their
disidentification with the nation. José Muñoz
defines disidentification as the process of
recycling and rethinking encoded meaning,
stating that disidentification "scrambles and
reconstructs the encoded message of a cultural
text in a fashion that both exposes the encoded
message's universalizing and exclusionary
machinations and recircuits its workings to

account for, include, and empower minority identities and identifications" (1999, 31). As the contestants performed their national dances, they not only made visible the exclusionary practices that continually denied their right to full citizenship but also simultaneously inserted themselves and insisted on their belonging.

In this category, Miss Honduras definitely outperformed her competitors. In general, the dance routines tended to be rather repetitive, but Miss Honduras displayed extraordinary originality and poise. Carrying a basket of roses, she sang along with the music and danced with ease and grace, prancing around the stage, rippling her dress and tossing roses into the audience. Her supporters responded happily, clapping, chanting her name, and catching the roses she threw to them. Without any sign of exhaustion or tentativeness, she exhibited a playfulness and ease with the dance steps that projected a sense of complete "at-home-ness."

Miss Costa Rica was less adept. With her eyes fixed on her feet, she seemed overly concerned with the dance steps, reflecting a lack of skill and confidence. Her steps seemed more prepared, more tentative, as if she were performing them by rote. Focusing on her dance steps, she was unable to engage the audience, and near the end of her performance, one could see the exhaustion in her face and her relief as the music came to an end. The two juxtaposed performances illustrated the contestants' contrasting degrees of expertise and comfort. As one audience member commented, "Miss Honduras looked comfortable ... as if she owned [the dance] ... Miss Costa, on the other hand, needed more practice." If this category were meant to establish one's relationship with the nation, Miss Honduras seemed to embody Honduran-ness, whereas Miss Costa Rica showed far less familiarity with her national identity.

The third category, the "self-introductions," featured the contestants in cheongsams. With Chinese music playing in the background, the contestants glided elegantly across the stage and introduced themselves in whatever languages they chose. Coming after the national dance category, this segment showcased performances of Chineseness. Overall, the rhythm and pace were slower; the contestants assumed a more reserved and more subtly coquettish demeanor. In contrast to the dance category, this one focused on overall comportment, gestures, and speech. It was in the stylized movements (the tilt of one's head, the swaying of hips and arms, the poses one strikes) and ways of presenting oneself (dress, hair, make-up, intonations, content and pattern of speech) that people discussed and judged their Chineseness. The seemingly simple act of walking across the stage took on immense meaning. According to my cousin, the reigning queen, the walk itself required arduous practice. She explained, "I watched videos of Hong Kong pageants to see how the women moved, walked with books on my head to check my balance. And once I learned the actual movements, I had to learn to be natural doing it." The subtle movements of the arms, hips, hands, and face, along with particular ways of looking and smiling all played a role in presenting a particular style of feminine sexuality. In their introductions, most of the contestants spoke in Spanish and Cantonese, but a couple of them also spoke in Mandarin. The use of different languages and the information they included and excluded all reflected their strategies of self-representation (cf. Besnier 2002).

Miss Costa Rica, dressed in a classic cheongsam, presented an archetypical image of idealized Chinese femininity. Slender, tall, with her hair tied in a bun and a few loose strands playing around her cheeks, she displayed an elegant, classic, and reserved femininity that clearly captivated the immigrant Chinese in the audience. Miss Honduras, with more voluptuous curves and wearing a less popular variation of the cheongsam, was less able to reproduce the conventional ideal of Chinese femininity. Despite this disadvantage, her performance was no less powerful.

Most contestants introduced themselves in Spanish and spoke at least a few words in Cantonese. Not surprisingly, since most were Latin American-born and/or raised, all of them spoke perfect Spanish. In the area of Chinese-language competency, Miss Costa Rica had an advantage. She spoke fluent Cantonese and Mandarin, while it was clear that the others had learned specific phrases for the purpose of the contest. When introducing herself, Miss Costa Rica spoke in Spanish, then repeated herself in both Cantonese and Mandarin. She had firm control of all three languages, coming across as truly multilingual. Miss Honduras, who clearly did not speak any Chinese, used her fan as a prop from which she read phonically a few words in Mandarin. As she struggled with pronunciation, audience members reacted with either mocking smiles or enthusiastic applause. A number of her supporters whistled, clapped, and shouted her name in support. To most Chinese speakers, her attempt was almost indecipherable. To monolingual Spanish speakers, her performance was courageous and commendable. In the intersubjective process between performance and reception, her sincere attempt to speak Chinese was interpreted as either mimicry or parody, as either "trying to be but not quite succeeding" or as criticizing and subverting the absurd notion that equated *being* Chinese with *speaking* Chinese. In my conversations with various audience members, I learned that most Chinese of the immigrant generation interpreted her attempt as an honest but failed effort, while most Panamanian-born Chinese saw it as a courageous act of subtle critique. In speaking with Miss Honduras after the contest, she commented, "I did what I could, what I was expected to do, but I am who I am, and there is nothing I can do to change that. People will judge me accordingly." Keenly aware of the judges' expectations, Miss Honduras understood both the possibilities and limits of performance. She knew all too well that one's socialization and embodiment also play a role in the contest.

Miss Honduras's performance highlighted the long-standing divide between immigrant Chinese speakers and Latin American-born Spanish speakers and enabled the latter to express openly their collective rejection of marginalization based on linguistic ability. As one audience member resentfully remarked, "Immigrant Chinese-speaking men dominate the leadership of this organization. They are the gatekeepers of the Chinese colony and determine the agendas and set the criteria of belonging in the diaspora. It is time to change

that." Clearly, Miss Honduras's insistence on speaking Chinese, however distorted it was, disrupted the dominant expectation that all contestants (and more generally, all diasporic Chinese) *should* speak Chinese with some degree of mastery. Her performance articulated disidentification. It created a break, a rupture, in representations of diasporic Chineseness, thereby allowing non-Chinese-speaking diasporic subjects to vocalize and confront the unspoken and unacknowledged marginalizing practices of the diasporic leadership. Indeed, diasporic formations are in part produced in response to the exclusionary practices of nation-states. Yet, in practice, diasporas often generate their own set of exclusions. In this particular case, the close relationship between diasporic Chinese and the ROC government undoubtedly shapes the manner in which idealized diasporic subjectivity is formulated and reproduced. Remarkably present throughout the contest, and the convention more generally, is the insistence on strong Chinese identifications, the ability to speak Chinese being the most significant of these. Speaking Chinese is also crucial for relations with the ROC, whose representatives are primarily monolingual Chinese speakers. The fact that business meetings in the annual conventions are conducted only in Mandarin and Cantonese further substantiates the importance of Chinese in sustaining diasporic communication and relations with the ROC.

The final segment of the pageant featured the contestants in Western-style evening gowns, and they were asked one question each, to which they gave impromptu answers. The questions varied: Who is your female role model? What would you say to your fellow contestants if you were to win the contest? Which of the three – intelligence, wealth, beauty – is the most important to you, and why? Most of the contestants answered in Spanish only. In 1996, the two exceptions were Miss Costa Rica, who answered first in Cantonese and then in Spanish, and Miss Honduras, who answered in Spanish and then in English. By displaying their ability to speak at least two languages, they performed and simultaneously affirmed the value of biculturalism. Miss Costa Rica reemphasized her ability to speak Cantonese and Spanish, and Miss Honduras surprised the audience with English. When I asked her later why she had answered in English, she responded, "I really wanted the judges to hear what I have to say. I know that some of them, especially the Taiwanese representatives, don't speak Spanish,[2] so I thought it would be a good idea for me to answer in English. I know most of them speak at least some English. Also, I wanted to show the judges that I can speak a language other than Spanish. I don't speak Chinese, but English has to count for something. I mean, just because I don't speak Chinese doesn't mean that I am closed-minded or provincial." While knowing that speaking Chinese is a quality valued in this competition, Miss Honduras also understood the significance of communication, and her strategic performance of English questioned the qualities associated with diasporic Chineseness.

In play here were the complexities of geopolitics. By speaking English, Miss Honduras subtly called attention to the role of American imperialism as the basis for relations between the ROC and Central America and Panama. America's Cold War campaign from the 1950s to the 1980s not only made impossible a mainland Chinese presence in this region but, in fact, encouraged and nurtured ROC relations with it and also with the diasporic Chinese there. While it may be difficult to assess Miss Honduras's intentions, her comment at the end of the contest reflects her understanding of politics in culture: "We [the beauty contestants] are mere pawns in their game of politics. It does not matter who we are or what we do. It's all about them and their political agendas." Succinctly, she unveils the beauty contest as a platform for political posturing and maneuvering.

Embodied Difference: Miss Costa Rica and Miss Honduras

The contestants' contrasting strengths in the beauty contest, conveying their degrees of cultural identification with the nation and Chineseness, were reinforced by their identity construction. Miss Costa Rica and Miss Honduras exemplified very different ways of being diasporic Chinese. Miss Costa Rica was born in mainland China and immigrated to Costa Rica about ten years ago. Both her parents are Chinese from the People's Republic. She speaks fluent Mandarin, Cantonese, and Spanish. Given these characteristics, she was considered the "most Chinese," both in racial and cultural terms. Light-skinned, svelte, and the tallest of all the contestants, she reminded me of a Hong Kong movie star. Her appearance, gestures, and mannerisms epitomized Chinese cosmopolitanism: her speech pattern and language abilities reflected a sense of worldliness, her choice of contemporary classic styles of dress marked her fashion consciousness, and her subtle yet effective make-up replicated contemporary Hong Kong aesthetics. She projected a reserved, slightly aloof aura of refinement and elegance. By way of gossip, I was told that her father has strong ties with the Taiwanese in Costa Rica, and a few people complained that she seemed arrogant because she did not mingle or "hang out" with the other participants in the convention. In her defense, however, another person responded that she has very protective, "traditional" parents and that she is not allowed to go out at night.

Miss Honduras is almost the polar opposite of Miss Costa Rica on the spectrum of Chinese Central Americans. She was born in Honduras and is racially mixed, her father being Chinese and her mother *mestiza* Honduran. Her facial features are unmistakably *mestiza*, and her shoulder-length brown hair is slightly wavy. Her style of dress was distinctively Latin American. Her outfits were vibrant in color and snug-fitting, so that they accentuated her feminine curves. She exuded a certain sensuality, confidence, and maturity that the other contestants had not yet developed. There was a quality of openness, warmth, and sincerity about her. She spoke neither Cantonese nor Mandarin but was fluent in Spanish and had a firm grasp of English. Furthermore, she was eloquent, thoughtful, and reflexive, qualities that came across not only in casual conversation but also throughout the beauty contest. She was very popular among her peers, who generally described her as friendly, warm, outgoing, and witty.

With the two women projecting such contrasting identities, one may ask how the winner could possibly have been in dispute? Unless, of course, there was little consensus to begin with, and, as a result, the votes were extremely polarized, with one group in favor of Miss Costa Rica and the other in support of Miss Honduras.

What is at stake in the beauty contest involves not only who gets to represent the Chinese diaspora, but also what qualities are deemed to be idealized characteristics of that diaspora. Which of the women best embodies Chinese Central American beauty, femininity, and community? What characteristics, standards, and values are being projected, affirmed, and reinforced? That the two winners occupy two extremes of the Chinese diasporic spectrum is hardly accidental. Chineseness, after all, is a homogenizing label whose meanings are multiple and constantly shifting (Ang 1994, 5). To understand the concerns negotiated on stage, I suggest we examine the larger debates among diasporic Chinese in this region. First, however, I want to highlight the tensions and contradictions inherent in diasporic formations and, more specifically, in the Chinese diaspora, in hopes that this may help clarify the persistence of certain irreconcilable struggles for diasporic citizenship.

Between "Here" and "There": Irreconcilable Tensions in Diaspora

In its simplest formulation, diaspora refers to the condition of a people who share a common "homeland," real or imagined, and who are dispersed throughout the world, either by force or by choice. Diaspora most commonly refers to "the doubled relationship or dual loyalty ... to two places – their connections to the space they currently occupy and their continuing involvement with 'back home'" (Lavie and Swedenburg 1996, 15). It is precisely this dual relationship, this tension between "where you are at" versus "where you are from" (Gilroy 1990; Hall 1990; Ang 2001) that constitutes the condition and the idea of diaspora and gives diasporic identifications the potential to be empowering as well as

disempowering. In a sense, diaspora embodies a third space where the "here and there," "now and back then" coexist and engage in constant negotiation, and it is within this time-space continuum that diasporic subjects interpret their history, position themselves, and construct their identity.

The Chinese diaspora has its distinct set of histories and complex relations with the Chinese "homeland." Three particular factors – China's immense presence in the global political economy, China's image as the "Other" in the Western imagination, and the symbolic construction of China as the cultural and geographical core of "Chinese identity" – together exercise an extraordinary pull on diasporic Chinese to always look to China for identity and a sense of belonging (Ang 1994). While such identification can provide a sense of pride and serve as a tool for empowerment, it also reconfirms the "impurity," the "lack," and/or the "in-authenticity" of diasporic Chinese. Measuring "Chineseness" by one's imagination and romanticization of China and at the same time recognizing the cultural difference that is informed by one's current location fuels the debates over what constitutes "Chineseness" in the diaspora. Furthermore, the situation for diasporic Chinese is rendered more complicated by the existence of two political entities – the PRC and the ROC – espousing two different official narratives and imaginaries of the Chinese nation-state and "homeland." (The conflict between the PRC and Taiwan, not explicitly apparent in this chapter, became much more significant after 1996.)

Most diaspora literature has focused on the predicament of trying to maintain dual relations with the nation of residence and the homeland (Louie 2004; Axel 2001; Raj 2003), with few exceptions.[3] In the case of diasporic Chinese, while it is certainly true that both the Chinese homeland and the nation of residence exert tremendous cultural-political influence, it is also important to recognize the interactions and relations among diasporic communities. Moreover, diasporic Chinese are not a homogenous group; distinctions in status and influence are evident within the diaspora (Tu 1994). As nation-based collectivities, each group's place of residence tends to determine its relative power in the diaspora. For instance, diasporic Chinese in the United States wield more influence and have higher status than those in Ecuador or Kenya simply because the United States is a wealthier and more powerful nation, which in turn lends diasporic Chinese living there more weight within the larger diaspora. As shown in this chapter, nationality serves as a primary identifier of difference among diasporic Chinese, because people are associated with their countries of residence. Nowhere is this clearer than in the beauty contest, where contestants represent and perform their national differences. As mentioned earlier, the convention of Chinese Associations in Central America and Panama facilitates social ties and intimate relations that the Chinese across this region sustain and actively seek to reproduce. In recognizing these lateral relationships between diasporic communities, however, I also want to underscore their unequal power relations vis-à-vis one another. Heterogeneity and unevenness within diasporas have not received sufficient attention; those of us engaged in diaspora studies would do well to shift our analysis to include conversations and interactions among diasporic subjects across national – as well as class, racial, gender, and generation – groupings.

National Differences and Inequalities within the Diaspora

Despite their common colonial histories and geographical proximity, Panama and these Central American countries each confront very different political-economic conditions. Consequently, in spite of their common ethnic status in this region, the Chinese communities have developed in contrasting ways. To a large extent, the beauty contestants reflected certain national differences. Just as Miss Honduras, Miss Nicaragua, and Miss Guatemala were Central American-born, racially mixed, and limited in their Chinese-speaking abilities, so are the majority of Chinese youth in these countries. Chinese immigration to El Salvador, Honduras, Nicaragua, and Guatemala has not been significant in the past few decades due to

these countries' volatile political and economic situations. Therefore, the Chinese population in these countries has dwindled, with more emigration from than immigration to these countries. Furthermore, Chinese cultural practices and institutions such as Chinese-language schools, Buddhist temples, and native place associations have become almost obsolete. The leadership of the Chinese associations of Honduras and Nicaragua is now composed mostly of Spanish-speaking, Central American–born Chinese. In contrast, Chinese immigration to Panama and Costa Rica has increased tremendously in recent decades. While the influx of Chinese immigrants to Costa Rica has largely been from Taiwan, most of Panama's immigrants are from the southern region of mainland China.

These differences are not free of power asymmetries. For one thing, all the formal meetings at the convention are held in Mandarin and Cantonese. This is so largely because the Taiwanese delegates from the Overseas Chinese Affairs Office do not speak Spanish. Also, members of the immigrant generation often feel more comfortable speaking Cantonese or Mandarin than Spanish. Hence, while these meetings can be empowering experiences for Chinese immigrants, they often exclude the non-Chinese-speaking population from participating. Let me draw on one ethnographic example to illustrate this point.

The official meetings of the Convention I attended were held in the following manner. The presiding officer would read an item of discussion in Mandarin, followed by open discussion in either Mandarin or Cantonese. After these discussions, the membership would vote. Throughout the meeting, the most outspoken members were from Panama, Costa Rica, and Guatemala. The Nicaraguan delegation sat there restlessly, looking around the room as representatives from different countries stood up and offered their opinions. It became clear that none of the Chinese Nicaraguans could understand the discussion. They were completely lost, unable to participate in any real way. The presiding officers, who had known about this problem, chose not to address it. Instead, a trilingual Chinese Panamanian, noticing the situation, walked over to the Chinese Nicaraguans and began translating for them.

Language has always been a central problematic in the politics of diaspora. Ien Ang argues that her inability to speak Chinese has become "an existential condition that goes beyond the particularities of an arbitrary personal history. It is a condition that has been hegemonically constructed as a lack, a sign of loss of 'authenticity'" (Ang 1994, 11). The privileging of Chinese languages in the official meetings of the Convention clearly reinscribes certain characteristics and even certain peoples as more "Chinese" and therefore more legitimate as participants than others. The Chinese Nicaraguan predicament also reminds us to be attentive to unequal power relations between the different Chinese communities in Central America and Panama vis-à-vis the larger diasporic organization. Although Chinese Nicaraguans are part of this network, they by no means participate to the same extent, with as much influence, as Chinese Panamanians or Chinese Costa Ricans, who are often bilingual. Similarly, the beauty contestants confront these same criteria for being diasporic Chinese. It is not surprising, then, that all the contestants attempted to say at least a few words in Chinese, with, of course, varying degrees of success. Clearly, the ability to speak Chinese is a salient factor in determining the level of participation in this diasporic organization, and more specifically, in gaining more leverage in the politics of diaspora.

Immigration and Competing Claims of Belonging

Aside from national differences, one of the most pronounced divisions within these communities, especially in Costa Rica and Panama, is between the recent immigrants, on the one hand, and the earlier immigrants and their descendants, on the other. It is important, moreover, to note that the category of "recent immigrants" is different in Costa Rica than in Panama. The controversy over the crowning of the queen brings these overlapping debates to the surface, as an examination of the

Panamanian response to the pageant's outcome makes clear.

Ricardo, a Panamanian-born Chinese in his forties who had been attending these conventions for the past twenty years, offered this analysis of the 1996 beauty contest:

Everyone wanted Miss Honduras to win. That was the talk around town the next morning. It's not that they felt pity [for her for what had happened], but it was the right thing to do. It has always been that a full Chinese, a Chinese-speaking girl, has the preference. In this case, that was Miss Costa Rica. Further[more], the vice president of the Costa Rican association, the one who organized the event, is Taiwanese. He leaned toward a more traditional Chinese outlook, so to speak. Behind all this, there is an old infight between the old [immigrants] and the new [immigrants] in Costa Rica, as usual in all [of] Central America. The new are the Taiwanese and the old, well, are the old established [Cantonese] folks. In Panama, the story is different. The new are the newcomers from mainland China, who consist mostly of people who work in the *tienditas* [little stores], while the old are the established old-timers and their Central American–born descendants, who are not interested in this kind of infighting. [The old immigrants and their children] are the ones who wanted Miss Honduras to win.

Ricardo was careful to point out that in Costa Rica, the recent immigrants are mostly Taiwanese, while in Panama, they are mainland Chinese who work in or own small stores. However, in the context of this Convention, both the Taiwanese and the store-owning mainland Chinese are categorized together as "recent immigrants" and are defined in opposition to the old immigrants and their Central American–born descendants.

A recent wave of Chinese immigrants to Panama in the 1980s has dramatically changed the demography of the Chinese population there, such that the recent immigrants now constitute about half of the total Chinese population in Panama. The two groups are characterized as complete opposites. While the old "Chinese Colony" (which includes the well-established Chinese immigrants and their descendants) are characterized as respectable, educated, and law-abiding citizens of Panama, the recent immigrants are portrayed as poor, uneducated, dirty, untrustworthy, and sometimes even criminal.

These negative images of recent Chinese immigrants are constructed alongside several other discourses, which may help elucidate how these images come into being and how the divisions between the immigrants and the Chinese colony are actualized and solidified. First, this group of newer arrivals is criminalized by being characterized as illegal immigrants. Shortly after the arrest of Manuel Noriega in 1990, the incoming government publicly announced that Noriega's military regime had sold Panamanian travel visas and passports to these immigrants. This information was then used to criminalize the immigrants, who quickly became scapegoats of Panamanian nationalism after the US invasion. Second, the narrative of the immigrant-as-victim was set against the image of the established-Chinese-as-victimizer. A series of sensational newspaper articles showed that many recent immigrants came as either short-term contract laborers or as wage workers who took on low-paying jobs as maids, caretakers, and cooks for established Chinese. Immigrants and established Chinese were thus pitted against one another as victims and victimizers respectively. Finally, recent immigrants were distinguished from the "Chinese Colony" along explicitly ideological lines, such that these immigrants were described as "communist Chinese," as if their undesirable behaviors were somehow inherently communist. These "communist Chinese" were deemed "a different breed of Chinese altogether," I was told repeatedly. The fact that many of the earlier immigrants and their families had been persecuted during the communist revolution in China partially contributes to their deep antagonism toward the recent immigrants, whom they associate with the communist regime. Another factor has to do with US imperialism and its use of Cold War anticommunist rhetoric to justify its military presence and political repression throughout this region. Although "communism" and the "Cold War" may not exist in those same terms today, in this age of so-called

globalization, ideological residues of the Cold War discourse are still firmly planted in people's memories and imaginations. Together, the three discursive constructions – the immigrant as criminal, as victim, and as ideological "deviant" – all feed into the formulation of the Chinese immigrant as an undesirable and dangerous subject.

Underlying these distinctions lies a certain fear that these new immigrants are transforming the "old Chinese Colony." According to Ricardo, the leadership of the Chinese Association in Panama is undergoing dramatic transformation. The representatives elected to office by the community are now reflecting the demographic changes in the Chinese population. More important, notions of "Chineseness" are changing faster than ever before. Since the 1980s, a number of new Chinese restaurants have opened, Chinese video rental stores have popped up in several places, cable television has given people easy access to Hong Kong media as well as American media, and Chinese karaoke performances are now being held regularly. In fact, at one of the Chinese Youth Association parties I attended, Chinese karaoke has now replaced salsa dancing, and a growing number of youth are speaking Cantonese with as much ease as Spanish. The members of the Youth Association convey their need to express their cultural pride and to affirm their difference. Salsa dancing no longer serves as a legitimate means of asserting their Chinese identity; rather, karaoke is their medium of choice to claim and reaffirm their Chineseness. It does not matter what language they sing in – Cantonese, Mandarin, Spanish, or English; what is significant is the act of singing karaoke and their participation in these performances. Karaoke has become the signifier of their Chineseness; it is the medium through which their diverse backgrounds and multiple identifications are enunciated. To be sure, this newfound Chinese confidence enacted by the recent immigrants threatens the established habitus of Panamanian Chinese who have survived culturally and economically by assuming a much more reserved and cautious comportment. The "Chinese Colony," overwhelmed by these changes and challenges to their prescribed notions of "Chineseness," feel as though they are losing control, losing their way of life, losing what was once an intimate community where everyone knew everybody else. To the extent that they are able to recreate their social networks and imaginings of a community that is connected by no more than two degrees of separation, the "Chinese Colony" has maintained its distinctive identity. However, even these boundaries are quickly eroding.

The debate over who should be the beauty queen embodied these anxieties and tensions, articulating not only divisions within the existing diaspora but also contrasting visions of what the diaspora should be. Discussions of standards of beauty are imbued with discourses of racial-cultural purity versus hybridity, discussions that express two divergent notions of "Chineseness" in the diaspora. I draw again from a conversation with Ricardo:

This year [1998], Miss Nicaragua was the winner, and she was certainly the best fit for the job. ... It is fair to say that she fits the Western standard of beauty, body, intelligence, and grace. Chinese standards are totally different. She has to speak [Chinese], look Chinese, her body doesn't matter, and above all [she] should and must be of Chinese [descent]. Costa Rica has always, to the best of my memory, chosen girls who met the Chinese standard. The Taiwanese are almost pure in Costa Rica, or at least ... they consider themselves as pure.

Ricardo claims that the recent immigrants prefer an aesthetic that is considered racially and culturally "pure" Chinese, suggesting that other Central American Chinese do not share this preference, but rather one that fits "Western" standards of beauty. By "Western," he means the Central American standard of beauty – that of a racially and culturally mixed woman (not the Western or European/North American idealized beauty). By preferring the "Western," Central American standard of beauty himself, he is in a sense reaffirming his own positioning in Central America and Panama. His location in Panama, hence, is what informs his notions of Chineseness in the diaspora. In contrast, he would assert that the

standards of beauty used by the recent immigrants are drawn from "China," from what he considers to be the repository of "pure" Chineseness. Their notions are informed, he suggests, by their strong ties to the "homeland," whether it is Taiwan or mainland China, not to Central America. Hence, Ricardo's preference for the Central American aesthetic is more than just a subjective reading of beauty. What he makes explicit is the politics of aesthetics in determining what it means to be Chinese in the diaspora. In stating his preference, he is asserting an ideological position as well as his resistance against hegemonic constructions of Chineseness.

In diaspora, notions of Chineseness change and evolve differently from those that are generated in China. Moreover, the play of difference within the diaspora also ranges tremendously. In the case of Chinese in Central America and Panama, these debates and contestations over Chineseness arise from the shifting power relations within the diaspora and the need for each community to assert belonging in relation to one another, to their nation of residence, and to the Chinese homeland. Indeed, at the center of the beauty contest controversy lies the struggle to determine what and who gets to represent diasporic Chineseness, at a time when the diaspora itself is undergoing rapid transformation.

At the end of a very long evening, after most of the audience had retired to their hotel rooms, Miss Costa Rica was formally named queen of the Chinese Colony. In an almost empty banquet hall, the officials awkwardly presented her with the prize of US$1,000 and a vacation package for two to Taiwan. The entire scene was somewhat surreal. The stage lights shone brightly on Miss Costa Rica, but there were only a few people left in the audience to witness her victory. Some people clapped, while others simple shuffled out of the banquet hall. With an awkward smile, Miss Costa Rica accepted her prize as if fulfilling an obligation.

Shortly after my return to Panama, I was told that the leadership of the Convention had decided to disqualify the 1996 competition altogether. Perhaps it was an admission of wrongdoing, but ultimately it was the only way to address the pain and hurt that had been inflicted on all those involved. The following year, Miss Costa Rica of 1996 did not attend the convention, and my cousin from Guatemala, the 1995 queen, crowned the incoming queen. It was as if the 1996 competition had never happened – but of course it had, and the tensions that erupted that night still persist within the diaspora today.

Conclusion

Initially established as a political and economic organization, the Federación de Asociaciones Chinas de Centroamérica y Panamá quickly incorporated an annual beauty contest to encourage multigenerational attendance at its annual convention and sociocultural inter-action across the region. In doing so, the leadership transformed the convention into a project of diasporic reproduction in political, social, and cultural terms. Using gender as a category of analysis, I have shown that both the organization and the convention are highly gendered. Building on established diasporic associations whose membership is determined by patrilineal descent, this organization rein-forces androcentric biases toward male participation and male dominance in formal spheres of diasporic politics. The beauty con-test, however, offers an opportunity for women to articulate and negotiate the tensions and contradictions within the diaspora. Disguised as a seemingly harmless competition of beauty and femininity, the beauty contest in actuality incites and facilitates passionate and highly politicized debates about belonging and the meaning of diasporic Chineseness. Though working within the framework of the contest, the contestants not only reveal and disrupt dominant expectations of diasporic subjec-tivity but insist on difference and belonging in the diaspora by embodying and performing divergent ideals of diasporic femininity. For while the contest seeks to convey the shared triadic identification with the nation of residence, the homeland, and the larger dias-pora – identifications that create the parameters of diasporic belonging and citizenship – it also

unveils the differences and inequalities within the diaspora. Although it attempts to generate "a structure of common difference," the indeterminacy of the 1996 beauty contest reflects the enduring tensions within the diaspora – tensions that arise from a struggle for relatedness based simultaneously on shared identification with the Chinese homeland and the region of Central America/Panama and on difference along the lines of national context and racial and generational backgrounds. The idealism of diasporic egalitarianism is fractured by the realism of unequal access to material and cultural resources, both in terms of national economic development and of relations with the homeland and homeland state. Indeed, their emplacement in specific geopolitical entities matters in the diaspora, and recognizing this illuminates the complex-ities of diasporic belonging beyond the homeland/nation-of-residence binary.

Diasporic citizenship points to this dynamic and contested process of subject formation. To examine its nuances requires a temporary crystallization in historical time, as if putting a film in slow motion or freezing a frame just long enough to analyze its details. Indeed, while diasporic citizenship addresses relations across cultural-geographical terrain, it also insists on historical specificity. To understand the significance of the beauty contest contro-versy fully, one must situate it in the context of recent migrations to Central America and Panama. With the new influx of Chinese immigrants and the new technologies of transnationalism enabling different diasporic subjectivities to emerge, notions of Chineseness in diaspora along with the conditions of living in diaspora are being reconfigured. In the past twenty years, Hong Kong movie videos and karaoke discs have found their special niche market in diasporic Chinese communities all over the world, including those in Panama and Central America. Unlike the earlier generations of Chinese immigrants and Panamanian-born Chinese, who did not have easy access to such media, the children of recent immigrants today are conversant with Hong Kong popular music and culture. These rapid changes in transna-tional media distribution have expanded the resources of diasporic identification as well as complicated the process of identity formation. Hence, what one sees in the Chinese diaspora of Central America and Panama today is *not* a structure of common difference, but rather, a debate, an ongoing argument about what the structure of common difference is or should be. Furthermore, membership in the Chinese diaspora is *not* defined by agreeing with this structure, but rather by participating in these debates and feeling that one has a stake in the argument.

Finally, while studies of diaspora have emphasized the popular mobilization of diasporic cultural productions (Gilroy 1987, 1993), they have not, for the most part, focused on the role of the homeland state in constructing diaspora. In the case of diasporic Chinese, the involvement of the Taiwanese state in transnational organizations such as the one discussed here underscores the state's influence in diasporic community formation. It not only shows the entrenched entanglement between the Taiwanese state and diasporic Chinese of this region but illustrates Taiwan's profound investment in ensuring the reproduction of both the diaspora and its identification with Taiwan via Chineseness. For diasporic Chinese serve as one vehicle through which Taiwan legitimates itself as a sovereign nation-state. Hence, as long as the ROC continues to struggle for state status and the People's Republic maintains its claims that Taiwan is a "renegade province" of the mainland, Taiwan will continue to seek to influence the diaspora.

NOTES

1   Panama's national dress is distinctly different from the other countries' national dresses because it is heavily influenced by Spanish colonial style. All the other Central American countries use indigenous dress forms to represent the nation.

2   About twelve judges are selected every year. Some are local representatives of diasporic Chinese communities, some are local embassy people, and some are diplomatic visitors from the ROC.

3   The exceptions include Paul Gilroy and Jacqueline Brown [1998], who explore connections amongst diasporic communities.

REFERENCES

Ang, Ien, 1994. On Not Speaking Chinese. *New Formations*, 24 (Winter): 1–18.

Ang, Ien, 2001. *On Not Speaking Chinese: Living Between Asia and the West*. New York: Routledge.

Axel, Brian, 2001. *The Nation's Tortured Body*. Durham, NC: Duke University Press.

Besnier, Nico, 2002. Transgenderism, Locality, and the Miss Galaxy Beauty Contest in Tonga. *American Ethnologist* 29(3) (August): 534–566.

Brown, Jacqueline, 1998. Black Liverpool, Black America and the Gendering of Diasporic Space. *Cultural Anthropology* 13(3): 291–325.

Cohen, Colleen Ballerino, Richard Wilk, and Beverly Stoeltje, eds, 1996. *Beauty Queens on the Global Stage: Gender, Contests, and Power*. New York: Routledge.

Gilroy, Paul, 1990. It Ain't Where You're From, It's Where You're At … The Dialectics of Diasporic Identification. *Third Text*, 13 (Winter): 3–16.

Gilroy, Paul, 1991 [1987]. *"There Ain't No Black in the Union Jack": The Cultural Politics of Race and Nation*. Chicago: University of Chicago Press.

Gilroy, Paul, 1993. *The Black Atlantic: Modernity and Double Consciousness*. Cambridge, MA: Harvard University Press.

Hall, Stuart, 1990. Cultural Identity and Diaspora. In *Identity: Community, Culture and Difference*, Jonathan Rutherford, ed. London: Lawrence & Wishart, pp. 222–237.

Lavie, Smadar, and Ted Swedenburg, 1996. *Displacement, Diaspora, and Geographies of Identity*. Durham, NC: Duke University Press.

Louie, Andrea, 2004. *Chinese Across Borders: Renogtiating Chinese Identities in China and the United States*. Durham, NC: Duke University Press.

Muñoz, José, 1999. *Disidentifications: Queers of Color and the Performance of Politics*. Minneapolis: University of Minnesota Press.

Raj, Dhooleka, 2003. *Where Are You From? Middle-class Migrants in the Modern World*. Berkeley: University of California Press.

Scott, Joan, 1999. *Gender and the Politics of History*. New York: Columbia University Press.

Tu, Wei-ming, ed., 1994. *The Living Tree: The Changing Meaning of Being Chinese Today*. Stanford: Stanford University Press.

Wilk, Richard, 1996. Connections and Contradictions: From the Crooked Tree Cashew Queen to Miss World Belize. In *Beauty Queens on the Global Stage: Gender, Contests, and Power*, Colleen Ballerino Cohen *et al.*, eds. New York: Routledge, pp. 217–233.

19

Transborder Citizenship

An Outcome of Legal Pluralism within Transnational Social Fields, 2005

Nina Glick Schiller

In this paper I will discuss the implications of migrants' transnational connections and networks for the concept of citizenship and propose the concept of the transborder citizen. Transborder citizens are people who live their lives across the borders of two or more nation states, participating in the normative regime, legal and institutional system and political practices of these various states. As all other citizens, they claim rights and privileges from government but transborder citizens claim and act on a relationship to more than one government. The fact that within the past decade an impressive number of states have adopted some form of dual citizenship or dual nationality is an important foundation of the development of transborder citizenship. But an understanding of the development of transborder citizenship takes us beyond legal definitions of citizenship into the subject of social and cultural citizenship and the multiple experiences of living within plural systems of laws, customs and values. The political ideas, practices and claims-making of transborder citizens confront

us with the task of assessing an important and unexplored outcome of legal pluralism within a transnational social field. By living their lives across borders, transborder citizens can become a social force in reshaping the workings of legal domains in more than one state. This does not make transborder citizens a single political force. Because the same transnational social field may contain individuals with differing interests and agendas, the degree of unity and purpose of a transborder citizenry must be assessed empirically, as with the study of any citizenry.

The paper begins with an exploration of the intersection of concepts of citizenship and legal pluralism. I next delineate two different contexts in which transborder citizenship is experienced and exercised. [...] To illustrate these contexts, I draw examples from my own research in the United States and Germany and from the work of other researchers on transnational migration. Underlying this review of transborder citizenship is the argument that the practices and discourse of transborder citizens complicates our discussion of legal pluralism.

Nina Glick Schiller, Transborder citizenship: an outcome of legal pluralism within transnational social fields. In *Mobile People, Mobile Law: Expanding Legal Relations in a Contracting World*, F. von Benda-Beckmann, K. von Benda-Beckmann and A. Griffiths, eds (Aldershot: Ashgate, 2005), pp. 27–49.

The paradigm of legal pluralism calls on social analysts to recognize the operation of more than one system of norms, values and customs within a single polity. When we begin to look at mobile people we note the complexities introduced to the study of pluralism when the actors are migrants. First of all, if migrants remain citizens of their homeland they may be governed by the rights and restrictions of that homeland in regard to a variety of practices such as marriage, divorce, child custody and the inheritance of property. Secondly, incoming populations bring within them different modes of family, social welfare, gender relations and means of organizing claims and rights. Whether or not they maintain citizenship in their homeland or obtain citizenship in the new land, they may live in the new land within a system of customary law.

The concept of transnational migration and transnational social field introduces an additional level of complexity (Faist, 2000). Transnational migration is a form of mobility in which migrants and their descendants choose to live their lives across borders, simultaneously becoming incorporated into a nation state of settlement while maintaining social relations that embed them in other nation states. These individuals, whom I have called 'transmigrants', live their lives across borders making daily decisions in relationship to actors and institutions that are not only within the new nation state but are also within other states (Basch, Glick Schiller and Blanc-Szanton, 1994, p. 7). Legally, migrants may arrive as immigrants, refugees, asylum seekers, students, or undocumented migrants. Having arrived they begin to take social actions, make decisions, and develop subjectivities and identities ensconced in networks of relationships that connect them to locations in which they live and across borders. Transmigrants build fields of social relations that engage others into indirect transborder connections although they do not have direct personal transborder links.

The realization that migrants both past and present have maintained home ties or transborder ties has led to a new paradigm with which to study migration, one that focuses attention on transnational social fields (Glick Schiller, Basch and Blanc-Szanton, 1992, 1995; Morokvasic, 1992; Rouse, 1991). Building on

work by the Manchester school of British social anthropology, I have defined 'social field' as an unbounded terrain of multiple interlocking egocentric networks (Glick Schiller, 1999, 2003; Epstein, 1967; Mitchell, 1969). 'Social field' is a more encompassing term than 'network', which is best applied to chains of social relationships that are egocentric and are mapped as stretching out from a single individual. The concept of social field directs attention to the simultaneity of transmigrant connections to two or more states. It provides the conceptual space to investigate the ways in which transmigrants become part of the fabric of daily life in their home state, including its political processes, while simultaneously becoming part of the workforce, contributing to neighbourhood activities, serving as members of local and neighbourhood organizations, and entering into politics in their new locality. Transnational social fields are not metaphoric references to altered experiences of space but rather are composed of observable social relationships and transactions. Multiple actors with very different kinds of power and locations of power interact across borders to create and sustain these fields of relationships

In the 1990s migrant-sending countries began to respond to the increased significance of transmigrants and their remittances by extending forms of dual citizenship or nationality to the sector of their population settled abroad. Today a broad range of states that currently send large numbers of emigrants, or have done so in the past (including Greece, Ireland, Portugal, Spain, Jamaica, Brazil, the Dominican Republic, the Philippines and Colombia) allow dual citizenship. The United States and many other migrant-receiving countries (including France, Canada, Israel and the UK) also allow dual citizenship either by law or practice. States such as Mexico find a legal middle ground by passing laws that recognize those who have emigrated and their descendants as 'nationals' of their homeland. Nationals are members of the nation in terms of some of its rights to own property but do not have full citizenship rights such as voting. Governments such as Haiti have found ways to recognize persons abroad as nationals without changing any of their laws.

Whatever their legal rights in their homeland, new land or the other lands into which their networks may extend, people who live within transnational social fields live in a legally plural world. This legally plural world contains not just customary law but also the constraints, possibilities, rights and restrictions of more than one set of official laws, institutions and governmental regulations, organizations and practices (Foblets, 2002). People who live within this transnational social field may react to this experience by becoming what I have called transborder citizens (Glick Schiller and Fouron, 2001). Transborder citizens build on their social connections to form multiple systems of values, laws and familial practices, and to generate concepts and ways of relating to other people and to the state that differ from those operative in any one of the states to which they are linked. Because of their generative practices of citizenship, transborder citizens have the potential to play an important role in reshaping the workings of several systems of law and governance.

The fact that within the past decade an impressive number of states have adopted some form of dual citizenship or dual nationality is an important foundation for the development of a transborder form of citizenship. But an understanding of the development of transborder citizenship must take us beyond legal citizenship into the subject of cultural and social citizenship and its transnational extensions.

[...]

Transborder Citizenship

The concept of transborder citizenship builds on the idea of social and cultural citizenship and expands the examination of citizenship practices and claims transnationally. Scholars, political leaders and the media most frequently discuss the politics of transborder citizens who may vote, lobby or finance campaigns in more than one system. But transborder citizenship has implications that extend beyond the domain of direct political action and the distinction between legal citizens and non-citizens. Whether or not transmigrants have legal rights in more than one country through dual citizenship or nationality, they may claim social or cultural citizenship in more than one country, although the success of their claims is mediated by their legal status. They may also follow customs, norms and values that regulate marriage, interpersonal relations, inheritance, diet, dress, childrearing, modification of the body, etc., that differ from prevailing legal or cultural norms in one or more of the states to which they are connected. And they may follow these alternative ways of being within a transnational social field that exists beyond the territorial borders and regulation of any one government.

Public policy makers, as well as scholars, often interpret the continuation of alternative ways of being and the establishment of a migrant *habitus* within a new land of settlement as a failure to incorporate. Ethnographic research shows that migrant incorporation is much more dynamic and interactive where migrants make claims to more than one state, using concepts of rights, culture and citizenship they experience and shape within an unbounded transnational social field. In this way, migrants become incorporated into more than one state at the same time, constructing forms of legal pluralism that differ from the predominant legal system. In all locations they are shaped by the constraints and possibilities of each governmental system into which their transnational social field extends.

To study transnational processes is to enter a domain in which crucial elements of social, economic, cultural and political life take place across borders but in which nation states and their borders influence and shape such movements. Many scholars of globalization emphasize that, although social, cultural and economic processes may cross borders, states are players in transnational processes, maintaining and watching borders, defining access to rights and benefits, and shaping or limiting the movements of people (Sassen, 1998; Brenner, 1998). They stress that while states have been altered by the recent high degree of global and regional economic interconnections, the nation state persists and borders are increasingly difficult to cross for large categories of people who do not hold citizenship rights in core capitalist states.

Increasingly researchers are examining the institutionalized legal pluralism that accompanies the continued role of states within globalization as they interact with transnational organizations. Soysal (1998, p. 206), for example, argues that there is now an 'institutionalized duality between the two principles of the global system: national sovereignty and universal human rights'. However, her focus has been on the legal pluralism that exists within the borders of a single state as a result of its penetration by global institutions and discourses of human rights. The argument here is that transmigrants are another important set of actors who establish a form of legal pluralism within the transnational social fields in which they live. Scholars of legal pluralism such as von Benda-Beckmann (2001) are increasingly noting the transnational dimensions of legal pluralism, including the ways in which religious law as transnational law is invoked by various local actors to counter local law and values. This new discussion can help highlight the ways in which transmigrants affect the broader social field, both within a country of settlement and across its borders. Governments and officials of institutions that regulate the actions of persons within the borders of the state also are actors within these social fields. And the actors within these fields respond to specific national forms of 'governmentality' that shape the daily experience, the 'everyday forms of state formation', cultural subtexts and identity markers that constitute nation-state building. Explorations of the significance of transborder citizenries must take into account the continuing role of states. This recognition was missing in some of the first writing on transnational migration that argued that transnational networks produced liberated social space (Kearney, 1991).

Two Different Contexts of Transborder Citizenship

1 The practice of citizenship between homeland and the nation state of settlement

Homeland politics usually constitutes the most visible transnational involvement of migrants and their descendants so scholars and policy makers have paid increasing attention to this form of cross-border connection. Current concerns, heightened after 2001, centre on dual loyalties, the formation of political lobbies in a country of migrant settlement in the interests of a homeland, and the right of migrants and their descendants to shape the political agendas of an ancestral homeland. What is most striking to the observer is the long-distance nationalism of some migrants. Long-distance nationalism is an ideology and set of practices in which persons declare that they not only identify with an ancestral land but also organize their daily activities on behalf of that land (Anderson, 1993; Fuglerud, 1999; Glick Schiller and Fouron, 2001; Glick Schiller, 2005; Skrbiš, 1999).

However, the study of legal pluralism raises a somewhat different set of questions. It examines the extensions of transnational social fields, exploring the ideas and practices of a broader set of people than those people who actively participate in politics on behalf of a homeland. Through the lens of legal pluralism, we can see that transborder citizens are individuals whose ideas about rights, the relationship between citizens and government, and actions as social citizens are shaped by their living in a transnational social field that spans more than one legal and normative system. They make demands, in relationship to alternative sets of rights, norms and expectations about governance, as legal or social citizens in more than one state.

The experience of Haitians settled in the US provides a case study of the development of a transborder citizenry. I have been conducting fieldwork with this citizenry for more than thirty years. Haitians began coming to the US in large numbers, beginning in the 1960s. They fled from the political repression and economic upheaval that accompanied the coming to power of François Duvalier in 1957. Among the migrants were members of the political opposition to the Duvalier regime. However, until the growth of a transnational grassroots political movement in the 1980s, most Haitian migrants tried to distance themselves publicly from the Haitian political opposition while continuing to maintain kinship and friendship connections with Haiti. That is to say, people experienced more than one system of governance within a transnational social field but there was initially no strong public discourse of long-distance nationalism.

Haitians brought to the US certain expectations about the relationship between citizens and the state and continued to experience this through the personal networks that connected them to Haiti. Two hundred years of Haitian history shaped ideas about governance which were communicated within this social field. Since the founding of the Haitian state in 1804, as a result of the success of the Haitian revolution against the French colonization and slavery, Haitian governments have sought to legitimate their regimes through constitutions that promise positive rights. In an ironic twist of history, this view that the government has responsibility towards the people was strengthened in the twentieth century during the US occupation of Haiti in 1915–34. The US began providing public services to major towns. These services, including latrine inspections, sewer cleaning, health clinics and food supplements for the poor, were continued into the 1970s by successive Haitian governments, including the Duvalier regime.

Together with political repression, the Duvaliers continued (through the promulgation of constitutional law and daily rhetoric) the long-established promises that the state would protect and provide for the people. The fact that very few of these promises were ever fulfilled did not take away from the potency of the vision. When the Haitian government began to abandon even the semblance of social services and price supports in response to pressures to implement the US neoliberal agenda of the 1980s, non-government organizations, funded by private foundations, churches and foreign governments (including that of the US), increasingly began to provide health, education and development programmes in Haiti. As a result, many Haitians felt confirmed in their belief that the state should be responsible to the people and that other governments did provide the programmes and services needed by the population. As discourses about human rights and women's rights came into Haiti through the non-government organizations and these organizations set up programmes to implement these values, Haitian peasants fused the new articulation of norms with their own understanding of democracy that equated with a retributive economy in which the poor had access to the wealth of the nation (Smith, 2001). They directed their anger at their own government's failure to live up to its responsibilities and began in the 1980s to build a grassroots movement to uproot the old system and implement basic social and economic change. Haitians of all class backgrounds, whom Georges Fouron and I interviewed in Haiti in the 1990s, spoke readily and eloquently about the 'responsibilities of the state' to the people as a basic aspect of democracy (Glick Schiller and Fouron, 2001).

The first waves of Haitian migrants to the US in the 1960s arrived expecting a state which, unlike the Haitian state, would be responsible for its people. Instead they found limited programmes for the poor, wretched unsafe inner-city housing, low-paid service or factory work, inadequate education and racism. While glad to earn larger sums than were possible in Haiti, Haitians began to view the US with critical eyes. They joined the struggles for civil, political, social and economic rights developed by African Americans and other people of colour. Haitians brought to struggles for justice their frustration with the treatment they received from the US government. Despite the fact that they faced a repressive regime at home, relatively few Haitians were given refugee status by the US, while Cubans were welcomed, celebrated and given special benefits. While many Haitian migrants managed to eventually obtain permanent residence with eligibility for citizenship, tens of thousands of others lived as undocumented workers. When in the 1970s Haitians began to risk their lives fleeing to the US in small wooden sailboats, they were imprisoned if they were fortunate enough to survive the journey. Haitians were almost uniformly defined as unwelcome economic migrants, and stigmatized as poor, illiterate and carriers of disease.

In the US, by the 1980s, Haitians began to take to the streets by the tens of thousands, united as 'the Haitian community' to protest mistreatment in the US and political repression in Haiti. Undocumented workers, who in previous decades had feared even reporting dangerous building conditions or injuries in traffic accidents, joined other Haitians in street protests. After 1986 when the Duvalier regime was overthrown by the transnational mass movement, transnational communication became more open and diverse and protests became frequent in both New York and Port-au-Prince (the capital city of Haiti). The New York Haitian newspapers began to be printed in Haiti. Radio broadcasts became transnational; Haitians in the US bought special receivers that gave them access to Haitian radio frequencies and radio shows accepted calls from both Haiti and the US. In both locations, protests were marked by demands on the state for freedoms of expression and democratic procedures experienced in the US and for rights to education and health care promised in Haitian constitutions. In April 1990, most of lower Manhattan was brought to a standstill when an estimated 80,000 Haitians demonstrated against the incorrect labelling of Haitians as carriers of AIDS by the US Center for Disease Control: a simultaneous demonstration was held in Port-au-Prince. The sense of social citizenship expressed through these demonstrations was reinforced through Haitian radio programmes in New York and Miami and Haitian newspapers produced in New York and distributed in a number of cities in the US where Haitians settled. Newly made citizens, second-generation youth born in the US (and consequently US citizens), permanent residents and the undocumented all actively participated in the demonstrations. The sensibilities expressed resonated with the grassroots movement developing in Haiti, as information about actions, concepts of democratic actions and ideas about rights and entitlements were communicated within various kinds of networks.

By the 1990s, both men and women, and Haitians of poor and middle-class backgrounds living in Haiti and in many cities of the US shared this sense of citizenship through direct engagement. They shared a political culture that differed from the US mainstream. The Haitian understanding and practice of citizenship built on both movements for empowerment of poor people in the US and developments in Haiti that included both

Haitian and transnational actors. Haitians learned from the US historical experience of the past and continuing labour movement, the US civil rights movement, the black activism of the 1960s, the US anti-imperialist movement and the immigrants' rights movement of the 1970s; at the same time, Haitians drew from Haitian revolutionary history, liberation theology, the international women's movement, the proliferation of non-government organizations in Haiti, UN discourses on rights, and the anti-Duvalierists' grassroots movement that developed in Haiti in the 1980s.

The movement that emerged in Haiti was a nationalist movement that demanded political empowerment for the poor, social justice, solidarity with oppressed peoples around the world and the liberation of women. It certainly built within Haitians settled in the US a sense of long-distance nationalism. But the ideologies contained within this nationalism and the forms of political practice contained within it are products of the pluralism that was constructed and experienced transnationally. People engaged in this movement brought political lessons about citizens' rights and social action learned in the US and Haitian notions of the state together in a potent mix as they constituted themselves as a consciously transborder citizenry. After the movement led to the electoral victory of Jean Bertrand Aristide in 1990, Aristide recognized this fact and tried to harness it by creating a Ministry of Haitians Abroad and labelling those settled abroad as the 'Tenth Department of Haiti', an addition to Haiti's nine territorial departments. In so doing he projected Haitian emigrants as a continuing part of Haiti, envisioning the Haitian state as existing wherever Haitians settle, regardless of geography or differing legal systems. He recognized their social citizenship and the particular voice that the Haitian transborder citizens had created. When the state still did not deliver on its promises of rights and benefits, a transborder citizenry helped topple the Aristide government in 2004.

It is very important to note that, although in particular instances it is possible to speak of a Haitian transborder citizenry, there is very often more than one voice that emerges within transnational social fields. Moreover, while the US–Haitian connection was the focus of this case study, the pluralism of the field is generated from bases in multiple nation states because Haitians have also settled in Canada, France, Mexico, the Dominican Republic and a host of other states. In addition the Haitian transnational social space contains multiple political actors and understandings, the differentiated experiences of gender, a rural–urban divide and sharp class divisions.

[…]

2   Transborder networks that stretch between migrants in multiple states to create global forms of identity and practices rooted in diverse legal systems and states and justifying entry into all

An entirely different form of social movement, based on global religious missions, is also fuelled by transnational migration. In this form of migrant incorporation, people build religious organizations and identities that allow them to become actors within their new state, while simultaneously building transnational networks and social fields that extend into many states. Rather than organize themselves in terms of an ethnic identity or as long-distance nationalism, migrants highlight a religious identity, their responsibility to proselytize within their new state of settlement, and their connections to co-believers worldwide. To illustrate this process I draw on research I conducted in Halle/Salle, Germany, with Evangelos Karagiannis and Ayse Calgar. We attended and studied two churches in Halle composed almost entirely of African migrants, most of whom are asylum seekers. Both churches preach a version of 'born-again' Christianity, identified by the members of these congregations as Pentecostal. One church is primarily Nigerian with services conducted in English. This congregation has grown to more than 150, encompassing most of the Nigerians living in Halle. The second congregation is primarily Congolese who worship together with some Lingalla-speaking Angolans: the

language of prayer is French. Both congregations are attended by a few German women. Some of the women who attend the French-speaking church have relationships with African members. In the English-speaking church, a few women also participate without such relationships. However neither church identifies by nationality or language. They see themselves as Christians bringing God's word to a Godless land. When the Congolese pastor was asked whether he regarded his congregation as a Congolese one, he answered:

> No, no. It isn't a Congolese Church. This is not the origin of the Word of God. I have told you about my origin. I have come from Congo where I met my Lord, where I worked for the Lord. And now I am here, in Germany, where I had the feeling that the inhabitants were in need of the same message. So I've clearly said that this church is not a Congolese Church. I've clearly said it is a church of Jesus.

The role of these churches in Halle has to be understood in relationship to German migration policy, particularly the policy towards asylum seekers that set the frame of the living conditions of the majority of the congregants. This is a policy of deterrence. Since 1980, when it was first introduced in the state of Baden-Württemberg, German policy is organized to make asylum seekers feel unwelcome in Germany, and to complicate their lives as much as possible. They are often housed in camps or asylum 'homes' that are bleak, isolated, overcrowded and dehumanizing. The federal government provides no opportunities for them to learn German; they are not allowed to work or to move, and they have considerably less money than the social welfare payments allocated to permanent residents and citizens (that is, less than the bare minimum needed to maintain a decent life). In short, they are not allowed to become incorporated. As an immigrant from Sudan said 'We are only allowed to eat and to sleep.'

The churches challenge this policy, offering activities that allow migrants to see themselves as part of Germany, to become connected through the churches to other institutions in Germany, and to thereby maintain their sense of self-respect and continue the struggle to obtain a secure foothold in Germany. Both pastors in Halle help congregants meet the contingencies and pressures of daily life created to a high extent by the German policy towards them. The churches represent the primary network of social support for their congregants. A member of the French-speaking congregation such as François, who could not obtain a flat or money, found both through the church. He also used the connections of the pastor with the German Protestant Church and got further social benefits. One church organizes various offerings to support specific congregants in difficult situations; the other uses its collections to provide financial support for members in need. At the same time, through regular and special events, the churches organize everyday life. They fill their members' days by challenging the irrationality of German asylum policy – the policy of 'eating and sleeping'. They create sociability and provide the congregants with the opportunity of enjoying normality, which secures them self-esteem and dignity. In short, they establish exactly what the German state policy intends to consciously circumvent.

In countering German policies the churches find ways to connect the congregants to social fields that stretch into Germany and beyond. Both pastors call upon the congregants to learn German and attach great importance to the translation of the services into German, even if there is only one monolingual German among the worshippers. They meet with German pastors in other cities and invite them to give sermons. The congregations are legally registered in Germany. Both pastors have worked with a white German Pentecostal Church in Magdeburg to become formal members of a German Pentecostal organization (*Bund Freikirchlicher Pfingstkirchen*). They desire this level of official incorporation, even though it means changing some of their internal organizational procedures.

Both churches are also transnationally connected. Among the visiting preachers to the English-speaking church was an Indian pastor, based in western Germany but linked to a global Pentecostal network of pastors. This Indian pastor has visited more than once and

has convinced the church to support his missionizing work in India by sending funds on a regular basis. Through another global Christian ministry, this one located in the US, the church sends funds to Christianize Israel. Members of this church attend pan-European Pentecostal conferences such as the one held in Berlin in June 2003 that sought to form a European-wide Pentecostal organization. A core member of the English-speaking church returned from the Berlin conference saying that the presence of people from all over the world at the conference was for her evidence of the power of God and the rightness of her beliefs.

In constructing their belief system and their religious practices members of both congregations draw on elements of a Pentecostal Christianity as it is practised in Africa and in Germany, and on the global religious networks to which they are connected through Christian organizations and networks. In a time of increasing restrictions on immigration to Europe, they forge an ideology of entitlement that legitimates their claims to rights in Germany as part of their relationship to Jesus.

Both churches preach that they represent God's agenda for the local city, for Germany and for Europe, and that they speak in the interests of both asylum seekers and native Germans. Whatever German and European politicians claim, in the view of the pastors of both these churches, the message of the Bible is clear: 'Every place whereon the soles of your feet shall tread shall be yours' (Deuteronomy, Chapter 11, 24). It is about a promise of God to the true believers: 'For ye shall pass over Jordan to go in to possess the land which the LORD your God giveth you, and ye shall possess it, and dwell therein' (ibid., 31). The Bible provides evidence of the difficulties immigrants meet in a strange world as well as the God-given right to claim the land for the Lord. Daniel, congregants are told, was 'in a strange land like you and me and never gave up. He only paid attention to what God said. He practised effective prayer.' Then you 'will speak and it will come to pass'. 'Nothing will be impossible. You can climb to any height.' This message is linked to the need of the parishioners for German passports, legal residence papers and marriages to Germans. Increasingly, the miracles promised include jobs, but in all cases Germany is envisioned as part of a terrain in which God, not the German state, has dominion. In the name of Jesus, according to the pastors, believers will obtain what they desire.

The individual members of these churches, including both pastors, live within transnational social fields composed of family members, friends and persons connected through shared religious beliefs. The organizations to which these migrants belong increasingly also have institutional transnational connections. The persons connected transnationally live within states with different legal systems and cultural and social practices. The transnational Christian networks impart to their participants an alternative set of values, practices and beliefs. They provide a vision of a different set of rights to membership in nation states and a different agenda for the practices of these states. The two migrant churches in Halle that I described do not critique the economic system they find in Germany and the high valuation of wealth, commodities and secular education. Members pray for prosperity and the achievement of prosperity is seen as a manifestation of the will of God. However, they do critique other sets of values they find around them. In some instances they preach against the growing pluralism of family forms and sexual preference in Germany, denouncing homosexuality and gay marriage. In other instances, they advocate a more tolerant society, targeting racism and the oppressive restrictions on asylum seekers. In their advocacy and in their claims to permanent residence in Germany, members of these churches build a form of transborder citizenship, differing in its content and rhetoric from the Haitian case, but equally built within a transnational terrain that spans borders and makes claims on states.

Summation and Analysis

Transborder citizens are people who not only live their lives across the borders of two or more nation states, participating in the daily life of various states, but also bring to bear a citizenship in these states, whether on the basis of legal rights or being substantively members of those states (Glick Schiller and Fouron, 2001). As with all other citizens, they claim rights and privileges from governments, but transborder citizens claim a relationship to more than one government. As transmigrants within a transnational social field they experience legal pluralism; that is to say their lives are shaped by more than one set of laws, social norms and values as they are embedded within the relationship between people and institutions.

Transborder citizens are more than the object of plural systems. They are actors within them. As they participate in the political processes and political cultures of more than one state, they draw on concepts of the state and the ideas of civil and political rights of more than one polity. This kind of citizenship practice may arise within different kinds of transnational contexts and identities. In this paper, for purposes of analysis, I have highlighted two different contextual situations that shape transborder citizenship. While I have illustrated these situations with examples of different sets of migrant actors, the situation is of course more complex. Migrants can be shaped by a transnational politics that stretches between one homeland, by transnational religious networks in which they are embedded, and by the particularities of citizenship practices in their city of settlement at the same time. [...]

Into their own performance of transborder citizenship, each migrant player brings notions of state, citizenship and cultural performance developed within their own transnational social fields. Similarly, the particularities and history of each city also enter into their understanding and performance of transborder citizenship. The examination of different contexts of transborder citizenship are offered here to strengthen the argument that when we examine citizenship through a transborder lens and within transnational social fields, scholars and policy makers can identify dynamics of change that are invisible if they look only at the ways in which social fields connect people within different states.

To conceptualize a transborder citizenry is to begin the analysis of a significant and generally unmarked type of social being. This is a citizenry whose relationships to legal regimes are shaped by multiple memberships and interconnections within and across nation states. Transborder citizens form different conceptions of legal institutions because they live in a social field that is legally plural. They come to see the nature and role of various institutional and organizational frameworks, including social welfare offices, local and national governmental bodies and non-governmental organizations (whether it is a church, a charity or a scouting association), with a gaze that differs from that of persons embedded in any one state. The various legal regimes in which transborder citizens are incorporated remain distinct; they do not merge into something else. But transborder citizens respond to their multiple positioning by approaching the institutions, laws and social policies of each state and local society in which they live in novel ways. The changes wrought by transborder citizens are not necessarily ones that I would consider progressive, that is, contributing to social and economic justice. In the Haitian experience some transborder citizens serve as a voice for privatization of public services in Haiti, a policy which makes services like electricity and water less accessible to the poor. Various forms of fundamentalism are shaping citizenries in many states. On the other hand, as the Haitian grassroots movement or the international women's movement has demonstrated, transborder citizens can contribute to new everyday forms of state formation from below that incorporate agendas for social justice (Antrobus and Peacocke, 2001).

Transborder citizens extend our understanding of governmentality. Building on work in anthropology and cultural studies that extended and interrogated the study of the disciplining of the social subject initiated by Michel Foucault, governmentality has been understood to include the multiple practices through which we all live our lives. In quotidian activities, individuals learn who they are and what social life looks and feels like as they interact with a range of state institutions and national symbols, and as they participate in various forms of political discourse about state, society and self. This understanding of the embeddedness of governing processes, however, should not turn our attention from the ways in which subjects become active agents within political processes that contest and reformulate structures of power. As Paul Willis (1977, p. 175) reminds us, social agents 'are not passive bearers of ideology, but active appropriators who reproduce existing structures only through struggle'.

Transborder citizens affect the public culture of the various states to which they are connected. Their presence is therefore important to acknowledge and their influence is important to assess. The implication of the development of transborder citizens is that new concepts of political life and responsibility and new forms of political action develop in locales around the world not by the actions of public policy makers in one locality, but with diverse sets of actors. These include transmigrants responding to very diverse sets of circumstances and public policies in disparate locations around the world.

If concepts of citizenship are being constructed across borders, then we have all entered a new and challenging political arena, where states remain significant and some states such as the US increasingly penetrate into the transactions of all others. However, people who live in transnational social fields raise new questions about the purpose and uses of government, pose new political agendas and contribute to new struggles against oppressive conditions. [...] Rather than question migrant loyalties, I suggest we examine whose conceptualizations of the rights and responsibilities of citizenship, whether based within one state or constructed across borders, best protects human well-being. The search for the meaning of nationality and citizenship in an epoch of globalization is an inquiry that confronts and beckons us all.

Acknowledgements

The research in Halle was supported by the Max Planck Institute of Social Anthropology, the MacArthur Foundation, the Sidore Foundation and the Humanities Center of the

University of New Hampshire. Research on Haitian transborder citizenry was supported by the Wenner Gren Foundation and USNICHD. Special thanks to Dr Burt Feintuch and Dr Günther Schlee.

NOTE

Organizational names in this paper are pseudonyms.

REFERENCES

Anderson, B., 1993. The New World Disorder. *New Left Review* 193: 2–13.

Antrobus, P., and N. Peacocke, 2001. "Yabba still empty": Comments on Holger Henke's "Freedom Ossified: Political Culture and the Public Use of History in Jamaica" and Rothbottom's response to Henke. *Identities: Global Studies in Culture and Power* 8(3): 441–450.

Basch, L., N. Glick Schiller, and C. Blanc-Szanton, 1994. *Nations Unbound: Transnational Migration, Postcolonial Predicaments, and the Deterritorialized Nation-State.* London: Gordon and Breach.

Benda-Beckmann, K. von, 2001. Transnational Dimensions of Legal Pluralism. In *Begegnung und Konflikt. Eine Kulturanthropologische Bestandsaufnahme*, W. Fikentscher, ed. München: Verlag der Bayerischen Akademie der Wissenschaften, pp. 34–48.

Brenner, N., 1998. Global Cities, Glocal States: Global City Formation and State Territorial Restructuring in Contemporary Europe. *Review of International Political Economy* 5(1): 1–37.

Epstein, A. E., ed., 1967. *The Craft of Social Anthropology.* London: Tavistock.

Faist, T., 2000. Transnationalization in International Migration: Implications for the Study of Citizenship and Culture. *Ethnic and Racial Studies* 23(2): 189–222.

Foblets, M.-C., 2002. Muslims, a New Transnational Minority in Europe? Cultural Pluralism, Fundamental Liberties and Inconsistencies in the Law. Paper prepared for the conference 'Mobile People, Mobile Law: Expanding Legal Relations in a Contracting World', Max Planck Institute for Social Anthropology, Halle, Germany, 7–9 November 2002.

Fuglerud, Ø., 1999. *Life on the Outside: The Tamil Diaspora and Long Distance Nationalism.* London: Pluto.

Glick Schiller, N., 1999. Transmigrants and Nation-States: Something Old and Something New in the US Immigrant Experience. In *The Handbook of International Migration: The American Experience*, C. Hirshman, P. Kasinitz, and J. DeWind, eds. New York: Russell Sage, pp. 94–119.

Glick Schiller, N., 2003. The Centrality of Ethnography in the Study of Transnational Migration: Seeing the Wetland Instead of the Swamp. In *American Arrivals*, N. Foner, ed. Santa Fe: School of American Research, pp. 99–128.

Glick Schiller, N., 2005. Long Distance Nationalism. In *Encyclopedia of Diasporas: Immigrant and Refugee Cultures around the World*, vol. 10, M. Ember, C. R. Ember, and I. Skoggard. New York: Springer Science and Business Media, p. 20.

Glick Schiller, N., L. Basch and C. Blanc-Szanton, 1992. *Towards a Transnational Perspective on Migration.* New York: New York Academy of Sciences.

Glick Schiller, N., L. Basch and C. Blanc-Szanton, 1995. From Immigrant to Transmigrant: Theorizing Transnational Migration. *Anthropology Quarterly* 68: 48–63.

Glick Schiller, N., and G. Fouron, 2001. *Georges Woke up Laughing: Long Distance Nationalism and the Search for Home.* Durham: Duke University Press.

Kearney, M., 1991. Borders and Boundaries of the State and Self at the End of Empire. *Journal of Historical Sociology* 4(1): 52–74.

Mitchell, J. C., 1969. *Social Networks in Urban Situations: Analyses of Personal Relationships in Central African Towns.* Manchester: Manchester University Press.

Morokvasic, M., 1992. Une migration pendulaire: Les Polonais en Allemagne. *Hommes et Migrations [Men and Migrations]* 1155: 31–36.

Rouse, R., 1991. Mexican Migration and the Social Space of Postmodernism. *Diaspora* 1: 8–23.

Sassen, S., 1998. *Globalization and Its Discontents: Essays on the New Mobility of People and Money.* New York: New Press.

Skrbiš, Z., 1999. *Long Distance Nationalism: Diasporas, Homelands and Identities.* Aldershot: Ashgate.

Smith, J., 2001. *When the Hands are Many: Community Organization and Social Change in Rural Haiti.* Ithaca: Cornell University Press.

Soysal, Y. N., 1998. Towards a Post National Model of Membership. In *The Citizenship Debates: A Reader,* Shafir, G., ed. Minneapolis: University of Minnesota, pp. 189–217.

Willis, P., 1977. *Learning to Labor.* New York: Columbia University Press.

20

Difficult Distinctions

Refugee Law, Humanitarian Practice and Political Identification in Gaza, 2007

Ilana Feldman

The almost four-and-a-half million people who are formally registered with the UN Relief and Works Agency for Palestine Refugees in the Near East (UNRWA), and who are therefore eligible for the agency's educational, health, and (for hardship cases) rations services, serve as a reminder of the longevity of what is often referred to as the "Palestine problem." Since 1948, when the former territory of British Mandate Palestine was divided by war into three distinct areas – the Egyptian-controlled Gaza Strip, the West Bank (quickly annexed to Jordan), and the newly established state of Israel – much of the former population of the country, along with their descendants, have been in exile: displaced from their homes and dispossessed from their lands. How to resolve the status of Palestinian refugees has proven to be a major sticking point in negotiations between Israel and the Palestinians, as well as a source of political contestation within the Palestinian community. As large as the group of registered refugees is, however, it does not account for all those Palestinians who suffered

losses in what they remember as the *nakba* [catastrophe] of 1948. The UNRWA mandate, for instance, is limited to those who "lost both their homes and means of livelihood" and does not, therefore, cover the native population of the Gaza Strip, many of whom were dispossessed, but not displaced, by the 1948 war.

Gaza, home to one-and-a-half million people of whom two-thirds are refugees, is a place that is at once exceptional and paradigmatic – of the broader Palestinian condition and of refugee situations more generally. As such, it offers a particularly good site for investigating refugee-dom, as well as its "partner" status, citizenship. Gaza is an anomalous space in that since 1948 it has not been the sovereign territory of any state – a condition that has meant that its residents have not been citizens of any existing state. Egypt, which governed the territory until 1967, saw itself as a caretaker of a Palestinian space and never claimed sovereignty. It is further distinguished by its demographics. The fact that refugees far outnumber the native inhabitants is only one of its unique features. Unlike many

Ilana Feldman, 2007. Difficult distinctions: refugee law, humanitarian practice, and political identification in Gaza. *Cultural Anthropology* 22(1): 129–169.

The Anthropology of Citizenship: A Reader, First Edition. Edited by Sian Lazar.
© 2013 John Wiley & Sons, Inc. Published 2013 by John Wiley & Sons, Inc.

other refugee situations, in which refugees are "out of place" not only because they are away from home, but also because they have different nationalities, ethnicities, and/or material conditions from the native population, in Gaza the entire population is Palestinian.

Gaza's transformation from a provincial district of Palestine under the British Mandate (1917–48) to a new almost indefinable sort of territory (the Gaza Strip) also threw its population categories into confusion. During the British Mandate, Gaza City was a reasonably prosperous town, not Jerusalem or Jaffa, but a major trade port for the southern part of the country and the administrative capital of the region. In the course of the 1948 war, the approximately 80 thousand original inhabitants of the area were joined by nearly 250 thousand refugees. Whereas many Palestinian refugees went to neighboring countries like Lebanon, Syria, or Jordan, fleeing to Gaza or the West Bank constituted a temporal rather than geographic border crossing. It was after the fact, with the signing of armistice agreements, that a boundary line was marked between people's home villages and their space of refuge. At the war's end, the Egyptian army was in control of the small portion of the Gaza district that became the Gaza Strip; its borders were delimited in the 1949 armistice agreement between Egypt and Israel. The rest of the Gaza district, including the land of many native Gazans, came under Israeli control. To this day, the Gazan landscape remains dominated by refugee camps – there are eight major camps in the Strip – even as only half the refugees have ever lived in them.

Given the contraction of Gazan space, the enormous influx of people, and its isolation from its former hinterland, it is not surprising that the economy of the area was utterly devastated in 1948. There was almost no one in Gaza who was not in need of assistance in the aftermath of the war. And, yet, the aid regimes that were emerging at the same time – both the international refugee regime and the Palestine-specific assistance program – depended on making distinctions among people in terms that were patently inadequate to capture these conditions. Although identifying people as "refugees" (displaced and dispossessed) or "natives/citizens" (the "merely" dispossessed)

did not say anything about their level of need, these were the terms that governed relief.

Beyond these distinctive features, the Gazan case illuminates the difficult decisions that are part of any humanitarian operation and indicates their long-lasting effects on the population. Some of these effects were evident to me when I was doing fieldwork in Gaza in the late-1990s, particularly in the ongoing significance of "refugee" and "native" as categories of identification. I tried to explore strains in these relations in my conversations with people, with varying degrees of success.[1] Some people were reluctant to acknowledge any problem, insisting that "we received the refugees as brothers" or "all of us are Palestinians. There is no difference between a refugee and a citizen." Others, however, were quite explicit about tensions. As one native Gazan commented: "When the boys of the camps were throwing stones (during the first intifada), they said that the boys of the city (i.e., nonrefugees) cover the stone with tissue before they throw it at the Israelis." Even as Hanan wondered why refugees would judge harshly those who had aided them, her own view of refugees as "wretched" and from the "most backward class in Palestine" suggests a scorn that might explain some of the hostility.

It is important to note that, despite this claim to a preexisting difference, before 1948 these two groups did not exist as such. Palestinian society during the British Mandate was highly stratified, but these distinctions do not correspond with precision to the post-1948 categories "refugee" and "native." Natives included both urbanites from Gaza City and villagers from places like Deir Belah and Jabalya. Refugees likewise came both from cities like Jaffa and small towns like Hammama and Yibna. Some were financially secure; others lived in more precarious conditions. The largest majority among both groups was formerly dependent on agriculture for their livelihoods, whether working their own land or employed as farmworkers on others. It was the accidents of geography and war (and the subsequent humanitarian projects), rather than preexisting distinctions, that divided the population of the former Gaza District of Palestine into refugees and natives.

As I have sought to better understand these distinctions among Palestinians in Gaza, it has become clear to me that they cannot be explained simply by the difficulties of the nakba, or of life, in overcrowded Gaza but are also rooted in the early relief provided to Palestinian refugees, relief guided, albeit in a somewhat unusual manner, by the emerging post-WWII international humanitarian regime. Population distinctions have been central to the international regime and, as refugee law developed in the postwar era, citizenship was the normative condition against which the exceptional status of being a refugee was defined. To explore the emergence of these distinctions in Gaza, as well as their relation to the wider humanitarian endeavor, in this article I turn my attention to the first years after the massive Palestinian dispossession – the period before new legal and bureaucratic apparatuses were codified – and explore the first organized relief in Gaza, a project managed by the American Friends Service Committee (AFSC) from late 1948 to 1950 at the behest of the United Nations.

This liminal period, which was a crucial moment for both refugee law and Palestinians, provides an opportunity to examine how humanitarian practice, the relief projects that sought to provide assistance to those in need, participated in the development of distinguishing population categories. It further shows how dependent this practice was on categorizations that were not always – and in the Gazan case not at all – adequate to the tasks of defining need. In this exploration, I make use of both archival records of this early relief work and ethnographic research I conducted in Gaza in 1998 and 1999. Both conversations held long after the fact and documents produced in the moment reflect the tremendous uncertainties and anxieties that accompanied this relief work.

Although neither AFSC volunteers nor the people they came to aid had the authority to determine humanitarian policy, their on-the-ground negotiations and interactions were crucial for shaping the refugee condition. Humanitarian practices were self-consciously narrow in their focus – intended to respond to immediate need, to avert full-blown crisis, rather than to define social policy – but their effects were often far reaching. The categorization of population for relief purposes, for instance, contributed to developments in political vocabulary and identification. Close investigation of the experiences of this period highlights the emergence not only of enduring distinctions within the Gazan population, but also of tentative enactments of political claims about rights, community, and citizenship that have had broad import for Palestinians. In these enactments, the category of "refugee" proved to be important not only for managing relief, but also for the rearticulation of Palestinian political identity in the aftermath of dispossession.

The Developing Postwar Refugee Regime

Palestinian exile occurred in a moment that witnessed a number of significant population displacements. Europe was still dealing with WWII displaced persons. Independence for India and Pakistan in 1947 was accompanied by one of the largest population movements in history. Fighting between nationalist and communist forces in China created significant refugee flows into Hong Kong. Although European refugees received the most attention, population instability was a global phenomenon, and potentially a global crisis. Hannah Arendt, writing at precisely this moment, believed that these conditions posed a fundamental challenge to the nation-state and to the idea of "the Rights of Man." These rights, she suggested, turned out to be so entangled in the rights of citizenship as to be "unenforceable – even in countries whose constitutions were based upon them – whenever people appeared who were no longer citizens of any sovereign state" (Arendt 1973: 293). It was in part to contain the effects of this crisis, as well as to formalize mechanisms for providing assistance to these masses of people, that postwar humanitarian apparatuses such as the 1951 International Convention Relating to the Status of Refugees and the UN High Commission for Refugees (UNHCR) were established.

In this development, beyond the identification of a "well-founded fear of persecution," it was the departure from one's home country that most defined refugee status. As Michael Barnett argues in a study of the UNHCR, "Only a world of sovereign states that had categories of people called 'citizens' and were intent on regulating population flows could produce a legal category of 'refugees'" (2001: 251). Not only did the category "refugee" require its counterpart citizen to be a sensible account of loss, the elaboration of this category seemed to be a way to limit the dangers such people might pose to states. Limiting relief to people who had left their countries served "to limit [states'] obligations and honor their sovereignty, restricting the numbers that might ask for international assistance and prohibiting the international body from intruding on domestic affairs" (Barnett 2001: 252).

The years of the AFSC project in Gaza coincided with international efforts to develop a new general definition of a refugee. Before WWII, refugees – Armenian, Russian, and German (Jewish), for example – and the regimes designed to aid them had been defined by particular circumstances (Hathaway 1984; Skran 1995). In its aftermath, efforts were made to provide a universal definition of a *refugee*, efforts that culminated in the 1951 Convention. Despite the move from particular to general in refugee law, the Convention was far from universal. Faced with the threat of limitless obligations to accept displaced persons, the drafters developed clearly specified parameters for acquiring refugee status (persecution on the basis of race, religion, nationality, or membership in a particular social group) and limited the Convention's applicability to those who left their countries "as a result of events occurring before 1 January 1951," with individual signatories given the option of interpreting that clause to mean "events occurring in Europe" or "events occurring in Europe or elsewhere" (Takkenberg 1998: 56). It was not until the convention was amended in 1967 that temporal and geographic restrictions were removed.

Although aid to Palestinians was in large part governed by this international refugee regime, it is important to note that Palestinians have an awkward place within it. After protracted discussions about the importance of acknowledging special UN responsibility for the Palestinian refugee problem, as well as concerns about extending the convention beyond European populations, the 1951 Convention "temporarily" excluded Palestinian refugees. Given the restrictions built into the convention, Palestinian exclusion does not appear so exceptional but, rather, was an experience they shared with other non-European refugee populations. They did not come under the authority or protection of the UNHCR but, instead, received aid from UNRWA, which was established in 1950. To the extent that Palestinians receive legal protection, and it is a very limited extent, this protection is derived from UN Resolution 194 and its demand for a resolution of the refugee condition.

Furthermore, there is no legal definition of a Palestinian refugee, just the working definition formalized by UNRWA in 1952 to determine eligibility for relief. The definition states that "a Palestine refugee is a person whose normal residence was Palestine for a minimum of two years preceding the outbreak of the conflict in 1948 and who, as a result of this conflict, has lost both his home and his means of livelihood" (UNRWA 1955). This definition of eligibility for relief does not, and was not intended to, cover all those who were displaced from their homes and who might qualify for return. It did not, for instance, include those persons who either left the area of UNRWA operations or who were not in need. Rather, it was an instrumental definition, intended to assist UNRWA in responding to the enormous humanitarian crisis among displaced Palestinians. In the absence of anything else though, it has de facto served to define Palestinian refugee status. The longevity of what might seem like a stopgap measure is a common feature of the Palestinian experience.

The Gazan instance thus illuminates a more general capacity of legal regimes to order conditions that fall outside their direct control. Despite all the ways Palestine has been rendered exceptional to the broader international refugee regime, the terms of this regime – with its emphasis on making clear distinctions between refugees and citizens – profoundly shaped the Palestinian experience. Gaza's population categories have been derived from legal definitions that do not quite apply in this territory (international refugee conventions), shaped by institutions that do not have jurisdiction over it (UNHCR), and influenced by long absent political forms (the sovereign state). That these instruments are not exactly applicable has had important consequences for the ways they have affected Gaza, but it has not been a relation of simple exclusion. My focus here is precisely on these consequences – on the ways that Gazans came to see themselves in the terms used by humanitarian practitioners and, in turn, on the ways that these practitioners were guided not just by the concrete needs of the situation but also by the demands of an emerging arena of international humanitarian law.

[...]

Who Is Not a Refugee?

In the years since WWII a highly elaborated international refugee regime – consisting of law and practice, institutions and agencies – has come into being. This regime has been subject to considerable critique, by both practitioners (Hyndman 2000; Kennedy 2004; Terry 2002) and observers (Malkki 1995; Rieff 2002), in part for its failure (or better said, refusal) to address the political dimensions of refugee crises. This question of politics is one of the endemic challenges of humanitarian relief and law. Its nonpolitical stance is often what makes humanitarianism possible – permitting access to populations in need of aid, convincing countries to sign on to refugee conventions – but it also gives humanitarianism a sometimes cruelly narrow focus, able to keep people alive but entirely incapable of changing the conditions that have put them at such great risk.

This stance has had important consequences, not only for the resolution of refugee crises but also for the consolidation of the figure and subject of the refugee (Daniel and Knudsen 1995; Malkki 1996). Refugees, it has been noted by many, seem the quintessential embodiment of what Agamben calls "bare life" (Agamben 1995, 1998; Pandolfi 2003): granted assistance to the extent, and only to the extent, that they appear as apolitical subjects. Although, as Miriam Ticktin argues, this "restricted humanity" (2006) also produces its own political forms (see also Fassin 2005). As humanitarianism has been reconfigured in the

post–Cold War period, its relationship to state sovereignty has become more complicated (Redfield 2005). Proponents of the "new" humanitarianism, for instance, have claimed a right of intervention across these previously inviolate boundaries (Chandler 2001; Holzgrefe and Keohane 2003; Rieff 1999). Just as significantly, though, efforts to keep people from moving across borders – with the effect frequently of rendering them "internally displaced," but not refugees – have also introduced new forms of humanitarian practice such as "preventative protection" and the creation of "safe havens" inside countries at war (Hyndman 2000: 17–18).

When the AFSC was working in Gaza, discussions about the new postwar refugee definition were underway, but it must be remembered that neither the general nor the Palestinian specific refugee definition had been codified. In the absence of a clear framework to define their work – whether universal (such as the 1951 convention would provide for other cases) or particular (such as the 1926 League of Nations Arrangements had for Armenian and Russian refugees) – practitioners had to improvise. Faced with immense need and limited resources, relief workers had to develop their own mechanisms for managing delivery and determining eligibility, mechanisms that often went against their own view of their mission.

While in the legal domain the distinction between the categories refugee and citizen may seem clear and sharp, for Quaker aid workers on the ground, it was not obvious who should count as a refugee. As one AFSC worker put it:

> It is becoming increasingly difficult to make a legitimate distinction on the basis of food need as between the refugees and the inhabitants of the area. Since the area produces very little food apart from oranges and a few vegetables, and since the bulk of normal economic life in the area is becoming progressively more stagnant, and the local food situation is progressively deteriorating ... when refugees receive a relatively steady and adequate diet, while the local population sees its own diet progressively restricted, an important source of conflict is added.[2]

Based on these observations, AFSC officials concluded that "*all* Arabs with their homes in Palestine were destitute and proper subjects for public assistance .... The category "refugee" is not only difficult to apply, but is quite unjust."[3] Reiterating this position in a July report to Philadelphia headquarters, the chief of mission stated: "We now feel the necessity of broadening our definition of the term refugee to include a considerable number of people who still live in their own houses but have been completely deprived of any source of livelihood due to the fact that their land is in the hands of the Jews."[4]

As long as the United Nations did not allow them to expand their definition to include these dispossessed people, and it did not, the AFSC was constrained by what it viewed as an inadequate account of who qualified as a "proper subject" of assistance. This refusal to expand the eligibility for aid – which was in essence a refusal to do away with the categories refugee and citizen as a guiding principle of relief – was, I argue, fundamentally connected to the emerging humanitarian regime. To be sure, the United Nations had budget constraints and concerns about setting precedents that would make it difficult to contain its aid programs, but without an international refugee regime – with its respect for state sovereignty – that depended precisely on making a distinction between those who were at home and under the protection of their governments and those who were uprooted from their states, it may not have continued to "steadfastly [resist] persistent and persuasive efforts to have it become responsible for the care and feeding of citizens of the various countries who are merely needy or destitute as a result of the war in Palestine."[5] In the domain of population distinctions, that is, relief to Palestinians seems to have been ordered by emergent legal regimes from which Palestinians were to be formally excluded.

Although the AFSC did not share the same outlook as the United Nations, because it was working under contract to this body it was compelled to operate within this framework. Despite the fact that one of its "nineteen points" was that it would work to "preserve life and health and provide shelter for those whose destitution arises from the present troubles, without any discrimination except that of human need,"[6] the organization was compelled precisely to discriminate based on "kind" not "need." In fact, even as the AFSC pressed for a change at the level of UN policy, it was often a strict enforcer of the distinction in planning its own work. Decisions about what projects to undertake were made by category of person to be helped. That the AFSC found itself acting in ways that often seemed to contradict its own principles further highlights the radiating effects of the emerging international refugee regime.

The need for a sanitation project in Jabalya, for example, provoked a typical sort of decision. The Quakers decided that because Jabalya was "an established village, it was not felt that it should be the particular responsibility of the Quakers to see this accomplished, nor should any funds come from [the United Nations]. Through some rather painful meetings with mukhtars, the District Officers [Egyptian officials], and a Quaker representative, money is being collected by the village to at least partially care for the situation."[7] As the Quakers understood the limits of their intervention in the lives of natives, they could be involved in elaborating a sanitation plan, and in pressuring Gazans to undertake and fund this plan, but could not offer financial assistance themselves. As this case makes clear, then, even as natives were not included in the refugee service domain, they had their own complicated relations with refugee-service providers.

The question of eligibility was not put to rest during the AFSC's time in Gaza. Even when UNRWA took over, it reminded the larger UN body of the inadequacy of its aid. In 1955, the UNRWA director prepared a report for the General Assembly on "other claimants for relief," which detailed the conditions of Gaza's natives. The report noted that of 95,000 natives, 70,000 were registered with the Egyptian authorities as being in need of assistance, stating: "Nearly the whole population is therefore in need as a result of the establishment of the demarcation line and of the impossibility of moving goods and persons across it legally" (UNRWA 1955: 10). Despite this strong statement, the General Assembly did not extend the mandate. UNRWA practice, therefore, was also bound by a policy that its own leadership ultimately found inadequate.

Rights to Relief

As this section will explore, the sense of relief as a right became central to how Palestinian refugees understood their receipt of this aid. It was also crucial to humanitarian practice, which had to sort out eligibility in essentially these terms. Like other aspects of Palestinian refugee experience, though, relief was not exactly a codified legal right. Given these ambiguities, for service providers in Gaza, the process of defining who was a "proper subject of assistance," and the difficulties therein, was only one step in a relief process that was fraught with difficulty, and moral quandaries, at almost every turn. As suggested above, these quandaries were in part a consequence of Gaza's particular location within a broader humanitarian context. Although Quaker relief workers were dissatisfied with the limitations of their mandate, the success of their relief project – for which they had only the limited resources provided for "refugees" – demanded that they enforce those limitations, that they carefully police the boundaries of this category. Crucial to this policing was careful documentation and record management, as it was the registration of population, and the rations lists created from that registration, that gave particular persons "rights" to relief (see Figure 20.1).

Ration cards were central components of the distribution of supplies and their accuracy was perceived as vital. Developing accurate refugee rolls was a problem that plagued the AFSC, and that remained a challenge for UNRWA for many years. One significant problem was the persistence of fraud in the lists. This fraud was of several sorts: the registration of native Gazans as refugees, the inflation of family size, the retention of the deceased on the lists, and the related multiple registration of births. As a Quaker report on the refugee camp in Maghazi noted in February 1949: "The death of a small child is easily concealed ... And no refugee is anxious to report a

Figure 20.1 *Ration cards were a central part of the AFSC relief distribution system. Eligibility for rations was determined by UN criteria that mandated that only "refugees" and not "natives" could receive UN aid. This distinction among the population has had enduring effects on political identity in Gaza. Source: AFSC Archives, 1948–50.*

death in another's family – he does not know how soon he will be anxious to conceal one in his own household."[8] When UNRWA took over the relief project, it reported the same sort of practice: "To increase or to prevent decreases in their ration issue, they eagerly report births, sometimes by passing a new-born baby from family to family, and reluctantly report deaths, resorting often to surreptitious burial to avoid giving up a ration card" (UNRWA 1952: 3).

Quaker volunteers were sympathetic to the pressures that might lead people to underreport deaths, but they nonetheless sought to discover the truth whenever possible. Former relief workers recall some of the methods they used. In an oral history conducted under the auspices of the AFSC archives, Paul Johnson explained that "at one point some brilliant character discovered that when someone died if you offered his family a winding sheet, a shroud, when he came in to collect the shroud you could work one number quickly."[9] The pressures that the AFSC felt to have accurate lists – pressures that were directly connected to limited resources – compelled them to make use of control methods that raised difficult moral questions. Although Johnson insisted that "that isn't trickery," he did note that "there were people who were terribly upset and were so sympathetic with the refugees that it was difficult for them to admit the circumstances were forceful and something had to be done."[10]

Although individual subterfuge may have elicited sympathy, the Quakers were more frustrated by fraud on the part of *mukhtars* (village leaders). Mukhtars had considerable responsibility for registering families, and Gazans remember how they sometimes registered people for money. Abu Hassan, a retired school principal, told me that a mukhtar "used to tell the family of 7 members that he would register them as 8 if they gave him 7 pounds, or he would make them 9 for 10 pounds …. Some native Gazans registered their names as refugees by giving the mukhtar something …. Some of them receive rations from UNRWA until today." Quakers in the field noted this same practice. As one commented: "They [mukhtars] will sell their signatures on virtually every occasion, shaking the refugees down if a complaint is to be submitted with their confirmation, if the mukhtar is to confirm the membership of a certain family in his village, confirming a certain number of children, etc, etc. What is sold for truth can equally be sold for falsehood, and that is frequently the practice it appears."[11] Through this process of sorting out the "honest" from the "dishonest," what came to identify a person as deserving of assistance was whether that person was in a category eligible for relief. One effect of these efforts, then, was that natives who made their ways onto the relief lists came to appear as the "undeserving poor," a judgment that seems divorced from the Quaker awareness that these people were in as much genuine need as refugees.

As time went on, factors other than immediate need contributed to reluctance to be removed from the refugee rolls. Palestinians quickly came to see this aid, not as charity, but as a right: a reflection of international responsibility for their conditions. Quakers noted this sense of entitlement right from the beginning, and Gazans I knew certainly felt it. As a letter

to AFSC headquarters in Philadelphia from the Gaza unit put it:

> Since it is very difficult for refugees here to communicate with the outside world, we feel we have an obligation to convey what we can of their opinions and thinking at the present time. They feel strongly that the United Nations are responsible for their plight, and therefore have the total responsibility to feed, house, clothe, and repatriate them …. Accordingly the relief we bring them appears to them to be their right, and in no way an act of humanitarian charity on the part of the United Nations.[12]

Relief services came to serve as "evidence" both of dispossession and of international responsibility for it. It is in part for this reason that even as time passed and some refugees began to earn income and become self-sufficient in the eyes of UNRWA, people remained reluctant to be removed from the rolls. As the 1956 report noted: "The Agency's ration card was regarded by refugees as their only evidence of refugee status" (UNRWA 1956: 3). Receiving aid seemed the only way to formally claim dispossession and, perhaps, even to claim the right to Palestine.

Palestinians were not wrong to see significance in their relief status. Being defined as a refugee not only gave a person access to a variety of services from which those whose losses were different were excluded, it also offered a recognition of this loss itself, which natives were denied. Given the lack of a legal definition of a Palestinian refugee – one that could guarantee, or at least confirm, their rights – it was humanitarian relief through which loss was recognized. Even as Quakers and UNRWA officials documented the tremendous need among natives, it was only refugees whose dispossession was given international standing by their work (though given the total lack of resolution such standing has proven to be of limited value).

However sensible local efforts to remain on the rolls may have been, the AFSC and then UNRWA were under tremendous pressure to bring the numbers down. In October 1949, the United Nations asked for an immediate reduction of the lists by 20,000 names. This demand further highlighted for the Quakers one of the difficulties inherent in their work – how to balance between the need for efficient and effective aid delivery and the importance of providing that aid in the Quaker way – a way that emphasized individual relations between aid provider and recipient. To try and reduce the rolls in this Quaker way "through careful individual investigation of every case"[13] would take years – and would mean in the meantime that new "legitimate" names could not be added to the lists. To reduce the rolls in an efficient manner required both making use of informants to identify false names and withholding food to villages whose mukhtars were recalcitrant about correcting the lists. Some mukhtars were jailed by Egyptian authorities until they could be compelled to cooperate. Many of the Quakers working in Gaza felt quite strongly that "using food as a weapon" in this way was entirely contrary to Quaker principles.[14] For these people, the very real need for more accurate accounting created an equally real crisis of conscience:

> Should we, as Friends, be asked to continue in this programme when we feel we are compromising Quaker principles? On the other hand, the Service Committee has taken on this obligation to the United Nations, to feed these masses of people, and we as individuals have come as AFSC representatives. Therefore, though we cannot reach the individual, should we not carry out to the best of our ability this relief programme, with whatever tools we are given, for as long as the need still exists?[15]

This was not a conflict that could be satisfactorily resolved. Unable to walk away from the crisis, the Quakers had to proceed in an un-Quaker manner.

The staff report on the successful reduction of rations recipients to around 210,000 from 245,000 reflected this uneasy method. Commenting on the withholding of rations, the report noted: "In using such measures it was recognized that honest refugees were made to suffer along with the dishonest ones." Reflecting on the use of informants, it stated: "While the AFSC worker attempted to insure

himself that real refugees were not removed from the lists, this undoubtedly happened in some instances where time and staff did not permit adequate investigation." Despite these problems, the report concluded: "the above mass methods of reducing lists were necessary, though undesirable from many points of view."[16] This process was troubling to AFSC volunteers, and highlighted persistent difficulties in being both Quaker and a relief worker. For the population of Gaza, it further contributed to tensions among the different parts of that population.

People in Relief: Tension, Conflict, Cooperation

Although humanitarian work needed to keep different sections of the Gazan population distinct, conditions on the ground had sometimes contradictory effects on such relations. Refugees sometimes came to the aid of natives by giving them (or selling them) some of their rations. As one person told me, "refugees lived on rations" and natives "shared the rations of refugees who lived with them." Natives opened their houses (or rented them) to refugees, and helped them get settled as best they could. As one woman remembered: "All women participated in receiving refugees and in helping them by putting them in schools, mosques, and empty places – until we had the Quaker organization." A refugee echoed this sentiment, saying: "when we came here, those from Gaza hosted and helped us as much as they could." These memories of mutual assistance are matched by other memories of a more tense reception. Im Amir, a refugee from Yibna, remembered moving around a great deal within Gaza searching for a place to stay: "The people of Gaza did not tolerate us, and kicked us out …. They wanted money for renting houses, and we had no money." These different memories of relations between refugees and natives are certainly colored by the experience of 50 years together in Gaza, but they also reflect the complexity of social relations at the time.

AFSC volunteers commented frequently on both the assistance provided by the local population and the burden that the influx of refugees necessarily represented. As I noted above, the fact that refugees receiving rations had a diet that was increasingly better than that of natives created an "important source of conflict" between the groups. That refugees were "naturally resented"[17] by natives is noted throughout the archival record, although so is the fact that Gazans extended themselves to assist these refugees when possible. The difficult conditions in Gaza both demanded and stretched to the breaking point existing practices of mutual aid, frequently thought of in terms of *zakat* (charity). According to a report on conditions in the Gaza City area: "There has been cooperation, decent in spirit but limited by necessity, on the part of local officials and plain citizens. A woman's group, under the direction of the mayor's wife … has furnished volunteers." The same report also noted: "Besides their own great and everpressing misery, the refugees are creating problems, both current and future, for the permanent population."[18] Among these problems was the fact that "lack of fuel has driven refugees to denuding the land of every burnable thing, especially trees and shrubs."[19] In an effort to stop or at least slow down this destruction, Gazans sometimes resorted to withholding what assistance they had been giving refugees: "This drove a nearby landowner to shut off camp water taps until refugees promised not to cut anymore from his trees."

Even as AFSC officials worried about the impact of refugees on natives, they also worried about the negative effects of being a refugee on refugees themselves. Reports from the field regularly commented on the low morale in Gaza: "As the refugees in the Gaza strip entered a second winter of miserable living conditions with no relief in sight, the deterioration of morale, evidenced by an increased feeling of discouragement and disillusionment, has continued."[20] These worries continued under UNRWA: "A refugee who has lost, or has never acquired, the habit of self-reliance and self-supporting work will be a useless burden on the community, whether he is later to be repatriated or resettled" (UNRWA 1956: 6). By the later years of the administration, the immediate threat of starvation or exposure was much diminished, but the threat of idleness

remained: "One of the tragic aspects of the life of a refugee is that he often has nothing to do. This is true of many Palestine refugees and is particularly true in the Gaza strip, where 300,000 people in all are concentrated in a small area of largely unproductive, desert land. … Although a man may not be aware of it, the debilitating effect of ten years without regular work is considerable" (UNRWA 1958: 19).

Although unemployment was also high among native Gazans, they saw themselves as at lesser risk for moral deterioration than refugees who lived on rations. As Salim Rashid, a native Gazan, said to me: "From my point of view, and I say it to everybody, it would have been better if there was no agency. Prophet Mohammed said 'the high hand is better than the low hand.' What does this mean? It means that the one who gives is better than the one who takes." Another Gazan contrasted the dignity of Palestinians before 1948 with their conditions after receiving UNRWA aid: "After UNRWA started to distribute rations, the Palestinian started to take; he started begging. And the morals were destroyed." As much as an expression of concern, these comments have to be understood as part of a discourse of differentiation, wherein Gazans sought to distinguish themselves from refugees.

This kind of discourse was by no means one sided. If natives thought refugees might be morally deficient, refugees often pointed to their educational and professional successes to suggest that they might be "better" than Gazans. As one refugee remarked to me: "The Gazans mocked us until we became educated and proved that we the refugees are better than the Gazans in education and craftsmanship." As the Quakers monitored their school program, they noted with some surprise that refugee children sometimes outperformed Gazans. In one school in which both groups were in classes together, "the refugee boys in the regular classes have higher average records than do the local boys, and the high ranking student in the four secondary grades is a refugee."[21] As educational opportunities in Gaza expanded, most dramatically under Nasser, the opportunities for refugees to improve their conditions also increased. As one Gazan native put it: "In my house I have water and electricity, but he is living in a shack, so he says to himself 'why don't I go to Saudi Arabia and earn money?' Of course he studied and worked. They appreciated education more than we did." As people struggled, both for survival and for their future, they quite understandably sought ways of improving their positions. Given the difficulties in affecting either the political conditions or the service environment in which they lived, these efforts were often directed against people who were as vulnerable as themselves. As the examples of refugees sharing food with Gazans and Gazans housing refugees highlights, though, these conditions also provided new grounds for cooperation.

As the complicated relations between refugees and natives suggest, an outcome of the limited UN relief mandate was not only that it did not encompass all "proper subjects" for aid, but also that it helped produce and sustain new sociological and regulatory categories within the population, which – especially with time – acquired significant symbolic charge. The "natural" resentment of refugees by natives that the Quakers noted was, at least in part, produced by their own practices. Quakers clearly felt that the distinctions they were forced to make among the population were unfair – unhumanitarian in their view. Given how overwhelming conditions on the ground were, though, it is not surprising that they were more cognizant of the ways that humanitarian work might impede political resolution than of the ways its distinctions helped produce political identifications. As the following section explores, the social resentments, cooperation, and contestations that emerged from the intersection of humanitarian relief and difficult conditions also proved important for the elaboration of political values and modes of civic identification.

What Is a Citizen?

One of humanitarianism's significant consequences in Gaza – with the division of the population along the lines of refugees and natives – was the emergence of new claims about rights and articulations of community values. Indeed, if for policymakers at the time,

"the chief factor in the determination of the concept of a refugee in the proper sense of the term [was] citizenship," it might equally be said that for Gazans, and Palestinians more generally, a key factor in the concept of a "citizen" came to be refugeedom. What I explore here is less the legal status of Palestinian citizenship or its formulation by organized political movements, and more the life of this concept among ordinary people living in extraordinary circumstances. I want to suggest that familiar ideas about Palestinian citizenship have roots not only in the actions of political movements and articulations of intellectuals but also in people's responses to conditions of displacement and relief. Indeed, humanitarianism provides a lens through which one can see enactments of still inchoate ideas. Although these early years after the nakba have often been seen (by Palestinians and others) as a moment in-between politics (a time of mourning and anguish over the loss of Palestine, but before the capacity to organize against this loss had been regained), investigation of this period in Gaza reveals tentative articulations of ideas that would later prove important for Palestinian politics. Further, humanitarianism – with refugee and citizen its key terms – helped ensure that the language of citizenship remained part of Palestinian vocabulary, even in this difficult time.

As difficult as codifying refugee status proved to be in Gaza, though, defining *citizenship* has been almost more challenging. Since the end of the British Mandate – and the loss of the Palestinian citizenship that this state had conferred – the category of a "Palestinian citizen" has had no legal standing. There have been, to be sure, some efforts in this direction. The first, in the immediate aftermath of 1948, was the never really functional establishment of the All-Palestine Government, which declared Palestine an independent country (Shlaim 1990). In the latter years of the Egyptian Administration, the Palestine Liberation Organization (PLO) was founded to serve as a representative for the Palestinian people, and given nominal (although not actual) authority in Gaza. In recent years, the creation of the Palestinian National Authority (PNA) as part of the Oslo Accords seemed at one point to be a step toward actual Palestinian independence and legal citizenship. As conditions in the territories become worse, however, and the PNA ever less viable as an entity, it is difficult to imagine when and how this will happen.

Given the continued absence of a Palestinian state and the deep uncertainty about the political future of Palestinian territories and population, Palestinian citizenship necessarily remains a changing and contested category. Looking at Cambodian refugees in the United States, Aihwa Ong argues that we should consider citizenship not only as a "bundle of rights – a legal condition" (2003: 79) but as a "social process of mediated production of values concerning freedom, autonomy, and security" (2003: xvii). From this perspective, citizenship has as much to do with the enactment and management of social relations as with codified relations with the state. This suggestion is very helpful for considering Palestine's uncertain condition, in which policies of the various countries in which Palestinian refugees have lived (Kassim 2000; Massad 2001), the emergence of independent Palestinian political movements (Sayigh 1997; Schulz and Hammer 2003), the daily experience of life under Israeli occupation (Jean-Klein 2001; Tamari 1991), and, more recently, the establishment of state-like institutions in Palestinian territories (Jad et al. 2000; Milton-Edwards 2000) have all contributed to ideas about Palestinian citizenship.

Palestinian political vocabulary has, over the years, included a variety of key terms – terms that have, in turn, ascribed prominence at the forefront of the struggle to different segments of the Palestinian population. Given that much of the population is in exile, it is not surprising that geographic location has been of considerable importance in this dynamic. Indeed, the distinction of inside and outside has mattered a great deal, although what particular territory is called "inside" has changed over time. Before 1967 it referred to the part of Palestine that had become Israel; after, it expanded to include the West Bank and Gaza. To be inside has also been differently valued, first, as Edward Said noted, "someone you might easily be suspicious of [for living

with Israel]" and later "privileged [as] 'already there'" (1985: 51). At times there have been political contestations across this divide – as Palestinians in the West Bank and Gaza who led the first intifada resented the takeover of political leadership by PLO "returnees" after Oslo; or as refugees living outside objected to the PNA seeming to ignore their demand to return home. In the aftermath of 1948, Gaza remained "inside" in important ways: it was after all part of the territory of Palestine. At the same time, the majority of its new population was now "outside" their proper place in this territory. This mismatch in place and population highlights both the loss of the "stability of geography" (Said 1985: 19) that has been so central to the Palestinian experience and the multiplicity of forces at work in shaping political valuations.

In the absence of a state, to be a Palestinian citizen has meant to be a member in the national community – a community defined as existing in struggle. What constitutes proper participation in this struggle – and what therefore are seen as the values of citizenship – has, not surprisingly, been contested. The question of which Palestinians, located where, are best placed to speak for Palestine has also been connected to challenges about how they should speak and act – what sorts of claims should be made, what methods adopted for achieving their aims. Political values like *sumud* (steadfastness), armed struggle (exemplified by the *fida'iyyin*), nonviolent resistance (a significant tactic of the first intifada), and more recently *martyrdom* (a term applied to both suicide bombers and civilians killed by Israel), have each played an important role in Palestinian politics. I do not trace this long and complex history here but, rather, consider the first enactments of post-nakba citizenship values, paying particular attention to the role of humanitarianism, and humanitarian distinctions, in this process. In identifying people as natives or refugees – as being "of" or "out of" place – Quaker relief practices unwittingly participated in locating people in an emerging political geography and in shaping new political values connected to this geography.

In Gaza the challenge was not only to determine what citizenship could be, but who should be considered a citizen. In the categorical terms of humanitarianism, Gaza's citizens were those who were excluded from the category of refugee, and Gaza's natives were indeed referred to – by both Quakers and refugees – as citizens (*muwataniin*). Although to some degree this label was a default term, it did also invoke a particular notion of membership, not principally in a nation-state, but in a more local, civic space. This sense of citizenship indexed a particular kind of belonging to which not everyone could lay claim. When native Gazans were called "citizens" (by themselves, refugees, or Quakers), their different investment in the locality and its civic life was acknowledged. This appellation, furthermore, referenced a corresponding set of civic obligations – such as the obligation to assist the refugees coming into the area.

Humanitarian practice, though, also contributed to ideas about citizenship that included the entire population. At the national level, everyone in Gaza was appropriately included in the category of a potential Palestinian citizen, and in this arena refugees sometimes occupied a privileged location. Indeed, as important as was civic citizenship, the idea of national citizenship remained paramount, in both the humanitarian field and in Gazan sensibilities. Rogers Brubaker notes that: "Debates about citizenship, in the age of the nation-state, are debates about nationhood – about what it means, and what it ought to mean, to belong to a nation-state" (1998: 132).[22] And, yet, being a native or a refugee – with distinct statuses and relations to the place of Gaza – did have considerable impact on how people fit in this category. Refugees and nonrefugees alike shared a strong ongoing attachment to Palestine. Refugees were focused on their desire to return to their homes. Gazan natives were equally interested in the return of their lost lands, but the fact of living in their houses did make a difference. In moving to the national level, local community is not entirely left behind, however. Claims about national membership – about participation in a political community – are often enacted through struggles over local belonging. In asserting their status as Palestinian citizens, refugees effectively claimed a place in Gaza's social and political landscape.

If we think about citizenship as an expression of rights and obligations, the ways that these attributes did not easily map onto the population become immediately clear. To understand Gazan struggles over Palestinian citizenship, it is important to remember that in the Palestinian context the idea of "citizenship" represented a claim to the rights and obligations that are generally associated with this term, rather than a condition of formally having such rights. Hannah Arendt, exploring the challenge that refugees and stateless persons posed to the nation-state with its citizen-subject, argued that even more fundamental than the particular rights of citizenship is the "right to have rights," to have "a place in the world which makes opinions significant and actions effective" (1973: 296).

In the Gazan context it was to refugees that this right most directly applied. As we have seen, refugees had the "right" to relief, to the benefits of UNRWA services – and to the political claims that (against the agency's own wishes) derived from that status. Gaza's natives had no such access. Natives, who were no longer citizens but who did not qualify for refugee status, seem to lie outside the domain of any category that might offer them such protection. One Gazan, describing their anomalous condition, told me that when natives lost their land "they became neither citizens nor refugees." This political aspect of native exclusion from the "humanitarian space" – leaving them without a place from which to claim rights – was ultimately more significant than their lack of access to UN rations. It was in part, although not only, because of the significance of refugee status in making rights claims that the figure of the refugee has come to occupy such a large role in the Palestinian political imaginary.

Although refugees had more immediate access to "rights," both natives and refugees could be said to have national obligations. Not surprisingly, this was a terrain on which conflict between these groups was sometimes enacted. In the first years after 1948, Palestinian political culture was highly fragmented and conceptualizations of citizenship were still inchoate. As we have seen, existing ethical and social values were equally in disarray. In the difficult conditions in which Palestinians were living, values that would later be held up as mechanisms for unifying the population in struggle were often means through which people distinguished themselves from each other. The tentative articulations of citizenship that emerged in Gaza in this period were very much shaped by conflicts and conditions on the ground, which as we have seen were themselves shaped by the relief practices that dominated life in Gaza at that point.

Humanitarian distinctions came to have political significance within the Palestinian community, as people sought to claim a space for themselves in the post-nakba landscape. Having been dispossessed of much of their property, with the local economy entirely disrupted, native Gazans had little to cling to as a means of preserving their dignity. That they remained in their homes was one of the few things that distinguished them from the masses of people who had poured into Gaza. Among these Gazans, there were incipient expressions of ideas that would later become an explicit facet of Palestinian citizenship – the notion of steadfastness (*sumud*), the value of staying put. This was not a formal articulation of *sumud* – a term elaborated after 1967 to describe Palestinians living under Israeli rule – but, rather, an ad hoc response to difficult circumstances. The early stirrings of this value that were evident in Gaza immediately after 1948 suggest that even before the language of sumud entered the Palestinian vocabulary, staying put was identified as an obligation of citizenship. In Gaza, these inchoate ideas were in part a means through which natives sought to differentiate themselves from, and claim superiority to, refugees. At the same time – also foreshadowing later developments in the politics of sumud, when it came to be criticized as an excuse for bourgeois inaction (Tamari 1991) – refugees challenged these claims.

Refugees I knew in Gaza described how natives sometimes accused them of being traitors for having left their land and used the term refugee as an insult, "saying 'you refugee, you left your village.'" Refugees responded with their own accusations. As Abu Khalil, a refugee living in Rafah camp, told me:

They used to say that we sold our land and came to ruin theirs. They accused us of being spies. But they are the ones who sold the land …. They used to say to the donkey, "your face is like the refugee's." The relation was good in the first weeks. We were guests. They thought that we would stay for a limited short period, but when they realized the situation, tension increased and they started differentiating between a citizen [*muwatan*] and a refugee [*muhajir*]."

If natives sometimes argued that refugees had been "bad" citizens by leaving their homes, the counterclaim in Abu Khalil's remark was that staying put had no value if it was not accompanied by "good" politics. Given a context in which their claims to fulfilling the obligations of citizenship had to rest on action, it is not surprising that, in the years since 1948, Gaza's refugees have developed a reputation for political activism and that many significant Palestinian political movements have emerged from Gaza. Just as the sumud of the 1970s and early 1980s was later overshadowed by active resistance in the intifada (1987–93), these accusations and counteraccusations constitute competing claims not only about who counted as a good Palestinian citizen but also what the values of that citizenship should be. In contrast to later discussions among the Palestinian leadership about these ideas, these early contestations in Gaza were embedded more in struggles for survival than in political ideologies.

Even as natives and refugees sometimes challenged each other across the difference of displacement, other, in some ways competing, ideas about citizenship also began to play out. In this process, the figure of the refugee came in many ways to be seen as the embodiment of Palestinian possibility. The subject who would be a citizen of the future Palestinian state has often been conceived of in the present as a refugee. Fawaz Turki argues that it was the transformation of the refugee from an "oppressed wanderer" – "who wander around the refugee camps, the Arab capitals and around the world, disinherited of homeland and an ability to share their humanity with others" (1974: 7) – to a fighter (*fida'i*) that enabled the exile to be a political figure. The establishment of fida'iyyin was indeed important, but, as I have explored here, experiences in Gaza in the early years after the nakba suggest both that the self-consciously nonpolitical practice of humanitarianism played a role in this development and that the refugee should not be seen as simply a prepolitical figure of exile.

The emergence of the figure of the refugee as crucial to the idea of the citizen was directly connected to the details of humanitarian practice. It was in part through these practices that the "worn dog-eared Palestine passport issued in British Mandate days by a government that no longer legally exists" (UNRWA 1952: 3) was supplanted as "evidence of nationality" by the ration card, a document that became, UNRWA officials commented, "so much a part of the life and economy of refugees that it is not unusual for it to be used as a tangible asset upon the strength of which substantial sums can be borrowed" (UNRWA 1954: 15). If being recognized as a refugee was also what recognized people as dispossessed, it is not surprising that refugee identification – as complicated as it was – would be politically important.

As Quakers noted throughout the course of their relief project, even in these "years of hunger" (Abu Naml 1979) Gazan refugees expressed themselves politically (even if they had little opportunity to act effectively on this expression). We have seen that they identified relief as a right, challenging their relegation to the humanitarian corner. As one Quaker reported back from an exploratory trip to Gaza: "The refugee's role is not always passive. As we were driving through one swarm of refugees in the town of Khan Yunis in our UN Observer, white-flagged jeep our Arab guide heard one of the tattered old ladies in the crowd say, 'We don't want your flag; let your pockets speak.'"[23] Further, as organized political life began to reemerge, and Gazans pressed the Egyptians for an opportunity to take up the fight for their homes, refugees occupied an important place. When refugees in Gaza did become fida'iyyin, their knowledge of their home villages acquired a tactical significance in the national struggle as people were often sent on missions

to their former homes. Although this participation in struggle did not end tension between natives and refugees – tension which, after all, was in part rooted in humanitarian practice – it did underscore how important refugeedom was to emerging practices of Palestinian citizenship.

The challenges of citizenship in Gaza were evident in the travel documents that the Egyptian Administration eventually and reluctantly issued for Gazans. These papers were necessary for international travel because their British Mandate-era passports were no longer valid and no non-Arab country had ever recognized the documents issued by the All-Palestine Government. To counteract the possibility that these Egyptian documents (even if they were not passports) might further the legal dissolution of Palestinian national identity, they identified the bearer as a Palestinian national, and a refugee.[24] Not surprisingly, some native Gazans objected to this demand that they travel as refugees. It was a stigma they did not want, especially as they did not receive the benefits of this status. Despite these objections, the demand that citizenship documents mark a collective nationality mandated this shared identity. In the Gazan context, the citizen had also to be a refugee, with all the contradictions that implies.

Conclusion

Although humanitarian principles – with their commitment to assist people in need without regard for political distinctions – seem at odds with the kinds of value judgments that are inherent to citizenship discourses, the Palestinian experience highlights how interconnected they can be. In Gaza the effects of humanitarianism were complicated, at once contributing to tensions among the population and affecting the development of a political vocabulary that has been important for everyone. Even as considerable current debate about humanitarianism centers on the question of how engaged with politics this enterprise should seek to be – whether or not, for instance, humanitarianism should "aspire to restructure underlying social relations" (Barnett 2005: 724) – the history I have explored here suggests that it may be impossible for humanitarianism to avoid such broad effects. Humanitarian operations are frequently compelled to make distinctions among people that seem antithetical to their core principles, with significant and often long-term implications for those populations. Further, however narrowly these organizations may seek to focus their interventions, humanitarian practice – the work of providing for people's needs – inevitably impacts the wider social order.

For Palestinians in the aftermath of displacement, what it meant – and would mean – to be a citizen or a refugee (or even a native) was clearly in flux. The requirements of relief ensured that these would be the dominant categories through which international organizations and workers viewed the population of Gaza. Conditions on the ground, including those produced by these organizations, meant that these distinctions were also meaningful for the population itself. The complexity of these categories in Gaza is also a reminder of the often awkward relation between legal regimes and relief projects – between human rights and humanitarianism. The development of a regime of refugee protection has required the careful and clear delineation of who is a refugee. Humanitarian aid projects are then governed by these categories which may not – and in Gaza clearly did not – reflect either conditions of need or loss on the ground. The inadequacy of these distinctions to the tasks they seek to fulfill is clear, as is their effectiveness in shaping people's lives in sometimes unexpected ways. The difficult political, social, and economic conditions in which Palestinians have lived for more than 50 years has ensured that these categories have continued to be fraught.

This exploration of early humanitarian efforts in Gaza further shows how multivalent the category of refugee can be. In the Palestinian case, even as it does not capture the full extent of Palestinian loss, and is thus not a fully adequate category through which to make political claims, it has also offered

the only formal recognition of this loss, and therefore has in practice been tremendously important for Palestinian politics and for claims made to the "international community" for Palestinian rights. Within the Palestinian community, it is not only the large percentage of the population who are refugees but also the tremendous importance that the idea of refugeedom has played in Palestinian political vocabulary that has made the question of how, now, to "solve" the refugee problem so vexed. That it has not been so easy to turn "refugees into citizens" (as one book (Arzt 1997) that proposed a regional resettlement plan was entitled), is a result not just of what is often called Palestinian "intransigence" but also of the complex role the "refugee" has played in Palestinian experience.

Although for Palestinians the first claim embedded in the refugee category was for a right to go home, they have never, in fact, been permitted to return. This history has made the Palestinian case a paradigmatic instance of displacement and refugeedom. While in the early postwar period the distinction between refugee and citizen was paramount in international humanitarianism (and remains important), new problems and henceforth new mechanisms of distinguishing among people in need have now emerged. Since the 1990s, the category of Internally Displaced Persons (IDPs) has become a subject of considerable debate and concern (Cohen 2006; Hyndman 2000). Not having crossed a border, such persons did not traditionally fit in the UNHCR mandate and they did not constitute a formal category. Decisions to extend UNHCR aid to two groups of such people – in Yugoslavia and northern Iraq – while not ending debate about jurisdiction, ensured that this category would henceforth have a place in the humanitarian field (Barnett 2001; Phoung 2005). The complex and radiating effects of inclusion in, and exclusion from, particular regimes and categories evident in the Palestinian instance provides a lens through which to consider current trends in refugee recognition.

Even as new categories of need are being acknowledged, we are also witnessing greater restrictions on qualifying for protections (one effect of aiding people as IDPs can, in fact, be to keep them from the protections provided by refugee status). The September 11, 2001, attacks on New York and Washington seem to have accelerated a process that was already underway to further restrict entrance into Europe and the United States (Hyndman 2005). This environment affects not only refugee status but also citizenship. As codified by both the 1996 immigration reforms and the Patriot Act, people living in the United States who lack formal citizenship are being more firmly excluded from the benefits of substantive citizenship. Although this lack of formal legal protection can leave people in very precarious positions, able to rely only on compassion for assistance (Ticktin 2006), the Palestinian case indicates that, sometimes at least, people may be able to use such precarious conditions as a starting point for more expansive claims. Not only refugees but also other kinds of victims as well have claimed relief (of various kinds) as a right and used that claim to make broader demands for recognition (Fortun 2001; Ong 2003; Petryna 2002).

The Palestinian instance, with its unique apparatuses and institutions, thus provides important insight into more general understandings of refugeedom and citizenship. This case illuminates – not a space apart from politics – but a liminal state of political formation. Just as population categories were operative, although not codified, political practice was evident, although tenuous. Even as the absence of citizenship as a "legal condition" has had deleterious and often devastating impact on the lives of Gazans (and all Palestinians), the inchoate ideas about citizenship I have explored here have also been important in forging community and shaping political action. Further, even as legal and practical definitions of refugees in humanitarianism have often sought to excise a discussion of rights, and of justice, from this domain, Palestinian experience illuminates the ways that the idea of the refugee can also operate politically (if not always effectively). This quintessential category of a supposedly apolitical humanitarianism appears, on close inspection, to have been crucial to the re-formation of Palestinian political identity in the wake of displacement.

NOTES

1 These conversations took place in the course of research I was conducting on government and bureaucracy in Gaza during the British Mandate and Egyptian Administration (1948–67). Unless otherwise cited, all quotes from Gazans (natives and refugees) are from interviews I tape recorded in the course of this research.
2 AFSC, #40 FS Sect Palestine, Memo from Howard Wriggins, March 18, 1949.
3 AFSC, #75 FS Sect Palestine, Memo from Howard Wriggins to Colin Bell, May 15, 1949.
4 AFSC, #72 FS Sect Palestine, Monthly Report from Emmett Gulley to AFSC, July 18, 1949.
5 UNWRA 1950.
6 AFSC, #174, "Nineteen Points."
7 AFSC, #106 FS Sect Palestine, Monthly Sanitation Report, July 1949.
8 AFSC, #36 FS Sect Palestine, "Background Material on Magazy," February 16, 1949.
9 Paul Johnson, AFSC Oral History Interview #601, September 19, 1992.
10 Paul Johnson, AFSC Oral History Interview #601, September 19, 1992.
11 AFSC, #41 FS Sect Palestine, letter from Howard Wriggins to Colin Bell, February 18, 1949.
12 AFSC, #53 FS Sect Palestine, letter from AFSC Gaza Unit to C. Pickett, AFSC Headquarters, October 12, 1949.
13 AFSC, #24 FS Sect Palestine, letter from Charlie Reed to Philadelphia AFSC office, October 15, 1949.
14 AFSC, #128 FS Sect Palestine, letter from Donald Stevenson to Bronson Clark, October 24, 1949.
15 AFSC, #80 FS Sect Palestine, "Concerns Expressed at Campleaders Meeting and at Staff Meeting," October 13 and 14, 1949.
16 AFSC, #83 FS Sect Palestine, "Measures Employed by the American Friends Service Committee to Reduce the Number of Rations Issued Refugees in the Gaza Strip," December 1949.
17 AFSC, #117 FS Sect Palestine, Background material on Gaza City area, January 28, 1949.
18 Background material on Gaza City area.
19 AFSC, #63 FSC Sect Palestine, "Background Material on Rafah," February 1, 1949.

20   AFSC, #67 FS Sect Palestine, "Operational Report of AFSC Palestine Refugee Unit for December, 1949."

21   AFSC, #60 FS Sect Palestine, Report on Education Activities for December 1949.

22   The most common word for citizen – *muwatan* – is directly tied to the idea of nation – *watan* in Arabic, although *muwatan* is also widely used in the more local civic way described above.

23   AFSC #84 FS Sect Palestine, Memo from John Devine to Ambassador Griffis, December 13, 1948.

24   DW, *Qawā, 'im Al-Mushır*, Group 41, file 90505, Memo from Governor General, November 15, 1958.

REFERENCES

Abu Naml, Husayn, 1979. *Qitā' Ghazzah, 1948–1967: Tatawwarat Iqtisadiya wa-Siyasiya wa-Ijtimaiya wa-Askariya*. Beirut: PLO Research Center.

Agamben, Giorgio, 1995. We Refugees. M. Rocke, trans. *Symposium* 49(2): 114–119.

Agamben, Giorgio, 1998. *Homo Sacer: Sovereign Power and Bare Life*. Stanford: Stanford University Press.

Arendt, Hannah, 1973 [1951]. *On Totalitarianism*. New York: Harcourt Brace Jovanovich.

Barnett, Michael, 2001. Humanitarianism with a Sovereign Face: UNHCR in the Global Undertow. *International Migration Review* 35(1): 244–277.

Barnett, Michael, 2005. Humanitarianism Transformed. *Perspectives on Politics* 3(4): 723–740.

Brubaker, Rogers, 1998. Immigration, Citizenship, and the Nation-State in France and Germany. In *The Citizenship Debates*, Gershon Shafir, ed. Minneapolis: University of Minnesota Press, pp. 131–164.

Chandler, David, 2001. Road to Military Humanitarianism: How the Human Rights NGOs Shaped a New Humanitarian Agenda. *Human Rights Quarterly* 23(3): 678–700.

Cohen, Roberta, 2006. Developing an International System for Internally Displaced Persons. *International Studies Perspectives* 7(2): 87–101.

Daniel, E. V., and J. C. Knudsen, 1995. *Mistrusting Refugees*. Berkeley: University of California Press.

Fassin, Didier, 2005. Compassion and Repression: The Moral Economy of Immigration Policies in France. *Cultural Anthropology* 20(3): 362–387.

Fortun, Kim, 2001. *Advocacy after Bhopal: Environmentalism, Disaster, New Global Orders*. Chicago: University of Chicago Press.

Hathaway, James, 1984. The Evolution of Refugee Status in International Law: 1920–1950. *International and Comparative Law Quarterly* 33(2): 348–380.

Holzgrefe, J. L., and Robert Keohane, eds, 2003. *Humanitarian Intervention: Ethical, Legal, and Political Dilemmas*. Cambridge: Cambridge University Press.

Hyndman, Jennifer, 2000. *Managing Displacement: Refugees and the Politics of Humanitarianism*. Minneapolis: University of Minnesota Press.

Hyndman, Jennifer, 2005. Migration Wars: Refuge or Refusal? *Geoforum* 36(1): 3–6.

Jad, Islah, Penny Johnson, and Rita Giacaman, 2000. Transit Citizens: Gender and Citizenship under the Palestinian Authority. In *Gender and Citizenship in the Middle East*, Suad Joseph, ed. Syracuse: Syracuse University Press, pp. 137–157.

Jean-Klein, Iris, 2001. Nationalism and Resistance: The Two Faces of Everyday Activism in Palestine during the Intifada. *Cultural Anthropology* 16(1): 83–126.

Kassim, Anis, 2000. The Palestinians: From Hyphenated to Integrated Citizenship. In *Citizenship and the State in the Middle East*, Nils Butenschon, Uri Davis, and Manuel Hassassian, eds. Syracuse: Syracuse University Press, pp. 201–224.

Kennedy, David, 2004. *The Dark Sides of Virtue: Reassessing International Humanitarianism*. Princeton: Princeton University Press.

Malkki, Liisa, 1995. Refugee and Exile: From "Refugee Studies" to the National Order of Things. *Annual Review of Anthropology* (24): 495–523.

Malkki, Liisa, 1996. Speechless Emissaries: Refugees, Humanitarianism, and Dehistoricization. *Cultural Anthropology* 11(3): 377–404.

Massad, Joseph, 2001. *Colonial Effects: The Making of National Identity in Jordan*. New York: Columbia University Press.

Milton-Edwards, Beverley, 2000. Internal Security and Citizenship under the Palestinian National Authority. In *Citizenship and the State in the Middle East*, Nils Butenschon, Uri Davis, and

Manuel Hassassian, eds. Syracuse: Syracuse University Press, pp. 338–367.

Ong, Aihwa, 2003. *Buddha Is Hiding: Refugees, Citizenship, the New America.* Berkeley: University of California Press.

Pandolfi, Mariella, 2003. Contract of Mutual (In)Difference: Governance and the Humanitarian Apparatus in Contemporary Albania and Kosovo. *Indiana Journal of Global Legal Studies* 10(1): 369–381.

Petryna, Adriana, 2002. *Life Exposed: Biological Citizens after Chernobyl.* Princeton: Princeton University Press.

Phuong, Catherine, 2005. Office of the United Nations High Commissioner for Refugees and Internally Displaced Persons. *Refugee Survey Quarterly* 24(3): 71–83.

Redfield, Peter, 2005. Doctors, Borders, and Life in Crisis. *Cultural Anthropology* 20(3): 328–361.

Rieff, David, 1999. Humanitarian Intervention. In *Crimes of War: What the Public Should Know,* Roy Gutman and David Rieff, eds. New York: W. W. Norton, pp. 181–185.

Rieff, David, 2002. *A Bed for the Night: Humanitarianism in Crisis.* New York: Simon and Schuster.

Said, Edward, 1985. *After the Last Sky: Palestinian Lives.* New York: Pantheon.

Sayigh, Yazid, 1997. *Armed Struggle and the Search for State: The Palestinian National Movement, 1949–1993.* Oxford: Oxford University Press.

Schulz, Helena Lindholm, and Juliane Hammer, 2003. *The Palestinian Diaspora: Formation of Identities and Politics of Homeland.* London: Routledge.

Shlaim, Avi, 1990. The Rise and Fall of the All-Palestine Government in Gaza. *Journal of Palestine Studies* 20(1): 37–53.

Skran, Claudia, 1995. *Refugees in Inter-War Europe: The Emergence of a Regime.* Oxford: Clarendon Press.

Takkenberg, Lex, 1998. *The Status of Palestinian Refugees in International Law.* Oxford: Clarendon Press.

Tamari, Salim, 1991. The Palestinian Movement in Transition: Historical Reversals and the Uprising. *Journal of Palestine Studies* 20(2): 57–70.

Terry, Fiona, 2002. *Condemned to Repeat? The Paradox of Humanitarian Action.* Ithaca, NY: Cornell University Press.

Ticktin, Miriam, 2006. Where Ethics and Politics Meet: The Violence of Humanitarianism in France. *American Ethnologist* 33(1): 33–49.

Turki, Fawaz, 1974. To Be a Palestinian. *Journal of Palestine Studies* 3(3): 3–17.

United Nations Relief and Works Agency for Palestine Refugees in the Near East, 1950. *Interim Report of the Director, A/1451/Rev.1.*

United Nations Relief and Works Agency for Palestine Refugees in the Near East, 1952. *Annual Report of the Director, Covering the Period 1 July 1951 to 30 June 1952, A/2171.*

United Nations Relief and Works Agency for Palestine Refugees in the Near East, 1954. *Annual Report of the Director, Covering the Period 1 July 1953 to 30 June 1954, A/2717.*

United Nations Relief and Works Agency for Palestine Refugees in the Near East, 1955. *Special Report of the Director Concerning Other Claimants for Relief, A/2978/Add.1.*

United Nations Relief and Works Agency for Palestine Refugees in the Near East, 1956. *Annual Report of the Director, Covering the Period 1 July 1955 to 30 June 1956, A/3212.*

United Nations Relief and Works Agency for Palestine Refugees in the Near East, 1958. *Annual Report of the Director, Covering the Period 1 July 1957 to 30 June 1958, A/3931.*

Urban Citizenship

21

The Implosion of Modern Public Life, 2000

Teresa P. R. Caldeira

São Paulo is today a city of walls. City residents will not risk living in a house without fences and bars on the windows. Physical barriers enclose both public and private spaces: houses, apartment buildings, parks, squares, office complexes, shopping areas, and schools. As the elites retreat to their enclaves and abandon public spaces to the homeless and the poor, the number of spaces for public encounters between different social groups shrinks considerably. The everyday routines of those who inhabit segregated spaces – guarded by walls, surveillance systems, and restricted access – are quite different from their previous routines in more open and mixed environments.

Residents from all social groups argue that they build walls and change their habits to protect themselves from crime. However, the effects of these security strategies go far beyond self-protection. By transforming the urban landscape, citizens' strategies of security also affect patterns of circulation, habits, and gestures related to the use of streets, public transportation, parks, and all public spaces. How could the experience of walking on the streets

not be transformed if one's environment consists of high fences, armed guards, closed streets, and video cameras instead of gardens and yards, neighbors talking, and the possibility of glancing at some family scene through the windows? The idea of going for a walk, of naturally passing among strangers, the act of strolling through the crowd that symbolizes the modern experience of the city, are all compromised in a city of walls. People feel restricted in their movements, afraid, and controlled; they go out less at night, walk less on the street, and avoid the "forbidden zones" that loom larger and larger in every resident's mental map of the city, especially among the elite. Encounters in public space become increasingly tense, even violent, because they are framed by people's fears and stereotypes. Tension, separation, discrimination, and suspicion are the new hallmarks of public life.

This chapter analyzes the changes in public space and in the quality of public life that result from expanded strategies of security: segregation, social distance and exclusion, and the implosion of the experience of public life in

Teresa P. R. Caldeira, The implosion of modern public life. In *City of Walls: Crime, Segregation, and Citizenship in São Paulo* (Berkeley: University of California Press, 2000), pp. 297–335.

the modern city. First, I discuss the modern notion of the public, framed by ideals of openness and accessibility both in the city space and in the polity. I analyze two critiques of industrial cities that remain committed to modern values: modernism and the Garden City. Both have influenced the fortified enclaves. Next, I compare the spaces of the new enclaves with those of modernist city planning, showing that the former use modernist conventions with the intention of creating what the latter produced unintentionally: segregation and fragmentation. Third, relying on ethnographic data and on my own experiences in São Paulo, I discuss the relationship between changes in the built environment and changes in the everyday life in the city, showing how the latter is increasingly shaped by incivility and enforcement of social distance. A comparison with Los Angeles shows that São Paulo's pattern of segregation is in fact not unique. In São Paulo and Los Angeles the new urban experience is structured not by the modern values of openness and tolerance to heterogeneity but rather by separation and the control of boundaries. Finally, I address some of the political consequences of these spatial changes in terms of the expansion and restriction of democracy itself.

Of course, the public spaces of cities and the types of relationships that exist there represent only one aspect of public life. Pervading the discussions in this chapter is one of the most challenging questions in urban analysis: how to conceive of the relationships between urban form, politics, and everyday life. These relationships are very complex and usually disjunctive: simultaneous processes with opposite meanings may take place in the same public sphere. São Paulo offers a compelling example of disjunction: its walling process has coincided with the organization of urban social movements, the expansion of citizenship rights for the working classes, and political democratization. By emphasizing this type of disjunction, I differ strongly from environment determinists who would see in the walls and the pattern of segregation crystallized in the urban environment the determinant origin of political processes.

Nevertheless, the built environment is not a neutral stage for the unfolding of social relations.

The quality of the built environment inevitably influences the quality of the social interactions that take place there. It does not determine them completely; there is always room for diverse and sometimes subversive appropriations of spaces and for the organization of social actions that counter those shaped by spatial practices. However, the material spaces that constitute the stage for public life influence the types of social relations possible on it. Against a backdrop of walls and technologies of surveillance, life on the sidewalks is quite different from what Jane Jacobs described in her famous defense of urban public space (1961: 50–54). The "metaphorical" cities people construct in their everyday practices of space (de Certeau 1984: 93) are inevitably different in an open modern city and in a city of walls. Usually it takes organized political action to resist walls or to dismantle patterns of segregation. In everyday life, it is a difficult matter to contest walls and rituals of suspicion and humiliation, as the residents of São Paulo know so well.

The Modern Ideal of Public Space and City Life

Streets open to the free circulation of crowds and vehicles represent one of the most vivid images of modern cities. Although there are various and sometimes contradictory accounts of modernity in Western cities, the modern experience of urban public life is widely held to include the primacy and openness of streets; free circulation; the impersonal and anonymous encounters of pedestrians; spontaneous public enjoyment and congregation in streets and squares; and the presence of people from different social backgrounds strolling and gazing at others, looking at store windows, shopping, sitting in cafes, joining political demonstrations, appropriating the streets for their festivals and celebrations, and using spaces especially designed for the entertainment of the masses (promenades, parks, stadiums, exhibition spaces). These are elements associated with modern life in capitalist cities at least since the remodeling of Paris by Baron Haussmann in the second half of the nineteenth century. Haussmann's state-promoted transformation of Paris was strongly criticized and opposed by citizens and analysts alike, but no one denied that the new boulevards were readily appropriated by huge numbers of people eager to enjoy both the street life, protected by anonymity, and the consumer possibilities that came with it. The flaneur described by Baudelaire and the consumer of the new department stores became symbols of the modern use of urban public space, as Paris became a prototype of the modern city.

At the core of this concept of urban public life are two related notions: city space is open space to be used and enjoyed by everyone, and the consumer society it houses is accessible to all. As Young puts it, in the ideal of modern city life "borders are open and undecidable" (1990: 239). Of course, this has never been entirely the case in Paris or anywhere else. Modern cities have always been marked by social inequalities and spatial segregation, and their spaces are appropriated in quite different ways by diverse social groups, depending on their social position and power. Paris itself demonstrates the perpetuation of inequality: the remodeling of the city under the Second Empire was in fact a transformation in the mode of spatial segregation and of the organization of class differences, as Engels (1872) noted early on (see also Harvey 1985). As a result, the literature on modern cities has often emphasized their negative aspects, from crime and violence to the danger of the mob, anomie, excessive individualism, congestion, and disease. However, in spite of persisting inequalities and social injustices, Western cities inspired by this model have always maintained signs of openness in circulation and consumption, signs that sustained the positive value attached to an open public space. Moreover, the sometimes violent appropriations of public spaces by different categories of excluded people – the most obvious example being the barricades erected during workers' rebellions – also constituted the modern public and simultaneously contributed to its expansion. Contestation is an inherent component of the modern city.

Some analysts of modern city life have been especially compelling in enumerating the positive values of the city and in defending modern public space. In general, they neglect the fact that the contemporary notion of the public is, in fact, a type of space and an experience of city life that was constituted only in the process of nineteenth-century industrial urbanization. The historical specificity of this notion of the public is essential in understanding its current transformation.

Jane Jacobs is one of the most famous advocates of the values of modern public life in cities. Her analysis of the use of sidewalks emphasizes not only openness and accessibility but also the etiquette and the conditions that make interactions among strangers possible and secure. These conditions include the complex and voluntary control exercised by city dwellers that she labels the "eyes upon the street" (Jacobs 1961: 35); density; continuous use; a wide diversity of uses; and a clear demarcation between public and private space. When these conditions disappear, she argues, the freedom of the city and its civilization are threatened. This happens, for example, when the "institution of the Turf" (1961: 47–50) orients urban constructions and people build barriers that enclose some areas and fence the others out. It also happens when the separation between public and private is confused. Privacy, Jacobs argues, is "indispensable" in cities (1961: 58). "Civilized public life" is maintained on the basis of dignified, formalized, and reserved relationships – what we can call civility – kept separate from people's private lives. Where no vivid sidewalks and public spaces exist, and when relationships in public start to extend into private life and require close sharing among neighbors, then city freedom is threatened; people tend to enforce common standards, creating a sense of homogeneity that leads to insularity and separation. When public life is absent, the alternative to sharing too much may be sharing nothing, and suspicion and fear of neighbors are the expected outcomes. For Jacobs, both the drawing of lines and boundaries in city space and the extension of the private into the public threaten the values of a good urban public life.

Iris Marion Young (1990) starts from Jacobs's analysis to construct a "normative ideal of city life," which she conceives as an alternative to existing cities and as one way of redressing their many social injustices. Young creates her model as an ideal and therefore does not elaborate on its historic and specific modern character. However, her arguments and criticisms of some Enlightenment views reveal its modern character. Young defines city life as "the being together of strangers," whose ideal is "an openness to unassimilated otherness." "As a normative ideal," she argues, "city life instantiates social relations of difference without exclusion" (Young 1990: 237, 227). By principle these ideals are incompatible with any kind of hierarchical order (such as the medieval, status-based order) and can be conceived only under the assumption of a universal equality of citizens that constitutes modern Western societies.

[...]

Modern ideals of the public do not refer only to city life but are always coupled with conceptions of politics. The promise of incorporation into modern society includes not only the city and consumption but also the polity. Images of the modern city are in many ways analogous to those of the liberal polity, consolidated on the basis of a social contract among equal and free people. The ideal of the social contract based on a principle of universality is quite radical – like that of the open city – and it helped destroy the feudal social order that preceded it. But, clearly, it is only through struggle that the definition of "free and equal" has been expanded. As with the open city, the polity that truly incorporates all citizens equally has never existed. Yet its founding ideals and its promise of continuous incorporation have retained their power for at least two centuries, shaping people's experience of citizenship and city life and legitimating the actions of various excluded groups in their claims for incorporation.

In contemporary politics, the unfulfilled liberal promises of universal citizenship and, simultaneously, the reaffirmation of some of these promises have been articulated best through social movements. These have taken various forms, either affirming the rights of specific groups (such as blacks, indigenous populations, gays, and women) or trying to expand the rights of excluded social groups (as in the case of São Paulo's movements of poor residents of the peripheries demanding their "rights to the city"). In general, especially in their liberal incarnations, social movements have mounted what one might call a positive attack on modern liberal ideals: their aim is still to expand rights, freedom, justice, and equality, and they search for models that include the excluded and, therefore, achieve those goals in a more effective way. In other words, their attack maintains and reinforces basic liberal values, especially those of universality and equality. What distinguishes these liberal social movements from a second type is the treatment of difference. In the liberal version, which Charles Taylor calls a "politics of universalism," social movements mark differences in order to expose injustice. For social movements that emphasize "the equal dignity of all citizens," to call attention to difference means to struggle for the expansion of rights and "the equalization of rights and entitlements" (Taylor 1992: 37). Ultimately their goal is the erasure of difference by the incorporation of the groups discriminated against into full citizenship. These movements aim at a public life and a polity in which equal respect for everybody's rights would eliminate the need to stress differences and inequalities. Because of their emphasis on universal principles, they do not view difference as something to be maintained and valorized.

A second type of social movement has brought to the forefront the question of difference. In this second category, which Taylor calls a "politics of difference," minority groups, especially feminists, argue that liberal notions of universalism have always been constituted on the basis of the exclusion of some. They insist that the rights of minority groups can be addressed only if approached from the perspective of difference rather than that of sameness. Although they still refer to a principle of universal equality, they demand recognition of the unique identity of each group and its distinctiveness from all others (Taylor 1992: 38–39). Iris Young's understanding of a politics of difference and of city life as the realm of social relations of "difference without exclusion" represents one version of this criticism (Young 1990). In her model, differences should remain unassimilated; they should not disappear under any fiction of a universal belonging. Although the break with liberalism in this view is explicit, it still constitutes an attack based on the principles of rights, freedom, justice, and equality and, therefore, within the parameters of modernity.

Other theorists of democracy such as Claude Lefort, Chantal Mouffe, Ernesto Laclau, and Étienne Balibar offer similar analyses. What they have in common, in addition to an emphasis on the nonassimilation of differences, is an insistence on a democratic polity and on a public space founded on uncertainty and openness and marked by the negotiation of meaning. As Lefort puts it, democracy is instituted and sustained by "the dissolution of the markers of certainty" (Lefort 1988: 19). In a democracy, the basis of power, law, knowledge, and social interactions is indeterminate, and the public space is the locus for negotiation about the meaning of the social and the legitimate.

These ideals of the democratic polity – openness, indeterminacy, fluidity, and coexisting, unassimilated difference – have found some of their best expressions in the public spaces of modern cities. Such spaces promote interactions among people who are forced to confront each other's anonymity on the basis of citizenship and therefore to acknowledge and respect each other's equal rights. Of course, there are many ways of subverting that equality and invoking status and hierarchy. Nevertheless, the modern city space, more than any other, forces their confrontation and therefore has the potential to challenge and level those hierarchies. In the space of the modern city, different citizens negotiate the terms of their interactions and socialize despite their differences and inequalities. This ideal of the open city, tolerant to social differences and their negotiation in anonymous encounters, crystallizes what I call the modern and democratic public space.

Cities such as contemporary São Paulo display a strikingly different type of public urban space. The difference is not of the kind expressed by the demands of social movements (of either type) or by criticisms of the numerous dysfunctions of modern cities, which aim to improve the modern public space and make it live up to its promises. Rather, the public spaces being created in these cities negate the main characteristics of the modern democratic ideal of urban public space. They represent a type of public space that makes no gestures toward openness, indeterminacy, accommodation of difference, or equality, but rather takes inequality and separation as organizing values. It contradicts the principles of modern city space and brings into existence some of Jacobs's and Young's worst scenarios of incivility, inequality, and privatization of public space. Cities of walls and fortified enclaves are cities of fixed boundaries and spaces of restricted and controlled access.

Garden City and Modernism: The Lineage of the Fortified Enclave

The fortified enclaves and the type of public space being created in São Paulo and Los Angeles are the result of complex and heterogeneous influences. Some of them can be traced to a number of critiques of inequalities, segregation, and social injustices that have plagued industrial cities. Two of these views especially influenced the new segregation of enclaves: the notion of the Garden City, and modernism. This analysis will help us to understand how what once constituted a critique of the problems of industrial cities became the source of the destruction of its democratic ideals.

The Garden City model was first articulated by Ebenezer Howard in nineteenth-century England.[1] Considering the problems of large industrial cities insoluble, he proposed replacing them with small towns. Residents, especially the poor, would live close to nature, on a basis of mutuality and collective ownership of land. Howard imagined the Garden Cities as self-reliant and therefore different from traditional suburbs where workers go only to sleep. In fact, the cities he imagined, with their combination of office and industry jobs and residences, are closer to the idea of the new suburbs. Howard envisioned his towns as round, encircled by a greenbelt (like those adopted by many British cities), and connected to other small towns to form another circle (as in the concept of satellite cities). Economic activities, residence, and administration were to be separated by green areas. At the center, public buildings would be clustered to create the "civic spirit." The town was to be planned as a totality – according to a concept that became the synonym for planning itself – and would be controlled by the public authority to prevent speculation and irrationality in its use. Garden Cities were to be governed by a democratically controlled, corporate technocracy, and its main members were to be elected by the renter-residents.

The Garden City model has been extremely influential, generating numerous "new towns" both in England and in the United States since the early twentieth century (Fishman 1988: chapter 1). Contemporary Paulista closed condominiums and American common interest developments (CIDs) exemplify the influence of the Garden City model and also the extent to which it has been modified. The enclosing walls and the private character of today's developments, the absence of a preoccupation with urban order, and the exclusive and exclusionary lifestyle directly contradict the original ideals. However, the Garden City imagery is still significant. In the United States, this model has been frequently associated with communitarian political ideals, although these were not necessarily a part of Howard's vision. It is not difficult to trace to this concept the origins of the CID, administered by a homeowner's association, which is becoming the main type of middle-class residence in the outer cities of the United States. Similarly, as my analysis of advertising shows, Brazilian closed condominiums were inspired by the Garden City model. In contrast with American CIDs, however, Brazilian condominiums do not emphasize the values of community. In São Paulo, communitarianism is not an important ideology, and the Garden City inspiration is expressed in a cruder way. Without the (presumably positive) discourse on the values of local community, its discriminatory intentions are the only ones to stand out.

Le Corbusier and modernist city planning represent another critique of the industrial city and its modern public space that has been appropriated and transformed by the new enclaves. In spite of many differences, Le Corbusier's Radiant City had some links with the Garden City model. In fact, he himself described it as a "vertical garden city" (Jacobs

1961: 22). His ideas about density were the opposite of Howard's, and he introduced the skyscraper into his plans; he also brought in the automobile and considerations about the rapid flow of traffic. Nevertheless, his plans reveal a dislike of the street and destruction of its unity; spatial segmentation of functions; emphasis on the city as a park and on the existence of green areas intercalated among built ones; and the need of a total plan that is continuously controlled by public authorities.

Modernist planning and design were influential everywhere in the world, but especially so in both modern Brazil and Los Angeles. As Holston shows (1989), the construction of modernist Brasilia in the late 1950s crystallized an international modernism in its transformation of public space and communicated it to the rest of the country. Modernism has been the dominant idiom of Brazilian architecture and planning to this day. As such, it is associated with prestige and has been helping to create elite spaces and sell residences for the Brazilian elite since the 1950s. In the closed condominiums, however, modernist architecture becomes not only a status symbol for the bourgeoisie, for whom this architecture is still fashionable, but also a principal device of segregation. To achieve their goals of isolating, distancing, and selecting, the fortified enclaves use instruments of design drawn from modernist city planning and architecture. One striking characteristic of both modernist city planning (and the Garden City) and the fortified enclaves is the attack on streets as a form of public space. In Brasilia, as Holston shows (1989: chapter 4), as in new parts of São Paulo and Los Angeles, modernist conventions of architectural and urban design eliminate pedestrians and anonymous interactions from the streets, which become dedicated to the circulation of motor transport. The street as a central element of modern public life in the city is thus eliminated. However, even if the results tend to be the same, the original projects of modernism and current enclosures are radically different. It is worth investigating how such different projects have ended up using similar strategies and producing similar effects.

Modernist architecture and city planning arise from a criticism of industrial cities and societies, which they intend to transform through the radical remodeling of space. Their ambition is clear: the erasure of social difference and the creation of equality in the rational city of the future, designed by the avant-garde architect. In this scheme the corridor street is perceived as a source of disease and an impediment to progress because it fails to accommodate the needs of the new machine age. Moreover, modernist architecture attacks the street because it opposes the architectural organization of the public and private embedded in the corridor street (Holston 1989: 103) and its related system of public spaces, including sidewalks and squares: a solid mass of contiguous private buildings frames and contains the void of public streets. Modernist planning and architecture invert these solid-void/figure-ground relationships. In the modernist city, "streets appear as continuous voids and buildings as sculptural figures" (Holston 1989: 125). By subverting the existing code of urban order, modernist planning aims at and succeeds in blurring the representational distinction between public and private. The result is the subversion of modern public space.

Modernist city planning aspired to transform the city into a single, homogeneous, state-sponsored public domain, to eliminate differences in order and create a universal, rationalist city divided into sectors by functions: residential, employment, recreational, transportation, administrative, and civic. Brasília is the most complete embodiment of this new type of city. The result, however, has turned out to be the opposite of the planner's intentions. Brasília is today not Brazil's most egalitarian city but its most segregated (Holston 1989: chapter 8; Telles 1995). In destroying the street as the space for public life, modernist city planning has also undermined urban diversity and the possibility of the coexistence of differences. The type of space it creates promotes not equality, as was intended, but only a more explicit inequality.

Ironically, then, the instruments of modernist planning, with little adaptation, are well suited to producing inequality. Streets designed for vehicles only, the absence of sidewalks, enclosure and internalization of shopping areas, and spatial voids isolating sculptural buildings and wealthy residential areas effectively generate and maintain social separation. These modernist creations radically transform public life. In the new fortified enclaves, they are used not to destroy private spaces and produce a total, unified public, but explicitly to destroy public spaces. Their objective is to enlarge some private domains so that they will fulfill public functions, but in a segregated way.

Contemporary fortified enclaves use essentially modernist instruments of design, with some notable adaptations. The treatment of circulation and commerce is quite similar: pedestrian circulation is discouraged, vehicular traffic is emphasized, sidewalks are absent, and shopping areas are kept away from the streets, discouraging meaningful public interaction. The large spaces separating sculptural buildings are another common feature. The surrounding walls are the clearest departure from the modernist idiom, but their effects are not strange to the modernist city. In modernist planning, as in Brasília, residential, commercial, and administrative areas were to have no fences or walls but were to be delimited by green areas and expressways, as in the Garden City model and in various contemporary American suburbs. In São Paulo, walls are considered essential to demarcate all types of buildings, especially the new enclaves. However, this demarcation of private property does not create the same type of (nonmodernist) public space that characterizes the industrial city. Because in contemporary enclaves the private universes are kept apart by the voids of open spaces (as in modernist design), they break the street line and no longer generate street corridors. Moreover, when there is a street line created by walls and enhanced by sophisticated technologies of security, the residual public space it produces is at odds with modern public life.

A significant difference between modernist design and the fortified enclaves occurs in the use of materials and forms of individual buildings. The plain modernist façades might be eliminated in favor of ornaments, irregularities, and ostentatious materials that display the individuality and status of their owners.

The technologies of security can also help assure the exclusivity of the already isolated buildings. The architecture of these buildings is also at odds with modernist notions of transparency and disclosure of private life, expressed in its use of glass façades. In other words, contrary to modernist publicness, the enclaves enhance internalization, privacy, and individuality, but they are disconnected from its modern counterpart, the formal public sociability, as the building façades no longer constitute a solid frame for meaningful public life in the streets.

The surviving elements of modernist architecture and city planning in the new urban form are those that destroy modern public space and social life: dead streets transformed into highways, sculptural buildings separated by voids and disregarding street alignments, walls and technologies of security framing public space as residual, enclaves turned inward, separation of functions, and destruction of heterogeneous and diverse spaces. The devices that have been abandoned are those intended to create equality, transparency, and a new public sphere (glass façades, uniformity of design, absence of material delimitations such as walls and fences). Instead of creating a space in which the distinctions between public and private disappear – making all the space public, as the modernists intended – the enclaves use modernist conventions to create spaces in which the private quality is enhanced beyond any doubt and in which the public, a shapeless void treated as residual, is deemed irrelevant. This was exactly the fate of modernist architecture and its "all public space" in Brasília and in all cities that have used modernist urban planning to make and remake themselves (Holston 1989). However, while in Brasília the result was a perversion of initial premises and intentions, in the closed condominiums and fortified enclaves it represents a deliberate choice. In the enclaves, the aim is to segregate and change the character of public life by transferring activities previously enacted in heterogeneous public spaces to private spaces that have been constructed as socially homogeneous environments, and by destroying the potential of streets to provide spaces for anonymous and tolerant interactions.

Today, in the new spaces in cities such as São Paulo, we tend to find no gestures toward openness and freedom of circulation, regardless of differences, nor a technocratic universalism that aims to erase differences. In São Paulo, the old modern urban design has been fragmented by the insertion of independent and well-delineated private enclaves (of modernist design) that are focused entirely inward. The fortified fragments are not meant to be subordinated to a public order kept together by ideologies of openness, accessibility, tolerance for differences, or promises of incorporation. Heterogeneity is now to be taken more seriously: fragments express irreconcilable inequalities, not simple differences. Public space expresses the new intolerance. The modernist conventions of design used by the enclaves help to ensure that different social worlds meet as infrequently as possible in city space: that is, they belong to different spaces.

In a city of walls and enclaves such as São Paulo, public space has undergone a deep transformation. Experienced as dangerous, framed by fences and walls, fractured by the new voids and enclaves, privatized with chains closing off streets, armed guards, and guardhouses, public space is increasingly abandoned by the well-to-do. As the spaces for the rich are enclosed and turned inward, the remaining space is left to those who cannot afford to go in. Because the enlarged, private worlds of the better-off are organized on the principles of homogeneity and exclusion of others, they are by principle the opposite of the modern public space. Yet neither can the leftover public spaces, territories of fear, aspire to modern ideals. Everyday life in the city of walls reinforces exactly the opposite values: incivility, intolerance, and discrimination.

In the ideal modern city life, "borders are open and undecidable," suggests Young (1990: 239). Fixed boundaries create nonmodern spaces, an undemocratic public space. However, the relationships between urban form and politics are complicated, as are the effects of a nonpublic space on civil life. My reflections on these complexities are all framed by the fact that the consolidation of the city of walls in São Paulo has coincided with the process of political democratization. It was exactly at the moment when social movements were booming in the periphery, when trade unions were paralyzing factories and filling stadiums for their meetings, when people were voting for their leaders for the first time in twenty years, that city residents started building up walls and moving into fortified enclaves. While the political system opened up, the streets were closed, and the fear of crime became the talk of the city.

Street Life: Incivility and Aggression

In São Paulo, as in any city, the urban environment is heterogeneous and shows the signs of different layers of construction, uses, and interventions. The current process of building up walls affects all types of spaces in the city but transforms them, and the experiences of public life, in different ways. I describe different types of material transformation caused by the walling process and discuss how they affect the quality of public life. Although the changes are of different types and have diverse effects, they all reinforce boundaries and discourage heterogeneous encounters. They all create policed borders and consequently leave less space for indeterminacy in public encounters. They all promote intolerance, suspicion, and fear.

As people move around the city, they use the space in individual and creative ways and, as de Certeau reminds us, make fragmented trajectories that elude legibility (1984: chapter 7). Therefore, any account of these spatial practices can be only fragmentary and particular. I draw here on what people have told me and on what I have read and seen, but I rely mostly on my own observations, experiences, and memories of the city. I want to indicate changes and suggest different experiences in the use of the city, but I have no pretension to being exhaustive.

In contemporary São Paulo, the public space is emptiest and the use of streets, sidewalks, and squares rarest exactly where there are the most fortified enclaves, especially residential ones. In neighborhoods like Morumbi, streets are leftover spaces, and the material quality of public spaces is simply bad. Because

of the inward orientation of the fortified enclaves, many streets have unpaved sidewalks or none at all, and several streets behind the condominiums are unpaved. The distances between buildings are large. Walls are high, out of proportion to the human body, and most of them are topped by electric wires. Streets are for cars, and pedestrian circulation becomes an unpleasant experience. The spaces are intentionally constructed to produce this effect. To walk in Morumbi is a stigma: the pedestrian is poor and suspicious. People on foot may be workers who live in nearby favelas and who are treated by their richer neighbors with distance and disdain – and, evidently, with fear. Since middle- and upper-class people circulate in private cars while others walk or use public transportation, there is little contact in public among people from different social classes. No common spaces bring them together.

The paths inside the favelas are spaces for walking, but the favelas too end up being treated as private enclaves: only residents and acquaintances venture in, and all that is seen from the public streets are a few entrances. The favelas can be seen in their entirety only from the windows of the exclusive apartments above them. When both rich and poor residents live in enclaves, passing within the walls is obviously a carefully policed activity, in which class signs are interpreted in order to determine levels of suspicion and harassment. Empty streets of fixed boundaries and scrutinized differences are spaces of suspicion and not of tolerance, inattention to differences, or wandering around. They are not enjoyable urban spaces.

Various strictly residential neighborhoods for the upper classes (older parts of Morumbi, Alto de Pinheiros, and Jardim Europa, for example) tend to have empty streets as well, but older neighborhoods, some of them designed as garden cities, have good streets and sidewalks. In these areas, however, other devices restrict circulation. Residents have privatized public streets and closed them off with gates, chains or, less ostensibly, with gardens, vases, and plants. In the United States, the same practice is becoming common; the spaces thus produced are called "security zone communities" by Blakely and Snyder (1997). Because the street is still considered open space, its privatization still generates opposition. A few years ago, when this trend started in São Paulo, the city government reacted and removed the chains. However, as support for the practice grew, the city incorporated enclosure into its policies: in 1990, the city government of the PT [Partido dos Trabalhadores, Workers' Party] started offering the services of its architects and construction workers to middle-class neighborhoods interested in the enclosures.

Although these neighborhoods still have nice streets full of trees and sidewalks, a form of entertainment enjoyed by my family when I was a child has now become impossible: to go around the streets of Jardim Europa admiring the mansions of the rich. They are no longer visible; the houses have been concealed behind walls and protected by electric wires and other security equipment. To walk in the area has become unpleasant, as the streets are now dominated by private guards installed in guardhouses, trained dogs barking at passers-by, and devices blocking circulation. The few people walking become suspects. I tried it, with my camera, and drew many guards aggressively in my direction, in spite of my middle-class appearance. The sense of being under surveillance is unavoidable, because the guards position themselves on the sidewalks (instead of inside the buildings, as in Morumbi); they observe everyone passing by, and directly address anyone they find suspect. Well, they are paid to suspect and to keep away strangers. This private army is there to privatize what used to be reasonable public spaces.

I spent my childhood in the late 1950s and early 1960s in a new middle-class neighborhood, Sumaré, which since the late sixties has been completely urbanized and is today a central neighborhood. When we moved there, the streets were unpaved; there was no sewage system and no telephone. We were just two blocks away from the headquarters of the city's department of trash collection, that is, the stable for the horses that pulled the collection carriages through our street every morning, to the great amusement of the children. Sometimes when it rained, my father's beautiful blue '54 Chevrolet, directly imported from the United States and designed for other roads, got stuck in the mud, and he had to walk the one

kilometer from our house to the School of Medicine of the University of São Paulo, where he was a professor. There weren't many houses on our street; some resembled little *chácaras* (country houses), with their vegetable gardens and chickens. Although it was a middle-class neighborhood, in the late 1950s it was still in the process of becoming, like Jardim das Camélias, on the periphery, when I first went there in the late 1970s. The city grew so rapidly, and Sumaré is today so urban, that it is strange to remember that not too long ago it was so undeveloped.

For many years my family's house was separated from the street by a low fence. The gate was only closed at night. In the 1970s, when the neighborhood was built up, the sidewalks became full of people, and traffic increased considerably, my parents built a wall and started to close the gate during the day. They were bothered by passers-by looking into their living room. But we always walked around freely and without fear, even at night. In the early 1980s, my father's house was robbed, and after that the gate was kept locked. Today my father has a private guard inside the walls during the night, and the gate is locked twenty-four hours a day. He asks us to call him in advance when we visit at night so that the guard can be prepared to open the gate promptly and we do not have to wait outside. All the surrounding houses and apartment buildings have been remodeled and have added gates and walls. There are several other private guards on the block. The street, which today combines residences, offices, and commerce, is intensively used during the day (in fact, parking has become a problem), but I would feel uneasy walking around after dark.

A working-class neighborhood such as Jardim das Camélias still has an intense street life, although it has changed in many ways since the late 1970s. On the one hand, the neighborhood has expanded, the houses have improved, the trees have grown, and the streets have been paved, illuminated, and equipped with sidewalks. But as the neighborhood was urbanized and its material quality improved, fences went up as well, and people became more scared and suspicious. Crime increased in the late 1980s, from thefts to homicides, some of these involving boys who had grown up together playing on the streets. Nevertheless, everyday life is still marked by a public sociability among neighbors, the kind of formal and polite interchange on the sidewalks that gives life to a neighborhood and makes public space meaningful. Traffic is light, and the streets are still constantly used by groups of children and adolescents playing, people who stop for a little chat and maybe sit down on the sidewalks to watch those passing by, people taking care of their cars or building something, people who stop at a little shop to catch up on the local news or, if they are men, to play *sinuca* or have a drink on their way home. The houses are enclosed, but by fences that allow visibility and interaction, not by high walls. This is the kind of neighborhood kept safe by intense use, mixed functions, and the "eyes upon the street" (Jacobs 1961: chapter 2). In other words, safety is maintained by engagement, not by isolation.

In spite of the continuing local sociability, people do not feel the neighborhood is as safe as it used to be. They have fortified their houses, are more suspicious, talk to strangers on the street from behind their bars, more carefully choose the people they relate to, and control their children. Many children are now prohibited from playing outside the fences of their houses, and adolescents are restricted from going out. As everywhere else, people focus their concerns on the poorest areas; they are especially afraid of the favela nearby and another area recently invaded by participants in the Movimento dos Sem Terra. Suspicion toward people seen as "other" or as "inferior" is not exclusive to the upper classes. The frequency of public parties and celebrations sponsored by the local associations has decreased, and the activities of social movements have slowed down. Collective life and political activities have weakened in the last decade, but the public space of the streets still sustains local interactions and public interchanges.

Most central neighborhoods of São Paulo, those with good urban infrastructure that the elite have maintained for themselves, have traditionally had mixed functions and maintain a relatively intensive and heterogeneous use of public space. Some of these neighborhoods are quite sophisticated, with luxury shops and restaurants (especially Jardins, but also Higienópolis and Itaim-Bibi). In these areas the streets are still used by people of various social backgrounds, and the rich rub elbows with the poor. Now, however, the streets are policed by an army of private guards and video cameras (each building has at least one), and interclass relationships have become nastier. Moreover, in this kind of neighborhood, as well as downtown, property owners have been creative in installing devices to keep undesired people away. In entranceways and *marquises*, sprinklers come on at odd times to discourage the homeless from lingering; chains are placed across patios, entryways, and sidewalks, and public parks are fenced off. The main target of these techniques is the increasing number of homeless people inhabiting the streets. Nevertheless, because the streets are generally crowded, the effects of the constant suspicion are not as severe as in emptier areas.

In these areas of intensive mixed use, the material obstacles at street level are complemented by a series of less visible practices of surveillance that reinforce social differences. The residents and users of these areas are not interested in indeterminacy. Their tools include video cameras, electronic pass systems at the entrances of any major office building, metal detectors at bank doors, and guards who demand identification of anyone entering office buildings and, increasingly, residential condominiums. Systems of identification, screening, and control of circulation are considered central to good business management and feed the rapidly growing industry of private security services. These systems are a matter not only of security but also of discipline and social discrimination. The image of the suspect is made up of stereotypes, and therefore systems of screening discriminate especially against poor and black people. The entrance guards do not bother people with the right class signs, but they give a hard time to everyone else.

Thus for many people everyday life in the city is becoming a daily management of barriers and suspicion, marked by a succession of little rituals of identification and humiliation. These including forcing office boys, who are invariably stopped by metal detectors in bank entrances, to open their backpacks in front of a long line of people waiting to get in; sending workers to the "service" doors; and physically searching maids when they leave their jobs at the condominiums. It is true that rich people also have to identify themselves and that they too are under surveillance, but the differences in the levels of control exercised over different people are obvious. Managers do not wear the same kind of ID tags, and upper-class people know how to use their class signs (including arrogance and disrespect) to avoid interrogation and go quickly past the guards, who respond with deference instead of the disdain they reserve for poorer people. In a city in which systems of identification and strategies of security are spreading everywhere, the experience of urban life becomes one of social differences, separations, exclusions, and reminders of the limitations of one's possibilities in the public space. It is, in reality, a city of walls, the opposite of the boundless public space of the modern ideal of city life.

São Paulo's streets may still be full of people, especially in central neighborhoods of commerce and service and in regional centers, but the experience of the crowd and the quality of anonymous interactions have changed. People are afraid of being robbed, and their fear of *trombadinhas* (muggers) is taken for granted. Nobody wears jewelry or valuable watches; people carry limited cash and if possible only photocopies of documents, for their replacement requires hours of dealing with various bureaucracies. Women carry their purses tied in front of their bodies, and people embrace their back-packs on their chests. People in cars drive with closed windows and locked doors. They are especially afraid of stopping at traffic lights, for the news is filled with tales of muggers who use knives or pieces of glass as weapons to rob drivers, especially women. It is hard to distinguish these muggers from the increasing number of beggars and street vendors disputing the same street corners.

Not only are the attitudes in the crowd changing, but so is the crowd itself. The middle and upper classes try to avoid the crowded streets and sidewalks, preferring to shop at enclosed shopping centers and hypermarkets. As the middle and upper classes circulate by car, the use of public transportation is becoming a lower-class experience. Still, it remains a mass experience, since the elite constitutes hardly 5 percent of the population of the metropolitan region.

The centers of public transportation – subway and train stations and the hubs of bus lines – have a culture of their own. They are mostly working-class spaces, filled with the sounds of popular music and the smell of fruits and all kinds of food. Every day, masses of people pass through these stations and spend a considerable amount of time commuting on public transportation. These always packed areas are great spaces to sell anything, from religions to food, from cures to electronic gadgets, from herbal medicines to lingerie. This intense informal commerce of the *marreteiros* or *ambulantes* – as the street sellers are called – takes up most of the sidewalk space downtown, filling it with small stands. The experience of taking a bus, a train, or the subway at rush hour (something the middle and upper classes have stopped doing) entails fighting for space in crowded cars and being squashed against others. This is nothing new; if anything, the quality of public transportation in São Paulo has improved, especially as far as the subway is concerned. Nevertheless, frequent users of public transportation, such as the residents of Jardim das Camélias, feel that things today are more tense and unpleasant than in the past: there is little courtesy and a lot of aggression. And there is certainly more prejudice, as the middle classes teach their children that buses are dangerous and hire private drivers for them.

Traffic is by consensus considered to be one of the worst aspects of public life in São Paulo. Disregard of rules and of other people's rights is the norm. There is no civility, as a significant part of the population seems to consider traffic regulations merely as obstacles to the free movement of individuals. The media has investigated and reported frequently on behavior in traffic. The findings are amazing, not only because of the extent of the disrespect they reveal, but also because they have become routine and lost the capacity to provoke any reaction. DataFolha, the *Folha de S. Paulo* research agency, found in April 1989 that 99 percent of São Paulo's drivers consider its traffic dangerous and that one in every four drivers had been involved in at least one accident the year before.[2] Another survey from DataFolha, in April 1986, found that city residents saw the main cause of car accidents as "the lack of responsibility and imprudence of drivers."[3] In October 1989, the research department of *O Estado de S. Paulo* interviewed a sample of drivers and discovered that 85 percent of them agreed that São Paulo's drivers do not respect pedestrian crosswalks and frequently make prohibited turns. Moreover, eight in ten people interviewed thought that drivers park in prohibited areas, double park, go through red lights, and ignore speed limits.[4] In 1991, DataFolha decided to observe an important intersection of the city (Avenue Paulista and Brigadeiro Luís Antonio). There were an average of thirteen prohibited left turns per hour, in spite of physical obstacles on the road, and most of the drivers never got a ticket because most of the time no policemen were there. They also found that one car ran one red light in every five, that 41 percent of the cars that stopped for a red light disregarded the pedestrian crosswalk, and that only 3 percent of the drivers used seat belts.[5] An additional problem is that of teenagers driving before they legally qualify for a license. Until the 1970s, middle-class adolescents like myself used public transportation to go to school and run their errands around the city. Today this is considered too dangerous or too uncomfortable for the kids, and they are transported exclusively by car, driven by private drivers or their parents – or else they are simply allowed to drive themselves.

São Paulo's traffic reveals that people use the public streets according to their private convenience and do not seem to be willing to conform to general rules or respect other people's rights. There is little respect for others or for the public good. There is also some sense of omnipotence in this behavior, for people do not seem to fear being injured by the same kind of transgressions they commit. The results are dramatic: during the 1980s, more than two thousand people died in car accidents every year in the municipality of São Paulo. Between 1992 and 1994, the numbers decreased, but not significantly. In addition, more than fifty thousand people are injured in car accidents annually in the metropolitan region of São Paulo. In 1996, there were 195,378 reported car accidents in the MSP, which means an average of 535 accidents per day. Of these, 13.16 percent resulted in injuries. According to one source, the total number of accident victims was 59,679, and of these 1,113 were fatalities.[6] Very few people responsible for accidents are prosecuted.

Traffic is a strong indicator of the quality of public life. In Brazil, traffic behavior constitutes only the most obvious example of the routine disrespect for the law and the difficulties in enforcing it. Traffic policemen disregard some violations simply because they have become the norm. When they issue tickets, traffic enforcers usually hide in places where they cannot be seen by drivers. They try to avoid confronting upper-class people, who do not hesitate to challenge their authority. This is done on the basis of manipulation of class signs, but sometimes, when the signs are ignored or misunderstood, drivers resort to violence. The most violent attacks seem to be made against parking wardens, usually women, who control the restricted parking areas called the *zona azul* (blue zone). Some have been beaten by men when they refuse to void tickets, and one ended up in the hospital after an enraged motorist ran his car over her. These behaviors indicate how violent people can become when they are asked to conform to the law and cannot use their class position as a source of privilege, that is, to evade the law. Since the working classes usually cannot avoid the law, these behaviors reveal once more how class differences not only rule public interactions but also are reproduced by the elements that shape the public space.

Traffic is obviously not exclusively São Paulo's problem, but it is a national problem. In 1996, around twenty-seven thousand people died in car accidents in Brazil. The situation has acquired such dramatic dimensions that the federal government decided to revise the national traffic code (*código nacional de trânsito*). After six years of debate in Congress, the new code took effect in January 1998. It establishes high fines and serious penalties and a system of demerit points that may lead to suspension of one's license. All violations, from not carrying the car registration to drunk driving, earn points and entail a fine (from R$40 to R$800). A more severe code is expected to increase civility in traffic. But it remains unclear whether the authorities can enforce these regulations, especially in a context in which public civility is deteriorating, not improving.

Experiencing the Public

Different social groups experience the transformed public spaces of the city in contradictory ways. The young middle-class and upper-class children who are coming of age in the city of walls do not seem unhappy with their experience of public spaces. Nor should they, perhaps, with private drivers on hand and no need to fight their way in crowded public buses. Moreover, they seem to love the secure spaces of shopping malls and fast food stores, of discotheques and video-game arcades. These are for them "cool" spaces in which to display their knowledge of a global youth culture of style labels and fashion trends. They connect to "global youth" but not to the youth of their own periphery. The Paulista working-class youth does not have the privilege of avoiding public transportation or the congested streets on which they commute and where some of them work. They do, however, share with rich kids some of the signs of a global youth culture, especially in clothes: sneakers, blue jeans, T-shirts. Nevertheless, they gather not in the upper-class malls but in spaces on the periphery itself (including malls), and they favor some subcultures (punk, skinhead) and some styles of music and dance (especially funk) not shared by the middle classes. Moreover, they experience violence and harassment in their use of the city and in their neighborhoods. In their musical gatherings themes such as police abuse, murders, and disrespect are constant. For working-class kids, the experience of the city is one of injustice, not of privilege.

In contrast to the experience of these younger groups, older people, who grew up in São Paulo when progress was the goal and the use of streets and parks was more open, are nostalgic in their discussions of public space. Their descriptions of the city in the past have a quality similar to those recalling the period before the trauma of a crime. The old city is remembered as better, more beautiful, and more civilized than it is now. I spoke to two sisters about changing habits, specifically going to the movies.

People don't go to the movies anymore?
L: They don't. Now, after the video, they won't really go.
W: And it is too difficult! It all starts with parking: there is no place to park: parking is as expensive as the movie. If you leave the car on the street, either it is stolen or there are the "owners of the street" to take care of it. So it is a problem to go out with the car, we cannot relax. You go to a shopping mall; sometimes we go to the movie in a shopping center.
L: We park the car inside. When we go to movie theaters, it is in the Lar Center, Center Norte, because it is more convenient.
W: Thirty, forty years ago we could go out. We used to dress well to go out, with gloves, all beautifully arranged, to go to the city, the downtown. Ipiranga, Metro. ... Metro was the greatest ...
L: Lido, at the Lido a man could not enter without a tie. Would not enter.

When was this?
W: Like forty years ago.
L: I think it was thirty years ago. We would only go to the movies downtown. We used to go to the movies, and then go out, look at some shop windows – Barão de Itapetininga was a good street, with good stores. You would have a snack ... would have dinner out. Nowadays you cannot go downtown on a Sunday, on weekends, it is impossible because there are the homosexuals, the transvestites ... the little stalls (*barra-quinhas*). Well, downtown is horrible now with all those street vendors (*marreteiros*).

(L and W are both widowed and in their fifties. They spent their lives in Moóca and now live

together to allow W's son to live with his family in her house without paying rent.)

Older people recall with nostalgia the formality involved in the enjoyment of the public space, the gloves and the ties they wore, the distinctiveness of the old movie theaters, and the "good" streets of old downtown in which one walked among elegant people – "It was so chic!" said one woman. These are signs of distinction and rules of class separation that have been lost. In today's downtown, the "chic" population has been replaced by "marginals," nothing guarantees distinction, and the feeling that remains is uneasiness with the proximity of the poor. Many years ago, when the downtown area was used by the upper classes, joining the crowd (through the use of the right clothes and accessories, for example) was a matter of identification with social superiors, a sign of distinction for the working-class residents of Moóca. Today, however, the same people feel the need to promote distance rather than identification with the downtown crowd, for it is now made up of poor and marginalized people – vendors, street children, transvestites, prostitutes.

The expansion of mass consumption makes matters of distinction more complicated. Easy symbols of superiority, such as gloves and ties, have disappeared, and frequently the middle and upper classes feel irritated by poor people's consumption of goods considered to carry some form of status but which are no longer exclusive. It is more difficult for the elite to impose their own code of behavior – including rules of deference – onto the city. Moreover, with democratization, the poor forced the recognition of their citizenship, and they occupied spaces – physical and political – previously reserved for the elite. With fewer obvious signs of differentiation at hand and with more difficulty in asserting their privileges and codes of behavior in the public space, the upper classes turn instead to systems of identification. Thus, spaces of controlled circulation (such as shopping centers) come to assure that distinction and separation are still possible in public. Signs of social distance are replaced with material walls.

The transformations in the various spaces in the city all seem to lead to more rigid and policed boundaries, and consequently less indeterminacy and fewer spaces for contact between people from different backgrounds. These experiences engender fear and intolerance rather than expectation and excitement. Experiences in public space seem to run counter to a modern and democratic public life. However, the politics of urban public spaces in São Paulo are still more complex, and two uses of public space contradict the dominant tendency of boundaries and segregation.

The few major parks in the city are intensively used in quite a democratic way. When a park is located on the periphery, such as Parque do Carmo, its users are mostly from the working classes, but the parks of Ibirapuera and Morumbi, both in rich neighborhoods, are used by people from all social classes. Although most of them are fenced, they are large, and they are the few green areas remaining in the city. In the last few years, the parks have been appropriated by thousands of people who go there, especially on weekends, to jog, bicycle, roller-skate, play ball, or simply be outside. These oases of intensive and mixed use are very few in São Paulo, and it is interesting that they are usually spaces used for the leisure of the masses. If what happens in other areas of the world is any indication, spaces for leisure and entertainment continue to have a mixed massive use – as in American waterfront areas, rebuilt historical districts, and theme parks, for example – even when all other public spaces deteriorate.

The second example is Praça da Sé, São Paulo's central square. Praça da Sé is the powerful symbol of the center of the city, whence all roads and streets are imagined to radiate. Today, the landmarks of this big square are the Catholic cathedral, the central subway station, and the "zero mark" of the city, indicated by a stone erected on top of a compass engraved on the ground. The square is mainly a working-class space. Every day, a mass of commuters crosses Praça da Sé. Many people work there: vendors of every type of popular product, preachers of different religions, musicians, and policemen – the same types of people who fill any major hub of public transportation. The square has many residents, too: a contingent of street children and homeless people. Men dressed in suits and carrying briefcases, usually lawyers who have to reach the Central Forum next door, are frequently seen in the square, but they no longer give the place its identity. Praça da Sé is fundamentally a space for poorer residents, both in its everyday uses and in its symbolism. Residents of Jardim das Camélias I interviewed in the late 1970s considered going to Praça da Sé a special activity for the holidays, such as New Year's Day: it was their way of enjoying the city and feeling that they belonged in it. Today, they feel that the square has become a dangerous space, and although they still use it, for leisure they instead go somewhere like a shopping mall. As the working classes rule the square with their sounds and smells, the wealthy avoid it as a dangerous and unpleasant space.

But Praça da Sé has a second layer of symbolism: for both rich and poor Paulistanos it is the main political space of the city, a meaning that has been fixed by various events in the process of democratization. During the military years, the few political demonstrations that took place were held in Praça da Sé mainly because of the presence of the cathedral. The Catholic Church was at that time the only institution able to offer a relatively safe space for protests against the abuses and human rights violations practiced by the military regime. For the same reason, Praça da Sé became the site of numerous demonstrations by social movements during the *abertura* process, most visibly the huge gatherings of the Movimento do Custo de Vida in the second half of the 1970s. When the movement for free elections was organized in the early 1980s, it was only natural that mass demonstrations be held in the square. On 25 January 1984, the day of the city's anniversary, around three hundred thousand congregated in Praça da Sé to demand free elections. Middle- and upper-class people who had not been downtown for years (the main economic activities and all luxury commerce had moved southwest) found out how to take the subway and emerged in the middle of the square to demand democracy. Demonstrations were moved to Vale do Anhangabaú on only two occasions, when the square was too small for the expected crowd of one million: the last rally for direct elections in April 1984, and

the demonstration for the impeachment of President Collor in September 1992.

On the one hand, Praça da Sé symbolizes the political reappropriation of public space by the citizens in the transition to democracy. On the other hand, it represents the deterioration of public space, danger, crime, anxieties about downward mobility, and the impoverishment of the workers who continue to use it for commuting, working in the informal market, and consuming its cheap products. It symbolizes both the strength and the deterioration of public space and, therefore, the disjunctive character of Brazilian democracy (Holston and Caldeira 1998).

The example of Praça da Sé is another indication that political democratization is not contradictory to the deterioration of public spaces. In fact, democratization may have helped to accelerate the building of walls and the deterioration of public space. This does not, however, occur in the simplistic way some right-wing politicians want us to believe it does: that democracy creates disorder and crime and therefore generates the need for walls. If democracy gave rise to walls, it was because the democratization process was unexpectedly deep. Until the end of the military regime, politics had been the exclusive realm of the elite. With the *abertura*, however, the poor residents of the periphery became important political players, taking Praça da Sé to present their demands and assert their rights to the city. Their trade-union movements and social movements surprised everybody; and they were able to claim a political space that was being opened, but not necessarily for them. In the imagination of those who prefer to abandon the city, the fear of crime intertwines in complex ways with other anxieties provoked by change. It intertwines with the fear of electoral results (especially the fear that the PT might win elections, as it did); the fear that one might decline socially because of inflation and economic crisis; the fear that certain goods no longer serve to create social distance or confer status; and the fear that the poor can no longer be kept in their places.

The coincidence of democratization with the deterioration of public space and more obvious processes of social segregation, as well as the ambiguous symbolism of Praça da Sé, precludes any easy associations between the material public spaces of cities and forms of polity. São Paulo shows that the polity and the public space of the city can develop in opposite directions. This disjunction between the political process and urban form is meaningful. On the one hand, because recent urban transformations are mostly not the result of imposed state policies but rather of the way in which the citizens engage with their city, they can be seen as the result of a democratic intervention. Although this engagement may be seen as a form of democratic action, it has produced mainly undemocratic results. The perversity of this engagement of the citizenry is that it leads to segregation rather than to tolerance. On the other hand, as citizens build all types of walls and controls in the city space, they create limits to democratization. Through the creation of walls, residents re-create hierarchies, privileges, exclusive spaces, and rituals of segregation where they have just been removed from the political sphere. A city of walls is not a democratic space. In fact, it counters democratic possibilities. Fortunately, however, this process is not monolithic, and there is always the possibility that spaces such as Praça da Sé will fill again with people from all classes, as it did when they gathered to overthrow the military regime.

[...]

Contradictory Public Space

In spite of their specificities, São Paulo and Los Angeles are today more socially unequal and more dispersed than they used to be, and many of the changes to the urban environment are causing separation between social groups, which are increasingly confined to homogeneous enclaves. Privatization and rigid boundaries (either material or symbolic) continuously fragment what used to be more open spaces and serve to keep groups apart. Nevertheless, the experience of the urban environment is not the only experience of the residents of these cities, and it is certainly not their only experience either of social difference or of democracy. One of the qualities of Los Angeles repeatedly

emphasized by its analysts is its multiculturalism, the presence of expressive numbers of different ethnic groups changing the makeup of a once predominantly Anglo city. These are the characteristics highlighted by those who, like Soja and Dear, look at its postmodern urbanism from a positive perspective instead of emphasizing its bleaker side, as Davis tends to do. Soja, for example, talks about a new cultural syncretism (Latino, Asian American), cross-cultural fusion, and coalition building (1996). There is also talk about hybridity and border cultures. Some mention the importance of the mass media and new forms of electronic communication and their role in blurring boundaries and bridging distances, not just in LA but everywhere. In São Paulo, opposition to the segregationist and antidemocratic impulses of the built environment comes partly from the media but mainly from other sources: the democratization process, the proliferation of social movements, and the expansion of citizenship rights of the working classes and of various minorities.

In both São Paulo and Los Angeles, therefore, we can detect opposing social processes, some promoting tolerance of difference and the melting of boundaries, and some promoting segregation, inequality, and the policing of boundaries. In fact, we have in these cities political democracy with urban walls; democratic procedures used to promote segregation, as in the NIMBY movements; and multiculturalism and syncretic formations with apartheid zones, promoted by segregated enclaves. These opposing processes are not unrelated but rather tensely connected. They express the contradictory tendencies that characterize both societies. Both are going through significant transformations. Both have been unsettled by the opening and blurring of boundaries (migration and economic restructuring in Los Angeles, and democratization and economic crisis and restructuring in São Paulo). If we look for a moment at other cities around the world where enclaves are increasing, we see that some are going through similar processes of deep transformation and democratization: Johannesburg and Buenos Aires, for example. The unsettling of social boundaries is upsetting, especially for the elite. Their movement to build walls is thus

understandable. The problem is that the consequences of fragmentation, privatization, and
walling are severe. Once walls are built, they alter
public life. The changes we are seeing in the
urban environment are fundamentally undemocratic. What is being reproduced at the level of
the built environment is segregation and intolerance. The space of these cities is the main arena in
which these antidemocratic tendencies are
articulated.

Among the conditions necessary for democracy is that people acknowledge those from different social groups to be co-citizens, having
similar rights despite their differences. However,
cities segregated by walls and enclaves foster the
sense that different groups belong to separate
universes and have irreconcilable claims. Cities
of walls do not strengthen citizenship but rather
contribute to its corrosion. Moreover, this effect
does not depend directly on either the type of
political regime or on the intentions of those in
power, since the design of the enclaves and walls
itself entails a certain social logic. The new
urban morphologies of fear give new forms to
inequality, keep groups apart, and inscribe a
new sociability that runs against the ideals of
the modern public and its democratic freedoms.
When some people are denied access to certain
areas and when different groups do not interact
in public space, then references to ideals of
openness, equality, and freedom as organizing
principles for social life are no longer possible,
even as fiction. The consequences of the new
separateness and restriction of public life are
serious: contrary to what Jencks (1993) thinks,
defensible architecture and planning may promote conflict instead of preventing it, by making explicit the social inequalities and the lack
of common ground. In fact, we may argue that
the Los Angeles uprising was caused by social
segregation rather than by the lack of separation and defenses.

If the experiences of separateness expressed
in the urban environment become dominant in
their societies, people will distance themselves
from democracy. However, given the disjunc-
ture between different types of experiences in
cities such as Los Angeles and São Paulo, there
is also hope that the reverse could happen: that
the experiences of the blurring of boundaries
and of democratization will one day extend
into the built environment.

NOTES

1 Howard's book *To-Morrow: A Peaceful Path
  to Social Reform* was first published in 1898.
  It was retitled *Garden Cities of Tomorrow* in
  1902.
2 *Folha de S. Paulo*, 13 May 1989.
3 *Folha de S. Paulo*, 11 May 1986.
4 *O Estado de S. Paulo*, 8 October 1989.
5 *Folha de S. Paulo*, 21 May 1991.
6 Data on the number of victims are from the
  military police, although they are underestimated, and probably the data for injuries as
  well. According to the civil registry, the
  number of fatalities was 2,368.

REFERENCES

Blakely, Edward J., and Mary Gail Snyder, 1997.
  *Fortress America: Gated Communities in the
  United States*. Washington, DC: Brookings
  Institution Press and Lincoln Institute of Land
  Policy.
Certeau, Michel de, 1984. *The Practice of
  Everyday Life*. Berkeley: University of
  California Press.
Davis, Mike, 1990. *City of Quartz: Excavating
  the Future in Los Angeles*. London: Verso.
Dear, Michael, 1996. In the City, Time Becomes
  Visible: Intentionality and Urbanism in Los
  Angeles, 1781–1991. In *The City: Los Angeles
  and Urban Theory at the End of the Twentieth
  Century*, Allen J. Scott and Edward W. Soja,
  eds. Berkeley: University of California Press,
  pp. 76–105.
Engels, Friedrich, 1872. *The Housing Question*.
  New York: International Publishers.
Fishman, Robert, 1988. *Urban Utopias in the
  Twentieth Century: Ebenezer Howard, Frank Lloyd
  Wright, Le Corbusier*. Cambridge, MA: MIT Press.
Harvey, David, 1985. Paris, 1850–1870. In
  *Consciousness and the Urban Experience:
  Studies in History and Theory of Capitalist
  Urbanization*. Baltimore: Johns Hopkins
  University Press, pp. 63–220.
Holston, James, 1989. *The Modernist City: An
  Anthropological Critique of Brasília*. Chicago:
  University of Chicago Press.
Holston, James, and Teresa P. R. Caldeira,
  1998. Democracy, Law, and Violence:
  Disjunctions of Brazilian Citizenship. In
  *Fault Lines of Democracy in Post-transition
  Latin America*, Felipe Agüero and Jeffrey

Stark, eds. Miami: University of Miami North-South Center Press, pp. 263–296.

Howard, Ebenezer, 1902. *Garden Cities of Tomorrow*. London: S. Sonnenschein and Co., Ltd.

Jacobs, Jane, 1961. *The Death and Life of Great American Cities*. New York: Vintage Books.

Jencks, Charles, 1993. *Heteropolis: Los Angeles, the Riots, and the Strange Beauty of Hetero-Architecture*. London: Ernst and Sohn.

Lefort, Claude, 1988. *Democracy and Political Theory*. Minneapolis: University of Minnesota Press.

Soja, Edward W., 1996. Los Angeles 1965–1992: From Crisis-Generated Restructuring to Restructuring-Generated Crisis. In *The City: Los Angeles and Urban Theory at the End of the Twentieth Century*, Allen J. Scott and Edward W. Soja, eds. Berkeley: University of California Press, pp. 426–462.

Taylor, Charles, 1992. The Politics of Recognition. In *Multiculturalism and the Politics of Recognition*. Princeton: Princeton University Press, pp. 25–61.

Telles, Edward, 1995. Structural Sources of Socioeconomic Segregation in Brazilian Metropolitan Areas. *American Journal of Sociology* 100(5): 1199–1223.

Young, Iris Marion, 1990. *Justice and the Politics of Difference*. Princeton: Princeton University Press.

22

Contesting Citizenship
in Urban China

Peasant Migrants, the State and
the Logic of the Market, 1999

Dorothy J. Solinger

Introduction: Citizenship, Markets, and the State

Appearing to urbanites as aimless and ominous as errant waters, China's sojourning peasant transients in the cities are outsiders, out of place. In their millions, they seem to city folk and their supervisors to be streaming in, as if incessantly, out of control. In the minds of their metropolitan detractors, they are aptly labeled: they are unrooted noncitizens, wanderers; they are the elements of the "floating population."

The march of markets into the municipalities from the early 1980s – with the transition from socialism and the steady evisceration of the rules and institutions of the planned economy – is precisely what made this peasant migration possible. But the many attendant externalities of this spread of capitalism were double-edged: they served to heighten the feelings among settled residents of a negative impact issuing from the arrival in town of the transients. This process is still unfolding, as of the second half of the 1990s.

This volume charts the complex clash in Chinese cities between incoming noncitizens, the markets that bore them, city residents, and the officials and changing institutions of the old Communist urban political community. Its major point is that citizenship does not come easily to those outside the political community whose arrival coincides with deepening and unaccustomed marketization.

Thus it challenges formulations, such as those associated with the work of T. H. Marshall (1950: 29), that predict a positive and unilinear connection between the rise of capitalism and the creation of citizens; it also engages theories, like those of Barrington Moore (1966) and S. M. Lipset (1963, 1959), that correlate commercialism or urbanization with the birth or the presence of democratic institutions (see also Turner 1986). Even if these scholars are proven correct over the very long run, my story paints a portrait of the often ugly time in between.

In China in the 1980s and 1990s, this pair of forces – markets and migrants (both, initially, intentionally summoned up by top state

Dorothy J. Solinger, *Contesting Citizenship in Urban China: Peasant Migrants, the State, and the Logic of the Market* (Berkeley and Los Angeles: University of California Press, 1999), pp. 1–7, 14, 241–243, 249–256, 269–275.

The Anthropology of Citizenship: A Reader, First Edition. Edited by Sian Lazar.
© 2013 John Wiley & Sons, Inc. Published 2013 by John Wiley & Sons, Inc.

officials) – was sharply unsettling to popular perceptions among city people and to the agents and institutions of the state as well. It was so because of the collision of these forces with entitlements and expectations long and inextricably bound to the institutions of the prior regime. But, to complicate the picture, the state-in-transition continued for a time to dispense its wonted welfare to its own employees. If migrants could get a temporary job in a state firm, the job might lend them a modicum of mercy while in town and even offer a lowly, second-class citizenhood.

For the institutions that comprised the socialist-era urban political system in China had a distinctly compassionate cast, certainly for their urban charges. They enabled the system to ground its legitimacy in two key functions, both of which the state was prepared to fulfill for urbanites, the "proper" citizens (*gongmin*) of cities: it provided and it watched. That is, socialist city managers for decades administered their system through a combination of welfare and control, in the terms of Andrew Walder (1986), a kind of "organized dependence"; or, alternatively, a solicitude paired with surveillance, to quote from Janos Kornai (1992: 315).

This organized solicitude was made possible as urban administrations granted all officially lodged residents a badge of proper affiliation, the urban household registration or *hukou*, and assigned all working residents to a "unit," a *danwei*, charged with overseeing their sustenance and their behavior. In addition to the welfare benefits and an array of services afforded employees by their work units after the mid-1950s, the city also allocated all the daily necessities of city residents via rations. In the pre-reform-era days, no one was eligible for the perquisites of urban life who was not a registered member of that municipality's population. While urbanites from another city could sometimes transfer their official household register among cities (with official approval or at official behest), ordinary peasants could almost categorically never do so.[1]

As later chapters reveal, with the coming of the country cousins, in the main (but not under all circumstances) municipal gatekeepers sought to withhold the usual, and quite substantial, privileges – the welfare – of urban existence from them. At the same time, the outsiders themselves, when not employed by any city "unit," typically slithered away from the controlling constrictions that had customarily tied "regular" urban dwellers to their moorings. Thus, toward the great bulk of the peasants newly in the cities, there was a bonding of the state's refusal to grant sustenance and security with its inability to dominate. At the same time there was a reciprocal effect: because of the peasants' presence, the former rules and norms about community and inclusion, and about the official allocation of public goods in the city, came under assault.

In many ways this so-called floating population joined an ancient saga. Leaving home and becoming "other" is an experience known to multitudes of millions around the globe and over the centuries who stepped across the borders that defined their identities to brave a life in a realm unknown. Like migrants elsewhere, China's mobile peasants appeared to be cut loose and drifting, seemingly pouring out in waves, sometimes in torrents, into regions whose citizens and their governors – though usually well cognizant of the economic contributions of these sojourners – often reacted to them with distaste and repulsion at worst, with profound ambivalence at best.

For migration throws up a specter of an overwhelmed state, of assaulted citizenry, and of rampant social turmoil: the vision of the optimists – that it can simply deposit docile toilers who will become assimilated settlers, acquiescent and conforming to the mode, enriching the nation – seems to many to be just a mirage. Put starkly, the immigration of "foreigners," whether internal farmers or truly "other" folks from afar, frequently entails confrontation. That confrontation, while not without its benign dimensions, is often fraught, surely at first, with dangers and hostility for both parties. The broadest themes (and even many of the details) are everywhere the same: these people are viewed as an incursion on locals' perceived deserts; they quite typically carry the brunt of discriminatory treatment.

I present this encounter in the urban areas of China at the end of the century as a contest over citizenship (and its changing content) waged primarily between the state – with its socialist system disappearing – and an enormous set of seemingly interloping peasant migrants who jostled uneasily with it, in a context of accelerating market transition.

Citizenship

Why citizenship? In late twentieth-century urban China, markets and the migrants they bore together challenged the city *hukou*, a most fundamental political institution, one that really amounted to an emblem of (urban) citizenship. The very presence of this pair of newcomers in town precipitated a crucial systemic alteration. As one Chinese writer phrased it,

> The floating population is summoning the household registration system, which is based on stable management, to transform into [one of] dynamic management. (Ding 1987: 103)

After migration took off in the early 1980s, Chinese journalists explicitly compared outsiders making their lives in the city to inferior citizens. One, discussing a governmental decision of 1984 that permitted peasants to acquire a new special *hukou* (household registration) for residing in towns, wrote of "the third kind of citizen, who had left the ranks of the peasantry and become an urbanite, but whose *hukou* is not the same as a real urban *hukou*." Another sympathized with "peasants in the city" who, "because they still have the rural *hukou* while living in the city, have a very low social position, no house, no grain and oil supply, no labor guarantee, and who, therefore, become second-class citizens."[2]

Indeed, the exclusion of peasants from state-sponsored benefits in cities entailed their rejection from what Harry Eckstein (1991: 346) terms "civic inclusion," or "access to institutions that provide capacities and resources." For, as a Chinese scholar remarked, the *hukou* – very much as a badge of citizenship in a Western society would do – determined a person's entire life chances, including social rank, wage, welfare, food rations (when these were in use), and housing (Gong 1989).

Any individuals living in a Chinese city without urban registration there were denied free compulsory education, deprived of many of the perquisites that went with permanent employment in state-owned factories, could normally not receive free health care, and could not even be conscripted into the army from their urban home (Dutton 1988: 8). Without the *hukou*, transients were virtual foreigners within the cities of their own country because this elemental fact of urban life guaranteed citizenship there and the "goods and opportunities that shape life chances" (Brubaker 1992: 21). Indeed, at the March 1995 session of the National People's Congress, then minister of labor Li Boyong actually proposed establishing a "system similar to international passport and visa requirements," with the purpose of curbing transprovincial migration (Saiget 1995: 33)! Thus, even as there were similarities between, on the one hand, the reactions and behavior of Chinese urbanites toward incoming peasants in China and, on the other, those of national citizens toward aliens in other "host" environments around the world, in this case the "strangers" who were despised were China's own people; peasants from China's own countryside were put outside the pale (Solinger 1999).

Perhaps most centrally, as with residence requirements aimed at excluding foreign immigrants from political participation in liberal states, the Chinese *hukou* even served as a means of preventing floating farmers from exercising the franchise in a city (for whatever it was worth in socialist China), no matter how long they lived there, and thus from being genuine members of the municipality. In other contemporary states, as Rogers Brubaker surveys them, a grant of the perquisites of "citizenry excludes only foreigners, that is, persons who belong to other states" (Brubaker 1992: 21).

By contrast, in many regards the level of discrimination experienced by China's ruralites residing in its metropolises exceeds that visited upon urbanizing peasants in Latin American, Southeast Asian, or African cities. In the first place, the various perquisites of urbanhood in China formally marked city folk off from ruralites much more decisively than is generally the case in other societies. Indeed, ordinary urbanites at all levels of income in China were recipients of benefits that made for a much wider gap than we see elsewhere.

But in addition in those other places, it is obstacles that might theoretically be overcome – such as poverty, class, low skills and lack of education, or inadequate social connections – that stand in the way of incorporation (Solinger 1995). Certainly these same factors isolated farmers in Chinese municipalities, but they were not at the core of the problem. Instead the Chinese peasants' lot in the city was much more akin to that of black people in South Africa before the 1990s or of blacks and Asians in the United States throughout the first half of the twentieth century.

In these similar cases, native residents were not just thrust to the bottom of a ladder of social mobility, as are ordinary rural transients upon arrival in third-world towns; instead – as in China – they were denied basic civil and even human rights as well (Solinger 1999). What all such outcasts have in common is that they all bore the brunt of a form of institution-alized discrimination so stringent that it barred them from becoming full citizens in their own home countries (Feagin and Feagin 1993: 15; Chan 1996: 145–47).

So sojourners from China's rural areas entered the cities (unless ushered in with a post arranged for them in a Chinese work unit) not just temporarily bereft of state-granted where-withal for their daily existence in town. In addition, they arrived altogether and categori-cally ineligible for this sustenance as well; this was so since their lack of association with the city *hukou* barred the great lot of them from enjoying any of the welfare benefits and social services that urbanites received as their natural birthright. For these reasons, to view Chinese peasants in the metropolises as foreign immi-grants there – as noncitizens – is fully in line with the general literature on citizenship.

Citizenship has been variously defined. Most fundamentally, as Bryan S. Turner (1993: 2) frames it, "the modern question of citizenship is structured by two issues," which are much the same as those that pertain to possession of the urban register in China. The first of these has to do with social *member-ship*, or, one might say, with belonging to a community; the second concerns the right to

an *allocation of resources*. From another angle, the hallmark of citizenship (and of the urban *hukou*) is exclusivity, as it "confers rights and privileges" just to those legally living within specifically designated borders (Soysal 1994; Meehan 1993; Brubaker 1992; Layton-Henry 1990). The boundaries that define members are usually drawn around the geographical community. But they may also delineate only some of the groups within it.

Various scholars term citizenship primarily a legal-cum-social status; a source of political identity; a claim for fulfilling duties and civic responsibilities; or a guarantee of social or welfare services, and of political rights. For some, the triad of citizenship rights attained by British citizens by the mid-twentieth century – civil, political, and social (in that order, histor-ically) – identified in T. H. Marshall's seminal essay on citizenship must all be present and reciprocally reinforcing for the status to become truly operational (Marshall 1950; Meehan 1993). Others underscore the access to goods that its ownership affords, its entitle-ments or privileges, and the expectations that accompany these (Brubaker 1992; García 1996; Turner 1993; Barbalet 1988).

Whatever the disagreements among ana-lysts on the content of citizenship, up to now the literature on this topic has been dominated by Westerners and, for the most part, evinces a Western perspective. That is, writers have anchored their definitions in a European/American understanding, one that connects the practice of citizenship primarily with par-ticipation in the political life of the community, whether in decision making or in taking part in the electoral process, and roots it in a civil and legal status (Barbalet 1988; Meehan 1993; Heater 1990; Freeman 1986).

But there is also sometimes a recognition that the meaning of the concept and the nature of its content may vary from one place to the next (Meehan 1993; Marshall 1963); and also that the phenomenon itself is part of or subject to a changing process (García 1996; Hollifield 1992). Across societies, such differences may be a function of how the status is acquired – whether it is attained through struggle or bestowed as a gift from above; over time, the push of new peoples for entry, alterations in the supposed "global political culture" and attendant worldwide ideas about rights, and economic crisis all may result in contractions or expansions of the eligible population or of the treatment its possession accords (Turner 1993; Soysal 1994; Barbalet 1988; García 1996; Hollifield 1992).

These insights help in generalizing about the specific substance of citizenship in any given context. It will vary in accord with the nature and with the prevailing conception of the political community in which it appears (Barbalet 1988; Meehan 1993). Correspondingly, and most critically, the values and behaviors that citizenship endorses in a society will reflect the norms of whatever might be the dominant participatory and allocatory institutions in the community with which the citizen is affiliated. And the society's receptivity to international influence is a function of the nature of the institutions already in place. Accordingly, the alleged shift in the "discursive order of rights at the global level" – a shift that Yasemin Soysal (1994) heralds as reshaping the practice of and eligibility for citizenship in Western Europe – is one that by no means necessarily takes root in all national soils, at least not with dispatch.

Turning to China, we find that the latest version of the state constitution, adopted in 1982, leaves the specific content of the country's citizenship vague. For this document simply announces in Article 33 that "All persons holding the nationality of the People's Republic of China" are citizens, equal before the law, and enjoying the rights while performing the duties prescribed in the constitution and the law.

For our purposes – since the chance for meaningful political participation in law making or in the electoral process was yet negligible to nonexistent for the urban resident in late 1990s China; and since gross disparities in social status and benefits exist between members of urban and rural communities – I follow the characterization offered by Turner and emphasize, as he does, not the political but just the identity/membership and distributive components of citizenship.

Accordingly, I consider as full, official, state-endorsed urban citizens those who had a form of valid, official membership or affiliation in the city, and who consequently were the recipients of state-disbursed goods. We will see that at century's end, though some peasant transients (those working, temporarily, in state-owned institutions) obtained a portion of these privileges and so could be viewed as half- or second-class citizens, officially ruralites in big cities were still denied genuine membership, the right to belong officially. Nonetheless, with the progression of marketization and economic "reform," socialist distribution steadily declined for *all* residents of the nation's municipalities. As this occurred, unentitled farmers subsisting on the fringes experimented with a new style of urban living, an untried model of city citizenship, in post-1949 China.

[...]

[This section shows] how urban peasants, excluded by the state institution of the *hukou* and working within incipient markets, participated in writing new rules of urban life. I focus on the peasants' persistent occupation of urban spaces (made possible by markets) that called into question the exclusivity of official urban citizenship. For – to return to Turner's usage – both the highly limited belongingness and the customary patterns of distribution (i.e., the marks of citizenship) that had existed before economic reform were threatened when outsiders appeared on the premises. The conclusion draws out comparative insights inherent in the study and spells out the implications of the analysis for the future forms of peasant citizenship in urban China. It also formulates conclusions about the larger relationship between incipient capitalism and the bestowal or acquisition of citizenship.

The data for the study come from nearly 150 hours of interviews in China with city officials, with scholars, and with over fifty migrants in six major cities (Tianjin, Harbin, Wuhan, Nanjing, Guangzhou, and Beijing) during trips to China in 1990, 1991, 1992, and 1994. The study also draws on extensive documentary research in Chinese governmental reports and in scholarly Chinese journals – which in recent years contain a wealth of academic scholarship, statistical data, and results of surveys – and on the new genre of reportage and journalistic accounts. Its focus is the period 1983 to 1996.

[...]

The Urban Rationing Regime: Coping Outside It and Alternate Citizenship

Not only in their working lives but also in their daily lives – their housing, medical care, education, and welfare services – many rural migrants in the cities through the mid-1990s had to make do without the trappings of formal, state-bestowed citizenship. For they had to live outside the third institutional wall the socialist state erected against them, the urban rationing regime. Thus, except for laborers contracted to state-owned organs who, as we have seen, did attain a modest second-tier citizenhood, the official system refused to grant most outsiders membership in the legitimized urban community by barring sojourners from access to the city services remaining within its grasp.

Indeed, through the mid-1990s it was official policy that "citizens" not in possession of a local *hukou* were to be prevented from receiving education and health care treatment and were ineligible for state-allocated housing and grain allocation (Q Zhang 1988). So, despite the imaginings and agitation of urbanites, in fact most migrants subsisted in a style that did much less to challenge city people's privileges than the official municipal residents supposed.

Transients found their own mode of urban life, one that often clashed with or diminished regular urban services very little. One after another, markets for all the requisites of daily subsistence came into being, and many peasants in the cities found their own solutions to the problems of meeting their daily needs; in their market activities they also discovered the means for generating new, unofficial intermediary groups outside the state. As they did, and as, accordingly, the meaning of life without formal citizenship in the city was transformed, the exclusivity of urban citizenship was altered as well.

A common conception is that the rural newcomers to Chinese cities existed in an administrative vacuum, scavenging, hanging on without the urban citizens' rights to housing, education, and health care, and

without any management responsible for their concerns.[3] And yet many of these people managed to stay on, some even to thrive. So the effect of their coming was a permanent collective urban presence (one, albeit, whose members were constantly shifting) of unlicensed sojourners not ratified by the regime. Over time, their joint success at survival without state endorsement posed a frontal challenge to the authority of the government and to its capacity to encompass and enclose the economic activities of entire municipal populations (Xiang 1996).

But we cannot generalize their solution: as we have seen, transients included a set of laborers employed by the state, a hierarchy of native-place-based communities, and finally a range of stragglers – the state-protected; the community-connected; and the anomic isolates. Where individual newcomers fell within this range was a function of the nature of their bonds. This chapter looks primarily at the community-connected and the isolates, referring only occasionally to the state-protected laborers as a point of reference. It asks how the two groups fared without any access to state-conferred services.

Those at the top of the hierarchy of noncitizens benefited from having cash or other capital, a well-endowed community, and, most of all, informal connections with state cadres (Xiang 1996); those progressively lower down the social pyramid lacked some or all of these sources of strength. Despite the continuing power of ties with officialdom, the novelty of market society recast the urban milieu, such that outsiders were not newcomers gradually assimilating into an established framework. Instead, they formed a patchwork of people in "parallel communities," plus some stragglers, all of them eking out existences for the most part outside the state (Portes and Stepick 1993).

Thus, a layering of "citizenship" emerged among those not considered proper citizens. Some, mainly coming from the inland, found a second-class citizenship through official contracts; others, chiefly from the talent-generating east, carved out a separate belongingness as they accumulated resources and benefits of their own through what one scholar terms their "auto-integration" (C Wang 1995); and it was only a motley residual, totally marginalized mass that stagnated, abandoned and bereft.

This picture complicates standard (and, at a more macro level, entirely correct) formulations, according to which Chinese society of the late twentieth century was one with a "dual nature," whereby "urban and rural sectors operat[ed] under different economic systems and enjoy[ed] different social and economic benefits ... living in two different worlds"; or where "socioeconomic dualism" (urbanites and ruralites living by different rules) characterized the city itself (Wang and Zuo 1996; Chan 1996: 146–47). Once peasants entered the city and interacted with state institutions and with the markets there, the metropolis had no longer just one, but rather manifold modes of "living on the edge," all "completely separate from local society" (Han 1994: 10; Ba jia 1995: A-02, 11).

This chapter describes the solutions different groups among this population found to the everyday problems of housing, education, food, and health care. It also explores the nature of organizational life among them. It concludes by reexamining the situation of citizenship for the urban transients. But first we ask about the gender ratio among these people, their marital status, their success in landing jobs, and the level of satisfaction they experienced.

[...]

Villages

When migrants first appeared in the cities, many settled in a murky world of suburban rentals, where land was more open, housing available, daily living costs lower, and management more lax (Xie 1990). These regions offered the outsiders a chance to set up facilities for commerce and business in used articles, handicrafts, manufacture, and processing; there they could sleep, conduct business, and store their carts and tools and raw materials, in rentals generally starting at around 50 yuan in 1990. There the peasant interlopers made common cause with local peasants-turned-landlord, and a mutual deal was struck (Li and Hu 1991). Native homeowners sectioned off a

portion of their own dwellings to rent to the newcomers; abandoned their older home to rentals, constructing a finer one for themselves; or else built an inferior shack to house migrant tenants.[4] In these situations, it was to the advantage of both to accommodate one another: the residents got wealthy while the transients enjoyed a relatively cheap and protected abode. Meanwhile, everyone skirted regulations, the migrants failing to register and the landlords saving tax money they should have been paying (Tang and Chen 1989; Li and Hu 1991; NFRB, March 30, 1990).

By the end of 1993, outsiders who were part of migrant communities or "villages" were "buying or building houses in Beijing and acquiring properties in the hopes of settling down and striking root in the city."[5] This was especially true in the Zhejiang Village in Fengtai district, Beijing, where peasants took to buying old, broken-down dwellings for use as combined living and working quarters. Some transients had even bought real estate there by mid-1993.[6] Even more flagrantly, in 1992, the local authorities (illegally, since without higher-level consent) in the Zhejiang Village region actually permitted wealthier, share-pooling residents to construct some forty buildings in large courtyards on village land and had signed leases with them (Xiang 1996; Beja and Bonnin, 1995).

In Guangzhou and Shenzhen as well in the early 1990s the practice of throwing up structures and shantytowns had taken root, even as an observer categorized it as "illicit" (Wong 1994). In Shanghai's Pudong district in 1994, at least 933 "illegal structures" had been erected by – or rented or lent by locals to – alien workers (X Wang 1994). And so with the reform era, China's cities came to appear more and more similar to those elsewhere in the third world, as slumlike spaces reappeared for the first time in post-1949 China; a specialist in Chinese urban studies remarks on the total absence of such areas – and of pavement dwellers – in 1980, before the migration had begun (Ma 1981).

It was not the poverty found among shantytown dwellers elsewhere that placed Chinese floaters in these out-of-the-way sites (Tang and Chen 1989). Indeed, many of the members of the Zhejiang Village had annual incomes of more than 10,000 yuan in the mid-1990s, and yet they continued to live there (C. Wang 1995). As the sociologist Li Qiang asserted in 1993, "Even those with money live in shacks and save all their money. These same people may own a three-story house in the rural area."[7] The concentrated location just outside the municipality for many thousands of them was instead a form of segregation that reflected – and also reproduced – the state-imposed isolation of the city-sojourning, rural-registered from the proper urbanites. And it forced upon the former a substitute form of urban subsistence as it deprived them of citizenship.

Outskirts outside the state

In these suburban areas incoming peasants – to varying extents in different communities – fashioned worlds of their own, where they made an accommodation outside the rules and restrictions thrown up by the registration system. The Chinese named these settlements after the provincial homelands of their dwellers. Though all the settlements were dubbed "villages," in fact, they existed in three different gradations by the mid-1990s. The most elementary in terms of structure and organization were ones that simply served as residential areas where people from the same province predominated. The second, more sophisticated form, entailed concentration of the inhabitants by profession, and those dwelling in them developed some economic cooperation as well as a degree of mutual aid in daily life.

Only in the third, most advanced, type did some leading residents arrange for the provision of community services and create informal, unofficial public welfare organizations. In Beijing, it was just the Zhejiang Village, to be discussed below, that qualified as the third kind of grouping by the mid-1990s (Yuan et al. 1995). This third, advanced form of occupational community was akin to what are called "ethnic enclaves" (Portes and Rumbaut 1990: 21) elsewhere, especially if we take the term "ethnic" in its special, spatial Chinese sense (Honig 1992). These settlements are universally the product of chain migration, a

system functional both in informing ruralites of the location of pockets of urban opportunity and in placing them in lodging and work upon arrival in town. As students of migration in other countries note, where newcomers have business acumen, they generally generate collective entrepreneurial ventures. A relatively complex division of labor within their trade also works to enhance the potential for the provision of community welfare (Yuan et al. 1995).

The very existence of these co-provincial villages openly challenged the state's capacity to overwhelm – indeed, to prohibit – the formation of unofficial, informal groups outside its aegis. For here just beyond the once tightly regimented urban areas, places where officialdom had for decades been able (with the exception of the period at the height of the Cultural Revolution) rather quickly to contain and suppress incipient nonstate organizations, were burgeoning an array of what amounted to contender, if nascent, ascriptive and corporate associations.

The people here were able to live so independently because the state did not – indeed could not – fit floating and often very transient migrants into the neighborhood associations that had customarily structured and kept up a steady surveillance over the "proper" urban residents' domestic existences. Neither were any of these itinerants on the outskirts members of any workplace danwei, the "units" that had long directed daily behavior at the office or the plant. City services were not supplied to their areas of congregation; nor were there any official associations that could absorb their energies or see to their social needs.

Left abandoned to scramble on their own, quite sizable concentrations of outsiders pooled their resources and carved out a means of subsistence over time. Thus a great paradox characterized floaters living in such collectivities. The state's registration system constrained them, excluded them from its privileges, and neglected them in its service network. And yet at the same time they were freed, if to a limited but growing extent, by their abandonment outside the pale of the state's organizations of administration and surveillance; they were also increasingly empowered by their own numbers.

There were two crucial differences in the Chinese case from the usual pattern elsewhere, in part a result of the *hukou* system and in part connected with the transition from socialism. One was that these people, though nationals, were barred by the *hukou* prohibition from acquiring city citizenship and so were denied any means of pressing their needs legally on urban and higher-level governments (Yuan *et al.* 1995). By way of contrast, in other polities in the developing world, where competitive party systems were present, native migrant squatters obtained the ballot and could sometimes bargain for city services and facilities in exchange for votes, at least around election time (Gunes-Ayata 1987; Cornelius 1974; Gallin and Gallin 1974; Lloyd 1979; Roberts 1995).

The result of this lockout from the urban system for Chinese rural sojourners was that those with the wherewithal to do so were forced to form wholly alternate societies, nearly totally unconnected with the mainstream. As one researcher explains, "The population [of the Zhejiang Village in 1995] has no sense of belonging to Beijing society" (C Wang 1995: 18). Of the respondents in a sample of 290 transients, 83 percent had not established any relations whatever with Beijing people as of 1992. Treated as foreigners, and seeing themselves that way too, some even felt they would benefit from setting up an ambassadorial organ to protect their interests! (S Zhu 1992)

The other important distinction was that, as we have seen, because of the continuing – if declining – presence of a powerful state-sponsored framework amid many fading socialist institutions, this mode of subsisting by living collectively was just one of three ways of existing found among urban outsiders. Though it offered more benefits and services than those available to unconnected stragglers, it proved inferior in this regard to the lot of the state-employed and bonded.

Co-provincial colonies

By 1985, an "ethnic" cluster had clearly emerged in one district within the jurisdiction of Beijing City. The large number of hotel beds

(24 percent of those in the city were there), open markets (about 20 percent of those in the whole city at that time), and business opportunities in the city's northwestern Haidian and Chaoyang districts had already drawn in groups of transients (Du 1986). By the middle of the next decade, one source cites twenty-five compact communities in Beijing housing at least ten thousand out-of-towners each (Zhang 1995). These included temporary colonies of Xinjiang Uighurs, along with natives of Hebei, Sichuan, Anhui, Tianjin, Henan, Jiangsu, Shandong, and, most conspicuously, Zhejiang.[8]

These areas each had their place in an informal hierarchy of social status: a Henanese informant on the streets of Beijing confided that he refused to live with his fellow provincials because of the low social status of their neighborhood.[9] For the spot the Henan natives, largely from Gushi county, occupied, the Erlizhuang neighborhood in Haidian's Dongsheng, was colloquially dubbed "garbage village," since most of the inhabitants lived off gathering and buying scrap material and junk. Within the site, a filthy market for old goods formed the foundation for the livelihood of over two thousand peasants, a mart barely distinguishable from the rubbish heap that constituted both the inhabitants' mine and their refuse.[10]

There were reports of migrant colonies in many cities besides the capital, including Shanghai, Guangzhou, Tianjin, Chengdu, and even Urumqi, to name a few (C Wang 1995; Quan 1994; Sun 1997). People from Jiangsu's Nantong congregated as long-term residents along particular streets in Xinjiang's Changji district, in Heilongjiang's Daqing, and in Shanghai (Wu 1990). In Urumqi, close to the train station, there was located a *mangliu* (blind wanderers') village, allegedly made up of some twenty-seven thousand outsiders from the inland, formed into five natural villages as of late 1989 (Yuan and Tang 1990).

In the vicinity of Zhongshan University in Fenghecun on Guangzhou's outskirts a whole village of ten thousand peasants had rented more than two thousand rooms from the locals and outnumbered them in a ratio of three to one by the early 1990s (F Zhu 1992). In that city's Sanyuanli district, Xinjiang people lived together in a hotel, eating lamb and carrying knives, according to local lore.[11] Squatter settlements graced several other areas around the city.[12] Scrap collectors settled in Huizhou city's Huicheng district; close to the Guangzhou zoo, cotton fluffers stayed in plastic shacks. In border areas along the city's streets, by the mountains, near the fields, and along the villages, outsiders opened shops, repaired shoes, did odd jobs, and collected scraps.[13] Guangzhou's natives disdained these areas for their decrepit appearance and sickening hygiene; but transients set up their own temporary day-care centers, schools, and markets there (Wong 1994).

By the late 1980s in Shanghai, too, migrants had gradually moved to the border streets and suburbs of the cities, finding the city center saturated (Shanghai shi 1989). One suburb became a center for food-processing factories; a 1990 government investigation uncovered as many as thirty subterranean such workshops, engaged in catering and baking for city residents (K Zhou 1996). In the early 1990s when a new development zone was established in the city's eastern Pudong section, colonies of fellow provincials quickly followed (Sun 1997).

The Zhejiang Village

But it was the Zhejiang Village that was by far the most massive and articulated; it was also the place that was best researched.[14] Its location was in Fengtai district's Dahongmen, eight kilometers south of the city. One journalist traced the first Zhejiang tailors in Fengtai to 1983 (B Liu 1989), though the later-famous Zhejiang Village only became fully constituted around 1986 (Xiang 1996). By late 1988, the ratio of outsiders to locals was already as high as 2.33 : 1 (Y Zhang 1989). The great majority – perhaps up to 80 percent[15] – of these transients were taken upon arrival by their co-county folk into the fold of the tailoring trade, assembling, manufacturing, and selling garments. The remainder were there to service the needs of the seamstresses and salespeople.

Over the years 1986 to 1990, the numbers of inhabitants sprang from twelve thousand to thirty thousand, and newcomers continued to increase at the rate of 50 percent per year after

1990 (Xiang 1996). Most sources agree that by the mid-1990s about one hundred thousand transients, mostly from Zhejiang's Wenzhou prefecture, had taken up residence in Beijing's five administrative villages, corresponding to twenty-six natural villages.[16] According to one report, the conglomeration was composed of four districts, with villagers residing in them according to native place (Piante and Zhu 1995).

Dahongmen has been compared to an American Chinatown, but in fact it was even more a self-contained community, sealed off as it was from the main life of the city by government intention, with city authorities restricting its residents to specific boundaries. For years the official administration of the city left the enclave to its own dictates. The exception was the city's demands for fees for residency papers and for hygiene services (without the transients deriving any benefit therefrom), and its requisition of taxes on their business and on every sewing machine, among other charges (Magritte 1994).

As the inhabitants built up a life of their own, their original need for outside assistance steadily decreased (Xiang 1996). Instead of waiting vainly for the Beijing authorities to service their wants, by 1993, residents of the village had established their own restaurants (catering exclusively Zhejiang dishes), some hundred barbershops, repair shops, twenty clinics and hospitals, day-care centers, five kindergartens, and markets, along with some two thousand small shops, all doing business in their Zhejiang dialect.[17]

Entrepreneurs also arranged daily buses to and from the home counties, set up rudimentary toilets, and installed long-distance phone lines. And in the large courtyards mentioned above that were constructed in 1992, water, electrical, sewerage, postal, educational, and recreational facilities came into being. Despite these efforts, in general sanitation infrastructure and educational institutions remained terribly deficient, and sewerage, electrical power, and postal services "could hardly meet the needs of the place."[18] Still, the residents of this community had found a way to sustain themselves with scarcely any backing from the bureaucracy.

By contrast, the region of Beijing peopled by peasants hailing from Anhui was less compact, though two-thirds of those living there came from just three counties of that province. As more and more Anhuinese arrived, by 1992, the place took on the visage of a true village, with trash scattered liberally, young children scampering about as if on open fields, indoor toilets lacking or broken down or ignored, and vegetables sprouting. Because of the paucity of living space and of people's incomes, residents shared household goods and tended one another if they should fall ill (Yuan *et al.* 1995).

There, as opposed to the Zhejiang Village, the much poorer level of the populace, plus the simplicity of its main profession – trash-picking done one by one, which did nothing to train its operators in division of labor and cooperation – discouraged, or at least failed to motivate, people from working together to create and perform community services beyond the most basic mutual assistance. That area managed to boast as its only joint undertakings a few small retail shops and a very basic restaurant (ibid.). Still, the resource of community that the residents shared gave them a potential for organization that transients living in a less concentrated fashion elsewhere in city lacked. [...]

Organization and leadership

In a 1994 survey of migrants in Beijing and Shanghai, only 9.4 percent responded that they belonged to a "spontaneous" (*zifa*) grouping of some type (Yuan *et al.* 1995). Yet an infinite number of quite informal associations, based on lines of blood and place of origin, succored those among the floating population who had access to them (Ba jia 1995; Yuan *et al.* 1995). If nothing else, these groupings served as refuges when transients encountered trouble. For their purpose was to provide mutual assistance in daily life and in work (Ba jia 1995).

Cliques (*bang*) of migrants from the same native place and working at the same kind of job thus became networks for self-protection, mutual care, and joint action against outsiders, when necessary. But their scale remained very small, their degree of organization elementary

and loose. For such bodies lacked fixed structure or any definition of internal relations. Moreover, unless members of such a group knew someone able to provide job opportunities, their mobility was endemic, their work life quite unstable (Yuan *et al.* 1995; Shi 1992; D Zhou 1994).

This feebleness of secondary associations was partly a reflection of the hazards that transient, scattered migrant workers encounter the world around (Huntington and Nelson 1976; Piore 1979). But, more important, its chief source was the specific restraints against migrants' affiliation imposed by the Chinese government, restrictions not generally found in other societies. Indeed, despite the obstacles, in other places associations among outsiders in cities gave them the means to launch themselves into urban society (Cornelius 1974; Perlman 1976; Lloyd 1979; Chandra 1977; Glazer and Moynihan 1963; Feagin 1978; Roberts 1995; Harris 1982; Hollifield 1992). In reform-era China, by contrast, the administrations of large cities refused to register or legally to incorporate – whether as part of a state organ or as an independent entity – any potentially sophisticated association among the sojourners. Not only that; individual migrants usually could not even become formal members of an urban organ in Beijing, up through the mid-1990s (Yuan *et al.* 1995).

Regardless of this official denial, some enterprising transients went on building collective connections, to promote the coordination, if not the defense, of their interests. Indeed, if we consider the several chief occupations in which transients in the cities engaged, we find that in each of them at least some of the practitioners participated in group activity of one sort or another.

A most intricately orchestrated effort was one several wealthy traders from Rui'an City, Zhejiang, mounted in Beijing after the mid-1980s. Their aim was to create a trade association among well-known fellow entrepreneurs from home holding sizable assets and running a steady business. They hoped at a minimum to consolidate the economic power of Rui'an businesspeople in Beijing, protect their legal interests, and exchange market information. But ultimately they hoped to use the full weight of their combined capital to enter the city's mainstream market as a force powerful enough to face the city's own entrepreneurs in any potential conflict (ibid.).

The story is a decade-long string of disappointments. For the Beijing city government persistently rebuffed their efforts, in spite of their having won the strong backing of Rui'an's liaison office in Beijing and the support of their hometown government, plus that of both the Rui'an and Beijing Communist Parties' United Front Departments and both cities' industrial and commercial federations (ibid.).

The circuitous path these pioneers traveled in trying to win permission was multipronged in spite of repeated setbacks along the way. It began with the creation of a "preparatory group," which, though acquiring legal approval, did not manage to thrust the movement further. Another avenue of approach was to set up Beijing branch offices of two professional associations already in operation in Rui'an; yet another was to form a Rui'an *tongxianghui*, composed of influential Rui'an locals who had successfully been doing business or who had been part of the Rui'an cultural and intellectual circles in Beijing for at least three years.

They proceeded to hold evening parties to which they invited city district police and taxation officials, whom they requested to lecture, and with whom they promised to cooperate in controlling their errant fellows. There was also a plan for a joint defense committee that was to cooperate with the local public security in handling merchants from Rui'an who were behaving illegally (ibid.).

One last maneuver entailed a number of Rui'an individual business people entering district-level industrial and commercial federations in Beijing as individual members and then composing a special group of Rui'an merchants within the federation (ibid.). Though none of these steps had led to the final, very minimal but essential goal of registration for their association as late as 1995, the ingenuity of the ringleaders and the multiplicity of entry points against which they pressed were impressive. Probably the aims, if not all the imaginative tactics, of this group were representative. For of the 9.4 percent of migrants professing

to belong to some kind of organization in 1994, 33.9 percent were businesspeople. Their groups worked to divide up turf and coordinate prices (ibid.).

Bosses dominated the teams among construction and other manual laborers and operated through a core of close lieutenants plus a second ring of activists, surrounded by a flexible body of frequently shifting followers (ibid). The bachelors who usually made up such teams often belonged to small-scale loyalty gangs, sometimes headed by an influential senior figure. These youths swore brotherhood oaths and passed their scant free hours in one another's company (ibid.; Ba jia 1995). Scuffles were commonplace among such gangs, but they were over territory and held no larger political appeals.[19]

Nursemaids formed *baomu* associations for pursuing their needs; beggars and trash collectors organized bands (Yuan *et al.* 1995; Ba jia 1995). Outsider beggars battled over sites with local ones (Liu 1986). And sometimes competition and economic interest split up a provincially homogeneous urban settlement by county or hometown, and again economically based conflicts were common (X Wang 1995). There were tales of jealousy and battles among the subregional groups, setting up their own tiny fiefdoms, often using extortion against competitors, and milking their turf for its meager yield, as this vignette suggests:

Many places in Guangzhou are carved out and occupied by gangs who set up separatist regimes; blackmailing each other becomes a way of life. If someone in such an area collects wine bottles, trash paper, and so on, the occupants levy a tax upon it. (Ba and Ma 1989: 54)

There were also rings that made their way within an underclass and reportedly dangerous underworld of "black" and secret societies.[20] These shady groups thrived as protection rackets, using extortion to collect monthly "security money" and dealing in crime, prostitution, and narcotics (Piante and Zhu 1995; D Zhou 1994; Guangdong wailai 1995; Ba jia 1995; Beja and Bonnin 1995; Kaye 1994).

Besides these occupationally based bodies, there was also a Christian organization composed of several thousand Zhejiang businesspeople in Beijing; though allegedly limited to religious affairs, it became a conduit through which business deals with locals were arranged (Yuan et al. 1995). All of these organizational forms and formats were clearly preliminary foundations for aggregating and asserting individual and group welfare and economic rights. Moreover they persisted in their actions even as both the top political elite and local urban administrations struggled to limit their significance.

What sort of leadership held these various groups together? Researchers' findings on the groups are mixed. Since there was "no legal organizational leadership" among the migrants (Guangdong wailai 1995), some write of a total "absence of authority and administrative management" in the villages (C Wang 1995: 18). Still others speak of community elites with "authority, power, and a certain degree of control," plus prestige among the residents, at least in the Zhejiang Village. This dominance, they claim, made for a sort of self-administration within the village. But it lacked the clinching legitimation of the state and so was forced to exist parallel to but not as a part of it (Xiang 1995: 16, 36; L Zhang 1998).

Reportage literature and hearsay focus on the seamiest, most authoritarian, aspects of local rule. They assert that bosses held sway in areas such as the Zhejiang Village, ruling in factionalized, well-structured cliques. One source refers to "tribes," tightly controlled internally (Tang and Chen 1989: 19); another describes "small independent kingdoms," led by the chiefs of "black societies," and dominated in the Zhejiang Village by a "Wenzhou clique," whose members gained their wealth through illicit activities (Ming 1994: 27). This kind of account resonates with a report from a bureaucrat in Guangzhou, who refers to local villains or bullies running the shack settlements of his city.[21]

But other Chinese scholars who are deeply familiar with such areas uncover a realm of internally recognized and law-abiding authority in them. These researchers adjudge that the ability to adjust disputes among their confreres, experience, fairness, and wealth are some of the main qualities that conferred such leadership. Most important, however, are seniority within the village (as measured by length of time living there) and the abilities to provide employment opportunities and to manage crises for their fellows (Yuan, Zhang, and Wang 1996; S Zhang 1998).

Here we see the persisting effect of the state on power formation at the grass roots, even in communities largely beyond its reach. For these latter, decisive, skills were ultimately a function of these elites' having developed informal connections with local official organs, especially the police station, and with relevant departments in their rural home counties – but not with the central-level politicians who could have made major decisions on their fate and place within Chinese urban society. Because of their lack of a genuine, formal political imprimatur, these leaders could sometimes handle the transients' daily needs but exercised no administrative powers that stretched beyond their own people (D Zhou 1994; Ba jia 1995; Piante and Zhu 1995; Xiang 1996; and Yuan et al. 1995).

Thus, the clout that had been nurtured among migrants by the mid-1990s was quite a circumscribed one, very much internal to the migrant communities themselves. That limitation was demonstrated in transients' powerlessness to stave off the Beijing City's demolition of many of the buildings of the Zhejiang Village in November 1995 (Beja and Bonnin 1995; L Zhang 1998). But even as this move triumphed physically (and temporarily), the autonomous and internally consolidated business dealings and networks among the village's commercial leaders built up over the previous years persisted nonetheless.[22] So once again we see the creation of lifestyles, solutions, and association outside and parallel to the state.

The floating population is generally depicted as an undifferentiated mass of people, one at a loss because of its deprivation of all of the perquisites and permissions the state bestowed on the urban citizenry. This stereotype is misleading in several ways. In particular, significant disparities within this population made for a great deal of difference in the conditions of a migrant's daily life. As in the case of their departure from the countryside, or in their insertion into urban labor markets, among their everyday lives once in the city we can starkly distinguish three broad modes of existence among these people. One urban lifestyle was protected by affiliation with the official framework or with its individual deputies; another was enclosed within the relative (and variable) safety of native-place enclaves; and only the third mode was drawn from itinerants who were forsaken, by dint of lacking any sort of useful bond at all.

We have examined these distinctions when it came to the housing arrangements, chances for getting grain and medical attention (and for getting sick), and educational opportunities enjoyed (or not enjoyed) by the members of these three gross sets of migrants. Some of those who were linked by place of origin (especially parts of Zhejiang), though deprived of even a minimum of the state-conferred benefits offered to the second-class citizens laboring in state firms, developed their own, sometimes quite sizable, villages in the cities, furnished with at least rudimentary city services, facilities, and infrastructure.

In all these dimensions of dailiness, possession of any of the resources pertinent to a time of transition from a planned, bureaucratically managed political economy to a market-based one could smooth the shocks of placement into a very unfriendly milieu. These resources were, respectively, cash (useful in the new, marketizing environment); connections to cadres (a legacy of the weight of the old, statist system); and membership in outsider communities (whose very institutional ambiguity was an emblem of a society in motion, undergoing change).

In the transitional era when China was forsaking its socialist pattern, by the very act of sanctioning markets, its leadership was also involuntarily relinquishing its monopoly on the bestowal of the trappings of urban citizenship, insofar as these amounted to a share in the distribution of public goods and a right to membership in a community. The state was also thereby abandoning (if similarly unintentionally and surely unwillingly) its stranglehold over forms of association outside its own aegis. In short, because of their exclusion by the state institution of the *hukou*, combined with the workings of incipient

markets, peasants in the cities – just by their presence alone – were participating in writing new rules of urban life.

These outsiders might not prefer to be the long-term recipients of just the unauthorized badge of belonging offered by the Zhejiang Village or rest content forever with the quality of the public goods they were dealt there. Still, for the interim, in their daily praxis these "villagers" were forging an alternative, nonauthoritative, ersatz form of urbanhood for themselves – one that for many was materially poorer than that of state-paid temporary workers, but better than that of vagabonds.

Theirs was a brand of citizenship that the government would eventually have to acknowledge, beyond the leadership's repetitive and ultimately useless coercive campaigns for driving migrants out of their settlements. Far more than migrants in other forms of polity, sojourners living in autonomous villages posed a most palpable challenge to a state with authoritarian pretensions, a state that had for years anchored its authority in its monopoly of supplying all needs, and controlling all activities, in the city.

NOTES

1 *NMRB*, November 23, 1988, 3.
2 *NMRB*, May 11, 1989, and November 23, 1988, 3.
3 For instance, see *The Independent* in cooperation with *Yomiuri shimbun* (Tokyo), November 13, 1994, 7A; *NMRB*, March 30, 1995, 4, in FBIS, May 26, 1995, 64.
4 Author's interviews, Harbin, July 19, 1991; GASS, May 10, 1992; Department of Sociology, Nanjing University, May 21, 1992; and talk with Gu Shangfei, a Chinese social scientist, New York, February 14, 1994; Tang and Chen 1989: 19; and Vogel 1989: 218.
5 JPRS-CAR-93-091 (December 29, 1993), 45; Xu and Li 1990.
6 FBIS, July 14, 1993, 53.
7 Lecture, Columbia University on November 10, 1993.
8 *Eastern Express* (Hong Kong), August 20–21, 1994, 8; B Liu, 1989; *CD*, June 18, 1992, 3.
9 Author's interview, Beijing, August 7, 1994.
10 JPRS-CAR-091-93 (December 29, 1993), 45; Zhu 1992: 22.

11 Author's interview, Guangzhou Urban Planning Automation Center, May 11, 1992.
12 *NFRB*, August 24, 1989, 2.
13 *NFRB*, March 30, 1990, 2.
14 S Zhu 1992; FBIS, November 16, 1992, 38 (from *South China Morning Post* (Hong Kong), November 16, 1992, 10); JPRS-CAR-93-091 (December 29, 1993), 45; Johnson 1994; my interviews with Gu Shangfei, New York, February 14, 1994, and Beijing, August 5, 1994; Ming 1994; Magritte 1994; Min 1995; C Wang 1995; Beja and Bonnin 1995; Piante and Zhu 1995; and Xiang 1996.
15 This is the estimate of Gu Shangfei.
16 JPRS-CAR-93-091 (December 29, 1993); Xiang 1996: 4.
17 Ming 1994; S Zhu 1992; JPRS-CAR-93-091 (December 29, 1993); Min 1995.
18 Xiang 1996; also S Zhu 1992; and my interview with Gu Shangfei, February 14, 1994.
19 Author's interview, social scientist, Harbin, July 25, 1991; Wang, Wu, and Jiang 1990: 2; and Zhang 1987: 25.
20 United Press International, March 2, 1993.
21 Author's interview at Guangzhou Urban Planning Automation Center, May 11, 1992.
22 Information from Li Zhang, and from L Zhang 1998.

REFERENCES

Ba, Liang, and Ma Lun, 1989. The dream of the gold panners [in Chinese]. *Tequ wenxue* [Special zone literature] 4: 48–66.

Ba jia, 1995. Eight "rural labor force mobility research" tasks commissioned by the Ministry of Agriculture, Rural Economic Research Center Task Group [in Chinese]. *Nongcun laodongli jingji yanjiu tongxun* [Bulletin of rural labor mobility studies]. N.p.

Barbalet, J. M., 1988. *Citizenship: Rights, Struggle, and Class Inequality*. Milton Keynes: Open University Press.

Beja, Jean Philippe, and Michel Bonnin, 1995. The Destruction of the 'Village.' *China Perspectives* 2: 21–25.

Brubaker, Rogers, 1992. *Citizenship and Nationhood in France and Germany*. Cambridge, MA: Harvard University Press.

Chan, Kam Wing, 1996. Post-Mao China: A Two-Class Urban Society in the Making.

International Journal of Urban and Regional Research 20(1): 134–150.

Chandra, Subhash, 1977. *Social Participation in Urban Neighbourhoods*. New Delhi: National Publishing House.

China Daily (CD) (Beijing). Selected issues, 1988–96.

Cornelius, Wayne A., 1974. Urbanization and Political Demand Making: Political Participation among the Migrant Poor in Latin American Cities. *American Political Science Review* 68: 1125–1146.

Ding, Shuimu, 1987. A preliminary view of our present household registration management system [in Chinese]. *Shehui* [Society (Shanghai)] 1: 18–19.

Du, Wulu, 1986. An inquiry into the question of the floating population in Beijing's urban district [in Chinese]. *Renkou yu jingji* [Population and economy (Beijing)] 1: 12–14.

Dutton, Michael R., 1988. Editor's introduction to "Basic Facts on the Household Registration System," by Zhang Qingwu. *Chinese Economic Studies* 22(1): 3–21.

Easter Express (EE), Hong Kong. Selected issues, 1994.

Eckstein, Harry, 1991. Civic Inclusion and Its Discontents. In *Regarding Politics: Essays on Political Theory, Stability, and Change*, Harry Eckstein, ed. Berkeley: University of California Press, pp. 343–377.

Feagin, Joe R., 1978. *Racial and Ethnic Relations*. Englewood Cliffs, NJ: Prentice-Hall.

Feagin, Joe R., and Clairece Booher Feagin, 1993. *Racial and Ethnic Relations*, 4th edn. Englewood Cliffs, NJ: Prentice Hall.

Foreign Broadcast Information Service (FBIS). *Daily Report: China*. Springfield, VA, 1989–96.

Freeman, Gary P., 1986. Migration and the Political Economy of the Welfare State. *Annals of the American Academy of Political and Social Science* 485: 51–63.

Gallin, Bernard, and Rita S. Gallin, 1974. The Integration of Village Migrants in Taipei. In *The Chinese City between Two Worlds*, Mark Elvin and G. William Skinner, eds. Stanford: Stanford University Press, pp. 331–358.

García, Soledad, 1996. Cities and Citizenship. *International Journal of Urban and Regional Research* 20(1): 7–21.

Glazer, Nathan, and Daniel Patrick Moynihan, 1963. *Beyond the Melting Pot*. Cambridge, MA: MIT Press.

Gong, Xikui, 1989. A perspective on China's present household register system [in Chinese]. *Shehui kexue* [Social science (Shanghai)] 2: 32–36.

Guangdong wailai nongmingong lianhe ketizu [Guangdong outside peasant workers joint task group], 1995. In floating choose the select migrants – Guangdong province outside workers investigation report [in Chinese]. *Zhanlue yu guanli* [Strategy and management (Beijing)] 5: 112–120.

Gunes-Ayata, Ayse, 1987. Migrants and Natives: Urban Bases of Social Conflict. In *Migrants, Workers, and the Social Order*, Jeremy Eades, ed. London: Tavistock, pp. 234–248.

Han, Jun, 1994. It's Imperative to Reform Household Registration. *Ban Yue Tan* [Biweekly chats (Beijing)], 11. Translated in Foreign Broadcast Information Service, August 5, 10.

Harris, William, 1982. *The Harder We Run: Black Workers since the Civil War*. New York: Oxford University Press.

Heater, Derek, 1990. *Citizenship: The Civic Ideal in World History, Politics and Education*. London: Longman.

Hollifield, James F., 1992. *Immigrants, Markets, and States: The Political Economy of Postwar Europe*. Cambridge, MA: Harvard University Press.

Honig, Emily, 1992. *Creating Chinese Ethnicity: Subei People in Shanghai, 1850–1980*. New Haven: Yale University Press.

Huntington, Samuel P., and Joan M. Nelson, 1976. *No Easy Choice: Political Participation in Developing Countries*. Cambridge, MA: Harvard University Press.

Johnson, Marguerite, 1994. Bright Lights, Pink City. *Time*, February 21, 47.

Joint Publications Research Service (JPRS). Selected issues, 1985–96.

Kaye, Lincoln, 1994. Conflicts of Interest. *Far Eastern Economic Review* (Hong Kong), August 4.

Kornai, Janos, 1992. *The Socialist Service: The Political Economy of Communism*. Princeton: Princeton University Press.

Layton-Henry, Zig, 1990. The Challenge of Political Rights. In *The Political Rights of Migrant Workers in Western Europe*, Zig Layton-Henry, ed. London: Sage Publications, pp. 1–26.

Li, Mengbai, and Hu Xin, eds, 1991. *The influence of the floating population on big cities'*

development and countermeasures [in Chinese]. Beijing: Economic Daily Publishing.

Lipset, Seymour Martin, 1959. Some Social Requisites of Democracy: Economic Development and Political Legitimacy. *American Political Science Review* 53 (March): 69–105.

Lipset, Seymour Martin, 1963. *Political Man: The Social Bases of Politics*. New York: Doubleday.

Liu, Bingyi, 1989. Floating 'city people' [in Chinese]. *Qing Chun* [Youth] 6: 31–32.

Liu, Hantai, 1986. China's beggar community [in Chinese]. *Wenhui yuekan* [Encounter monthly (Shanghai)] 10: 197–234.

Lloyd, Peter, 1979. *Slums of Hope? Shanty Towns of the Third World*. Manchester: Manchester University Press.

Ma, Laurence J. C., 1981. Urban Housing Supply in the People's Republic of China. In *Urban Development in Modern China*, Laurence J. C. Ma and Edward W. Hanten, eds. Boulder, CO: Westview Press, pp. 222–259.

Magritte, N. A., 1994. 'Trashpickers' Urban Wasteland. *Eastern Express* (Hong Kong), August 20–21.

Marshall, T. H., 1950. *Citizenship and Social Class and Other Essays*. Cambridge: Cambridge University Press.

Marshall, T. H., 1963. *Sociology at the Crossroads and Other Essays*. London: Heinemann.

Meehan, Elizabeth, 1993. *Citizenship and the European Community*. London: Sage Publications.

Min, Kangwu, 1995. A Village in the Capital. *China Focus* 3(8): 4.

Ming, Lei, 1994. The "Zhejiang Village" of Beijing that I have seen [in Chinese]. *Zheng Ming* [Contend (Hong Kong)] 2: 25–27.

Moore, Barrington, Jr, 1966. *Social Origins of Dictatorship and Democracy: Lord and Peasant in the Making of the Modern World*. Boston: Beacon Press.

Nanfang ribao (NFRB) [Southern daily (Guangdong)]. Selected issues, 1989–90.

Nongmin ribao (NMRB) [Peasants' daily (Beijing)]. Selected issues, 1987–89.

Perlman, Janice E., 1976. *The Myth of Marginality: Urban Poverty and Politics in Rio de Janeiro*. Berkeley: University of California Press.

Piante, Catherine, and Zhu Haibo, 1995. Life and Death of "Zhejiang Village": A Law unto Itself – Peking's "Zhejiang Cun." *China Perspectives* 2: 12–15.

Piore, Michael J., 1979. *Birds of Passage: Migrant Labor and Industrial Societies*. Cambridge: Cambridge University Press.

Portes, Alejandro, and Ruben G. Rumbaut, 1990. *Immigrant America: A Portrait*. Berkeley: University of California Press.

Portes, Alejandro, and Alex Stepick, 1993. *City on the Edge: The Transformation of Miami*. Berkeley: University of California Press.

Quan, Lixin, 1994. Beware! Mafia-Type Organized Crime – A General Crackdown on Organized Crime in Beijing in Recent Years. *Xuexi yu yanjiu* [Study and research] 24: 35–37. Translated in Foreign Broadcast Information Service, February 14, 1995, 22–25.

Renmin ribao (RMRB) [People's daily (Beijing)]. Selected issues, 1954–96.

Roberts, Bryan R., 1995. *The Making of Urban Citizens: Cities of Peasants Revisited*. London: Arnold.

Saiget, Robert J., 1995. Beijing Exiles the Floating Population. *Kyodo* (Tokyo), March 25, 1995. Reprinted in Foreign Broadcast Information Service, March 27, 33.

Shanghai shi tongjiju bian [Shanghai City statistics bureau], ed., 1989. Shanghai's floating population [in Chinese]. Shanghai: Chinese Statistical Publishing House.

Shi, Xianmin, 1992. The categorization and development history of Beijing City's private entrepreneurs – research on Beijing Xicheng district's private entrepreneurs [in Chinese]. *Zhongguo shehui kexue* [Chinese social science (Beijing)] 5: 19–38.

Solinger, Dorothy J., 1995. The Floating Population in the Cities: Chances for Assimilation? In *Urban Spaces in Contemporary China*, Deborah S. Davis, Richard Kraus, Barry Naughton, and Elizabeth J. Perry, eds. New York: Cambridge University Press, pp. 113–148.

Solinger, Dorothy J., 1999. Human Rights Issues in China's Internal Migration: Insights from Comparisons with Germany and Japan. In *The East Asian Challenge for Human Rights*, edited by Joanne R. Bauer and Daniel A. Bell, eds. New York: Cambridge University Press.

Soysal, Yasemin Nuhoglu, 1994. *Limits of Citizenship: Migrants and Postnational Membership in Europe*. Chicago: University of Chicago Press.

Sun, Changmin, 1997. Floating Population in Shanghai: A Perspective of Social Transformation in China. In *Floating Population and Migration in China: The Impact of Economic Reforms*, Thomas Scharping, ed. Hamburg: Institut für Asienkunde, pp. 201–215.

Tang, Xiaotian, and Chen Donghu, 1989. Forced residence away from home and urban society's criminals [in Chinese]. *Shehui* [Society (Shanghai)] 9: 19–21, 41.

Turner, Bryan S., 1986. *Citizenship and Capitalism: The Debate over Reformism*. London: Allen and Unwin.

Turner, Bryan S., 1993. Contemporary Problems in the Theory of Citizenship. In *Citizenship and Social Theory*, Bryan S. Turner, ed. London: Sage Publications, pp. 1–18.

Vogel, Ezra, 1989. *One Step Ahead in China: Guangdong under Reform*. Cambridge, MA: Harvard University Press.

Walder, Andrew G., 1986. *Communist Neo-Traditionalism: Work and Authority in Chinese Industry*. Berkeley: University of California Press.

Wang, Chunguang, 1995. Communities of 'Provincials' in the Large Cities: Conflicts and Integration. *China Perspectives* 2: 17–21.

Wang, Feng, and Zuo Xuejin, 1996. Rural Migrants in Shanghai: Current Success and Future Promise. Paper prepared for presentation at International Conference on Rural Labor Migration in China, Beijing, June 25–27.

Wang, Xiamin, 1994. The Public Order Situation in Pudong's Alien Worker Gathering Points Demands Immediate Attention. *Shehui* [Society (Shanghai)] 118: 27–29. Translated in Foreign Broadcast Information Service, January 26, 1995, 23–24.

Wang, Yanling, Wu Yekang, and Jiang Jianping, 1990. Get enlightenment from a bloody lesson [in Chinese]. *Shehui* [Society (Shanghai)] 8: 2–3.

Wong, Linda, 1994. China's Urban Migration – The Public Policy Change. *Pacific Affairs* 67(3): 335–355.

Wu, Li, 1990. The facets and effects of the migratory bird population and an assessment [in Chinese]. *Renkou xuekan* [Population bulletin (Changchun)] 6: 37–43.

Xiang, Biao, 1996. How to Create a Visible "Non-State Space" through Migration and Marketized Traditional Networks: An Account of a Migrant Community in China. Paper presented at European Science Foundation Workshop on European Chinese and Chinese Domestic Migrants, Oxford, July 3–5.

Xie, Bailing, 1990. An investigation into the question of the floating population in the cities – a summary of the Shanghai "Research forum on the problem of the floating population" [in Chinese]. *Shehui kexue* [Social science (Shanghai)] 2: 73–75.

Xu, Xue-qiang, and Li Si-ming, 1990. China's Open Door Policy and Urbanization in the Pearl River Delta Region. *International Journal of Urban and Regional Research* 1: 49–69.

Yuan, Xin, and Tang Mingda, 1990. A preliminary investigation of Xinjiang's floating population [in Chinese]. *Renkou yu jingji* [Population and economy (Beijing)] 3: 46–52.

Yuan, Yue, *et al.*, 1995. *The exposed – a research report on the condition of the organization of migrants in Beijing* [in Chinese]. Beijing: Beijing Horizon Market Research and Analysis.

Yuan, Yue, Shouli Zhang, and Xin Wang, 1996. Self-Organize: Finding Out the Way for Migrants to Protect Their Own Rights. June and July, Beijing and Oxford.

Zhang, Li, 1998. Strangers in the City: Space, Identity, and the State among China's "Floating Population." PhD dissertation, Department of Anthropology, Cornell University.

Zhang, Qingwu, 1988. Basic Facts on the Household Registration System. *Chinese Economic Studies* 22(1).

Zhang, Wenyi, 1995. The Mobile Population Should Not Have Free Reign of the Cities. *Minzhu yu Fazhi* [Democracy and the legal system (Shanghai)] 208: 16–18. Translated in Foreign Broadcast Information Service, March 21, 1996, 23–24.

Zhang, Ying, 1989. An investigation of the problem of planned birth among the individual firms in 'Zhejiang Village' in Beijing City's Fengtai district [in Chinese]. *Renkou yu jingji* [Population and economy (Beijing)] 3: 23–25.

Zhang, Youren, 1987. Respecting 'outsiders' should become social public morality [in Chinese]. *Shehui* [Society (Shanghai)] 6: 25–26.

Zhou, Daming, 1994. An investigation and analysis of 'outside casual labor' in Guangdong [in Chinese]. *She-huixue yanjiu* [Sociological research (Beijing)] 4: 47–55.

Zhou, Kate Xiao, 1996. *How the Farmers Changed China: The Power of the People.* Boulder, CO: Westview.

Zhu, Fengchun, 1992. Keeping tabs on rented housing to curb excessive childbirths among the migrants [in Chinese]. *Nanfang renkou* [Southern population (Guangzhou)] 2: 12–13, 7.

Zhu, Suhong, 1992. Peasants in the city: An investigation of the peasant population temporarily living in Beijing [in Chinese]. Master's thesis, Department of Sociology, Beijing University.

II.3 The Citizen and the Non-Citizen

Introduction

The non-citizen has historically been as important to the formation of specific citizenship regimes as the citizen has. The readings in this final section therefore explore citizenship regimes of exclusion and alterity, of immigrants (Mandel and de Genova), and non-'autochthonous' others (Marshall-Fratani). By giving greater prominence to citizenship as exclusionary, this section incorporates post-Foucauldian approaches to power, violence and citizenship. Ruth Marshall-Fratani discusses the crisis in Côte d'Ivoire, and the importance of notions of autochthony and belonging in articulating the different sides in the conflict. The 'war of "who is who"' was not 'mere' discourse but had extremely violent consequences, despite a far more complex history of regional mobility than that acknowledged by the producers of extremist discourse. Ethnicity and race are important elements also in Ruth Mandel's chapter, which examines how Turkish migrants to Germany have engaged with the legal construction of German citizenship; and the legal framework is also central to Nicholas de Genova's chapter on Mexican migrants to the USA. De Genova examines some of the implications and disciplining effects of 'protracted vulnerability in everyday life' that results from immigrant illegality, for example the connection between the insecurity of immigrant illegality and exploitative labour practices. Both pieces outline the historical development of specific legal citizenship regimes, and remind us that legal citizenship is still a central question for significant numbers of people outside of legality, despite the analytical emphasis that we might want to place on social, political and cultural construction within citizenship theory as well.

SUGGESTIONS FOR FURTHER READING

Ceuppens, Bambi, and Peter Geschiere, 2005. Autochthony: local or global? New modes in the struggle over citizenship and belonging in Africa and Europe. *Annual Review of Anthropology* (34): 385–407.

Cooper, Frederick, 2009. From imperial inclusion to republican exclusion? France's ambiguous postwar trajectory. In *Frenchness and the African Diaspora: Identity and Uprising in Contemporary France*, C. Tshimanga, D. Gondola and P. Bloom, eds. Bloomington: Indiana University Press, pp. 91–119.

The Anthropology of Citizenship: A Reader, First Edition. Edited by Sian Lazar.
© 2013 John Wiley & Sons, Inc. Published 2013 by John Wiley & Sons, Inc.

de Genova, Nicholas P., 2002. Migrant 'illegality' and deportability in everyday life. *Annual Review of Anthropology* 31(1): 419–447.

de Genova, Nicholas P., 2004. The legal production of Mexican/migrant 'illegality'. *Latino Studies* 2(2): 160–185.

Gilroy, Paul, 2002 [1987]. *'There Ain't no Black in the Union Jack': The Cultural Politics of Race and Nation*. London: Routledge.

Hansen, Thomas Blom, and Finn Stepputat, 2005. *Sovereign Bodies: Citizens, Migrants, and States in the Postcolonial World*. Princeton, New Jersey: Princeton University Press.

Kipnis, Andrew, 2004. Anthropology and the theorisation of citizenship. *Asia Pacific Journal of Anthropology* 5(3): 257–278.

Partridge, Damani, 2008. We were dancing in the club, not on the Berlin Wall: black bodies, street bureaucrats, and exclusionary incorporation into the new Europe. *Cultural Anthropology* 23(4): 660–687.

23

The War of 'Who is Who'

Autochthony, Nationalism and Citizenship in the Ivoirian Crisis, 2006

Ruth Marshall-Fratani

Introduction

People of the Greater West,

The current political situation of our country is linked to its recent history lived by the sons and daughters of our tribes. For forty years, misfortune, injustice, inequality and crimes have been inflicted on our tribes.

For forty years the Akans and the despot Houphouët-Boigny, the greatest thief of all time, have fought our tribes without respite. Odious crimes have been ordered and executed. One of our illustrious sons, Kragbé Gnagbé, aka Opadjélé was decapitated, and with him perished nearly 4,000 of our people. A genocide such as this cannot remain unpunished.

Our lands, our most precious possession, were torn from us by force by the Akans, led by Houphouët-Boigny with the treacherous collusion of the Dioula and a handful of our own people.

The people of the Greater West must thus unite around one of their own, Laurent Gbagbo, the reincarnation of Opadjélé. It is through him we shall be saved.

The 24 December 1999, God, in giving the power to one of our sons, wanted to show us the way. Daughters and sons of the Greater West, link hands together, the hour has come for us to be heard. The hour has come to kill the Akans and chase them from our lands. The hour has come to recuperate our land. The hour has come to clean our villages and towns of the Dioulas (Mossi) and the Akans, who are objective allies.

Yes, the hour of grand vengeance has struck. We too want our cities to become capitals like Abidjan, Yamoussoukro and Daoukro.

People of the Greater West, unite, so that power will never leave us again. We must use our guns, our machetes. Get ready. Let us kill for the survival of our tribes, to prevent the confiscation of power.

Union of the Greater West.

This extremely virulent tract was found circulating in Abidjan in April 2004 and then again in the summer of 2005. Echoing the discourses of the so-called Young Patriots, fervent supporters of President Laurent Gbagbo, the

Ruth Marshall-Fratani, 2006. The war of 'who is who': autochthony, nationalism, and citizenship in the Ivoirian crisis. *African Studies Review* 49(2): 9–43.

tract not only expresses violence toward political enemies determined along ethnic lines, but also makes direct reference to one of the central issues in the Ivoirian crisis, that of land tenure and relations between autochthonous and "allogenous" populations.[1] The Côte d'Ivoire, once famous throughout the continent for its peace and political stability, now finds itself teetering on the brink of explosion. Since the failed coup attempt of September 19, 2002, and the division of the country into a rebel-held north and loyalist south, thousands of strangers have been chased from their lands, many killed in the process. While this call to "ethnic cleansing" of villages and towns throughout the central and southwest regions reflects the views of an extremist minority, during three years of war the Front Populaire Ivoirien's (FPI) map of territorialized identity has become a partial reality, paradoxically reinforcing the very ideology the rebellion claims to be fighting against.

The Gbagbo regime has, as it were, undertaken to "turn back the clock" of Ivoirian history (Chauveau 2000), marked during Houphouët's forty-year reign by determined state policy favoring migration and migrants' rights and promoting an ideology of an Ivoirian "melting pot." The FPI has revived a long tradition of political opposition based on autochthons' rights and nativist identity that first emerged during the colonial period and whose construction has been determined by colonial and postcolonial state policies. In this sense, the Gbagbo regime's accusation that the rebellion is a "foreign terrorist attack" is heavy with meaning. Who is a "foreigner" and who is an Ivoirian in the country today? This distinction is at the heart of the conflict, and this debate, perpetually postponed since independence, and exacerbated both by economic crisis and the process of democratization, has become increasingly radicalized over the years of the conflict. Interviewed shortly after the September 19th attacks, the radical Mamadou Koulibaly claimed that he thought the war would be salutary for the nation: "At last we'll be able to know who is who" (Hoffnung, interview, 2002).

In what will necessarily be a cursory attempt to trace the long and complex trajectory of the

outbreak of this war of "who is who," I argue that what is at stake in the current Ivoirian crisis is not only a struggle for state power, but also, and more importantly, the redefinition of the content of citizenship and the conditions of sovereignty. This conflict concerns de facto the population from countries that have furnished the majority of immigrants (in particular the northern neighbors of Burkina Faso, Mali, and Guinea), not to mention the Côte d'Ivoire-born children of non-nationals or the huge mass of Ivoirians of mixed heritage. Not surprisingly, the conjunction between nativism and nationalism also involves the revitalization of an anti-imperialist discourse directed against the French presence, both civilian and military, and the demand for a "second independence," which likewise expresses itself in terms of autochthony. While in some senses the Ivoirian conflict appears to be a war without borders – in particular because of the "spillover" of the Liberian war in the west – it is, nevertheless, above all a war *about* borders, crystallizing in liminal spaces and social categories and practices. Despite the ongoing ravages of "Ivoirité," Ivoirian "representations of self," as Mbembe says, "are edified at the interface of autochthony and cosmopolitanism. ... The disjunction and interlinking of a multiplicity of principles and norms is now the rule. It is in the interstices that the central historical action now unfolds. And the occupation of the interstices does not happen without violence" (2000: 16, 43).

The current revitalization of discourses of autochthony, as Bayart, Geschiere, and Nyamnjoh have argued, is no doubt intimately linked to current processes of democratization and liberalization (Bayart and Geschiere 2001; Bayart, Geschiere, and Nyamnjoh 2001). Some claim that the rise of autochthony as a political category is directly related to the wide vistas opened up by processes of globalization: that a "need for closure" is the flip side of intensified global flux and openness (Geschiere and Meyer 1999). Others see it as a result of the weakening or breakdown of the nation-state in this context. One of the questions that this article will address is the centrality of the colonial and postcolonial state to the process of the construction of autochthony as a political category. Following Geschiere *et al.*, it appears in the Ivoirian case that the explosion of violence and counterviolence provoked and legitimated by the mobilization of autochthony does not necessarily signify either the triumph of those monolithic identities "engineered" during the colonial occupation, nor the disintegration of the nation-state in the context of globalization. Contrary to contexts in which the mobilization of autochthony can be analyzed as supranational, subnational, or "postnational," "by-passing" the state or testifying to its "weakness" in a context of globalization, the Ivoirian case appears to show the continued vitality of the nation-state, not only as the principal space in terms of which discourses of authochtony are constructed and make sense (*fait sense*), but also in terms of the techniques and categories that the political practice of autochthony puts into play. The mobilization of discourses of autochthony and nationalism can be seen as a strategy for the redefinition, closure, and control of liminal or mobile spaces and categories. Yet while the relations of power that underwrite autochthony find their roots in the long history of state formation and epistemological structures and techniques of government accompanying colonialism, and while the current context gives autochthony new force and performative power, there is no reason to presume that it is a "winning" strategy (*stratégie gagnante*) (Foucault 1994: 241–42). Geschiere *et al.* are no doubt right to underline the performative power of discourses of autochthony in Africa, as the Rwandan genocide reminds us. Nevertheless, its phantasmagorical projections and totalitarian ambitions are subjected to the messy and uncertain logics of struggle and experiences of the self. The project of government expressed in the FPI's discourse can only be strategic and programmatic – and as such, "it never works" (Foucault 2004: 405). This means that we cannot prejudge the outcome, nor reject the idea that "in the long run," and despite the violence, this confrontation will found "a new imagined community, rather than being a simple mechanism of disintegration" (Bayart, Geschiere, and Nyamnjoh 2001: 194).

The Colonial State and the "Search for Autochthons"

The first question that we need to ask when thinking about the revitalization of autochthony is why, in Africa at any rate, does political confrontation so often wear "primordialist" clothing? While this question is by no means new, I think we need to go further than recent discussions concerning the construction of ethnicity and identity by the colonial state. Historians and anthropologists have rightly drawn attention to the ways in which colonial powers constructed a hierarchy of ethnic categories among local populations: how through a variety of techniques (including colonial ethnography), colonial power inscribed, via overwhelming processes of subjectification, primordialist assignations that were in turn appropriated and made performative. While the colonial encounter thus gave rise to a "conversion process," as Talal Asad calls it (in the sense of induction into modern life) and while, as is always the case in historical change, such a process built on the past, we should not underestimate the nature of the epistemological rupture such a process entailed for the colonized. This "profound displacement" cannot be grasped by tracing the origins of an amalgam (Asad 1996: 264). The political contestation of "consciousness" only becomes possible when forms of self-representation are publicly represented as the sign of an authentic identity. Something new emerges, which can be determined by asking "what new possibilities for constituting themselves [did] these subjects now encounter ...? Given that there was now a possibility of recognizing themselves as *authentic*, what part did this new fact play in their constitution? ... The changed epistemic structure brought about by the conversion to modernity articulates a new range of possibilities not adequately captured by the simple alternatives of passive reception by subjects or active resistance by agents, of unoriginal reproduction or synthetic originality" (Asad 1996: 265).

If colonial power subjectifies natives in terms of primordialist categories whose fundamental logic is one of biological race, we must ask ourselves under what precise circumstances these categories are in turn appropriated and set to work under the imaginary of authochthony, as the sign of an *authentic* identity. Of course, other forms of categorization and subjectification are operative, but I think it is fair to say that the most powerful, the most overwhelming, are indeed all those assignations that have a biological form of racism at their heart and operate not only according to the old binary black/white distinction (upon which will be based the principle of indigeneity, autochthony, and the possibility of conceiving of an African specificity, of its radical difference) but that also will form the bases of internal ethnic categorizations and normative classifications, upon which diverse cultural, political, and social attributions will be attached as emanations of a fundamental, genetic, and authentic form. The most striking example of this is of course Rwanda and Burundi, as Jean-Pierre Chrétien (1997) has argued, but one can also recall Lord Lugard's penchant for the Hausa-Fulani, and his claims that they emerged from a superior racial source. In colonial Côte d'Ivoire, the same sorts of categorizations were operative, with the French policy of creating administrative units based on "pure autochthonous races" for which they spent a considerable amount of time searching. This question merits a much lengthier discussion than these few words here, but to state my view in brief, I do not think it is satisfying to claim that colonial racism is simply "one of power's lies," nor a simple and old form of contempt or hatred among races, nor, in Foucault's terms "a sort of ideological operation by which states, or a class, attempt to displace towards a mythical adversary hostilities which would otherwise be turned on them or which are at work in the social body." I agree with Foucault when he argues that "it is much more profound than an old tradition, much more profound than a new ideology, it is something else. The specificity of modern racism, that which constitutes its specificity, is not related to mentalities, to ideologies, to power's lies. It is related to the technique of power, to the technology of power" that is at the heart of the modern state (1997: 230).

What is striking are the ways in which these categorizations and distinctions are appropriated

and made operative not only in colonial, but also in postcolonial, politics. In the case of the Côte d'Ivoire, numerous studies have examined at length the central role played by the colonial state – and in particular the plantation economy it developed – in structuring civil society and crystallizing forms of political identification (Raulin 1957; Chauveau 1997, 2000, 2002; Chauveau and Dozon 1987; Chauveau and Bobo 2003; Losch 2000; Dozon 1985a, 1985b, 1997, 2000; Bobo 2002; Zongo 2001; Dembélé 2002). As Chauveau and Dozon (1987) persuasively argue, the plantation economy provided the context in which the colonial state was to "produce" ethnic identity, giving rise to a territorialized and ethnicized definition of citizenship and national identity. It was precisely through the processes of the "ethnographer state" that the opportunities for social mobility and for assimilation – or on the contrary, the possibility of exclusion, violent coercion, or death – were determined. As Karel Arnaut (2004: chap. 3) notes, as early as 1901, Maurice Delafosse explained how the Mandé, settling in northern Côte d'Ivoire and eventually covering large territories, nowhere constituted "the autochthonous element." Delafosse and other colonial agents following him noted the socioeconomic and "mental" mobility of the Dioula, their political "superiority," "energetic character," and aptitude for becoming agents of French trade and civilization. By contrast, the autochthonous peoples of the southern forest belt were considered savage, backward, and ill-suited for productive economic activity.

As Geschiere and Nyamnjoh argue, both the freeing up of labor and its categorization and compartmentalization have been essential processes of capitalist development everywhere, and a vital part of the colonial power's project of pacification and economic exploitation. As they put it, "the seesaw of mobility and fixing has been crucial in setting the stage for the emergence of autochthony movements and communal violence in recent times" (2000: 444). In the Côte d'Ivoire, colonial policy involved a complex process of both mobilizing and fixing labor and populations. Plantations were developed first in the east among the Agni in the 1920s and '30s, then during the 1940s and '50s in the underpopulated central and southwest regions, where land was extremely well suited to growing cocoa and coffee. Alongside the French plantations, local small-holders threw themselves into the new economy with great energy, and migrants from the center (Baoulé) and especially the north (Malinké, Dioula, Senoufo), brought into towns to provide labor and services, sought to acquire land themselves. The French also orga-nized the transport of Voltaïques (Burkina Faso) to provide manual labor. In the 1930s a debate about land tenure and national repre-sentation had already begun. An indigenous association with Agnis at its head was created – the Association of Defence of Autochthons Interests of Côte d'Ivoire (ADIACI) – and pro-tested to the colonial government about the excessive use of Senegalese and Dahomeans in the administration, asking for their replacement by "evolved indigenes." They also complained that the Baoulé and Dioula were not content with commercial activities or manual labor, but wanted land, and they called for respect of customary law on the nonalienability of land, even though they had themselves ceded consid-erable amounts.

The model throughout the southwest was the institution of the *tutorat*, in which autoch-thonous stakeholders ceded land to clients in exchange for various social, cultural, and economic payments and services, such as pres-ents, assistance at weddings and funerals, labor, and money. According to Chauveau (2006: 219), "In the western part of the forest belt of Côte d'Ivoire, however, the extent of the rights conceded by *tuteurs* and the corresponding obligations of 'their' strangers have varied. In many cases, such transfer rights verge[d] on, or [hid], largely commercial transfers of land – except for the important difference that the commercial aspect [did] not erase the social relation stemming from the 'gratefulness' that the migrant (or his heirs) owe[d] to his *tuteur* (or to the latter's heirs)." As Dozon (1985a: 289) argues, the cession of land by autochthons does not imply prior property rights; rather, from the optic of customary communal land tenure (whose modern terms and representa-tions are set out through the ethnographer state), it is through the process of cession that the autochthon acquires the status of landowner – thus it is not "I am a property owner, therefore I sell," but "I sell, therefore I am a property owner."

Colonial policy thus distinctly favored migrant and mobile populations, even if the explosion of local production far surpassed what the colonial state had intended or even desired. By the late forties, indigenous planting largely outstripped that of Europeans, which survived only through subsidies from the colo-nial state. The struggle for indigenous planters' rights and the abolition of forced labor gave birth to the Syndicat Africain Agricole (SAA), which represented principally those interests of wealthy indigenous planters of Baoulé and Agni origin. Under the leadership of Houphouët-Boigny, it prepared the ground for the creation of the political party that was to rule Côte d'Ivoire for over forty years, the PDCI-RDA (Parti Démocratique de la Côte d'Ivoire-Rassemblement Démocratique Africain). In both the SAA and subsequently the PDCI, autochthonous western planters and adminis-trative heads were unrepresented, the majority of the adherents being Baoulé and "Dioula." From the thirties on in the west, associations were formed, such as the Mutuelle Bété, followed in 1944 by the Union des Originaires des Six Cercles de l'Ouest de la Côte d'Ivoire (UOCOCI), as well as other associations whose social composition reflected regional and ethnic affiliations – Agni, Ebrié, Mossi (Voltaïques).The activities of these associa-tions, which were based in urban centers (particularly Abidjan), perpetuated the links between rural and urban populations and kept alive a territorialized identity among those living in the highly mixed neighborhoods of the city. Over time, the large, mobile northern group – straddling the territories of what would become Mali, Burkina Faso, Guinea, and Côte d'Ivoire, and made up of distinct ethnolinguistic groups that nevertheless shared a vehicular language and often religion – came to be known by the generic term "Dioula," whose signification and valorization would vary over the colonial and postcolonial periods. Esteemed by the French for their mobility, their "civilizational advance," and their industry, the Dioula in the postcolonial period would increasingly be associated not only with piety and industry (albeit circumscribed to the realm of manual labor), but also backwardness (lack of education, high levels of reproduction, archaic hygiene and health practices) and criminality, especially in urban centers.

Thus it is through these combined processes and activities of colonial ethnography, colonial government, and economic policy that a politicized territorial identity began to take shape. As Dozon (1985a, 1985b) points out, it is through the ongoing presence of strangers and their demands for land that the autochthon not only comes to consciousness of himself as such and reclaims rights (notably, land) conferred by this identity, but also becomes aware of his relatively disadvantaged position, both in his own "home" and also in emerging national politics. Already visible in the 1930s through the creation of the ADIACI, this early crystallization of "civil society" representing autochthonous interests was to increase dramatically in the postcolonial period. From this point on, territoriality and citizenship would become organically linked in political discourse. The initiation of this process would have been unthinkable outside the colonial state, even if, as many have noted, the process is not necessarily exercised by the institutions of the state itself, but can be found in instances of "décharge" (missions, schools, medical institutions, *comptoirs*), as Bayart (2004) and Hibou (1999) argue.

The processes of liberalization mean that today, as during the colonial period, state functions are increasingly the object of various forms of "décharge" – in particular with the rise of international aid, but also with the privatization of certain sovereign functions, such as the right to kill, to extract wealth, and so on. Thus liberalization may certainly be related to new confrontations between groups and the revitalization of arguments of autochthony (Geschiere and Nyamnjoh 2000; Bayart, Geschiere, and Nyamnjoh 2001). However, while such forms of privatization may involve transformations of the state, they nevertheless do not undermine its centrality or principal modes of power. The technologies of power and mode of government that produced autochthony and ethnicity during the colonial period were not fundamentally called into

question with the advent of independence. This position situates the historicity of ethnicity and autochthony differently from that claimed by those who interpret it as the sign or an effect of the crisis or effacement of the state.

The Postcolonial State: The "Geo-politics" of Immigration and Autochthony

Mbembe argues that the moment of independence does not imply a rejection of colonial power's principal modes of representation or functioning: "When, under the colonial period, the autochthonous discourse on the emancipation of indigenous peoples and their right to self-determination emerges, the relation between leaving barbary and entering civilization does not become the object of a fundamental critique. In the justification of the right of sovereignty and self-determination, and in the struggle for power, two central categories will be mobilised: on the one hand, the figure of the African as a victimised subject, and on the other, the affirmation of his cultural singularity" (2000: 24). Pan-Africanism, says Mbembe, is a "discourse of inversion, in which its fundamental categories will be drawn from the myths it purports to oppose and the dichotomies which it will reproduce" (2000: 30). Even if the process of rehabilitation involves refusing the distinction in terms of which Africans are determined as inferior on the scale of humanity, this process does not question the fiction of race or the original, cultural difference "based on the principle of repetition (custom) and the values of autochthony" (2000: 27).

If we examine those representations produced in the Côte d'Ivoire during the nationalist struggle, we find the same uncritical appropriation of these racial constructions, glorifying cultural difference and the principle of territorial autochthony as the basis not only of self-determination, but also of national belonging, citizenship, and authentic identity. The terms of opposition to the colonial state were perpetuated following independence, not least because of Houphouët's "French turn" in the 1950s, in which he turned his back on his left-wing nationalist allies and renewed the "colonial compromise" between the French and the migrants. According to the terms of this compromise his group, the Baoulé, had pride of place, but it also involved a political pact between the Baoulé and northern migrants and immigrants. His critics, who invariably mobilized cultural nationalist and nativist arguments against this compromise, developed an extensive literature of cultural nationalism, bemoaning the alienation of Ivoirians under the leadership of the white man's puppet (Amondji 1988). The renewal of this compromise also left many Ivoirians with the impression of an incomplete or phantom form of self-determination, one in which the principle of autochthony was denied its full expression and which required the advent of a "second independence."

In his discussion of the construction of the category of "foreigner" in postcolonial Côte d'Ivoire, Ousmane Dembélé (2002) shows how claims to exclusive local and regional forms of citizenship were integral to the construction of the concept of citizenship in general. The advent of the independent state introduced a new notion of foreigner, against which that of citizen, as articulated in positive law, would be expressed from now on (as opposed, theoretically, to previous definitions of citizenship based on notions of autochthony). However, the relationship between foreigner and citizen continued to be thought of in terms of territorialized ethnic spaces, and an absolutist conception of the foreigner, or stranger, as anyone from outside these territorialized communities was perpetuated. According to Dembélé, "In order to affirm his status as Ivoirian citizen of a local territory (*terroir*), the autochthon ends up reducing to himself and his group the attributes of the national citizen. This reduction allows him to return to an absolutist conception of foreigner, who is neither a member of his ethnic group nor a national" (2002: 161). This conception of citizenship complements the one set out by Mbembe, who argues that it is in the combination of the ideological categories of origins and belonging and the spatial categories of territory and locality that citizenship emerges: defined as "essentially, the possibility of benefiting [from] a home (*chez soi*); the possibility of excluding strangers from it; the right to protection of and access to a range of collective goods and resources situated in the designated space. In this context, the expression of grievances and complaints, the claiming of rights and the legitimation of struggles over resources are made through the idiom of filiation, genealogy or heritage" (Mbembe 2000: 38).

Ivoirians represent immigration as the sign of Côte d'Ivoire's exceptional status in the region, and yet the society's acceptance of massive numbers of immigrants into its territories gives rise to highly ambivalent discourses. On the one hand, immigration is valorized as both the reason for the country's remarkable economic success and the sign of its moral superiority – promoting the values of pan-Africanism, fraternity, and generosity, as the national anthem declares. This argument has continued to be mobilized during the current conflict: "What? Ivoirians xenophobic?" they ask. "Who else has opened their arms so wide and with such generosity?" On the other hand, the theme of immigrants' "rapacity" and "ungratefulness" has increasingly been evoked from the 1990s on. Côte d'Ivoire is indeed absolutely singular in West Africa with respect to levels of immigration and internal migration, with 26 percent of the population currently composed of non-nationals. However, this official figure hides important territorial disparities concerning not only the geographical distribution of these foreigners, but also the demography of internal migration, which is no doubt as decisive in terms of the construction of national identity. Northern populations, such as the Malinké, Senoufo, and Dioula, have migrated massively south, becoming in some cases the dominant population in southern towns, particularly in the southwest, whereas migrants represent only 10 percent of the populations in the north (Dembélé 2002: 128). The question of the status of immigrants and migrants has never been resolved, making their self-identification as autochthons by virtue of longstanding residence practically impossible, and implying a refusal on the part of others to recognize the central role they have played in national development. How long before a stranger is no longer a stranger? The position of second- and third-generation immigrants in today's war is clearly tragic; not only do they consider themselves among the principal archi- tects of Côte d'Ivoire's economic success and the development of its southern towns and cities, but they have no other "home" outside of the country.

Houphouët and the PDCI have never directly addressed the question of citizenship, and the debate concerning national belonging has increasingly divided the national political space. The failure to accord citizenship rights to immigrant populations, even if they have benefited from some important de facto rights such as the vote, implies in and of itself a con- secration of the definition of citizenship in terms of territorialized ethnicity as opposed to positive law. Indeed, until 1972, citizenship could automatically be conferred on any person born in the Côte d'Ivoire regardless of the parents' nationality. However, in practice, very few naturalizations were granted. The question of citizenship turned first on the status of Burkinabé and Malian immigrants, more than a quarter million of whom arrived in Côte d'Ivoire before independence, some as early as the 1920s. Clearly they fell into a legal void, since neither the states of Côte d'Ivoire, Mali, nor Burkina Faso, upon whose creation legal citizenship depended, yet existed. Second, the southward migration of northern popula- tions of Ivoirian, Burkinabé, and Malian origin into regions where they had no cultural or religious affinity with their hosts created the grounds of an amalgam on ethnicist lines. Despite the fact that northern Ivoirians made greater efforts than the Baoulé to "integrate" into their host communities, they were identified along with other non-national northerners in terms of their perceived cultural and religious affinities. Indeed, for many Ivoirians, these cultural differences were merely the external signs of what were considered to be, more pro- foundly, *racial* differences, in which biological signs (height, facial morphology, skin tone) are the operative modes of identification. Indeed, when describing themselves and other ethnic groups, the term "race" is still popularly used by many Ivoirians today.

One of Houphouët's central state policies – which would fundamentally determine the ways in which ethnicity and autochthony would be politicized under forms of cultural nationalism

and would give rise to an opposition focused on autochthons' rights – was his decree of 1963 stating that "land belongs to those who make it productive." Until the passing of the 1998 rural land law, unclaimed rural land officially belonged to the state, while customary law considered it the unalienable property of autochthonous communities. Unable to pass a land bill in 1962 that would have consolidated migrants' position on ceded land, the state tolerated the coexistence of distinct land regimes but used a combination of intimidation and incentive to persuade local populations to allow increasing numbers of migrants to break new land. The state used the existing institution of the tutorat to provide a "cultural" argument for the installation of migrants, putting the accent on the "cultural obligation" to give land to strangers as a sign of "African fraternity." At the same time, as Chauveau (2006) points out, "up until the 1990s, village chiefs (who at the village level were recognized as state representatives), sous-préfets, district head men, PDCI members of parliament, and PDCI section and village secretaries were the ones in charge of passing on the instructions to receive and accommodate migrants in search of land. … [And] up to the 1980s, the dependence of urban elites and their associations on the clien- telistic political system did not allow those most opposed to official policy to debate these questions openly for fear of incurring repres- sion." As Alain Marie (2002) argues, the very structure of the patrimonial state and its clien- telist networks contributes to a sort of "sur- communitarisation," which in the Ivoirian context reinforced identity in terms both of ethnicity and autochthony as the principal grounds upon which access to the state and to resources could be obtained and legitimated.

While enabling a relative degree of rural integration and stability, the institution of the tutorat was nevertheless poor compensation for what was considered illegitimate state policy. Recurrent land conflicts between Baoulé and autochthons marked the first thirty years of independence in the southwest. Less willing than the northerners to participate in the social and ritual obligations of the tutorat, more arrogant in the knowledge that state political power rested on what was essentially a Baoulé monarchy at its heart, the Baoulé and their political party were the principal local producers of autochthonous ethnicity in the postcolonial period. The most striking example of violent dissension on the grounds of autochthony – which in many ways presaged things to come – was the Guébié uprising in Bété country in 1970 (Dozon 1985a: 344–48). In 1967 Kragbé Gnagbé, an urban intellectual with socialist leanings, had formed the Parti Nationaliste Africain (PANA) which, while theoretically legal under Article 7 of the Constitution, constituted in practice an unacceptable challenge to the sovereignty of the one-party state. Faced with the impossibility of legal representation, Gnagbé and a small group of Guébié, Zabia, and Paccolo (subgroups of the Bété) attacked the city hall in Gagnoa in October 1970, hoisting a flag and declaring the succession of the "independent state of Eburnie," and violently attacking several local state representatives and security forces in the process. The army savagely repressed the uprising (it was claimed that 3,000 to 6,000 were killed, although these numbers are no doubt greatly exaggerated). This incident, called in Bété country the "Guébié genocide," has remained fundamental in Bété collective memory.

As Dozon argues, the Guébié incident, while extremely localized and naïve in its aspirations, nevertheless revealed the crystallization of a political identity among the Bété intimately linked to territorial autochthony. As he notes, the fugitive "Republic of Eburnie," despite its extremely local manifestation, was projected to include all the southern forest peoples (the loose group commonly called Kru – Bété, Dida, Neyo, Bakwe, Kroumen, Guéré, etc.) sharing certain characteristics: precolonial patterns with regard to settlement and political structure; late colonial occupation, a plantation economy founded on smallholding, a territory that attracted tens of thousands of migrants; a socialist orientation and a weak level of representation at the state level. The transition from ethnic or tribal identity to regional consciousness had as its underpinning the principle of autochthony, and in the declaration of a "secessionist state," this characteristic became the symbolic condition for citizenship. Indeed, Kragbé's "program" involved not only the tripling of

prices paid to planters, but also the departure of the migrants, their presence being conceptualized as internal colonization and their occupation of land as theft (Dozon 1985a: 347–48). Since Gbagbo's rise to power, and particularly since the coup attempt in September, the Guébié affair has been evoked continuously; it was a central theme during the National Forum for Reconciliation held in 2001, and it continues to emerge in discourses and tracts such as the one cited at the beginning of this article. The ongoing political salience of the Guébié incident demonstrates that autochthony does not succeed ethnicity, either temporally or spatially. The rise of regional forms of autochthony does not necessarily depend upon a change of scale brought about, say, by globalization. Rather, regional forms of autochthonous identity can be understood as one projection of a mode of identification in which ethnic particularisms are simply another vehicle: representations of autochthony in Côte d'Ivoire are expressed on a continuum based on an original assignation whose terms go from the idealized village space or ancestral home to the black race. Indeed, the principle of autochthony itself is productive of increasingly localized and specific forms of ethnicity, since the dual principle of the purity of natural origins (filiation and authenticity) and territorialization tend to their smallest common denominator. It is here, I think, that we can situate not only the ambivalence of autochthony but also its plasticity as a politically effective discourse of exclusion.

The Struggle for the Nation: Democratization, Economic Crisis, and the Rise of "Ivoirité"

By the mid-eighties the edifice of the "Ivoirian miracle" was already crumbling. The decade was marked by the collapse of protectionist mechanisms and international alliances guaranteeing the stability of profit from agricultural production, the growing inability of the state to integrate both local and immigrant populations within a clientelist system now severely strapped for cash, a crisis in the educational system and the formal sector, serious land shortages in the rural central and southwest regions, and the social crisis provoked by the slashing of prices paid to producers in 1989. By the end of the eighties, civil society – including the trade unions, student groups, and political parties (in particular the FPI, formed among left-wing urban intellectuals) – was at the boiling point. Under intense pressure, Houphouët allowed multiparty elections in 1990 and found himself face to face with a certain Laurent Gbagbo, leader of the socialist FPI. The decade of FPI-led political protest that followed – in which the party was to take strong positions against "Ivoirité" – has often led observers to forget one of Laurent Gbagbo's principal campaign arguments in the 1990 presidential race. Accusing Houphouët of using northern immigrants as his "electoral cattle," he campaigned against their voting rights as well as foreigners' "preponderant" role in the national economy (Dozon 1997). The term "foreigners," as we have seen, was highly ambiguous in this context and open to local interpretation concerning the place of Ivoirian migrants in what was to become the urban FPI's rural fiefdom. It was at this time that the FPI press began to publish rumors that Houphouët's prime minister, Alassane Dramane Ouattara (1990–93), a northern technocrat from the IMF appointed in 1989 to apply the World Bank's austerity program, was in fact Burkinabé.

Houphouët's death in 1993 was preceded by two years of intense protest on the part of opposition parties, unions, and student groups, whose avant garde came from Laurent Gbagbo's FPI and the closely associated Fédération Estudiantine et Scolaire de la Côte d'Ivoire (FESCI). It was in this context of generalized contestation, along with the emergence of Alassane Ouattara, the first figure in postcolonial history capable of acting as a powerful representative of northern migrants, that Henri Konan Bédié launched the concept of Ivoirité. The exacerbation of ethnicity as a form of political self-identification and contestation went hand in hand with the revitalization of autochthony as the grounds for national belonging, and was elaborated in the "ideology" of "Ivoirité" from the mid-nineties on, thus rupturing the "community of destiny" that had tied together the north and the south from the colonial period.

The first aspect of Ivoirité was the use of legal mechanisms to exclude Bédié's principal rivals from power, which had the catastrophic consequence of creating, de facto, two types of Ivoirian citizen, those of "pure" Ivoirian origin and those of "mixed heritage." The electoral code, voted on November 23, 1994, provided for new, restricted conditions of eligibility for elected office. The candidate for president had to be "born in the Ivory Coast to mother and father themselves born in the Ivory Coast" (Obou 2000: 57–62). However, the profound echo that the elaboration of "Ivoirité" by a handful of intellectuals had among a large section of the population, and the performative capacity of these concepts, demonstrates that it was more than a simple electoral tactic. "Ivoirité" brings together a series of representations concerning both national sovereignty and the content of citizenship, in which autochthony is the central sign. A study/manifesto published in 1996 by a group of ideologues from the PDCI (the Cellule Universitaire de Recherche et de Diffusion des Idées et Actions Politiques du Président Henri Konan Bédié, or CURDIPHE) expounded a restrictive and ethnonationalist vision of citizenship: "the individual who claims his 'ivoirité' has as his country the Côte d'Ivoire and is born of Ivoirian parents themselves belonging to one of the autochthonous ethnic groups of the Ivory coast" (Touré 1996: 46). "It is not being segregationist," claimed the document, "to want to expose one's true roots. According to documents in our possession, we can group the ancestors of Ivoirians, or pure Ivoirians, into two groups: the autochthons with mythical origins, the autochthons without mythical origins. According to the table, the 10 March, 1893, at the moment the Côte d'Ivoire was born, the ancestors of all the great ethnic groups were already there." And finally, "the foreign presence [threatens] to rupture the socio-economic equilibrium of our country. ... The Ivoirian people must first affirm their sovereignty, their authority in the face of the threat of dispossession and subjection: be it a question of immigration or political and economic power" (Touré 1996: 50, 21).

Bédié's concept of Ivoirité profoundly reinforced the idea of territorialized autochthony as the ground upon which citizenship should be constructed. It also reopened the question of self-determination in the face of IMF conditionality and the ravages of structural adjustment and the continued, although largely diminished, French presence. In this sense, Ouattara was the perfect incarnation of the "danger" facing the "autochthons" of Côte d'Ivoire; he had spent his childhood in Burkina Faso, worked outside the country for most of his professional life, and not only was the prime minister who applied the World Bank's austerity program, but also had been the assistant director of the IMF itself. From 1999 on, Alassane Ouattara became, almost despite himself, a highly charged, larger-than-life symbol concentrating intense and contradictory passions on his person (Konaté 2003). As one FPI supporter of northern origin asserted following the violence against the RDR during the presidential elections of 2000, "If they don't say that Alassane is Ivoirian, I don't see who can make reconciliation work. If Alassane isn't Ivoirian, we're not Ivoirian either. Gbagbo isn't going to back down, and the people of the north aren't going to back down" (Vidal 2002: 252).

While Bédié and his party may have been the originators of "Ivoirité" as official state ideology, Laurent Gbagbo and the FPI's project of "refounding" the nation on nationalist lines was not developed merely as a response to political imperatives. Rather, Gbagbo appeared as the spiritual son of Kragbé Gnagbé, positioning himself and his party as the legitimate spokesmen for the aspirations and interests of the "autochthons." As a historian, Gbagbo had already displayed an intellectual interest in defending the idea of Bété autochthony, attempting to show in his work that the Bété, contrary to what many European ethnographers had claimed, had not in fact migrated from Liberia, but were among the original peoples present from time immemorial on Ivoirian territory. His vision of territorialized ethnic spaces, as well as techniques of government for controlling and producing them, was clearly stated in 1998, when he claimed that the violent land conflicts opposing autochthons and strangers had "nothing to do with ethnic problems, they are technical problems and should be treated as such," going on to suggest

that the northern zones could be developed "according to a rational programme which would fix autochthonous farmers in their zones" (La Voie, January 8, 1998). His political platform – which promised greater sovereignty for the Ivoirian state with respect to international capital and conditionalities (implying a rupture of the privileged postcolonial contract with the French), better control over the population (particularly with respect to immigration through new and modern forms of identification), universal schooling and medical insurance (projects which all involve massive processes of census-taking and inscription of populations) – shows that his political project depended upon a significant increase of administrative state power and control over the population.

The 2000 presidential elections, which saw Laurent Gbagbo elected under "calamitous conditions," as he put it, were marked by unprecedented violence in which attacks against northerners and immigrants by FPI youth and gendarmes were justified by their supposed support for the RDR, whose youth had taken to the streets demanding new elections (Le Pape and Vidal 2002). Speaking about the events a few months later, one FPI militant of northern origin lamented that as a northerner, he and his people would be obliged to join the RDR: "'I'll never be able to say that I'm not Dioula. It's not written on my forehead "FPI" ... Me, in my heart I'm FPI, but people treat me as RDR. You see, that's the whole problem ... No one distinguishes anymore. You're from the north, you're Malian, it's the same thing, once you wear a long boubou, you're from the north. They attack everybody.'" However, he considered the amalgam between foreign and Ivoirian northerners partly of their own making, showing the profound ambivalence nearly all Ivoirians have toward immigrants and the perceived importance of creating criteria for determining autochthony. "'They've done everything so that no one can tell them apart, Ivoirian Dioulas and foreign Dioulas. It's a problem: amongst themselves they can't identify one another. ... Foreigners came and moved in next to the Dioula from here. They were clever. They had ideas in the back of their heads. When they arrive, they pray together, do everything together. The guys say: we want the Ivoirian national identity card, they give it to them, and then they say they're Ivoirians. It's total confusion. … It's because the Ivoirian Dioulas don't make the distinction that everyone says now: you, you're Dioula, you're a foreigner'" (Le Pape and Vidal 2002: 242).

During the first two years of the Gbagbo regime, the cleavage between pro-FPI and pro-RDR populations continued to grow in the schools, the universities, the rural areas, and the army. The latent nationalism of the FPI became state policy and was echoed with increasingly xenophobic and radical accents by pro-FPI youth and student groups in Abidjan. Those in the army thought to be sympathetic to the RDR were downgraded, and following a witch hunt in response to an apparent coup attempt in January 2001, many young NCOs joined those soldiers in Ouagadougou exiled since 2000 under General Guei's junta. The amalgam between northerners and immigrants intensified. In the southeastern town of Bonoua (which, not incidentally, is also the home region of President Gbagbo's extremist wife, Simone), following a violent altercation between Abouré youth and the allogenous northern population, a group of young Aboures held a meeting on January 22, 2001, during which a document was drawn up and submitted to the municipal and traditional authorities. Along with prohibitions on mixed marriages, extramarital relations, and the building of mosques, the document stipulated, among other things, that all strangers must register with a photograph; that no shop, stand, or other commercial space may be used by strangers for any type of commercial activity; that no stranger may engage in any commercial transport activity; that two male strangers of the same sex are prohibited from occupying the same room; and that strangers must clean the streets and drains and pay a yearly head tax of 5000 FCFA to the royal court (Le Patriote, January 30, 2001). At the Forum for National Reconciliation, held between October and December 2001, Jean-Yves Dibopieu, Charles Blé Goudé's successor at the head of the FESCI, said the following in his declaration on behalf of the organization: "The FESCI demands that foreigners stay away from Ivoirian politics, since they've already got

their hands on our economy. We want to tell Ivoirians not to have a complex about being treated as xenophobic, as is commonly accused. They want to trick us so as to invade us. We must even acclaim xenophobia at the present time, since it is a normal and natural sentiment. Yes, brother Ivoirians. Being xenophobic is good" (FESCI, Forum de Réconciliation Nationale, October 9, 2001).

The War of "Who is Who"

This war, it's a war of identification. The Minister of State – rest in peace – Emile Boga Doudou, wanted us to be able to identify all the Ivoirians. And that caused a general outcry, 'cause there's lots that are foreigners, Malians and Burkinabè who came here. They've been here for such a long time, they managed to have the same documents as us, even the same birth certificates as us. Those people, they're the same ones who are opposed to identification. Because it's a problem for them. Because in the new formula of identification, when you go to get your card, you have to tell them the name of your village, so they can go and find out if you're really from that region. Because if I take the case of our Dioula brothers, when they arrive, as soon as they find a city like Yamoussouko and they settle there, have children there, do everything there, they don't return to their country of origin. And then they say they are Ivoirians. We saw that it isn't right, that we have to be able to tell who is Ivoirian, who isn't Ivoirian. That's why they're making war on us. (Interview in Banégas and Marshall-Fratani 2006)

For the political leaders of the Forces Nouvelles, longstanding collaborators of Laurent Gbagbo throughout the 1990s, the turning point was not principally the question of xenophobia, or Ouattara's nationality, or the victimization of northerners by state security forces (even if exclusion from the army was the principal motivation of the exiled soldiers who organized the military rebellion), but the FPI's program of national identification. The first thing their forces did once they had taken towns and cities in the northern part of the country was to destroy national identity records and state registries. When travelers presented the new "receipts" given out from the time the identification process had begun in the summer of 2002 at roadblocks in rebel-held territory, rebel soldiers often fell into violent rages, destroying the documents and menacing or physically attacking the individuals. When questioned about their motivation for joining the rebellion, many young recruits cited the national identification operation. As one traditional hunter (*dozo*) put it, "I joined the rebellion because the Malinké have been here since the twelfth century, and soon they'll be giving us a foreign resident's card to be able to live here" (interview, March 2003). Indeed, during the peace talks held at Linas-Marcoussis (France) in January 2003, the principal demands of the leaders of the rebellion were the abandonment of the national identification program in its current form, the revision of the constitutional conditions of presidential eligibility, a revision of the 1998 land law, and a new law on the naturalization of longstanding immigrants.

National identity records and the question of "usurpation" of citizenship have been a national obsession since the early 1990s, with the introduction of the foreign resident's card by the Ouattara government. The FPI's program differs from previous attempts to create reliable, unfalsifiable national identity records in its methodology and its conception. Motivated both by electoral calculations (national identity as the factor in determining voters' lists) and ideological conviction, the FPI's policy involves the clearest consecration in the history of the country of the principle of territorial autochthony as the grounds for national identity and citizenship. The enrollment of individuals in the exercise could result in their receiving a foreign resident's card instead of a national identity card (Al Moustapha, Radio et Télévision Ivoirien, August 18, 2002), even though a separate process of enrollment of foreigners for their resident's cards was to have been undertaken. The cost of the foreign resident's card was high (35,000 FCFA for ECOWAS, and 300,000 for other nationalities) and, in total contradiction to ECOWAS and UEMOA regulations, the law provided for hard-hitting penalties against those who were unable to produce the appropriate documents, including

heavy fines and expulsion. The announcement of these policies only served to reinforce the impunity with which security forces harassed northern populations, often destroying their documents in the process. The parliamentary commission set up to determine the operation's procedure claimed that since every Ivoirian had a village of origin, the best way to know who was Ivoirian was for each citizen to return to his or her village of origin to acquire the identity card. Abidjan was not to be considered a "village of origin" except for those belonging to the Ebrié ethnic group, "historical" autochthons.

Protest over this extremely onerous, exclusionary, and anachronistic method led to the adoption of a procedure that enabled the individual to establish the card in his place of residence, but with the obligation to cite local witnesses from his "village of origin" who could testify that either the applicant or one of his parents was indeed originally from the village in question. Local commissions were to be established, involving dignitaries such as traditional chiefs, land chiefs, members of leading families, and political parties, to verify the claims of autochthony. Decisions had to be unanimous, and receipts were to be issued until verification could be effected. Séri Wayoro, director of identification at the Opération Nationale d'Identification (ONI) explained the Operation's notion of "village of origin" thus: "The village of an Ivoirian, it's firstly from the ancient Côte d'Ivoire. ... Authentically [*sic*], people were sedentary, they stayed on their homelands, where their parents, their elders and ancestors were born. That's what we consider as a village, the place where a person finds members of his family at their origin, before the urban phenomenon" (*Le Patriote*, March 21, 2002). In the face of growing outcry from the opposition, Wayaro stated unambiguously several months later that "whoever claims to be Ivoirian must have a village. Whoever has done everything to forget the name of his village or who is incapable of showing he belongs to a village is a person without bearings and is so dangerous that we must ask him where he comes from" (*Notre Voie*, July 28, 2002).

What better illustration of the "re-enchantment of tradition," "the rehabilitation of authentic origins and belonging," and the idea that there can be no identity without territoriality, as described by Mbembe? Here we find clear confirmation of Mbembe's notion that "the territory par excellence is the locality, or the village; the 'chez soi' which includes the home, inherited land and where social relations are reinforced by a common genealogy and a cultural matrix (real or imaginary) which anchors the civic space" (2000: 36–37). The inanity of such a program goes without saying in this historical context marked by mobility, urbanization, and mixed ancestry. Nevertheless, the war waged by the Gbagbo regime against "dangerous persons without bearings" is all too real, as is the violence committed by the rebellion's soldiers and recruits.

Within six months of this war of "who is who," the southern populations had returned from the north. When it came to political enemies, the rebellion appeared to follow the policy of "take no prisoners." In the "cours communes" of Abidjan, veritable ethnic melting pots, neighbors eyed one another with suspicion, speaking in whispers. A reign of terror had taken hold of the city, with the infamous "death squads" roaming the streets after curfew, army officials encouraging citizens to report "suspicious activity" to telephone hotlines, and the destruction of poor neighborhoods and slums. Northerners in popular neighborhoods were subjected to regular roundups in which they were stripped to the waist, relieved of their documents, and carted off in trucks like cattle. It was not uncommon to drive by a naked corpse on the side of the road in the early morning, hands tied behind the back and a bullet in the back of the head. In what seemed like a form of collective madness, the only voices that made themselves heard were those of the "young patriots" filling the streets and neighborhoods with patriotic rallies, and the nationalist media, all screaming hate-filled insanities daily. As an observer present during this period, I was absolutely stunned by the daily escalation of events. On the one hand, it seemed that each new violent statement or act was an isolated event, one option among several, whose occurrence had nothing self-evident about it. On the other hand, the unfolding of events gave the impression of following an inexorable and terrifying logic, against which nothing could be done.

Three years later, while the reign of terror had become more sporadic or cyclical, the situation was one of radical opposition between two diametrically opposed camps, with the majority of the population fearfully watching from the sidelines. On the one side, a protean rebellion occupying the north of the country, supported by the major opposition parties grouped together since 2004 under a loose coalition, the G7; and on the other side the Gbagbo regime, supported by the "patriotic galaxy," a nebulous group of youth organizations and militias largely controlled by power holders at the presidency and in the FPI. While theoretically all working together in the reconciliation government put in place after the peace talks in Linas-Marcoussis and Accra, these two camps confronted one another in a zero-sum game of winner takes all. The loose and fragile G7 coalition has been attempting to project the image of a "republican response" to the political crisis brought to a head by the rebellion, an ambition seriously compromised by its alliance with armed rebels and its intransigence vis-à-vis Gbagbo. The Gbagbo regime, in an increasingly minority position, has from the outset refused any form of political compromise likely to weaken its grip on power. It proceeds with its program of ultranationalist radicalization via a vast propaganda apparatus, whose central themes are the values of autochthony and national self-determination and parallel forms of control, surveillance, and violence, most notably via informal militias and paramilitary forces. These forces have become the principal popular relays of ultranationalist and xenophobic government discourses, as well as the principal agents of the state's functions of surveillance, propaganda, and violence.

Youth, "Young Patriots," and "Self-Defense" Militias

The great majority of the principal actors in the current crisis are direct products of the same matrix of violent contestation that was formed in the schools and universities around the FPI and the FESCI throughout the 1990s (Konaté 2003). Many of the young noncommissioned officers who led the attacks – the rebellion's political leader Guillaume Soro, and Gbagbo's "young patriot" leaders – were all active participants in the initiatives designed to wrest power from the PDCI and its barons. The role of the youth in spearheading the confrontation over citizenship and national belonging should not be underestimated. This group, a liminal category par excellence, is the principal victim of the socioeconomic crisis. The current war provides a formidable opportunity for the renegotiation of their status, and the vital role they are playing constitutes nothing less than a small social revolution.

The "young patriots" are most highly visible in the streets of Abidjan, where, under the direction of extremely popular leaders, veritable stars of the pro-Gbagbo media, these die-hard Gbagbo supporters have taken the streets by storm. This movement, in all its organizational, sociological, and ideological complexity, is doubtless the most emblematic expression of the Gbagbo regime's evolution during the war; with neither a powerful army nor solid international alliances, the regime has used a process of paramilitarization of its youth to impose its political order through terror, and an ultranationalist radicalization in order to legitimate its resistance to any form of external interference. The "Alliance des Jeunes Patriotes pour le Sursaut National," led by the self-styled "General" Charles Blé Goudé, was born just after the attacks of September 19, 2002, as a movement supporting the government in its resistance against the assailants from the north. Benefiting from extremely generous presidential largesse, this movement managed to mobilize hundreds of thousands at rallies held in Abidjan in the first few months of the conflict. While the first rallies were attended by people from every political party, region, and age group, the increasingly ultranationalist, xenophobic, and pro-FPI discourse very rapidly discouraged the participation of more moderate populations and militants from other parties. Stigmatizing in the most virulent terms a whole range of "enemies" (the rebels and neighboring countries – in particular, Burkina Faso and their nationals) as well as the rebels' supposed external supporters (principally France, but also the UN), the young patriots rapidly

became central political actors in the crisis. They also developed into urban militia forces working for the regime, charged with surveying the opposition and denouncing "suspicious" or "enemy" behavior, controlling popular neighborhoods, and creating a climate of terror throughout the city, even assisting at times the famous "death squads" responsible for numerous disappearances and summary executions. From early 2003 on, squadrons of youths – heads shaved, clad in t-shirts and khakis – could be seen running and doing drills in every neighborhood in Abidjan. In January 2005, the infamous Groupement Patriotique pour la Paix (GPP) was involved in extremely violent confrontations between local traders and transporters enraged by the constant racket, violence, and extortion inflicted on them by the militiamen who had taken up illegal residence in a girls' boarding school. Several days later, a shootout between the GPP and students from the police academy left three dead.

These informal associations have been organized on a national level and are engaged in a process of establishing "grids" throughout southern cities and towns, enabling the least compound and its occupants to be identified and watched, even going as far as painting marks on some compounds. It was these associations that were instrumental in the identification of opposition militants during the demonstrations of March 24–27, 2004, which ended in the killing of some three hundred opposition marchers, many of them in their homes. This movement is growing, but it is also increasingly divided. As time has gone on, the "patriotic galaxy" has become increasingly schismatic, giving birth to a multitude of groups led by petty chiefs fighting for the monopoly of the patriotic label and especially the presidential largesse that accompanies it. As in the case of the rebellion, its internal divisions not only serve to weaken the movement, but also, and more dangerously, to radicalize it. Already in 2003, Charles Groghuet was chillingly clear about the GPP's mission:

National reconciliation is not going to happen with these divisive accords, you can count on me. All these RDR and MPCI ministers who are around Gbagbo are looking to kill him to finally take power. We're going to liberate Côte d'Ivoire; we want to tear Côte d'Ivoire away from the sons of immigrants who want to take everything away from the Ivoirians. We know that it's Alassane Dramane Ouattara, that son of immigrants, who opened the door of Côte d'Ivoire to his foreign brothers to invade us. ... The GPP has relations with senior military officers, we confirm it. We will not allow our country, full of strong youths, to accept the new form of colonisation that France wants to impose on us. ... We aren't fighting for a political party, even less for an individual, even if he is the President of the Republic; we're fighting to clean Côte d'Ivoire of its sons of immigrants and their spokesman, Alassane Dramane Ouattara. (*Soir Info*, June 3, 2003)

The rural south and southwest have also seen the rise of "patriotic" movements, "self-defense" groups, and militias. In the early months of the crisis, "self-defense" groups were developed, as a form of "patriotic resistance," in every southern town and village after members were publicly recruited by the regime. These informal patrols, composed of young autochthons, were rapidly organized with the help of local officials into hierarchic organizations. In many localities, one now finds highly structured village associations of "rural young patriots," complete with president, treasurer, and posts linked to activities such as security, fundraising, and mobilization. These groups are part of a loose national network, and often receive visits from the national "patriotic leaders" on tour. At times, groups coordinate their actions on a regional level. This process of politico-administrative organization is accompanied by the registration and identification of volunteers, as Chauveau and Bobo observe: "All possess an identity card proving that they are patriots serving their country, with their names, age and village of origin. These cards are used as laissez-passer on instructions given by the Préfet [local state administrator]" (2003: 20). With the encouragement of local authorities and regional dignitaries with important positions in Abidjan, groups of "young village patriots" have created a climate of terror in which strangers (northerners, Burkinabè, but

also Baoulé) are chased off their land, which subsequently is seized "legally" by local big men. In this process of expropriation, the youth use violence, but they also pose as defenders of a "tradition" which they accuse their elders of having abandoned. Thus they reaffirm not only their autochthonous rights to land but also their growing ascendancy vis-à-vis the older generations.

Beyond self-defense groups, regional militias made up exclusively of young autochthons have been constituted via networks leading from the president to local state officials and army officers. These groups also served as fighters proper during the war in the far west near the Liberian border. Both the rebellion and President Gbagbo recruited Liberian forces, resulting in a spillover of the Liberian war onto Ivoirian territory (Ero and Marshall 2003; Marshall-Fratani 2004). The Front de Libération de Grand Ouest (FLGO), a militia composed essentially of autochthonous Guéré youths, was recruited to fight alongside the national army (FANCI) and anti-Taylor forces, which were, through Gbagbo's support, to constitute the new Liberian rebel group, Movement for Democracy in Liberia (MODEL), in 2003. The Ivoirian rebel groups MPIGO (Mouvement Populaire Ivoirien du Grand Ouest) and MJP (Mouvement pour la Justice et la Paix) were themselves largely composed of pro-Taylor Liberian and Sierra Leonean fighters. Between November 2002 and May 2003, battles led by Liberian protagonists set fire to the west, with fighters on both sides committing atrocious acts of killing, torture, and rape. The confrontation between Ivoirian Yacoubas, fighting together in the MPIGO and the MJP with their Liberian Gio "cousins," and the Guérés, loyal to Gbagbo and forming a common front with their Krahn "cousins" from MODEL, provoked a deadly interethnic conflict among autochthonous populations who had always lived together peacefully.

Yet even more deadly has been the conflict between Guéré and northern Ivoirians, Burkinabé, and Malians. Motivated by a politics of xenophobia, the desire to avenge the hundreds of Guérés tortured and brutally murdered by the rebellion, as well as the hope of appropriating strangers' land and harvests, a systematic policy of targeting and murdering northerners has provoked a spiral of revenge and counter-revenge that continues to claim victims, despite the creation of a demilitarized "confidence zone" by UN and French forces. As Boubacar Diallo of the UN agency OCHA (Office for the Coordination of Humanitarian Affairs) noted, the "confidence zone" is a huge misnomer: "Not a week goes by without us being told of people being killed or of other serious human rights violations" (BBC World Service, February 8, 2005). The massacre of more than eighty villagers in the area of Duékoué in late May 2005 is the latest episode to date, and risks to derail the fragile accord hammered out by Thabo Mbeki in April 2005. In comparison to all the violence in the west, what is singular about this situation has been the complicity of state security forces and the active participation of local and national state officials and politicians. The leader of the FLGO is none other than the third assistant to the mayor of Guiglo, and many other local state officials and even ministers from the region are directly involved in the expropriation of land. Expropriations are legitimated through the idiom of autochthony and reclaiming the "lands of our fathers" from "rebel" hands. The nebulous term "rebel" not only evokes the menace and treachery of strangers but also reinforces the ethnicist amalgam between rebel fighters and northerners more generally.

These forces, as well as other groups like them from other cities and towns in the south, were mobilized during the fresh outbreak of hostilities in November 2004, when Gbagbo unilaterally broke the cease-fire and ordered the bombardment of rebel territory. In March 2005, a new militia attacked the rebel-held town of Logoualé in the west, leading to fears of a general mobilization of militia forces throughout the south. Finally, working under the doubtful hypothesis that the presidential elections would be held as planned in October 2005, the FPI and the presidency gave these militias a more political mission, consisting of preventing opposition party members from campaigning in, or even visiting, their electoral districts in the southwest. Thus UDPCI Health Minister Mabri Toikeusse was prevented on two occasions in late 2004 and early 2005

from entering the towns of Guiglo, Bloléquin, and Toulépleu, where he was attempting to deliver ambulances and medicines (*Le Nouveau Reveil*, February 28, 2005). As one observer, a militiaman from Diégonéfla, remarked:

> Failing an attack from the ex-rebels, the militiamen's mission has been modified to adapt itself to the current combat. In the forest zones of the south-west, the instructions given to the militias are clear. They consist, on the one hand, in protecting the zones held by the party in power [FPI] against any incursions from the opposition. In regions like Gagnoa, Guibéroua, Divo … the elective posts (MPs, Mayors, and Presidents of General Councils) must remain the exclusive property of the FPI. At the same time, the regime's militiamen are to "chase" all opposition parties from the zones where they hold elected posts. … In the upcoming elections, there will be no Mayor, no MP, nor President of the General Council from the PDCI or the RDR in our region. These parties are rebel parties, and we're going to prevent the votes of their militants. (*24 Heures*, February 16, 2005)

A year later, these groups have been mobilized in a struggle against the revised national identification process that is required to establish voters' lists for the elections now scheduled for October 2006. Given the FPI's political opposition to this process and the ongoing blockages by the "young patriots," as well as the refusal of the rebellion to disarm until the process has been completed, there is no chance that the elections will be held as planned.

These groups have operated throughout the south with complete impunity for the past four years. Even on the rare occasions when their activities have led to arrest and incarceration, their members inevitably have been released only weeks later. In his only public statement concerning the problem of urban militias in Abidjan, President Gbagbo claimed they were unarmed, only youth who enjoyed "running and doing exercise" (*Le Patriote*, May 19, 2003; *24 Heures*, May 20, 2003). On the problem of militias in the west, where it has been established by UN forces that several hundred militiamen were bused in to Logoualé from

Abidjan, Gbagbo claimed that the attacks were the work of "local farmers" determined to chase the rebels from the "lands of their ancestors" (interview with UN officer, DPKO, New York, November 18, 2005; IRIN, March 3, 2005). One can hardly be surprised by the vehemence of the youth when the president's wife, herself a leading MP in the FPI, calls the peace accords "an abomination" and Mamadou Koulibaly, the regime's number two, regularly makes statements on the crisis such as this:

It's called the invasion of our country by foreigners, amongst which the most vehement are the Burkinabé who have taken up arms in the rebellion. ... The logic behind the colonisation of the Côte d'Ivoire by its powerful neighbour, the Burkina Faso, is based on the false hypothesis according to which numerous Burkinabé live in the Côte d'Ivoire and have been here for 3 to 5 decades. They don't know where to go and want to live here. These Burkinabé don't want to be called "foreigners" since it sounds pejorative. Some of the most illustrious amongst them, such as "the mentor" [Alassane Ouattara] go so far as to consider the word "Burkinabé" an insult. ... Can we say that all those born in the Côte d'Ivoire are automatically Ivoirian?. ... We need to realise that a Burkinabé who lives in the Côte d'Ivoire continues to be Burkinabé, and his descendants continue to be Burkinabé *ad vitam æternam*. (*Le Temps*, November 21, 2003)

[...]

Conclusion

By way of conclusion, I pose the question of the performative capacity of these discourses. Given the "reality" of Ivoirian populations, the multiplicity of modes of subjectification, the diversity of their individual experiences and origins, and the multiplicity of their ancestries, the totalizations and reductions expressed in the ultranationalist hate propaganda seem simply insane. How is it that these discourses of exclusion were met so rapidly with such radical forms of mobilization and adhesion? No single response, or even series of responses, seems adequate. Even if the majority of the

Ivoirian population is horrified by the extremism of the president's followers, horrified by the violence perpetrated by both sides, horrified by the travesty their country has become, they appear singularly impotent in the face of the continued escalation. It is as if a profound doubt has seized the entire nation, paralyzing its capacity to react, to rally and pull the country away from the brink. Far from allowing Ivoirians to know, "once and for all, who is who," the war has only made the question more acute and terrifying. The war has shown that in the designation of political enemies and allies, ethnicity and autochthony prove to be highly unstable and deceptive. For the southern autochthons seduced by the "patriotic" awakening, among the huge mass of "Dioula" perceived as an invasive horde, how is one to tell who is an Ivoirian Senoufo, a Malian Malinké, who is a peaceable farmer and who a mercenary or a rebel, who an "infiltrator," who an unarmed civilian? And the Baoulé – are they not wolves in sheep's clothing? For years they have taken land, robbed the state blind, and mortgaged our future. They said they were with us against the Dioula, but now they too have joined the rebellion. The greatest sacrilege is the existence of traitors from our own homelands. The turncoats, like Dacoury-Tabley, Djédjé Mady, Bété "sons of the soil." How many more are hiding within our midst? How can we tell, for once and for all, who is who?

What is clear at least is that in this process of assignation and totalization, state power and its techniques have a capital role to play, as they did in the Rwandan genocide. The current violence is undoubtedly an effect of, rather than merely a reaction to, both nation-state formation and globalization (Bayart *et al.* 2001: 190; Bayart 2004). At the same time, today's representations of self are edified in the interstices, between global and local horizons, capturing nonisomorphic processes of flux. Particularly among the youth, representations of self are liminal and unstable. It is perhaps precisely the current ambivalence of autochthony that is at the heart of this racializing, biologizing tendency we can observe in the Ivoirian conflict, to the extent that individuals such as Mamadou Koulibaly find themselves producing discourses on the self that are quite delusional. Appadurai has drawn attention to the key role of this ontological uncertainty in situations of ethnocide. In his argument, he focuses on "bodily violence between actors with routine – and generally benign – prior knowledge of one another" in order to "illuminate 'threshold' or trigger conditions, where managed or endemic social conflict gives way to runaway violence." In an unstable situation of violence that is "explicitly about categories under stress and ideas striving for the logic of self-evidence," the identification of the enemy demands fixed criteria of classification and identification as well as taxonomical purity (Appadurai 1999: 310). Perhaps Appadurai is correct in suggesting that this very uncertainty itself triggers violence, as if the ultimate "certainty" can only be achieved through death and dismemberment. These brutal actions by no means establish certainty; indeed, they only exacerbate the frustrations of their perpetrators and lead to cycles of revenge and preemptive violence, as the ongoing killings between autochthons and strangers testify. Appadurai argues that the dead body as a form of closure in situations of categorical uncertainty is closely related to themes of deception, treachery, betrayal, imposture, and secrecy. He reminds us that the themes of trickery, secrecy, and hidden identity pervaded the prelude to the Rwandan genocide and other situations of ethnocide in recent history (1999: 313). The search for secure knowledge in the midst of cadavers has been taken to extremes in the Ivoirian context. Patricia Hamza-Attea, one of the lawyers leading the Collective of the Victims of the War financed by Gbagbo's wife, announced at an international conference on the Ivoirian conflict that their forensic scientists had collected bones and had identified the bodies of hundreds of the thousands killed in the fighting in the west.[2] To a stunned audience she declared; "We have the bones, and we've done tests, we know who is who, who is Wê, who is Dan, who is Malinké." The real postmortem has yet to come in Côte d'Ivoire. It should be recalled that the Rwandan genocide occurred not only through the revival of imaginaries of autochthony and the purity of origins, but also because the international community allowed the utopia of autarchy to become a reality, averting its eyes as the killings began.

NOTES

1 I will use the term 'stranger' to refer to the French ethnographic term *allogène*, which does not have an English equivalent, and which is used in contrast to the term *autochtone* as referring to populations of nonlocal origins, be they nationals or non-nationals.
2 "Côte d'Ivoire: Consolidation of a Fragile Peace," International Colloquium on the Côte d'Ivoire, Université Saint-Paul, Ottawa, February 23–24, 2003.

REFERENCES

Amondji, M., 1988. *Côte d'Ivoire: La dépendance et l'épreuve des faits*. Paris: Harmattan.

Appadurai, A., 1999. Ethnic Violence in the Era of Globalization. In *Globalization and Identity: Dialectics of Flow and Closure*, P. Geschiere and B. Meyer, eds. Oxford: Blackwell.

Arnaut, K., 2004. Performing Displacements and Rephrasing Attachments: Ethnographic Explorations of Mobility in Art, Ritual, Media and Politics. PhD diss., University of Ghent.

Asad, T., 1996. Comments on Conversion. In *Conversion to Modernities: The Globalization of Christianity*, P. Van de Veer, ed. New York: Routledge.

Asad, T., 2006. Côte d'Ivoire: Negotiating Identity and Citizenship through the Barrel of a Gun. In *Revisiting African Guerrillas: Actors, Issues, Sectors and Trends*, M. Bøås and K. Dunn, eds. Boulder, CO: Lynne Rienner.

Banégas, R., and B. Losch, 2002. La Côte d'Ivoire au bord de l'implosion. *Politique Africaine* 87: 139–62.

Bayart, J.-F., 2004. *Le gouvernement du monde: une critique politique de la globalisation*. Paris: Fayard.

Bayart, J.-F., and P. Geschiere, eds, 2001. "J'étais là avant": Problèmes politique de l'autochtonie. *Critique Internationale* 10 (January).

Bayart, J.-F., P. Geschiere and F. Nyamnjoh, 2001. Autochtonie, démocratie et citoyenneté en Afrique. *Critique Internationale* 10 (January).

Bobo, K. S., 2002. La question de l'accès à la terre des jeunes et des citadins de retour au village: Cas de Donsohouo dans la sous-préfecture d'Oumé. Master's thesis, Université de Bouaké.

"Bouaflé, Oumé, Diégonéfla, Hiré …: Les milices préparent un coup." 2005. *24 Heures* (February 16).

Chauveau, J.-P., 1997. Jeu foncier, institutions d'accès à la terre et usage de la ressource. Une étude de cas dans le Centre-Ouest ivoiriren. In *Le modèle ivoirien en questions. Crises, ajustements, recompositions*, B. Contamin and H. Mémel-Fotê, eds. Paris: Karthala-ORSTOM.

Chauveau, J.-P., 2000. Question foncière et construction nationale en Côte d'Ivoire. Les enjeux silencieux d'un coup d'État. *Politique Africaine* 78: 94–125.

Chauveau, J.-P., 2002. Une lecture sociologique de la nouvelle loi sur le domaine foncier rural. Formalisation des "droits coutumiers" et contexte socio-politique en milieu rural ivoirien. Documents de travail UR RÉFO Nr. 6. Montpellier: IRD.

Chauveau, J.-P., 2006. How Does an Institution Evolve? Land, Politics, Intra-household Relations and the Institution of the "Tutorat" amongst Autochthons and Migrant Farmers in the Gban Region of Côte d'Ivoire. In *Landrights and the Politics of Belonging in West Africa*, R. Kuba and C. Lentz, eds. Leiden: Brill.

Chauveau, J.-P., and K. S. Bobo, 2003. La situation de guerre dans l'arène villageoise. Un exemple dans le Centre-Ouest ivoirien. *Politique Africaine* 89: 12–32.

Chauveau, J.-P., and J.-P. Dozon, 1987. Au cœur des ethnies ivoiriennes … l'Etat. In *L'Etat contemporain en Afrique*, E. Terray, ed. Paris: L'Harmattan.

Chrétien, J.-P., 1997. *Le défi de l'ethnisme: Rwanda et Burundi, 1990–1996*. Paris: Karthala.

"Daloa, Duekoué, Guiglo et Bloléquin: L'Ouest militarisé se prepare à la guerre." 2004. *24 Heures* (November 4).

Dembélé, O., 2002. La construction économique et politique de la catégorie "étranger" en Côte d'Ivoire. In *La Côte d'Ivoire: L'année terrible, 1999–2000*, M. Le Pape and C. Vidal, eds. Paris: Karthala.

"Dons d'ambulance à Guiglo, à Bloléquin et à Toulepleu: Le ministre Mabri Toikeusse bloqué par les 'jeunes patriotes'." 2005. *Le Nouveau Reveil* (February 28).

Dozon, J.-P., 1985a. *La société Bété*. Paris: Karthala.

Dozon, J.-P., 1985b. Les Bété: une création coloniale. In *Au coeur de l'ethnie*, J.-L Amselle and M. Bokolo, eds. Paris: Editions la Découverte.

Dozon, J.-P., 1997. L'Etranger et l'allochtone. In *Le modèle ivoirien en questions. Crises, ajustements, recompositions*, B. Contamin and H. Mémel-Fotê, eds. Paris: Karthala-ORSTOM.

Dozon, J.-P., 2000. La Côte d'Ivoire entre démocratie, nationalisme et ethnonationalisme. *Politique Africaine* 89: 45–62.

Ero, C., and A. Marshall, 2003. L'ouest de la Côte d'Ivoire: un conflit Libérien? *Politique Africaine* 89: 88–101.

Foucault, M., 1994. *Dits et Ecrits*. Vol. 4. Paris: Gallimard.

Foucault, M., 1997. *"Il faut défendre la société." Cours au Collège de France, 1976*. Paris: Gallimard.

Foucault, M., 2004. *Sécurité, Territoire, Population. Cours au Collège de France, 1977–8*. Paris: Gallimard.

"Gagnoa, Ouragahio, Bayota, Sinfra …: Dans le couloir de la terreur." 2004. *24 Heures* (March 12).

Geschiere, P., and B. Meyer, eds, 1999. *Globalization and Identity: Dialectics of Flow and Closure*. Oxford: Blackwell.

Geschiere, P., and F. Nyamnjoh, 2000. Capitalism and Autochthony: The Seesaw of Mobility and Belonging. *Public Culture* 12(2): 423–452.

Hibou, B., ed., 1999. *La privatisation des Etats*. Paris: Karthala.

"Ivory Coast's Wild West." 2005. BBC World Service. August 2. http://news.bbc.co.uk/2/hi/africa/4244299.stm.

Konaté, Y., 2000. Le destin d'Alassane Dramane Ouattara. In *La Côte d'Ivoire: L'année terrible, 1999–2000*, M. Le Pape and C. Vidal, eds. Paris: Karthala.

Konaté, Y., 2003. Les enfants de la balle. De la FESCI aux mouvements des patriotes. *Politique Africaine* 89: 49–70.

Le Pape, M., and C. Vidal, eds, 2002. *La Côte d'Ivoire: L'année terrible, 1999–2000*. Paris: Karthala.

Losch, B., ed., 2000. *Côte d'Ivoire. La tentation ethnonationaliste*. (Special issue, *Politique Africaine* 78.) Paris: Karthala.

Marie, A., 2002. Une anthropo-logique communautaire à l'épreuve de la mondialisation: de la relation de dette à la lutte sociale. *Cahiers d'Etudes Africaines* 166: 207–255.

Marshall-Fratani, R., 2004. Liasons dangereuses: les implications régionales de la guerre ivoirienne. In *Côte d'Ivoire: Consolidation d'une Paix Fragile*. Ottawa: Partnership Africa Canada.

Mbembe, A., 2000. A propos des écritures africaines de soi. *Politique Africaine* 77: 16–43.

"Menace sur le processus de paix – Gbagbo prépare la guerre depuis le Libéria." 2004. *Le Patriote* (January 27).

Obou, O., 2000. *Requiem pour un code électoral*. Abidjan: Presses des Universités de Côte d'Ivoire.

Raulin, H., 1957. *Mission d'études des groupements immigrés en Côte d'Ivoire. Fascicule 3: Problèmes fonciers dans les régions de Gagnoa et de Daloa*. Paris: ORSTOM.

Touré, S., ed., 1996. "L'ivoirité, ou l'esprit du nouveau contrat social du Président Henri Konan Bédié." Acts of the CURDIPHE forum, March 20–26. In *Ethics*. Abidjan: Presses Universitaires d'Abidjan.

Vidal, C., 2002. Témoignages Abidjanaises. In *La Côte d'Ivoire: L'année terrible, 1999–2000*, M. Le Pape and C. Vidal, eds. Paris: Karthala.

Zongo, M., 2001. Etude des groupements immigrés burkinabè dans la région de Oumé (Côte d'Ivoire): organisation en migration, rapports fonciers avec les groupes autochtones et les pouvoirs publics locaux. Working paper, Unité de recherche "Régulations foncières," Montpellier, IRD.

24

Practicing German Citizenship, 2008

Ruth Mandel

"wir sind kein Einwanderungsland"
(we are not an immigration country)
jus solis: *law of the land: citizenship reckoning*
according to place of birth
jus sanguinis: *law of the blood: citizenship*
reckoning by one's parentage

Citizenship is inscribed on the German body politic in complex ways. Contrasting attitudes about citizenship in Germany come to the fore in mechanisms of inclusion or exclusion of outsiders. In light of changing juridical landscapes, "outsiders" range from "ethnic Germans" or Russian Jews from the former Soviet Union to the larger group of "foreigners" often exemplified by Turks. As already discussed, despite the economic participation of Turkish and other minorities in the German market, the cultural representation of them as essentially unintegratable into the German homeland, the *Heimat*, prevents their full political and social enfranchisement. A major hindrance to the cultural and political enfranchisement of these minority groups lies in a continued attachment to the ideal of an organic community, that is, of

belonging to a common people bound by language, history, and tradition. Although the very model of descent either from a common ancestry or a common people has been highly contested in much academic, political, and juridical discourse, the language of descent remains an enduring element in the legal identification of who can make claims to authentic Germanness (Brubaker 1992).

This criticism is levied from the perspective of the changes to naturalization law affecting Turks and other migrants, juxtaposed with the constitutional guarantees offered the Russian German "settlers." Comparisons between these groups are highlighted by debates over what constitutes a rightful German but also the right to become a German citizen – as opposed to becoming or being a *German*. It is noteworthy that "Turks" born in Germany have fewer rights in claiming to be accepted as Germans than do the so-called ethnic Germans born abroad. Hence a hindrance to political enfranchisement rests in the implicit acceptance of mimetic models of Germanness, that is, to prevailing correspondences with "images" of a common

Ruth Mandel, Practicing German citizenship. In *Cosmopolitan Anxieties: Turkish Challenges to Citizenship and Belonging in Germany* (Durham, North Carolina: Duke University Press, 2008), pp. 206–231.

people bound by language, history, and tradition, regardless of geography. This pervasive cultural mimetism available to the "ethnic Germans" banishes the minorities from the center of the political spectrum in the name of the exclusivist laws of the *Heimat*.

The Citizenship Conundrum: Romantic and Philosophical Roots and Consequences

Constitutional changes in citizenship and immigration laws have been at the center of political debates for decades. In the 1980s many advocates of minorities began to demand changes to anachronistic laws – some inherited from the Third Reich – governing foreign denizens' rights to reside, travel, reunite families, and naturalize. Most of these citizenship debates surrounded various interpretations of Article 116a of the *Grundgesetzt*, Germany's "Basic Law," containing the classic definition of German citizenship, the crucial paragraph of which is:

> A German in the sense of this constitution, unless stipulated differently by other legal regulations, is a holder of German citizenship [*Staatsangehörigkeit*], or a refugee or exiled person of German ethnicity [*Volkszugehörigkeit*], or his spouse or descendant, who was admitted to the territory of the German Reich according to its borders of December 31, 1937.

More than defining who is a citizen of the Federal Republic, Article 116 spells out exactly who has the right – and who does not have the right – to be considered a *German*, expressed in the term *Volkszugehörigkeit*, literally, folk- or people-belongingness (often inadequately glossed as "ethnicity"). The constitutional reference to the fiction of the German *Volk* constitutes the conundrum of citizenship, providing the criterion for including or excluding the foreign body. The genealogy of *Volkszugehörigkeit* can shed some light on its meaning for contemporary political discourse.

The reference to the *Volk* is a problematic remnant of the romantic belief that the origin of the Germans is an organic, supra-individual, and sometimes ethnicized concept of political community bound by common language, history, and culture. Carl Schmitt observed that the idea of ascribing special *Volksgeist* to people was not a specifically German phenomenon in itself but rather appeared already in French political thought. According to Schmitt, the specificity of German political thought – political romanticism in particular – is the view that the spirit (*Geist*) of the people is produced by a unique historical trajectory: "The new element was this: Now the people becomes the objective reality; historical development, however, which produces the *Volksgeist*, becomes the superhuman creator" (1985: 63).

This shift from the *origin* of community to the dream of producing a politically homogeneous body, a community, is at the heart of German political thought, including National Socialism. This logic was extended beyond the theoretical and philosophical implications of romanticism in the perverse interpretations and appropriations by National Socialists, whose vision of community was achieved by annihilating those who did not share in the Aryan essence. Agamben has observed that though the shift toward the production of the political body has concerned the fate of biopolitical modernity since the seventeenth century, it assumed catastrophic proportions under National Socialism (1999). In other words it characterizes the political project of modern nation-states to subsume the bare life of their citizens under a common recognizable sovereign body.

By contrast, Räthzel argues that "this prepolitical German nation, this nation in search of a state, was conceived not as a bearer of universal political values, but as an organic cultural, linguistic, or racial community – as a *Volksgemeinschaft*" (1991: 8). Whereas German romanticism had merely based the idea of the uniqueness of the German people in a metaphysical theory, the later biological construction of "race" not only maintained the idea of the specialness (or exceptionalism) of the German people (and likewise the specialness of all traditions, nations, communities); it reinforced this uniqueness, grounding it on the biological principle of racial superiority (Hodzic 2001: 32).

Blood, Proximity, and Racialization

The Aryan cult was based on the idea of an authentic, pure German essence reflected in the bloodline. The emphasis on symbolic blood heritage together with popular eugenics theories, consciously promoted "the fertility of the healthiest bearers of the nation" (Burleigh and Wipperman 1991: 40). Representations of blood were associated with the affirmation "of the genealogical ordering of society, in which blood functions as a verbal signifier of descent and citizenship" (Brubaker 1992), and through the violence inflicted upon subaltern bodies thereby affecting the transfiguration of the linguistic construct "race" into its physical signs: blood, pain, and contagion (Linke 1999b: 119).

Linke has shown that representations of the pure German people in current political discourse in Germany are tied to a metaphorics of blood and discourse of liquidation: the historical thread joining the politics of blood with the discourse of liquidation, equating blood with race, and therefore a concern with racial purity. This problematic legacy, she claims, remains unquestioned in the politics of postwar Germany; in particular it "has analogues in the postwar German understanding of alterity, an understanding shaped by a deep-seated revulsion to racial difference and facilitated by a vocabulary of race that originated during the Nazi period" (Linke 1999a: 217).

Documenting numerous instances of contemporary usages of these metaphors in the political and social spectrum, Linke cites the example of Bjoern Engholm, prime minister of the state of Schleswig-Holstein. This Social Democrat referred to asylum seekers "as a threatening 'counter race' (*Gegenrasse*) whose continued existence 'had become a question of survival for Germany'." In 1988 a former Bavarian head of state, Edmund Stoiber, "claimed that Germans were becoming 'hybridized and racially infested' (*durchmischt und durchrasst*)." A councilman from Dormagen in 1991 remarked, "Some people talk about integration, others about amalgamation. I speak about the adulteration and filthy mishmashing of blood (*Blutverpanschung und –vermanschung*)" (ibid.).

Themes of infestation and pollution travel beyond political rhetoric and trickle down to quotidian levels. An example of how a "foreigner" might perceive the reaction of a German to physical proximity was related to me by a Turkish German friend, Meral. A sophisticated professional woman, impeccably groomed and middle-aged, she had immigrated to Germany as a child in the 1960s. Meral saw herself as a quintessential Berliner, with as many if not more German friends and colleagues than Turkish. She long ago had received German citizenship. One day, in the late 1990s, we were meeting in a favorite cafe; she arrived visibly upset, having lost her usual nonchalance. She related what she had just experienced on the U-Bahn, the Berlin underground train. Meral had been flicking her long straight black hair behind her shoulder, pushing it out of her face. Suddenly the German woman seated beside her recoiled in disgust and let out a shriek. A few strands of Meral's hair apparently had made contact with the woman's arm; the woman, unable to contain herself, let out the spontaneous cry. "She thought I would contaminate her, that she would be infected somehow by me," Meral said, shaken. Meral saw herself as a Berlin insider; this incident struck a powerful blow at her sense of self and belonging. She only half-jokingly remarked that perhaps she would be better off in Turkey, a place she had not lived for over thirty years, but perhaps a place where her physical person would not cause offense.

On one occasion a Turkish German musician friend brought me along to a chamber music event at the spacious, elegant home of one of his German colleagues. With the exception of the two of us, all assembled were Germans, refined, genteel, classical music lovers. An elderly woman eagerly approached the two of us and began a conversation. She put her hand on my arm, explaining, "I wanted to speak with you, you see, since I've never touched a Turk before!"

These two instances, though contrasting reactions to the proximity, nonetheless converge in the unquestioned assumption of ontological difference. In Meral's episode, the proximity of perceived racialized difference threatened the

U-Bahn passenger; by contrast, the frisson experienced by the intrigued and excited German woman was equally animated by the notion of proximity to racialized difference, albeit positively inflected.

Jus Solis, Jus Sanguinis: *Aussiedler*, Mimesis, and Suffering for Germanness

The legal tradition of jus sanguinis, inclusion based on "law of the blood" and genealogy, with citizenship justified through ancestry, contrasts with jus solis, inclusion derived from place, with citizenship by virtue of where one is born. The permanence of this model and this legal tradition constitutes a violent act of exclusion of the foreign body from the German body politic. Indeed, it represents a dangerous entanglement of identitary thinking in the national construction of *Volkszugehörigkeit*. Consider, for instance, that Article 116a of the constitution mentions the possibility of losing the right to German *citizenship* while making it clear that it is impossible to disown oneself as a German *person*. It states:

Former German citizens whose citizenship was withdrawn [*entzogen*] on political, racial, or religious grounds between January 30, 1933, and May 8, 1945, and their descendants, shall be renaturalized [*einzubürgern*] on application. They shall not be considered as expatriated [*ausgebürgert*], if they took up residence in Germany after May 8, 1945, and have not expressed a different will.

The law sets in relief the legal demand that original citizenship status be withdrawn or requested to be withdrawn, as usually occurs in the case of naturalizing foreigners. While paragraph 2 of the constitution was written in order to account for the "ethnic Germans" who had been forced either to migrate away from German territory or from whom the German territory receded (in the radically recast borders before, during, and following World War II), these "exilic" Germans always were acknowledged as belonging to the ideal German community of destiny. While this is not comparable, from a strictly legal point of view, to the situation of Turkish Germans, it does pose questions concerning the biopolitical division of people and citizens.

Some authors, taking a critical view of the ideology of descent, have argued that it is based not on genealogy but ideology. Thus Senders finds the emphasis on the rules of descent secondary to a more complicated notion of representation. He argues that descent

is not a biological or genealogical relation, but is an ideology used to legitimate identification. It is a narrative strategy for designating a degree of likeness, of similarity, seen as necessary for full membership in the German nation. Such relationships of similarity and reproduction can be characterized in terms of mimesis or representation. More particularly, in the context of identity law, mimesis can be analyzed in terms of the organization and evaluation of identification and perceived resemblances among people and between people and identity categories. (1999: 178)

His argument derives from the specific case of the "ethnic Germans" living outside the Federal Republic whose claims to German ancestry need to be proven through a complex set of tests. Indeed, the entire discourse of their repatriation is permeated by mimesis, insofar as the repatriates must present themselves "publicly, freely, and truly as Germans, and ... when Aussiedler express that which within them is German; they manifest their 'true' identities as Germans" (92).

Since the 1990s it is increasingly the display of German cultural norms, proven in an "ethnicity" test administered by consular officials in the emigration countries, that comes to define who has the right to claim Germanness and hence German citizenship. However, with the awareness that close to two million ethnic Germans from the former Soviet Union might claim costly repatriation privileges, German authorities reconsidered the initial indiscriminant policies of acceptance of any and all claiming German descent. It became insufficient merely to be German on the basis of one's Soviet-defined "ethnicity" (*natsionalnost'*) stamped in an internal passport, as in the early postunification days, but additionally one had to prove affinity with and knowledge of German culture, tradition, and language. Applicants for repatriation were subjected to interviews in which they were quizzed, among other things, about their observance of holidays, such as the dates they celebrated Christmas (Russian Orthodoxy, the dominant religion in the former Soviet Union, follows a different calendar) and their knowledge of Christmas and Easter songs and foods. Furthermore, in accordance with the law on the persecution of exiled Germans, ethnic Germans had to have suffered as a direct result of their Germanness to qualify for repatriation.

In a sense, the experience of suffering came to define Germanness. Having suffered for one's ethnicity, for one's German identity, became an essential part of the staged performance at the interview but also of one's identity. It was this experience of having suffered at the hands of the Soviets, of having proved one's mettle, having been tested and passed the exam of Germanness, having tenaciously held onto Germanness and not denying or relinquishing it in times of adversity, that enabled one to "repatriate" to Germany. Past suffering justified the huge state expenditure on their behalf. All new *Aussiedler* had the right of two years of full state support in this initial adjustment period. Housing, monthly stipends, language classes, free health care, employment assistance, and other social services all represented an enormous commitment on the part of the state and its taxpayers.

Indeed, the newly imported Germans who arrived in the 1990s brought narratives of suffering and victimization. In some senses they were seen as the representation of the nation, having suffered for its sins. But they also carried the burden of the projected, idealized ur-German ancestor temporarily transposed to modernity. For the nostalgic, they represented authentic Germanness, untainted, uncorrupted, and pure. Animated artifacts, they increasingly were expected to infuse a hybridized Germany with its lost essence. Those who could spoke a quaint ancient vernacular and initially were welcomed as distant relatives. Yet this discourse of purity was entangled with the awareness that fraud might occur: as Senders observes, the *Aussiedler* have to perform their identity "in an institutional context that is based on the assumption that some applicants will try to act like Germans," that some will try to defraud the German government to acquire full benefits of German society (1999: 92). In addition, a major component of this institutional performance is the shock on the part of the German authorities and the population at large, when those who had romanticized these "urkinspeople" discover the ugly truth – the German authenticity the *Aussiedler* were assumed to have carried with them looked, sounded, and acted like foreign Russians.

This shock cannot be accounted for by a simple idea of mimesis that seems to presuppose the notion of a German essence that can be replicated or reproduced. To make sense of the shock experienced by the *Aussiedler* (as well as by the *Ausländer*) one needs to move away from the idea of resemblance and similarity to that of radical difference. Mimesis does not reflect a stable essence; rather, it is a creative and recreative process of self-making. This general mimesis, while supplementing the "real" instead of reflecting an image, can be understood as a more generative, creative process.

Similarly, Senders speaks of mimesis as augmentation of the real: "mimesis by augmentation in which the real is improved, heightened or corrected in representation. The figure (of Germanness) is offered as a prototype, a point from which to take measure, a model after which to pattern" (1999: 101). On the one hand *Aussiedler* are expected to conform to a given and stable prototype and try to pattern their own behavior after this given model. On the other hand, the dismay registered by the German authorities and population at large demonstrates that the prototype is recreated in the context of the mimetic performance itself. *Aussiedler*, in the very act of conforming to German standards of identity, present themselves with their own acquired characteristics. The German evaluators eventually base the judgment on whether or not such a self-presentation *possesses* the requisite German identity. What is dangerous in this apparently benign gesture of recognition is that mimetism is always already bound up with a troubling identity, supposed to be stable, essential, and authentic. The problem is that identity (whether

"German" or other) is never given as such; rather it is performed, hence unstable. In other words, the problem with mimetism is that a stable identity is presupposed which needs only to be reproduced through an act of representation. Any effort to demonstrate the mimetic signifiers of German identity (the sign of one's membership in the German folk is generally understood in the ability to speak the German language and the awareness of the folk traditions – religion, culture, ethics) comes down to questions of ideology. Political mimetism consists in the forced inscription of ethnos on the natural body of the citizen. Yet the inscription of ethnos is effective even when language is lacking.

The sign of one's membership in the German *Volk* (*Volkszugehörigkeit*) generally is constituted by fluency in German. Yet one of the most interesting cases discussed by the German courts concerns the problem of those repatriates who do not speak the language. In the case of the German minority from the USSR, the German court decided that the narrative of loss, dispossession, deportation, death, and repression was "more important in determining authentic identity claims than language. Identity was seen instead as a matter of 'consciousness,' 'identification,' and 'experience.' One of the primary experiences pointed to by the court as associated with Russian-German identity was the linguistic and cultural repression practiced by the Soviets upon the Germans. That is, a German's inability to speak German, as a sign of repression, is in itself a sign of 'German' identity." Behind the court's recognition of German identity despite the absence of language facility lies an idea that "to be German is to suffer for it" (Senders 1999: 133, 148).

The repatriates' self-presentation puts on stage the fragmentary remainders of another German body, namely, that of Germans as a victimized oppressed people. This discourse of victimization harkens back to the question of Jews, as the people who have historically undergone ignominious suffering, precisely at the hands of Germans. The reduction of the Jews to the subhuman, to bare life, was also a legal, constitutional act through which they were stripped of all nationality, and of all the rights of citizenship. If, as Senders seems to argue, the new citizenship law has made progress in expanding its idea of membership in the German *Volk*, by giving priority to cultural identifications rather than to descent claims, the question remains, to what "image" of Germany are the cultural identifications attached? What is the German essence that has to be "produced" as community? One which a priori excludes its outsiders?

Another contradiction in the appeal to common descent has been shown by Wilpert. Pointing out the inherent injustice of the descent principle, she compares the cases of the *Aussiedler* whose accepted proof of Germanness (for purposes of "repatriation" to Germany from Eastern Europe) is "membership of an ancestor" in the Nazi Party. Thus, persons whose fathers or grandfathers were Nazi Party members "are in a sense more privileged than those whose parents had nothing to do with these organizations. Inadvertently or not, this process could be considered a form of positive compensation for identification with the Nazi movement" (Wilpert 1995: 73; see also Wilpert 2003). Comparing such cases to one brought to the Berlin courts in 1991, whereby a Romanian Jew "claimed German language and culture and wanted to be recognized as a German with rights to German citizenship," he was obliged by the court to prove the cultural Germanness of his ancestors, as well as their having been *Bekenntnisdeutsche*, or having a sense of consciousness of national belonging. However, when the court learned that the claimant's father had been condemned to *Zwangsarbeit* (Nazi forced labor) from 1941 to 1944, he was deemed to be a member of the Jewish ethnic group and therefore could not be considered of German ethnicity (*Volkszugehörigkeit*). Thus, "the claimant could present his ancestors as Germans in practically all aspects, language, culture and education, but a Jew can never prove membership in the SS, the most common proof to be recognized as an Aussiedler" (Scheidges 1992: 3; quoted in Wilpert 1995: 74). Jewishness and Germanness in the eyes of the court were mutually exclusive, as, in effect, the court implicitly acknowledged the continued legitimacy of the Nazi Nuremberg racial laws. Wilpert concludes, stating that the "racist rationale, central to the system which Hitler exploited, remains a major principle for determining access to privileged rights within German society." Furthermore, it "supplies the logic for access to membership and provides legitimacy for racist ideologies and institutional discrimination toward the collective of foreign workers and their descendants, who are not recognized as having accumulated similar rights within German society" (ibid.: 74).

As this case makes clear, German identity is not assigned on the basis of common language but rather on the problematic idea of descent. The ability to speak German alone is not sufficient to establish proof of German ancestry. The same criteria that prove effective in including *Aussiedler* ultimately exclude those who are deemed non-ethnic Germans. In other words, one does not become German by speaking the language; rather one is *born* a German. In determining the rights to Germanness and membership in the German body politic, the German courts explicitly have recognized the primacy of descent over other attributes, such as language; they also have determined that, all else being equal, Jewish heritage can make the crucial, disqualifying difference. Therefore, if descent is the sign of an immediately communal belonging, those people unable to make this claim remain radically excluded. Similarly, where the courts ruled in favor of the *Aussiedler* woman who spoke no German, she was pronounced to be an ethnic German based on principles of inherited suffering and victimization – the descent principle at work once again. The implication is that had the Romanian Jew based his claim of rightful inclusion on having suffered, the court would have dismissed it, since he had suffered as a Jew, not as a German. These court rulings beg uncomfortable and troublesome questions.

The Politics of Race

The politics of exclusion of foreigners from the nation's body points to a vision of the non-German as unchangeable in nature. Gilman suggests that the doctrine of the nonconvertibility of the Jews, espoused by Reformation authors, constitutes the basis for discrimination. Behind this doctrine is the idea that there cannot be a true convert to Christianity; by extension there cannot be a true convert to a dominant culture. A story from Reuchlin's *Letters of Obscure Men* expresses doubt that the faith of the new convert to Christianity will persevere over time (cited in Gilman 1990: 49). Central to the story is the idea that the Jew cannot change his nature and thus reveals his true nature in moments of crisis. Hence the lesson that one can never trust a Jew – converted or not (50). In one of Luther's harshest statements, from *Against the Jews and their Lies*, he argues that Jews are liars and therefore dangerous to the social fabric (ibid.: 59). The significance of this is that these views reappear throughout the history of German attitudes toward Jews (57). The aim here is not to argue that Luther was an anti-Semite but rather to show how a theological doctrine could end up in the hands of ideologists and of the political proponents of Hitlerism. In addition to the racialism, the doctrine of the nonconvertibility of the Jews reflects an essentialist vision of the self and the community. Jews could be expelled from Hitler's German community of belonging because they could not truly be "changed" into ethnically pure German people.

Views of the unchangeable nature of foreign groups survive in contemporary Germany, albeit in less virulent forms. This is reflected in the rationale behind the distribution of entitlements to various minorities. While the Federal Republic's stretched budget commited enormous resources (e.g., nearly one-half billion DM per year in the 1990s) to teaching recently arrived *Aussiedler* to speak German as part of its "integration" policy, it spends virtually nothing assisting Turkish immigrants, for example, who have lived in the Federal Republic for decades, to speak German. Does it mean that the Turks' essential status as non-German prevents them from mastering the language, and thus from becoming full members of German culture, whereas the Russian-speaking post-Soviet incomers, categorized as German, do possess this capacity? Labeling them "settlers," not "foreigners," and treating them as repatriates buttresses this view. Political and cultural classifications play roles in determining and justifying budgetary expenditures. In most if not all of the official literature published by the interior ministry's department of overseas migration, the demographically inflected *Zuwanderung* is the operative term – not the overdetermined *Einwanderung*, immigration. The prefixitive difference insists that the former term, a more neutral rendering of migrant minus the intention to permanently settle, dominates the discourse. Notionally, if Turks are not permitted to be immigrants – and the decades-old slogan "We are not an immigration country" precludes the opening of a social and political space for immigrant status – then presumably they will return to Turkey at some point and are not in need of integration via language. Such beliefs are an indication of the dangers still present in any appeal to common culture and tradition on the basis of genealogy.

Citizenship Revisited

The debates accompanying the passage of the reformed citizenship law that took effect January 1, 2000, center on new definitions of belonging without resorting to the principle of genealogy. Indeed, as the German foreign ministry declared in an official statement, "With the reform of the citizenship law Germany recognizes itself by means of a realistic concept of the nation. The idea that it was possible to ground the idea of a nation on ethnic homogeneity was already an illusion. The definition of such a homogeneous society was and is a construct, and a representation of the nation defined by blood ties belongs to the tragic evils of our past" (1999).[1] The text continues to acknowledge that some progress has been made in the very enlightenment of the German nation.[2] This is because

what binds a society together cannot be reached only by a common language, geographic demarcation of borders or a common religion. A modern enlightened understanding of nation can only be built with a common will for peaceful living together, and a common shaping of the future and an understanding of the basic values of a free society. In this sense

the new citizenship law sets the basis for a peaceful and mutually enriching living together of different culture forms.

And, furthermore:

With the modernization of the citizenship law Germany finally meets European standards accentuating the vision of a united Europe understood as a place of freedom, rights and security. Thus in the new citizenship law Germany appears as tolerant and open to the world.[3]

Despite the lofty language, this vision of a tolerant Germany does not answer anxieties about the demands placed upon foreigners to comply with the new citizenship law, as applicants for citizenship are required to renounce their prior nationality. In doing so, they are expected to renounce their language and culture as well. How would this act embrace the tolerance and multiculturalism espoused? The suggestion by the Minister of Education of Baaden-Württemberg that imams in mosques throughout Germany preach in German is a further iteration of such an expectation.[4] The harshness of such expectations raises questions about the kind of society foreigners are called to embrace.

In June 1998 a Berlin Senator of the Interior complained publicly about "the detrimental influences" of the multicultural society he saw around him. Claiming that integration policies had failed, pointing to the excessive unemployment figures among the foreign population, ghettoization in urban areas, their poor mastery of German, and finally to Islam, he contended that this population was "alien to the majority culture" (John 2001: 45). This provoked a public debate first in Berlin and then nationally, calling for the mainstream German culture to be based on traditional and dominant German values.

A year later, a debate on culture and tradition entered into the public arena under the banner of *Leitkultur*, a term referring to a guiding, dominant culture (cf. leitmotif). Friedrich Merz, the leader of the Christian Democrat Union-Christian Social Union parliamentary group, invoked the term, bemoaning its loss in the context of the immigration debate. Merz's use touched a national raw nerve as major exponents of German *Hochkultur* entered the discussion, dominating nightly talk shows and other media debates. Vigorous defenses and attacks of the notion and definition provided an outlet for many to discuss feelings and attitudes about foreigners in Germany and, by extension, menacing visions of Germanness. Some questioned the validity of a single dominant high culture, *Hochkultur*, in its exclusivity and rejection of other cultural forms. For many, the term was deployed as a convenient euphemism for "xenophobia," as debate ensued on cultural pluralism versus the hegemonic implications of the term. Some tried to contort the compound word into a charter for an inclusive and plural civil society. Finally a bit of humorous closure was found: a linguistic-political contest declared *Leitkultur* to be the year's winning *Unwort*, the non-word of the year.

The closure proved incomplete. Several years later, in late 2004, *Leitkultur* re-emerged. Reacting to the killing of the controversial Dutch filmmaker Theo van Gogh by an irate Muslim, conservative politicians in Germany resorted to Huntington's "clash of civilizations" model to explain the murder, voicing concern that such violence easily could occur next in Germany. Markus Soeder, the leader of Bavaria's Christian Social Union party, took this event as justification for the urgent need of *Leitkultur* in Germany. He declared, "When we look at the recent events in the Netherlands, we see a clash of civilizations in full, and we must prevent anything similar from evolving here. We need a change in our integration policy which ought to be based strictly on the values and notion of a modern Christian society" (Deutsche Welle, November 16, 2004). To Soeder and his supporters, expressions of pluralism and cultural relativism have no role to play in Germany.

Dual Nationality – Divided Loyalty?

The debate about dual nationality evokes strong emotions and political action on both sides of the question. It often has been discussed within the debate on tradition and culture, identity and entitlement. On one side has been the Green Party, the foremost supporter of dual nationality. On the other, Christian Democrats remain vehemently opposed, generally citing their conviction that it inevitably would produce irreconcilable divided loyalties. The Social Democrats, in the middle, have tended to mediate and strike compromise positions. On the Green side, in the 1990s a highly publicized campaign was spearheaded by Ismail Koşan, a naturalized German from Turkey and a Green Party (Bündes 90) member of the Berlin Parliament. The campaign gathered one million signatures supporting legalization of dual nationality. The statement cited other European and North American examples where dual nationality is legal and called the German law anachronistic, a "folk relic." It demanded the repeal of Article 116 and of the legality of jus sanguinis. Bauböck interprets such demands for dual citizenship as an indication of "the emergence of a new model of membership that breaks with both ethnic and republican traditions of nationalism" (1994: ix). Though Bauböck sees Germany as more tolerant about the idea of dual citizenship than previously, he may have been overly optimistic.

Though in public policy rhetoric, dual nationality does not exist, in practice, even in legal fact, it does, and in all sorts of unexpected forms. An obscure example was that throughout the forty-five years of the GDR (East Germany: the German Democratic Republic), all its citizens were virtual citizens of the Federal Republic (West Germany). The nature of their citizenship was known as a "sleeping nationality," *ruhende Staatsangehörigkeit*. However, though GDR citizens had the right, from the perspective of West Germany, to "awaken" this recumbent nationality at any time, they were restricted by the contingencies of political geographies. If they could manage to get there, they could make their claim in West Germany (Hofmann 1998: 16).

These sleeping conationals, unactivated West Germans, were unproblematically dual citizens for the duration of the GDR. They were, after all, not *Blutsfremd* – foreign-blooded – but "co-blooded" Germans. Of course, once the GDR no longer existed and merged into the FRG, neither did GDR citizenship exist, and the former GDR nationals automatically became FRG mononationals. Furthermore, conceptually and legally the sleeping citizenry was only a half-step removed from the several million-strong *Aussiedler* population scattered throughout Eastern Europe and the former Soviet Union, who also could claim West German and then German citizenship. Despite the paradoxical precedent dual nationality did not become the law of the land. A diluted reform was passed instead.

In May 1999, the Bundestag approved an "option model," fundamentally amending its citizenship law and, by implication, challenging some of the inherited German ideologies of blood and soil. To many observers, this legislation has been the most important feat of the Social Democratic–Green Party coalition government, elected in 1998. The new citizenship legislation went into effect January 1, 2000, and provided for a temporary dual nationality to children born of foreign parents. The new law stipulated that these dual-national children, upon reaching their majority, were compelled to choose between nationalities; also, it reduced the minimum waiting time that a foreigner must reside in Germany in order to qualify to apply for naturalization. The law stopped far short of what some would have liked, that is, full rights of dual nationality. However, to others it was a shift of seismic proportions. After the law's passage the Bavarian Christian Social Union (CSU), historically right wing and anti-foreigner, announced that it would challenge its constitutionality in Germany's highest constitutional court.

The phrase *Null-Tarif* became popular among those opposed to any change in the law. *Null-Tarif*, glossed as "for free" or "for nothing," assumed the status of a catchword, its immediately pejorative implication obvious in the hearing. "The acquisition of citizenship 'for free' without comprehensive integration attacks the principles of identity of the people of the German state," wrote Wolfgang Zeitlmann in 1999 for the CDU/CSU:

Inner peace and integration in Germany are seriously at risk if SPD and the Greens insist on their ideological plans ... [t]he meaning of German citizenship will be changed radically and surrendering the principles of the German

National State. ... culture and history are consciously put at stake as the basis for community ... the inner peace of Germany is threatened by privileges for persons with dual citizenship.[5]

In a similar vein, at an informal gathering in Berlin in November 2000, a distinguished German professor of international and human rights law noted with puzzlement, "Isn't it curious how in other countries, they are pleased, even flattered, when foreigners want to take on citizenship? But here we do everything to make it difficult if not impossible. We don't want them to become German." He went on to explain to me how things had changed dramatically since the days of *Gastarbeiter* migration. "But there are differences between the migrants. Now, Greece, Italy, Spain, are all part of the EU; there are no problems any more with these European migrants – the Yugoslavs, all the others – they get along fine here. It is only the Turks who do not seem to wish to integrate. They are the real problem," insisted the jurist, who considered himself to be an enlightened intellectual and politically progressive.

The issue is highly charged; documents such as Zeitlmann's encourage anxiety about threats to the "principles, culture, history and inner peace" of Germany. From this perspective the only way to maintain the integrity of German culture is to demand the total renunciation on the part of *Ausländer* of both their original *Staatsangehörigkeit* and their *Volkszugehörigkeit*. Dual nationality would be cognitive dissonance, a violation of an accepted logic. The conventional excuses such as "Where would one's loyalty *really* lie?" or "It would prevent true integration" are iterated endlessly. Martin writes, "The persistence of a symbolic discourse on the perils of non-renunciation in the German public sphere reinforces a culture of exclusion, xenophobia and mistrust" (2002: 41).

Commissioning Germans from Foreigners

As dual citizenship has been a nonstarter, some critics have focused on naturalization as a solution to the "foreigner problem." An example of this effort is the modest leaflet produced by Berlin's foreigner commissioner, entitled *Erleichterte Einbürgerung junger Ausländer* (Simplified Naturalization for Young Foreigners). On its front is an illustration of a German passport, on which, above the "Bundesrepublik Deutschland," reads "Europäische Gemeinschaft," providing a visual reminder that a German passport serves at the same time as a pan–European Union passport. Published under the auspices of "Miteinander Leben in Berlin" (Living with each other in Berlin), the over-arching program of the commissioner's office, the leaflet opens up, asks catchy questions cast in advertising-speak.

Have you ever thought of becoming a citizen? Why should you do this?! Quite simply: You were brought up in Germany and belong here. Why shouldn't you be treated like a citizen?

It continues with a long list of the advantages to German citizenship, followed by the legal conditions:

- freedom of movement through EU
- visa-free travel in many countries also outside of Europe
- free employment choice (e.g., civil service) and right to establish a business, private practice (e.g., doctor or pharmacist)
- right of a German to take up independent employment
- protection against deportation
- protection against extradition to another country
- the right to vote and run for office
- your non-German spouse may join you and immediately receive a work permit
- when you have fulfilled the following legal conditions ...
- must apply between your 16th and 23rd birthdays
- give up or have lost your previous citizenship
- must have resided in Germany for eight years with legal residence permission
- must have attended school for six years in Germany, of which at least four years at a comprehensive, basic school
- must not have committed a criminal offence

Then You Have the Legal Claim to a Simplified Naturalization.

The brochure's intention is straightforward: Berlin, Germany, and Europe is foreigners' rightful place, whether by birth or by adoption, and they should become naturalized stakeholders in it.

As commissioner for foreigners, Barbara John set the precedent for using her role as an advocate for increased naturalization. She expressed pride in the fact that "more foreigners have been naturalized in Berlin than in any other German state."[6] Until foreigners attain citizenship, they will lack equality under the law; thus, the ultimate aim is as much naturalization as possible. And, following from naturalization presumably comes integration. Still, it may be somewhat disingenuous to promote citizenship as a panacea that will improve lives and solve problems overnight. It is clear that even if the newly German Turks gain suffrage, the color of their new passports is no guarantee of overcoming prejudice, discrimination, and social marginality.

Passport Stories and Pink Cards

The remarkable change in citizenship practice has occurred over the past several decades. When I first lived in West Berlin in the 1980s, virtually none of the Turks I knew had German citizenship. By the late 1980s the trend to acquire a German passport had begun, and currently it seems that *not* to be a naturalized German citizen is the exception. An official estimate for 2000 stated that forty thousand Turks had become German citizens.[7] Another change is that previously most newly naturalized Germans retained their Turkish citizenship, with the full blessing and assistance of the Turkish government. Now, though many still have both passports, the more recently naturalized citizens have complied with German law, fearful of severe penalties should they be caught with two passports. For example, the consequences for any civil servant – *Beamter* – would be permanent exclusion from future public-sector employment, and given the ubiquity of the civil service this could be serious indeed. One friend, a Turkish German professional, married to a German man, and the mother of four German and Turkish binational children, learned her lesson the hard way and had her German passport revoked.

Throughout the 1980s and into the 1990s, after relinquishing their Turkish passports to the German authorities, the newly minted German citizens simply fetched their Turkish passports from the local Turkish consulate. The German government was helpless in stopping this, though the practice was illegal, and Germany did not recognize *Mehrstaatigkeit*, multiple citizenship. Turkey, however, was not anxious to lose its citizens – they sent valuable remittances, for one thing, an important part of the Turkish economy. Furthermore, having over two million Turkish nationals in Germany could be used as political leverage in a whole host of arenas, not least in Turkey's bid for joining the European Union. At the same time the Turkish government, in response to pressure from Germany, arrived at a creative quasi-citizenship for Turks becoming German citizens but not wishing to cut ties with Turkey. Thus was born the *Pembe Kart*, Pink Card, in 1995, ushering in a status that one keen observer coined "citizenship light" (Çağlar 2004). The bearers of the *Pembe Kart* possess a slightly compromised citizenship status that allows them most rights of citizens of the Turkish Republic with the exception of suffrage, standing for election, or entering the civil service. Owning and inheriting property remain unrestricted. Nevertheless, news of the *Pembe Kart* has been slow to percolate through the Turkish population in Germany and many with whom I spoke had not heard of it. Deniz, a generally well informed, sophisticated woman was unaware of such a status. In her late forties, she came to Germany as a child in the 1960s, part of the first wave of *Gastarbeiter*. Deniz has "made it," holding a lucrative and responsible position in a German multinational firm. She told me her citizenship story:

I got my passport in 1980; I could have received it a few years earlier, but I was afraid what my parents would say. So finally I applied: I had to write an autobiography – where I'd been to school, when I'd left the country, where I'd worked. Back then you had to have worked about eight years before getting citizenship, and I had done this. I wrote

down all my travel, all my qualifications, and my German was impeccable. But I had to renounce my Turkish citizenship. I couldn't write the letter in Turkish – formal, written Turkish is so different and difficult – so I had some friends help me with that letter. I gave it to the Turkish Consulate, and in the letter had to explain why I wanted to give up my Turkish citizenship – I said for economic reasons, for work, considering my job. But I whispered to them that I really did not want to give up my passport, and they with a wink said "fine, no problem."

Deniz had few Turkish friends. She spoke Turkish somewhat haltingly, though she was fluent in German, French, and English; she read primarily English novels, vacationed in Spain, France, and the United States, and had invested in property in Germany. She did not bother to disguise her complete disinterest in people and things Turkish. Yet when asked if she was German, she reacted powerfully, as though the very idea filled her with distaste. Over several decades, German rhetoric about homogeneity and cultural belonging have succeeded in alienating her from being able to call herself German – despite twenty-five years of citizenship. The phrases "Deutsche mit türkischer Herkunft" or "Türken mit deutschem Pass" – German with Turkish background, Turks with German passports – echo an essentialist interpretation of German identity, whereby membership in the *Volksgemeinschaft* – the folk or "ethnic" community – ultimately is ascribed and not achievable. German citizen, yes; German, no.

Deniz explained that it was important to keep the Turkish passport. Unaware of the terms of the Pink Card, she mentioned that it was necessary to eventually receive her inheritance in order to own property. She could not expect to inherit much – at most a modest apartment in the outskirts of Istanbul, where her retired parents lived. This middle-aged woman, by certain standards as thoroughly "integrated" as one could be, having lived the bulk of her life in German and in Germany, still felt unequivocal about the desire not to become deracinated from a place she barely knew.

Contested Meanings of Citizenship

The citizenship conundrum has led many critics of German politics to revisit citizenship theories from antiquity to the present (e.g., Pocock 1998). Whereas some authors have returned to a Weberian understanding of the changing historical relationship between economic, political, and cultural citizenship (Shafir 1998: 5; Weber 1958: 43), others question the very idea of citizenship or call for a conception acknowledging the collapse of the European nation-states as we know them. Several of these positions try to make sense of the citizenship conundrum in German politics and elsewhere, developing a new vocabulary for what many consider our postnational or cosmopolitan epoch.

Recent critics of citizenship theory have observed the obsolescence of classical notions insofar as they recognize a radical shift in the modern invention of citizenship (Agamben 1998; Foucault 1994; Brubaker 1994). As historians of modernity commonly agree, a modern definition and conception of citizenship was the invention of the French Revolution (Brubaker 1992: 35), whereby the individual for the first time was seen as being born into the nation-state, inheriting the attendant rights and obligations. Commenting on Hannah Arendt's book on imperialism – the chapter on the decline of the nation-state and the end of the rights of men – Agamben observes that "a simple examination of the text of the declaration of 1789 shows that it is precisely bare natural life – which is to say the pure fact of birth – that appears here as the source and bearer of rights. 'Men,' the first article declares, 'are born and remain free and equal in rights'" (1998: 127). Agamben argues that "the very natural life that, inaugurating the biopolitics of modernity, is placed at the foundation of the order, vanishes into the figure of the citizen, in whom rights are preserved" (ibid.). Previously, there had been no conflation of individual and state sovereignty; since the individual was not considered the repository of sovereignty, there was no connection between nativity and nationality. It was perfectly possible, in the classic context, to be a nonpolitical being, unconnected to the confines and sovereignty of

the *polis* or state. Modernity's vision changed this, where the sovereignty into which the individual is born becomes one and the same and appropriated by the state.

However, the link between citizenship and nationality was shown to be inadequate after World War II, when millions of stateless people no longer could benefit from the protection of a nation-state and were discriminated against by the European nations. Arendt's radical critique of the Declaration of the Rights of Man and of the human rights tradition in general clearly shows to what lengths nation-states go to expel from their borders people whom they deem as dangerous and threatening to the social fabric (1951). Arendt makes clear that the exclusion of stateless persons, or aliens, from membership in nation-states reduced those persons to the nakedness of being just human beings and nothing else. Without the qualification of national belonging, aliens had no quality whatsoever that could be preserved, protected, and maintained. What then is the status of citizenship today after the experience of statelessness? To what extent should one hold on to the fiction of citizenship, loaded as it is with the ideal of an organic community, bound by common language, history, and tradition? To what political status could one appeal, lacking adequate, heterogeneous citizenship laws?

While harking back to the classics of citizenship theory, some have identified the perils of exclusively focusing on civil or political citizenship to the detriment of social citizenship. Thus Young proposed a liberal model of *differentiated citizenship* placing more emphasis on the social (1998: 264). Drawing from Rawls, she recognizes that certain practices of equality can suppress and even create inequalities, arguing that a genuinely heterogeneous concept of culture and citizenship is necessary to meet diverse needs without stigmatizing or marginalizing them. We might think of affirmative action or bilingual education as examples, whereby unequal distribution of resources serves the common good in its redressing asymmetrical social balances. Identifying a "dilemma of difference" (Shafir 1998: 24), Young shows how groups not yet having achieved the necessary level of universality are pressured into a denial of their difference in order to achieve "equal moral worth of citizens" yet find themselves disadvantaged. Thus, "formal equality, ironically, creates substantive inequality" (ibid.: 25). Her call for a reversal of perceptions of mainstream-to-marginal, whereby difference becomes embedded within normativity, is suggestive indeed and relevant to Germany.

In a similar liberal vein, Kymlicka also theorizes the need for an ethnically differentiated citizenship, particularly in the context of a state where "polyethnic rights and representation rights are primarily demands for inclusion, for full membership in the larger society" (1995: 85). He takes the primacy of states as we know them as a given, challenging them to strike a balance whereby they are not threatened by minority demands or rights but at the same time where the latter do not destabilize the former. Here the demand for minority rights must be reconciled with liberal definitions of justice and fairness. However, we might wish to question the assumption on which this is based, namely, the idea that stable ethnic groups can be identified through time and space. There is an inherent danger, both political and theoretical, when what is ultimately changing and unstable is delimited as a bounded, controllable entity. What is seen as a problematic and definable "ethnic minority" in Germany is in fact an unstable category, assuming different guises at different times and in different places. The same *Ausländer* in Berlin, are *almancı*, an emergent social group, in Anatolia; in addition, they may be part of other global networks such as an Islamic Sufi organization; or part of transnational casual labor migration based on extended kin from the same village. Furthermore, those who have become naturalized German citizens can lay claim to a vastly different set of rights from those with only Turkish nationality and temporary German visas. In the German case it is not a matter of recognizing the specifically ethnic rights of Turkish actors; rather, what is needed is a more realistic – not dependent on the tropes of ethnicity – and tolerant vision of their place in a society that is also subject to historical changes.

Soysal approaches the question of citizenship from the perspective of the supra-national configuration of a universalist discourse on human rights. Like Agamben, she suggests that the value of the modern idea of citizenship can be diminished in our postnational epoch due to the growing legitimacy of "discourses of universalistic personhood, the limits of nationness, or of national citizenship ... [which have] become inventively irrelevant" (1994: 162). Echoing the classic work of Marshall (with his tripartite description of civil, political, and social rights of citizenship), she privileges the social and civic achievements (enshrined by supranational bodies) over legal/political demands for protection; in other words, disenfranchisement, or non-enfranchisement, takes a back seat to other sorts of identities, affiliations, and rights. Positing that a contemporary repertoire of extensive memberships within Europe and the United Nations suggests that it is possible to hold on to the same package of universally valued rights without adopting an obsolete nationalistic model, Soysal's intention "is to highlight the emergence of membership that is multiple in the sense of spanning local, regional, and global identities, and which accommodates intersecting complexes of rights, duties, and loyalties" (166). Recourse to human rights and membership in the European Union she sees as exemplary of postnational citizenship. Yet even for those not indoctrinated in a "no taxation without representation" ideology (she cites examples of tax-paying non-citizens), the idealism of postnational citizenship might appear somewhat illusory at present. In a world that continues to resort to often humiliating visa requirements or stigmatizing resident restrictions, citizenship is still inextricably tied to national and state identities, borders, and powers. Though a suggestive notion, a postnational imaginary may not suffice for many Turkish German actors who have not yet found a credible hearing in the halls of Brussels. Perhaps the future will open paths for local civil rights disputes to be resolved within the bureaucracies of the EU or UN in the name of abstract universal rights.

Similarly, Dahrendorf imagines a supranational society based on a fundamental inclusivity, very much like Kant's world civil society. Adding to the universalistic model, he observes that "the true test of the strength of citizenship rights is heterogeneity" (1994: 17). The same litmus test of heterogeneity should apply as well to any postnational model of citizenship. Julia Kristeva notes that essential to the contemporary discussion of postnational citizenship is the possibility of "choosing" one's own membership and freedom of action, emphasizing the active voice of transnational migrant experience. This voice is born out of a critique of ethnicity-as-ascription: "When I say that I have chosen cosmopolitanism, this means that I have, against origins and starting from them, chosen a transnational or international position situated at the crossing of boundaries" (Kristeva 1993: 16). Kristeva invokes the freedom of modern cosmopolitan travelers to redefine the terms of their membership with new national configurations as well as the duty of states to enable that very freedom. "Beyond the origins that have assigned to us biological identity papers and a linguistic, religious, social, political, historical place, the freedom of contemporary individuals may be gauged according to their ability to choose their membership, while the democratic capability of a nation and social group is revealed by the right it affords individuals to exercise that choice" (ibid.). Alas, many nations and groups deny that democratic choice to large sectors of their denizens.

In the European context the Schengen and Maastricht agreements signed by many EU member states need to be considered in terms of their potential for overcoming citizenship constraints for non-nationals living in Germany as well as for enabling the freedom of movement Kristeva aspires to achieve. Some observers have seen EU changes as important steps toward a postnational, cosmopolitan citizenship that extends state sovereignty beyond state borders, whereby all Schengen passport holders become subject to a new, transnational set of rights and responsibilities (Soysal 1994; Held 1995; and Faulks 2000). However, others pose critical questions about a new sort of exclusivity of a fortress Europe, particularly affecting refugees and asylum seekers. O'Leary's argument disputes EU citizenship as a progressive postnational form;

rather, she argues that the recent legal strictures and structures of EU have made it more exclusive. She asks why, since "European is being defined not as a geographical but as an ideological concept with reference to a shared culture, heritage and history," has there been little regard paid to the "potentially negative impact which this citizenship might have on the non-Community nationals resident in the Union?" (1998: 100). By increasing rights and privileges of the European Union citizens, the non-citizen residents are, at the same time, increasingly restricted and forced into legally second-class status. Recognition of these fundamental contradictions has been one of the motivating factors of Berlin's Commissioner for Foreigners, in the campaign to convince all who qualify to apply for German citizenship.

Humans, Citizens, Exceptionalism

The paradoxical link between the human being and citizen inscribed in German legal and political culture reflects changes from its formulation of 1913 up to the amendments of the naturalization law of 1999. The common denominator throughout the modern debates is the unquestioned reference to the model of national belonging, based on the trope of the common people, common culture, and tradition. Sometimes this has linked the tradition of the common culture with the belief in a common ancestry, as under National Socialism; in other periods the two have been disaggregated, such as during the statist Bismarckian regime. Thus it should be recognized that not all arguments about common culture are reiterations of arguments about a mythical German ancestry.

Despite several attempts to change the constitution in the direction of the inclusion of the "aliens" in German territory, models of organic community have yet to be fully challenged. Though the 1999 citizenship law enables increased numbers of Turks and others to become citizens, it does not bestow on them the full visibility of social and cultural membership in the German nation. This incomplete status of Turkish German citizenship has been well documented through analysis of the forms of stigmatization and mystification that naturalized Turks have undergone over the past decades (e.g., Wilpert 1995, 2003). While it is now possible for a Turkish German to become a member of the German Parliament, certainly a major victory for the foreigners in Germany, it remains an exceptional case. The law of exception characterizes the German relation to the "alien" (the Turk, the foreigner on its soil), insofar as the process of naturalization and integration of the alien is itself seen as an exceptional event, a process that needs to be examined at the singular level again and again. It seems inevitable to question the status of the aliens in Germany today when they are not fully accepted into German society. What is the space they occupy between the loss of originary national identity (and nostalgia for their country of origin) and the demand for a new political "home"?

German political rhetoric (especially on the right) at times reduces aliens, Turks in particular, to figures of social misfits, of the threatening enemy from the Orient, despite their participation in German society for close to half a century. Is it possible to destroy the representation of the Turk as an enemy of German culture, history, and tradition? This Orientalist representation proves powerful in a certain part of the German political imaginary, perhaps linked to the persistent fear of a heterogeneous society. So much so that in 2005 a politician from the Free Democrat Party, Daniel Behr, called for more Germans from the educated classes to reproduce. "The wrong people in Germany are having children," Behr declared, betraying a eugenically informed bias (Deutsche Welle, January 24, 2005). Thus, if German representations of Turks remain bound up with the oppositions of friend and enemy, unproductive vs. overly fecund, what sort of experiences might Turkish Germans expect in their relationships with German politicians, bureaucrats, intellectuals, and people more generally? What sort of rapprochement can emerge from a situation where one is perceived only as "ethnically" Turkish, as if one's essence were essential and unchangeable? In the words of Kristeva, they need to be allowed to "choose" between alternative forms of cosmopolitan expression, forms that would reflect their capacities as transnational actors in transferring their skills, and even allegiances, across unstable boundaries.

NOTES

1 Foreign Ministry, Bonn, May 21, 1999, *Das Neue Staatsangehörigkeitsrecht*, 2.
2 Ibid., 2–3.
3 Ibid., 3.
4 See Deutsche Welle, November 24, 2004.
5 "Klares Nein zur rot-gruenen Doppelstaats-buergerschaft, '06/01.1999," January 6, 1999, http://www.cducsu.bundestag.de/texte/csu/dreuth99ze.htm (accessed November 2000).
6 Interview with Barbara John, September 14, 1995, Berlin.
7 Interview, Turkish Consul General, Berlin, December 19, 2000.

REFERENCES

Agamben, Giorgio, 1998. *Homo Sacer: Sovereign Power and Bare Life*. Stanford, CA: Stanford University Press.

Agamben, Giorgio, 1999. *Remnants of Auschwitz: The Witness and the Archive*. Translated by D. Heller-Roazen. New York: Zone Books.

Arendt, Hannah, 1951. *Origins of Totalitarianism*. New York: Harcourt Brace Jovanovich.

Bauböck, Rainer, ed., 1994. Preface to *From Aliens to Citizens: Redefining the Status of Immigrants in Europe*. Brookfield, VT: Avebury.

Brubaker, Rogers, 1992. *Citizenship and Nationhood in France and Germany*. Cambridge, MA: Harvard University Press.

Brubaker, Rogers, 1996. *Nationalism Reframed: Nationhood and the National Question in the New Europe*. Cambridge: Cambridge University Press.

Burleigh, Michael, and Wolfgang Wipperman, 1991. *The Racial State: Germany, 1933–1945*. New York: Cambridge University Press.

Çağlar, Ayşe S., 2004. "Citizenship Light": Transnational Ties, Multiple Rules of Membership and the "Pink Card." In *Worlds on the Move: Globalisation, Migration and Cultural Security*, Jonathan Friedman and Shalini Randeria, eds. New York: Palgrave Macmillan, pp. 273–92.

Dahrendorf, Ralf, 1994. The Changing Quality of Citizenship. In *The Conditions of Citizenship*, Bart van Steenberger, ed. London: Sage, pp. 10–19.

Deutsche Welle, 2004. Holland Prompts Soul-Searching in Germany. *Deutsche Welle*, November 16, 2004. Available at http://www.dw-world.de/.

Deutsche Welle, 2005. Politician Wants Academics to Have Kids. *Deutsche Welle*, January 24, 2005. Available at http://www.dw-world.de/.

Faulks, Keith, 2000. *Citizenship*. London: Routledge.

Foucault, Michel, 1994. *Dits et Ecrits: 1954–1988*. Paris: Gallimard.

Gilman, Sander, 1990. *Jewish Self-Hatred: Anti-Semitism and the Hidden Language of the Jews*. Baltimore: Johns Hopkins University Press.

Held, David, 1995. *Democracy and Global Order: From the Modern State to Cosmopolitan Governance*. Cambridge, MA: Polity Press.

Hodzic, Saida, 2001. Die Einbürgerung in Australien und Deutschland. Master's thesis, University of Cologne.

Hofmann, Rainer, 1998. Nationality Status and Minorities in Germany. In *Citizenship and Nationality Status in the New Europe*, Siofra O'Leary and Teija Tülikainen, eds. London: Institute for Public Policy Research, pp. 57–168.

John, Barbara, 2001. German Immigration Policy – Past, Present, and Future. In *A New Germany in a New Europe*, Todd Herzog and Sander L. Gilman, eds. New York: Routledge, pp. 43–48.

Kristeva, Julia, 1993. *Nations without Nationalism*. New York: Columbia University Press.

Kymlicka, Will, 1995. *Multicultural Citizenship: A Liberal Theory of Minority Rights*. Oxford: Clarendon Press.

Linke, Uli, 1999a. *Blood and Nation: The European Aesthetics of Race*. Philadelphia: University of Pennsylvania Press.

Linke, Uli, 1999b. *German Bodies: Race and Representation after Hitler*. New York: Routledge.

Martin, David, 2002. New Rules for Dual Nationality. In *Dual Nationality, Social Rights and Federal Citizenship in the U.S. and Europe: The Reinvention of Citizenship*, Randall Hansen and Patrick Weil, eds. New York: Berghahn Books, pp. 34–60.

O'Leary, Siofra, and Teija Tülikainen, eds, 1998. *Citizenship and Nationality Status in the New Europe*. London: Institute for Public Policy Research, Sweet and Maxwell.

Pocock, J. G. A., 1998. The Ideal of Citizenship since Classical Times. In *The Citizenship Debates: A Reader*, Gershon Shafir, ed. Minneapolis: University of Minnesota Press, pp. 31–41.

Räthzel, Nora, 1991. Germany: One Race, One Nation? *Race and Class* 32(3): 31–48.

Schmitt, Carl, 1985. *Political Theology: Four Chapters on the Concept of Sovereignty*. Translated by George Schwab. Cambridge, MA: MIT Press.

Senders, Stefan, 1999. Coming Home: Aussiedler Repatriation, History, and Justice in Post-Cold War Berlin. PhD dissertation, Cornell University.

Shafir, Gershon, ed., 1998. *The Citizenship Debates: A Reader*. Minneapolis: University of Minnesota Press.

Soysal, Yasemin Nuhoglu, 1994. *Limits of Citizenship*. Chicago: University of Chicago Press.

Weber, Max, 1958. *The Protestant Ethic and the Spirit of Capitalism*. New York: Scribner.

Wilpert, Czarina, 1995. Ideological and Institutional Foundations for Racism in the Federal Republic of Germany. In *Racism and Migration in Europe*, John Wrench and John Solomos, eds. Oxford: Berg, pp. 67–81.

Wilpert, Czarina, 2003. Racism, Discrimination and Citizenship: The Need for Anti-Discrimination Legislation in the Federal Republic of Germany. In *Challenging Racism and Discrimination in Britain and Germany*, Zig Layton-Henry and Czarina Wilpert, eds. London: Palgrave Macmillan, pp. 245–269.

Young, Iris Marion, 1998. Polity and Group Difference. In *The Citizenship Debates: A Reader*, Gershon Shafir, ed. Minneapolis: University of Minnesota Press, pp. 263–290.

25

The Legal Production of Mexican/Migrant 'Illegality', 2005

Nicholas de Genova

History, as Lefebvre suggests, is made in the present, and this is so in a double sense. On the one hand, we are historical actors inescapably engaged in the everyday work of producing our own sociopolitical circumstances and potentially making history by transforming the social relations that constitute our world. On the other hand, this historicity is inextricable from our distinct location within the tangled historical trajectories that we have inherited, which implicate us in either reproducing or rectifying the enduring consequences of the past. Throughout this book, I have repeatedly emphasized the historical specificity of the sociopolitical climate that prevailed in the United States during the precise period of my research, my ethnographic "present." That moment was distinguished by a fiercely anti-immigrant politics of racist nativism, targeting undocumented Mexican migrants in particular, that manifested itself in legal campaigns and was ossified in the law. Likewise, I have located the living and open-ended historicity of my ethnographic interlocutors at the decisive conjuncture formed by ongoing histories – most prominently, the racialization of Mexicans and the spatialization of their transnational condition as labor migrants in relation to US nationalism and "American" national identity. In all of this, the US nation-state has played a predictably powerful and inordinately important role. Having devoted so much of this study to the task of producing an archive of the ever-fleeting "present," that contemporary moment at the end of the twentieth century when I realized my ethnographic research, now, from the vantage point of the present and with the urgency of present purposes as my guide, I turn to the task of reconstructing the history that only in retrospect may be most clearly seen to have framed some of the defining parameters of race, space, and "illegality" in Mexican Chicago. And such a history of Mexican labor migration to the United States, as will be seen here, is inseparable from a history of Mexican migrants' sociopolitical relation to the US state, its immigration policies, and the law.

Nicholas de Genova, The legal production of Mexican/migrant 'illegality'. In *Working the Boundaries: Race, Space, and 'Illegality' in Mexican Chicago* (Durham, North Carolina and London: Duke University Press, 2005), pp. 213–217, 226–249.

The Anthropology of Citizenship: A Reader, First Edition. Edited by Sian Lazar.

Mexican migration to the United States is distinguished by a seeming paradox that is seldom examined: while no other country has supplied nearly as many migrants to the United States as has Mexico since 1965, most major changes in US immigration law during this period have created ever more severe restrictions on the possibilities for "legal" migration from Mexico. Indeed, this apparent paradox presents itself in a double sense: on the one hand, apparently liberalizing immigration laws have in fact concealed significantly restrictive features, especially for Mexicans; on the other hand, ostensibly restrictive immigration laws purportedly intended to deter migration have nonetheless been instrumental in sustaining Mexican migration, but only by significantly restructuring its legal status – as undocumented. Beginning precisely when Mexican migration escalated dramatically in the 1960s – and ever since – persistent revisions in the law have effectively foreclosed the viable prospects for the great majority who would migrate from Mexico to do so in accord with the law and thus played an instrumental role in the production of a legally vulnerable undocumented workforce of "illegal aliens."

The argument of this chapter is not simply that the category "illegal alien" is a profoundly useful and profitable one that effectively serves to create and sustain a legally vulnerable – hence relatively tractable and thus "cheap" – reserve of labor. That proposition is already so well established as to be irrefutable. This is undeniably an important critical insight into the *effects* of migrant "illegality." But by itself, this crucial insight is insufficient, precisely insofar as it may leave unexamined, and thus naturalized, the fundamental *origin* of this juridical status in the law itself – what I am calling the legal production of migrant "illegality."

This chapter, therefore, discerns the historical specificity of contemporary Mexican migration to the United States as it has come to be located in the legal (political) economy of the US nation-state, and thereby constituted as an object of the law, especially since 1965. More precisely, this chapter interrogates the history of changes in US immigration law through the specific lens of how these revisions have had a distinct impact upon Mexicans in

particular. Only in light of this sociolegal history does it become possible to elaborate a critical perspective that is not complicit in the naturalization of Mexican migrants' "illegality" as a mere fact of life, the presumably transparent consequence of unauthorized border crossing or some other violation of immigration law.

In addition to simply designating a juridical status in relation to the US nation-state and its laws of citizenship, immigration, and naturalization, furthermore, migrant "illegality" signals a specifically *spatialized* sociopolitical condition. "Illegality" is lived through a palpable sense of deportability – which is to say, the possibility of deportation, the possibility of being removed from the space of the US nation-state. Deportability is decisive in the legal production of Mexican/migrant "illegality" and the militarized policing of the US–Mexico border, however, only insofar as some are deported in order that most may ultimately remain (undeported) – as workers, whose particular migrant status has been rendered "illegal." Thus, the legal production of "illegality" provides an apparatus for sustaining Mexican migrants' vulnerability and tractability – as workers – whose labor-power, because it is deportable, becomes an eminently disposable commodity. In the everyday life of Mexican migrants in innumerable places throughout the United States, "illegality" reproduces the practical repercussions of the physical border between the United States and Mexico across which undocumented migration is constituted. In this important sense, migrant "illegality" is a spatialized social condition inseparable from the particular ways that Mexican migrants are likewise racialized as "illegal aliens" – invasive violators of the law, incorrigible "foreigners," subverting the integrity of "the nation" and its sovereignty from *within* the space of the US nation-state. As a simultaneously spatialized and racialized social condition, migrant "illegality" is also a central feature of the ways that the "Mexican"-ness of Mexicans is thereby reconfigured in *racialized* relation to the hegemonic "national" identity of "American"-ness. Before examining these more contemporary dimensions of the historicity of Mexican migration to the United States, however, it is crucial to locate these conjunctures of race, space, and "illegality" in terms of an earlier history of the intersections of race and citizenship in the United States.

Citizenship, Race, and the Racialization of Nation-State Space

Each new form of state ... introduces ... its own particular administrative classification of discourses about space ... and people in space.
    Henri Lefebvre, *The Production of Space*

Citizenship appears to be a universal, distinctive, and central feature of modern political life. Literally every modern state deploys the institution of citizenship as the political means by which it publicly identifies its official members, assigns them an enduring legal status as "individuals," and disburses to them specific rights, entitlements, and obligations. In this way, a state attaches a specific population to its particular politically enclosed space, usually equated with a bounded territory. Citizens are thus defined as a state's insiders. Indeed, most modern states largely derive their legitimacy from a claim that their power over people actually rests precisely upon the sovereignty of those same people, taken together to comprise a particular, bounded collective body – usually called a "nation" – presumed to be not some random collection of individuals but rather imagined to be a coherent community of "citizens" (B. Anderson [1983] 1991; see Agamben 1998). In short, modern states need citizens: a state must constitute people as its citizens in order to justify its power over them.

If the institution of citizenship defines a kind of membership to the state and so appears within purportedly democratic states such as the United States to be broadly directed toward inclusion, it is likewise always also a definition by default of those who are *not* citizens, and thus outsiders, "foreigners," or "aliens." Despite the liberal and egalitarian conceits of universalistic inclusiveness, then, citizenship – in the guise of sovereign self-government by the insiders – justifies the coercive rule of the state over the excluded, purportedly on behalf of its proper citizens.

National identities – whether they be hegemonic or subjugated – can therefore be understood to be "national" only because they have been produced *politically*, in relation to processes of state formation and the inclusions and exclusions of citizenship (see Balibar 1991; Wallerstein 1991). Thus, a brief examination of the history of the institution of US citizenship – a consideration of how exactly it has been defined and refined in law, historically – reveals much about what have been the real inclusions and exclusions shaping a US national identity of "American"-ness.

The first United States Congress mandated in 1790 that a person who was to become a naturalized citizen of the United States must be "white."[1] Before this Naturalization Act of 1790, there had been no official formulation of who would be considered the citizens of the new nation. The original US Constitution (1787) had nowhere defined who were citizens or what specific entitlements, privileges, or immunities they would enjoy, leaving it a prerogative of the individual states. Thus, this was the first legislative determination of access to US citizenship, and in effect, the first official definition of US nationality. Revealingly, it passed with no debate or dissension whatsoever. Much as whiteness was never a transparent, stable, or natural category and has been the object of a history of relentless ideological production and re-elaboration, there was nonetheless an intrinsic link between whiteness and access to citizenship within the US nation-state since its inception. What is perhaps most remarkable about this whites-only policy for migrant access to US citizenship, however, is that it remained in effect until 1952, with the passage of the McCarran-Walter Immigration and Nationality Act, and its practical effects largely persisted until the landmark overhaul of US immigration law in 1965, which then did not go into effect until 1968. In other words, the substantive decoupling of racial whiteness from migrants' access to US citizenship has been in effect for only a few decades. For roughly three-fourths of US history, despite the eventual extension of an ostensible (but palpably inferior) citizenship to racially subordinated "minorities" within the United States, the law declared that migrants representing the great

majority of the world's people would continue
to be strictly ineligible for US citizenship simply
and solely because of their presumed "race."
From the very outset, a nation that fashioned
itself as an asylum for liberty would be, at best,
a promised land only for *white* liberty.

[...]

The Visibility of
"Illegal Immigrants" and
the Invisibility of the Law

Due to the critical function of deportation in
the maintenance of the revolving-door policy,
the tenuous distinction between "legal" and
"illegal" migration was deployed to stigma-
tize and regulate Mexican/migrant workers
for much of the twentieth century. Originally
by means of *qualitative* regulations, "illegality"
has long served as a constitutive dimension of
the specific racialized inscription of "Mexicans,"
in general, in the United States (see Ngai 2004).
In these respects, Mexican/migrant "illegality,"
per se, is not new. Indeed, this reflects
something of what James Cockcroft (1986)
has characterized as the special character of
Mexican migration to the United States:
Mexico has provided US capitalism with the
only "foreign" migrant labor reserve so suffi-
ciently flexible that it can neither be fully
replaced nor be completely excluded under
any circumstances. What is crucial, however,
is to critically examine how the US nation-state
has historically deployed a variety of different
tactics to systematically create and sustain
"illegality," and furthermore, has refined
those tactics to generate ever more severe
constraints for undocumented Mexican
migrants living and working in the United
States. After all, the history of legal debate
and action concerning immigration is, precisely, a *history*.

This chapter is centrally concerned with
the task of denaturalizing Mexican/migrant
"illegality," and locating its historical specificity as an irreducibly social fact, *produced* as
an effect of the practical materiality of the
law. By emphasizing the law's productivity,
I aim to trace the historical specificity of

migrant "illegality" within the contemporary
US Immigration and Naturalization regime.
Furthermore, as this book has been emphatically
concerned with Mexican migration in particular
(in contradistinction to some presumably
generic immigrant experience), I also underscore the history of a distinct "illegality" that
predominates specifically for Mexicans.
Mexican/migrant experiences certainly have
meaningful analogies with the sociopolitical
conditions of other undocumented migrations,
but such comparisons will be intellectually
compelling and politically cogent only if they
derive their force from precise accounts of the
particular intersections of historically specific
migrations and complex webs of "legality" and
"illegality."

Legislation, of course, is in fact only one
feature of "the law" (see Lee 1999), but my
discussion will principally focus on the more
narrowly legislative history affecting "illegality"
for Mexican migration, because this subject
itself has been sorely neglected, if not misrepre-
sented altogether. The history of immigration
law is nothing if not a contradictory succession
of rather intricate and calculated interventions.
Indeed, the complex history of lawmaking is
distinguished above all by its constitutive rest-
lessness and the relative incoherence of various
conflicting strategies, tactics, and compromises
that the US nation-state has implemented at
particular historical moments, precisely to
mediate the contradictions immanent in crises
and struggles around the subordination of
labor. Thus, rather than a master plan, US
immigration laws have served more as a kind
of permanent crisis management, tactically
supplying and refining the parameters of labor
discipline and coercion. As such, immigration
laws are part of the effort to make particular
migrations into disciplined and manageable
objects, but the ongoing fact of class conflict
ensures that such tactical interventions can
never be assured of success. In other words,
immigration laws, in their effort to manage the
migratory mobility of labor, are ensnared in a
struggle to subordinate the intractability
intrinsic to labor's constitutive role within
capital as well as the capitalist state – the sort
of "protracted and more or less concealed civil
war" depicted [earlier]. As John Holloway

suggests, "Once the categories of thought are understood as expressions not of objectified social relations but of the struggle to objectify them, then a whole storm of unpredictability blows through them. Once it is understood that money, capital, the state ..." (and here I would add, emphatically, the law) "are nothing but the struggle to form, to discipline, to structure what Hegel calls 'the sheer unrest of life,' then it is clear that their development can be understood only as practice, as undetermined struggle" (1995, 176; see Bonefeld 1995; Pashukanis [1929] 1989). And it is this appreciation of the law – as undetermined struggle – that best illuminates the history of the US immigration law, especially as it has devised for its target that characteristically mobile labor force comprised of Mexican migrants.

Migrant "illegality" is ultimately sustained not merely as an effect of such deliberate legal interventions, however, but also as the ideological effect of a discursive formation encompassing broader public debate and political struggle. Social science scholarship concerning undocumented Mexican migration is itself often ensnared in this same discursive formation of "illegality" (De Genova 2002). The material force of law, its instrumentality, its productivity of some of the most meaningful and salient parameters of sociopolitical life, and also its historicity – all of this tends to be strangely absent. Yet, with respect to the "illegality" of undocumented migrants, by not examining the actual operations of immigration law in generating the categories of differentiation among migrants' legal statuses, scholars largely take the law for granted. By not examining those operations over the course of their enactment, enforcement, and revision, furthermore, scholars effectively treat the law as transhistorical and thus falsely presume it to be fundamentally unchanging – thereby naturalizing a notion of what it means to transgress that law. The treatment of "illegality" as an undifferentiated, transhistorical thing-in-itself colludes with state power in creating a remarkable visibility of "illegal immigrants" swirling enigmatically around the stunning invisibility of the law.

Legislating Mexican "Illegality"

Before 1965, [...] there were absolutely no numerical quotas legislated to limit "legal" migration from Mexico, and no such quantitative restrictions had ever existed. The statutory imposition of previously unknown restrictions that reformulated "illegality" for Mexican migration in 1965 and thereafter, furthermore, transpired in the midst of an enthusiastic and virtually unrelenting *im*portation of Mexican/ migrant labor. The end of the Bracero Program in 1964 was an immediate and decisive prelude to the landmark reconfiguration of US immigration law in 1965. Thus, a deeply entrenched, well organized, increasingly diversified, and continuously rising stream of Mexican migration to the United States had already been accelerating before 1965. As a consequence of the successive changes in US immigration law since 1965, therefore, the apparently uniform application of numerical quotas to historically distinct and substantially incommensurable migrations has become central to an unprecedented, expanded, and protracted production of a more rigid, categorical "illegality" for Mexican/migrant workers in particular than had ever existed previously.

[...]

[...] The very character of migrant "illegality" for Mexicans was reconfigured by what was, in many respects, genuinely a watershed liberalization in 1965 that dismantled the US nation-state's openly discriminatory policy of immigration control. The Hart-Celler Act of 1965 (Public Law 89-236; 79 Stat. 911, which amended the Immigration and Nationalities Act of 1952, Public Law 82-414; 66 Stat. 163) comprised a monumental and ostensibly egalitarian overhaul of US immigration law. The 1965 reforms dramatically reversed the explicitly racist exclusion against Asian migrations, which had been in effect and only minimally mitigated since 1917 (or, in the case of the Chinese, since 1882). Likewise, the 1965 amendments abolished the draconian system of national-origins quotas for the countries of Europe, first enacted in 1921 and amplified in 1924. Predictably, then, the 1965 amendments have been typically celebrated as a liberal reform.

US immigration policy suddenly appeared to be chiefly distinguished by a broad inclusiveness, but with respect to Mexico, the outcome was distinctly and unequivocally restrictive. This same "liberal" reform (taking effect in 1968) established for the first time in US history an annual numerical quota to restrict "legal" migration from the Western Hemisphere. Indeed, this new cap came about as a concession to "traditional restrictionists" who fought to maintain the national-origins quota system, and as Aristide Zolberg puts it (1990, 321), "sought to deter immigration of blacks from the West Indies and 'browns' from south of the border more generally." Although hundreds of thousands already migrated from Mexico annually, and the number of apprehensions by the INS of "deportable alien" Mexicans was itself already 151,000 during the year before the enactment of the new quota, now no more than 120,000 "legal" migrants (excluding quota exemptions) would be permitted from all of the Western Hemisphere. Notably, the Eastern Hemisphere quota – 170,000 – was higher than the 120,000 cap set for the Western Hemisphere, but the individual countries of the Eastern Hemisphere were each limited to a maximum of 20,000, whereas the quota for the Western Hemisphere was available to any of the countries of the Americas on a first-come, first-served basis, subject to certification by the Department of Labor. Nevertheless, although no other country in the world was sending numbers of migrants at all comparable to the level of Mexican migration – and this has remained true, consistently, ever since – the numerical quota for "legal" migrants within the entire Western Hemisphere (i.e., the maximum quota within which Mexicans would have to operate) was now restricted to a level far below actual and already known numbers for migration from Mexico.

Following more than twenty years of enthusiastic "legal" contract-labor importation, orchestrated by the US state, a well-established influx of Mexican migrants to the United States was already accelerating before 1965. The severe restrictions legislated in 1965 necessarily meant that ever-greater numbers of Mexicans who were already migrating increasingly had no alternative other than to come as undocumented workers. Beginning in 1968 (when the new law took effect), the numbers of INS apprehensions of "deportable" Mexican nationals skyrocketed annually, leaping 40 percent in the first year. Although apprehension statistics are never reliable indicators of actual numbers of undocumented migrants, they clearly reveal a pattern of policing that was critical for the perpetuation of the revolving-door policy: the disproportionate majority of INS apprehensions were directed at surreptitious entries along the Mexican border, and this was increasingly so. [...] These persistent enforcement practices, and the statistics they produce, have made an extraordinary contribution to the common fallacy that Mexicans account for virtually all "illegal aliens." This effective equation of "illegal immigration" with unauthorized border-crossing, in particular, has served furthermore to continuously restage the US–Mexico border as the theater of an enforcement "crisis" that constantly rerenders *Mexican* as the distinctive national name for migrant "illegality."

[...]

Immigration law, of course, was not the only thing that was changing in 1965. It has been widely recognized that the sweeping 1965 revisions of immigration policy emitted from a generalized crisis of cold war-era liberalism, in which US imperialism's own most cherished "democratic" conceits were perpetually challenged. Taking shape in a context of the international relations imperatives that arose in the face of decolonization and national liberation movements abroad, this crisis was further exacerbated within the United States by the increasingly combative mass movement of African Americans in particular, and "minorities" generally, to denounce racial oppression and demand civil rights, which is to say, their rights of *citizenship*. Thus, US immigration policy was redesigned in 1965 explicitly to rescind the most glaringly discriminatory features of existing law. Furthermore, the end of the Bracero Program had been principally accomplished through the restrictionist efforts of organized labor, especially on the part of the predominantly Chicano and Filipino farmworkers' movement. The specific historical conjuncture from which the 1965 amendments emerged was therefore profoundly character-ized by political crises that manifested themselves as both domestic and international insur-gencies of racialized and colonized working peoples. So began a new production of an altogether new kind of "illegality" for migra-tions within the Western Hemisphere, with disproportionately severe consequences for transnationalized Mexican labor migrants in particular – a kind of transnational fix for political crises of labor subordination.

Tellingly, the explicit topic of "illegal immi-gration" had been almost entirely absent from the legislative debate leading to the 1965 law. David Reimers ([1985] 1992, 207–8) notes the irony that the US Congress "paid little attention to undocumented immigrants while reforming immigration policy in 1965," but "as early as 1969 [i.e., the first year after the 1965 law had taken effect] Congress began to investigate the increase in illegal immigration along the Mexican border." By 1976, however, legislative debate and further revisions in the law had suc-ceeded to produce "illegal immigration" as a whole new object within the economy of legal meanings in the US Immigration regime – the explicit "problem" toward which most of the major subsequent changes in immigration policy have been at least partly directed.

In 1976, within days of the national elections, a new immigration law was enacted (Public Law 94-571; 90 Stat. 2703). [...] Then, after legisla-tion in 1978 (Public Law 95-412; 92 Stat. 907) abolished the separate hemispheric quotas and established a unified worldwide maximum annual immigration cap of 290,000, the Refugee Act of 1980 (Public Law 96-212; 94 Stat. 107) further reduced that maximum global quota to 270,000, thereby diminishing the national quotas to an even smaller annual maximum of 18,200 "legal" migrants (excluding quota exemptions). In the space of less than twelve years, therefore, from July 1, 1968 (when the 1965 amendments went into effect), until the 1980 amendments became operative, US immigration law had been radically reconfigured for Mexicans.

Beginning with almost unlimited possibilities for "legal" migration from Mexico (literally no numerical restrictions, tempered only by qualitative preconditions that, in practice, had often been overlooked altogether), the law

had now severely restricted Mexico to an annual quota of 18,200 nonexempt "legal" migrants (as well as a strict system of qualitative preferences among quota exemptions, with weighted allocations for each preference). At a time when there were (conservatively) well over a million Mexican migrants coming to work in the United States each year, the over-whelming majority would have no option but to do so "illegally."

There is nothing matter-of-fact, therefore, about the "illegality" of undocumented migrants. "Illegality" (in its contemporary configuration) is the product of US immigration law – not merely in the generic sense that immigration law constructs, differentiates, and ranks various cat-egories of "aliens," but in the more profound sense that the history of deliberate interventions beginning in 1965 has entailed an active process of inclusion through illegalization (Calavita 1982, 13; see Calavita 1998, 531–32, 557; Hagan 1994, 82; Massey, Durand, and Malone 2002, 41–47; Portes 1978, 475). Indeed, the legal production of "illegality" has made an object of Mexican migration in particular, in ways both historically unprecedented and dis-proportionately deleterious.

As the culmination of years of recommen-dations, a new kind of landmark in the history of US immigration law was achieved in 1986 with the passage of the Immigration Reform and Control Act, or IRCA (Public Law 99-603; 100 Stat. 3359), because its principal explicit preoccupation was undocumented migration. Once again, the law instituted a legalization procedure for those undocumented workers who had reliably (and without evident interruption) served their apprenticeships in "illegality," while intensifying the legal vulnerability of others. Indeed, IRCA provided for a selective "amnesty" and adjustment of the immigration status of some undocumented migrants, while it foreclosed almost all options of legalization for those who did not qualify, and for all who would arrive thereafter. [...]

The Immigration Reform and Control Act of 1986 also established for the first time federal sanctions against employers who knowingly hired undocumented workers. Nevertheless, the law established an "affirmative defense" for all employers who could demonstrate that they had complied with a routine verification procedure. Simply by keeping a form on file attesting to the document check, without any requirement that they determine the legitimacy of documents presented, employers would be immune from any penalty. In practice, this meant that the employer sanctions provisions generated a flourishing industry in fraudulent documents, which merely imposed further expenses and greater legal liabilities upon the migrant workers themselves, while supplying an almost universal protection for employers (Chávez 1992, 169–71; Cintrón 1997, 51–60; Coutin 2000, 49–77; Mahler 1995, 159–87; see US Department of Labor 1991, 124). Likewise, given that the employer sanctions would require heightened raids on workplaces, inspectors were required to give employers a three-day warning before inspections of their hiring records, in order to make it "pragmatically easy" for employers to comply with the letter of the law (Calavita 1992, 169). In order to avoid fines associated with these sanctions, therefore, employers would typically fire or temporarily discharge workers known to be undocumented before a raid. In light of the immensely profitable character of exploiting the legally vulnerable (hence, "cheap") labor of undocumented workers, moreover, the schedule of financial penalties imposed by IRCA simply amounted to a rather negligible operating cost for an employer found to be in violation of the law. Thus, IRCA's provisions primarily served to introduce greater instability into the labor-market experiences of undocumented migrants and thereby instituted an internal revolving door. What are putatively employer sanctions, then, have actually aggravated the migrants' conditions of vulnerability and imposed new penalties upon the undocumented workers themselves.

[...]

The Caprice of Sovereignty and the Tyranny of the Rule of Law

When undocumented migrants are criminalized under the sign of the "illegal alien," theirs is an "illegality" that does not involve a crime against anyone; rather, migrant "illegality" stands only for a transgression against the sovereign authority of the nation-state. With respect to the politics of immigration and naturalization, notably, sovereignty (as instantiated in the unbridled authoritarianism of border policing, detention, deportation, and so forth) assumes a pronouncedly absolutist character (Simon 1998). Such an absolutist exercise of state power, of course, relies decisively upon a notion of "democratic" consent, whereby the state enshrouds itself with the political fiction of the social contract in order to authorize itself to act on behalf of its sovereign citizens, or at least "the majority." This circular logic of sovereignty conveniently evades the racialized history of the law of citizenship, just as it sidesteps altogether the laborious history in the United States that has produced a "majority" racialized as "white." The racialized figure of Mexican/migrant "illegality," therefore, can be instructively juxtaposed to what is, in effect, the racialized character of the law and the "democratic" state, itself. Because the political culture of liberalism in the United States already posits and requires "the rule of law" as a figure for "the nation," the instrumental role of law in the work of racialization reveals its vital stake in the whiteness at the heart of what comes to be glorified as "American" sovereignty and "national culture."

In the dominant discourses of "immigration control," state sovereignty and "national culture" are invariably conjoined. Anti-immigration stalwart Alan Simpson (former US senator from Wyoming), for example, supplies a classic articulation: "Uncontrolled immigration is one of the greatest threats to the future of this nation, to American values, traditions, institutions, to our public culture, and to our way of life ... we intend to clearly exercise the first and primary responsibility of a sovereign nation which is to control our borders" (quoted in Harris 1995, 85). The standard cant of right-wing nativists in the United States of the late twentieth century incessantly invoked the menace of a stark and immanent immigrant peril facing this "American" national "culture" – its values and institutions. One such foreboding image was that of an inassimilable and inevitably separatist Mexican "Quebec" rapidly arising in the southwestern United States (Barrera 1979, 2; Rodríguez 1997).

Former CIA director William Colby raised the specter of this "Spanish-speaking Quebec" in 1978, insisting that Mexican migration posed a greater threat to the United States than did the Soviet Union (Cockcroft 1986, 39). During the nativist convulsions of the mid-1990s, in an article prominently featured in the *Atlantic Monthly*, immigration historian David Kennedy of Stanford University invoked the same metaphor:

Mexican-Americans ... will have sufficient coherence and critical mass in a defined region so that, if they choose, they can preserve their distinctive culture indefinitely. They could also eventually undertake to do what no previous immigrant group could have dreamed of doing: challenge the existing cultural, political, legal, commercial, and educational systems to change fundamentally not only the language but also the very institutions in which they do business. ... In the process, Americans could be pitched into a soul-searching redefinition of fundamental ideas such as the meaning of citizenship and national identity. ... There is no precedent in American history for these possibilities. ... The possibility looms that in the next generation or so we will see a kind of Chicano Quebec take shape in the American Southwest. (1996, 52–68)

Notably, Kennedy titled his essay's penultimate subsection with a question: "What Does the Future Hold?" On the opposite page, that question was juxtaposed to a color photograph depicting a mass protest mobilization, budding with brown faces and bristling with Mexican flags. (The caption identified Los Angeles – a march against California's anti-immigrant ballot initiative Proposition 187, which specifically targeted undocumented migrants and their children.) The concluding subsection from which the quote is extracted, furthermore, was ominously (and revealingly) called "The Reconquista." Clearly, for Kennedy, the immigration question had become a decidedly *Mexican* problem, in which what was at stake was nothing less than the prospect that the US nation-state might see its own history of conquest subverted through a reversal of its imperial fortunes. Baldly echoing the "Save Our State" rhetoric of Proposition 187's

campaign against "illegal immigration," Kennedy closed his essay with an appeal to "save our country." Who was, and who was not, included in that national *we* appears to have been long settled by conquest and colonization.

"Illegality" has thus been rendered to be so effectively inseparable from the Mexican/migrant experience, historically, that it should hardly come as a surprise that during the mid-1990s in Mexican Chicago, one could find for sale bumper stickers simulating an Illinois license plate that proudly announced, "100% Mojado" ("100% Wetback"), or caps and T-shirts that declared defiantly: "Ilegal – ¿Y Qué?" ("Illegal – So What?"). Despite such audacious Mexican/migrant expressions of their "illegal" identity, however, the considerable legalization provisions of the 1986 Amnesty had afforded Mexican migrants a rare opportunity to "straighten out" or "fix" [*arreglar*] their status that few who were eligible opted to disregard. The immigration status of "legal permanent resident" vastly facilitated many of the transnational migrant aspirations that had been hampered or curtailed by the onerous risks and cumbersome inconveniences of undocumented border crossing. By 1990, however, 75.6 percent of all "legal" Mexican migrants in the state of Illinois notably remained noncitizens (Paral 1997, 8). In other words, the rush to become "legal" migrants did not translate into an eagerness to naturalize as US citizens. By the mid-1990s, nonetheless, amid the political climate of heightened nativism and anti-immigrant racism that was widely associated with the passage of California's vindictive Proposition 187, Mexican migrants began to seriously consider the prospect of naturalizing as US citizens in much greater proportions than had ever been true historically. Whereas in 1995 only 19 percent of Mexican migrants eligible to become US citizens opted to do so, by 2001 the naturalization rate among eligible Mexicans had risen remarkably to 34 percent (Margon 2004).

During the spring of 1995, Meche, the worker at Die-Hard Tool and Die who had relocated from California only two years earlier (when the anti-immigration campaign had been gathering steam), was quite unequivocally determined to become a US citizen. She had already submitted her application to the INS and was regularly attending citizenship classes on Saturdays. "Who discovered America?" Meche laughed sarcastically as she mimicked the inane substance of the citizenship exam for which she was studying – "Christopher Columbus." Meche had no romantic illusions about "becoming an American"; rather, she was very clear about the pragmatic reasons for naturalizing. Meche had a sister who was still undocumented, and she hoped to be able help her sister to get her papers "straightened out." Notably, her sister was still living in California, now notorious for the odious Proposition 187, but was considering a move to Chicago. "Lots of people are coming from California now," Meche affirmed. Even as a "legal" migrant, Meche was also quite reasonably concerned about her own prospects in the United States. "Maybe the laws are changing," she hypothesized, "and if I get laid off, maybe they won't give me any unemployment money if I'm not a citizen." Furthermore, living in the two-thirds-majority Mexican suburb of Cicero, Meche was painfully aware of the extent to which noncitizenship meant political disenfranchisement. "I want to vote," she declared, "because my kids asked me why I can't vote, and why the only ones who can vote in Cicero are the old people, the citizens." Referring to recent electoral struggles in the town where she lived, which were quite baldly racialized, she explained further, "So a white person won the election with ten thousand votes, and the Mexican lost because he only had three thousand. The white people don't want to pay taxes for the schools, and we [Mexicans] can't do anything about it."

Later that year, when I was teaching English at the Pilsen community organization Casa del Pueblo, Faustino, a migrant in his fifties originally from a small town in San Luis Potosí who had been in Chicago for twenty-six years, initiated a conversation about citizenship that expressed strikingly similar concerns.

A lot of people are coming here for citizenship classes. Many say that the government is cutting out our rights and wants to try to deprive us and rob us of many of our rights and benefits, and so they're becoming citizens now to protect themselves. And it makes sense. All you have to do is look at the news. There are rumors that later they'll even deny us our social security pensions, that all this is happening little by little. There's a lot of racism against us, and they'll take anything they can from us. I've been here twenty-six years – I'm already entitled to something, I have my rights [ya tengo mis derechos]. Many of us have been here a long time working, but they want to take away the rights we've earned. So you start to worry. At the factory where I am now, I've been working five years with no health insurance for me or my family. We don't have anything. And when I retire I have my right to a pension, but maybe they'll try to take it from me.

Faustino went on to contrast hardworking migrants such as himself to "those who want welfare but don't have any right to it [quieren pero no tienen el derecho]," citing the example of young women whom he knew – "mostly they're Tejanas [Texas Mexicans], and they're always in the cantinas." These US-born Mexican women had "three, four, and five children." He contended, "They have them just to get the money. That money is supposed to be for your food and rent ... And because of them, the government wants to take away our rights that we've worked for. It's not right. But that's why I'm thinking about becoming a citizen." Resembling many Mexican migrants' discourses about Blacks and Puerto Ricans, Faustino insinuated that it was the laziness, debauchery, and welfare "abuse" of impoverished US-citizen Mexicans that was to blame for the persecution of migrant Mexicans, whose rightful entitlements were now in jeopardy (see De Genova and Ramos-Zayas 2003). Meaningfully coupled with his allegations of others' undeservingness, Faustino nonetheless also asserted, though agonistically, a positive politics of citizenship that affirmed that Mexican migrants had earned their "rights" through their labor and thus ought to be entitled to various social welfare benefits. His considerations of naturalization, notably, had been instigated only by the greater injustice of a system that sought to deny Mexican migrants what was already rightfully theirs.

As the veritable culmination of precisely the anti-immigrant campaigns that Meche and Faustino were confronting, the Illegal Immigration Reform and Immigrant Responsibility Act of 1996 (Public Law 104-208; 110 Stat. 3009) was quite simply the most punitive legislation to date concerning undocumented migration in particular (see Fragomen 1997, 438). It included extensive provisions for criminalizing, apprehending, detaining, fining, deporting, and also imprisoning a wide array of "infractions" that significantly broadened and elaborated the qualitative scope of the law's production of "illegality" for undocumented migrants and others associated with them. It also barred undocumented migrants from receiving a variety of social security benefits and federal student financial aid. In fact, this so-called Immigration Reform (signed September 30, 1996) was heralded by extensive anti-immigrant stipulations in the Antiterrorism and Effective Death Penalty Act, AEDPA (Public Law 104-132, 110 Stat. 1214, signed into law on April 24, 1996), as well as in the so-called Welfare Reform, passed as the Personal Responsibility and Work Opportunity Reconciliation Act (Public Law 104-193, 110 Stat. 2105; signed August 22, 1996). The AEDPA entailed an "unprecedented restriction of the constitutional rights and judicial resources traditionally afforded to legal resident aliens" (Solbakken 1997, 1382). The Welfare Reform enacted dramatically more stringent and prolonged restrictions on the eligibility of the great majority of "legal" migrants for virtually all benefits, defined as broadly as possible, available under federal law, and also authorized states to similarly restrict benefits programs. Without belaboring the extensive details of these acts, which did not otherwise introduce new quantitative restrictions, it suffices to say that their expansive provisions (concerned primarily with enforcement and penalties for undocumented presence) were truly unprecedented in the severity with which they broadened the qualitative purview and intensified the ramifications of migrant "illegality." Given the already well-entrenched practices that focused enforcement against undocumented migration disproportionately upon Mexican migrants,

there can be little doubt that this act, at least before September 11, 2001, likewise weighed inordinately upon Mexicans. Indeed, the language of this legislation, with regard to enforcement, was replete with references to "the" border, a telltale sign that could only portend a further disciplining of Mexican migration.

The Border Spectacle

Mexican migration in particular has been rendered synonymous with the US nation-state's purported "loss of control" of its borders and has supplied the preeminent pretext for what has in fact been a continuous intensification of increasingly militarized control (Andreas 1998 and 2000; Dunn 1996; Nevins 2002; see Chávez 2001; Durand and Massey 2003; Heyman 1999; Kearney 1991). And it is precisely the border that provides the exemplary theater for staging the spectacle of "the illegal alien" that the law produces. Indeed, throughout the twentieth century, US immigration enforcement efforts consistently and disproportionately targeted the US–Mexico border, sustaining a zone of relatively high tolerance within the interior. "Illegality" looks most like a positive transgression – and can thereby be equated with the behavior of Mexican migrants rather than the instrumental action of immigration law – precisely when it is subjected to policing at the border. The elusiveness of the law, and its relative invisibility in producing "illegality," requires this spectacle of enforcement at the border, which renders a racialized Mexican/migrant "illegality" visible, and lends it the commonsensical air of a natural fact.

The operation of the revolving door at the border that is necessary to sustain the "illegality" effect always combines an increasingly militarized spectacle of apprehensions, detentions, and deportations with the banality of a virtually permanent importation of undocumented migrant labor. This was remarkably illustrated in the narrative that emerged when I interviewed Carlos [...] with his wife Rosario in their home. I asked about their experiences in coming to the United States. Carlos joked that he had come on vacation, but decided not to go back. "But you had your adventures, when you crossed," Rosario prompted him. Carlos simply asked her, "Adventures?" Rosario continued (now addressing me), "Because they locked him up in jail – he was in jail!" Carlos clarified that he had been apprehended in 1976 when he sought to reenter the United States after a workplace raid that had led to his deportation, but noted simply that when he had first crossed, ten years earlier, it had been "really easy." Now, however, Carlos began to relate the story in earnest:

> I went three months in that adventure because Immigration had pushed me back all the way to Mazatlán, Sinaloa – and then I turned back again for Tijuana. [...] I didn't want to go home, because I didn't have even a nickel, and I was wearing my work clothes, and I was really filthy. So from there, I just turned back around and it took me like five weeks to get to Tijuana, hitching rides. And then I crossed, and they grabbed me, and they had me two months in jail, in Chula Vista ... Chula Vista, California, right there stuck on the line [at the border]. They were saying that I was the *coyote* [the migrant guide, or "smuggler"]. Because they caught us, some thirty people, and I told them, "Save yourselves, whoever can!" And everyone ran, and many saved themselves – they slipped right out from under the feet of the Immigration! But me, they succeeded to grab! And they said that I was the one who was bringing them across, and no, no, I wasn't. I was set back two months there, locked up. [...] The first days, like the first eight days, it was hard ... They had me in a cell by myself, in a tiny little room, just me, I stayed in there alone. And no, no, I couldn't even lie down because it was tiny. It was like a punishment cell. [...] It was so that I would say that I was the one who was bringing the people across. They had me like a month there in that cell. I slept sitting up because I couldn't lie down. And daily they pulled me out for a confession, three times a day, every day. And they were asking me the same questions ... but I couldn't say anything else because I didn't have anything else. Then when they pulled me out of there from that cell, they threw me in the one they called "the farm" [*la granja*] – and it is a farm, and they have it full of the people they go catching! And there they had me another month. [...]

And when I got out, they dumped me in Tijuana, and from there, I was already headed home. Because I didn't want to come here any more, not any more! I didn't have any thoughts of going back because of what had happened to me, and ... Well, it turns out that I was on the international bridge when a few people arrived – a van passed, and they knew me. I didn't know them. [...] I said, "You know what? I was just three months here, and now I'm a wreck, and I'm going home now." And he says, "No, wait right here for me, right at this same place, wait for me. I'm going back to Los Angeles and I'll be back in a little while." And from there he went and took one of his brothers across, and then he came back and said, "Let's go!" and "Here, use my brother's green card." And the brother didn't look anything like me, nothing! He was dark [*moreno*] and I'm a little more, more white [*más blanco*]. [...] No, well, so there we went, and crossing the bridge, I told the Immigration, "Here you go, I have it here. It's just the two of us, him and me," and he [the Border guard] just said, "I caught it," and he said, "It's not necessary, go ahead." And so we followed the road up to San Clemente, and there's another guard station, another checkpoint, and just as we were arriving – like some ninety feet before arriving, they left, and we passed freely. I arrived easily in Los Angeles with someone else's green card. And then from there, I decided to come here [to Chicago] because [...] because there were more jobs here that paid better, and there, in the ten years I spent, I almost always was earning the minimum wage, or two bits more than the minimum.

Carlos's narrative bears a distinct resemblance to those of many other Mexican migrants (especially men), in which stories of great hardship commonly alternate with accounts of quite easy passage (see Chávez 1992; Kearney 1991). It was not at all uncommon, furthermore, for Mexican migrants to tellingly conclude their border-crossing narratives – again, as Felipe also did – with remarks about low wages. The fact that Carlos was being originally deported in his filthy work clothes, of course, was yet another decisive detail. These narratives of the adventures, mishaps, as well as genuine calamities of border crossing seem to be almost inevitably punctuated with accounts of life in the United States that are singularly distinguished by arduous travail and abundant exploitation.

If Mexican/migrant "illegality" is truly produced by the law and *not* through "crime and punishment" at the border, this legal production of "illegality" nevertheless requires the spectacle of enforcement at the US–Mexico border. The border spectacle is necessary precisely in order for the spatial difference between the United States and Mexico to be socially inscribed upon Mexican migrants themselves, as their distinctive spatialized (and racialized) status as "illegal aliens," as Mexicans "out of place." The production of their difference in terms of both race and space is crucial, therefore, in the constitution of the class specificity of Mexican labor migration.

The "illegality" effect of protracted vulnerability in everyday life has to be recreated more often than simply on the occasion of crossing the border, however. Indeed, as noted above, the 1986 legislation that instituted employer sanctions was tantamount to an extension of the revolving door to the internal labor market of each workplace where undocumented migrant workers were employed. This became quite manifest on one occasion at the Czarnina and Sons factory. Karina, a Mexican raised in the United States, was in her mid-twenties and worked as the secretarial assistant to the personnel boss. On one occasion, she casually mentioned: "I'm calling Immigration to check on whether some of these people are legal residents." I was surprised, and said plainly, "I thought you hire illegal people here." Karina replied, now more theatrically, in a half-heartedly clandestine tone: "We *do*! But we're not supposed to, and we could get fined if we ever got caught, and I could get in a lot of trouble for not checking them when they look so fake. Look at some of these! They're really bad! You can tell they're fakes." "You're checking for Mexican people?" I asked, hoping to make some appeal to any residual sense of loyalty she might have had to people who, like her own parents, had migrated from Mexico. "Everybody! This one's Polish, this one's Mexican," Karina replied, "You don't think I should do it?" Now, careful to protect myself, just as Karina was simply hoping to safeguard

her own intermediary position in the larger structure, I rephrased my own implicit argument: "I'm not sayin' what you should or shouldn't do, *pero* ..." Now, switching to Spanish to perform my own semitheatrical clandestinity, I added, "But people have to work, they need the jobs." Karina admitted, "I know, but ... at least they should give me something that *looks* good – not this stuff where you can see the jagged edge around the picture, and you can see where they just stuck it on there! Because I can get in trouble for accepting it – at least make it look good, not this phony-looking stuff."

Much like their employers' policing of the jagged edges of their fraudulent "papers," the policing of public spaces outside of the workplace likewise served to discipline Mexican/migrant workers by exacerbating their sense of ever-present vulnerability (Chávez 1992; Heyman 1998; Rouse 1992; and see Coutin 2000; Mahler 1995). The lack of a driver's license, for instance, was typically presumed by police in Chicago to automatically indicate a Latino's more generally undocumented condition (Mahler 1995). In the Pilsen neighborhood, it was a commonplace to hear the menacing voices of police amplified over the loudspeakers of their patrol cars. On one occasion, outside the window of my apartment, I heard the police detaining a car. I peered out to see a tall, burly white cop bellowing to the Latino driver of the detained vehicle: "Do you have a license? Then why are you driving? Park this car or I'll take you to jail!" And it was precisely such forms of everyday "illegality" that confronted many Mexican migrants with quite everyday forms of surveillance and repression. During the spring of 1995, I was teaching an ESL course for a vocational training program intended to prepare people for work in hotel kitchens. Blanca, a migrant in her thirties from the city of Guadalajara who had been in the United States eight years, arrived late and reported that she had just been pulled over by the police. As she had no driver's license, nor any insurance card, the cop had written her a $200 ticket. Blanca had not been asked for a cash bribe to "settle" the fine for the infractions, but this incident inspired Estela to relate how, on multiple occasions, police had demanded payments of $100 in cash from her, as well as others she knew who were undocumented migrants without driver's licenses. Indeed, among undocumented migrants, similar stories were ubiquitous. Notably, although she had only spent five years in the United States, Estela was a US citizen, born to Mexican/migrant parents in Texas before the family returned to the small town in Durango where she had grown up. Estela told us that she had personally had to pay several hundred dollars in bribes of this sort. While her US citizenship had hardly shielded her from this pervasive sort of casual police corruption and abuse, it was precisely Estela's status as a Mexican/migrant woman who spoke virtually no English that facilitated the police's cynical presumption that she was legally vulnerable and therefore easily exploitable.

The illegalities of everyday life were often, literally, instantiated by the lack of various forms of state-issued documentation that sanction one's place within or outside of the strictures of the law (Cintrón 1997; Coutin 2000; Hagan 1994; Mahler 1995). But, as was already evident in Estela's case, there are also those illegalities that more generally pertain to the heightened policing directed at the bodies, movements, and spaces of the poor, and especially those racialized as not-white. On one occasion, my friend Salvador and his two brothers, migrants in their early twenties from a small town in Puebla, were waiting for their sister in the parking lot of a museum. A white man whose car was parked nearby decided that their mere presence was threatening and reported to the police that they were "gang members" and wanted to rob him. They were arrested for "loitering," and their protestations were met with the convenient additional charge of "resisting arrest." Many Mexican migrants' subjection to such quotidian forms of intimidation and harassment was ultimately intensified by their undocumented condition. In effect, there was virtually no way for undocumented migrants to not be always already culpable of some kind of legal infraction. Because any confrontation with the scrutiny of legal authorities was already tempered by the discipline imposed by their susceptibility for deportation, these mundane forms of harassment likewise served to relentlessly reinforce Mexican migrants' distinctive vulnerability as a highly exploitable workforce.

Yet the disciplinary operation of an apparatus for the everyday production of migrant "illegality" is never simply reducible to a quest to achieve the putative goal of deportation. There of course has never been sufficient funding for the INS to evacuate the country of undocumented migrants. Indeed, the Border Patrol has never been equipped even to "hold the line" and actually keep the undocumented out. Rather, it is *deportability*, and not deportation per se, that has historically rendered Mexican labor to be a distinctly disposable commodity. Douglas Massey and his research associates (2002, 41, 45) have understandably characterized the effective operation of US immigration policy toward Mexico since 1965 – "the era of undocumented migration" – as "a de facto guest-worker program." This is an inevitable and indisputable conclusion for any sober analysis of the facts. Here, however, one must also underscore what have been the real *effects* of a history of instrumental revisions in US immigration law. Presumptively characterizing the law's consequences as "unintended" or "unanticipated" amounts to an unwitting apologetics for the state that is even more reckless than conspiratorial guessing games about the good or bad "intentions" of lawmakers. In contrast, the challenge of critical inquiry and meaningful social analysis commands that one ask: What indeed do these policies *produce*?

At least until the events of September 11, 2001, the very existence of the enforcement branches of the now-defunct INS were always premised upon the persistence of undocumented migration and a continued presence of migrants whose undocumented legal status has long been equated with the disposable (deportable), ultimately "temporary" character of the commodity that is their labor-power. These contradictions were memorably illustrated when my friend María's grandmother, an elderly migrant visiting Chicago from California for the first time, related the story of how her husband had once come as an undocumented migrant to work in Chicago. When he decided that he had had enough, and that he wanted to return home to Mexico, he proceeded to turn himself in to the INS. He announced that he was none other than an "illegal alien," and requested that they deport him. His hopes that they would pay for his trip home, however, proved to be unfounded; the INS refused his repeated requests. Much as he tried to denounce himself as "illegal," the INS refused him the right to be deported. In its real effects, then, and regardless of competing political agendas or stated aims, the true social role of much of US immigration law enforcement (and the Border Patrol, in particular) has historically been to maintain and superintend the operation of the border as a revolving door, simultaneously implicated in importation as much as (in fact, far more than) deportation. Sustaining the border's viability as a filter for the unequal transfer of value (Kearney 1998; see Andreas 2000, 29–50), such enforcement rituals also perform the spectacle that fetishizes migrant "illegality" as a seemingly objective "thing in itself."

With the advent of the antiterrorism state and a deadly eruption of genuinely global imperialist ambition, the politics of immigration and border enforcement in the United States has been profoundly reconfigured under the aegis of a remarkably parochial US nationalism and an unbridled nativism, above all manifest in the complete absorption of the INS into the new Department of Homeland Security on March 1, 2003. Nevertheless, given US employers' intractable dependency on the abundant availability of legally vulnerable migrant labor, the Bush administration proposed on January 7, 2004, a new scheme for the expressly temporary regularization of undocumented migrant workers' "illegal" status and for the expansion of a Bracero-style migrant labor contracting system orchestrated directly by the US state. Such a legalization plan aspires only toward a more congenial formula by which to sustain the permanent availability of disposable (and still deportable) migrant labor, but under conditions of dramatically enhanced ("legal") regimentation and control. Like all previous forms of migrant legalization, and indeed, in accord with the larger history of the law's productions and revisions of "illegality" itself, such an immigration

"reform" can be forged only through an array of political struggles that are truly transnational in scale and ultimately have as their stakes the subordination – and insubordination – of labor.

NOTE

1   1st Cong., Sess. II; *Statutes at Large of the United States of America*, 1789–1873 (17 vols., Washington, DC, 1850–73), Ch. 3, 1 Stat. 103 (Act of March 26, 1790); see Haney López 1996.

REFERENCES

Agamben, Giorgio, 1998. *Homo sacer: Sovereign power and bare life*. Stanford, CA: Stanford University Press.

Anderson, Benedict, 1991 [1983]. *Imagined Communities: Reflections on the origins and spread of nationalism*, rev. edn. New York: Verso.

Andreas, Peter, 1998. The U.S. immigration control offensive: Constructing an image of order on the southwest border. In *Crossings: Mexican immigration in inter-disciplinary perspectives*, Marcelo M. Suárez-Orozco, ed. Cambridge, MA: Harvard University Press, pp. 343–356.

Andreas, Peter, 2000. *Border Games: Policing the US–Mexico Divide*. Ithaca, NY: Cornell University Press.

Balibar, Etienne, 1991. The nation form: History and ideology. In *Race, Nation, Class: Ambiguous identities*. Etienne Balibar and Immanuel Wallerstein, eds. New York: Verso, pp. 86–106.

Balibar, Etienne, and Immanuel Wallerstein, 1991. *Race, Nation, Class: Ambiguous identities*. New York: Verso.

Barrera, Mario, 1979. *Race and Class in the Southwest: A theory of racial inequality*. Notre Dame, IN: University of Notre Dame Press.

Bonefeld, Werner, 1995. Capital as subject and the existence of labour. In *Emancipating Marx: Open Marxism Vol. III*, Werner Bonefeld, Richard Gunn, John Holloway, and Kosmos Psychopedis, eds. East Haven, CT: Pluto, pp. 182–212.

Calavita, Kitty, 1982. California's "employer sanctions": The case of the disappearing law. Research Report Series, Number 39. San Diego: Center for US-Mexican Studies, University of California.

Calavita, Kitty, 1998. Immigration, law, and marginalization in a global economy: Notes from Spain. *Law and Society Review* 32(3): 529–566.

Chávez, Leo R., 1992. *Shadowed Lives: Undocumented immigrants in American society.* Fort Worth, TX: Harcourt, Brace, and Jovanovich.

Chávez, Leo R., 2001. *Covering Immigration: Popular images and the politics of the nation.* Berkeley: University of California Press.

Cintrón, Ralph, 1997. *Angels' Town: Chero ways, gang life, and rhetorics of the everyday.* Boston: Beacon.

Cockcroft, James D., 1986. *Outlaws in the Promised Land: Mexican immigrant workers and America's future.* New York: Grove.

Coutin, Susan Bibler, 2000. *Legalizing Moves: Salvadoran immigrants' struggle for U.S. residency.* Ann Arbor: University of Michigan Press.

De Genova, Nicholas, 2002. Migrant "illegality" and deportability in everyday life. *Annual Review of Anthropology* 31: 419–447.

De Genova, Nicholas, and Ana Y. Ramos-Zayas, 2003. *Latino Crossings: Mexicans, Puerto Ricans, and the politics of race and citizenship.* New York: Routledge.

Dunn, Timothy J., 1996. *The Militarization of the U.S.–Mexico Border, 1978–1992: Low-intensity conflict doctrine comes home.* Austin: Center for Mexican American Studies Books and University of Texas Press.

Durand, Jorge, and Douglas S. Massey, 2003. The costs of contradiction: U.S. border policy, 1986–2000. *Latino Studies* 1(2): 235–252.

Fragomen, Jr., Austin T., 1997. The Illegal Immigration Reform and Immigrant Responsibility Act of 1996: An overview. *International Migration Review* 31(2): 438–460.

Hagan, Jacqueline Maria, 1994. *Deciding to be Legal: A Maya community in Houston.* Philadelphia: Temple University Press.

Haney López, Ian F., 1996 *White by Law: the legal construction of race.* New York: New York University Press.

Harris, Nigel, 1995. *The New Untouchables: immigration and the new world worker.* New York: I. B. Tauris.

Heyman, Josiah McC., 1998. State effects on labor: The INS and undocumented immigrants at the Mexico–United States border. *Critique of Anthropology* 18(2): 157–180.

Heyman, Josiah McC., 1999. State escalation of force: A Vietnam/US–Mexico border analogy. In *States and Illegal Practices,* Josiah McC. Heyman, ed. New York: Berg, pp. 285–314.

Holloway, John, 1995. From scream of refusal to scream of power: The centrality of work. In *Emancipating Marx: Open Marxism 3,* Werner Bonefeld, Richard Gunn, John Holloway and Kosmos Psychopedis, eds. East Haven, CT: Pluto, pp. 155–181.

Kearney, Michael, 1991. Borders and boundaries of states and self at the end of empire. *Journal of Historical Sociology* 4(1): 52–74.

Kearney, Michael, 1998. Peasants in the fields of value: Revisiting rural class differentiation in transnational perspective. Unpublished ms., Department of Anthropology, University of California at Riverside.

Kennedy, David M., 1996. Can we still afford to be a nation of immigrants? *Atlantic Monthly* 278(5): 52–68.

Lee, Erika, 1999. Immigrants and immigration law: A state of the field assessment. *Journal of American Ethnic History* 18(4): 85–114.

Mahler, Sarah J., 1995. *American Dreaming: Immigrant life on the margins.* Princeton, NJ: Princeton University Press.

Margon, Sarah, 2004. *Naturalization in the United States.* Washington, DC: Migration Policy Institute, Migration Information Source, May 1.

Massey, Douglas S., Jorge Durand and Nolan J. Malone, 2002. *Beyond Smoke and Mirrors: Mexican immigration in an era of economic integration.* New York: Russell Sage Foundation.

Nevins, Joseph, 2002. *Operation Gatekeeper: The rise of the "illegal alien" and the making of the U.S.–Mexico boundary.* New York: Routledge.

Ngai, Mae M., 2004. *Impossible Subjects: Illegal aliens and the making of modern America.* Princeton, NJ: Princeton University Press.

Paral, Rob, 1997. *Public Aid and Illinois Immigrants: Serving non-citizens in the Welfare Reform era: A Latino Institute report.* Chicago: Illinois Immigrant Policy Project.

Pashukanis, Evgeny B., 1989 [1929]. *Law and Marxism: A general theory towards a critique of the fundamental juridical concepts.* Worcester, UK: Pluto.

Perea, Juan F., ed., 1997. *Immigrants Out! The new nativism and the anti-immigrant impulse in the United States.* New York: New York University Press.

Portes, Alejandro, 1978. Toward a structural analysis of illegal (undocumented) immigration. *International Migration Review* 12(4): 469–484.

Reimers, David M., 1992 [1985]. *Still the Golden Door: The Third World comes to America*, 2nd edn. New York: Columbia University Press.

Rodríguez, Néstor P., 1997. The social construction of the U.S.–Mexico border. In *Immigrants Out! The new nativism and the anti-immigrant impulse in the United States*, Juan F. Perea, ed. New York: New York University Press, pp. 223–243.

Rouse, Roger, 1992. Making sense of settlement: Class transformation, cultural struggle, and transnationalism among Mexican migrants in the United States. In *Towards a Transnational Perspective on Migration*, Nina Glick Schiller, ed. *Annals of the New York Academy of Sciences* 645: 25–52.

Simon, Jonathan, 1998. Refugees in a carceral age: The rebirth of immigration prisons in the United States, 1976–1992. *Public Culture* 10(3): 577–606.

Solbakken, Lisa C., 1997. The Anti-Terrorism and Effective Death Penalty Act: Anti-immigration legislation veiled in anti-terrorism pretext. *Brooklyn Law Review* 63: 1381–1410.

US Department of Labor, 1991. *Employer Sanctions and U.S. Labor Markets: Final report.* Washington, DC: Division of Immigration Policy and Research, US Department of Labor.

Wallerstein, Immanuel, 1991. The construction of peoplehood: Racism, nationalism, ethnicity. In Balibar and Wallerstein 1991, 71–85.

Zolberg, Aristide R., 1990. Reforming the back door: The Immigration Reform and Control Act of 1986 in historical perspective. In *Immigration Reconsidered: History, sociology, politics*, Virginia Yans-McLaughlin, ed. New York: Oxford University Press, pp. 315–39.

Index

The Anthropology of Citizenship: A Reader, First Edition. Edited by Sian Lazar.
© 2013 John Wiley & Sons, Inc. Published 2013 by John Wiley & Sons, Inc.